In Search of the Public Jesus

A SECULARIZED EXAMINATION OF THE GOSPELS

Other books by the author

Liberation Theology – The Political Expression of Religion

I'm Right, You're Wrong – Moral Values, Conflict, and Politics in America (online)

The Married Pope (a novel)

Ricardo Planas

IN SEARCH OF
THE PUBLIC JESUS

A SECULARIZED EXAMINATION OF

THE GOSPELS

In Search of the Public Jesus

Copyright © 2021 by Ricardo Planas

ISBN 978-0-578-82910-4

Artwork of Jesus by Ernesto Molina

Cover and book design by Hugo Chilo

Table of Contents

Preface

The purpose of this work is to attain a distinctive and more realistic image of the public Jesus than what emerges from apologists or detractors of the Christian faith; an image of who he was at the time, beyond what people might think, feel, or believe. A critical inquiry of the Gospels, I thought, would lead me to an unvarnished look at the man who billions refer to as the Son of God and to an examination of the texts upon which Christianity originated. Although a Christian (Catholic), I was interested in finding out how an outsider to the faith might react to the Gospels today, a reason why I chose to read the texts from a secularized standpoint.

Initially, the idea felt senseless, so I discussed the project with a good friend from whom I have always received sound counsel, Agustin Dominguez. He was my 'go-to' person when I needed specific answers about terms I did not understand. Although he would have written on the subject matter in less than one hundred words, he did not dissuade me from proceeding. I visited Professor Frederick Pearce at the University of South Florida's School of Mass Communications seeking advice. He provided me with affirmation and determination to persist in my endeavor and gave me general rules on dealing with a novel method I intended to use, content analysis. Next, I called former Professor Ole Holsti, a pioneer in the use of content analysis in political science, and discussed with him the possibility of using the method to examine the Gospels. He was intrigued by the idea and thought it was feasible although he warned me that it would be a complex and time-consuming venture; he was right. I wrote to Rev. John P. Meier, an expert in the use of the Historical-Critical Method at the University of Notre Dame who has written extensively about Jesus, to inquire if he knew of any work done on the Gospels while using this method. He told me that he could not recall anything similar being done and added that any innovative approach would serve as a worthy contribution to the subject matter.

With this information in hand, I wrote to Philipp Mayring, Professor of Psychology at the University of Klagenfurt in Austria, and a recognized authority in the use of content analysis in the social sciences, to solicit his view. He replied saying the project was thought-provoking but insisted that I needed to be guided by a research question that would tie the core of the work together and that I should pay close attention to identifying essential categories to do the qualitative portion of the work. He generously provided me with access to his software platform which I adapted to the intricacies of the project. I benefitted from the guidance he provides in his book as it led me to perform necessary adjustments to deal with an esoteric text such as the Gospels. He writes *that content analysis is not a standardized instrument that always remains the same; it must be fitted to suit the particular object or material in question and constructed especially for the issue at hand.*[1]

With these considerations in mind, I sought to distance myself from writing to an academic audience. At times, I wanted to use informal writing to become personally involved with the reader. However, I was aware I still had to provide the necessary data that would stand quantitative and qualitative scrutiny. The primary data used to quantify the various categories and upon which I depended for the qualitative section is too long to publish. Hence, I uploaded it online for anyone who wishes to peruse it. The website address is www.RicardoPlanas.com/notes.

The work has been arduous. I revised the manuscript several times to the point that probably I was reading (and not correcting) my own mistakes. I apologize to the reader for the oversight. Nonetheless, I think I have not overstated the academic boundaries in either the quantitative or qualitative use of the data. Ultimately, I stand by the results.

Notes:
1. Philipp Mayring, Qualitative Content Analysis. Theoretical Foundation, Basic Procedures and Software Solution, (Klagenfurt, Austria: 2014), p. 39, 4.1.2. https://nbn-resolving.org/urn:nbn:de:0168-ssoar-395173 (accessed January 20, 2017), (accessed January 20, 2017).

1 – Who is the Public Jesus

One day, on his way to the villages of Caesarea Philippi, Jesus turns to his disciples and asks them, *who do people say that I am?* They said, John the Baptist, Elijah, even one of the prophets. It appears that after having spent time teaching through Galilee and Judea the people still were not certain who Jesus was. Peter, however, seems unhesitant and replies, *you are the Messiah* (Mk 8:27-29). The account in Mark's Gospel does not say how Peter learns that Jesus is the Messiah. It is Matthew who discloses that Jesus tells them that his heavenly Father, i.e., God, had revealed Peter his secretive identity (Mt 16:17).

Supposedly, the Messiah is a temporal leader, anointed by God to unite the Jewish people, free the land of Israel from oppressors, and bring peace to the world. The idea of a Messiah is embedded in Jewish tradition, seemingly as a desire of people who have suffered hostility and repression. According to Jewish sources this concept has no explicit roots in the Old Testament,[1] and the term does not appear in the texts.[2]

The concept of Jesus as a temporal leader, however, is found numerous times in the Gospels. Perhaps the most notorious passage appears in Luke when Jesus attends a synagogue in Nazareth. Reading from the prophet Isaiah, he appears to proclaim that he has been anointed *to bring glad tidings to the poor, proclaim liberty to the captives, and let the oppressed go free* (Lk 4:16-18). Jesus, however, never assumes the role of a political liberator or messiah, nor does he ever explain why. This is one of the most disconcerting aspects of Jesus's mission on earth.

Who, then, is Jesus? The Gospels do not seem to provide an answer clear enough that the reader may be confident that God is in some manner responsible for their content. This book is about searching for the public Jesus from a secularized perspective.[3] The public Jesus refers to the man around whom a small group of Jews once came together to establish a community of worship based on a consensus of what he had taught them. This initial acquiescence to a set of beliefs surrounding his person enabled the Christian faith to expand from its humble origins in Palestine throughout the rest of the world. Although political legislation within the Roman Empire in the fourth century certainly contributed to the public recognition of the faith, the idea of Jesus being God had been gaining adepts since the middle of the first century while facing competing beliefs, namely Judaism, Gnosticism, Roman paganism, and Pelagianism.

The consensus that once had kept the faith united, nonetheless, began to erode during the next centuries. Conflicts arose between popes and kings over temporal authority based on diverse understandings of Jesus and his teachings. State and church contended with heresies and incorrect beliefs, followed by schisms, and often war. Monarchs became divided over their understandings of Jesus's message. Eventually, church unity splintered as new religious leaders began to confront popes with their versions of the Gospels.

Today, there are dozens of Christian denominations, each with its unique portrayal of Jesus. Unwilling to worship under the same roof, they remain divided, each pledging allegiance to their version of Jesus while allying themselves with political parties and organizations that suit their values. The inadvertent outcome of the politicization of religion has been to split the Jesus message into ideologies. This is true particularly in nations where the democratic process and individual freedom tend to prevail.

Amidst the divisiveness surrounding the public Jesus, there is among Christians a personal Jesus. This is the Jesus followers bond in silence with, pray to, cry and laugh with; the one who understands their hopes, disappointments, and shortfalls, and whose teachings inspire their daily lives. Millions of people find this intimate Jesus comforting. But the personal Jesus is not the problem. The problem lies when the personal Jesus emerges into the public square and confronts different personal Jesuses. Disagreements over his behavior and his teachings have led to enormous misfortunes, including dissension, personal and religious division, and even warfare. Today, religious polarization extends into the world of politics as divided Christians use their beliefs and behavior both as swords and shields to justify their actions.

The approach used in this book provides a unique method to examine the Gospels. Through content analysis, the study rearranges the texts into specific categories, thereby allowing the reader to focus on how others viewed Jesus and how he viewed himself; which themes or concepts the Gospels emphasize the most and which the least; which are the most glaring omissions and its most significant incongruences and contradictions; and, more important, how a secularized society might view and respond to Jesus's teachings once the texts are examined from a unique perspective.

The search for the public Jesus from a secularized viewpoint ought not to be regarded as trivial. The process of secularization is advancing at a rapid pace throughout the post-modern world. Inadvertently and willfully, secularization seeks to uproot or deny religion its own space in the marketplace of ideas as a guiding spiritual, ethical, and moral compass, both at the personal and social spheres. Ironically, secularism, which primarily emphasizes the separation of church and state in society, is among Christianity's main defenders, as secular states generate laws that guarantee its protection. Nonetheless, whether the Christian faith may survive the challenge of secularization and become merely one among various moral philosophies that are studied academically, or simply merge with current cultural and political ideologies and eventually disappear, depends on how Jesus and his teachings are understood today and in the coming future.

The rift among Christian denominations revolving largely around the interpretation of the scriptures, and the increasing indifference to Christian beliefs, particularly among younger generations, pose insurmountable challenges to the faith. Contributing to the problem is the fact that the New Testament was written within a culture that took for granted social, political, economic, and moral practices that were different from the ones we currently face. As the texts have not been actualized to reflect a post-modern understanding of today's issues,[5] it is not surprising that many passages might leave contemporary readers confused, estranged, or even downright disappointed.[6]

After more than two thousand years of seeking to understand the man whom Christians call the Son of God, we need to ask if we are any closer to attaining a consensus on who Jesus was, what he did, and what he said. Throughout the centuries, the Jesus message has been interpreted mostly through *apologetics* or the systematic (and at times intolerant) defense by supporters of the faith, relying on different interpretations of the texts. Modern-day agnostics, atheists, and non-Christians who oppose Christianity have sought to invalidate the Jesus message through unrelenting rhetorical and prejudicial attacks while entrenching themselves in quasi-scientific jargon. Others have proceeded more reasonably, advancing questions that become incomprehensible when raised from outside the faith.

Traditionally, two approaches have been utilized to understand the public Jesus, faith, and reason, although a third approach, science, has been involved in the discussion during the last four centuries. Given the gap that exists among them, can they be reconciled as partners in the search for truth? The answer depends on whether each field admits its limitations and respects the inherent characteristics and boundaries of the others; a reductionist approach by each will only lead to increased intellectual and moral conflict.

Although Catholicism and mainstream Protestantism consider reason a human asset, both recognize that the only true way to understand the scriptures is through faith. This view would seem to leave out the possibility of those outside the Christian faith ever knowing (much less) understanding Jesus. The premise 'first I must believe then I will understand' is tautological. Where and how are non-believers and non-Christians supposed to procure what is necessary to believe, as faith cannot be purchased in religious stores? Admittedly, a rational faith appears to be as difficult to attain as it is necessary. Meanwhile, believers still adhere to the scriptures despite lacking a sensible understanding of the texts. It is difficult to ask a person to believe in Jesus if he or she lacks faith or has an aversion to religion. This is where reason enters the realm of the supernatural. Nonetheless, if understanding the mysteries of Christianity (somewhat of an oxymoron) requires *a profound faith in God, nourished by prayer and contemplation,*[7] few are likely to succeed, in which case the future of Christianity looks increasingly bleak. Today's world is becoming less inclined toward this type of spirituality unless we are pushed toward it through fear of dreadful events, such as illness, war, and natural calamities. But is the sudden reliance on God under these circumstances a sign of faith; or is it a reaction to self-preservation that would reduce prayer to nothing more than spiritual Prozac? When faith becomes the primary requirement to be Christian, the sign on the door is clear: Christianity is off-limits to religious and non-religious foreigners.

The dilemma that Christianity faces when its premises are examined from a secularized angle seems inescapable: 1) God is responsible for creation, out of which human beings continue to evolve; 2) according to the scriptures, God creates human beings in his image, suggesting that we share the capacity to reason (higher level of intelligence, abstract thinking), and thus the ability to survive and control our own environment; 3) humans have enormous capacity to love and do good, but for reasons not necessarily of our own choosing (Original Sin or biological evolution), human nature has remained imperfect (the flesh—reason and feelings—is flawed and weak); 4) as a result, humans have a proclivity toward malice (sin), and initially were deemed by God of being unworthy of eternal life, suggesting that God's work somehow had become corrupted; 5) not giving up, God decides to cast a lifeline to humans—redemption through Jesus; 6) God's plan for salvation requires that humans fully understand how the redemptive process works, and what they have to do, if anything, to attain that which sin or human imperfection has denied us; 7) thus, God decides to communicate with humans through divine revelation, first through the prophets in the Old Testament, then through the incarnation of his son Jesus, and the recording of his teachings in the Gospels and the rest of the New Testament as the outcome of oral transmission; 8) the New Testament then becomes the most significant empirical evidence of God's willful desire to communicate his plan of salvation to humanity; 9) nonetheless, after two thousand years of research and study of the scriptures, Christianity has divided and subdivided itself over its inability to fully understand the mysteries that keep Christianity, well, so mysterious. Hence, the crucial question: why would God make his plan of salvation difficult to understand while knowing that human nature is extraordinarily limited and flawed? If God's message of salvation is difficult to comprehend, can human beings be blamed for failing to understand it? The conclusion is problematic; aware of human limitations, God is either an abysmal communicator or he has chosen to remain mysterious and hidden for unknown reasons. There is a third possible explanation that while unpleasant to believers would gratify non-believers, particularly those with strong anti-religious sentiments: if God exists, he is merely a spectator or indifferent to his creation.

The following analogy might help to explain the above statement. Imagine ourselves being lost in a dense forest and having no idea of where to go. Suddenly, someone who dwells in the forest and knows his way around it appears and offers to assist us. He says that he can show us the path to our homes. He proceeds to draw a map and provides us with instructions. But there is a problem; being novices at wandering through the woods, the map, and the instructions this good person provides are difficult to follow. It has symbols we do not understand; he tells us what to eat and what not to eat, but without any frame of reference or images; he makes us aware of obstacles and dangers we cannot relate to; he further recommends us what to do when we encounter difficulties but uses an outdoorsman's terminology proper to the locality where he lives that is difficult to comprehend. Once on our way, we begin to argue whether he meant for us to take path A or path B, and what the symbols in the map conveyed. Suddenly, nightfall comes. We stop, look around and realize that we are lost. What are we to conclude, other than we were fools for wandering into unknown areas completely unprepared; that the guidance this person offered us with good intentions was of little if any help? This realization suggests that God may have wanted his message to be cryptic.[8]

Many Christians might individually argue that the analogy does not apply to them. They will suggest that they fully understand God's message, even while they disagree with others, who too, would claim that they know what the Gospels tell them. This condition--call it subjectivism at its worse—hinders any comprehensive effort at understanding what God is trying to convey. My initial conclusion that God does not excel in his communication skills or that we do not have 'the smarts' to understand the divine, however, may be entirely misleading, a product of undisclosed bias or traumatic experiences that might have conditioned my thinking process. If this were the case, I can rely on being in good company, as we shall read in the next chapters. For now, it might suffice to say that the apostles themselves had incredible problems understanding Jesus despite deeds they witnessed with their own eyes.

A Personal Note

I am aware that searching for the public Jesus from a secularized standpoint may upset believers who might object to novel social science approaches to understand the Gospels. They may view these methods as a desecration of sacred texts that have stirred the passions of billions throughout history. This, however, is neither the intention nor the outcome. Systematically studying the public Jesus is far different than how believers—including me--approach the personal Jesus. As research tools, the approaches employed in this work (content analysis and empirical reasoning) require an unemotional and painstakingly rational-like attitude, but without necessarily being less faithful. I consider these approaches akin to the *historical-critical analysis* undertaken by exegetes and theologians today; to the dispassionate demeanor of a heart surgeon seeking to save the life of his patient; or the astrophysicist seeking to discover the mysteries of the universe. Within this context, faith is neither an obstacle in using these approaches nor a requirement. Nonetheless, I expect strong personal disagreement, even resistance, and opposition, to my examination; but as long as disagreements are reasonable and empirically based, they will be respected.

A detailed description of the method used in this work appears in Appendix A at the end of the book. Although rummaging through the appendix may help understand the results, its primary purpose is that others may be able to confirm or reproduce the study or parts of it by using the same steps. Otherwise, detailed knowledge of the approach is not necessary to be able to traverse through the various categories and the inferences that are discussed throughout the book.

Regarding the empirical evidence, I can say that there may be mistakes that I was not able to rectify, e.g., incorrectly incorporating passages into a category, thereby slightly increasing its significance; or more likely the inverse, leaving relevant passages out. There may even be a few numerical errors too. However, having reviewed the data several times, I can attest that such oversights will not affect the overall results.

Subjecting the Gospels to a quantitative and qualitative approach is a complex endeavor. It requires tallying specific words that appear in the texts and are important to the Christian faith. Since this study is being conducted in English, I have no other option but to rely on an English translation of the Bible, of which there are quite a few.[9] The number of translations reveals, not only the extent of discrepancy that exists among Christian translators, but the difficulties encountered in one language to find a common understanding of the texts. There being numerous translations, it is likely that words used in some versions may be substituted for their synonyms or even not used at all, as translated versions may reflect different (ideological) understandings altogether.[10] Since each category is compartmentalized, if the study were to be replicated utilizing different versions of the Bible, this issue is unlikely to affect the overall results.

In this work, I have chosen the New American Bible Revised Edition (NABRE) namely because of its concern to ensure a more literal translation of the scriptures according to the historical and cultural context in which they were written; and, because of its impressive contribution of nearly one hundred scholars and theologians, bishops, revisers, editors, [and] particularly the participation of scholars from various Christian denominations.[11] When called for, however, I rely on other versions found in BibleGateway.com.

Moreover, to remain credible to my original purpose, I did not submit the manuscript to experts for review, considering it inappropriate, insofar as my objective was to read and attempt to understand the Gospels as a non-Christian without outside assistance. Thus, the interpretation of passages is my own.

A caveat: the reader must bear in mind that this work does not focus on what Jesus said or what he did; rather, it aims to understand the sayings and actions that Gospels' authors attribute to Jesus. Christianity upholds that the Gospels are the word of God; that God either revealed or inspired the authors on what to write. This view carries an enormous risk because it holds God responsible for whatever the texts say. Ultimately, human beings are accountable for what appears in the texts. Thus, it must be understood that what Jesus says and does cannot be attributed necessarily to him, but to what the authors wrote.

Notes:

1. Joseph Telushkin, *Jewish Literacy,* (New York: William Morrow and Co., 1991), reprinted in *Jewish Virtual Library,* https://www.jewishvirtuallibrary.org/the-messiah (accessed November 29, 2020); Louis Jacobs, *Encyclopedia Judaica,* The Gale Group, 2008, reprinted in *Jewish Virtual Library,* https://www.jewishvirtuallibrary.org/messiah (accessed November 29, 2020). Some evangelical Christian scholars, however, have attempted to assert that the concept shows up in the Old Testament. Walter C. Kaiser Jr., *Messiah in the Old Testament,* Revised ed., (Grand Rapids: Zondervan, 1995).

2. NABRE Version, *BibleGateway.com.* Nonetheless, the Evangelical Heritage Version uses the term *Christ* in Mark's and Matthew's Gospels instead of Messiah. The term does appear twelve times in the Old Testament version, however, as inserts in subheadings, not as part of the text.

3. The terms *secularization* and *secularism* differ when they are theologically and secularly defined. In this work, neither term refers to the theological view. Thus, *secularization* refers to an ongoing historical process whereby religious authorities and institutions find themselves having less influence in society, namely because people are losing interest in religious matters. The significance of ecclesiastical authorities is waning in part because other social and cultural forces are at work, e.g., science, technology, and a predominant turn toward temporal realities that reject (willfully or not) religious authority or influence over a nation's cultural and political institutions and activities. In some cases, this process stands for active opposition to religion, advocating instead the prevalence of agnostic or atheist beliefs and stressing the temporal world as the only reality. *Secularism,* meanwhile, refers to outcomes of secularization, particularly the separation of church and state in society. This separation, however, does not necessarily entail a diminishing role of religion in the culture of a nation. The existing legal and tacit understanding in secular societies grants autonomy to each sphere, thus, governments do not have to seek permission from religious hierarchies to legislate; cannot favor one type of religion over another, or resort to attacks against one faith and/or denomination to persuade people to oppose said faith. Additionally, *secularism* allows for religious freedom or religious pluralism, both as a means to avoid conflict and as a symbol of respect toward the personal faith of its citizens. Because of their affinities, the use of the terms may be confusing at times; however, in most instances I will be dealing more with the impact of secularization. In liberal democratic societies, secularism has proven to be an ally of religion rather than an opponent.

4. Judaism is a monotheistic religion with Abrahamic origins and the precursor of Christianity. Its beliefs at the time of Jesus were based on the *Torah* (the first five books of the Old Testament), the more extensive *Tanak* or Hebrew Bible, and the *Talmud* (Rabbinic teachings on Judaism). Gnosticism refers to a philosophical or quasi-religious movement, initially relying on Jewish and Christian views that centered on the supreme value of self-knowledge obtained from a personal relationship with the divine, and the belief that the physical world demeans God's creation by responding to evil forces. Roman paganism primarily denotes polytheistic beliefs (various gods) and forms of pantheism or worship of nature that early Christians—including Jesus—attributed to those who did not believe in the one true God. Pelagianism was based on the belief that human free will was not adversely affected by Original Sin to the extent that it prevented humans from attaining salvation through their own efforts.

5. Actualization of the texts does not imply only the use of different words so that the Gospels may be better understood. Although words do matter, the Gospels reflect a faith and a socio-political way of life that were very different than life in the twenty-first century. There are issues that were relevant then that are not relevant today, and issues that were non-existent that since then have become central to Christianity. In fact, we may surmise that if Christians today are expected to communicate and act in the same manner Jesus did toward his opponents, they would become insufferable at times. In this context, actualization means having to modernize the Jesus in the Gospels as well as having to place and explain his teachings in a world that is much more secularized and relative than the one in which Jesus lived.

6. Data gathered by the World Religion Database and published in National Geographic.com indicates *"Religion is rapidly becoming less important than it's ever been, even to people who live in countries where faith has affected everything from rulers to borders to architecture."* Although religion is experiencing fast growth, particularly in parts of Africa, the data shows that a new category of religious

people unaffiliated with specific denominations referred to as *nones,* is rapidly surging. Today they constitute the second-largest religious group in North America and most of Europe. According to recent studies, *nones* make up twenty-five percent of the population in the United States, having overtaken Catholics, mainline protestants, and all followers of non-Christian faiths in recent decades." Gabe Bullard, "The World's Newest Major Religion: No Religion," *National Geographic.com*, 22 April 2016, https://news.nationalgeographic.com/2016/04/160422-atheism-agnostic-secular-nones-rising-religion/ (accessed 23 February 2016).

7. Following in the footsteps of John Paul II, Pope Benedict XI intimates that faith is *first and foremost a personal, intimate encounter with Jesus.* Benedict XI, General Audience at St. Peter's Square, 21 October 2009,//w2.vatican.va/content/benedict-xvi/en/audiences/2009/documents/hf_ben-xvi_aud_20091021.html (accessed 23 February 2016).

8. The Gospels and Paul continuously refer to the *mystery* of God and the mystery surrounding God's revelation. NABRE editors, henceforth NE, explain that *God's secret, known only to himself, is his plan for the salvation of his people ...* [and] *that this secret involves Jesus and the cross* (1Cor 2:1, Mt 11:25-27, Mt 13:10-13, Lk 9:43-45). NABRE, *New American Bible Revised Edition*, United States Conference of Catholic Bishops, 2010, online, https://bible.usccb.org/bible.

9. According to Bible.com there are currently sixty versions of the Bible in English. Bible Versions, English, https://www.bible.com/versions (accessed August 18, 2019).

10. The following examples, taken from seven versions at Biblegateway.com (six selected at random plus the NE version that is used throughout this work) reveal the degree of discrepancy. The term *love* appears 66 times (xt) in the 21 Century King James version (21KJ), 84xt in the Evangelical Heritage version (EH), 72xt in the Good News version (GN), 69xt in the International Standard version (IS), 68xt in the New Testament for Everyone version (NT4E), 100xt in The Voice version (V), and 66xt in the NE version; the term *sin* (that includes *sinfulness* plus all words containing those letters) appears 92xt in 21KJ, 163xt in EH, 128xt in GN, 170xt in IS, 117xt in NT4E, 163xt in V, and 134xt in NE; *devil* appears 76xt in 21KJ, 17xt in EH, 18xt in GN, 15xt in IS, 16xt in NT4E, 23xt in V, and 14xt in NE; *faith* appears 44xt in 21KJ, 41xt in EH, 57xt in GN, 41xt in IS, 37xt in NT4E, 92xt in V (it relies mostly on the term *believe*), and 52xt in NE.

11. NE, https://www.bible.com/versions/463-nabre-new-american-bible-revised-edition.

2 – The Roots of the Problem

The title of this book was going to be, *Jesus Christ - the God of Christians*. Suddenly I realized I was facing a conundrum. To which Jesus would I be referring? There is, to be sure, a host of Jesuses: Catholic, Eastern Orthodox, Oriental Orthodox, several Protestant Jesuses, a Jesus of the Church of Jesus Christ of Latter-Day Saints, and a Jehovah's Witnesses' Jesus, each claiming to be the authentic interpreter of the Christian faith. The title would have led to the presumption that Jesus is only the God of Christians; that Jesus, in effect, is Christian. Nonetheless, this view is not in line with basic Christian monotheistic theology affirming that there is one God and that all humanity, not only Christians, was redeemed through Jesus's death. Accordingly, Jesus is also the god of Jews, Muslims, Hindus, Buddhists, Sikhs, Shintoists, Taoists, Jains, Spiritists, less known pagan groups, agnostics, and atheists.

The public Jesus has been referred to as a prophet, temporal messiah, human rights activist, revolutionary, troublemaker, and as a mythical legend that never existed. Yet, by far the most crucial question about Jesus, even among non-Christians and non-believers, is whether he is or not divine. Ascertaining that Jesus is divine would go a long way toward resolving important religious, philosophical, historical, scientific, and moral issues. Unfortunately, we are far from attaining consensus on the answer and as mentioned in chapter 1, the fault might not be ours.

For centuries, many suppositions have been advanced rejecting Jesus' divinity. The issue is intriguing, for how was it possible for a less than highly educated person to become so enlightened about scripture, politically and philosophically astute, confident of his beliefs and mission, and capable of defining a reasonably well-articulated moral code, altogether while appearing to contradict himself at times, consciously wishing to remain an enigmatic public figure only to become known in history as God?[1] Who is this pretentious Jew who has captivated the human interest, evoked so much passion, intellect, and admiration and whom history has elevated to the pinnacle of humankind? The simple and intricate answer is that Jesus is who the New Testament says he is. This is where the problem begins because Christians and non-Christians alike are being asked to have faith, not in Jesus, but in what the Gospels say about Jesus.

Faith as a Source of Faith

In simple terms, faith means to believe without sufficient confirmation or evidence. To Christians, if faith is real, it means to have a personal relationship with Jesus because they believe that he still lives even if they cannot see him. Additionally, lest Christians consider it as a cultural or social status symbol, faith entails having to accept Jesus's teachings and behave accordingly. Certainly, this is asking too much of mere humans, a reason for which it is important to trust the source of the information believers are being asked to accept.

According to some Christian denominations, faith is a gift that God extends only to those he chooses. Nonetheless, most mainstream denominations affirm that faith is offered to every single human being that is born, given that Jesus's redemption knows no boundaries. Either way, this is problematic. If billions of people do not share the Christian faith, does it mean that God plays favorites with some, i.e., divine nepotism? Moreover, regarding those who have a different faith or no faith at all through no fault of their own, can it be assumed that they have rejected God's gift? The literature abounds on the significant role that social and geographic elements play in the acquisition of faith, suggesting that many or most non-Christians have not willfully turned their back on Jesus.[2]

Rationally one's beliefs ought to be predicated on the level of trust that exists toward the sources that in turn lead to faith in the person of Jesus. Interestingly, the opposite seems to happen more often; believers accept the sources as truthful because they have faith in Jesus. Many Christians even have faith without wanting to question copies of what the original texts say about Jesus since the original manuscripts have not been unearthed. This faith even presumes that the existing documents are authentic copies of the originals; that the content of the New Testament is the product of a trustworthy oral tradition that for decades preceded the writing of the texts, or as others believe, the result of direct divine revelation.

The belief that Jesus is God tends to be far removed from the sources. The initial source in the proposition would be Jesus himself, or God, or the Holy Spirit. Those who witnessed Jesus and listened to his teachings, i.e., his disciples, those who followed him around, and his opponents would be the secondary sources. A third and more distant source is the oral tradition or transmission, the unwritten and spoken word that was passed on to others who may not have had the occasion to meet Jesus and had to rely on what others had told them. There is another (yet unidentified) source, the original writings of the Gospels. Since there are only copies of the Greek version, we do not know what the original Gospels read like, or if they were ever written in other languages. Thus, copies of the Gospels are even more distant from being the word of God.

Those who believe that the written word corresponds, literally, to God's divine revelation (Fundamentalism) bypass the second and third sources, since it is God who supposedly recites word by word what the texts say. Non-Fundamentalists, on the other hand, acknowledge the three previous sources and believe that the authors of the Gospels were 'inspired' by the oral tradition, although the term *inspired* has lacked a clear definition.

Moreover, the Gospels do not appear to have been written at the same time. Scholars believe that the Gospel of Mark appeared first, thirty to forty years after Jesus' death, followed by the Gospel of Luke and the Gospel of Matthew fifteen or twenty years after Mark's, and the Gospel of John that may have been written ten to twenty years afterward. Only Matthew and John were disciples of Jesus; nonetheless, given their ages at the time the texts were written, it is questionable that they alone authored their gospels. Scholars today believe that none of the named authors penned the gospels that carry their names.[3]

Furthermore, given the period in which the Gospels appeared, it is interesting that there are no explicit references to each other, notwithstanding the amount of 'text borrowing' that takes place in the synoptic Gospels, i.e., Mark's, Luke's, and Matthew's texts.[4] Otherwise, we must improbably concede that verbatim oral transmission may have coincidentally occurred in the synoptic Gospels. Moreover, nearly all of Paul's letters in the New Testament seem to have been written long before the Gospels, yet Paul is not mentioned in any of the texts, despite the close relations between the first apostles and him. Therefore, it is likely that the real authors of the Gospels were tertiary and/or quaternary sources, presuming that there were no alterations when the first copies were made.

Nonetheless, even if direct divine inspiration or revelation is affirmed throughout the entire writing process, i.e., from God to each of the authors, the numerous suppositions, dating and geographical errors, incongruences, and out-of-context passages found in the texts, make it difficult to accept that an omniscient and omnipotent God could be the primary author of the Gospels. Hence, a close examination of the texts suggests that a *faith-in-faith* circular approach is ultimately responsible for Christians' beliefs.[5]

The Gospels and the Temporal World of Politics

There is in the New Testament a well-hidden message that has gradually surfaced throughout the history of Christian churches, but particularly forcefully during and after the Enlightenment period (the mid-1600s through early 1900s): the Christian doctrine, if soundly and appropriately implemented, would result in a more humane, just, and peaceful world. This view has provided Christianity with a significant temporal and social role. Aware of this task, Christian denominations formulate their interpretations of the scriptures to rationalize and/or justify their status as religious and moral institutions. These institutions use their public standing to exert social, political, economic, and cultural influence in their localities as well as around the world. Given the temporal supernatural importance of God's message, it would be reasonable to conclude that its correct interpretation and understanding would be of the utmost consequence. Nevertheless, after two thousand years, there is still no clear consensus on the message. Instead, the texts continue to elicit uncertainty, confusion, and discord, there being as many different interpretations of the scriptures as there are interpreters.

Lack of consensus on an authentic interpretation of God's message to humankind has led to serious predicaments. The Bible can be and has been treated subjectively by its users to selectively focus on preferred passages and interpret them to support preferred points of view. Besides the religious wars of past centuries, the American Civil War in the nineteenth century was a most unfortunate event as both the South and the North relied on passages from the New Testament to validate their moral and political actions.[6] Given the above conditions, what may non-Christians learn about Jesus by reading the Gospels? And at a time when the world is becoming highly secularized and drawn to technological and scientific progress, and moral and religious pluralism, is it prudent for church authorities to foster the study of the Gospels?[7]

Deciphering the Gospels
In the 2014 historically based film, *The Imitation Game,* young lad Christopher Morcom introduces his schoolmate Alan Turing to the practice of cryptography describing it as, *messages that anyone can see but no one knows what they mean ... unless you have the key.*[8] Cryptography provides a reasonable analogy to understanding the process of interpreting the scriptures, although with a caveat: intelligence messages are encrypted to prevent enemies from reading them. The assumption in this book is that it was not the purpose of the authors of the Gospels to hide God's message from his creatures, despite certain passages indicating that such was Jesus's intention. The point here is that, as the definition of cryptography suggests, those on the receiving end require a key to decipher the encrypted messages.[9]

It must then be asked, is it that complicated to understand the scriptures? According to experts, it is. For centuries, and despite several schisms, Catholic doctrine had managed to prevail over most of the Christian world; that is until in the sixteenth century the Protestant Reformation considerably undermined the doctrinal monopoly the Church's hierarchy had at the time. Rejecting the authority of the Catholic Church, Protestantism downgraded oral tradition, maintaining instead that the scriptures were the only source for authoritatively interpreting Jesus's message. As various Protestant denominations arose, each would set forth its own explanations upon which their authority would be validated. It was then that biblical interpretations began to flourish within the Christian faith.

It was not, however, until the seventeenth and eighteenth centuries that real confusion set in. Under the inspirational guidance of the French Enlightenment, agnostic and atheistic scholars began to question many aspects of the Bible. Devoid of personal faith and irritated by doctrinally safe devotional studies of the texts, these intellectuals popularized an interesting approach known today as the historical-critical method. They sustained that human reason could lead to a more precise understanding of God's word.

After all, if the divine had inserted itself in human history to communicate with humankind, what better instrument than reason to interpret what amounted to a historical document? Incisive questions were raised, much to the displeasure and concern of Catholic authorities, even though a few church scholars were doing something similar in private.[10] Reason by itself, however, failed to pierce God's mystery.

Following the Enlightenment, an attempt at establishing orthodoxy emerged within Protestantism toward the end of the nineteenth century, namely in the United States: Fundamentalism. Around 1910, a group of Protestant scholars defined through a collection of essays what they believed to be authentic Christian doctrine, leading to still another Christian interpretation of the scriptures. These scholars affirmed the inerrancy of the Bible and attacked doctrinal errors, such as Mormonism, Christian Science, modern philosophy, Darwinism and evolution, socialism, and even Romanism.[11] The yearning for orthodoxy among Protestants led to additional doctrinal understandings of the Jesus message; Evangelicals, Baptists, Methodists, Pentecostals, Adventists, were quickly becoming mainstream Christian denominations, each with their unique interpretations. At this stage, it might be reasonable to ask if there would be any fundamental reason (other than personal belief) for considering any interpretation correct, including those by agnostics and atheists?

Fundamentalism is based on the principle that since the Bible is the word of God it is free from error; therefore, it should (and can) be interpreted literally. It affirms that God would not allow humanity to be confused by his words, fully trusting God to find ways to overcome human limitations.[12] Non-fundamentalists, e.g., the Catholic Church, some mainstream Protestant denominations, agnostic and atheist scholars, object to this approach because it makes no attempt to go beyond the written text no matter how unreasonable or cryptic a passage may be. The consensus among them (including agnostics and atheists) is that the Gospels were preceded by decades of oral traditions that require serious interdisciplinary examination.[13] Facing these predicaments, the Christian faith finds itself cornered by highly critical religious and secular minds. Currently, church authorities believe that they have no choice but to continue to insist on the inerrancy of the scriptures as a source of moral truths despite significantly unanswered questions.[14] Although not openly stated, it is well-known that anything short of the inerrant claim made by church authorities could weaken even further Christianity's credibility and those who use the scriptures to support moral, social, and political policies. However, without additional information about the life of Jesus, the issue of his divinity--while it cannot be arbitrarily rejected--will remain problematic, and eventually could become a simple cultural devotion.

Notes:

1. The Gospels indicate that Jesus was not illiterate, but rather a student of the Jewish religion, shown by his ability to quote from the Old Law. Moreover, nothing--other than his prolific debates and knowledge of the scriptures—suggests that he was a scholar in the modern sense of the term, i.e., he attended schools of higher learning. For a more precise understanding of Jesus's social and intellectual background, see John P Meir, *A Marginal Jew: Rethinking the Historical Jesus*, Vol. I, (New Haven: Yale University Press, 1 November 1991), 276-285.

2. This does not mean that faith in God is merely a delusion; if it were, even scientists would be delusional too, as faith is not only an artificial construct but a trust one places in something or someone based on credible information. Those who study sociology of religion accept that people are reared in certain faiths, or acquire them, depending on various factors that include family, geography, and personal experiences. Hence, God's role in the acquisition of faith remains somewhat of a mystery. For an interesting argument on the subject, see Peter Berger, *The Social Construction of Reality: A Treatise in the Sociology of Knowledge,* (New York: Anchor, 11 July 1967); Berger, *The Sacred Canopy: Elements of a Sociological Theory of Religion,* Reprinted edition, (New York: Anchor, Reprint Edition, 1 October 1990; Timothy Keller, *The Reason for God: Belief in an Age of Skepticism,* Reprint Edition, (London: Penguin Books, 4 August 2009; Richard Dawkins, *The God Delusion,* (Boston: Mariner Books, Reprint Edition, 16 January 2008).

3. Information regarding approximate dates and authorship appears in the NABRE Version's Introductions to the Gospels of Mark, Luke, Matthew, and John.

4. The hypothetical Q Source that emerged at the turn of the twentieth century explains similar or identical sayings in the synoptics. Although the Q source does not extend to John's Gospel, it becomes evident that similar events and sayings appear in all four documents. Anthony Maas, "Jesu Logia ("Sayings of Jesus")," *The Catholic Encyclopedia*, henceforth, CE, Vol. 9, (New York: Robert Appleton Company, 1910), http://www.newadvent.org/cathen/09323a.htm (accessed April 3, 2020).

5. This process holds for any historical event, the difference usually lying on the veracity of the documents we possess. For example, what we believe to be the primary values and circumstances that led to American independence would hold to be true depending on whether we trust that we have in our hands the original signed and printed version of the Declaration of Independence and whether the written words accord with historical events.

6. Harry S. Stout, *Upon the Altar of the Nation: A Moral History of the Civil War,* Reprint Edition (London: Penguin Books, 27 March 2007); James H. Moorhead, *American Apocalypse: Yankee Protestants and the Civil War 1860-1869,* (New Haven: Yale University Press, 1 February 1978).

7. For centuries, Protestantism has argued in favor of the individual reading and understanding of the Bible, believing that God would speak to those who wish to communicate with him, i.e., without intermediaries. For centuries too, and until very recently, Catholicism rejected this approach realizing the inherent difficulties in understanding the scriptures. Instead, it suggested relying on church mediators who could more aptly explain the mysteries in the Bible. In the end, Catholicism has been able to extract a concise and unified public understanding of the scriptures (whether correct or incorrect), while, to a large extent, the interpretation of the scriptures in Protestantism has multiplied and become largely dispersed, forcing specific denominations to write their own set of beliefs that would distinguish them from others; in effect, establishing themselves as intermediaries of their own viewpoints. Since Vatican II, however, Catholics have been urged to read the Bible: "Easy access to Sacred Scripture should be provided for all the Christian faithful." Second Vatican Council, "Dogmatic Constitution on Divine Revelation," 18 November 1965, *22,*
http://www.vatican.va/archive/hist_councils/ii_vatican_council/documents/vat-ii_const_19651118_dei-verbum_en.html. There is also an opposite view. Philosophy professor David Kyle Johnson asserts that *the quickest route to atheism is to study the Bible.* This statement is offered without empirical evidence; other than anecdotal stories, no serious research study appears to have been undertaken to verify or disprove it. Moreover, at face value, the statement may be contradicted by millions who 'study' the Bible and yet continue to believe. Johnson's statement, however, may have tacit validity depending on what it means "to study the Bible," and how it is done. David K Johnson, "Book Review: Bart Ehrman's Jesus Before the Gospels," *Psychology Today,* 10 April 2016, https://www.psychologytoday.com/blog/logical-take/201604/book-review-bart-ehrman-s-jesus-the-gospels (accessed 16 March 2016).

8. *The Imitation Game,* directed by Morten Tyldum, The Weinstein Company, 2014. During World War II, Turing led a team that was able to break German encrypted messages enabling the Allies to shorten and eventually win the war against Hitler, thereby saving countless human lives. Andrew Hodges, *Alan Turing: The Enigma,* (London: Walker Books, 2000).

9. An article by Dr. Mark D. Roberts, Presbyterian pastor and Executive Director of the Max De Pree Center for Leadership at Fuller Seminary, provides an example of New Testament cryptography to facilitate the understanding of Jesus's divinity. The author, however, admits to its limitations, indicating that some early Jews began to believe in Jesus because others regarded or exalted him as God. Roberts identifies several *keys*: tracing the use of two words *marana tha* in Paul's 1 Cor 16:21-24 to the early days following Jesus's death; a passage in Paul's Phil 2:5-11 affirming Jesus's divinity; Jesus's affirmation of the Jewish *Shema* that appears in Deuteronomy 6:4-6; the *Wisdom Tradition* in ancient Judaism; John's Gospel' Jesus's behavior, and others. He concludes that *there isn't one simple answer to the question of why the earliest Christians came to see Jesus as divine... What is pretty clear from the historical records is that Jesus was not, by and large, regarded as divine during his earthly life... Rather, Jesus' true and full nature was revealed to the earliest Christians in a variety of ways and times, as they reflected upon the life, teachings, death, and resurrection of Jesus in light of the Old Testament, and as they served Jesus as Lord and even worshiped him.* Rev. Dr. Mark D. Roberts, "Was Jesus Divine," *Patheos*, 2011, patheos.com/blogs/markdroberts/series/was-Jesus-Divine/ (accessed 16 March 2016).

10. The Catholic Church gives credit to a seventeenth-century priest, Richard Simon, and a converted Catholic, Jean Astruc, in the eighteenth century, for being among those who spearheaded the method. Pontifical Biblical Commission, "The Interpretation of the Bible in the Church," *Origins*, 6 January 1994, I-1, History of the Method, https://catholic-resources.org/ChurchDocs/PBC_Interp-FullText.htm (accessed 18 March 2016).

11. R.A. Torrey, A.C. Dixon, and others, *The Fundamentals – A Testimony to the Truth*, Vol 4, (Madison: AGES Software Rio, 2000) Version 1.0, AGES Digital Library, http://ntslibrary.com/PDF%20Books%20II/Torrey%20-%20The%20Fundamentals%204.pdf (accessed 18 March 2016).

12. Evangelicals are among those who follow a literalist interpretation of the Bible. According to a 2011 survey, fifty percent believe *the Bible should be read literally, word for word* while forty-eight percent believe *not everything* is to be interpreted literally. Pew Research Center, "Global Survey of Evangelical Protestant Leaders," 22 June 2011, https://www.pewforum.org/2011/06/22/global-survey-of-evangelical-protestant-leaders/ (accessed 20 March 2016). Another poll released in 2017 indicates that twenty-four percent of Americans said the Bible should be taken literally while nearly half of Americans do not take the Bible literally. Lydia Saad, "Record Few Americans Believe Bible Is Literal Word of God," *Gallup*, 3-7 May 2017, http://news.gallup.com/poll/210704/record-few-americans-believe-bible-literal-word-god.aspx (accessed 9 September 2017).

13. Oral transmission suggests entails having to memorize a detailed description of Jesus's teachings and passing it forth intact while tradition involves a looser activity that allows for differences while focusing on major themes of Jesus's life. A detailed explanation of the various sources is found in Meier's *Marginal Jew*, vol. 1, and in Bart Ehrman's *How Jesus Became God*, (New York: Harper Collins, 2014); additional information on the sources is found in *Interpretation*, I, A-1, History of the Method.

14. The Catholic Church has declared that, since the Holy Spirit is said to be instrumental in the inspiration of the texts, *the books of Scripture must be acknowledged as teaching solidly, faithfully and without error that truth which God wanted put into sacred writings for the sake of salvation.* Second Vatican Council, *Dogmatic Constitution on Divine Revelation,* 1965, 11, http://www.vatican.va/archive/hist_councils/ii_vatican_council/documents/vat-ii_const_19651118_dei-verbum_en.html (accessed 23 March 2016). Critics (even within the Church), however, sustain that passages in the New Testament amounting to "truths," have changed throughout time.

3 – The Complexity of Understanding the Gospels

The reader may recall from the first chapter that difficulties in understanding the scriptures lead to the tentative conclusion that God's communications skills are wanting and/or that humans simply lack the wisdom or intelligence to comprehend the message. Following the Reformation, the Catholic hierarchy opposed any critical study of the scriptures. Despite recently crediting the Catholic Oratorian priest Richard Simon to be among the founders of the historical-critical method in the seventeenth century, Simon's work did not fare well in the hands of his superiors as he was persecuted and silenced.[1]

After nearly two centuries of unsuccessfully rebutting those who dared question the supernatural dimension of the New Testament and the divinity of Jesus through the historical-critical method, the Catholic hierarchy finally decided to rely on newer forensics.[2] In 1902 Pope Leo XIII decided to establish the Pontifical Biblical Commission, among other things, *to protect and defend the integrity of the Catholic Faith in Biblical matters; and to decide controversies on grave questions which may arise among Catholic scholars.*[3] In retrospect, it seems he had no idea of the future implications of his decision.

Jump ninety-one years to 1993, when this same commission gave Pope John Paul II a watershed document that referred to the historical-critical approach as *the indispensable method for the scientific study of the meaning of ancient texts.* The pope's approval meant that Catholic scholars finally were given official permission to critically examine the scriptures with the aid of science and reason in addition to their faith.[4] Their conclusions could be nothing less than shocking to the faith, although it is likely that the average believer is unaware of its findings.

After thoroughly studying the scriptures, these experts bluntly issue the following warnings:

- *The Bible bears witness that its interpretation can be a difficult matter* (Introduction, A).
- *The meaning of biblical texts [are] often very difficult to comprehend* (I, A-2).
- *In order to interpret scripture ... theologians need the work of exegetes* (III, D-2).

As if the outcome of these conclusions were not difficult enough to digest, these experts add that the New Testament itself is not easy to interpret *in the area of morality* (III, D-3). Was this God's intention; that believers needed religious cryptologists to decipher his message? The conclusions of the Biblical Commission carry an ominous message for the casual reader of the scriptures: *caveat lector*--let the reader beware—that he or she reads at their own risk; certainly, these are not words of encouragement when it comes to understanding how to behave morally to pursue one's salvation.

Amidst such a disheartening outlook, I discussed the issue with a good friend who has helped me in the past to repair my ignorance of the scriptures. He outright dismissed my exposition and replied to the question, "What is Jesus's message," by citing five brief passages: Matthew 22:35-40, Mark 12:28-31, Luke 10:25-28, Deuteronomy 6:4-8, and Leviticus 19:18. The message in Mt 22:35-40 reads:

> *Teacher, which commandment in the law is the greatest?" He said to him, "You shall love the Lord, your God, with all your heart, with all your soul, and with all your mind. This is the greatest and the first commandment. The second is like it: You shall love your neighbor as yourself. The whole law and the prophets depend on these two commandments.*

Needless to say, I almost gave up on writing this book.

Readers who dispense with the assistance of experts tend to rely on a basic approach; they rummage through the scriptures out of devotion or curiosity, tending to disregard passages they do not understand or may lead them to confront certainties they much prefer to avoid because of the uneasiness they may cause. Instead, they selectively interpret the scriptures in a manner that gratifies them or their ideologies.

Non-Fundamentalists assert that the entire Bible is not to be interpreted literally. Nonetheless, they do not indicate which parts are to be taken at face value and which others are questionable. Thus, readers have to oscillate between the non-fundamentalist and the fundamentalist approaches, confused by passages that do not seem to make sense or by others that seemingly contradict themselves. The task is left up to them to formulate their own interpretations.[5] Interestingly, if read critically, the New American Bible, Revised Edition (NABRE), shows instances among the *endnotes* that raise questions about the inerrancy of the New Testament as well as the concept of divine inspiration or revelation.

Setting aside the assistance that theologians and exegetes could provide me, the task in this work is to read the Gospels like millions of people do every day while seeking to decipher God's message. Nonetheless, in the Gospels Jesus acknowledged that things hidden from the wise and learned have been revealed to *the childlike*, suggesting that those whom the world considers people of lowly status are privileged hearers of the word of God (Mt. 11:25, Lk. 10:21).[6] Probably, he was referring to Pharisees, Sadducees, and scribes as being the wise and learned (whom he casts as hypocrites and proud), as opposed to a group of fishermen who became his apostles.

But interpreting Jesus nowadays presents problems, as his criterion would disqualify most if not all highly educated religious scholars, theologians, and philosophers who scrutinize the scriptures.

Hence, would it be possible for humble believers to find the truth after spiritually invoking God's assistance? How would they know? What guarantees are there that the personal approach will not result in countless different interpretations (as it has happened) often in contradiction with one another? It may be recalled that the input of personal religious beliefs in public policy can have extraordinary outcomes in our socio-economic and political cultures. With this perspective in mind, do we not know of voters, Protestants or Catholics, who claim that God has told them to vote for a certain candidate that still loses, or of public officials that start a war based on God's guidance, only to make things worse?

Intriguingly, if we recur to the scriptures, we find evidence that Jesus promised to assist the Apostles and their successors in the interpretation of his message (Jn. 14:26). If this was his promise, how is it possible that after more than two thousand years we are still debating Jesus's teachings? At this stage, my friend's advice keeps humming in my ears, 'stick to those five passages and forget everything else.'

Biblical cryptologists, however, contend that their work is not futile. The literal sense of the scripture, they say, can be discovered, although it will require the combined efforts of experts *in the fields of ancient languages, of history and culture, of textual criticism and the analysis of literary forms, and who know how to make good use of the methods of scientific criticism.*[7] They indicate, however, that all that can be expected after their laborious effort is to arrive only at *the greatest possible accuracy.*[8] If these experts are correct, then contrary to what Jesus said, God has hidden things not only from the high and the mighty or those who do not have faith in him, but also from the lowly faithful and his church too.

The message these scholars provide us, aside from being dispiriting, is exceptionally meaningful and honest. They are indicating how complex it is to produce a clear and concise interpretation and understanding of *the Jesus message.*[9] Non-Catholic exegetes who rely on the historical-critical method are likely to agree with these conclusions. But it is precisely their realism and honesty that inexorably cast doubts upon God's ability or willingness to communicate with his creatures or with humans' inability to understand God. After thousands of years of painstaking effort, scholars--Catholics, Protestants, even atheists—can only conclude that the content and meaning of the scriptures remain a mystery; a mixture of historical truth and legend, drawn up by human hands, and maybe under divine inspiration.

Presenting a mysterious document to incredulous and critically minded generations and telling them it encloses eternal truths seems like a Sisyphean task. To these generations and the ones to come, the New Testament is likely to appear as an archaic tract, even if it encloses significant—yet contradictory and obsolete--moral teachings. Already, we start reading the proverbial writing on the wall: since 1976, the percentage of Americans who view *the Bible in purely secular terms--as ancient fables, legends, history, and precepts written by man*--rose from thirteen percent to twenty-six percent in 2017. In Central and Eastern Europe most people believe the Bible is the word of God, and yet religious observance is low; and in Western Europe regardless of how people view the Bible, the majority no longer believes in heaven or hell.[10] Another research poll contrasted church-attending Christians and people who consider themselves Christians, despite little or no attendance to religious services. The results among the fifteen European countries that were polled indicate trends that might concern Christian religious authorities.[11]

As the historical-critical method began to gain acceptance, social scientists began to ask questions that had not been proposed largely because the social sciences had not been highly regarded among Christian religious authorities. But despite incessant pushbacks, the *historical-critical method* has been accepted by many mainstream Christian denominations despite its extraordinary complexity.[12] Clearly, something is seriously amiss. As a friend once told me with a certain irony, who would have thought that rocket science would be easier to grasp than to unveil God's message! This is the condition that pervades the Christian faith.

Therefore, what will this book seek to accomplish? Do I dare say that it will succeed where experts have failed? No. Only pride and arrogance would let me go that far. Instead, this work seeks to study Jesus from a different angle to understand what his message might mean in today's world.[13] Transparency, candor, and temporal relevance regarding the Jesus message are among the most significant objectives to be pursued in this work. Amid the continued and absurd cacophony of biblical interpretations, each disputing their validity, it sets its goals high and expectations rather low. Not being a historian, a theologian, or a biblical scholar (but a social science researcher and analyst), I set out to read the Bible from a secularized perspective and in the manner that casual readers might do, i.e., accepting the written word literally, but while subjecting it to an in-depth and more empirical examination. Indeed, Jews living in the city of Beroea in northern Greece to whom Paul preached *the word, examined the scriptures daily to determine* if Paul was being truthful about Jesus (Acts 17:10-11). The Acts contrast these people's fair-mindedness with Jews in Thessalonica who were unwilling to listen to Paul. Ironically, although he persuaded many, Paul may have unintentionally misled them. He had been *expounding and demonstrating that the Messiah had to suffer* (Acts 17:2-3), a view that Jesus told his disciples (Lk 24:26, 46) that does not show up in the Old Testament or Jewish literature prior to the New Testament. [14]

Notes:
1. Richard Simon, *Critical History of the Texts of the New Testament,* trans. Andrew Hunwick (Leiden: Koninklijke Brill NV, 2013), xxvii –xxxvi. http://www.scribd.com/doc/166004234/Richard-Simon-Andrew-Hunwick-Transl-Critical-History-of-the-Text-of-the-New-Testament-Wherein-is-Established-the-Truth-of-the-Acts-on-Which-The#scribd (accessed 8 April 2016).
2. Protestant theologians and philosophers, namely from Germany, already had been using the historical-critical method since the late eighteenth century and likely played an influential role in the Catholic

Church's decision. Among them, Friedrich Schleiermacher, Ferdinand Christian Baur, and Adolf von Harnack.

3. John Corbett, "The Biblical Commission," (CE), http://www.newadvent.org/cathen/02557a.htm (accessed 8 April 2016). The commission operates under the authority of the pope; it does not retain independent publication rights, and in 1971 became a consultative group to the Congregation for the Doctrine of the Faith entrusted with preserving the integrity of the Catholic faith.

4. Interpretation. Underneath the title of the document it reads, *Presented by the Pontifical Biblical Commission to Pope John Paul II on April 23, 1993.* http://catholic-resources.org/ChurchDocs/PBC_Interp-FullText.htm. The entire document is worth reading, although it may require a strong mental disposition to avoid being disillusioned by these scholars' admission about the complexity of God's message. Note: Citations are given according to their location within the body of the text and not the Table of Content, as the latter differs from the former.

5. There are various translations of the Bible in contemporary English that attempt to facilitate its reading and understanding. None of these versions, however, have been historically and theologically actualized, i.e., given a modern interpretation of the significance or application of Jesus' teachings in today's world. See *New Living Translation,* (Carol Stream: Tyndale House Publishers 2015), https://www.biblestudytools.com/nlt/ (accessed 8 April 2016). There is also a Catholic version consisting of a paraphrased translation: *The Catholic Living Bible: Paraphrased - A Thought-for-Thought Translation,* (Carol Stream: Tyndale House Publishers, 1979). A third version, Eugene H. Peterson, *The Message – The Bible in Contemporary Language,* (Colorado Springs: NavPress, 2002).

6. *Interpretation,* III, B-3, Role of Various Members of the Church in Interpretation; Commission's emphasis.

7. Ibid., III, B-3.

8. Ibid., II, B-1, The Literal Sense.

9. *Interpretation* is being defined as the actions we undertake to understand something. *Understanding* refers to the outcome of interpretation; that which is attained after successfully penetrating the essence or core of an idea, an action, or a text.

10. *The shift is most pronounced among young adults, indicating the trend is likely to accelerate in the years ahead.* Saad, "Record Few Americans..." In Central and Eastern Europe religious observance is very low, although the majority of countries believe the Bible is the word of God. Pew Research Center, "Religious Belief and National Belonging in Central and Eastern Europe," May 2017, http://www.pewforum.org/2017/05/10/religious-beliefs/ (accessed 9 September 2017); Stoyan Zaimov, "Most Western Europeans No Longer Believe in Heaven and Hell," *Christian Post,* Dec. 2017, https\\www.christianpost.com/news/most-western-europeans-no-longer-believe-heaven-hell-survey-209270/ (accessed 9 September 2017).

11. Among the conclusions reached are the following:
- Church-attending Christians are in the minority in all countries except for Italy.
- While non-Church attending Christians *do not believe in God "as described in the Bible," they do tend to believe in some other higher power or spiritual force.* A third group polled, those with no religious affiliation whatsoever ('none') averaging 24 percent, *do not believe in any type of higher power or spiritual force in the universe.*
- Non-Church attending Christians have *more positive than negative views toward churches and religious organizations* though less than Church attending Christians, *saying they serve society by helping the poor and bringing communities together.*
- Both Church attending and non-attending Christians *are associated with higher levels of negative sentiment toward immigrants and religious minorities* than 'nones.'
- Non-Church attending Christians are less likely to express nationalist views than Church-attending Christians, but more than 'nones.'
- Non-Church attending Christians (along with 'nones') tend to favor legal abortion and same-sex marriage, although there is still *substantial support* for these issues among the more conservative Church-attending Christians.
- Both Church-attending Christians and non-attending Christians are more sympathetic toward raising their children in the Christian faith. 'None' parents, however, tend to raise their children with no religion. Pew Research Center, "Being Christian in Western Europe," May 2018, http://www.pewforum.org/2018/05/29/being-christian-in-western-europe/ (accessed 30 May 2018).

12. To acquire a feeling of what is being done in this field today, refer to *Interpretation,* I-3 Description. Purposefully, I omitted the commission's depiction of its methodology including semiotic analysis, for fear that the reader may despair. A description of semiotics is found in I, B-3 Semiotic Analysis.

13. In the 1980s and 90s a colorful method of finding out what Jesus may have said emerged. Known as the *Jesus Seminar*, a group of about two hundred scholars discussed the Gospels and, following rigorous discussions of the issues, voted through colored beads on the degree of authenticity of hundreds of passages attributed to Jesus. Several books were published. The seminar completed its work in 1998 concluding that, about 18 percent of the sayings and 16 percent of the deeds attributed to Jesus in the gospels are authentic. *The Jesus Seminar*, Westar Institute, https://www.westarinstitute.org/projects/the-jesus-seminar/ (accessed 8 April 2016).

14. NEs note, Luke 14:26.

4 – New Methods to Examine the Gospels

Along with the historical-critical method, the social sciences have spawned various approaches useful to the in-depth examination of cultures, languages, and history. Two distinctive methods will be employed in this study: Content Analysis and Empirical Reasoning. Both are proper for examining any type of communication whose purpose is to convey messages to an audience, which was precisely the intention of the authors of the Gospels. By closely examining the content of the Gospels we may be able to uncover significant issues that are not visible to the naked eye or the naked ear for that matter. These approaches are not a substitute for historical criticism or any other approach; they may, however, complement other techniques.

The primary function of any message that seeks to persuade people to change their hearts and minds is to rely on several practices that humans engage in both consciously and subconsciously. One technique involves the repetition of key concepts throughout the message. This may best be appreciated in advertising and the marketing of products, in political speeches and writings, and in religious sermons. In communications, the author or speaker seeks repetition to ensure that the audience would remember its significance.

Marketing is mostly about repetition. So, anyone who wishes to sell a product to make a profit, mobilize voters to win an election, or attempt to save souls will seek to stay on message. It would be unwise and nonsensical for a messenger who wants to instill his/her views about policy x to devote most of his time writing or speaking about y and z. For this reason, authors use similar words or concepts repeatedly; rely on synonyms; use metaphors that support their central ideas; rephrase a concept to express the same view without changing its overall meaning; alternate between positive consequences of accepting the message and the negative ones of rejecting it. These techniques can be easily observed in the Gospels.

Content analysis accounts for the human tendency to reveal a portion of ourselves when we communicate with others. Nowadays, the content of political speeches is methodically analyzed to unveil the author/speaker's *cognitive or mental map*, i.e., an internal rational scheme through which the author/speaker willfully or inadvertently discloses his or her intentions. These intentions can be identified and analyzed by examining the content of the message. This approach provides additional information about the messenger and the message because, in their desire to persuade their audiences, authors/speakers emphasize concepts and themes they regard as significant by repeating them (as I am doing here).

As a research technique, content analysis seeks to systematically quantify the content of communication to make inferences from selected messages.[1] Content analysis contends that numbers are significant. A primitive version is often used to indicate the number of times a term appears in a specific text. The results, in and of themselves, are truly meaningless, however, since numbers become relevant mostly when related to other numbers. For example, a term or a concept that appears fifty times in a thousand words article would suggest that it is more meaningful to the author than if it is mentioned only ten times. In the Gospels, the authors emphasized certain themes more than others either because they deemed them to be more important, or because they were divinely guided or inspired; otherwise, why would they have done it?

The approach in this work, nonetheless, goes beyond a simplistic count of terms. Instead, it begins by reorganizing the texts into categories that are easily recognizable in Christianity, selecting and systematically quantifying passages that correspond to the categories, and ultimately ranking and designating them according to their significance. In the absence of quantifying the texts, all we have left is a subjective interpretation, which is precisely what we are seeking to minimize. For example, although Christian believers presume that nothing Jesus said or did was insignificant, a systematic review of the texts lead to the realization that he did not pay equal attention to everything he said or did, and that he left out or failed to address issues that have become exceedingly important today. Instead, he (or the authors of the Gospels) concentrated on what they deemed to be important at the time.

Nonetheless, Jesus's instructions to his disciples to spread the good news to all nations of the world lead to the view that the Gospels are timeless. If this is the case, unearthing the significance or insignificance of his deeds and his words would signal what he desired his legacy to be. This, however, is somewhat problematic because Jesus did not write his autobiography or any treatise on his teachings. Everything we know Jesus said or did comes from those who wrote the Gospels, indicating that we may not have the entire story. On the other hand, since Christians believe that divine guidance is responsible for the Gospels, we must assume that the content of the texts coincides with God's wishes. But could God have left anything important out of the Gospels while leaving in the texts other matters that in time became irrelevant? The results of content analysis and empirical reasoning indicate that this is precisely what may have happened on several occasions.

Empirical reasoning will be used primarily for explanatory purposes to validate significant concepts found in the texts. It suggests that ideologies, historical events, and everyday statements can be examined in terms of their empirical, i.e., observed validity and/or logical soundness. For example, the statement "cows do fly" can be empirically tested and rejected without much fanfare. Religious concepts, such as prayer, the existence of divine providence, and other moral recommendations may be subjected to empirical reasoning too, by examining the historical record and recurring to everyday human experiences.

Take Jesus saying in Matthew 5:29:

> *If your right eye causes you to sin, tear it out and throw it away. It is better for you to lose one of your members than to have your whole body thrown into Gehenna. And if your right-hand causes you to sin, cut it off and throw it away. It is better for you to lose one of your members than to have your whole body go into Gehenna.*

Was this passage meant to be taken literally, as Fundamentalism might do, or was Jesus seeking to instill fear by being distressfully hyperbolic about the evil consequences of sin? From an empirical standpoint, history ought to have recorded these extreme cases, and in the age of information-sharing, we must have heard or seen incidents detailing believers severing their body parts to avoid sin; but we do not.[2] This means that believers do not heed Jesus's warning; they are afraid of admitting it, or they simply never sin.

Even then, if we conclude that Jesus was being hyperbolic, the message is horrifying, likely leading believers and non-believers nowadays to disregard it as being too bizarre. Throughout, the purpose of empirical reasoning is to contribute toward a more realistic theology (may we call it "theological realism"?) that is in tune with a more credible view of faith, human nature, and Jesus' teachings.

The usefulness of content analysis and empirical reasoning lies in that they may validate and/or reject in a more precise manner traditional premises and assumptions that have been made about the public Jesus. To the extent that a more detached interpretation of the Gospels is attained, it will, in no uncertain terms, shed light on the relevance of Christianity on worldly or temporal matters as well as suggest a prognosis of what awaits the Christian faith in the years ahead. Examining the Gospels through the use of these two approaches may unearth the hidden message behind the written letter that in turn may lead to noteworthy questions: a) which are the most significant themes and concepts dealt with in the Gospels; and which are the least important ones; b) how are these themes described and used in the texts; c) what were their relationship with the Old Testament and with Mosaic Law; did Jesus boldly veto God's laws; d) are there conflicting teachings in the Gospels; e) how relevant are passages found int the texts in today's secularized world; f) and do the wording and the tone in the texts enhance or diminish the Gospels' appropriateness and acceptability to a postmodern audience.

In this work, content analysis and empirical reasoning operate as a social science barometer that quantitatively and qualitatively indicates the substance, magnitude, and relevance of the Gospels. Content analysis, as with any quantitative method, follows two essential rules of the scientific method: it allows for verification of the data and for the entire study to be reproduced by others, provided the same rules used in this work are employed. Additionally, the project is self-evolving; that is, new concepts that interest other students, or passages that may have been omitted, may be added to unearth a multiplicity of sub-messages that may otherwise remain hidden.

Notes:

1. Bernard Berelson, *Content Analysis in Communication Research,* (Glencoe: Free Press, 1952); Ole Holsti, *Content Analysis for the Social Sciences and Humanities,* (Reading: Addison-Wesley, 1969).

2. Eusebius, Bishop of Caesarea in the fourth century, suggested that Origen (184 AD-253AD), today a Father of the Church, had castrated himself to prevent the sin of lust. Origen denied the charge, going as far as to denounce the literalist interpretation of Jesus's words. John Anthony McGuckin, ed., *The Westminster Handbook to Origen,* (Louisville: Westminster John Knox Press, 2004), 65, https://books.google.com/books?id=riEdrWEDFq0C&pg=PA69&source=gbs_toc_r&cad=4#v=onepage &q&f=false (accessed 24 June 2016).

5 - A Profile of the Public Jesus

The first step in quantifying the results was to prepare a Profile of Jesus that would provide an overall portrayal of who he is according to how others perceived him and how he perceived himself. This was done by identifying, ranking, and examining eleven titles that are accorded to Jesus in the texts, ten of which are cited consistently in the Gospels. The eleventh title shall be dealt with separately at the end, as its relevance lies in its numerical insignificance despite being, perhaps, the most important title, suggesting a gradual evolution of the Christian faith. Numbers are expressed as *xt* for the times each title appears in the Gospels. The method note at the end of Table 1 describes how the data was set up.

The Public Jesus
Who is Jesus? How do others perceive him in the Gospels? Who does he say he is? The answers to these questions are complicated. As parallel examples, the President of the United States, albeit a very important person today, is known as President, Head of State, Commander in Chief, Head of the Free World, and Chief Executive. In public, however, no one calls him by any of these titles; instead, he is publicly addressed as 'Mr. President.' The pope is accorded at least eleven titles: His Holiness the Pope, Bishop of Rome, Vicar of Jesus Christ, Successor of St. Peter, Prince of the Apostles, Supreme Pontiff of the Universal Church, Patriarch of the West, Servant of the Servants of God, Primate of Italy, Archbishop and Metropolitan of the Roman Province, and Sovereign of Vatican City State. Yet, although the titles relate to the theological and historical designations of his duties, the pope is simply addressed as Holy Father or Your Holiness.

Jesus, on the other hand, is on a different scale. The various designations used in the Gospels reveal someone who is regarded by others (as well as someone who regards himself) as an extraordinary person. Surely, an account needs to be taken of the inherent bias in all four Gospels since, aside from being uncritical of Jesus, they were written to favorably spread a message about someone the authors revered as a remarkable human and/or divine being.

A simple Word Find procedure shows that the name Jesus (by itself) appears 593xt, i.e., times, in all four Gospels (Table 1D). His name is used almost exclusively by the authors in their narratives. But the people Jesus encounters throughout his public life seldom call him by his name. Instead, he is addressed by others, sees himself, and responds to or acknowledges others through ten different titles: Son of God, Lord, Teacher/Rabbi or Master, Son of Man, Savior/Redeemer, Messiah, King, Prophet, (M)aster—not a title but a self-projection of a powerful person with authority over others, and Son of David. Altogether, the Gospels mention these titles about Jesus 915xt (Table 1A). See Notes at the beginning of the Notes Section, chapter 5 for an explanation of how the tally was performed.

Additionally, the texts often depict Jesus as a fierce opponent of the Jewish religious authorities; (less often) as a magician, a super being, or a ghost; a religious teacher; an agent of Beelzebul; a disruptor of family institutions; an enigmatic person; a famous healer; being misunderstood by his disciples; being doubted by John the Baptist; favored by God, and fearless by Pontius Pilate. Overall, the data reveals multiple sub-personas all subsumed into one person.

Son of God

The title mostly attributed to Jesus in the Gospels is Son of God. Tallying this term includes similar titles, such as Son of the Most High, son of the Blessed One, Son of the Living God, Father's only son; being called my beloved/chosen Son by God; passages in which he forgives sins, an attribute of divinity in ancient Judaism; and instances in which Jesus identifies himself as Son of God through his close relationship with the Father, saying that he was sent by his Father, and that whoever knows him knows the Father.

In all four Gospels, people refer to or perceive Jesus as Son of God (38xt) while he perceives himself as Son of God (216xt). Such disparity in numbers is astonishing enough to raise questions; it suggests that despite Jesus's revealing himself to others incessantly, people do not seem to apprehend the message. Hence, what does it mean for Jesus to be the Son of God? Why is there such disproportion in numbers?

First, we must bear in mind the length of each Gospel (according to the NABRE Bible); the longest being Luke (23,745 words), followed by Matthew (21,932 words), then John (18,025 words), and the shortest being Mark (13,546 words).[1] **Table 1 Online** (www.RicardoPlanas.com/notes) offers a breakdown by author indicating that people perceive or address Jesus evenly: Mark (6xt), Luke (9xt), Matthew (8xt), and John (15xt), a total of 38xt. The authors' portrayal of how Jesus perceives himself (mostly in his own words), on the other hand, shows a surprising disparity. In Mark, there are (9xt) references to Jesus's divinity; in Luke (20xt); in Matthew (35xt); and in John (145xt). Although John's Gospel is considerably shorter than both Luke's and Matthew's, it records a disproportionate number of attributions to Jesus's divinity (3-4 times more) than each of the other authors mostly because of the number of times

John's Gospel references the Father-Son relationship. The term Son of God occurs only 9xt in John's Gospel. Nonetheless, there are approximately 145xt instances in which Jesus alludes to his intimate relationship with the Father. Why?

John's Gospel has a definite purpose in mind that the authors candidly expressed, and the results of content analysis confirm. This is found toward the end of the text:

> *Now Jesus did many other signs in the presence of [his] disciples that are not written in this book. But these are written that you may [come to] believe that Jesus is the Messiah, the Son of God, and that through this belief you may have life in his name (Jn 20:30-31).*

In line with the author's purpose, the text supports the oneness that exists between Father and Son. It is difficult not to notice as one goes through the text that John's Gospel seeks to deliver the message that, despite his incarnation and humanity, Jesus is divine and the only begotten son of God. The disproportionate number of references in John's Gospel seems to entail an effort at ensuring that the message would leave no doubt in the minds of its readers.

Being vastly different in style and purpose (exceedingly theological), does John's Gospel present a reasonable understanding of Jesus as the Son of God? Its forceful tendency to stress Jesus's divinity goes far beyond the already acknowledged predisposition of the synoptic texts to educate people in the faith. As might be expected, the results raise questions. Why would God reveal something so dissimilar decades after the synoptic texts were written? Was John's Gospel an attempt by God's hand to hammer into the human mind a certainty the synoptic texts did not adequately deliver? Biblical experts provide a reasonable explanation: *the fourth gospel is not simply history; the narrative has been organized and adapted to serve the evangelist's theological purposes as well... Such theological purposes have impelled the evangelist to emphasize motifs that were not so clear in the synoptic account of Jesus' ministry, e.g., the explicit emphasis on his divinity.*[2] This observation—aside from not speaking well about God's selection of those who wrote the Gospels, or the effectiveness of revelation--suggests that John's Gospel is a late clarification to the earlier texts, in which case, who is doing the clarification, God or human beings?

From a literary standpoint, John's Gospel is enlightening—despite its deeply mysterious opening--and rich in symbolism. To the pious or the uncritical mind, it is enthralling and highly believable. What makes the text effective rhetorically is the burst of repetitions of the same theme coming at the reader from different angles with the express intention of making the narrative noticeable, thus credible.

John's Gospel proved to be useful at the Council of Nicaea in 325 CE, two centuries after being written. The central problem brought to the council by bishops and Emperor Constantine had to do no less than with solving the theological question surrounding the divinity of Jesus and dealing with the Arian heresy that had divided Christianity and become a source of political instability within the empire. At Nicaea,

Jesus was officially (dogmatically) declared to be divine; it is challenging to imagine the adoption of the Nicene Creed—the crux of the Christian faith--without relying on John's Gospel.[3] This text was able to accomplish what the oral tradition and the three synoptic texts apparently had failed to do at the time. If this interpretation is accurate, it adds to the intellectual skepticism regarding Jesus's divinity; John's Gospel appears more as an instrument in settling a vexing religious dispute than to show God's revelation at work.

What Does it Mean to Be the Son of God?
Presbyterian pastor Mark Roberts believes that the historical records indicate that people did not regard Jesus as divine while he was alive; that when others referred to him as Son of God, *they were thinking of him as royalty, not divinity.* He finds the keys that according to him unveil evidence that Jesus is divine in the writings of Paul, who claims that Jesus is the Son of God.[4] Biblical experts also point to significant annotations revealing some inconsistencies with the use of the term Son of God. [5]

During the time of Jesus, Egyptian Pharaohs, Greek heroes, and Roman emperors were accorded the title Son of God and were worshipped as divine beings. The uniqueness and absurdity of these instances lie in temporal creatures being deified by other temporal creatures; that is, humans elevating other humans to a level of existence that is superior to them simply by acquiescing to the notion. In the case of Augustus and other Roman emperors, divinity was conferred by the Senate on basis of the individual's most notorious deeds. The title also applied to women. [6]

These attributions do not mean that Greeks and Romans did not believe in the existence of a supernatural being; they did, and in more than one, as polytheism characterized their beliefs. Judaism and Christianity rejected the worshipping of a multitude of gods. And while polytheism was not able to alter the monotheistic nature or the main tenets of the two religions, when the leaders of the emerging Christian sect moved to Rome, they co-opted many of the rituals, titles, and institutions from the Roman Empire, the Greeks, and the Egyptians. Historian Will Durant—once a Catholic seminarian turned unbeliever--kept an evenhanded affection toward the institution. He emphasized the syncretic nature of the nascent religion by observing, alas with some exaggeration, that "Christianity was the largest creation of the ancient pagan world." [7] Perhaps, a more accurate historical assessment would have indicated that Christianity grew and evolved within a non-Christian and anti-Christian social environment, and was, despite its attributed divine guidance, influenced and conditioned by those elements, just as it would have happened with any other human institution. Given the history of Christianity, the problematic evolution of its doctrine culminating with the Council of Nicaea in the fourth century, and the skepticism surrounding John's Gospel, theories suggesting that Christianity followed the Roman path in deifying Jesus acquire reasonable validity. [8]

The Son of God in the Gospels

In Mark, those who refer to Jesus as Son of God are the evangelist himself; the Spirit along with a voice from heaven; demons; and a Roman centurion. Jesus acknowledges the title by holding a conversation with a demon and does not object to the voice from the heavens referring to him as God's beloved son (Mk 1:9-11). Moreover, when he is brought before the Sanhedrin and asked by the high priest if he is the Messiah, the son of the Blessed One, Jesus does not hesitate in saying, *I am* (Mk 14:61-62). His admission sealed his fate; the religious authorities accused him of blasphemy, an offense punishable by death.

In Luke, angels, the holy Spirit, a voice from heaven, the evangelist, the devil, and demons refer to Jesus as Son of God too (Lk 1:30-35; 3:21-22; 3:23-38; 4:1-13; 4:41; 8:26-36; 9:35). When Jesus appears before the Sanhedrin, however, he does not sound as confident as in Mark. When asked if he is the *Son of God* he replies, *You say that I am* (Lk 22:70), a less than an affirmative statement that could be interpreted as saying, 'If you say so,' or 'You are the ones saying it.'[9] The Spanish translation is in contradiction with the English translation as it is noticeably more assertive--*Dicen bien, yo lo soy* (*You speak correctly, I am*).[10]

There is a passage in all three synoptic texts, however, in which Jesus indicates he is someone different from God, thereby seemingly contradicting his assertion about his divinity; when an official asks Jesus what he needs to do to inherit eternal life, Jesus replies, *Why do you call me good? No one is good but God alone* (Mk 10:17-18, Lk 18:18-19, Mt 19:16-17). Jesus, it appears, does not consider himself to be divine in this passage. Are the three authors of the synoptics aware of a discrepancy between the two passages, or is it possible that subsequent revisions of the texts simply circumvented these inconsistencies?[11]

In Matthew, as in Mark and Luke, angels, the *Spirit of God*, the devil, demons, and a centurion identify Jesus as Son of God (Mt 1:21; 3:16-17; 4:1-11; 8:28-34; 17:5; 27:39-43; 27:54). Additionally, during the crucifixion, a crowd and members of the Council of Elders mock Jesus by tossing the title to his face, *if you are the Son of God, come down from the cross!* (Mt 27:39-40). The disciples too, refer to Jesus as the Son of God after he appears before them walking on the sea and saves Peter from drowning: *Those who were in the boat did him homage, saying, Truly, you are the Son of God* (Mt 14:24-33). If Jesus has done something so amazing as to walk on the sea, it would be reasonable to conclude that he is endowed with superior powers. Nonetheless, it is possible that God gives Jesus these powers in the same manner as Jesus passes them down to his disciples.

In Matthew, Jesus asks the disciples who they believe he is. Peter does not seem to hesitate to answer, *You are the Messiah, the Son of the living God*. Jesus tells them that Peter's answer did not come from within him but was revealed to him by God (Mt 16:13-17). Peter's reply in Mark and Luke, however, is different; they only refer to Jesus as *the Messiah* (Mk 8:27) and *the Messiah of God* (Lk 9:20). If, indeed, Peter's answer came from God, as Jesus said, why would God reveal different versions to the authors of the Gospels? After all, it does make a difference if Jesus is a temporal or an eschatological Messiah, or if he is the *Son of God.* Matthew's addition (*the Son of the living God*), to Mark's assertion, is in line with the view held by many scholars that Matthew's statement is *a post-resurrectional confession of faith in Jesus as Son of the living God.*[12] If such is the case, can Matthew's citation be considered divine revelation, or is it simply an emotional reaction of faith?

It appears that either God reveals things differently to each author, which complicates human understanding, or that each author takes liberties in the name of revelation by adding words and ideas of their own. For example, in Matthew's narrative of Jesus's appearance before the Sanhedrin, Jesus is ordered to state *under oath* if he is *the Messiah, the Son of God.* On this occasion, as in Luke 22:66-70, Jesus issues a tepid reply, *You have said so,* except he follows by adding that he is the Son of Man (Mt 26:63-64).

Moreover, in Matthew, Jesus refers to God as his Father numerous times, indicating a strong and intimate relationship. Under these circumstances, it is perplexing that at the time of his death Jesus appears to forget who he is. Immediately after he pleads to *my Father* twice at Gethsemane not to allow him to be crucified (Mt 26:39-42), Matthew quotes Jesus calling on his father by his generic name: *My God, my God, why have you forsaken me?* (Mt 27:46). The use of the term *my God* sounds detached--something anyone would say nowadays—but not someone who regards himself as the Son of God, and certainly not at that moment. If Christian doctrine indicates that Jesus is divine since the beginning of time (John 1:1-5, Council of Nicaea), could the suffering he endured led him to forget he is God?[13]

It is likely that the postmodern (critical) reader will perceive major differences in Jesus's behavior through these answers and will fail to understand the rationale behind them. These doubts, however, are absent in John's Gospel. In John, it is Jesus who most often identifies himself as being one with the Father, although the author of the text contributes to attributing divinity to Jesus more than the synoptics' authors. Without delving into the veracity of the term, the way John bestows the title may be interpreted either as a religious honor or as inspired revelation:

> - *And the Word became flesh and made his dwelling among us, and we saw his glory, the glory as of the Father's only Son (Jn 1:14).*
> - *No one has ever seen God. The only Son, God, who is at the Father's side, has revealed him (Jn 1:18).*
> - *For God did not send his Son into the world to condemn the world, but that the world might be saved through him. Whoever believes in him will not be condemned, but whoever does not believe has already been condemned, because he has not believed in the name of the only Son of God (Jn 3:17-18).*
> - John indicates that the religious authorities are witnesses to Jesus admitting to being the Son of God (Jn 19:7), thus making him a rival of the Roman Emperor.

- Now Jesus did many other signs in the presence of [his] disciples that are not written in this book. But these are written that you may [come to] believe that Jesus is the Messiah, the Son of God, and that through this belief you may have life in his name (Jn 20:30-31).

It is difficult to surmise what to make of John's Gospel. Certainly, as the text indicates, its purpose is to persuade people to believe that Jesus is the Son of God. Biblical scholars gracefully refer to this gospel as a *developed theological reflection.*[14]

Additionally, John the Baptist testifies that Jesus *is the Son of God* (Jn 1:32-34) along with Nathanael who is suspicious that anything good could come from Jesus's childhood place; yet he seems flabbergasted when Jesus recognizes him before being introduced and exclaims, *Rabbi, you are the Son of God; you are the King of Israel* (Jn 1:45-49). Is Nathanael the unexpected subject of a private divine revelation, as it happened to Peter, or is he simply returning a temporal compliment? We simply do not know, although Jesus did not seem to mind being referred to as *Son of God.*

The same occurs with Martha, Lazarus's sister, who admits to Jesus that she believes he is the Messiah and the Son of God (Jn 11:25-27). The miracle of Lazarus's resurrection has not occurred yet, thus what is the basis for Martha's statement, divine revelation or hope amid sadness? Or is it perhaps that she feels confident having heard about Jesus's other miraculous deeds? Again, we do not know.

Returning to the content analysis tally, Jesus explicitly admits that he is the Son of God in all four Gospels. Six of these instances are strong affirmations (Mk 14:61-62; Mt 16:13-17; Jn 5:17-18; 5:25; 10:36-38; 11:4). But these are followed by two tepid replies (Lk 22:70; Mt 26:63-64); a passage which seems to contradict his previous affirmations by disavowing being God (Mk 10:17-18, Lk 18:18-19, Mt 19:16-17); and another in which he refers to 'his' father at the moment of his death simply as *my God* (Mt 27:46). Overall, these results weaken the meaning of the title.

The data supporting this title is similar to the Attributions of Divinity category in Table 2 that shows a significant ranking. This tally does not necessarily provide evidence that Jesus is God, but in line with the purpose of this work, it suggests what the Gospels say beyond what we think, feel, or believe they say.

Notes:
1. Once each gospel is copy and pasted as if it were one lengthy paragraph (no blank lines), Word will indicate the approximate number of words of each text.
2. Introduction to the Gospel of John, NEs' Bible.
3. For a line by line comparison of the original Nicene Creed in 325 and changes made at the First Council of Constantinople in 381, see New World Encyclopedia Contributors, "Nicene Creed," *New World Encyclopedia,* 8 January 2015,
http://www.newworldencyclopedia.org/entry/Nicene_Creed#The_original_Nicene_Creed_of_325
(accessed 18 December 2016).
4. None of Paul's letters cite that he was the subject of personal revelation from Jesus, other than his initial encounter with Jesus through a vision. Hence, Paul's affirmations are only the outcome of his faith. Roberts's view is found in, "Was Jesus Divine." For his use of these keys see note 9 in Chapter 1.
5. NEs' note, Mk 1:1 states that *some important manuscripts here* (in the passage) *omit the Son of God;* another note on Mt 16:13-17 indicates that Matthew's *addition of this exalted title* (Son of God) *to the Marcan confession eliminates whatever ambiguity was attached to the title Messiah.* That is, the terms

Messiah and Son of God connote the same meaning, although this 'revelation' does not come across so clearly in some manuscripts relating to Mark. Moreover, they point to a note on Jn 1:49 in which they agree half-heartedly with Roberts indicating that *this title* (Son of God) *is used in the Old Testament, among other ways, as a title of adoption for the Davidic king (2 Sm 7:14; Ps 2:7; 89:27), and thus here, with King of Israel, in a messianic sense.*

6. Henry Fairfield Burton, "The Worship of the Roman Emperors." *The Biblical World*, vol. 40, no. 2, 1912, 80–91. JSTOR, University of Chicago Press Journals, www.jstor.org/stable/3141986 (accessed 15 December 2016).

7. For glimpses of cultural syncretism see Will Durant, Vol III, pp. 575-672.

8. Bart Ehrman discusses several possible answers to the title of his book, all of which he claims to find some evidence in the historical past and the Gospels. His answers point to human, not divine, intervention: a) the human Jesus was exalted to be God by credulous followers with an agenda of their own; b) Jesus was human but his followers believed that at some point in time prior to his death he was adopted by God into his divinity; c) or that for political reasons (Emperor Constantine's concerns about the stability of his empire) and the Church's inability to theologically explain scriptural contradictions that had given rise to the Arian heresy, the theology of the Synoptic Gospels was marginalized in favor of the Gospel of John. Ehrman, *How Jesus Became God.*

9. In Luke, Jesus replies to the Elders that he is the *Son of Man* who *will be seated at the right hand of the power of God,* but his answer to the question about being the *Son of God* would sound evasive in today's era. Jesus makes a similar remark to Judas though in a different context: *You have said so.* NEs' note, Mt 26:25 qualifies the remark as being *a half-affirmative. Emphasis is laid on the pronoun and the answer implies that the statement would not have been made if the question had not been asked.*

10. *Biblia Latinoamericana,* (Madrid: Editorial San Pablo), http://www.sanpablo.es/biblia-latinoamericana (accessed 15 December 2016).

11. NEs provide an explanation that creates more doubt than certitude. In Mk 10:18 they state, *Jesus repudiates the term "good" for himself and directs it to God, the source of all goodness who alone can grant the gift of eternal life.* Does this mean that Jesus cannot do the same? If so, the statement seems to cast doubt on the concept of the Trinity.

12. Ibid., note Mt 16:13-17.

13. Catholic priest Raymond E. Brown, S.S., one of the first modern biblical scholars to utilize the historical-critical analysis, appears to have reached this view in "Does the New Testament Call Jesus God?" Theological Studies, 549, http://cdn.theologicalstudies.net/26/26.4/26.4.1.pdf (accessed 15 December 2016). John's Gospel appears to have been written forty to one hundred years following the death of Jesus. The Nicaean Council in 325 CE confirmed Jesus's divinity as expressed in the Nicene Creed it issued. The creed appears on the United States Conference of Catholic Bishops website, http://www.usccb.org/beliefs-and-teachings/what-we-believe/ (accessed 17 December 2016). The creed is shared by all major Christian denominations, albeit a significant controversy on the origin of 'the Son' that led to the East-West Schism in 1054 that remains to this date.

14. While pointing out in the Introduction to John's Gospel that this text was not the product of one author, NEs add that, *to a much greater degree, it is the product of a developed theological reflection and grows out of a different circle and tradition. It was probably written in the 90s of the first century. Critical analysis makes it difficult to accept the idea that the gospel as it now stands was written by one person.*

Lord

The term *Lord* is the second most used title in the Gospels when referring to Jesus. Usage of *Lord*, however, is riddled with inconsistencies. The term appears (171xt) in the texts; not all of them referring to Jesus. Approximately (70xt) refer to God, (93xt) to Jesus, and 8xt do not seem pertinent to its use in this work. At times, it is difficult to differentiate if the term applies to God or Jesus. For example, when John the Baptist cries out *Prepare the way of the Lord* (Mk 1:3), is he referring to God or Jesus? Presumably to Jesus,[1] but there is no certainty. While quoting David, the passage uses the term once in upper case, likely referring to God, and twice in lower case (Mk 12:36-37). Do any of the terms refer to Jesus? Probably not.

People refer to (or speak about) Jesus as *Lord* (90xt) while Jesus acknowledges the title (60xt). In a few instances, the term appears in lower case, and only those related to Jesus as lord are considered.

Since the term *Lord* is not only attributed to the divine in the Gospels but was (and is) used today as an expression of honor—akin to sire, it is difficult to understand when others regard Jesus as divine or if he is called *Lord* as a sign of respect, e.g., Vice-Admiral Horatio (Lord) Nelson, or Members of the House of Lords. In Spanish, we note similar predicaments. The term *el Señor* means the Lord in English and it is accorded not only to God and to Jesus, but even to the Virgin Mary, *Nuestra Señora,* as in Our Lady, even though divinity is not ascribed to Mary.

As we examine various passages, the differences in usage become apparent. Jesus picks grain on the Sabbath (supposedly a violation of Mosaic Law), and when he is criticized by the Pharisees, he tells them that as Lord of the Sabbath he has authority to do it (Mt 12:8), suggesting that he outranks the Jewish religious authorities. Is Jesus aware that he is acting in his capacity as God, or as a temporal messiah or prophet? He is not only referred to as *Lord* but even as *Lord and Messiah* (Lk 2:11). Yet, on one occasion he acknowledges that *The Lord our God is Lord alone* (Mk 12:29), supposedly not referring to himself but God. When the devil tempts Jesus to worship him, he replies that only *the Lord, your God* is to be worshipped (Lk 4:8, 12, Mt 4:7, 10). Jesus seems to be setting himself apart from God; unless he is saying that he alone should be worshipped as God. Moreover, as Jesus enters Jerusalem people chant, *Hosanna! Blessed is he who comes in the name of the Lord* (Mt 21:9, Mk 11:9-10), indicating that people perceive Jesus as someone who comes as God's representative, whether as the temporal messiah they are expecting or as a prophet, but not as God.

Being empirically reassured of the resurrection, Thomas says to Jesus, *My Lord and my God* (Jn 20:28), thereby attributing divinity to Jesus. Is Thomas the subject of a special revelation or does he conflate the two terms astonished by what he sees? Additionally, several people, including strangers, the father of a lunatic, a Roman centurion, a blind man, a Gentile woman, all call Jesus *Lord* (Mt 17:14, Lk 7:6, 18:35, Mk 7:26-28). Are these people subjects of divine revelation, or are they expressing respect? Neither the texts nor the Bible notes provide explanations to these questions.

It appears the term *Lord* is used in the texts interchangeably as an attribution of honor toward someone people hold in high regard; to designate the presence of the divine in the person of Jesus, and to refer to the God of the heavens. Almost everyone, the authors of the texts, his disciples, close relatives and friends (Elizabeth, Martha, Mary Magdalene), even pagans accord Jesus the honor. There are notable exceptions: Jesus never calls himself *Lord*, and never says *I am your Lord*; however, he acknowledges the honor by conversing with those who accord him the title. As may be expected, the texts indicate that the religious authorities show no deference to Jesus; it would have been nonsensical to show Jesus respect since they would be honoring someone they loath and wish to kill.

What does it mean to call Jesus Lord? Is there any significance in voicing this title? Two passages in the texts reveal an interesting trait in Jesus; he tells the crowd, *Why do you call me, 'Lord, Lord,' but not do what I command?* (Lk 6:46); and, *Not everyone who says to me, 'Lord, Lord,' will enter the kingdom of heaven, but only the one who does the will of my Father in heaven* (Mt 7:21-22). The sheer authority and power these words project are secularly speaking, more appropriate of a self-righteous, autocratic human person bent on making his authority felt; but within the context of the Gospels, the passages recall someone who believes has an intimate relationship with God. Is the combination of these two traits possible in Jesus? Perhaps the review of the other titles might suggest an answer. For the time being, it is important to recognize the duality that exists in the title and the confusion it may create among readers regarding his divinity.

Notes:
1. NEs' note on Luke 1:76 indicates that when Zechariah tells John the Baptist, you will go before the Lord, *the Lord is most likely a reference to Jesus* (Emphasis mine). However, in John 1:23, John the Baptist's remark, *I am the voice of one crying out in the desert, make straight the way of the Lord*, is attributed to Isaiah 40:3, and NEs suggest that the Lord, in this case, is God.

Teacher/Rabbi or Master

The terms Teacher/Rabbi/Master is the third most used title accorded to Jesus in the texts. These three terms have the same connotation, that of a religious educator. According to the count, others see Jesus as a Teacher (70xt); and by responding or simply acknowledging the title Jesus views himself as a teacher (75xt). Its total is almost identical to the Lord title.

Being called *teacher or master* at the time was particularly important (as it is today too) because it carried a combination of authority and power that were central in a theocratic society. As *teacher/master,* Jesus rivaled the religious authorities in Israel and was followed and listened to by thousands of people. According to the texts, the crowds *were astonished at his teaching*, for *he taught them as one having authority, and not as their scribes* (Lk 4:32; Mt 7:29).

How did Jesus become knowledgeable in 'Judaic Studies' has been the subject of speculation, as he was not known to have received a degree in higher education or been ordained. The texts suggest he had some schooling in his religion.[1] His professorial demeanor was surprising even to his neighbors who wonder where he had obtained so much wisdom. After all, *Is he not the carpenter's son?* (Mt. 13:54-55).

There is no doubt that Jesus saw himself and acted as a teacher. Others too perceived him as a teacher once his fame as a preacher extended throughout the land. He used his knowledge and personal interpretation of Judaism to articulate God's path to righteousness. He spent a greater part of his time combating religious deception, the teachings of the religious authorities that distorted God's image among his people. Eventually, his teachings contributed to his death.

Almost everyone called him *teacher*, including Pharisees, Herodians, scribes, Sadducees, even Judas, at the moment he delivered Jesus to the religious authorities (Mk 12:13, 12:18, 12:28, Lk 11:45,19:39, Jn 8:3, Mt 22:23-24, 26:47). He asserted himself—*You call me 'teacher' and 'master,' and rightly so, for indeed I am* (Jn 13:13), even though he was reluctant to call himself *Lord*. Nevertheless, he tells his disciples not to use the title among them, indicating that there is to be only one teacher, supposedly him (Mt 23:8).

Jesus's teachings are among his greatest legacies. His role as Teacher/Master retains extraordinary relevance nowadays, being advocated by all Christian institutions and over two billion people. As a title, *Teacher* is certainly not as controversial as *Lord*, although perhaps it has less religious significance when compared with the other titles. It is his teachings, however, that are more questionable today because they are presented as absolute truths arising from being the Son of God. Secularization and theological pluralism (perhaps lesser evils than religious wars) today present themselves as major challenges to the absoluteness of his teachings. Their future relevance may depend on what people believe to be Jesus's identity.

Notes:
1. Meier, *A Marginal Jew*, vol I, chapter 9.

Son of Man

The term *Son of Man* appears (82xt) in all four texts; it is fourth in the count ranking. It is also the most puzzling of Jesus's titles, largely because of its meaning, its attributes, and because it is the name he chooses for himself over all others (79xt). Only in three instances do others refer to Jesus as the Son of Man; Mark (Mk 8:31, 9:9), and *two men in dazzling garments* following the resurrection, in Luke (Lk 24:7).

It is beyond the objective of this book to unravel God's mysteries, but it is worth noting the enigmatic and incomprehensible sense behind the term. The term appears over 200xt in the Old Testament namely to designate a human being; someone different from a supernatural entity that had no special relevance in Ancient Judaism other than a respectful way to address a prophet, or possibly in reference to Michael, an angel with a human appearance.[1] Nonetheless, as indicative of a messiah who will rule over all nations on earth, the term is found in an obscure passage in the Book of Daniel seemingly derived from visions that Daniel had regarding the liberation of Israel from oppression six centuries before the birth of Jesus:

As the visions during the night continued, I saw coming with the clouds of heaven One like a son of man. When he reached the Ancient of Days and was presented before him, He received dominion, splendor, and kingship; all nations, peoples and tongues will serve him. His dominion is an everlasting dominion that shall not pass away, his kingship, one that shall not be destroyed (Dn 7:13-14).

Daniel does not indicate what he means by *One like a son of man.* If the term implies a sovereign king who would liberate Israel, Daniel's vision had to wait 2500 years before Israel became a sovereign state, although without Jesus as king. Even now, Jesus remains an obscure figure in Judaism and other parts of the world. Furthermore, as it will be noted ahead, throughout his lifetime, Jesus remained utterly unconcerned about the temporal plight of his people.

Why would Jesus choose a cryptic title for himself (so common yet so unique) to communicate his plan of salvation to humans with a limited capacity to understand? In the Gospels, the term indicates that Jesus was not simply 'a human being.'[2] While calling himself Son of Man, Jesus:

- insinuates he is greater than Solomon (Mt 12:42).
- claims authority to forgive sins on earth, an attribute understood to belong only to God (Mk 2:10; Lk 5:24; Mt 9:26).
- considers himself to be Lord of the Sabbath, with authority to bend the rules (Mk 2:28; Lk 6:5; Mt 12:8).
- predicts his passion and resurrection (Mk 8:31; Lk 9:22; Mt 12:40; Jn 12:23-24).
- declares that anyone who denies the Son of Man would be condemned (Mk 8:38; Lk 12:8).
- manifests that his mission is to redeem many (Mk 10:45, Lk 19:10, Mt 20:28); whether such a mission is temporal or eschatological will be discussed later.
- indicates that he not only would initiate and lead the Second Coming (Mk 13:26-27, Lk 13:27, Lk 17:30, Mt 13:41) but would preside the Final Judgment too (Mt 25:31-32).
- claims that everything written by the prophets about the Son of Man will be fulfilled (Lk 18:31), even though no other prophet, other than Daniel, speaks specifically about the Son of Man.
- acknowledges being given the possession of life in himself, and the power to exercise judgment because he is the Son of Man (Jn 5:26-27).
- claims that unless people *eat the flesh of the Son of Man and drink his blood,* they have no life within them. (Jn 6:52-54); his teachings bewilder people who ask, *Who is this Son of Man?* (Jn 12:34).
- combines (or conflates) being the Messiah and/or the Son of God with the Son of Man several times (Mk 14:61-62, Mt 16:13-20 Lk 22:67-70, Mt 26:63-64, Jn 9:35-37). In one instance, being told by a disciple that he is the Son of God and King of Israel, he does not object but instead describes himself as the Son of Man (Jn 1:48-51).

Titles are supposed to tell us something about the identity or demeanor of the person. Jesus opts to address himself as Son of Man in the third person, which if done today would be unquestionably odd. Moreover, it is ironic that Jesus's most favored title is practically ignored nowadays, suggesting its irrelevance, even though it remains significant within small theological circles.

Notes:

1. *BibleGateway.com* (for the count); Emil G Hirsch, "Son of Man," *Jewish Encyclopedia,* *http://www.jewishencyclopedia.com/articles/13913-son-of-man* (accessed April 11, 2020).

2.Apologists indicate that during Jesus's time, people did not seem to recognize or understand the term, and even today its meaning remains uncertain. "Jesus the Son of Man," *Loyola Press,* https://www.loyolapress.com/our-catholic-faith/scripture-and-tradition/jesus-and-the-new-testament/who-do-you-say-that-i-am-names-for-jesus/jesus-the-son-of-man (accessed April 11, 2020). According to Roberts, Jesus *seems to take the attributes of God* himself. Roberts, "Was Jesus Divine;" NEs agree that the term defines not only a human being but *a unique figure of extraordinary spiritual endowments, who will be revealed as the one through whom the everlasting kingdom decreed by God will be established.* Note, Mk 8:31.

Savior and Redeemer

In this section, the terms Savior and Redeemer are used synonymously, as they both have similar religious and worldly implications. The dictionary defines a savior as, *someone who saves from danger or destruction or harm*, and the term redeemer as *to free from what distresses or harms* or *to free from captivity by payment of ransom.*[1] The titles denote valor, heroism, and selflessness, as the person chooses to place the wellbeing of others ahead of his or her own, even being willing to give up his life to redeem, thus save them. In secular terms, a soldier, a police officer, or even a civilian who gives up his life to save his companions, hostages, or innocent people may be properly regarded as a temporal savior and a redeemer.

According to the Gospels, these titles seem to befit Jesus's eschatological and temporal roles as well as his role as Messiah, thus complicating the understanding of the three titles. Being Savior and Redeemer arguably outweighs the significance of all other titles (perhaps including Son of God), namely because they convey a mission that in the Christian religion has portentous consequences; in Christianity, Jesus is referred to as Savior and Redeemer because he saves humankind (or part of it) from the possibility of eternal condemnation while offering the opportunity to enjoy eternal happiness. This is a desire or hope likely shared by billions throughout the world, including non-Christians.

The two titles are interrelated; Jesus is savior because he redeems.[2] This view presumes that Jesus not only died for the sins of some, many, or all of humanity but that he must undergo death to atone for the offenses committed either by perfect beings (the first generation of humans as told in Genesis) or by flawed humans that commit wrongdoing while evolving into a higher species (the evolutionary process).

Tallying these two titles presents some difficulties because the Gospels conflate temporal and eschatological connotations with the Messiah title. Luke, for example, narrates a passage in which the angel of the Lord refers to Jesus as Savior, Messiah, and Lord (Lk 2:10-11). The official definition of the titles Savior and Redeemer according to the Christian faith dispenses with their earthly role, accepting instead a process that finds its conclusion at the end of time. As it will be noted in the Messiah section, the texts are less than clear, as they present two types of Messiahs, the one many Israelites are awaiting to liberate them from temporal oppression, and the one that sidesteps subjugation in favor of eternal bliss after death.

If Jesus is presumed to have given humanity (or a part of it) the opportunity to be saved eternally, it would be reasonable to think that all four Gospels would stress the two titles. Yet the opposite is true. The term *savior* occurs only (3xt) while *redeemer* does not appear in any of the texts, except perhaps indirectly as an expected temporal redeemer (Lk 24:21).

There are several passages in which Jesus describes himself as the giver of eternal life and as having power over life. If we add these passages together, this title would rank fifth, behind Son of God, Lord, Teacher, and Son of Man. Doing it, however, requires special attention because the numbers are highly skewed due to the disproportionate number of passages in John's Gospel (as opposed to the synoptics), in which Jesus refers to having the power to grant eternal life to those that believe in him. Table 1A (online) indicates that in John's text, other people perceive Jesus as savior/redeemer 7xt (mostly in temporal terms); Jesus, however, presents himself in this role 35xt in John's Gospel alone, as opposed to 19xt in the synoptics. The numbers indicate that the ranking of Jesus as Savior and Redeemer increases mainly on account of John's Gospel, suggesting that its authors (or God) made an awkward correction to the synoptics.

Temporal or eschatological savior?

How are these two titles used in the Gospels? In Luke, the angel Gabriel tells Mary that she will bear a son who is to be a temporal ruler of the house of Jacob and assume the throne of David; however, she refers to God as *my savior* on earthly terms, as a divine power that will oppose the enemies of Israel.[3] Zechariah too refers to God in temporal terms, as the one who *brought redemption to his people* whom he *rescued from the hand of enemies.* Moreover, although this passage states that Jesus will provide *knowledge of salvation through the forgiveness of sins,* (Lk 1:67-79),[4] replying to the disciples' question, *who then can be saved?* Jesus admits that he is not the one who saves, but God (Mt 19:24-29). In these passages, God, not Jesus, is Savior. Understanding of the term is further complicated by the many times Jesus uses the phrase *You are saved*, not to indicate that the person has attained eternal salvation, but merely healed from his or her infirmities (Mk 5:25-34, 10:49:52, Lk 7:1-10, 7:36-50, 8:36, 8:43-48, 17:11-19, 18:35-42, Mt 9:18-22).

The passages in Luke dealing with Simeon, the prophetess Anna (Lk 2:25-32, 2:36-38), and the two disciples on the road to Emmaus (Lk 24:13-27), denote a temporal savior or redeemer, the type of earthly redemption and salvation the Israelites were expecting of a temporal Messiah. John the Baptist is an exception in Luke when he refers to Jesus as someone in which *all flesh shall see the salvation of God,* suggesting eternal salvation through the forgiveness of sins (Lk 3:1-6). In Matthew, the angel of the Lord is more explicit, although he contradicts John the

Baptist by pointing to Jesus as someone who *will save his people* (not all flesh) *from their sins* (Mt. 1:18-21), thereby denoting Jesus as a supernatural savior. Additionally, Matthew mistakenly attributes Jesus a redemptive role by healing human infirmities (Mt 8:16-17), a passage similar to a character in Isaiah (chapter 53); except that no resurrection occurs in the latter.[5]

John's Gospel, meanwhile, presents a brief and mixed view of how others view Jesus. In his narrative, John the Baptist twice refers to Jesus as the *Lamb of God who takes away the sin of the world* (Jn 1:29-35), an allusion to a sacrificial ritual of animals practiced by many Israelites at the time to atone for their sins. Moreover, John's Gospel refers to Jesus as a savior (Jn 3:17). Although the passage does not indicate what type of salvation Jesus is offering, it may be surmised (given the overall content of John's Gospel) that he is not referring to an earthly activity, but to a process that begins on earth and is finalized on Judgment Day.

Nonetheless, there is a group, of Samaritans no less, that upon meeting Jesus are so captivated by his teachings that they proclaim him, *truly the savior of the world* (Jn 4:39-42). This is surprising since Jesus previously slights the way Samaritans worship God by insinuating that Jewish worshipping is superior to that of the Samaritans since *salvation is from the Jews* (Jn 4:22). In the same chapter, Jesus acknowledges to the Samaritan woman that he is the Messiah (Jn 4:25-26). Since Samaritans at the time shared the Israelite view of the earthly Messiah, they likely understood the *savior* title as having temporal connotations.

It is Jesus, however, who in John's Gospel emphasizes his roles as Savior and Redeemer, albeit he does not specifically refer to himself by any of these two titles. Instead, his sayings constantly refer to a supernatural salvation (eternal life) that only he can concede (Jn 3:14-15, 4:13-14, 5:21-22, 24-29, 39-40, 6:27, 35-40, 48-51, 53-58, 7:37-38, 8:12, 51, 10:11-18, 27-28, 11:25-26). Additionally, Jesus's own words attest to part of his mission; as the Son of Man, he does not come to be served but to give his life as a ransom for *many* people (Mk 10:45, Mt 20:28, Mk 14:24, Lk 22:20, Mt 26:28).[6] But what exactly is this type of ransom? It may very well be that his death will atone for the sins of humanity. How or why humans sin, however, is not clear, since Jesus never refers to Original Sin. All he says is that he will give his *flesh for the life of the world* (Jn 6:51), and the sheep (Jn 10:11-18). Metaphorically, John the Baptist depicts Jesus as the sacrificial *Lamb of God who takes away the sins of the world* (Jn 1:29), a concept that would not be understood by Jews because its supernatural undertones were not part of their beliefs.

A human sacrifice to satisfy humanity's offense would not be regarded today as being original, since it was practiced to placate the gods, particularly among the Mayans and the Aztecs in North America. Neither would it be unique as a willful act personally undertaken to save others (as it has happened during wartime). What may distinguish Jesus's action from temporal acts is the scope and magnitude of the outcome, i.e., all of humanity or many are being saved for all eternity. Nevertheless,

Jesus does not explain why he is doing it (other than it is the Father's will or to fulfill the scriptures); nor does he make any references to the cosmic offense committed by the Adams and Eves in Paradise against God. This lack of clarity does not reject a supernatural redemption, but neither does it affirm it.

To compound the question, the passage when Jesus enters the synagogue and states that he is fulfilling Isaiah's prophecy has temporal connotations (Lk 4:18-19). Countering this passage, Jesus becomes an eschatological savior when upon noticing Zacchaeus's repentance of his sins he observes that, *salvation has come into his house ... For the Son of Man has come to seek and to save what was lost,* (Lk 19:1-10); a possible cosmic allusion to salvation. Furthermore, Jesus speaks about events resembling the Second Coming stating that when it happens, one's *redemption is at hand* (Lk 21:25-28), though it is not clear what his words mean since redemption already takes place once his blood is initially shed.

In Luke, following his resurrection, Jesus corrects the Emmaus disciples indicating that, according to the scriptures, it was *necessary that the Messiah should suffer these things and enter into his glory* (Lk 24:26). This idea, however, does not appear in the Old Testament or any other Jewish literature at the time.[7] Moreover, it does not denote a clear reference to eschatological redemption.

In John's Gospel, Jesus is emphatic that his mission is to obey the Father's will, which is to perish for the sins of (some, many, or all). His statements suggest he is a savior and a redeemer (Jn 6:51). He insists he is the good shepherd who *lays down his life for the sheep* (Jn 10:11-18). He recognizes that he needs to die—like a grain of wheat—to produce much fruit (Jn 12:24), and he assures others that he does *not come to condemn the world but to save the world* (Jn 12:47).

Is Jesus Redeemer and Savior? It is far from clear within the context of the texts if his words have a temporal or an eschatological significance. If his mission had a temporal purpose, it did not materialize; if it was eschatological, it shall become known in the afterlife.

In Matthew, Jesus tells us more, albeit in a cryptic manner, about his title as redeemer. He tells his disciples that he will be executed, and when he is about to be apprehended by the Jewish religious authorities, he offers no resistance. He makes a statement indicating that he cannot or will not fight off the process that is leading up to his crucifixion because *all this has come to pass that the writings of the prophets may be fulfilled* (Mt 26:56). His words suggest that he is allowing himself to be crucified just to prove the prophets right, a motive that devalues his redemption. It would have been different, however, if he had said that the Father had given him a mission that he had to follow, regardless of how much he disliked it.

Additional evidence pointing to an eschatological Savior and Redeemer shows up when Jesus points to the Father's will in several instances by relying on an Old Testament term, *cup,* referring to the destiny God assigns to Jesus. He tells the sons of the Zebedee (their mother in Matthew) that he has been given the task to drink from

God's cup of wrath, God's punishment to the wicked, as a means to take upon himself their sins to redeem (save) them (Mk 10:39, Lk 22:41-42, Mt 20:22-23, Jn 18:11).[8]

Moreover, Jesus tells his disciples that everything written about him in the law of Moses, in the prophets, and the psalms must be fulfilled; accordingly, repentance, for the forgiveness of sins, would be preached in his name to all the nations, beginning from Jerusalem (Lk 24:44-47). This is an enigmatic statement. It alludes to an eschatological savior and redeemer stemming from a Jesus who cannot make up his mind as to whether his mission is to save the Israelite people or all humanity, and whether to save them temporally or eschatologically.

A Secular Outlook

The traditional Christian answer for the last two millennia is that humanity's offense to God, something akin to a bacteria (a living organism) infecting (disobeying) his master, could only have been remedied by eternally condemning the bacteria or by the master demanding that his son be executed as a means to satisfy the bacteria's offense. Is there in human history a similar act—even an imagined one—to which humans might be able to relate? The Christian explanation, accepted by billions as the ultimate act of love, provides atheists and agnostics with fodder to exploit. God asks Abraham to prove his loyalty by asking him to sacrifice his son; now the same God asks for the ultimate sacrifice of his son. Could God be as egocentric as the Old Testament tells us? Given the enormous gap that according to Christian standards exists between humans and God, it seems incongruous that God's ego could be bruised by human action to the point of having to ask his son to die to repair what flawed humans do. What would billions of non-Christians think of this God?

There is, on the other hand, a theological explanation that suggests that Jesus's crucifixion was not cosmologically necessary. His death, according to the Christian faith, is simply proof that God's love for humanity is so great that he offers his son's life *as the ransom that would free men from the slavery of sin.*[9] Clearly, this statement requires further explanation since it is evident that humanity is still enslaved to sin.

Content analysis results indicate that the Gospels did not regard these titles as significant, except for the corrective action taken by John's Gospel. Instead, it has been up to church authorities to accord these titles to Jesus, raising an interesting question; who is responsible for the correction? Having to rectify himself would not speak highly of God; if, on the other hand, human intervention is responsible for the correction, the reliability of revelation comes into question.

Notes:

1. *Merriam-Webster Dictionary,* online, s.v. "savior, redeemer."

2. *Christ paid the price of his own sacrificial death on the cross to ransom us, to set us free from the slavery of sin, thus achieving our redemption.* Glossary from the Catechism of the Catholic Church, Diocese of Madison, https://madisondiocese.org/documents/2016/10/Glossary.pdf (accessed 22 March 2017). The statement, although coming from an official Catholic document likely finds agreement among all mainstream Protestant denominations.

3. *He has shown might with his arm, dispersed the arrogant of mind and heart. He has thrown down the rulers from their thrones but lifted up the lowly. The hungry he has filled with good things; the rich he has sent away empty. He has helped Israel his servant, remembering his mercy, according to his promise to our fathers, to Abraham and to his descendants forever.* (Lk 1:51-54).

4. NEs' note, Luke 1:68-79 reads, *Like the canticle of Mary (Lk 1:46–55) the canticle of Zechariah is only loosely connected with its context. Apart from Lk 1:76–77, the hymn in speaking of a horn for our salvation (Lk 1:69) and the daybreak from on high (Lk 1:78) applies more closely to Jesus and his work than to John. Again like Mary's canticle, it is largely composed of phrases taken from the Greek Old Testament and may have been a Jewish Christian hymn of praise that Luke adapted to fit the present context by inserting Lk 1:76–77 to give Zechariah's reply to the question asked in Lk 1:66.* It should be noted that NEs attribute these insertions to the hands of humans to fit their narratives. Their motives question whether divine revelation takes place.

5. Ibid., note on Mt 8:17 indicates that Matthew considers the infirmities as physical afflictions. However, Is 53:3-13 regards these infirmities as sins.

6. Whether the term 'many' means that Jesus was limiting redemption to some people or not is unnecessarily confusing. Popes Benedict and Francis chose, for the sake of authenticity, to leave it confusingly rather than to actualize it. As it stands doctrinally, the term implies 'for all,' despite other passages in the texts that clearly indicate otherwise. Pope Francis's explanation, however, gets in the way of what redemption means, suggesting a two-stage process. See "Pope Francis sides with Benedict by saying Christ shed blood 'for many,'" *Catholic Herald*, November 4, 2017, https://catholicherald.co.uk/pope-francis-sides-with-benedict-by-saying-christ-shed-blood-for-many/ (accessed 26 March 2017).

7. NEs' note, Lk 24:26.

8. Ibid., note, Mark 10:38-40: *In Jesus' case, this involves divine judgment on sin that Jesus the innocent one is to expiate on behalf of the guilty (Mk 14:24; Is 53:5). His baptism is to be his crucifixion and death for the salvation of the human race; cf. Lk 12:50.*

9. *Although one single theandric operation, owing to its infinite worth, would have sufficed for Redemption, yet it pleased the Father to demand and the Redeemer to offer His labours, passion, and death.* Joseph Sollier, "Redemption." *Catholic Encyclopedia*, www.newadvent.org/cathen/12677d.htm (accessed 26 March 2017). *As the ransom that would free men from the slavery of sin* is found in *The Catechism of the Catholic Church*, 601, CCC (Vatican City: Vatican Editorial Library, English version, 1994), http://www.vatican.va/archive/ccc_css/archive/catechism/index/a.htm (accessed 26 March 2017).

Messiah

From a Jewish and Christian perspective, the term *Messiah*, i.e., the anointed one, means not only that someone is chosen or appointed to a specific position of great authority and historical significance, but that it is God who does the anointment. While Jews do not believe that Jesus is the Messiah, Christians do, largely because there are innumerable voices in the Gospels, including Jesus, that say so. Table 1A shows that others in the Gospels believe or refer positively to Jesus as Messiah 31xt, and Jesus acknowledges the title 26xt. Despite its theological importance, this title is less significant in the Gospels than Son of God, Teacher, Lord, Son of Man, and Savior and Redeemer. Jewish belief in the Messiah at the time of Jesus was crucial because it not only created an earthly hope among the Israelites; it also tested God's credibility since he had promised his people a liberator.

There seem to be numerous prophecies in the Old Testament regarding a God-sent Messiah. Among the most cited are, Isaiah 7:14, 40:3, and 53:3-7, Micah 5:2, and Zechariah 9:9. A former president of an evangelical seminary cites authors, including himself, who have identified hundreds of messianic predictions, adding that, *few will dispute that there are at least six direct Messianic predictions in the Pentateuch.*[1]

These passages describe, to some extent, aspects that appear to fit Jesus's life. The question, however, is whether they provide evidence beyond a reasonable doubt that Jesus is the Messiah. It is possible that an exegete deeply engaged in cryptoanalysis may arrive at these conclusions, although it would suggest that Christianity requires that believers and non-believers become theological experts to grasp what seems well hidden in the texts. Once again, the texts' enigmatic nature betrays a sensible understanding of something supposedly so vital to humankind and faith.

The texts indicate (as previously seen in the last sections) that Jesus admits to being Son of God, Son of Man, and Messiah, all at once, each one having temporal and supernatural connotations that tend to complicate the identity of his public persona. The usage of the term, nonetheless, as with previous titles, is inconsistent. It is well-known in Christian tradition-- and passages abound in the texts--that God had promised a temporal Messiah to the Jewish people. They had been suffering oppression for a long time, and now the yoke of the Roman Emperor subjugated them. It is within this context that Mary in her Canticle refers to God's promise in earthly terminology:

> [to help Israel his servant] ... *to use his power to disperse the arrogant of mind and heart ... throw down the rulers from their thrones and lift up the lowly ... fill the hungry with good things and send the rich away empty (Lk 1:46-55).*

Zechariah too, in his Canticle to God, once he is made aware of God's plans for his son John the Baptist, refers to God's temporal actions:

> *the God of Israel has visited and brought redemption to his people. He has raised up a horn for our salvation within the house of David his servant ... salvation from our enemies and from the hand of all who hate us, to show mercy to our fathers and to be mindful of his holy covenant and of the oath he swore to Abraham our father, and to grant us that, rescued from the hand of enemies...* (Lk 1:67-76).

Strangely, Zechariah's canticle indicates that God's design is to attain peace (which the Israelites had not been experiencing), *through the forgiveness of sins* (Lk 1:77). This phrase is an anomaly, as it pertains more to an eschatological or supernatural Messiah. Also, it is difficult to see how forgiveness of sins would have brought about temporal peace, unless it referred to the possibility that, had the Israelites repented, God would have sent a plague to destroy Roman oppression, as he did with the Egyptian rulers.

Simeon, a righteous and devout man eagerly awaiting the consolation of Israel (Lk 2:25-32), and Anna the prophetess, give thanks to God and refer to the child that all had been waiting to redeem Jerusalem, likely from the subjugation they were suffering (Lk 2:36-38). Again, this view refers to what the Jewish people had been promised: liberation from oppression.[2] Luke tells us about Jesus who, upon entering a synagogue in Nazareth, is handed a scroll of Isaiah announcing *glad tidings to the poor; proclaiming liberty to captives, recovery of sight to the blind,* and *to let the oppressed go free....* Upon finishing reading the scroll, he says, *today this scripture passage is fulfilled in your hearing,* seemingly indicating that the nature of Jesus's mission is temporal and that he intends to fulfill it (Lk 4:16-21).

Other passages, however, appear to cloud Jesus's role as Messiah. At one point, Jesus is concerned that the religious authorities share the notion that David is the Messiah, but Jesus confronts them with a riddle dispelling this view (Mk 12:35-37, Lk 20:41-44, Mt 22:41-46). He does not clarify the riddle, suggesting that his statement is more of a rhetorical question he uses to confuse the authorities. Furthermore, in a most vexing passage that has repercussions in postmodern times, Jesus makes it a point to warn about false messiahs indicating these impersonators *will perform signs and wonders in order to mislead.* Nonetheless, he offers no indicators that would allow people to identify these false impostors (Mk 13:21-22, Mt 24:4-5, 23-25). As a result, there have been countless prophets since his death, each suggesting different interpretations of his words, causing confusion and division among Christians.

In Matthew's genealogy of Jesus, the evangelist writes, *of her* (Mary) *was born Jesus who is called the Messiah* (Mt 1:16 emphasis mine). Does this description suggest divine revelation or is it a rumor that is being spread? And what kind of Messiah will Jesus be? According to Herod's chief priests and scribes, he is to be a temporal leader, *a ruler, who is to shepherd my people Israel* (Mt 2:1-6). On the other hand, three synoptic texts allude to John the Baptist who, per the 'the angel of the Lord,' (Lk 1:17) calls for preparing *the way of the Lord* by making his paths straight. These passages do not mention Jesus as Messiah and are not included in the tally. The passages do not clarify whether the way of the Lord refers to God or Jesus; much less whether Jesus is within this context a divine or a human envoy (Mk 1:2-3, Lk 3:4, Mt 3:1-3).[3]

Other passages reveal uncertainty about Jesus's role. Andrew, the disciple, while referring to Jesus, is credited with finding the Messiah first (Jn 1:40); both Peter and Martha confess Jesus is the Son of God and the Messiah (Mt 16:16, Jn 11:27). Some people tend to believe Jesus is the Messiah (Jn 6:14, 7:31, 7:46, 11:27); others are not certain (Jn 4:29, 7:25-27, 7:41-2); some are fearful to acknowledge it fearing reprisals from the Jewish religious authorities (Jn 9:20-22); some even want to kill Jesus, perhaps for either impersonating or believing he is the Messiah (Jn 7:25-26); and yet others simply do not believe him (Jn 10:24-26, 12:34-37). Jesus, on the other hand, insists that he is the Messiah (Mt 23:10, Jn 4:25-26); but he *rebukes* his disciples telling them not to divulge his identity (Mk 8:27-30, Lk 9:18-21, Mt 16:13-20). The secret, however, is not well kept, for the crowd that welcomes Jesus into Jerusalem identifies him as someone resembling a temporal Messiah: Mark relates him to David's kingdom (Mk 11:8-10); Luke adds a new title, king, (Lk 19:38);[4] in Matthew, the crowd identifies Jesus only as the Son of David and the prophet from Nazareth (Mt 21:9-11); but in John, he is welcomed in the name of the Lord and as king of Israel (Jn 12:12-14). These are all earthly—not eschatological--titles.

Pontius Pilate publicly refers to Jesus as the Messiah, likely not caring or believing it (Mt 27:17, 22). Interestingly, on the cross, the religious authorities mock Jesus, daring him to come down from the cross if, indeed, he is the Messiah (Mk 15:31-32). And in Luke, one of the criminals who is being crucified with Jesus tells him derisively, *Are you not the Messiah? Save yourself and us* (Lk 23:35-39). This is significant because it suggests that the Messiah is not a temporal being, but someone with supernatural powers (or someone God would protect) that would enable him to save himself and others from physical death. Thus, it appears that Jesus's identity as a type of eschatological Messiah had become well known.

Luke provides additional evidence that Jesus's followers are aware of his earthly expectations. Disguised as a resurrected Jesus, he encounters two of his disciples on the route to Emmaus, feigns ignorance about himself, and asks them who this Jesus is. They tell him that he was the one they were hoping *would be the one to redeem Israel,* in the temporal sense of the term (Lk 24:19).

Many of the above passages suggest that Jesus intends to fulfill Jewish social, political, and religious expectations of being freed from oppression so they can worship their God in peace. Is this the way Jesus proceeds? According to other passages in the texts, the answer is a resounding No. To begin with, if Jesus were to have fulfilled Jewish expectations, he would have been vociferously critical of Roman oppression and led the Israelites to an insurrection—or at least civil disobedience-- anything that would show that he empathized with the plight of his people. Probably these actions would have led him to be crucified by Pontius Pilate much sooner, but likely he would have been remembered as a hero to his people.

The religious authorities bring the accusation to Pontius Pilate that Jesus is the Messiah (not that Pilate could care since he is not Jewish), and that he calls himself a king (something that would worry Pilate). Regardless of whether Pilate takes him seriously or not, he simply bows to the wishes of the Jewish authorities-led mob. Jesus is going to be crucified because, after being apprehended and taken before his accusers, he admits without hesitation that he is *the Messiah, the son of the Blessed One* (in Mark only), although the authorities refuse to believe him (Lk 22:67). Nonetheless—without being asked—Jesus adds that he is the Son of Man who would lead the Second Coming while seated at the right hand of God (Mk 14:61-62, Lk 22:66-71, Mt 26:64). This extraordinary remark transforms his temporal messianic role. From then on, any talk about temporal redemption, consolation, or liberation becomes tied to eschatological salvation from sin that will include Gentiles as well. This remark leads to the following question: if Jesus emphasizes that he is doing the Father's will and does not want to deviate from it, why would God promise his people a temporal liberation, then send his Messiah, who happens to be his son and in whom he is well pleased, to do something entirely different? The Gospels do not explain what appears to be a 'bait and switch' tactic that alters Jesus's mission.[5]

There are additional instances in the texts suggesting temporal salvation that will be reviewed under the category dealing with Salvation; however, passages referring to an eschatological Messiah require further attention. In Luke, an angel is the first one to proclaim the good news *for all the people. For today in the city of David,* the angel tells shepherds, *a savior has been born for you who is Messiah and Lord* (Lk 2:8-11). Strangely, Luke is the only evangelist who refers to Jesus as a savior that will rescue humanity from sin (Lk 2:2-11). Unquestionably, this is an eschatological characterization. Matthew, meanwhile, reinforces Jesus's eschatological objectives in Luke, but seemingly contradicts him by asserting that the angel tells Joseph that this Messiah *will save his people* (the Jewish people) *from their sins* (Mt 1:21). John the Baptist too, while denying he is the Messiah, announces that someone else soon will appear to *baptize with holy Spirit and fire* (Lk 3:15-16, Jn 1:19-33, Jn 3:28), also an eschatological symbol. The Baptist too, makes an unusually early allusion to the Parousia and the Last Judgment—both expressions of eschatology in Jesus— indicating that this someone has a *winnowing fan ... to clear his threshing floor and to gather the wheat into his barn, but the chaff he will burn with unquenchable fire* (Lk 3:17). Additionally, the Baptist cryptically refers to Jesus in eschatological terms as the sacrificial *Lamb of God,* suggesting that God—out of love--has asked him to die for the sins of all humanity (Jn 1:29).

After baptizing Jesus and listening to a voice from heaven calling him his beloved son, John the Baptist is still uncertain if Jesus is the Messiah (even though their mothers knew each other closely), and he sends his disciples to ask him in person. Jesus insinuates he is the Messiah, pointing to the deeds he has been performing (Lk 7:18-22, Mt 11:2-6). Moreover, there is an unusual passage in Luke that points to Jesus as the eschatological Messiah. When told about Pilate's ruthlessness for the killing of a group of Galileans (Lk 13:1-3),[6] Jesus not only seems indifferent to Roman oppression but uses this episode to tell the crowd that a similar punishment would befall them if they do not repent. As someone with direct connections with God, Jesus regards repentance from sin—an eschatological term--far more important than physical, emotional, and religious oppression.

Luke is the only one that tells us that demons know that Jesus is the Son of God and the Messiah (Lk 4:41). Is this a conflation of terms or is Luke telling the reader that both terms refer to the same person? Is Luke the subject of personal revelation (or personal insertion)? In addition to using the titles *savior* and *king* in referring to Jesus, he cites Jesus as indicating that his messianic role entails suffering, a remark that is not found in the Old Testament or any other Jewish records at the time.[7]

Amid ample affirmations, doubts, and denials about Jesus's role as the Messiah, John's text establishes the most forceful characterization regarding Jesus's eschatological role. There are no temporal nuances in John even when in only four occasions does Jesus appear to admit (twice clearly) that he is the Messiah (Jn 4:26, 7:26-27, 10:24-25, 11:27). This has to do with John's disproportionate references to Jesus's divinity, no doubt, and his overall purpose to persuade believers that Jesus is the Messiah (Jn 20:30-31).

Can we establish beyond a reasonable doubt that all four texts see Jesus's role either as an earthly or an eschatological Messiah? It would be difficult, given the ambiguous way the authors use the term. Is there enough evidence to suggest that the authors attempted to change oral tradition to deceive? If they did, they seem to have failed. Their vague use of the term suggests confusion in gathering the information; revisions that were not followed by thoughtful investigation; or simply the complexity that an imperfect oral tradition provided well-intentioned writers.

Is it possible that Jesus's deeds and his teachings led people to receive him so triumphantly as a messiah? Other Jewish prophets had come along before Jesus, but no one had ascended to Jesus's status. Why else would Jesus be acclaimed as a combination of temporal king and messiah? None of the evangelists indicate he was able to initiate strong opposition on the part of the population toward the chief priests and the Pharisees, and no significant mounted protests led by Jesus are recorded in the texts against them. Jesus seems to be a Palestinian Lone Ranger who not only stirs passion among a fearful and well-intentioned group of disciples but arouses the interest and expectations of many Jewish people. This view leaves us with the possibility that his miraculous healings may have happened, in which case he would be entitled to a ticker-tape parade. If this is the case, one can only wish there could be additional evidence about these feats beyond the texts and the oral tradition. In its absence, the term Messiah raises serious questions about God's real intentions and his kingdom; is it temporal or eschatological?

As Jesus enters Jerusalem triumphantly as a plenipotentiary, many believe he is sent by God. Jesus himself believes it, acts upon it, and dies for admitting it. The concluding view is that Jesus proves to be no temporal hero who frees Israel from oppression despite passages to the contrary. His behavior must have proven disappointing to many Israelites who had placed their trust in God's promise of a temporal savior.

Notes:

1. Genesis 3:15; 9:27; 12:2-3; 49:8-12; Numbers 24:15-19; and Deuteronomy 18:15-18. Walter C. Kaiser, Jr., "Jesus in the Old Testament," Gordon-Conwell Theological Seminary, 2009, http://www.gordonconwell.edu/resources/Jesus-in-the-Old-Testament.cfm (accessed 2 February 2017).

2. NEs indicate in their Note on Lk 2:25 that the type of redemption both Simeon and Anna were expecting *represents the hopes and expectations of faithful and devout Jews who at this time were looking forward to the restoration of God's rule in Israel.* They add *the birth of Jesus brings these hopes to fulfillment.* What exactly this last sentence means is difficult to say, as Jesus transforms his earthly messianic role into a completely different one.

3. Ibid., *John's ministry is seen as God's prelude to the saving mission of his Son,* and that, *John the Baptist is to prepare the way for him.* Note on Mk 1:2-3. The editors, however, point out that Mark's reference to Isaiah's prophecy is not entirely correct: *the text is a combination of Mal 3:1; Is 40:3; Ex 23:20; cf. Mt 11:10; Lk 7:27.*

4. Ibid., *only in Luke is Jesus explicitly given the title 'king' when he enters Jerusalem in triumph*, Note on Lk 19:38. Nonetheless, the crowd also refers to Jesus as the king of Israel in Jn 12:13.
5. Despite clearly referring to the consolation of Israel, Simeon alludes to an enigmatic type of salvation that will be, *a light for revelation to the Gentiles, and glory for your people Israel.*" (Lk 2:30-32). NEs indicate that *the political overtones of the title* (Messiah) *are played down in Luke and instead the Messiah of the Lord or the Lord's anointed is the one who now brings salvation to all humanity, Jew and Gentile.* Note Lk 2:11. NEs do not explain why Jesus (or God) switches plans.
6. NEs' note, Lk 13:1 shows this episode is only known to Luke, adding, *from what is known about Pilate from the Jewish historian Josephus, such a slaughter would be in keeping with the character of Pilate.*
7. Ibid., note on Luke 24:26. It adds that the idea of a suffering Messiah *is hinted at in Mk 8:31–33.* Emphasis mine.

King

Is Jesus King of the Israelites or King of the Jews? Or is he the King of Christians, as Christians refer to him? Or is he the king of all humanity? Is he king by acclamation or does he come from a royal succession? Furthermore, is Jesus's a temporal or an eschatological kingdom? These are the questions that come to mind when examining the title of Jesus as king.

The term *king* relating to Jesus appears 52xt, and 1xt to God. As with other titles, it offers no less confusion. This count includes instances in which Jesus is perceived, questioned, or accused of making himself king, or when he is referred to as king by those who mock him, or by him. He acknowledges or calls himself king 24xt while people refer to him as a king 28xt, including instances in which he is mocked.

Content analysis results (Table 1A) show that Jesus's kingship is on par with Savior and Redeemer, Messiah, and Prophet, but it is less significant than Son of God, Lord, Teacher, and Son of Man. Given that the authors of the texts wrote what they believed was being revealed, inspired, or transmitted from oral tradition, the numbers confirm that they did not regard Jesus being king as significant as his other titles, the more so when in many instances the term is used mockingly or with hostility.

The term *King of Israel* appears 4xt and the title *King of the Jews* shows up 18xt. Pontius Pilate and his soldiers treat the title with contempt; Jewish crowds, and the religious authorities with hostility. King Herod and the chief priests and scribes, on the other hand, give credence to the title when three wise men from the east, guided by a star, inquire about the newborn king of the Jews to pay homage to him (Mt 2:1-11).

In the Gospels, the title *King of the Jews* is used only by pagans,[1] in part because the religious authorities did not regard Jesus as their king. The term *pagan,* however, acquires a derogatory connotation among early Christians within the Roman Empire, referring to people who adhere to polytheistic beliefs. Awkwardly, Jesus uses the term[2] disparagingly five times even though pagans are the first to pay homage to him, and knowing that eventually they would constitute the source of the Christian faith. Nonetheless, somewhat ironically, there are four instances in which Jesus chooses to reply to the pagan title in the affirmative, perhaps indicating that he is not ashamed of being called King of the Jews (Mk 15:2, Lk 23:3, Mt 27:11, Jn 18:33-34).

The texts provide us with diverse and contradictory information regarding Jesus as king, King of Israel, King of the Jews, the temporal king/Messiah that Jewish believers are expecting, and a transcendental or supernatural king of all people:

- Three wise men (not Jewish) arrive in Jerusalem inquiring about *the newborn king of the Jews,* referring to a temporal ruler. The Jewish religious authorities tell a suspicious King Herod that the reference is about, *a ruler, who is to shepherd my people Israel* (Mt 2:1-6). Believing it, Herod orders the massacre of innocent children (Mt 2:16).

- Early in his public life Nathanael equates Jesus with being the Son of God and the King of Israel; Jesus not only agrees but adds that he is the supernatural Son of Man (Jn 1:49-51). Then, following the multiplication of the loaves, Jesus becomes aware that the crowd wants to *carry him off to make him king,* but he refuses (Jn 6:15).

- Jesus tells his disciples that as Son of Man he possesses a kingdom of his own (different from that of God's kingdom), and one day he will separate evildoers--whom he will condemn--from the righteous who *will shine like the sun in the kingdom of their Father,* referring apparently to a different eschatological kingdom (Mt 13:41-43, 16:27-28).[3]

- Believing Jesus has a supernatural kingdom, the mother of the sons of Zebedee asks him to grant preferential seating to her children. Jesus replies disconcertingly, indicating that that decision is not up to him but the Father (Mt 20:20-23). At this point, there appear to be two kingdoms each with a different judge.

- Jesus tells his disciples that God has *conferred* him a kingdom and he is going to allow them to partake in what appears to be both a temporal and a supernatural realm, but whose mission is to judge only *the twelve tribes of Israel* (Lk 22:29-30). Nonetheless, in Matthew, Jesus tells his disciples that upon his Second Coming *the Son of Man ... will sit upon his glorious throne, and all the nations* (not just the twelve tribes of Israel) *will be assembled before him* (Mt 25:31-33).

- Jesus appears before Pontius Pilate and remarks that his kingdom, *does not belong to this world*; otherwise, he would call on his soldiers to rescue him. He then tells Pilate that he was born to be a king, and his mission was to come into the world to *testify to the truth* (Jn 18:33-37). His remarks point to an eschatological kingdom, his mission being to be king both on earth and beyond.

- The Jewish religious authorities perceive that the title, whether King of the Jews or King of Israel, has political and religious repercussions because it is being legitimized by public acclamation. When Jesus triumphantly enters Jerusalem, he is welcomed by the crowd chanting that he comes in the name of God, but people cheer him too because he comes to occupy the throne *of our father David that is to come,* both temporal acclamations (Mk 11:9:10, Lk 19:38, Mt 21:8-9, Jn 12:13). The narratives indicate that Jesus is being recognized as an Israelite king--the successor to King David--and the earthly Messiah that many Israelites are expecting.[4]

- Some Pharisees are concerned that the Roman governor might perceive Jesus as threatening his authority that in return would lead to further repression of the Israelites. Hence, when they ask Jesus to rebuke his disciples (who were leading the parade into Jerusalem) he pays scant attention and tells them *if they keep silent the stones will cry out* (Lk 19:39-40)*;* a message of defiance in which he tacitly indicates that he is rightfully a (temporal) king.[5]

The religious authorities appear to take Jesus's claim seriously enough that they despise him for admitting being King of the Jews before Pilate. As Mark indicates, *the chief priests stirred up the crowd* to ask Pilate to release Barabbas and *crucify* Jesus (Mk 15:11-13). Once Pilate gives the order for Jesus to be crucified, Roman soldiers, along with the chief priests and scribes, scornfully salute Jesus as *King of the Jews,* signifying too, that the religious authorities have refused to accept both the title and the person who calls himself king (Mk 15:18, 15:25-26, 15:31-32, Lk 23:36-37, Mt 27:27-30, 27:37, 27:41-42).

Jesus maintains his conviction until the last moment on the cross. Dramatically, a repenting criminal being crucified with him believes Jesus is a king and asks him to be remembered in his kingdom; forgivingly, Jesus tells him, *I say to you, today you will be with me in Paradise* (Lk 23:39-43)*,* an allusion to a celestial realm.

As previously observed, Pontius Pilate, his soldiers, and the Jewish religious authorities use the term King of the Jews several times, derisively and with animosity. Therefore, it is awkward that Jesus—who at times remains silent in the presence of the Roman governor—now decides to answer Pilate's question on whether he is or not the king of the Jews. He replies with his well-known half-affirmative, *you say so,* and *You say I am a king* (Mk 15:2, Lk 23:3, Mt 27:11, Jn 18:37). Does Jesus take the question seriously? It is difficult to accept that Jesus admits to an uncomplimentary title; as a Jew, he would be mocking his own religious and ethnic ancestry. His admission to Pilate appears more like a scornful response--a 'think whatever you want to think,' type of reply to someone whose authority he does not find legitimate.

It is remarkable that despite the title's pagan origin, John's Gospel acknowledges it with a sense of reverence (or is it defiance?) by describing the scene in which Pontius Pilate orders the acronym INRI (Jesus the Nazarene King of the Jews) to be placed atop the cross. To this day this symbol continues to appear in crucifixes in churches throughout the world. Following the revision to the Nicene Creed in 381, Jesus was officially invested as a Christian king by the then catholic (universal) church. An excerpt was added at the time to the initial creed that today reads, He (Jesus) will come again to judge the living and the dead, *and his kingdom will have no end.* Since early in the twentieth century Catholics and Protestants observe the Feast of Christ the King as part of their liturgy.

How would the narratives of Jesus as king be read today? Although he allows himself to be acclaimed as king, his kingly mission is perceived as being temporal, i.e., the successor to King David who would lead the battle against the Roman goliath and succor the needy. Yet, perhaps suggesting that he does not intend to confront him, Jesus tells Pontius Pilate that his kingdom *is not of this world*. The expression on Pilate's face must have been priceless.

Those who welcomed Jesus and were counting on his support as an opponent of the Romans must have felt disappointed that he offered no resistance; he did not ask his angels to protect him, and instead allowed his crucifixion to take place. As a king, he would fit into one of Shakespeare's plays. Throughout history, no one comes to mind that would have reacted in this manner. Is it pacifism that drives Jesus? Is it resignation to the Father's will to redeem humanity? Or is his motive simply to allow the prophecy of his death to be fulfilled for the sake of his followers' faith? There being no contradiction, it may be a combination of all three circumstances.

What likely would strike the reader of these passages today are Jesus's derisive comments about pagans. Bearing in mind that Jesus is a public role model, conducting oneself in a self-righteous manner is most unappealing nowadays, even if one has the truth. It might be difficult for many to accept that Jesus made those comments. After all, pagans were not necessarily at fault for being raised in the belief of various gods; they knew nothing better. Perhaps if Jesus had appeared on earth centuries before, many of those pagans would have believed differently. However, at the time, the new to-be Christians needed to seek their own identity by separating themselves from those who believed differently, and oral tradition likely forced the authors' hand into using these derogatory terms. Today, religious tolerance and respect for a diversity of faiths (even when it awkwardly results in some form of theological, moral, and political relativism) are paramount and compels us to frown on those remarks.

Notes:

1. NEs' note, Mt 27:11.

2. Jesus considers pagan religious practices inferior or less righteous than his teachings; he prevents his disciples from going into pagan lands, seeking instead to save only *the lost sheep of Israel;* and he compares pagans to evil Jewish people who will persecute his followers (Mt 5:47-48, 6:7-8, 6:31-32, 10:5-6, 10:17-18).

3. NEs point out that the kingdom of the Son of Man in Mt 13:41 is distinguished from that of the Father's in Mt 13:43, apparently accepting the idea of two separate kingdoms. Note on Mt 13:41.

4. Luke's passage refers to the multitude calling Jesus 'king,' but without the Davidic connection.

5. NEs' note, Lk 19:39.

Prophet

The term *prophecy*, including specific names of prophets, appears prominently throughout all four Gospels. It scores high in the overall ranking, (Table 2). The count suggests that the authors viewed anything related to prophesy or prophets as being significant, namely because, in Christianity, the fulfillment of the prophecies in Jesus reinforces claims to his divinity. However, the Database Profile of Jesus indicates that the title of prophet is not as significant, despite Jesus's prophetic role and his own affirmations as a prophet. People in the Gospels perceive or believe Jesus to be a prophet 23xt, and Jesus acknowledges too, directly and indirectly, 23xt.

Christian apologists abound eager to provide reasonable arguments indicating that prophecies were fulfilled in Jesus; one author even provides evidence based on mathematical probabilities. Critics, however, indicate that the evidence is not reliable.[1]

At the time of Jesus (and today in Christianity), a prophet was someone appointed by God to transmit two types of knowledge to humanity: a) denunciation of wrongdoing or sinfulness against people and their rulers, and b) foretelling of events that would take place in the distant future. In the Gospels, Jesus's role as teacher and prophet is often indistinctive. Therefore, for purposes of the count in this category, Jesus's self-references as prophet exclude his confrontations with the religious authorities (as these would be treated separately) and include only the instances in which he identifies himself as a prophet or with God's emissaries in the Old Testament, when he emits prophecies, and when others perceive him as a prophet.

For example, people mistake Jesus thinking he is John the Baptist raised from the dead. Some say he is Elijah; others see him as any of the other prophets (Mk 6:14-16, 8:27-28, Lk 9:7-8, 9:18-10); they even say he is Jeremiah (Mt 16:13-14). The religious authorities despise his fame as a prophet, yelling, *prophesy!* as they punch him before being executed (Mk 14:63-65, Lk 22:63-65, Mt 26:65-69).

His deeds earn him fame as a prophet while disregarding more significant titles. As Jesus resurrects the son of a widow, witnesses are seized with fear and exclaim that *a great prophet has arisen in our midst* (Lk 7:13-17). After Peter admits that Jesus is the Son of the living God during the transfiguration, he accords Jesus the same status as Moses and Elijah (Mk 9:5, Lk 9:33, Mt 17:4). The crowd that welcomes him into Jerusalem is certain that *this is Jesus the prophet, from Nazareth in Galilee* (Mt 21:10). The Pharisees are afraid to arrest Jesus because the crowds regard him as a prophet (Mt 21:45-46). A Samaritan woman tells Jesus, *I can see you are a prophet* (Jn 4:19). Following Jesus's multiplication of the loaves and fishes people exclaim, *this is truly the Prophet, the one who is to come into the world* (Jn 6:14). A crowd of people who upon hearing him preach say, *this is truly the Prophet* (Jn 7:40). When the Pharisees ask a man that Jesus has cured of his blindness what he thinks of him, he replies, *he is a prophet* (9:15-17). Even the disciples on the road to Emmaus, not realizing they are speaking to Jesus, refer to him as a prophet (Lk 24:19).

His remarks do not help to clarify his public mission; upon his return to Nazareth, his own people view him with disdain and take offense at him. Disappointed, Jesus compares himself with a prophet (Mt 13:55-57, Mk 6:3-4, Lk 4:24, Jn 4:44); the hypocrisy of the Pharisees leads him to quote Isaiah as if the passage applies to him: *Well did Isaiah prophesy about you hypocrites, as it is written: 'These people honor me with their lips, but their hearts are far from me; In vain do they worship me, teaching as doctrines human precepts.'* (Mk 7:6-7);[2] at the synagogue in Nazareth, Jesus claims that a passage from Isaiah he reads is being fulfilled in him (Lk 4:16-21); even Luke cites Jesus defending the prophets Elijah and Elisha, likely to emphasize that Jesus's role is similar to theirs (Lk 4:25-26).[3] Moreover, Jesus compares himself with past prophets who had suffered at the hands of their ancestors (Lk 6:22-24).

Inexplicably, when told that he should leave Jerusalem because Herod wants to kill him, Jesus refuses, and the reason he gives is, *I must continue on my way … for it is impossible that a prophet should die outside of Jerusalem* (Lk 13:31-33). As opposed to referring to himself as the Son of God or the Messiah, Jesus chooses to die as *a prophet* (one among many whose responsibility is to die in Jerusalem). Moreover, he claims that he intends to continue the role of past prophets by seeking to fulfill Mosaic law (Mt 5:17); he insinuates being a rightful prophet by warning others, *of false prophets, who come to you in sheep's clothing* (Mt 7:15, 24:11, 24:24). Moreover, when the Pharisees ask Jesus for a sign, he contrasts himself with the prophet Jonah, indicating that he is even greater than Jonah, without offering any explanations (Lk 11:32, Mt 12:41).

Understandably, people would perceive Jesus as a prophet. Jewish history has a rich tradition that suited Jesus's role. His behavior and deeds likely led people to regard him as another of God's envoys.[4] What becomes difficult to understand is why Jesus would identify himself with and acquiesce to a title that, as important as it may be, lacks the status of being the Son of God, Savior, and Redeemer, or the Messiah.

Moreover, the proposition that prophecies made centuries before the birth of Jesus appears to have been fulfilled in him throughout his life, while extraordinary (though uncertain), does not constitute evidence of Jesus's divinity; only that he is special. Even prophecies about God sending a temporal savior to redeem the Jewish people do not necessarily mean that the savior is or must be divine. Furthermore, no prophecy in the Old Testament indicates that the Son of God would become incarnated and be asked to sacrifice his life to compensate the Father's anger to provide humanity with another opportunity to attain eternal life. Why, then, would the authors of the Gospels accentuate Jesus's role as a prophet so often unless people believed it, and Jesus would not deny it? On the other hand, it may be possible that they were well-intentioned, but in their naiveté, they may have not noticed that their writings were contributing to confusion over who the public Jesus was. While Jesus appeared to have prophesized the destruction of Jerusalem, the end of time, and Judgment Day, it was his willingness to identify himself with those who denounced evil in the name of God that adds to the enigma of his public persona.

Notes:
1. See Peter W. Stoner, *Science Speaks: Scientific Proof of the Accuracy of Prophecy and the Bible*, (Chicago, Moody Bible Institute of Chicago, online revised edition 2002), http://sciencespeaks.dstoner.net/index.html#c0 (accessed 15 March 2017). Questioning aspects of the theory of evolution, Stoner mixes religious creationism with scientific probability and personal reasons for accepting Christian 'truths.' His chapter 3, "The Christ of Prophecy" seems to be statistically impressive; not being a statistician, however, I cannot vouch for its accuracy. Other works supporting the

fulfillment of the prophecies include Lee Strobel, *The Case for Christ: A Journalist's Personal Investigation of the Evidence for Jesus*, 1st edition, (Grand Rapids: Zondervan, 1998); Josh McDowell, *Evidence That Demands a Verdict: Life-Changing Truth for a Skeptical World*, (Nashville: Thomas Nelson Publisher, 2017). Arguments by critiques of Stoner's and McDowell's books appear online and are less persuasive. "Science Speaks by Peter Stoner and Robert Newman," "Religious Lies Refuted, http://www.testreligion.com/sciencespeaks.html (accessed 15 March 2017); Steven Carr, "Critique of Josh McDowell's Non-Messianic Prophecies," https://infidels.org/library/modern/steven_carr/non-messianic.html (accessed 15 March 2017).

2. The passage may also refer to Jesus speaking as the Son of God since Isaiah was referring to God.

3.Twice, NEs point out that, *the references to Elijah and Elisha serve several purposes ... they emphasize Luke's portrait of Jesus as a prophet like Elijah and Elisha;* Note on Lk 4:18 and in Lk 4:25-26.

4. The definition of a prophet is *one who speaks in the name of God.* NEs' note, Mt 10:41.

Master

The connotation of the term *Master* in this section is different from its initial meaning as Teacher and Rabbi. The term appears in Luke's and Matthew's parables[1] where Jesus characterizes himself as someone with great authority over his subjects, be they slaves, servants, or tenants. In postmodern times this master would resemble a powerful landowner or a wealthy businessman with authority over his workers. There is little doubt that Jesus was referring to someone other than to him or God in these parables. At the time, the term's connotations were an integral part of societies whose ethos favored excessive reliance on power and authority while requiring meekness and servility off those under a master. Today, the image of a *master* denotes absolute rule over subservient workers and recalls the history of slavery. Overall, this image would make Jesus's persona as a master quite unappealing in postmodern secular society.

In the texts, Jesus does not call himself *master,* and no one refers to him by that term (in lower case). Nonetheless, he projects himself as *master* 40xt through his parables, using this term to instruct people on God's teachings. These passages are vivid examples of 'What Would Jesus (or God) Do' situations. He presents a moral dilemma, judges human conduct, and decides on appropriate punishments. In some instances, his judgments are rather unpleasant and incomprehensible.

The master in Jesus initially appears as an honorable person, just, reasonable, sensitive to the needs of his workers, merciful, and forgiving. In return, he requires those under his authority to be attentive to his wishes, obedient, prudent, and loyal; the master simply expects his kindness and just rule toward others to be reciprocated. Yet, when disobeyed—if those under him become irresponsible, abusive, lazy, or drunk--the master feels an immediate sense of betrayal. He becomes enraged as if his dignity has been crushed and his person publicly humiliated. He does not restrain his impulses and promptly make his wrath felt; unexpectedly, there is no mercy, no understanding, and no forgiveness in him. Without there being no laws or limitations to the ways he inflicts retribution, the master hurls insults and punishes severely, even permanently condemning those who defy him. He sells a servant along with his wife and children because he has been delinquent with his credit. Begging for a second chance the master accedes out of pity, but upon finding out that the servant later becomes unkind to someone else he is tortured eternally (Mt 18:23-35). In another instance, a servant acts irresponsibly with the talents (funds) given to him to negotiate. The master feels his employee has violated their contract, calls him wicked and lazy, and orders to *throw this useless servant into the darkness outside, where there will be wailing and grinding of teeth* (Mt 25:14-30).

Even those outside his authority (neighbors, strangers) are supposed to acquiesce to his demands and whims. In one passage, the master gives a great dinner and invites many. One by one, however, the invitees make excuses and decide not to attend. The master becomes furious and orders his servants to force strangers to attend his feast so that his home *may be filled*, and his ego satisfied. As for those who choose not to attend, they are likely to expect the worst punishment (Lk 14:16-24).

Furthermore, an inexplicable behavior on the part of the master occurs when he becomes aware that one of his foremen has been *squandering his property*. Upon being dismissed, the foreman decides to correct his misdeed and pay the master out of his own pocket. What seems startling is that the master not only *commends that dishonest steward for acting prudently*; he instructs that we ought to learn from the children of this world (children of darkness) whom he regards as being more prudent—a cardinal virtue no less—than the children of light whom he views as naive. He recommends *making friends for yourselves with dishonest wealth, so that when it fails, you will be welcomed into eternal dwellings* (Lk 16:1-9). There are imaginative interpretations to Jesus's words today, but having dishonest people as friends is not something that may find sensible explanations coming from the pulpit.[2]

One unique feature about this master is that he judges his workers' behavior and decides on the punishment while answering to no one. He is different from a CEO or a business owner who nowadays is limited by government laws in applying inhumane disciplinary measures to his employees. Ironically, the master's wrath would find no limits in most countries today were it not for Christian and other religious and human values extolling understanding, justice under the law, compassion, and forgiveness.

The master's wrath seems humanly understandable once he realizes he is being taken advantage of by his kindness. He is reasonable and altruistic, but his benevolence is met with rejection, derision, and indifference. Who would not feel despondent and downright angry?

Perhaps what is mostly at odds with postmodern society is that Jesus presents God through the figure of a master that, having no limits to his authority, appears to make little or no distinction among various misdeeds (sins), ranging from drunkenness to physical abuse, corruption, laziness, or indifference to his kindness. This attitude is somewhat inconsistent with the same Jesus who is aware of human proclivity to sin, even admitting that the flesh is weak. Thus, a more empathetic and merciful Jesus would have been in line with his understanding of the frailty of human nature. Instead, the kind master now becomes an irascible authoritarian who enforces law and order without limitations. The fact that people may have been once in his company no longer counts; as soon as their weaknesses lead them astray the response is eerie: *I do not know where you are from. Depart from me, all you evildoers!* (Lk 13:25-27).[3]

It is reasonable that if Jesus's master were to be only kind, merciful, and forgiving, his moral laws would lack credibility making their implementation impossible. This attitude is no different in human society. Quite often, fear conditions good behavior and averts serious misdeeds. Jesus's master parallels society's understanding of human behavior: without deterrence—the fear of punishment—and law and order, any semblance of civilization would not be possible on earth.

Moreover, a most perplexing question arises concerning the implementation of these teachings. On the one hand, they suggest that the master's excessively violent parables may be applicable on earth as these parables relate to temporal behavior. However, one of Jesus's least quoted parables—the Weeds Among the Wheat-- presents an opposite scenario. In this parable, the master instructs his servants not to combat evil by utilizing punishment on earth to deter sinful behavior because of the probable collateral damage that may result. Instead, he tells them to wait until the end of the harvest (Judgment Day) at the end of time (Mt 13:24-30).[4]

A plausible consequence in this parable is that injustice, crime, and aggression would be allowed to continue rampant, as there would be no significant measures to deter evil behavior. People would have to resort to the values of the beatitudes-- peacemaking, compassion, meekness, and forgiveness—that, while laudable, would render society defenseless. This view is not farfetched; it is revealed in the texts through Jesus's apparent indifference toward injustice and oppression on earth, preferring instead to focus on the afterlife. The difficulty in accepting this aspect of Jesus's teachings is that, while many of his parables condemn injustice, murder, theft, and greed, the prescribed answer to these evil actions in this parable is to accept suffering while continuing to forgive one's enemies. Individually, this behavior may be dignified and heroic, although it would degrade Jesus's other teachings, including the love of neighbor that entails defending others from injustice. This seemingly contradictory behavior is examined in other categories.

In the meantime, it is useful to observe that from its beginning and throughout the medieval period, Christian education placed great emphasis on the fear of God as a way to condition behavior on earth; the fear of God's punishment was deemed to be a more effective means to teach proper moral behavior because people deeply believed in hell and eternal condemnation. Nowadays, perhaps aware that God's wrath in the texts has overshadowed his love and mercifulness—or that an increasing number of people are no longer afraid or believe in hell--Christian teaching has shifted its focus toward a kind and loving God, likely because it is more appealing and less stressful to the believer. Another plausible explanation is that the divine's invitation to eternal bliss is losing its significance as temporal progress has changed humanity's conception of happiness to the extent that it no longer values delayed gratification.[5] Today, the 'God loves us' mantra has become an integral part of all Christian denominations, likely because it is more hopeful and enticing than living under the endless anxiety of being eternally condemned for being lazy or getting drunk.

Notes:

1. The exception appears in Lk 2:29 when the prophet Simeon, given the opportunity to see the child Jesus before his death calls God *Master*. The term is also used in Jn 15:14, 15:20, but the passages do not relate to the master in this section.

2. According to NEs, *the first conclusion recommends the prudent use of one's wealth (in the light of the coming of the end of the age) after the manner of the children of this world, represented in the parable by the dishonest steward*; note on NEs, Lk 16:8b-9. *The second conclusion recommends constant fidelity to those in positions of responsibility*; NEs' note, Lk 16:10-12.

3. Although this passage relates to the Israelites' rejection of Jesus, the consequences are the same: the gate is narrow. Note on NEs' note, Mt 8:11-12.

4. Ibid., note on Mt 13:24-30 editors interpret this parable as suggesting that, *Until then there must be patience and the preaching of repentance.*

5. Upon learning that based on the Gospels there might not be sexual intercourse in heaven (Mt 22:30), a cynical acquaintance said to me, 'That's why I'm trying to indulge in it while on earth.'

Son of David

That the title *Son of David* occurs only 15xt in the Gospels (John mentions the term once indirectly) belies its significance at the time. Before Jesus's birth, there were expectations that a temporal leader from the house of David (a descendant from the tribe led by David that became known as the Kingdom of Judah), would emerge and unite the Israelite people. Prophecies in the Old Testament allude to this leader becoming the Messiah; Isaiah 16:5 indicates that *in love a throne will be established; in faithfulness a man will sit on it—one from the house of David—one who in judging seeks justice and speeds the cause of righteousness.* In Luke, Zechariah, John the Baptist's father, glorifies God upon learning that his son will pave the way for someone from the house of David who will rescue the Israelites from their enemies (Lk 1:68-77). Also in Luke, the angel Gabriel, upon visiting Mary tells her that she will give birth to a child who *will be called Son of the Most High, and the Lord God will give him the throne of David his father, and he will rule over the house of Jacob forever, and of his kingdom there will be no end (Lk 1:32-33).* Luke and Matthew show that Jesus is that leader, thereby equating the Son of David with the Messiah. Thus, the term was extraordinarily important to the Jewish people.

In the texts, other people refer to Jesus as Son of David 13xt while Jesus responds and/or alludes to the title 8xt. The numbers indicate that among the ten titles selected in this work, Son of David has the lowest count, suggesting that for some reason the authors did not deem it important to highlight Jesus's relation to the Davidic line, but merely to acknowledge it. This is awkward, since calling Jesus Son of David implies that he is the temporal Messiah the Israelites are hoping for. The significance of the title, however, is attenuated by the fact that there are many descendants from the house of David, including Joseph who is called Son of David by the angel of the Lord (Mt 1:20) and possibly Mary (Lk 1:32-33).

Both Luke and Matthew seem the most interested in underlining Jesus as Son of David in their respective and extensive genealogies of Jesus; Matthew explicitly refers to Jesus as the Son of David (Lk 3:23-31, Mt 1:1-1). The genealogies are not without problems. The Catholic Encyclopedia states, *it is granted on all sides that the Biblical genealogy of Christ implies a number of exegetical difficulties.*[1] These issues will not be dealt with since they lie outside the scope of this work.

Among those who refer to Jesus as Son of David are: a blind man who pleads with Jesus to restore his sight and Jesus agrees to do it; Matthew, who tells the same story twice adding a second blind man to each one (Mk 10:46-52, Lk 18:35-42, Mt 9:27-31, Mt 20:29-34); a crowd that questions the possibility of Jesus being the Son of David after he cures a demoniac (Mt 12:22-23); a Canaanite woman who engages Jesus in an interesting conversation in which she practically begs him to cure her daughter, which he does (Mt. 15:21-28); a large crowd that welcomes Jesus in Jerusalem chanting *Hosanna to the Son of David; blessed is he who comes in the name of the Lord* (Mt 21:8-9); and children in the temple who praise Jesus—*Hosanna to the Son of David*—after he cures people with disabilities (Mt 21:14-17).[2] It appears that the view that associates Jesus with being the Son of David, a temporal concept, was well known among the Jewish people.

Jesus does not have any reservations responding every time to those who call him Son of David, just as he had done when called upon by other titles (except master). He sees himself comfortably using multiple identities, but he does not call himself Son of David. Instead, he uses a riddle to dispel the notion that the Messiah is the son of David and to suggest that he is more significant than merely being a descendant of the Davidic line (Mk 12:35-37, Lk 20:41-44, Mt 22:41-46).[3] John's Gospel chooses not to affirm the title; instead, it questions it by indicating that some people are not certain if Jesus is the Messiah (Jn 7:40-42).

Despite the insignificance shown in the Gospels to the Son of David title, nowadays it has acquired new relevance. It is important to orthodox Jews who await a future king whose lineage may be traced to the Davidic line. In Christian theology, this title is also a reminder of Jesus's ties to the Jews—the apple of God's eye—and the Old Testament. Both views increased Christianity's esteem for Judaism, leading the faith to reject the concept of Jewish deicide. It also guided the Catholic Church to its act of contrition for the anti-Semitism perpetrated by Christians throughout the ages. Additionally, for some evangelical Christians the Davidic line has apocalyptic implications that bond them to the military security of the State of Israel based on biblical reasons.[4]

What are the consequences of Jesus being identified by various titles in the Gospels? Titles usually have two connotations: they are used as an indication of respect for people who have earned the admiration of others, or as a designation related to the position they hold in society or to their functions. In the Gospels, Jesus acknowledges and refers to himself using ten titles. Although these titles may relate to Jesus's mission, each one has different meanings that when viewed together provide incongruent images that cloud who he is. In this sense, the Gospels raise more questions than they answer, including, why would God reveal documents that are so appallingly confusing to his creatures?

In most cases, a title contradicts, weakens, or even negates other titles because their significance varies considerably at times. Likely, the terms whose significance is reduced the most are Savior/Redeemer, simply because they define who Christians believe is Jesus's most important attribute. Is the term *Lord* simply an honor bestowed upon him, or is it an attribution of divinity? Messiah and Son of David have mostly theological relevance but, except for Jews, Christians largely ignore them. Jesus's role as a master depicts an impatient and insensitive god. As for Son of Man, Jesus's preferred title, aside from its irrelevance today, may require additional cryptologists to decipher its meaning. Some titles convey strictly a temporal mission for a specific group of people; other titles depict a more supernatural and inclusive mission at the expense of betraying God's promise to liberate the Jewish people from oppression.

There is little doubt that Jesus (or the texts' authors) is responsible for the confusion on account of the variety of titles he relied on and their significance, insofar as he failed to clarify who he was. Some titles project a temporal mission while others emphasize the eschatological nature of his work. Humanly speaking, the evangelists only attempted to record what had been said about Jesus throughout the years. Their research appears disjointed at times, as if the authors were not aware of the identity problems they were creating for the future in their eagerness to spread the new faith.

Secularly speaking, the Jesus of the Gospels is a complex personality. He can be caring and forgiving, rude and with a limited understanding of human nature, violent and non-violent. The multiplicity of titles, each portraying a different Jesus, does not increase our understanding of an already mysterious person; instead, it leads to questioning the wisdom of divine revelation.

Notes:
1. Anthony Maas, "Genealogy of Christ," CE, http://www.newadvent.org/cathen/06410a.htm (accessed 29 March 2017).
2. NEs highlight that in several of the passages Jesus responds to the title while curing people, thereby associating the title to a healing Messiah. Nonetheless, it must be noted that Jesus cured others without responding to the term.
3. Ibid., editors indicate that Jesus's motive is not to deny the Davidic descent of the Messiah, but to imply that he is more than this. NEs' note, Mark 12:35-37. In Mark this question is posed to people in the temple area; in Luke, it appears that he is addressing the Sadducees, or possibly to the scribes and the Pharisees; and in Matthew, the question is put to a gathering of the Pharisees.
4. Christians United for Israel is an evangelical movement in the United States that seeks to defend and strengthen Israel politically and militarily basing its motives on biblical issues https://www.cufi.org/impact/about-us/ (accessed 30 March 2017)

Christ – The Missing Title
The significance of relying on content analysis as an approach to study the Gospels lies not only in finding what is in the texts but what is not as well. This is the case with the term *Christ*. But first, it is important to examine what the name Jesus means. In Greek the name Iesous, given at the angel Gabriel's subtle command to Joseph (Mt 1:21), is the transliteration in Hebrew of Jeshua, meaning Jehova that translated into English and other languages signify that God *saves* or *salvation*.[1] Through the

examination of the ten previous titles it was noted that in the Gospels Jesus is supposed to save the Jewish people (or some or all humanity) from their temporal afflictions and/or from sins or offenses committed against God. Being a savior must be regarded as an important role, and yet the name Jesus was quite common at the time.[2] Is it possible that parents who named their child Jesus were aware of its portentous meaning? Probably that was not the case; how many Jesuses acted the role at the time? Hence, why would God choose a common name whose cultural meaning had no exceptional supernatural connotations beyond the ordinary? Admittedly, this is just a rhetorical question.

The texts project conflicting versions of Jesus as savior: who is he supposed to save, only the Jewish people or all humanity; is he human or divine, or both; is his mission purely temporal or eschatological? The Gospels indicate all the above. It is within this context that *Christ* appears as one of Jesus's titles. Christ or Christos is a Greek translation of the Hebrew term Messiah that means 'anointed' by God, in which case we may ask, why was Jesus not named Christ from the beginning? Having written the texts in Greek, the authors of the Gospels had to be aware of the meaning of the term. Yet, *Christ* is scarcely present in the Gospels and under dubious circumstances. According to the Catholic Encyclopedia, Christ or *Messias* was not a proper name, but a title; and it was only following Jesus's resurrection that the title *gradually* became a combination of name and title into a single name.[3] If this assessment is correct, it does not speak highly of a direct divine revelation. This title, however, did not simply pass gradually.

Table 1D shows that Christ, seemingly as a name, appears only 6xt; in four instances the full name appears only at the beginning of three Gospels (Mk 1:1, Mt 1:1, 18, Jn 1:16).[4] Oddly enough, in the other two passages it is Jesus who calls himself Christ (Mk 9:41, Jn 17:3), likely an insertion by the authors, as it would seem awkward for Jesus to have called himself Christ and for the authors not to have noticed it.[5]

Therefore, the question remains; why the Gospels hardly used the term, *Christ,* despite it was already quite prominent at the time since Paul's letters were written before the Gospels? The contrast between the Gospels and Paul's letters in this regard is striking. In all letters attributed to Paul, regardless of authorship, all written prior to the Gospels (approximately between 48-63 CE), the name Jesus by itself seldom appears while Christ, whether by itself or tagged to the name Jesus (Christ Jesus or Jesus Christ), shows up 386xt (Table 1E).

The tally indicates that there is no Christology without Paul. The question of why Paul chooses to refer to Jesus mostly as Christ is outside the boundaries of this work. The question of why Christ as a name or title is practically absent from the Gospels, however, is far more intriguing. In Luke's Acts of the Apostles, written decades after Paul's letters, the term Jesus Christ or its reverse appears 12xt while the term Jesus, associated with the title Lord and with the resurrected Jesus, shows up 56xt, suggesting some hesitation on Luke's part in using Christ as a title or a name.

Using Christology as a way of explanation, Paul's emphasis on Christ intimates that to him Jesus Christ is more divine than the authors of the Gospels believe. For example, the Catholic Encyclopedia bases its Christology primarily on Paul's letters, followed in their importance by James's, Peter's, and Jude's letters, John's Gospel, and the synoptics.[6] This interpretation is manifested today in the index of the Catholic

Catechism issued by the Vatican Library with the full endorsement of the Congregation for the Doctrine of the Faith and the Pope. The Index shows that the name Christ appears 1699xt, twice as many times as Jesus, 855xt.[7] Given the meaning of the title Christ, Paul's letters minimize the significance of Jesus's divinity in the Gospels (John's Gospel notwithstanding), suggesting that it is Paul, who based on a spectacular vision and other revelations, is responsible, at least temporally, for anointing Jesus as a resurrected Messiah, despite he seldom uses the term.

The discontinuity of the Jesus name suggests that there are issues with a flawed oral tradition prior to the writing of the New Testament. Jesus's revelation to Paul ought to have influenced (or clarified) deficiencies in this regard in the Gospels, since Paul already had met, at least twice, with Jesus's disciples prior to the writings of the Gospels. Why the Gospels did not assimilate Paul's views on Jesus is puzzling.

Today, Jesus is said to be regarded as divine because he *accomplished perfectly the divine mission that "Christ" signifies.*[8] But, supposedly, God anointed the greatest prophets, including Moses, Isaiah, and John the Baptist to pursue divine missions too, and none of them are considered divine. It may be granted that Jesus's anointment appears to be more significant, but anointment by itself provides insufficient evidence of Jesus's divinity or non-divinity. As noted previously, the question of whether Jesus was a temporal or eschatological Messiah is not clearly explained in the texts; nor why Jesus transformed God's promise of a temporal Jewish liberator into an eschatological and universal savior. Altogether, despite various revisions, the authors of the Gospels did not use *Christ* as a name or a title for Jesus because they did not regard it as significant, which, again, does not speak highly about the process of divine revelation.

Notes:
1. Anthony Maas, "Origin of the Name of Jesus Christ," CE, Vol 8, http://www.newadvent.org/cathen/08374x.htm (accessed 4 April 2017). Also (CCC) 430.
2. Maas.
3. Ibid.
4. NEs note that some texts leave out the designation *Son of God* next to the name; NEs' note, Mk 1:1.
5. NEs point out that the verse in John *was clearly added in the editing of the Gospel,* indicating that *Jesus nowhere else refers to himself as Jesus Christ.* Note on Jn 17:3.
6. Maas.
7. (CCC), Index, Alphabetical Word List, http://www.vatican.va/archive/ENG0015/_STAT.HTM. (Go to Alphabetical occurrence distribution--by first letter--and look up the word). A partial review of what the Catholic Catechism is about according to its index shows that this text is mostly about God (2788xt), Christ (1699xt), Church (1382xt), Holy Spirit (1040xt), prayer-related (967xt), life (935xt), Jesus (866xt), Father (mostly God 803xt), sin-related (755xt), faith (737xt), Lord (689xt), Son (mostly Jesus 555xt), love (521xt), and salvation-related (431xt). Other notable terms that caught my attention include kingdom (212xt), Resurrection (193xt), and Mary (166xt). A count of personal pronouns and nouns reflects today's patriarchal Church culture as it did in the decades following the New Testament: man/men (1104xt), woman/women (108xt), he (1414xt), she (237xt), him (894xt), her (405xt), himself (444xt), herself 38xt), his (2386xt), her (405xt).
8. (CCC) 436.

6 – What the Gospels are About

The next sections encompass the results of applying content analysis and empirical reasoning to over one hundred categories that are relevant to the Christian religion. By ranking these categories, and discussing how they are used in the texts, a more coherent appreciation of the public Jesus emerges. It tells us which aspects of Jesus's life and his teachings the Gospels emphasize the most, which ones he speaks about the least, which ones he (or the authors) chooses to disregard while focusing on their incongruences.

Table 2 shows the overall tallies and the ranking of all examined categories. Among the most noticeable results is a shift in emphasis over the centuries whereby certain themes the Gospels did not regard as significant have become noteworthy so that Christianity has adopted them in one way or another. Moreover, issues the authors considered relevant enough to be included in the Gospels are barely mentioned today. Thus, if asked what the major themes of the Gospels are, results indicate that they relate primarily to Jesus, not to Christ; the highest ranking issues were Righteousness, Faith, Sinfulness, Afterlife, the Jewish Religious Authorities, the Jewish People, Jesus's Use of Power, Love, and Reason. Among the less significant categories in the Gospels are Baptism, Marriage, Sexual Behavior and other sins, Justification, Redemption, War and Peace, Adultery, and Soul. A separate section deals with Contemporary Significant Categories whose significance does not stem from the Gospel, but from valuable inputs from a secularized world that includes non-believers and believers. A consensus seems to have emerged over the last two centuries that these themes were so important that Christian denominations have had to accept their tenets. Among these are, temporal freedom, anti-slavery, equality, human rights, democracy, gay rights, feminism, abortion, secularism, and climate change.

A postmodern reader of the Gospels may be surprised by how much space is consumed by the conflict between the Jewish religious authorities and Jesus—hardly a relevant topic today except when discussing anti-Semitism (that is noticeably depicted in the texts), the sin of hypocrisy, or Jesus's confrontational role as an example to be followed in a secularly polarized world characterized by religious pluralism. Furthermore, Jesus's (or the authors') disparaging emphasis on a sinful temporal world, and the necessity to concentrate on eternal salvation (the core of Jesus's message), indicate there has been a 120-degree shift today, whereby many of Christianity's themes now relate to improving the overall quality of life on earth. For example, the Peace and War category does not rank high in the Gospels while today it is regarded as an existential matter. The high ranking of Reason or Intellect was unexpected, particularly when contrasted with Jesus's description of the Heart as a sensorial organ capable of 'thinking' or at least providing intuitive moral conclusions. It is appropriate to remind the reader, however, that the texts may not necessarily reflect all that Jesus may have said, but rather what the authors gathered from oral tradition, and what they thought was important (or were inspired by God) to include in their texts.

(Note): Throughout all category narratives that follow, xt stands for the number of times a term appears in a category; p stands for the number of passages; and sp stands for the space the Gospels accord to each category. The reader may wish to refer to the Method Notes for each category in Chapter 6 prior to the Index to understand how the tally and ranking were done.

Gospel

Since this work addresses an examination of the Gospels, it seems reasonable to begin with the Gospel category. To Christians, the Gospels represent the word of God. Most denominations regard its content to be infallible and/or inerrant in teachings dealing with doctrine and morals. Some denominations even accept the content of the Bible as being literally true, connoting that nothing that appears in the texts can be factually wrong. Overall, Christians accept the Gospels, along with the rest of the New Testament and the Old Testament, to be divinely revealed or inspired. There is much at stake in this belief. Jesus indicates that those who believe in him and his teachings will be saved, and those who fail to believe will be condemned (Mk 16:15-16).

There is a notable difference between the terms *gospel* and Gospels that need to be addressed at the outset. What is known today as the Gospels is different from that which the Jewish people were exposed to during Jesus's lifetime. The term *gospel* refers to events taking place in real-time relating, not to the life of Jesus, but namely to his public mission while preaching about the kingdom of God. Thus, Jesus's historical/biographical data, e.g., where he traveled, the people he met, or events surrounding his death and resurrection would not be considered part of the gospel. All four Gospels, on the other hand, are a partially written compilation about the life of Jesus and his teachings undertaken by several people, possibly dozens, who sought to create a legacy of Jesus decades following his death and resurrection (Lk 1:1-5). Hence, we learn about the gospel through the Gospels.

The Gospels began with recollections about aspects of the lives of John the Baptist and Jesus, and their public undertakings that had been handed down to people through oral transmission over decades. This process ended with the Gospel of John. It was followed by probing stages that questioned the canonicity, i.e., church validation, of the texts according to what tradition dictated at the time. The texts of the New Testament were vehemently contested by apocryphal versions. Nonetheless, after the Reformation, the various denominations officially recognized the four Gospels, Paul's Letters, and the rest of the New Testament in the order they appear today.[1]

During Jesus's time, the word gospel signified good news, announcement, or unfamiliar information that he was providing to the Israelite people. In addition to the word gospel, the authors of the Gospels include other terms that were probably meant to include the gospel that Jesus began to preach, and which eventually became a partial biography of Jesus.[2]

This category tallies and examines the gospel, although its discussion inevitably will relate to parts of the Gospels. As a category, it ranks modestly among the less significant in Table 2. Nonetheless, the authors' determination to go beyond the *gospel* suggests that events about the private and public aspect of Jesus's life constituted a transcendental experience not only for the Jewish people. Today, the *gospel* and the Gospels are meant to address all humanity. Hence, the Gospels include aspects of Jesus' life, including his birth, the angel's announcement to Zechariah and Mary as well as its announcement about the birth of a savior, John the Baptist's preaching, Jesus's teachings and miracles, his confrontation with the religious authorities, and his arrest, trial, crucifixion, and post-resurrection. In the gospel, Jesus is the bearer of good news about the kingdom of God and the afterlife. In the Gospels, however, the authors (and/or God) put in writing the gospel's testimony for posterity to indicate that Jesus is different from other human beings; that he is the Messiah, savior, and the Son of God. What exactly Jesus expected of his gospel is puzzling; at no time he tells his disciples to make notations of his sayings or his miracles, perhaps anticipating that the kingdom of God would extend without the assistance of others, as he foretold in one of his parables.

At the time of Jesus's birth, the Jewish people were being morally governed by the same Mosaic Law that had been handed down to them thousands of years before. Jesus confronts this law indicating that his mission is to fulfill it rather than to abolish it (Mt 5:17); nonetheless, this seems to be an understatement. It is correct that, technically, Jesus does not abolish the entire Old Law, but he alters it substantially; enough that Paul considers it worthless. Had Jesus not transformed Mosaic Law considerably, the gospel (and the Gospels) would have been just recycled news rather than good news. Thus, when Jesus begins to preach the latest news, i.e., his interpretation of God's word, people become amazed at his words (Mk 10:24, Mt 7:28), despite they are hearing something uncomfortably different from Mosaic Law.

The reader may want to ask if there is anything newsworthy in the Gospels? Surprisingly, there are new revelations. The texts tell about the coming of the kingdom of God (Mk 1:14-15); the fulfillment of God's promises including the much awaited Messiah (Lk 2:10-11); the promise of eternal salvation to those who choose to believe in Jesus (Mk 8:35); a redefinition of righteous conduct stressing humility, i.e., the last shall be first and the first shall be last (Mt 20:15-16); a new way to love God by obeying Jesus's commandments (Jn 14:23-24); an inclusive reformulation of the commandment to love one's neighbor with an emphasis on those who are in dire need (Lk 10:25-37); the necessity to seek repentance and acknowledge one's sins (Lk 5:32); the importance of mercy, compassion, caring, and forgiveness over the rigidity that Mosaic Law demanded (Mt 23:13-33); the significance of prayer (Mt 17:14-21); and the unexpected revelation that Jesus is not only the Messiah but savior and Son of God (Mk 14:61-62). The continued belief in the kingdom of God throughout history is the outcome of increasing faith in Jesus's resurrection as depicted in the Gospels; its temporal expansion would have been impossible without such a belief.

Among the most notable observations in this category is that all four texts present the gospel, in varying degrees, as an extension of the person of Jesus. Thus, when he is critical of the scribes because they nullify the word of God in favor of human tradition (Mk 7:13, Mt 15:6), Jesus is referring to his very own interpretations of God's teachings. He tells the scribes that by rejecting his teachings they are rejecting him and the Father. Examples of Jesus's personification of God's words abound in the Gospels:

> - *Whoever is ashamed of me and of my words in this faithless and sinful generation, the Son of Man will be ashamed of when he comes in his Father's glory with the holy angels* (Mk 8:38, Lk 9:26).
> - *Whoever rejects me and does not accept my words has something to judge him: the word that I spoke* (Jn 12:46-49).
> - *There is no one who has given up house or brothers or sisters or mother or father or children or lands for my sake and for the sake of the gospel who will not receive a hundred times more now in this present age* (Mk 10:29-30).
> - *Heaven and earth will pass away, but my words will not pass away* (Mk 13:31, Mt 24:34).
> - *Everyone who listens to these words of mine and acts on them will be like a wise man who built his house on rock.... And everyone who listens to these words of mine but does not act on them will be like a fool who built his house on sand* (Mt 7:24-26).
> - *Whoever hears my word and believes in the one who sent me has eternal life* (Jn 5:24).
> - *If you remain in my word, you will truly be my disciples, and you will know the truth* (Jn 8:31).
> - *Whoever keeps my word will never see death* (Jn 8:51).
> - *If you remain in me and my words remain in you, ask ... and it will be done* (Jn 15:7).

None of the authors go to as great an extent in personifying the *gospel* as John. It is John who reveals that Jesus is *the Word* ... that was with God in the beginning, through whom *all things came to be*, including life (Jn 1:1-4).[3] This *Word* becomes flesh and dwells among humans, and his glory was that of *the Father's only Son* (Jn

1:14). Whether under divine inspiration or exact revelation, John equates Jesus with God and his words with the words of his Father, occasionally indicating that the words he teaches are not Jesus's but his Father's (Jn 14:10-11, 17:6-8). Since Jesus is the Word, this Word makes itself known when he communicates with others. Thus, the Word becomes a living *gospel*, words being a mere reflection of the person. Neither the words nor the Word is easily understood in John's writings (or in the other Gospels), suggesting that only God is responsible for our ability to understand.

The Parable of Sower would seem to be an adequate (if puzzling) depiction of Jesus and his mission to spread the *gospel*. Jesus is the sower who sows the seed, i.e., God's word, among people. He tells the crowd that many will be incapable of holding on to the word while those that are made of *rich soil* are gifted or gracious enough to accept the word and bear fruit. A literal reading of the parable indicates something troublesome; the sower does not appear to be competent in his occupation. He seems to know where the rich soil that will bear fruit is, and yet he indiscriminately, i.e., wastefully, tosses the seed in unsuitable areas, and then becomes critical of both the outcome and the areas where the seed lands. This is not the traditional understanding of this parable. Its apologetic interpretation is that humankind is responsible for rejecting the word, despite in one instance it is Satan who steals the word from people.

Jesus acknowledges that the *gospel* will be delivered in many instances through parables, which at times become riddles; mysterious ways of communicating the word with the intention *that* [others] *may look but not see, and hear but not understand* (Mk 4:11-12, Lk 8:10). In effect, if some parables are meant to confuse people, can they still be considered *good news*? According to Mark, when Jesus finishes narrating the Parable of the Sower, he realizes that not even his disciples (along with others present) can understand; *do you not understand this parable*, he asks them. *Then how will you understand any of the parables* (Mk 4:13)? Jesus seems to be encountering problems with his favorite pedagogical tool to deliver the *gospel*. This would not be the first instance, however, in which *the word remained hidden from them* (Lk 18:31-34). People's lack of understanding, including the disciples, occurs often while Jesus preaches the *gospel*. In Matthew, on the other hand, Jesus suggests something entirely different; while the disciples appear to understand the word, such an understanding is (disconcertingly) denied to many people including *many prophets and righteous people* (Mt 13:10-17). Is this the proper way to deliver good news, and what is Jesus trying to accomplish by doing so?

Does it matter that there are four somewhat distinctive versions of the *gospel*? Yes and no. Certainly, it would have helped had there been consensus on minor and major details (there is not) to avoid the charge that God makes mistakes or the Christian defense that God cannot be held responsible for human error. Nonetheless, given that each author has a different audience in mind, each version represents a part of a puzzle that adds unique aspects to the entire picture. Needless to say, there must be agreement among major issues, namely who Jesus is as well as on his teachings. In this regard, there are still significant variations.

The primary concern in this work is to critically examine the substance of who Jesus is said to be along with the empirical and logical consistency of his teachings from the standpoint of a secularly minded person typical of future generations. In this regard, some questions will be raised throughout this work about both Jesus and his teachings, including their suitability with human nature as well as inconsistencies in the *gospel*. It would be possible for Jesus's teachings to provide a pivotal moment across societies if they were to be generally understood and accepted. For this to happen, the Gospels, i.e., a probable inexact extension to Jesus's *gospel*, will need to undergo a process of actualization; that is, it would require their revision to the point of being updated in light of current historical understandings so that their essence might be better understood. Failure to actualize the texts may lead new generations to develop an archaic opinion of the Gospels that may only spark historical interest.

The Gospels and Paul
There is in the Gospels an inherent and problematic conundrum that weakens their trustworthiness as being divinely ordained or inspired: their relationship with Paul's letters. The Gospels are at the center of Christian liturgy for a specific reason: they express, literally, the words of Jesus. Presuming that oral transmission worked as intended to echo Jesus's sayings with divine assistance or inspiration, the Gospels are as close as we might expect to the *gospel* that Jesus preached. Nowhere else do Jesus's words come alive as they do in the Gospels; not even in Paul. There is supposed to be little or no room for misunderstanding or misinterpreting his sayings or how events transpired at the time. Candidly, the Gospels even reveal their apologetic tone, including the anti-Jewish predisposition that existed at the time; a normal human reaction to a conflict regarding different views on crucial religious issues.

Nonetheless, the way the Gospels appear in the Bible does not follow a chronological order, which means that for purposes of studying them, they are historically misleading. It is Paul who authors the first accounts of Jesus. His accounts are more like characterizations, features that define, not so much the historical as the resurrected Jesus and the implications of that event. Christianity has accepted his musings as being divinely inspired too, thus inerrant. But what are his sources? It appears that Paul had been an indirect recipient (or inquirer) of oral transmission. He zealously begins to persecute Jesus's followers because he had learned or heard that his sayings were desecrating Pharisaic Judaism, his religion (Acts 9:21, 22:1-5). Paul, however, does not indicate that he relies on oral transmission to reflect on who Jesus is. His primary sources, he says, are visions and revelations.

Paul appears to be well versed in the scriptures, having studied under Gamaliel, a renowned doctor of Jewish Law. He begins to persecute Jesus's followers likely after Jesus's death in the mid to late 30s CE. Nonetheless, following a most memorable episode, he starts to preach in the synagogues that Jesus is the Son of God. The Acts indicate that on his way to Damascus he falls (or is brought down) from his horse. He alleges that he hears a voice that asks him why he is persecuting him (Jesus). Blinded (by the fall or by Jesus), he asks who the voice is, and Jesus replies, *I am Jesus, whom you are persecuting.* Jesus tells him to go into the city where he will be told what to do. The men who accompany Paul also hear the voice, but they see no one. In the city, he is led to Ananias, a disciple of Jesus, who is told in another vision to visit Paul and lay his hands upon him so he may be healed. Once he regains his sight, Paul is filled with the Holy Spirit and is baptized (Acts 9:1-20). The story is repeated in Acts; Paul alleges that his companions do not hear the voice; however, he admits falling into a trance and having a vision in which Jesus tells him to leave Jerusalem (Acts 22:6).

He recounts his experience for the third time before Jewish King Agrippa I, saying that he may have seen Jesus, at least partially; Jesus tells him, *I have appeared to you for this purpose, to appoint you as a servant and witness of what you have seen [of me] and what you will be shown.* Paul adds that Jesus tells him he will be his instrument to guide the Gentiles, *that they may turn from darkness to light and from the power of Satan to God* (Acts 26:12-18).

Differences in Paul's story, i.e., whether his companions heard the voice (Acts 9), or not (Acts 22), may be set aside as a mental lapse (we all have them). Far more important are Paul's revelations and visions. He asserts that the gospel he proclaims is not from a human source, but *a revelation of Jesus Christ* (Gal 1:11-12). He is the subject of a vision that leads him to Macedonia *to preach the good news to them* (Acts 16:7-10). Jesus speaks to him, telling him, *do not be afraid. Go on speaking, and do not be silent, for I am with you. No one will attack and harm you, for I have many people in this city* (Acts 18:9-10). He indicates that God has revealed to him through the Spirit *what eye has not seen and ear had not heard* (1 Cor 2:10). Moreover, he states that God has revealed his Son to him (Gal 1:15-16). He speaks of visions and revelations (2 Cor 12:1, 17). He travels to Jerusalem with Barnabas and Titus *in accord with a revelation* to present the apostles the gospel he has been preaching to the Gentiles (Gal 2:1-2). He tells the Romans that he preaches the gospel that God has revealed to him (Rom 1:16-17). Moreover, Paul's insight into Christ's mystery is being revealed to his apostles and prophets by the Spirit (Eph 3:4-5), and although unworthy, he is given the grace to preach to the Gentiles the plan of the mystery hidden from ages past (Eph 3:8-10). He claims that the gospel he preaches about Jesus Christ is in accord *with the revelation of the mystery kept secret for long ages* (Rom 16:25). Although modern scholarship questions the authorship of the letters to Timothy and Titus, the texts state that God has entrusted him with the gospel (1 Tim 1:11, Titus 1:1).

Following Jesus's death and Paul's conversion, Paul begins to establish what were to become Christian communities, sometime between the mid-30s to 50s CE. Three years after his conversion he travels to Jerusalem and meets with Peter and James to explain what already he has been preaching to the Gentiles (Gal 1:18). Paul's letters, whose authorship are not questioned (1, 2 Thessalonians, Galatians, Philippians, 1, 2 Corinthians, Romans, and Philemon), are written approximately between 48 and 63 CE, years and decades before the Gospels.[4]

Given the significance of his letters to Christian theology, morals, and dogma, Paul must have received the equivalent of a graduate degree in Christology from the Holy Spirit. He writes on justification, the basis of which led to a schism and religious wars, while Jesus hardly mentions the term. His musing on redemption is different (no reference to temporal redemption) and more extensively elaborated than in the Gospels. He writes about Original Sin and a new Adam while Jesus does not. For Paul, the future of Christianity lies in paganism, the Gentile world. In Jesus, says Paul, there is *neither Jew nor Greek* (Gal 3:28). In the Gospels, however, Jesus tells his disciples to seek only the lost sheep of Israel and not go into pagan territory; (Mt 10:5-6), although he does; and he even derides pagans' behavior (Mt 6:7, 32). Paul does not write about the Son of Man, Jesus's mysterious moniker. He practically rebaptizes Jesus, referring to him as Christ numerous times, something the Gospels ignore. Paul seems to be the originator of the term *grace,* mentioned 81xt in his letters while the Gospels hardly mention it.

Because of these (and other) important notations, Paul's letters tend to undermine both the *gospel* and the Gospels, despite the latter is considered the centerpiece of Christianity. Since Paul wrote much earlier than the authors of the Gospels and told the disciples of his views, is it possible that God would allow such an enormous information gap (in both time and content) between Paul's revealed musings and the Gospels? Why would Jesus not tell Paul (or perhaps Paul thought it was not important) to write extensively about his arrest, death, his resurrection, his sayings, or his miracles? Christian morality at times is not as elaborate in Paul's teachings as it is in the Gospels; however, the opposite is true too.

Paul's letters would have become more authentic or legitimate if he had had the benefit of relying on the Gospels about the *gospel.* Whatever historical and empirical evidence there is in the Gospels would have provided Paul with a stronger foundation for his Christology. Viewed chronologically, Paul's letters weaken the Gospels' claim that it is divinely inspired.

Setting aside divine revelation, the Gospels' historicity, based on claims of oral transmission, would be more believable and serve as a firmer foundation to the Christian faith today (despite its flaws) than being asked to accept Paul's theology based on a vision (that may very well have happened).

Although Paul may have heard about Jesus's deeds, teachings, and resurrection, his objective was not to engage in an elaborate investigation from which he then could make plausible inferences. Perhaps the Holy Spirit reveals the faith to Paul, but his theology lacks solid premises, other than continuous revelations about which he says little. Hence, his interpretations of Jesus become gratuitous apologetics that Christians have accepted based on personal claims that he was the subject of God's revelation.

As a result, there is little that can be corrected in Paul's letters, since his theology is a reflection based on supposed revelation. His views on political authority and women are hardly compatible with Jesus's *gospel*. Hence, it is difficult to explain the *gospel* given Paul's letters, since the method he employs cannot bridge the Gospels and vice-versa. He does not necessarily describe the *gospel*; instead, he interprets it. As a result, the Gospels appear as being less divinely inspired and based more on human hands.

Notes:

1. George Reid, "Canon of the New Testament," CE, Vol. 3, http://newadvent.org/cathen/03274a.htm (accessed November 15, 2019). All texts in the New Testament appear in the same order in the NABRE and the King James versions.

2. Usage of the terms varies slightly according to each version of the Bible.

3. According to NEs, the term *the Word* has a profound connotation. Stemming from the Greek *logos, this term combines God's dynamic, creative word (Genesis), personified preexistent Wisdom as the instrument of God's creative activity (Proverbs), and the ultimate intelligibility of reality (Hellenistic philosophy)*. Note on John 1:1.

4. Timeline for Paul's letters and the Gospels are taken from the introductory chapters to each text in NABRE.

Righteousness

The term *righteousness* appears only 38xt in the Gospels,[1] suggesting that it might not have been a significant subject matter either to Jesus or the texts' authors. When viewed from a different angle, by relying on its true meaning, righteousness becomes the highest-ranking category in this study. As used throughout the Bible, righteousness means proper moral behavior in the eyes of God. Therefore, the Gospels are a compendium of moral and ethical *dos* and *don'ts* answering to the phrase *righteousness is ... or is not.*

Going through the list of categories in Table 2, it may be noticed that several of the most significant ones relate directly to moral teachings or righteousness; for example, the *Sinfulness* and *Sins* categories, i.e., the don'ts of moral behavior; *Faith,* the quintessential element of being righteous, along with *baptism*, the internal/external imprimatur of the Christian faith; the *Love* category, including its cognates; *Mosaic Law*, the initial concept of righteousness; *Prayer*, Jesus's major spiritual practice; the teachings on *Poverty* and *Wealth, Repentance, Forgiveness, Non-violence, Humility, God's Will, Righteous Sexuality,* and the *Parables.* Hence, once these categories were tallied, they were combined into a super-category, although each was still counted and examined as independent categories. Such an exercise was done only to state the obvious; that in their essence, the Gospels are a call to righteousness, a combination of proper belief and proper behavior, i.e., orthodoxy and orthopraxis, in the eyes of God.

In the Bible, righteousness is used rather evenly. Nonetheless, as with other terms in the scriptures, its examination reveals major differences. In the Old Testament, God is an ever-present and personal being, thus righteousness has little if anything to do with belief in God; its existence is presumed and acknowledged. Righteousness is about proper conduct. There are no gray areas in the meaning of the word, and no explanations or definitions become necessary, largely because the term has been described through the multitude of moral and civil rules and regulations handed down by God (supposedly to Moses) and contained in the Torah; thus, the reference to Mosaic Law. Accordingly, righteousness is used throughout various books of the Old Testament, its authors seemingly possessing the same tacit understanding of its meaning; the term is equivalent to conduct according to Mosaic Law.

Righteousness in the Gospels
Prior to Jesus's public life, the Israelites lived according to the interpretation of the term their ancestors had. Righteousness implied *observing all the commandments and ordinances of the Lord blamelessly,* like Elizabeth, Zechariah, Mary, John the Baptist, Simeon, Anna the prophetess, and even Jesus did, as he allowed John the Baptist to baptize him *to fulfill all righteousness* (Lk 1:5-6, 30, 76-80, 2:25-32, 36-38, 3:21-22, 4:16, Mt 1:19, Mt 3:15). This means that Mosaic Law had remained the prevailing standard of Israelite moral conduct. Deviating from commands that were considered to be divine was proscribed, thus rigidity became a distinctive (and perhaps necessary) feature of complying with the Law. During Jesus's infancy, the religious authorities were responsible for administering moral conduct in the Jewish theocratic state, and did so, following the Torah or the first five books of the Bible. It is not incidental that Mary and Joseph take Jesus to the Temple to present him to the Lord, *according to the law of Moses, just as it is written in the law of the Lord* (Lk 2:22-23).

From the moment Jesus begins his public life, however, he provides an understanding of righteousness that the religious authorities find incompatible with their own. Obstinacy on both sides is reasonable, as the religious authorities question Jesus's legitimacy. The conflict arises over the validity of each other's interpretations. It is not surprising that the religious authorities refuse to accept someone determined to keep company with sinners and tax collectors rather than being with the righteous (Mk 2:17, Mt 9:13).

A most interesting aspect about the Gospels, however, is that, in effect, Jesus disregards God's Mosaic Law, but there is no mention of the reaction on the part of Jesus's righteous characters, including his disciples, all of whom would have been stunned when Jesus contravenes the Law's central features and its human traditions. Another noteworthy feature of the Gospels is that this is not the only time that Jesus departs from God's plans. These instances happen so often that it raises questions about the continuity between the Gospels and the Old Testament.

Once Jesus begins to preach his views about the kingdom of God, his interpretation of righteousness becomes the new wine that would burst the old wineskin (Mk 2:22, Lk 5:37-38, Mt 9:17). When he tells people that only those who do the will of God are his real brothers and sisters (Lk 3:31-35), his audience has every right to reply that they have been doing God's will for centuries. Instead, the Jewish people do not seem to complain about the unorthodox claims Jesus is making. Only the religious authorities are willing to confront the itinerant preacher who is seeking to overturn the status quo.

Jesus confirms his role as the primary interpreter of righteousness when he goes into a synagogue in Nazareth and claims before the attendees that the Spirit of the Lord is upon him, and that God has anointed him *to bring glad tidings to the poor, proclaim liberty to captives and recovery of sight to the blind, to let the oppressed go free, and to proclaim a year acceptable to the Lord* (Lk 4:18-19). The Israelites, however, including the righteous ones, do not become alarmed when they see Jesus violating the Sabbath and calling their religious authorities hypocrites; when he tells the well-to-do that, contrary to the promises that God made to his people about material prosperity, now they are called to practice material poverty; that his followers are to forgive their enemies and pray for them. He tells the crowds that prostitutes and tax collectors have a place in the kingdom of God. He engages in a pleasant conversation with a Samaritan woman that must have astonished his disciples since it was contrary to Jewish religious custom. Moreover, indicating that he has authority to amend the Law, he forgives an adulteress that should have been stoned to death.

As the new interpreter of God's righteousness, Jesus's teachings represent a radical change. Overnight, the poor, the meek, those who hunger and mourn, those who are persecuted and *reviled* because of Jesus along with peacemakers and the merciful, they now become the new righteous people (Lk 6:17-38, Mt 5:1-12). As Mosaic Law applied only to the Jews, it suggests that, until then, God had no visible plan of eternal salvation for humanity. Now, Jesus teaches that eternal life awaits those who eat his flesh and drink his blood (Jn 6:54-59). He indicates that his relationship with the Father is unique; that in fact, he is God's son, and only those who follow him will merit eternal salvation (Jn 5:23-24, 6:40). The Jewish Bible includes the stories of the many prophets that God sends to make his people aware of their sins. Conversely, the Gospels appear to present Jesus as being the latest and seemingly the last one to denounce sin, redefine righteousness, and preach about a cosmic kingdom of God that awaits those that follow him.

Nonetheless, throughout two millennia, aspects of Jesus's concept of righteousness have changed. Despite the affirmation by the leaderships of the various Christian denominations that the absoluteness of moral truth lies with their faith, the mere fact that divisions exist among them belie its confirmation. Jesus's departure from God's original Mosaic Law is mystifying. Perhaps, moral truth needed adaptation to the times. Jesus, however, does not explain why God initially would hand down a set of moral guidelines to the Jewish people and then ask him to redefine many of its elements. Amidst the vast modifications he makes, the Gospels do not explain Jesus's saying that he comes not to abolish the Law but to fulfill it.

The responsibility to make changes to Jesus's teachings fell upon the apostles, since Jesus granted them authority to tie and untie things on earth along with the promise that he would respect whatever modifications needed to be undertaken. This is a most important element in Christianity that seems to have lost relevance. Calling himself *the light of the world* (Jn 8:12), and *the way and the truth* (Jn 14:6), it would have been reasonable for Jesus to extend his teachings and make them universal. Although there are glimpses of this intention in the texts, his mission is to reinterpret *righteousness* only to the Israelites.

Initially, Jesus seems to have a provincial understanding of his mission despite brief statements in the texts to the contrary. His instruction to his disciples not to *go into pagan territory or enter a Samaritan town, but go rather to the lost sheep of the house of Israel* (Mt 10:5-6) is, at the very least, in contradiction with the universality of Jesus's mission. There are exceptions. There is the centurion, a pagan whose faith is greater than anything Jesus has seen in all of Israel; and his encounter with the Samaritans, and few others. Innumerable explanations have been discerned that would clarify Jesus's intention at the time, but here lies the problem: discernment has led to innumerable explanations. Ironically, it is Paul (a Jew) who persuades the disciples to expand Jesus's teachings and the notion of eternal salvation beyond the Jewish people.

Jesus's concept of righteousness has continued to evolve most unexpectedly. Some of his most radical teachings have been ignored or set aside because they did not seem compatible with human nature. Perhaps they were unrealistic or not properly understood. Nonetheless, although the roots of his teachings contributed to the advent of new moral rights and wrongs throughout the centuries (as will be seen in other sections), different ones have emerged that have little to do with the Christian church in general. The term *moral progress* today has Christian, humanist, and non-Christian elements, suggesting that righteousness in the eyes of God continues to evolve.

Notes:
1. There are numerical differences in this category depending on biblical versions. The term righteousness appears more times in the 21st Century King James Version (512xt) than in the NEs' Version (294xt), because NEs' version uses other synonyms for righteousness such as justice, innocent, and right in the Old Testament while KJV21 relies on the word *righteous*. There is practically no difference between the two New Testament versions.

The Temporal World

The Nicene Creed, accepted by most Christian denominations,[1] begins by affirming *I believe in one God, the Father almighty, maker of heaven and earth, of all things visible and invisible.* Since its origins, Christianity has asserted that matter and creation are the work of a loving God, not the product of an evil act. During the first centuries, the faith had to struggle against heresies stressing the opposite, namely Gnosticism that held *matter to be a deterioration of spirit, and the whole universe a depravation of the* Deity; and Manichaeism that advanced the belief that two opposing elements, good and evil, each ruled by a supreme being, prevailed on earth.[2] Centuries later, the faith fought Catharism in France. As a popular religious movement with gnostic roots, Catharism (a form of neo-Manichaeism) affirmed the existence of two gods, an evil one responsible for the creation of the visible or temporal world, and a good one that created the invisible or spiritual world.[3]

This section looks primarily at how Jesus viewed physical or human existence on earth as opposed to the spiritual or supernatural realm. The results show that this category enjoys a significant ranking. It ought not to be surprising since the Christian drama takes place in this world, and it is here where God sends Jesus on a special mission. Since the term *world* is mostly used in the texts, particularly in John's Gospel, we need to ask what Jesus meant by it, and who constituted this world.

When the authors of the Gospels and Jesus use the term *world,* they are denoting the earthly or temporal dimension, physical matter, or that which decays and dies. However, in most instances, they are referring to the people who inhabit Planet Earth.[4] Information provided by a Greek geographer, Strabo, who lived and wrote during Jesus's time, suggests the possibility that Jesus might have been aware of a world that today includes Ethiopia to the South, Germany, and Britain to the North, and India to the Far East. His work, *Geography*, did not include the entire North and South American continents, China, most of Africa, Oceania, and provided only negligible information about Scandinavia.[5]

Appearing to be well-versed in the Old Testament, at the very least Jesus had to know about the existence of numerous and diverse groups of people that interrelated with the Israelites centuries before, including Assyrians, Chaldeans, Amorites, Hittites, Canaanites, Phoenicians, Persians, Elamites, Urukians, Babylonians, and Medes, all of which are mentioned in the Bible. Narrowing it down, the world that Jesus probably knew corresponds today to the countries of Israel, Iraq, Jordan, Lebanon, Palestine, Syria, Turkey, Egypt, and Iran, although it is likely that he may have heard accounts about the peoples under the Roman Empire living in Western Europe and the northern coast of Africa. This world was, for the most part, inhabited by Gentiles (non-Jews) with different religious beliefs than Pharisaic Judaism. People (including the Israelites to an extent) had become Hellenized due to the spread of Greek culture throughout the region following the conquest of territories by Alexander the Great in the late fourth century BCE.[6]

As the Gospels do not capture the true extension of the world Jesus lived in, it is difficult to know the exact meaning of his words *Go into the whole world and proclaim the gospel to every creature* (Mk 16:15); and in Matthew, *Go, therefore, and make disciples of all nations* (Mt 28:19). These words, appearing at the end of the two texts, suggest the desired universality of Jesus's mission and the need to reach, at least, people living in this part of the world.

Jesus's dramatic words in John's Gospel, *the world hates me* (Jn 7:7), are more problematic. What world is he referring to, the Israelite people who are not willing to accept him? A passage in John, *God did not send his Son into the world to condemn the world, but that the world might be saved through him* (Jn 3:17), in which he seems to give a broader view of the world, still does not delineate what Jesus meant. Although these are not Jesus's words (but John's), it is difficult to conceive that John only had Jews in mind. It must be remembered that Jesus said that he only came for the Jewish people, and the texts do not explain what provoked Jesus to alter God's mission.

Although Jesus does not travel too far from his land, his parents must have told him about their stay in Egypt. He also experienced the Roman occupation of Judea, and even interacts at least with one centurion whose servant he cures (Lk 7:1-10, Mt 8:5-13). The texts indicate that he visits towns in Samaria, where he heals ten lepers and his words convert many (Lk:17:11-19, Jn 4:7-42). He travels to Gentile territory visiting Tyre, where he cures the daughter of a Greek woman of Syrophoenician extraction (Mk 7:24-30), Sidon, and the Decapolis, where he heals a deaf man with a speech impediment resulting in his fame spreading throughout the region (Mk 7:31-37). He visits the territory of the Gerasenes (Gadarenes in Matthew), inhabited by Gentiles under Greek influence where he destroys a herd of swine to heal a demoniac (or two in Matthew). The people, filled with fear, ask him to leave the area (Mk 5:1-17, Lk 8:26-37, Mt 8:28-34).

Today, Christianity has expanded Jesus's conception of the world to encompass the entire planet and perhaps even transcending the Earth. Does it then matter that Jesus might have not been aware of the existence of two-thirds of the world's lands, or that the world would grow and become what it is today? Was he aware of the implications and difficulties of acculturation, i.e., accommodating his teachings to the various cultures on earth, and actualization, i.e., the rewriting of the texts to maintain his teachings relevant throughout history? Did he envision divisions within his faith and warfare among his followers; or the outcome of an existing heterogeneous and highly secularized world culture and its symbiotic relation with a divided Christianity?[7]

Jesus's Concept of the World

The Gospels' references to the temporal world are anything but appealing. As *the ruler of the world* (Jn 12:31), the devil subjects the temporal realm in a manner that is inimical to God. According to Jesus, the world generates behavior that leads to condemnation (Mk 8:35-36, Lk 9:23-25). He says that earthquakes, wars, and famines will take place (Mk 13:7-8, Lk 21:9-11), and although it is not clear if these are Satan or God-related incidents, there are no supernatural cures for these tribulations.

The Gospels appear to undervalue human activity. Jesus suggests that salvation is difficult if not impossible as the world constitutes a temptation for many (Lk 18:24-27, Mt 19:25-26); the kingdom of God begins as something small and then expands on its own, seemingly unrelated to what humans may do (Mk 4:26-29);[8] poverty will not be eradicated, regardless of human efforts (Mk 14:7); combatting evil deeds committed by others is not a worthwhile activity and is not recommended (Mt 13:24-43); since the body causes sin, it may be mutilated to avoid condemnation (Mk 9:43-48); human precepts and traditions are of no value unless they reflect God (Mt 15:1-8, Mk 7:1-9); from within the human heart comes behavior that defile--evil thoughts, unchastity, theft, murder, adultery, greed, malice, deceit, licentiousness, envy, blasphemy, arrogance, folly (Mk 7:21-23, Mt 15:16-20); the flesh, although created by God is weak and prone to sin (Mk 14:38); human thinking may be discarded since it is inferior to God's judgment (Mt 16:21-23, Mk 8:33). These passages suggest that Jesus regards the world with disdain.

According to the texts, the temporal world is ruled by a wicked entity that relishes in opposing God's plan by inducing humans to sin. In the desert, Jesus confronts the devil who admits that *all the kingdoms of the world ... with all this power and their glory* are his to give, *as it has been handed over to me, and I may give it to whomever.* Although Jesus rejects the offer, he does not contradict the devil in its assertion that it rules the world (Lk 4:6-7). Only God could have given the devil these earthly powers, which is the notion portrayed in the Book of Job (Job 1:7-12), or else God allowed it to take them. Jesus explicitly refers to the devil as the ruler of the world three times (Jn 12:31, 14:30, 16:11), even though in an apparent contradiction, in one instance he prays to God as being *Lord of heaven and earth* (Lk 10:21).

Satan's jurisdiction over the world is reinforced by the belief that its abode—the netherworld—a term Jesus uses, lies in none other than deep inside the earth. Moreover, Jesus's contempt for the world is detected through his teachings that detachment from the world is necessary to enter the kingdom of God. He tells his disciples that being concerned with the bare necessities of life is precisely what *all the nations of the world seek* but it is not what God wishes. Instead, we should place our dependence on God who in turn would fulfill humanity's needs (Lk 12:29-30). To survive in this world, Jesus praises maintaining good relations with dishonest people—even learn from them. Since they are craftier than *the children of light,* it might be beneficial to have ties to the children of darkness (Lk 16:1-13).

According to the Gospels, the temporal world is more likely to lead people to hell than to heaven. The gruesome example in Luke is that of the rich man who is seduced by the devil into being indifferent to poor Lazarus and ends up being engulfed in flames from which there is no exit (Lk 16:19-31). Sweeping generalizations, such as saying that anything that *is of human esteem is an abomination in the sight of God* (Lk 16:15), suggest that nothing of value can exist in the world; and no matter what is of human origin, it will be less worthy than that which is heavenly (Lk 20:1-6). Earthly values exalt the grandiosity of humans, their pride, and self-righteousness, while Jesus instead values meekness, i.e., those who acknowledge their imperfections rather than hiding them (Lk 18:9-14). The human body dies, he tells us, thus we ought to be more concerned with eternal life (Lk 12:4-5). These are strong words that even if they were to reveal a physical, spiritual, and moral truth, belittles an existence that happens to be the temporary dwelling that God provides to humanity. Today, Christian doctrine asserts that God's created earth is important because it safeguards and nurtures human life, and ultimately serves as the springboard into eternal salvation.

The section on hell suggests that Jesus entertains two causes of evil: the first is supernatural—Satan; the second one is the flesh, i.e., corrupted or weakened matter.

Both elements are present in Jesus's Parable of the Sower. Accordingly, once God sows his word among humans there are four types of responses among people; only one group is made up of people whom God has willed their understanding of the word, so the *word bears fruit and yields a hundred or sixty or thirtyfold* (Mt 13:18-23, Lk 8:4-8, 11-15, Mk 4:1-34).

This parable is highly instructive on how the two forces, Satan and the flesh, supposedly work to the detriment of God's plan. Jesus seems to be referring to the various dispositions with which people receive the word of God, though this is left unclear. For unknown reasons, it appears that humans are not equally created in terms of their likelihood to receive or reject God's word. Some do not understand God's word either because they are not well prepared or because God's word is so mysterious that it is beyond their comprehension. The act of Satan stealing the word supposedly stands for those who simply refuse to accept Jesus,[9] in which case, why blame Satan? In the second group, a fearful flesh is at work. However, would not Jesus understand that fear is a normal emotional reaction inherent among humans? Where is God when one needs him most, we would ask? The third group is made up of anxious people whose worries are too recognizable. While a minority of the world population driven by greed is mostly involved in accruing riches, the majority is concerned with unemployment, low wages, sickness, medical care, working hard to provide their children with education or simply having to raise the family's standard of living from poverty. Millions must deal with war, corruption, and famine; all understandable anxiety-producing events. The fourth group, however, is special because, somehow, they can understand God's word. It may be surmised that the parable refers to people who have a disposition toward prayer and possess beatitude qualities; yet how do they become so fortunate? What drives the first three groups to reject God's word? We know that Satan and the flesh were partially responsible; but what about structural inequalities that would induce people to behave in sinful ways? What degree of free will exists among the four groups? These questions address Jesus's understanding of human nature that at times seems naïve or harsh and in other instances merciful and understanding.[10]

What stems from this parable is the view that the world is not a safe place because Satan and the flesh seem to be more powerful than God. Beyond these two possibilities, Jesus provides an explanation that overwhelms faith and reason. In Mark, the disciples ask Jesus why he speaks to others in parables. Christian educators today would indicate that parables were among Jesus's tools to teach people. Jesus, however, tells his disciples that the kingdom of God is a mystery that he is willing to reveal only to a few, although to outsiders (the majority?) everything becomes more difficult to understand, *so they may not perceive, not understand, in order that they may not be converted and be forgiven.* (Mk 4:11-12). If taken literally, it appears that Jesus is not willing to spend time converting—and saving--precisely those who might need it the most. Moreover, although the statement may be addressed to people whose hearts are hardened beyond repair (is redemption not always possible?), in Matthew Jesus even wishes to confuse *the large crowds* (that) *gathered around him* by speaking to them in parables (Mt 13:2-3).

Not Everything Temporal is Evil
No matter how inferior and degrading is the flesh and the temporal world, and how contemptuous Jesus feels about physical existence, there are examples in the texts that express an opposite view of the world. For example, John celebrates Jesus's flesh as it *made his dwelling among us* (Jn 1:14). His body seems magical--*If I but touch his clothes, I shall be cured*—says the woman whose body is healed of her afflictions (Mk 5:25-34). Furthermore, before he departs the world Jesus leaves us with his body and blood to consume (Mk 14:22-24, Lk 22:19-20),[11] supposedly because there is value in them. Jesus sees so much value in his flesh that he is willing to give it up *for the life of the world* (Jn 6:51).

Despite their sinfulness, John the Baptist suggests that humanity is worth being redeemed, proclaiming that in Jesus *all flesh shall see the salvation of God* (Lk 3:6). The primary example occurs following the resurrection. Although Jesus could have ascended as a live spirit into heaven, it is important to the faith of his disciples and others that they see him again, not merely as a ghost, but in his flesh and bones (Lk 24:38-39). He still asserts that the body (and its limbs) can lead to sin by becoming attached to the world, and if necessary, must be ridden of rather than risk condemnation (Mk 9:43-48, Lk 12:4-5). However, if used wisely the body becomes a conduit to a superior level of existence (Mt 6:21, Lk 11:33-35). Moreover, despite the disquiet that daily living produces, there is some beauty in the world (birds, trees, flowers, children, and a few good people) that can best be appreciated by not becoming too attached to an existence that eventually will come to an individual end (Mt 6:26-34).

Jesus's mission entails setting *the earth on fire ... how I wish it were already blazing!* He also wishes to create division among families (Lk 12:49-53, Mt 10:34-38). These are unusual words from someone who is referred to as the Prince of Peace. But read between the lines his remark indicates that he is referring to a demarcation line between the temporal and the supernatural; between what dies and what lives forever. What divides people is the promulgation of the truth Jesus teaches. If *the Son of Man has come to seek and to save what was lost* (Lk 19:10), it is because he believes there is a significant value in what God created.

Jesus's words, nonetheless, are confusing to a temporal world populated by countless beliefs and 'truths.' The last time humans attempted to absolutize truth began early in the twentieth century and led to the forceful imposition of a Garden of Eden on earth; it was called communism. It too set the earth on fire throughout several decades after which it became recognizably useless and ineffective. It appears that although Jesus may want to set the world on fire, the way he goes about is different.

Another example indicating that Jesus has high regard for the temporal world is found in Luke, as he tells the Pharisees not to wait for the arrival of God's kingdom because it is already *among you* (Lk 17:21). The implication is that Jesus is willing to set God's kingdom on earth and allow humans to conduct their affairs while offering his protection (Mt 16:18-19); this would not happen had he not regarded the temporal world worthy. Despite this consideration, it is incomprehensible that he allows devastating events and promises to head the destruction of the world that God created (Mt 24:1-44, Mk 13:1-37, Lk 21:7-34).

Jesus is adamant that the earth is God's footstool (Mt:5-35), a useful sacred device that suggests that the earth must be appreciated and highly regarded. In one of the many perplexing passages in the Gospels, we learn that the earth is an extension of God's love, and that Jesus delegates authority to his disciples to set up a community of followers and grants them absolute authority over it (Mt 16:19). Why Jesus would delegate unfettered power to flawed human beings to make decisions in his name is difficult to understand. Would he defend all actions that high-level ecclesiastics make in his name even if they were evil?

In John's Gospel, the world appears even more alien to Jesus (and likely becomes more confusing to today's readers) than in the synoptic texts. The world originates through Jesus (Jn 1:9), yet it is sinful, as John the Baptist tells us (Jn 1:29); thus, God's desire to send his son to save it (Jn 3:16-17). Nonetheless, despite the light, i.e., Jesus, coming into the world, *people preferred darkness to light, because their works were evil* (Jn 3:19). In this passage, John takes a limited view of the world (unless he was anticipating the future), restricting it to the Jewish religious authorities and their followers. It is Jesus who tells Nicodemus that those who come from *the world* do not understand him, seemingly because being born of the flesh makes them inferior: *The one who is of the earth is earthly and speaks of earthly things. But the one who comes from heaven [is above all]* (Jn 3:31-36). The only recourse for people to be saved from this sinful world is to *eat the flesh of the Son of Man and drink his blood* (Jn 6:51-56).

The world hates Jesus because he testifies *that its works are evil* (Jn 7:7). But which world is this? Does today's world—all of it—hates Jesus, or is he referring to the small circle of people to whom he preached; or could it be those who, given the opportunity, choose to reject Jesus? It is difficult for Christians to read this passage and not feel antagonism toward a *world* that hates Jesus. This is the type of feeling that leads to neo-crusades and contempt for the world at the time we are looking for solutions to coexist peacefully. Jesus tells the religious authorities that he does not belong to this world because it is evil (Jn 8:23-24). Therefore, his followers must hate their lives and the world if they want to attain eternal life (Jn 12:25). Seclusion and a hostile posture toward the world would seem the logical response to be saved.

Furthermore, Jesus claims that *now the ruler of this world* (Satan) *will be driven out* (Jn 12:31). The statement weakens Jesus's credibility, as he said it two thousand years ago, yet people continue to empirically observe and feel the presence of that wicked ruler among us. Prior to his departure, he wishes his disciples his peace; not the world's peace, however, because the world does not understand about peace (Jn 14:27). *The world hates you,* he tells his disciples again, which is why he removes them (spiritually) out of the world (Jn 15:18-21). Physically, nonetheless, he not only keeps them in the world but tells them that they are likely to undergo the same fate as his, which will require the same courage as the soldier that likely will be killed on the battlefield. Thus, it is difficult to understand what Jesus meant when he said that he *has conquered the world.* What do these words mean from a temporal standpoint? In his last discourse, he asserts again that the world hates his disciples, just as it hates him; yet he purposefully keeps them in the world to continue his mission: to convince the world that God truly has sent him to authenticate his teachings (Jn 17:9-26). It seems like a futile ordeal; but then, why would he insist that God sent him *to give life to the world* (Jn 6:31)?

At the beginning of this section, I noted that Christianity has had to struggle with beliefs that describe the temporal world as a depravation of God's work and a source of evil generated by a god that rules the earth. Nonetheless, it would be challenging for the postmodern reader not to view Jesus's notion of the world as having Manichaean and Catharist traits. Both the Old Testament, and namely, Jesus in the Gospels, admit that God sustains or allows evil and its source; that God allowed Satan to wrest control of the earth from his hands and become a formidable force that would successfully oppose the divine. In the Gospels, the term *world* and *earth* stand for those who do wicked things as well as for a lower sphere of existence that due to its ignorance and the malevolent forces that guide it may lead good people to do evil acts that will eternally condemn them. The remedy to counteract evil, according to Jesus, starts with the belief that truth lies in him, and only through him and with him can evil be resisted (Jn 14:6).

In his confrontation with the devil, Jesus succeeds because he is *filled with the holy Spirit* (Lk 4:1), a powerful force from above. 'No wonder,' someone may quip today; if people, particularly those who have faith and have been baptized were given the same dosage of the Holy Spirit as Jesus, they might be able to successfully resist temptations and make this a better world. Noticing that humankind is ill-equipped to deal with evil, however, suggests that the dosage they receive is not high or powerful enough, hence they are at a disadvantage. It should be noted that while Jesus overcomes the temptation to do evil and is able to forge ahead with his message, evil forces win the physical battle. In purely secular terms (although with a religious foundation) the example that comes to mind is that of Martin Luther King who despite being assassinated, his followers were able to uphold his dream while they continue to fight and make progress toward racial justice and equality. This is similar to what Jesus commands his followers to do, even though several passages in the texts suggest that human action may be futile.

From a temporal perspective and regardless of belief, a person does not have to be Christian to notice there is evil in the world. Everything that Jesus says about the wicked forces that operate among us accords with empirical reality. Whether the devil exists or not may be beside the point for some people; however, what cannot be ignored is that something in the world causes humans to do evil. The obstacle to a sensible solution is that the existing plurality of 'truths,' including the many Christian denominations, poses an obstacle to a consensus. This is the challenge that Christianity faces today to salvage its truths.

The task is arduous. It begins with a divided faith unable to agree on concepts and views that Jesus might regard as trivial, but that has kept Christians at bay from each other. Logically, a divided faith would not be able to persuade others' beliefs. We may ask, however, if it is necessary to unify the faith to persuade others. Although helpful, is it possible to attain consensus on teachings and values that may counteract a common and detailed understanding of evil? Today, this venue does not enjoy much consideration as each set of beliefs seeks to prevail at being more legitimate than the others; unification would have to be attained at the expense of each denomination losing its identity. Given this pessimistic view, it is remarkable that the mundane world of politics that guides the behavior of nations (albeit imperfectly) has been able to reach far greater consensus on domestic and international norms of good and evil than religious denominations.

Probably the confusion over Jesus's teachings about the world makes it more difficult to spread his truth. While seeking spiritual dependence on God may be necessary, translating it into practice to the point of being unconcerned with the necessities of life might be unrealistic, since there is no evidence that food, shelter, and clothing descend from heaven. It would be interesting to see the reaction of the millions of people who worry about what they might eat on a given day to Jesus's remarks, and whether Jesus might consider these people worthy of him despite their daily concerns and struggles.

By rejecting the values that the temporal world offers without discriminating among them, we run the risk of discarding much of the positive activity that is common to all humans, including industriousness, inventiveness, common security, laws, government, globalization, science, technology, and many others. There is empirical evidence that supports the Gospels' view that the temporal world can be a potential path to perdition. The texts, however, overlook, to a large extent, the beauty, love, and caring that people with different beliefs can provide; simple human love (perhaps God-instilled) that while imperfect, can generate Good Samaritans among non-Christians and non-believers.

It is generally accepted that the thirst for material acquisition creates a great deal of anxiety, particularly when powerful minorities control most of the world's wealth leading to existing inequalities and daily struggles for billions of people. Nations are forced into competing with one another seeking to lure the production of goods and services away from others to provide for their own. Unruly competition was found to be desirable by Herbert Spencer when he coined the phrase 'survival of the fittest,' despite the nefarious consequences it would create. Nonetheless, the temporal world has taken matters into its hands, having to come to terms with rules of commerce and trade to ameliorate these consequences.

The other side of production is consumption. Temporal reality dictates that we must produce to satisfy human needs. It appears that this view was God's idea, as read in Genesis. Moreover, it appears to be empirically correct that the production process has gained the upper hand by creating artificial needs through the seductive process of branding and marketing that almost inevitably leads to consumerism. This has led to unsustainable inequality, corruption, social upheaval, crime, famine, and military conflicts. Nonetheless, it is also an undeniable reality that until humanity figures out a way to allocate resources and the outcome of one's work in a more just or balanced manner to avoid these social problems, the production-consumption process, i.e., the struggle for existence, becomes a necessary component of daily life even though it detracts—and at times renders obsolete—Jesus's teachings on world detachment.

Another incongruence that postmodernity may find in Jesus's teachings on the world is the dichotomy that exists in his actions. He views the temporal world as an evil place controlled by an evil ruler that he is willing to confront by establishing God's kingdom on earth. He redeems humanity by giving up his own life, and instructs his followers to spread his teachings, however, not to improve the human condition as an end in itself (since life on earth is temporal), but mainly for the glorification of God (Mt 5:14-16) and as a test of individual salvation. This behavior seems to be at odds with God's initial plan for humanity in Genesis to populate and cultivate the earth, whose people will inhabit a kingdom that has been *prepared for you from the foundation of the world* (Mt 25:34). Once the fall of humanity takes place, God's plans change; they now include the final destruction of his creation at the end of time. Human activity and progress become a 'something to do while we wait for the end;' a futile endeavor that serves merely as a test of loyalty (Book of Job). Thus, while we wait, it may be noticed that the outlook of the postmodern world, including that of most Christian denominations, has drastically changed from stressing the afterlife (salvation and condemnation) to building the earth, regardless of Jesus's teachings. Consequently, temporal needs and desires seem to be overtaking eternal yearnings. This is observed in the world of politics where ideologies compete for power oblivious to the end of time.

For Jesus, the temporal world is inherently evil because God has chosen not to (visibly) intervene and instead has allowed humans to figure out their affairs while offering Jesus as a teacher. His bipolar (or Manichean) views of the world range from subtle worthiness, to confusion, and exasperation. It leaves a weakened and flawed humanity thirsty for consensus on knowledge about good and evil, something that God initially forbids humankind from acquiring (Gen 2:16-17). Further ahead, other passages will be examined suggesting that despite God's wishes, salvation is more difficult to attain than many would expect, leaving people to wonder if Satan has not already won the battle in the temporal world.[12]

Notes:
1. The Catholic version of the Creed: usccb.org/beliefs-and-teachings/what-we-believe/ (accessed 10 October 2017); the Protestant version: christianitytoday.com/biblestudies/articles/ churchhomeleadership/ nicene-apostles-creeds.html (accessed 10 October 2017); the Orthodox Christian version: http://www.orthodox.net/services/symbol-es.html (accessed 10 May 2018). Jehovah's Witnesses reject parts of the Nicene Creed while accepting others. "What do Jehovah's Witnesses Believe," JW.org, https://www.jw.org/en/jehovahs-witnesses/faq/jehovah-witness-beliefs/ (accessed 10 October 2017); Mormonism (the Church of Jesus Christ of Latter-day Saints) accepts certain aspects of the creed and rejects others, particularly the Trinity: Daniel C. Peterson and Stephen D. Ricks, "Comparing LDS Beliefs with First-Century Christianity," March 1988, The Church of Jesus Christ of Latter-Day Saints website, https://lds.org/ensign/1988/03/comparing-lds-beliefs-with-first-century-christianity?lang=eng (accessed 10 October 2017).
2. John Arendzen, "Gnosticism," CE, http://www.newadvent.org/cathen/06592a.htm (accessed 10 October 2017); Ibid., "Manichaeism," (CE), http://www.newadvent.org/cathen/09591a.htm (accessed 10 October 2017).
3. For one hundred fifty years [Catharism] had a reasonable prospect of becoming the dominant religion. Church councils proved incapable of putting an end to the heresy and had to rely on military and inquisitorial power requested by the pope and carried out by French forces. Henry Charles Lea, *A History of the Inquisition of the Middle Ages*, Vol. 2, (New York, Harper and Brothers, 1887), 107-108, online at https://books.google.com/books?id=WeLb1vh84rkC&printsec=frontcover&source=gbs_ge_summary_r& cad=0#v=onepage&q=cathar&f=false (accessed 10 October 2017). See also Nicholas Weber, "Albigenses." CE, http://www.newadvent.org/cathen/01267e.htm (accessed 10 October 2017). According to this Catholic author, Pope Innocent III was justified in saying that the Albigenses were "worse than the Saracens"; and still he counseled moderation and disapproved of the selfish policy adopted by Simon of Montfort. Weber adds that what the Church combated were principles that led directly not only to the ruin of Christianity but to the very extinction of the human race.
4. At the time of Jesus our planet was not known as Planet Earth, but was referred to simply as *earth*, or ground. Alastair Gunn, Ph.D., "How did Earth get its name?" *Science Focus,* sciencefocus.com/planet-earth/how-did-earth-get-its-name/ (accessed February 19, 2020).
5. Sarah Laskow, "How The World Looked When Jesus Was Born, According to Roman Geographers," *AtlasObscura.com*, December 16, 2015, www.atlasobscura.com/articles/how-the-world-looked-when-jesus-was-born-according-to-roman-geographers (accessed 11 October 2017). Also, Strabo, *The Geography,* initially written in 7 BCE, trans. H.C. Hamilton, Esq., W. Falconer, M.A., Ed. (London: George Bell & Sons, 1903), Perseus Digital Library, http://www.perseus.tufts.edu/hopper/text?doc=Perseus%3Atext%3A1999.01.0239%3Abook%3Dnotice (accessed 11 October 2017).
6. For a detailed look at various civilizations and their beliefs existing before Jesus, see Chester G. Starr, *A History of the Ancient World,* Fourth Edition, (New York: Oxford University Press, 1991), chs 2-9.
7. If Jesus considered himself divine, including possessing divine attributes, then he would have had to know that his mission transcended the Israelites and peoples surrounding Judea as well as the conditions that were to affect the growth of the kingdom of God.
8. NEs' note, Mk 4:26-29: *Only Mark records the parable of the seed's growth. Sower and harvester are the same. The emphasis is on the power of the seed to grow of itself without human intervention (Mk 4:27). Mysteriously it produces blade and ear and full grain (Mk 4:28). Thus the kingdom of God initiated by Jesus in proclaiming the word develops quietly yet powerfully until it is fully established by him at the final judgment.* (Emphasis mine).
9. Ibid., note Mt 13:18-23.
10. Ibid., note Mt 13:18-23: *In this explanation of the parable the emphasis is on the various types of soil on which the seed falls, i.e., on the dispositions with which the preaching of Jesus is received. The second and third types particularly are explained in such a way as to support the view held by many scholars that the explanation derives not from Jesus but early Christian reflection upon apostasy from the faith that was the consequence of persecution and worldliness, respectively. Others, however, hold that the explanation may come basically from Jesus even though it was developed in the light of later Christian experience.*

11. Whether symbolic or not, it suggests a form of spiritual and physical cannibalism widely accepted throughout the Christian world, although it was viewed—and still is--as a bizarre act among non-Christians. The difference in Christianity, particularly in Catholicism and Anglicanism, is that believers do not kill the body of Jesus but consume his live body as an act of worship that he had requested as a means for believers to stay close to him and to receive spiritual graces that would assist them during times of hardship. In cannibalism, the victimizers commit homicide for various reasons, including a symbol of victory over their enemies. It should be noted that there are examples of cannibalism in the Bible in which God would force such acts upon those who defied his commandments (Deut Ch 28, 2 Kings 6:28-29, Jeremiah 19:9.).

12. In a Letter to the Bishops of the Catholic Church issued by the Congregation for the Doctrine of the Faith, Pope Francis views the temporal world in a very different light than that expressed at times by Jesus. The document asserts that *according to biblical faith, the origin of evil is not found in the material, corporeal world,...* but that *all the universe is good because it was created by God and that the evil that is most damaging to the human person is that which comes from his or her heart.* The letter, however, leaves out the role of Satan and limitations imposed by an imperfect temporal world created by God in causing sin. Congregation for the Doctrine of the Faith, "Letter Placuit Deo," 4, February 22, 2018, www.vatican.va/roman_curia/congregations/cfaith/documents/rc_con_cfaith_doc_20180222_placuit-deo_en.html (accessed 12 May 2018).

The Afterlife

The most important revelation in the Gospels is the existence of an afterlife. The texts assert that human life does not end with physical death, and, instead, continues with two types of eternal existence, salvation, or condemnation. This section tries to examine the implications of the Gospels' concept of an afterlife in a secular society characterized by religious pluralism. Content analysis results rank this category as highly significant, primarily because other categories that pertain to the afterlife are being incorporated into it. The emphasis on the afterlife in the Gospels provides the texts with an inescapable divine or supernatural tone. The results, however, do not constitute evidence of an afterlife; only that Jesus's message, as narrated by the authors of the Gospels, centers on the eternal continuation of human life in some form after death.

The Afterlife and the Resurrection of Humans

The resurrection of humans and their continued eternal existence is a fundamental tenet of the Christian creed.[1] For humanity, it is likely the most appealing aspect of the New Testament, perhaps because death is the worst tragedy that people experience in their lives; the death of their loved ones or the unforeseen slow ending of their own lives. According to Genesis, death is the penalty humanity must suffer because of the indiscretion of our progenitors (Gen 3:19). Despite its inevitability, the expectation of death creates a level of anxiety in most people; what will happen once dead; where would their loved ones go; will they see them again. From this perspective, human life is like a tragic comedy; something good is offered to them, only to be taken away. Many who have enjoyed their lives, likely would prefer to extend it into eternity; to those less fortunate, the existence of an afterlife would be as exhilarating as finding a permanent oasis in the middle of the desert.

Throughout the texts, Jesus is emphatic that there will be a resurrection of humans at the time of the Parousia or following his second coming to earth. Perhaps the most direct affirmation found in the synoptics is the passage in which the Sadducees, who do not believe in the resurrection, ask Jesus about it. He tells them they are misled, insisting they do not know the scriptures. To refute their view, Jesus refers them to a passage in the Book of Moses about the dead being raised (Mk 12:18-27, Lk 20:27-38, Mt 22:23-32). Awkwardly enough, there is nothing in this passage that relates to the resurrection. Moreover, Jesus's quote that God *is not the God of the dead but of the living*, does not appear in Exodus (Ex 3:1-17).

In John's Gospel, Jesus is more daring, using phrases like *never die* (Jn 11:26), *will never see death* (Jn 8:51), *never taste death* (Jn 8:51), *will never hunger, never thirst* (Jn 6:35), *not die* (Jn 6:50), *will live forever* (Jn 6:51, 59). He emphasizes the term *eternal life* far more than the synoptics and uses the term *life* by itself continuously, suggesting *eternal life*. It is, indeed, interesting that Jesus speaks at length about the resurrection of humans, given that not much is said in the Old Testament. Again, this is another profound gap, particularly on the theme that likely has given Christianity its biggest promoting advantage: the promise of eternal life.

While some people may be bored with their existing lives, they might still be afraid of dying, in which case the possibility of eternal life comes with mixed blessings. Everlasting life supposedly includes joy and happiness, which makes the promise more alluring, despite not knowing if joy and happiness in heaven will be similar to how people define it on earth. It does not appear that there will be sexual intercourse, one of humanity's favorite pastimes. Will people be able to go to the beach, play golf, fire up a grill, and drink beer? Will there be competitive sports, perhaps the largest audience-oriented activity on earth? Will people be able to attend the theatre; to see what, exactly? Will they have to work for a living, or will a divine socialist provider satisfy their basic needs? Will there be a need or a desire to sleep, a biological and pleasurable necessity on earth; or the desire to enjoy a warm bath? Even more important, will humans be resurrected at the same age they died? If a baby, will it reach old age? Will the elderly stay old, or will they be rejuvenated? Will there be a preferred age (20s-to30s) after which humans will no longer grow old?

Jesus speaks about the resurrected living like angels, except that we do not know how angels live; hence, the notion that it may turn out to be a boring life. Moreover, depending on how merciful Jesus is on Judgment Day, if many are saved where will they live? Will the earth be able to accommodate so many people? On the other hand, there will likely be peace; people will not become sick or go hungry at bedtime, and there might not even be a need for politics. It is not surprising that even Jesus's disciples seem clueless when he speaks to them about the resurrection of the dead. As he comes down from the mountain with Peter, James, and John following the Transfiguration, he tells them not to tell anyone what they have witnessed until after the Son of Man had risen from the dead. The three disciples kept the matter to themselves, questioning what rising from the dead meant (Mk 9:9-10, 31-32).

Announcing eternal life is an extraordinary selling point on Jesus's part. No other religion makes so much emphasis on the resurrection of humans. Nonetheless, what we understand by the resurrection of humans may be different from existence in the afterlife. Jesus does not mention (explicitly) the resurrection of the flesh or the physical body anywhere in the Gospels. Instead, he insinuates that the body will be resurrected through the use of the verb *raise* or *rise* (Jn 6:44, 54, 11:24).[2] It was the Christian (catholic) hierarchy that affirmed without reservations, as an article of faith, that the resurrection includes the resurrection of the body (the flesh in Latin and Greek) in the Apostles' Creed (date unknown). However, the Nicene Creed (325) did not refer to the resurrection of humans; this passage was added to a modified creed during the Council of Constantinople in 381. It then became part of most Christian denominations.[3]

The Crux of the Discussion About the Afterlife
The afterlife deals mostly with eternal salvation and eternal condemnation, who gets to be saved, who does not, and why. Answers to these questions are complicated. To begin with, it is difficult to find roots to eternal salvation in the Old Testament unless someone with a great deal of imagination engages in sophisticated extrapolations.[4] Although the term *salvation* appears (78xt, BibleGateway.com) throughout the Old Testament, it tends to have a temporal (not an eternal) connotation. Furthermore, the term *eternal life* that suggests an afterlife existence does not appear in the Old Testament, in contrast with the New Testament where the term shows up 29xt, mostly in John's Gospel.

Divisions within Christianity about who may be saved or condemned places the faith in an awkward position. Likely, there are dozens of official answers and even more unofficial responses to this question. Although each Christian denomination has its own distinctive set of beliefs on salvation, all rely on the Bible. Therefore, how is it possible that different answers can flow from the same source? Once again, either God is excessively mysterious (to our detriment) on an important issue; Christians are not canny enough to decipher God's message, or they are too self-righteous regarding their connections to God. There is yet another reason; the Gospels do not offer a precise treatise on the subject. The rest of the New Testament does not clarify the issue any further. Paul, for example, while seeking to add to Jesus's teachings on the subject, has become the primary source of reference regarding salvation, often taking Jesus's place as a spokesperson for God. Hence, it would not be surprising if non-Christians were to view this conflict with amusement and bewilderment, thus justifying their cynicism and indifference to Christian teachings.

The problem begins with the term *salvation;* it is seldom, and yet, ambiguously used in the texts. The term shows up (1xt) in Mark (16:20), and it is characterized as being of dubious origin.[5] In Luke, it appears (6xt), four of them having temporal connotations (Lk 1:69, 71, 77, 2:30); a fifth passage in which John the Baptist cites Isaiah, proclaiming that *all flesh shall see the salvation of God* (Lk 3:5), suggesting either temporal or eschatological implications; and another (possibly eschatological) passage in which Jesus points to the repenting attitude of a tax collector and remarks, *today salvation has come to this house because this man too is a descendant of Abraham* (Lk 19:9-10). In Matthew, the term does not appear at all. In John, the term occurs once while Jesus belittles the way Samaritans worship God, telling a Samaritan woman that *salvation is from the Jews* (Jn 4:22). Altogether, the term *salvation*, as used in the Gospels, does not always suggest eternal life.

The term *condemnation/condemn* (an aspect of the afterlife) also has a dual meaning in the texts, leading the reader to confound Jesus's words. He uses the term *condemnation* when he censures behavior that he considers sinful. In other instances, however, the term refers to a punishable sentence or conviction he will apply in the future, e.g., *they will receive a very severe condemnation* (Mt 12:24). These words can only be understood if condemnation takes place in the afterlife, a notion that he keeps repeating in many instances through the parables and in John's Gospel.

Furthermore, in the texts, Jesus uses the verb *to save* several times, not about eternal salvation, but while healing the sick. There are passages in which the sick come to Jesus, not necessarily because they have faith in the divine; rather, they believe he can cure them in the same manner a sick person trusts his doctor to heal him (Lk 8:50). At times, Jesus does not even ask for faith, and he heals without asking for repentance (Mk 2:2-12, 5:34, 10:51-52, Lk 17-19, 18:41-43 Mt 9:20-22). He associates healing with a temporal act of compassion, i.e., *saving* (physical) *life rather than destroying it* (Mk 3:1-6); while in other instances he cures through the forgiveness of sins even without the person asking for forgiveness (Mk 2:2:12, Lk 7:48-50). There are passages, however, in which *save*-related words are indicative of an afterlife (Mk 8:35, 10:26, 16:15, Lk 8:12, 9:24, 17:33, Mt 1:20, 10:21, 16:25, Jn 3:17, 10:9, 12:47).

Jesus identifies four basic requirements for eternal salvation: 1) repentance, i.e., acknowledgment and contrition of one's sins, 2) baptism, a physical act symbolizing the supernatural reality and necessity of being born from above (Jn 3:5-7),[6] 3) faith, implying trust in the person who by performing miraculous deeds and forgiving sins would be accepted as Son of God, and as savior and redeemer, and 4) righteousness, i.e., behaving in accordance with Jesus's teachings.

What becomes clear is that most passages in the synoptic texts emphasize good works or righteous behavior as meriting eternal salvation while John's Gospel highlights belief in Jesus as the preeminent path to eternity. Condemnation occurs when the opposite, i.e., sinful behavior or unbelief, takes place. In the synoptics, following Jesus seems to have been the outcome of personal trust. Having spent time with him and witnessing his miraculous deeds, his disciples believe that Jesus's teachings would be conducive to eternal salvation; indeed, a human aspiration possibly found even among atheists. John's Gospel, although it revolves around a series of miracles, is mostly about the necessity to believe in Jesus while moral behavior based on his teachings is seldomly mentioned. The synoptics, on the other hand, do not emphasize believing in the way John's text does; they are more about the act of being righteous, i.e., doing the right thing.[7]

Moreover, the issue of who will be saved and how, according to the four Gospels, provide incongruent answers, indicating that Jesus (or the texts' authors) is simultaneously operating on a two-track approach. According to Matthew, God sends Jesus to save only the Jewish people *from their sins*. This may explain why Jesus is prophesized to be the ruler of Judah; why he instructs his disciples not to go into pagan territory but instead seek only *the lost sheep of the house of Israel*; and possibly, why in John's Gospel he tells the Samaritan woman that *salvation is from the Jews,* meaning that any salvation would come through or from them (Mt 1:21, 2:6, 10:6, 15:24, Jn 4:22).

Other passages, nonetheless, indicate that non-Jews might be eligible for salvation: Jesus goes into gentile territory and cures pagans (Mt 8:5-13, 15:24); he praises and meets with Samaritans (Lk 10:29-37, Jn 4:39-41); the texts claim that *all flesh shall see the salvation of God* (Lk 3:5-6); that *repentance for the forgiveness of sins would be preached in his name to all the nations* (Lk 24:47), and that the Son of Man was sent ... so that *the world might be saved through him* (Jn 3:17). Jesus's change of heart is not explained in the texts, although through some of his parables he tells the Jewish religious authorities and their people that the kingdom of God would be taken away from them and given to others if they insist on rejecting him.

If Jesus was instructed to seek only the Jewish people, it would be difficult to imagine that he would disobey God's will and go on his own to seek the salvation of all nations. However, there are several passages in the Old Testament indicating that (subject to what their authors understood by the world, earth, and Gentiles at the time) all nations throughout the earth are to be included in God's plan of salvation, irrespective of what the plan may entail since it is not clearly described in the Old Testament.[8] The question that arises is, why despite having considerable knowledge of the Old Testament, would Jesus make contradictory statements, and why would Matthew's revelation include accounts that oppose passages in the Old Testament, all of which would render Jesus's parables regarding the Israelites meaningless? His attitude about salvation in the parables alternate between forgiveness and unforgiveness, salvation and condemnation, at times referring to the Israelites, sometimes with a view of Gentiles in mind. In some instances, he is merciful until the last minute; at other times he loses patience and is unwilling to widen the narrow gate.

An interesting passage contradicting the notion that salvation is extended only to Jews, and that eternal life may be attained through righteous behavior as opposed to belief, is found in the Parable of the Good Samaritan. This Samaritan does not profess the Jewish faith, and may not even be a believer, and yet Jesus sets him as an example of what it means to be righteous. This is likely the most inclusive and ecumenical of all parables in the Gospels. We do not know if Lazarus, in the Parable of the Rich

Man, is a believer or not. Jesus, however, says that he will be saved namely because of the suffering that he endured while the rich man will not. His description of who will be saved on Judgment Day (Mt 25:31-46) reaffirms these parables, suggesting that salvation is open to all.

The synoptic texts, I indicate, emphasize righteous behavior while John's Gospel practically ignores it, highlighting instead faith or belief in Jesus. The difference is awkward. Jesus makes it distinctively clear that *the Son of Man ... will repay everyone according to his conduct* (Mt 16:27), which is why he spends so much time (in the synoptics) teaching what this conduct ought to be like. His behavior presumes that believers act according to his teachings because they see in him an extraordinary teacher, the temporal Messiah, a prophet, or even perhaps the divine Son of God. Meanwhile, in John's Gospel, the emphasis is on believing, as shown in most of the passages outlined in note 4; hence, the message that *everyone who believes in him might not perish but might have eternal life* (Jn 3:15).

As questions surrounding the nature of Jesus arose years after his death, the nascent church struggled to insist on his divinity mostly based on Paul's letters and John's Gospel. Two centuries later, political, and canonical resolutions settled the issue at the Council of Nicaea. Proclamation of Jesus's divinity is important, as it would differentiate him from mere human philosophers, an event that would eventually lead *the catholic church* to assert that Jesus's teachings unveil absolute moral truths. It is at that time that insistence on Jesus's divinity becomes a dogma of faith and the essence of the Christian faith. The outcome appears to be a reversal of the synoptics; while righteous conduct (good works) is supposed to flow from Jesus's teachings, following the Nicaean Creed, righteousness, defined as good works, becomes secondary. Moreover, it is significant that the so-called first council in Jerusalem in or about 50 CE was not about orthodoxy or proper belief but orthopraxis, i.e., rightful conduct stemming from belief. The key statement issued by the Apostle James that led to the expansion of Christianity asserted that the existing community of believers *should not make it difficult for the Gentiles who are turning to God* by imposing unnecessary restrictions on practices (behavior), such as requiring circumcision of Gentiles. Ironically too, the council kept some restrictions including the non-consumption of certain foods and meat of strangled animals and forbidding acts that are deemed being sexually immoral, all decisions relating to behavior or deeds.[9]

Eventually, nothing seems to restrict the primacy of faith in Jesus from becoming the foundation of the Christian faith. But the primacy of faith over righteous behavior or good works becomes controversial when it is accompanied by the belief that there is no salvation outside of faith in Jesus, or even outside the Catholic Church. In other words, the Christian faith is reduced to the formula found in Mark--*Whoever believes and is baptized will be saved; whoever does not believe will be condemned* (Mk 16:16), and in John, *for God so loved the world that he gave his only Son, so that everyone who believes in him might not perish but might have eternal life. Whoever believes in him will not be condemned, but whoever does not believe has already been condemned, because he has not believed in the name of the only Son of God* (Jn 3:15-18). The understanding that comes down through history is that, while righteous behavior is important, belief in Jesus's divinity becomes the true path that leads to the afterlife; even then, only if God wishes it to happen since according to Jesus, it is impossible for humans to attain salvation by themselves (Mt 19:25-26).

The formula that only faith in Jesus can lead to salvation has kept some degree of unity among all Christian denominations while indicating that non-Christians cannot benefit from this 'entitlement' unless they convert. This doctrine of religious exclusion, mostly based on John's Gospel, is contradicted by other passages reiterating the significance of righteous behavior found in all four texts (and in Paul's letters), thereby creating a true dilemma within the Christian faith; not only does it alienate nations and peoples that have been raised under different religious beliefs, but 'forces' non-Christians to change their beliefs to be saved. Since Christian denominations have different standards of salvation among themselves, from a secular viewpoint the salvific process becomes a farce.

It may be accurate to say that religious inclusivity based on righteous behavior could dilute the identity of the Christian faith regardless of denominations. Two passages in John's Gospel illustrate the problem. Its authors assert that *whoever believes in him* (Jesus) *will not be condemned, but whoever does not believe has already been condemned, because he has not believed in the name of the only Son of God* (Jn 3:18). Meanwhile, John the Baptist states that *no one can receive anything except what has been given him from heaven* (Jn 3:27). These passages seem to indicate that those who believe in Jesus are chosen from heaven, thereby leaving those who are not selected in a precarious situation. It is well-known, however, that most people have little if any control over what they believe. Many choose not to believe because they see no empirical evidence to support believing; others are not offered the choice of believing in Jesus because they are raised under different faiths or philosophies. In these cases, is salvation being denied to people even if they comply with Jesus's standard of righteousness? Based on a literal understanding of the texts, the answer seems to be an unqualified Yes.

Paradoxically, sustaining these teachings suggests that Jesus was unduly unreasonable regarding who would be saved. In Matthew, Jesus tells people that salvation is not easy to attain, thus one must enter through the narrow gate that leads to eternal life, adding that only a few can find this path (Mt 7:13-14, Lk 13:24). He adopts a strict attitude about the observance of Mosaic Law as the path to salvation (Mt 5:17-19), and his words become more severe as he indicates that, *on the day of judgment people will render an account for every careless word they speak* (Mt 12:36-37). In Luke, Jesus is even harsher as he denies the already condemned rich man's request to send someone to alert his relatives about the torment he is experiencing in hell (Lk 16:19-31). At the same time, somewhat inconsistently, Jesus sets a rather low bar to attain salvation indicating that one's righteousness must surpass that of the scribes and Pharisees (whom he would condemn), or *you will not enter into the kingdom of heaven* (Mt 5:20).

Today, Christianity is beginning to realize that, despite conflicting circumstances, religious tolerance and religious freedom are based on Christian precepts: love of neighbor, respect for the dignity of all of God's children, and a Christian version of peace that forbids killing in the name of God. It is undeniable that acceptance of these precepts places belief in a divine Jesus in a challenging situation. Within this context, the Parable of the Good Samaritan is *de facto* anathema to the strict view that only faith in Jesus saves or that faith is more important than good works.[10] On the other hand, Christianity could adopt the Good Samaritan approach under the presumption and belief that everyone who is saved (including non-Christians) is due to Christ's salvific grace. In this manner, Christianity would become a more inclusive faith, as it regards all Christian-like good works by non-Christians as part of God's plan.[11]

Change is already noticeable. In a Letter addressed to all bishops of the Catholic Church, the Congregation for the Doctrine of the Faith with the approval of Pope Francis, concedes difficulties by the contemporary world to confess the Christian proclamation of faith that Jesus is the only one who saves. Without overtly contradicting Ratzinger's Declaration emphasizing deficiencies in salvation according to beliefs, the Letter states that Christ mediates *the salvation of God for all of the sons and daughters of Adam.*[12] In two extraordinary paragraphs, the Letter combines faith with *the care of all suffering humanity through the spiritual and corporal works of mercy,* indicating that *Christians must also be prepared to establish a sincere and constructive dialogue with believers of other religions, confident that God can lead "all men of good will in whose hearts grace works in an unseen way" toward salvation in Christ.*[13] It thus appears that the Catholic hierarchy is acknowledging the presence of God's grace in all good works regardless of faith or beliefs.

Beyond the Gospels' emphasis on an afterlife, given the incongruences found in the texts, no one knows who will be saved. Is it possible for God to grant salvation to non-Christians, or even non-believers? Would Christians accept the possibility that Jihadist soldiers could reach paradise since they follow what they sincerely believe is their true convictions? If someone believes in his heart that he must kill in the name of God (as Christians have done) can he be saved? These questions, which will be examined ahead, relate to other aspects of Jesus's teachings, including God's supposed mercy and compassion, his understanding of human nature, and his concept of justice or retribution, which at times seem to be at odds with one another.

The Afterlife in a Secularized Society
Jesus's core teachings are simple; all who wish to live forever, need to repent, become baptized, accept Jesus, and behave righteously in accordance with his teachings. Jesus's promise, however, has failed to persuade massive conversions from other

religions, those with no religion, or Christians who pay little or no attention to this promise. The teaching itself has become uninspiring, largely because of a prevailing and seemingly unavoidable materialist mindset indicating that humanity is mostly concerned with the present that is occupied by issues dealing with the excesses we seek or the deprivations we suffer. Additionally, and maybe as important, is the absence of an extraordinary incident that would jolt humanity's attention back to Jesus's promise. Circumstances in the world suggest that humans no longer fear God; that God's presence is not felt as it was felt in the Old Testament; and even then, God was less than persuasive. It is difficult to imagine how a merciful and benevolent God will deal with his creatures at a time when Jesus no longer seems to arouse the interest of his teachings among human beings.

Notes:

1. The Catholic version of the Creed: www.usccb.org/beliefs-and-teachings/what-we-believe/ (accessed 10 October 2017); the Protestant version: www.christianitytoday.com/biblestudies/articles/churchhomeleadership/nicene-apostles-creeds.html (accessed 10 October 2017); the Orthodox Christian version: http://www.orthodox.net/services/symbol-es.html (accessed 10 May 2018). Jehovah's Witnesses' version: "What do Jehovah's Witnesses Believe," JW.org, https://www.jw.org/en/jehovahs-witnesses/faq/jehovah-witness-beliefs/ (accessed 10 October 2017); Mormon version: Daniel C. Peterson and Stephen D. Ricks, "Comparing LDS Beliefs with First-Century Christianity," March 1988, The Church of Jesus Christ of Latter-Day Saints website, https://www.churchofjesuschrist.org/study/ensign/1988/03/comparing-lds-beliefs-with-first-century-christianity?lang=eng (accessed 10 October 2017).

2. Jesus tells the religious authorities, *No one can come to me unless the Father who sent me draws him, and I will raise him on the last day;* and again, *Whoever eats my flesh and drinks my blood has eternal life, and I will raise him on the last day.* When Martha tells Jesus that she knows that her brother Lazarus *will rise, in the resurrection on the last day,* Jesus seems to affirm the view saying, *I am the resurrection and the life; whoever believes in me, even if he dies, will live.*

3. In his *De Virg., vel 1.,* written around 200, Tertullian synthesizes the articles of faith that were believed at the time, and includes as the last article, the following: *destined to come to judge quick and dead through the resurrection of the flesh as well (as of the spirit).* The words in parentheses are awkward as they suggest that the soul is not immortal and thus needs to be resurrected. *Trinity in you.* https://trinityinyou.com/tertullian-de-virg-vel-1/ (accessed June 4, 2019).

4. Some Christian denominations have attempted to unravel the mysteries of God, a reason for which there have been so many modern-day "prophets," and divisions within Christianity. An example is the doctrine of Dispensationalism that claims to remove the cloud from the eyes of Christians by asserting that everyone else other than Dispensationalists is mistaken in the interpretation of the Bible. Charles C. Ryrie, *Dispensationalism,* (Chicago: Moody Publishers, 2007); about *faulty* "dispensationalism," Pastor J. C. O'Hair, *The Unsearchable Riches of Christ,* https://www.bereanbiblesociety.org/wp-content/uploads/2012/08/unsearchable-riches-of-christ-the.pdf (accessed February 20, 2020).

5. According to NEs, the Gospel of Mark *ends in the most ancient manuscripts with an abrupt scene at Jesus' tomb, which the women find empty* (Mk 16:8). They add, *other hands have attached additional endings after Mk 16:8;* Introduction to the Gospel According to Mark. They indicate that the longer version (Mk 16:9-20), although officially defined as canonical by the Council of Trent may have been added during the second century; NEs' note, Mk 16-9:20.

6. At the time, only adults or those who were old enough to distinguish good from evil were baptized, as small children and babies lacked such capacity. Later on, the Catholic Church concluded that baptism constituted a spiritual immunization against *the consequences of having been born with a fallen human nature and tainted by original sin that likely would predispose the believer to do evil.* (CCC 1250).

7. Below are examples of passages indicating the ambiguity of the term salvation as the outcome of faith, works, or both. Moreover, some passages underline the temporal nature of salvation while others its eschatological dimension.

Inconclusive passages:

- Mt 1:21, Mk 10:26-27, Lk 18:27-30, Mt 19:25-29.

Passages from the synoptic texts stressing that believing is necessary for salvation:

- Mt 8:10, 21:31-32, Mk 8:38), Lk 12:8-9, Mt 10:32-33.

Passages from the synoptic texts stressing that both believing and behavior (baptism/conversion) are necessary for salvation:

Mk 16:16, Mt 28:18-19, Mk 12:28-34, Lk 10:25-28, Mt 22:34-40, Mk 13:12-13, Lk 21:16-18, Mt 10:21-22, Lk 23:42-43.

Passages from the synoptic texts emphasizing that righteous or proper moral behavior in accordance with Jesus's teachings are essential for salvation:

Mk 8:34-35, Lk 9:24-25, Lk 17:33, Mt 16:24-28, Mk 9:43-48, Mt 5:29-30, Mt 18:8-9, Mk 10:15, Lk 18:16-17, Mt 18:2-4, Mt 19:14, Mk 10:17-21, Lk 18:18-23, Mt 19:16-22, Mk 10:29-30, Lk 1:76-77, Lk 3:3-4, Lk 3:5-6, Lk 3:9, Mt 3:10-11, Lk 15:7, 10, 11-32, Lk 6:20-22, Mt 5:3-12, Lk 6:37, Mt 7:1-2, Lk 10:29-37, Mt 5:20, Mt 5:17-18, Mt 12:36-37, Lk 9:59-62, Lk 13:22-30, Mt 7:13-14, Lk 14:13-14, 16:19-31, Lk 19:1-9, Lk 24:47, Mt 4:17, Mt 5:34, Mt 5:44-48, Mt 6:1, Mt 6:14-15, Mt 13:43, Mt 13:47-48, Mt 16:27, Mt 25:34-40.

Passages in John's Gospel that appear to stress behavior as opposed to believing:

Jn 1:23, Jn 5:29, Jn 12:25.

Passages emphasizing that believing is more significant than good works or righteous behavior: Jn 3:15-18, Jn 3:36, Jn 4:15, Jn 5:24, Jn 5:39, Jn 6:27, Jn 6:40, Jn 6:47, Jn 6:51, Jn 6:53-58, Jn 6:68, Jn 10-9, Jn 10:27-28, Jn 11:25-26, Jn 17:3.

8. The terms *nations* and *all nations* that supposedly include Gentiles, appear numerous times in the Old Testament indicating that a) the Jewish people are the favored nation, and b) that, eventually, all nations will bow before the Lord. However, the existence of an afterlife in these passages is not clear since many seem to refer to the temporal world.

9. Florentine Bechtel, "Judaizers," CE, http://www.newadvent.org/cathen/08537a.htm (accessed 18 May 2018).

10. The attribution of the Parable of the Good Samaritan to Jesus, along with other parables, has been questioned by none other than Fr. John P. Meier, a Catholic priest, and an expert in the historical-critical analysis of the Gospels. Accepting this view would have radical consequences, and possibly lead to a first step into the actualization of the Gospels. Meier, *A Marginal Jew: Rethinking the Historical Jesus, Volume V: Probing the Authenticity of the Parables,* (New Haven: Yale University Press, 2016).

11. Ratzinger's document proposed something similar: *Theology today, in its reflection on the existence of other religious experiences and on their meaning in God's salvific plan, is invited to explore if and in what way the historical figures and positive elements of these religions may fall within the divine plan of salvation…. The content of this participated meditation should be explored more deeply, but must remain always consistent with the principle of Christ's unique mediation. Although participated forms of mediation of different kinds and degrees are not excluded, they acquire meaning and value only from Christ's own mediation, and they cannot be understood as parallel or complementary to his. Hence, those solutions that propose a salvific action of God beyond the unique mediation of Christ would be contrary to the Christian and Catholic faith.* Declaration "Dominus Iesus" on the Unicity and Salvific Universality of Jesus Christ and the Church, 14, *Congregation for the Doctrine of the Faith,* 2000, http://www.vatican.va/roman_curia/congregations/cfaith/documents/rc_con_cfaith_doc_20000806_domi nus-iesus_en.html (accessed 18 May 2018). (accessed 18 May 2018).

12. Congregation for the Doctrine of the Faith, "Letter Placuit Deo," 2, 10, February 22, 2018, http://www.vatican.va/roman_curia/congregations/cfaith/documents/rc_con_cfaith_doc_20180222_placui t-deo_en.html (accessed 18 May 2018).

13. Ibid, 14, 15.

Love and Its Synonyms (miracles excluded)

Although Jesus's revelation of an afterlife is the central message in the Gospels, love of God and love of neighbor is his most significant legacy and the measure by which he will judge humankind. His audacity to transform these seemingly inconsequential rules and place them above God's Ten Commandments (see Mosaic Law), perhaps deserve more historical and religious recognition than what has been accorded.

This category pertains to the use of the word *love* in addition to terms that express love in the Gospels, e.g., *blessed, generosity, pity, mercy, compassion, caring,* and *forgiveness*. It does not take miracles into account (even though miracles may be considered acts of compassion), as this is done separately. The term *love* is used 91xt in the texts; John relies more on the word than the three synoptic authors (Jn 55xt, Lk and Mt 14xt each, and Mk 8xt). However, once its synonyms are taken into account (Lk 82xt, Mt 69xt, Jn 65xt, and Mk 25xt), the Love category becomes highly significant; it ranks even higher when miracles are added (Table 2).

In understanding the term *love* as constituting the core of Jesus's teachings along with the afterlife, it is important to delineate how it is used in the Gospels. The words *generosity, pity, mercy, compassion, caring,* and *forgiveness* are action-words, i.e., overt manifestations of love. The word *blessedness* is also included although it is separately examined to indicate how it relates to *love. Forgiveness*, owing to its significance in the Gospels, requires an even more detailed explanation and will be dealt with in a separate section. Additionally, there are other terms that despite being related to love, such as *truth* and *light* or transparency, are not accounted for in this section, although both show up in the Gospels.

Blessedness

The *love* category includes the term blessedness because it refers to an expression of God's love toward people who act in a manner that God approves. Blessedness refers to specific conduct that is to be emulated; for example, the types of behavior suggested in the beatitudes in Luke (Lk 6:20-22) and Matthew (Mt 5:3-12). It is commonly used in the synoptics, but scarcely in John (only 3xt), each instance suggesting a different meaning: as a greeting to Jesus's entrance in Jerusalem (Jn 12:13), as a reward if the disciples are capable of understanding Jesus's concept of humility (Jn 13:17), and when people believe without being provided evidence (Jn 20:29). As an independent category, it ranks as among the less significant, its noteworthiness being dependent on a variation of the term *love*.

Love of God in the Old Testament

In the Gospels, love of God is not the opposite of hatred; it is the opposite of sin, i.e., an offense in which the person rejects or is indifferent to God and his teachings (Lk 6:27-35, Mt 6:24, Jn 3:16-17, 5:23, 14:21-24). A thorough reading of the Gospels suggests that Jesus purposefully wants to make love among the central points of his teachings. He succeeds by radically amending God's rules contained in Mosaic Law. In Genesis, for example, God shows up as a supreme being who through trials (on his part) and errors (by his people) begins to deal with his creation on earth. By the time Exodus, Leviticus, and Numbers appear, God has become a Hobbesian Leviathan seeking to establish law and order in a theocratic society. In Exodus, the death penalty is in full vigor even for offenses that would not merit it today (Ex 19:12, 21:12, 14-17, 29, 22:1, 22:18, 31:14-15, 35:2). There are laws on the treatment of slaves, property damage, trusts and loans, and social laws to govern interpersonal relations and religious laws about feasts in God's honor.[1]

Leviticus illustrates that the reward for obedience to the law is ample: good weather, bountiful harvests, peace, and victory against enemies in case of war (Lev 26:3-9); if God's decrees are disobeyed, however, the punishment is gruesome:

> *I will bring terror upon you—with consumption and fever to dim the eyes and sap the life. You will sow your seed in vain, for your enemies will consume the crop.... Your land will bear no crops, and its trees no fruit... I will unleash wild beasts against you, to rob you of your children and wipe out your livestock, till your population dwindles away and your roads become deserted.... I will send pestilence among you, till you are delivered to the enemy.... I myself will discipline you for your sins sevenfold, till you begin to eat the flesh of your own sons and daughters.... I will lay waste your cities and desolate your sanctuaries, refusing your sweet-smelling offerings. So devastated will I leave the land that your enemies who come to live there will stand aghast at the sight of it. And you I will scatter among the nations at the point of my drawn sword, leaving your countryside desolate and your cities deserted* (Lev 26:16-33).

These breathtaking powers are accompanied by meticulous designs of artifacts and rules through which God describes how he would like to be worshipped including materials to be used in building the Ark of the Covenant, sacred vestments, and regulations governing the sacrifice of animals (Ex ch 25-29). Nowadays, this type of worshipping would be more in line with a cult of personality that would be the envy of modern-day dictators. Ironically, God's emphasis on ritualism likely conditioned the Jewish religious authorities' strict adherence to Mosaic Law at the time, an attitude that Jesus would harshly criticize.

Jesus's Amendments to God's Commandments
Jesus drastically transforms Mosaic Law by making *love* its central focus. He alters God's commandments given to Moses at Mount. Sinai, i.e., *you shall have no other gods besides me,* and shall not bow down or serve them (Ex 20:1-5), with a new and more forceful one: *You shall love the Lord, your God, with all your heart, with all your soul, and with all your mind.* Then, he binds two decrees from Leviticus, i.e., to love one's neighbor and to love the foreigner (Lev 19:18, Lev. 19:33-34), and adds a third one, to love one's enemy (Mt 5:43-47), thereby presenting three commandments, together with love of God, as the foundation and the core of his teachings.[2]

Although love of God seems to be the most important commandment, what exactly does this mean in practice? Jesus does not offer instructions to implement the part of the commandment that reads, *you shall love the Lord, your God, with all your heart, with all your soul, and with all your mind* (Mt 22:34-40). It may be surmised that loving God entails going to the temple, offering sacrifices, and praying. Nonetheless, Jesus seems to purposefully set aside all rules God had established for the Israelites to worship him to focus on the second part, *you shall love your neighbor as yourself,* as the empirical indicator of love of God.

There are in the Gospels numerous indicators of love in addition to the first two commandments: God's love for his son on whom he is pleased (Mk 1:11, 9:7, Lk 3:21, Mt 3:17, 17:5, Jn 3:16, 5:20); Jesus's love of the Father by doing his will (Mk 14:36, Lk 22:42, Mt 7:21, 26:39, Jn 10:17); Jesus's praises of the Father (Lk 19:45-46, Mt 11:25-27); and the close relationship between father and son, particularly in John's Gospel. Moreover, he teaches to pray for those who persecute his followers instead of retaliating; to turn the other cheek when struck; to assist those in need (Lk 6:27-36, Mt 5:33-44); and to forgive others' misdeeds (Mk 11:25, Lk 6:37-38, 17:3-4, Mt 6:12-15, 18:21-35). Lastly, love is defined in terms of fidelity to Jesus by keeping his commandments and acting upon them (Mk 3:35, Lk 8:21, Mt 12:50, Jn 14:15, 21-24).

The action words blessedness, pity, mercy, compassion, generosity, caring, and forgiveness are to be emulated by followers of Jesus. These words appear throughout the synoptics rather casually (Table 2). On the other hand, in John's Gospel, the term *love* appears four times more than in the synoptics, but the command to love the stranger (neighbor) or one's enemies does not show up; instead, John limits himself to citing Jesus's command to love one another only to his disciples (Jn 13:34-35, 15:12, 17). Moreover, none of these terms appear as commandments in John, although a few concrete actions reflecting these words are present (Jn 4:4, 5:1, 8:1).[3] In John, the search reveals that the term *love* usually refers to the relationship between Father and Son; God's and Jesus's love of the world and the Israelite people; the religious authorities' lack of love for God and Jesus; and Jesus's love for his disciples.

Temporal Love and Jesus's Teachings
In secular culture, *love* is among the most used words in the English language[4] The term connotes a variety of meanings. It indicates instinctively liking, being attracted, showing affection or desire toward something or someone; or it may suggest intensity of attraction, i.e., infatuation or obsession. It is culturally used to avoid using the term 'to have sex,' perhaps because of the failure of the sexual revolution that was supposed to end personal guilt and social shame.

More specifically, *love* suggests direction, from the self to an object, to another being, or even toward the self (pathological narcissism, selfishness, or a healthy self-centered concern). Even when described in non-Christian terms, as when applied to interpersonal relations, the word *love* denotes *goodness, unselfishness,* and *caring.* These traits likely are the most frequent manifestations of love, as they occur when there is a natural attraction toward someone we like (a parent, a spouse, a child, a friend). There is, on the other hand, a more challenging aspect of love; as ideal conduct, it is not supposed to be short-lived but enduring; its most purposeful characteristics are being unrequited, committed, willful, and self-sacrificing, i.e., having to love when love becomes an ordeal.

From a secularized viewpoint, the primary objectives of an act of human love toward those we like may include alleviating suffering and sorrow, protecting others from harm, fostering happiness and security, nurturing cooperation and generosity, and being sensitive to the needs of the other. This behavior is relatively easy to act out, insofar as relations do not become disagreeable; when they do, love becomes a challenge. As humans, we can repress these feelings (purposefully or as a reaction) when the self feels hurt. At that point, the act of love declines, sometimes temporarily, sometimes permanently.

Moreover, the human act of love is not limited to those we like. Whether moved by a sense of humanity or by God's teaching, many people feel a sense of solidarity that motivates them to feel a level of empathy toward others that surpasses even national boundaries, or religious, ethnic, gender, and racial differences. We have observed countless instances in which sentiments of pity, mercy, compassion, generosity, caring, and forgiveness are externalized following sudden awareness of people in distress as a result of natural or human disasters or conditions of poverty. Love (and its action-related words) is inherently human; we feel and experience it when it takes place within us.

Viewed temporally, Christian love is the opposite of hatred, indifference, prejudice, selfishness, or any other type of conscious or subconscious behavior that results in harm or injury (physical or emotional) toward others. When these sentiments prevail, love can be stifled or smothered. Within this context, given the amount of suffering humanity has undergone throughout the centuries, one wonders why love (which is not only a religious commandment but a human drive too) has not become culturally entrenched given its supposed personal and social benefits. At times, it appears as if human hatred and indifference are preferred despite their detrimental or downright evil effects. Although there may be psychological explanations that help to indicate why humans react with hatred and indifference to the plight of others, there seems to be a cultural aspect involved: the words *love, mercy, pity, compassion, caring,* or *forgiveness*, particularly when applied toward people unknown to us, have been debased, i.e., stripped of their proper value, by secular connotations as well as by traditional religious behavior.

The Downfall of Love

The ethos of the Roman Empire that preceded the rise of Christianity as a religion in Europe looked upon leaders that were driven by public pride and personal glory. Demonstrating superior capability over others would earn public admiration and reverence to the point of being worshipped as gods. The paths to attain popular admiration were boundless ambition, the capacity to be merciless, performing good deeds for personal glorification, power as a means and ends, and conquest and domination. A leader's prestige required respect for the empire's religion; except that its religious values conflicted with Jesus's teachings. Love, pity, mercy, kindness, and forgiveness were perceived (and still are today) as the outcome of emotional weakness, mushy sentimentalism, and romantic softness; values that were detrimental to a culture that relied on the symbols of military power and grandeur.

Nonetheless, once Christianity becomes the official religion of the empire, church leaders borrow pagan ethos, incorporating practices and beliefs into its rituals.[5] A telling example is one of the titles the Pope uses today; *Pontifex Maximus* was used initially to refer to the high priest of the Ancient Roman College of Pontiffs and was later adopted by the Catholic Church.[6] However, having expanded beyond its capabilities, besieged by barbarian invasions, and its ethos no longer able to inspire the loyalty of its people, the Roman Empire implodes. Almost simultaneously, Christian religious values begin to take hold, backed by the likes of Emperor Constantine and King Charlemagne.

As the church acquires lands that transform the institution into a temporal theocratic kingdom, it realizes that the only way to wield its authority as God's representative on earth and confront its existential threats is to rely on the same pagan ethos it previously combatted (the aura of power and authority, alliances, warfare). A contradictory dualism emerges in which the teachings of Jesus were juxtaposed to the necessity of dealing with power politics. No concrete church doctrine appears to deal with the problem. The teachings of Jesus, primarily envisioned to address interpersonal relations, are deemed impractical to deal with state-to-state conflict. Personal evil and sinfulness now must contend with individual behemoth monarchies that often question papal authority. Popes become adept at the uses of temporal power, having to enjoin holy alliances to maintain their earthly authority and guarantee the survival of the institution.

These are seedy times; Europe has become a continent riddled with turmoil, intrigue, domestic instability, and constant military conflict. Under those conditions, Jesus's teachings on love find outlets primarily through charitable works. The church hierarchy seems unprepared to deal with a new specter: sinfulness at the state and international levels. There were, for sure, significant theoretical developments in the ethics of warfare throughout the Middle Ages that were incorporated into the United Nations Charter; among the most noteworthy ones being the prohibition of military action for preventive purposes.[7] Nonetheless, the harm could not be undone. A normative doctrine (attributed to Machiavelli) claiming to offer a realistic picture of world affairs emerges, asserting that human behavior at the state level requires special rules of conduct. Since then, pagan ethos. e.g., power, force, and self-interest, become dominant; the church, overtaken by events, is not only unable to suppress them; it uses them for its own survival.

Continued warfare (including religious wars among Christians), the development of ruthless capitalism, mercantilism, colonialism, communism, nazism, two world wars, the Cold War, the atomic era, ICBMs and Mutual Assured Destruction, and a warped version of Islam resulting in terrorism, have reinforced the view that the world still remains in a dysfunctional state of nature. The emergence of other serious issues, such as continued poverty, political corruption, environmental degradation, human trafficking, religious persecution, the possibility of another arms race (this time in space), relate to the widening of a path to the possible destruction of civilization. Amid these existential issues, there now appears a potentially lethal human attitude, domestic and international *polarization.* Seemingly accepted as inevitable, polarization may be likened to infested waters out which emerge hatred, divisiveness, and social conflict.

As fear and insecurity take over, large sectors of populations worldwide have come to accept that the teachings of Jesus, preached and believed by millions, are useless and not to be taken seriously when dealing with current worldwide conditions. Instead, existing circumstances call for a set of opposite values, including a certain level of callousness and mercilessness simulating level-headedness, firmness, and resolve. Embedded within the practical efficiency of pagan ethos is a type of human conduct that Jesus addresses that hinders the resolution of domestic and international problems: human pride or hubris. At the personal and national levels, human pride induces self-righteousness, a myopic reaction that prevents us from recognizing mistakes within ourselves. At the national level, it is perhaps the greatest unrecognized political evil. As of today, the effectiveness of the existing set of secularized values capable of transcending rivalries that would allow the solution of world problems, such as the United Nations Charter, is marginal at best. We seem unable to escape the view that only power politics offers a sensible set of values to ensure human survival.

Human Poverty, Love, Pity, and Compassion
It appears that a primary reason for which Jesus makes love the central core of his teachings is to address human suffering and to create peaceful living conditions. Nonetheless, under the current political culture, there is a sizable sector of the world population that holds the view that addressing poverty by formulating policies based on love, mercy, compassion, generosity, kindness, and caring demeans those who support such policies as well as those toward whom the action is directed. Helpless people are seen as indulging in self-sorrow, as miserable beings unable to raise themselves by their bootstraps, or shameless persons that take advantage of the welfare state and the generosity of the faint-hearted. As long as this language prevails, Jesus's commandment (or its humanist version) to love would fall on deaf ears.

Philosophically, this view was espoused in the nineteenth century by philosopher Friedrich Nietzsche who believed that *an unwillingness to help* [those in need] *may be nobler than the virtue that rushes to do so.*[8] He viewed kindness and pity as the type of weakness that would be intolerable to his conception of a "Superman," characterized by a dominating will to power capable of resisting frail emotions in order to assert oneself in life. This view is shared today in the form of attitudes and political ideologies by millions of people within the most advanced (and less developed) nations that call themselves Christians. These values and ideologies tend to express disdain for inclusivity and acceptance of those who confront human suffering, racial, religious, gender, or ethnic discrimination, and people fleeing misery and crime at home. They tend to exacerbate divisiveness, intolerance, and violence. In reaction to this behavior, a narrow-minded opposition exhibiting similar conduct seems to be creeping worldwide.[9]

Irrespective of the circumstances that incapacitate some people, e.g., whether poverty, crime, lack of education, disability, unemployment, health issues, age, or gender, it is a verifiable reality that distress and misfortune have occurred since creation, and likely will continue to befall humanity in the foreseeable future. The question is, how do we as human beings deal with such issues; what should be the attitude of the more powerful or fortunate people toward those in need of assistance? Several alternatives have been placed in practice over the years, including eugenics policies to reduce sectors of the population deemed to be physically, mentally, or conceivably morally deficient by improving the quality of the human population through selective practices, euthanasia, and genocide[10] as well as the temporal conception of the new man that Marxist-Leninist totalitarianism sought to recreate.

If the above approaches appear to be distasteful, the body politic might need to forge a stronger social contract in which policies based on compassion are formulated to deal with the more helpless sector of the world population as a means to prevent the unpalatable consequences of human indifference. Altogether, it is possible to see in the Gospels the foundation of an acceptable social contract (despite its contradictions). The love-pity-mercy-compassion-generosity-caring/kindness-forgiveness behavioral linkage might be useful to overcome the discriminatory and divisiveness tendencies in contemporary society. However, there only seems to be a slim chance for this conduct to emerge as long as the stigma of weakness attached to these Christian terms prevails in a secularized culture.

Nothing in the Gospels explains the psychological undertones of Jesus's teachings, despite their profound implications. Empirical studies focusing on the fields of social psychology, sociology, health, economics, and politics linking love of others to personal and social outcomes are lacking at the academic and cultural levels. In the Gospels, Jesus indicates inclusivity among races, ethnic groups, nationalities, gender, and people of different socio-economic backgrounds. But his teachings have additional features. He is intolerant of practices that would disfigure his version of worshipping God while being willing to maintain relations with peoples of other religions, including pagans. He clearly favors sinners who repent (as he wishes to save them, Lk 15:1-7, Mt 9:13); those who suffer (the sick, the poor and the meek, those who mourn, victims of injustice and persecution); followed by those who pursue peace, and people who possess a clean heart (Lk 6:20-23, Mt 5:1-12). Although among his followers there are wealthy persons and intellectuals (Nicodemus, Joseph of Arimathea, a scribe, a scholar of the law), Jesus exhibits disdain toward rich and proud people (Lk 6:24-26) who seek to serve both mammon and God together.

He abhors hypocrisy (Mk 7:5-7, Mt 6:2,5,16, 23:13-30), and feels contempt for those who decline God's invitation (Mt 22:1-14). The love he feels enrages him when he notices people who are indifferent to human suffering, to the point that he makes assistance to those in need the ultimate standard on Judgment Day (Mt 25:31-46). Reconciliation, repentance, forgiveness, mercy, and a clean heart are inherent to his commandment to love one another. It is the attitudes of those who ignore these teachings that he seems to despise, supposedly because they are conscientiously rejecting God.

This brings us to an inherent difficulty in understanding the commandments to love God and to love one's neighbor. If a non-Christian or an atheist were to ask, which commandment is more important, what would the reply be to those who do not believe in God or were not raised in the Christian faith; would they meet Jesus's criteria of righteousness? Would the Parable of the Good Samaritan asserting love of stranger by a non-Christian be the practical application of the commandment to love God *with all your heart, with all your being, with all your strength, and with all your mind* (Lk 10:25-37)?

Love as Jesus's Dilemma
Jesus's teachings on love (unless they are only regarded as an individualistic test to attain salvation), pose a puzzling incongruence. The commandment to love predisposes the believer to turn his or her attention to the temporal world; the same world that is governed by Satan and whose fleeting existence stands in contrast with an afterlife that lasts forever. Jesus's seeming contempt for the world is real, leading him to say, *do not store up for yourselves treasures on earth, where moth and decay destroy, and thieves break in and steal. But store up treasures in heaven, where neither moth nor decay destroys, nor thieves break in and steal* (Mt 6:19-20).

On the other hand, the commandment to manifest human love on earth places the value of temporal life alongside that of the afterlife in a delicate balance, if not into an outright contradiction. Neither Jesus nor the authors of the texts attempt to solve the dilemma, presuming they are aware of its existence. Initially, it was God's design that humans populate and build the earth. We must assume that it was not God's wishes for humans to behave like Cain and Abel, although that has been humanity's history. In the Old Testament, however, God appears to be more concerned about the way he wishes his people to worship him and how they behave toward one another. In his teachings on love, Jesus seems to be earnest that his followers obey his commandment to love God and one another. Many passages confirm this view. Nevertheless, it is difficult to negate the incongruences in Jesus's remarks on the temporal world and the afterlife.

Christianity's Inability to Love
The question must be raised: why has the application of God's commandment to love one another failed to become more deeply embedded within cultures where Christian

majorities prevail, i.e., in Europe (including Russia and excluding Estonia and the Czech Republic), North, Central, and South America, the Caribbean Islands, most of Oceania, the Philippines, and Sub-Saharan Africa? Altogether, these peoples constitute the world's largest religion (thirty-one percent of the world's population or 2.3 billion).[11] Despite the complexity of the question, a simplistic yet not philosophically unfounded answer exists. Since the essence of Christianity is love, and Christians are supposed to become *the salt of the earth* (Mt 5:13), and *the light of the world* (Mt. 5:14), a reasonable conclusion is that Christian salt has lost its flavor and its light is slowly burning out.

From a non-Christian outlook, a most serious contributing factor to the slow demise of the Christian faith is its centuries-old divisiveness that has evolved into religious tribalism. Despite esoteric ecumenical conversations, Christian denominations appear contented to maintain their independence and their identity, seeking to spread a unique message that owing to the various interpretations has resulted in a politically fractionalized faith.

Thus, it may not be surprising that the Christian God (prematurely declared dead one hundred twenty years ago) is indeed dying a gradual death as younger generations are losing interest in searching for a unified truth in a specific set of values. It appears that newer generations are joining the ranks of the *nones* (no religious affiliation) in droves; since divisiveness seems to matter little to the various religious tribes, these new generations appear to be randomly creating their own secularized version of Christian love. This view finds support in recently conducted polls in the US where most *nones* have chosen no religious affiliation because they have questions over religious teachings, i.e., the message is incoherent; because social and political polarization has taken over the faith; because they simply find religious organizations irrelevant, meaning they lack credibility; and because they dislike religious leaders.[12] These conditions point to a troublesome issue. Love, along with faith and hope, is said to be infused by God in people, meaning that it is God who is ultimately responsible for these virtues. Nonetheless, if the trend seems to be moving toward love of neighbor as an indication of human solidarity, is the love expressed by these generations less worthy because the faith factor is absent, or could it be that it is God who drives people to love one another regardless of faith?

Another more recent and traumatic issue that non-Christians must find highly disturbing is the recurrence of child sexual abuse incidents in various parts of the world, particularly by members of the Catholic clergy. Notwithstanding that these sad, sick, and felonious acts do not stem from anything found in the Gospels, rather the opposite (Lk 17:1-2), it is conceivable that this crisis will affect Catholicism (and perhaps Christianity in general) for generations to come. Given the emotional way humans perceive these events, this behavior has unintentionally corrupted the Christian message in the eyes of outsiders. Already, the crisis is drowning the Christian messages on poverty, marriage, religious persecution, wars, and environmental degradation. While no in-depth polling has been undertaken, it would not be surprising if a response akin to 'don't talk to us about Jesus while his representatives engage in these crimes' polls high.

Another Impediment to Love (Lost in Translation)
There is another explanation for love's inability to go beyond loving those we like. Since Jesus does not seem to impose limitations on love, theoretically, love of neighbor is an open field that has been fenced in by its definition. It is problematic that the commandment to love is often taken too literally, suggesting that love of neighbor is limited to one's neighbor, or as in the case of the Good Samaritan, to the stranger we meet on the road. While reviewing the Gospels, it is easy for the reader to suppose that Jesus's teachings fall under the personal morality category; that his teachings are limited to one's conduct toward people with whom we interact (family members, neighbors, work colleagues, or those we run into in our streets).

Since many Christians lead racially, ethnically, and religiously isolated lives, this interpretation would allow them to justify and support discriminatory practices toward diverse groups of people with whom they have little or no contact. This view would be an excellent excuse for believers to avoid feeling compassion toward migrants they have not met, or toward the poor and the sick they seldom encounter. National political, civic, and religious leaders carrying the Christian label could foster contempt toward other nationalities, races, and ethnicities to score points at home. The rationale seems tight and impeccable; unless Christians confront strangers physically, they will not be under the obligation to care about them. If this were to be the outcome of Jesus's teaching, Christianity would seem shortsighted as a moral doctrine. There is no doubt that the commandment to love one's neighbor, as it appears in the Gospels, requires substantial extrapolation from physical closeness to the remote existence of people we do not know. Today, it is virtually impossible to ignore the existential crises of strangers in other parts of the world. Thus, it becomes apparent that Christians who express indifference or contempt toward those they know are in dire need but have not met physically, likely do so deliberately.

Christian Love in the Age of Pandemics
At a time when the world is beginning to face pandemics, are Jesus's teachings of any help? There are knots in the Gospels that seem difficult to untie. Throughout the world, the impact of the Covid 19 pandemic brought these knots out into the open. Many people wanted to continue to attend religious services despite the elevated level of contagiousness and transmission of the virus. At the personal level, a conflict ensued involving religion, politics, morality, and science, only to find that the conflict may reflect contradictions in the Gospels. Some among the faithful would take a cue from Jesus telling them, *do not be afraid of those who kill the body but cannot kill the soul; rather, be afraid of the one who can destroy both soul and body in Gehenna* (Mt 10:28). These people would attend religious services to pray to an end of the pandemic

(a selfless act), at the risk of becoming contagious and spreading the disease to others who might not even be Christians or wish to become sick or die. Other Christians, however, no less faithful, would follow Jesus's commandment to care for one's neighbor (which would include relatives, friends, and strangers), and decide not to congregate in places of worship for fear of becoming infected and passing the disease to others. Who is right?

In many countries, secular political ideologies would ultimately decide, some in favor of religion and others in favor of science (presuming science has indicated that attending religious services contribute to the spread of the disease). What would Jesus do under these circumstances? Nothing prevents the faithful from praying for others in solitude at home. Nonetheless, by isolating oneself willingly, the faithful would also be caring for others (love of neighbor) in a more reasonable (scientific) manner. I could see Jesus scratching his head on this issue. It is one thing to not be afraid of dying, but should this expression of faith be displayed at the expense of being indifferent to others?

Notes

1. Ex 21, 22, 23.

2. In Matthew and Mark, their respective passages indicate two distinct commandments while in Luke both love of God and love of neighbor constitute one commandment. In John, Jesus speaks to his disciples about the need to keep commandments, i.e. teachings, although twice he refers to a new commandment, to love one another as he has loved them. Furthermore, it is important to recognize that Jesus's commandment to love one's enemy is partially based on Matthew's inaccurate citation of Jesus (otherwise it is Jesus's mistake). Jesus teaches that enemies are to be loved in part because of the preceding sentence in the passage: *You have heard that it was said, 'You shall love your neighbor and hate your enemy.'* Nonetheless, as NEs point out, *there is no Old Testament commandment demanding hatred of one's enemy, but the "neighbor" of the love commandment was understood as one's fellow countryman.* NEs' note, Mt 5:43-48; it adds that *both in the Old Testament (Ps 139:19–22) and at Qumran (1QS 9:21) hatred of evil persons is assumed to be right.*).

3. Some of Jesus's miracles in John's Gospel are not primarily motivated by pity or compassion, but namely to foster faith in him: 2:1 Cana, 4:46 healing the official's son, 6:5 feeding thousands, 6:16 walking on water, 9:1 healing the blind man, 11:1 raising Lazarus.

4. *Word Frequency Data*, English-Corpora.org (accessed July 22, 2018).

5. CE admits Christianity's fertilization of ideas with the Roman world that Christianity *did not disdain to use, to transcend, and to transform.* Cyril Charles Martindale, "Paganism," CE, Vol. 11, http://www.newadvent.org/cathen/11388a.htm (accessed on August 21, 2018).

6. "Pontifex Maximus," *New World Encyclopedia*, *http://www.newworldencyclopedia.org/entry/Pontifex_Maximus#Credits* (accessed online August 21, 2018). *As regards the title Pontifex Maximus, especially in its application to the pope, there was further a reminiscence of the dignity attached to that title in pagan Rome.* George Joyce, "The Pope." *Catholic Encyclopedia* Vol. 12, 1911), http://www.newadvent.org/cathen/12260a.htm (accessed online 21 Aug. 2018).

7. Thomas Massaro SJ, Thomas A. Shannon, *Catholic Perspectives on Peace and War*, Chapters 1-2, (Lanham: Rowman & Littlefield Publishers, 2003). On the prohibition of military force for preventive purposes see United Nations Charter, Article 2(4), online http://www.un.org/en/sections/un-charter/un-charter-full-text/ (accessed August 23, 2018).

8. Friedrich Nietzsche, *Thus Spoke Zarathustra*, LXVII, The Ugliest Man, The Project Gutenberg EBook https://www.gutenberg.org/files/1998/1998-h/1998-h.htm (accessed on August 4, 2018).

9. Nowadays these extreme ideologies (that will rely on violence and actions to repress free speech) are identified with Nazism, white supremacy or white nationalism, alt-Right, and the KKK on one end, and the Antifa or anti-fascist groups made up of neo-Marxists, anarchists, and progressive elements on the other. Interestingly, conservative and progressive Christians militate on both sides.

10. Hesketh T, Lu L, Xing ZW., "The consequences of son preference and sex-selective abortion in China and other Asian countries," CMAJ : Canadian Medical Association Journal. 2011;183(12):1374-1377. doi:10.1503/cmaj.101368. https://www.ncbi.nlm.nih.gov/pmc/articles/PMC3168620/ (accessed August 15, 2018); Also, China's 'one-child' policies led to forced abortion. Mei Fong, *One Child: The Story of China's Most Radical Experiment,* (Boston: Houghton Mifflin Harcourt, January 5, 2016). In the United States and many developed and semi-developed countries, abortion has become legal for the reasons outlined in the document. Regarding infanticide, *the US has the highest rates of child homicide (8.0/100,000 for infants, 2.5/100,000 for preschool-age children, and 1.5/100,000 for school-age children). The problem of child homicide transcends national boundaries. These rates of child murder are probably underestimated due to inaccurate coroner rulings and some bodies never being discovered.* Other countries in addition to the United States that were part of the study included Australia, Austria, Brazil, Canada, Finland, France, Hong Kong, Japan, Ireland, New Zealand, Sweden, Turkey, and the United Kingdom. Susan Hatters Freidman, Phillip J Resnick, "Child Murder by Mothers: Patterns and Prevention." World Psychiatry 6.3 (2007): 137–141,
 https://www.ncbi.nlm.nih.gov/pmc/articles/PMC2174580/ (accessed on August 15, 2018).
Euthanizing the disabled was practiced by Hitler's regime prior to the genocide of Jews. See Michael Berenbaum, "T4 Program," *Encyclopedia Britannica,* Encyclopedia Britannica, Inc., January 2, 2014,
https://www.britannica.com/event/T4-Program (accessed August 15, 2018); and Deborah Schurman-Kauflin Ph.D., "Killing the Disabled: The danger of the wolf pack mentality," *Psychology Today,* June 19, 2012. https://www.psychologytoday.com/us/blog/disturbed/201206/killing-the-disabled (accessed August 15, 2018).
In terms of genocidal crimes on account of political ideology, we find the atrocities committed by the Pol Pot regime in Cambodia, Ben Kiernan, *The Pol Pot Regime: Race, Power, and Genocide in Cambodia under the Khmer Rouge, 1975-79,* First edition, (New Haven: Yale University Press, 1996); on account of ethnicity, see Gérard Prunier, *The Rwanda Crisis: History of a Genocide*, (NY: Columbia University Press, 1997). As to recent religious conflicts, the ongoing Muslim Rohingya people is suffering from persecution by the Buddhist majority in Myanmar, the Uyghurs in China, Christians, and Yazidis at the hands of ISIS in Syria, Christians and Muslims in the Central African Republic, and the religious/ethnic conflict in which Serbian (Orthodox Christians) persecuted Bosnian Muslims in the Balkans during the 1990s, and Christian repression in North Korea and some Muslim countries.
11. Conrad Hackett, David McClendon, "Christians remain the world's largest religious group, but they are declining in Europe," Pew Research Center, 5 April 2017. http://www.pewresearch.org/fact-tank/2017/04/05/christians-remain-worlds-largest-religious-group-but-they-are-declining-in-europe/ (accessed August 14, 2018); PBS, "World Religions Map," www.florida.pbslearningmedia.org/ resource/ sj14-soc-religmap/world-religions-map/ (accessed August 14, 2018); Pew Research Center, "Global Christianity – A Report on the Size and Distribution of the World's Christian Population," 19 December 2011, http://www.pewforum.org/2011/12/19/global-christianity-exec/ (accessed August 14, 2018).
12. Becka A. Alper, "Why America's 'nones' don't identify with a religion," Pew Research Center, August 8, 2018, http://www.pewresearch.org/fact-tank/2018/08/08/why-americas-nones-dont-identify-with-a-religion/ (accessed August 17, 2018).

The Jewish Religious Authorities

It may seem odd that in the Gospels, the most important sacred texts in the Christian religion, the authors (or God) assigned so much space to the Jewish religious authorities and Jewish people. Table 2 indicates that these themes rank among the most significant categories. The results disclose that the story of the public Jesus is the story of his interactions with the Israelites. Without these narratives that originally were historically inconspicuous, the Christian faith might never have occurred.

Viewed from the perspective of the Israelites, the most pertinent themes in the Gospels might have included a detailed account of Jesus's public mission, his preaching activity, and his conflict with the Jewish religious authorities that eventually led to his death at the hands of Pontius Pilate. Nonetheless, when viewed from a

Christian angle, the Gospels become the written record about a messiah sent by God to save the Israelites (and the world), who performs miraculous deeds, but in the end is crucified at the behest of his own people and resurrected from the dead, in effect, making Jesus a historical legend as well as divine.

This section, and the next one, examine how the four Gospels portray the contentious relationship between Jesus and the Israelites. While this section tends to view the conflict from each side, a word of caution is in order; when reading Jesus's attacks against the Pharisees, it is important to bear in mind that his words may not have been his own. Exegetes today tend to accept that passages in Matthew reflect *an opposition that goes beyond that of Jesus' ministry and must be seen as expressing the bitter conflict between Pharisaic Judaism and the church of Matthew at the time when the gospel was composed.*[1] The conflict, however, extended beyond Matthew and into the other three Gospels. This view is critical because the Gospels are the outcome of an oral tradition that was divinely downloaded (according to Fundamentalism) into the hands of its authors; or at the very least inspired (according to non-Fundamentalists) by God. A critical reading of the texts will not be able to ignore temporal manifestations of anti-Jewishness that found their way into the texts, the early Christian Church, and up to our times, thereby raising serious questions about the quality of divine revelation.

There is insufficient information about how the conflict between Jesus and the Jewish religious authorities begin. The narratives start once the quarrel is well underway, although we do not know for how long it had been going on. Nothing during Jesus's infancy indicates any antagonism between Jesus's parents, relatives, friends, and the religious authorities. If anything, all of them were faithful observants of Mosaic Law. Mark provides a glimpse of the conflict when he writes that people admire Jesus's teaching authority in contrast with that of the scribes (Mk 1:22), suggesting the oral tradition he incorporated in the text indicated that these men were not well looked upon by the people. However, appearing so early in the first chapter, the passage does not say what the scribes have done to earn their disrepute. It is Jesus, nonetheless, who notices. After he forgives a paralytic's sins, some of the scribes begin to murmur that he is blaspheming, since it is their understanding that only God can forgive sins. The scribes do not appear to know who Jesus is. Nonetheless, Jesus thinks that their attitude is sinister, and he uses the incident as a teaching moment by invoking his title, Son of Man, and healing the paralytic. He tells them that the deed he just performed is equivalent to his authority to forgive sins and they simply must accept it (Mk 2:3-12).[2]

In the incident (that appears in all synoptic texts) it appears that Jesus already dislikes the scribes (or begins to), and although he may have good reasons for not being fond of them, he does not tell us. As for the scribes, presuming they have not witnessed any previous miracles, it seems reasonable for them to feel indignant about someone they consider an 'intruder' or a false prophet who is attributing to himself divine characteristics. Following his deed, they are probably mesmerized, yet annoyed, about someone who has overshadowed them. The distinctive characteristic in this incident is not the forgiving of sins, since any impostor can utter the same words, but the healing of the paralytic.

Following the sequence of events in Mark, Jesus further alienates the religious authorities when another group of scribes (who are Pharisees) sees him eating with sinners and tax collectors, a type of behavior that is frowned upon because it goes against their customs (Mk 2:15-16, Lk 5:30, Mt 9:11), and complain to his disciples. Overhearing them, Jesus tells the scribes that he seeks their company because they are spiritually and morally sick and in need of his assistance. His remark, *I did not come to call the righteous, but sinners,* is interesting, since he regards the religious authorities as sinners, yet he does not seek to establish a rapport with them. The scribes and the Pharisees do not appear to understand Jesus's metaphor, as they seem to have a different understanding of how to deal with sinners in accordance with Mosaic Law and customs they themselves have developed over time (in similar fashion as Christian denominations have done throughout history).

Likewise, the Pharisees question Jesus's unwillingness to fast. They and the Baptist's disciples fast as a ritual to please God; a custom practiced today by many Christian denominations. Jesus, however, rebukes the practice, replying to them with a parable (Mk 2:18-22, Lk 5:30-38, Mt 9:14-17) about pouring new wine into an old wineskin. The texts do not indicate if the Pharisees understand Jesus's riddle, particularly since he uses parables at times to confuse those who lack faith.[3] By now, their displeasure toward Jesus would seem to grow.

As he goes about his mission to convert sinners, Jesus antagonizes the Pharisees when they notice him and his disciples picking heads of grain on the Sabbath because they are hungry. According to the religious authorities' understanding of Mosaic Law, the Sabbath is sacred, but Jesus practically brushes them aside and tells them that he lords over the Sabbath (Mk 2:23-28, Lk 6:1-5, Mt 12:1-8). He believes he is interpreting God's law properly while the Pharisees beg to differ. Jesus would violate the Sabbath again by curing a man with a withered hand (Lk 6:6-11, Mt 12:9-14). By now, the reader might have the impression that Jesus truly has demonstrated a strong sense of antipathy toward the Pharisees. The Pharisees are probably becoming exasperated because, not knowing Jesus, they realize that God's law is not meant to be broken, much less by someone who so far has not authenticated his mission.

In Mark, it does not take long for the conflict to reach a monumental resolution; by the third chapter the Pharisees begin to conspire to put Jesus to death (Mk 3:1-6). In Luke, the Pharisees decide they need to take action against him too (Lk 6:6-11), for the same reasons, but without offering much detail. Meanwhile, Matthew is more forthcoming. While he tells us in the words of John the Baptist that the religious authorities are not righteous people, he does not provide any explanations. Baptizing Jews in the Jordan River the Baptist sees *many* Pharisees and Sadducees approaching, and he suddenly erupts into a tirade calling them a *brood of vipers,* censuring words they have not yet verbalized, and warning them of eternal condemnation if they fail to change their behavior (Mt 3:7-10). Happening so early in the text suggests that the Baptist's and Jesus's discontent with the religious authorities had been brewing for some time, although there is no explanation regarding any specific incidents that might have prompted either one to confront the Jewish religious authorities.

There is no other account about them until Jesus, while preaching to the crowds during the Sermon on the Mount, teaches that their behavior must surpass that of the scribes and Pharisees if they wish to enter the kingdom of heaven (Mt 5:20). Although no reason is yet given why these persons are so loathsome, by the time Jesus violates the Sabbath for the second time, Matthew writes that the Pharisees have decided to *take counsel against him to put him to death* (Mt 12:9-14).

John's view of the religious authorities is one of suspicion since the beginning. When *the Jews from Jerusalem* (presumably referring to the religious authorities) send priests and Levites to find out who the Baptist is, he is not talkative and tells them that he is simply *the voice of one crying out in the desert* seeking to persuade people to repent and become righteous. He adds, however, that he is preceding someone far more important than him (Jn 1:19-27). By the second chapter, Jesus is already enraging the religious authorities by disrupting the area of the temple where merchants and moneychangers gather to conduct temple-related business. He angrily overturns their tables and whips them out of the area feeling they have converted his Father's house into a marketplace. *The Jews* (the religious authorities in this instance) ask him under what authority he is doing these deeds. Jesus sidesteps the question, replying instead with another cryptic remark, daring them to destroy the temple, which he will then raise in three days. According to the text, the religious authorities appear bewildered (Jn 2:13-21).[4]

The reader may be startled when John tells us in chapter 5 that *the Jews began to persecute Jesus* for curing a paralytic man during the Sabbath and *tried all the more to kill him* for calling God his father, thus *making himself equal to God* (Jn 5:10-18). As in Mark's text, these Jews probably interpreted Jesus's remark correctly as a blasphemy. The deed itself, indicating supernatural powers, would not have been enough for the authorities to accept that Jesus is who he claims to be. After all, God also granted Moses special powers that he used against the Egyptians. On the other hand, it is surprising that the religious authorities did not attempt to rethink Jesus's claim and initiate a serious exchange with him. Instead, the text tells us that Jesus ensues on a cosmic explanation about his relationship to God that, likely, keeps the authorities even more confused:

> *For just as the Father raises the dead and gives life, so also does the Son give life to whomever he wishes. Nor does the Father judge anyone, but he has given all judgment to his Son, so that all may honor the Son just as they honor the Father. Whoever does not honor the Son does not honor the Father who sent*

him.... I say to you, the hour is coming and is now here when the dead will hear
the voice of the Son of God, and those who hear will live. For just as the Father
has life in himself, so also he gave to his Son the possession of life in himself.
And he gave him power to exercise judgment, because he is the Son of Man (Jn
5:21-27)

Given the limited knowledge the religious authorities have about Jesus, his
words seem unintelligible to them. At times, the exchanges between Jesus and the
religious authorities are similar to two groups of people speaking to each other in
different languages. At no time do the texts tell us that Jesus ever reaches out to the
religious authorities as he does toward tax collectors.

Nonetheless, a serious exchange takes place between Jesus and a reasonable
Pharisee, Nicodemus, who seems to express an open-minded attitude toward him.
Nicodemus is a man of faith and believes that Jesus's incredible feats are the product
of someone who has a very close relationship with God. Nonetheless, he seems
perplexed by Jesus's explanation about the need to be *born from above*. Twice
Nicodemus tells Jesus that he does not understand, to which Jesus replies with a self-
righteous affront: *You are the teacher of Israel and you do not understand this?* (Jn
3:1-12). Is Nicodemus supposed to grasp through reason what Jesus is seeking to
convey? Even today, all that humankind can do is to accept his remark in faith, as
there is no other conceivable way to understand what Jesus is saying.

Who Are the Religious Authorities?

The authors of the Gospel portray the religious authorities as being insidious, either
for not understanding or for rejecting Jesus. But, once again, we need to see these
events from the perspective of the religious authorities to find out what makes them
react to Jesus the way they do. The Gospels identify Jesus's main opponents as being
Pharisees, scribes, Sadducees, the council of elders, the chief priests, and the head
priest. The texts allude to what motivates their anger toward Jesus; he is usurping their
authority, and in their eyes, committing blasphemy. Jesus does not respect them. We
learn at some point that the main reason is that some of them, i.e., the Pharisees, are
hypocrites who malign the word of God. Possibly, they are aware of their behavior,
but they are not prepared to cede their authority to a stranger.

Although the term *Pharisee* is today regarded as a pejorative term by many
Jews, likely because of Jesus's harsh denunciations against these men, the Pharisees
are considered the spiritual fathers of modern Judaism. Their origin dates to the
second or third century BCE. They were devoted followers of the Oral law that God
gave to Moses at Sinai and were primarily responsible for codifying this law into the
Talmud upon which Jewish religious behavior is based.[5] It is interesting and
seemingly incongruous that the Catholic Encyclopedia (an apologetic yet scholarly
source published at the turn of the twentieth century) holds this group in high esteem,
attributing to them *a certain moral dignity and greatness, a marked tenacity of*
purpose at the service of high, patriotic, and religious ideals. Their religious and

political functions were vital in a theocracy, where it constituted the most important priestly class that ruled during the time of Jesus, to the point that its *pedagogical influence* paved the way for the advent of Christianity.[6]

Among their affinities with the Christian faith, the Pharisees believed in the afterlife and the coming of a Messiah. They were known for their religious purity or the necessity to separate themselves from non-Jews to prevent being influenced by the cultural forces of paganism, a reason for which they would eat separately from Gentiles. However, despite narratives in the Gospels indicating proneness toward violence, historically, the Pharisees had adopted a policy of abstaining from the use of military force, in contrast with the Zealots, a political faction that sought armed insurrection against the Roman Empire.[7]

The scribes too were as important as the Pharisees, and likely exercised a conditioning effect on Judaic Pharisaism through their function as interpreters of the Law and teachers of the Torah to the Jewish people.[8] What stood them apart from the others was their formality and their legalistic expressions of Jewish piety, revering the Law *as the precise expression of God's will.* Their adherence to the Law was the measure of righteousness in the eyes of God.[9]

Anyone who browses the Pentateuch (the Torah or first five books of the Hebrew Bible) likely would conclude that an intricate web of laws entangles Jewish religious behavior. It was the scribes' responsibility to interpret these laws in the spirit of Pharisaic Judaism. These were pious men whose worshipping of God was based on their devotion to his laws.

The Chief Priests constituted an exclusive fellowship. In the Gospels, they appear mostly in the company of the elders, scribes, and Pharisees together conspiring against Jesus (Mt 26:3-4). Their primary functions were ritualistic, and many were members of the Sanhedrin. Presided by the Head Priest, the Sanhedrin was the foremost religious assembly among the people, having *final authority on Jewish law.*[10]

The elders were a group of men who enjoyed a high social status on account of their wisdom. They are mentioned in Exodus where Moses is said to establish *a judicial-social organ in order to help him judge the people.* Among the attributes that made them outstanding in their community were fear of God, trustworthiness, divine inspiration, and intellectual capacity.[11]

The Sadducees were one of the three major political-religious sects at the time along with the Pharisees, and the Essenes (who are not mentioned in the Gospel). They were not as popular as the Pharisees namely because of their self-ascribed aristocratic background and close relationship with political rulers. They distinguished themselves from the Pharisees in their denial of an afterlife, although they appear in the Gospels conspiring with the Pharisees (Mt 16:1, 5). Their minor influence in the Gospels, as reflected in the content analysis tally, presents a problem.

The Sadducees had an important role in Judaism that is not covered in the Gospels. They oversaw the Temple's maintenance that included supervision of sacrificial rituals, a fundamental element of Judaism. They were considered an elitist and wealthy group appealing to the rich, suggesting that they too, were involved in issues, such as taxation, law enforcement, and relations with the Roman Empire. They were members, along with the Pharisees, of the Sanhedrin, with whom they interacted and whose views differed sharply from those of the Pharisees.[12] This would signify that they must have had considerable influence in Jewish life, even though the Gospels seldom refer to them or their activities in detail. In terms of numbers, the Sadducees are hardly mentioned in the texts (10xt), as opposed to the Pharisees (90xt).

Jesus would seem to be as opposed to the Sadducees as he is to the Pharisees. Wealth, for example, appealed to the Sadducees, just as to the Pharisees (Lk 16:14). Yet, there are no major invectives against the Sadducees in the texts. Jesus's violent reaction in the outskirts of the Temple regarding money changers and merchants had to do with the supervision of these practices, supposedly by the Sadducees; however, there is no critique of them in the texts. The only major encounter with the Sadducees has to do with the resurrection of humans that they reject (Mk 12:18-27, Lk 20:27-39, Mt 22:23-33), which happens to be the most important aspect of Jesus's mission. It appears, then, that we only have a partial understanding of the religious authorities; the view the authors (or God) chose to include.

The main protagonists (the Pharisees) would not seem to be initially as evil as the Gospels portray them. Their historical background does not suggest that they were members of anything resembling an organized crime cartel. They were probably like today's high profile religious and political leaders, some of whom behave improperly at times. A major difference perhaps may lie in the religiosity of the time, something that is lacking in today's secular societies. These men were devoted to God; they abided by centuries of oral and written tradition that had been handed down to them. Their highly relevant religious and political status made them feel important; a conditioning factor that at times may vitiate good intentions. In other instances, fear possibly made them compromise with superior political powers; but then, they did not have armed forces. They were taught that their most important behavioral feature to become righteous was adherence to God's laws.

Although the Gospels tend to generalize about the wickedness of the religious authorities, they present occasional exceptions: well-intentioned elders ask Jesus to assist a Roman centurion who is building a synagogue for the Jews (Lk 7:1-5); a group of Pharisees alerts Jesus about Herod's desire to have him killed (Lk 13:31). Others question if Jesus is really evil (Jn 9:16, 10:21); some guards appear persuaded by Jesus's teachings (Jn 7:46-47); a scribe is willing to follow him (Mt 8:19), and Jesus even praises one of them (Mk 12:28-34). Nonetheless, as indicated by the content analysis tally, the image the Gospels portray of the religious authorities is overwhelmingly negative (Table 2).

From the standpoint of the religious authorities, the incidents surrounding Jesus's condemnation and the questions they themselves raise about Jesus lead to the plausible conclusion that they act according to how they were taught. They accuse Jesus of blaspheming because he calls himself Son of God; he meets with sinners (Lk 15:2) and violates the Tradition of the Elders (Mk 7:1-5, Mt 15:1-9). They question him about divorce laws established by Moses (Mk 10:2-4, Mt 19:3); paying taxes to the emperor (Mk 12:12-17, Lk 20:20-26, Mt 22:15-22); and ask him if there is a resurrection (Mk 12:18-27, Lk 20:27-40, Mt 22:23-32). They quiz him about the commandments (Mk 12:28-34, Lk 10:25-28); they even feel enraged when he calls God *my Father* (Jn 8:12-59); they ask him about the validity of Moses' law on stoning an adulteress (Jn 8:3-11); they demand an explanation to his violent outburst when he throws out the merchants from the temple area and ask for signs that might legitimize his authority (Lk 11:29, Mt 12:38). From their perspective, they feel they cannot remain passive amidst Jesus's affront to God's religion, to his laws, and their customs. According to them, Jesus's behavior is in opposition to their understanding of God's way as manifested in their scriptures.

One day, this son of a mason, born in a small inconsequential town (aside from the prophecy in Mt 2:6) makes his public appearance and begins to ignore these notable persons. He notices that something is seriously amiss in the behavior of the religious authorities and their understanding of the Law. He is severely critical of the ruling establishment, telling them they will face condemnation from God. He violates laws and traditions that righteous people follow, the likes of Mary, Joseph, Zechariah, Elizabeth, the virtuous Simeon, the prophetess Anna, Nicodemus, Joseph of Arimathea, and many others who have been living according to the same Law being observed by the religious authorities. Nonetheless, Jesus proceeds to arbitrarily impose his own interpretation of the Law while insinuating he is the Messiah, a king, and the Son of God. Why would the religious authorities believe him?

Jesus spends more time denouncing the religious authorities than reasoning with them. He hardly explains the logic behind his rejection of the Tradition of the Elders, except to his disciples (Mk 7:17-23, Mt 15:10-20). He is unconvincing about his reason to meet with sinners and tax collectors, particularly when he refuses to sit down with those who he regards as the greatest sinners, the Pharisees. Moreover, he even tells his disciples to treat those who refuse to listen to them as Gentiles and tax collectors, i.e., scum (Mt 18:17). At times he explains his reasons for violating the Sabbath by appealing to their compassion, but his attacks drown his explanations. Rather than converse with them he debates them with the power of logic. When told that he works his deeds through the devil, his response is powerful, a kingdom divided against itself becomes weakened (Mt 12:25). He rejects their opposition, calls them a brood of vipers, and tells them they will be condemned by their words (Mt 12:22-37).

The Pharisees' question about divorce and adultery is reasonable; yet Jesus offers no explanation other than it is God's Law and must be accepted (Mt 19:1-9). He deflects their question about paying taxes to the emperor because he believes they are seeking to entrap him (Mk 12:13-17, Lk 20:20-39, Mt 22:15-33). Jesus appears to act unnecessarily confrontational, particularly when his exchanges with them are filled with threats and condemnation. As his opponents do not enjoy being publicly excoriated, the probabilities of persuading them decrease exponentially. Does Jesus understand the difficulties involved in confronting a legalistic culture that has existed for centuries? His attitude is like some of the prophets that preceded him, a fresh version of Isaiah and Jeremiah who is more into fierce denunciation and humiliation of his enemies, than a Plato who is willing to sit and wittingly hold lengthy conversations with his opponents. What possible explanation could Jesus provide to his followers today in dealing with an opposition that feels is not legitimate? His harsh denunciations in the public square make him appear like a madman. His behavior would preclude him from having access inside the halls of government. If by any chance he develops a group of followers, his zealousness might even inspire violence.

Jesus simply is not prepared to accept any compromise. Three times he tells his disciples that the religious authorities will kill him, but he keeps doing what eventually will take him to the cross. His own civil disobedience tacitly undermines the authority of the religious leaders. He refuses to provide signs to those who ask; perhaps because they have not yet seen any; otherwise, why would they keep asking? In the synoptics, he often refuses to engage his opponents in a dialogue; he regards it as a waste of his time since they will not listen, in which case what other objective is he pursuing? In John, he engages the religious authorities several times, but they do not believe him. The things he says and does are simply too outrageous. He threatens to take away their authority (Mk 12:1-11, Lk 20:9-19), but what authority does he have other than his claim? In his mildest moment he addresses a parable to their face telling them that tax collectors will be welcomed into God's kingdom ahead of them (Lk 18:9-14). In time, the religious authorities find themselves in a difficult situation. Jesus is critical of them, and they do not understand why, or perhaps prefer not to understand. They are aware that he has caught the attention of many followers and he is no longer a lonely voice crying in the wilderness.

That the Gospels show little empathy toward the religious authorities may be culturally understandable since they are apologetic manuals for religious instruction. However, seeking adequate explanations for any type of behavior requires examining said behavior from the opponent's point of view. If today someone were to appear from nowhere to incite massive crowds by questioning the validity of a country's laws and the legitimacy of their rule, be it across the U.S. Capitol, the British Parliament, the Knesset, or St. Peter's Square, how would these leaders react? Would they not feel compelled to defend themselves against the radical behavior and charges of a stranger? Would they not demand signs that would legitimize his teachings?

Reactions to a contemporary Jesus would depend on the type of political systems he faces. In a true democracy where the rule of law, separation of powers, and extensive freedom rights prevail, the issue presumably would be settled at the ballot box, assuming Jesus would not mind running for office or sponsoring his own candidates and issuing his platform on the issues. The response by autocratic governments and theocracies might be different. These types of political systems prefer their status quo. When confronted by strong vocal opposition or massive protests their first inclination is to resort to violence. Under these systems Jesus likely would be crushed. This is what happens to him in Jerusalem.

The religious authorities and their followers feel that Jesus is imperiling their standing in society. They fear for the existence of the nation if the Romans decide to take military action (as they did in 70 CE). But it is not only a matter of their existence; as hypocritical as they may have been (presuming Jesus's charges against them are accurate), they are passionate about their beliefs and their social status in the community. As the ruling class, they would like to keep the entitlements to which they have become accustomed. Following his violations of their laws and customs, Jesus offends their intelligence by saying that he exists even before Abraham and by making himself God. In return, they seek to stone him (Jn 8:59, 10:31). Several times they plot to arrest him (Mk 11:18, Lk 22:1-6, Mt 26:3-5, Jn 7:30, 32). When they do, they gather false witnesses, provide false charges when he is brought before Pontius Pilate (Mk 14:5, Lk 23:1-5, Mt 26:60, Jn 11:57), and finally incite the crowds to press Pilate to crucify him (Mk 15:13, Lk 23:23-25, Mt 27:20-22, Jn 19:6, 15).

What makes Jesus acts the way he does? According to the texts, God entrusts him with a mission that will cost him his life; that mission is not to atone for humankind's offense against God, since he never makes references to Original Sin. His mission is to do the Father's will to spread the good news about the kingdom of God and eternal salvation, to ask for repentance of peoples' sinful behavior, and to believe in him. Although the texts do not provide information about the origin of Jesus's conflict with the religious authorities, it is clear that it is Jesus who provokes the crisis by confronting the religious authorities; however, his woes against the Pharisees and the scribes provide a plausible explanation for Jesus's behavior.

Had Jesus come to earth and remain indifferent to the incongruities and complexity found in the Law, and the incompatible behavior of those entrusted with its implementation and interpretation, his crucifixion might not have taken place. The texts tell us, however, that Jesus is certain of how his life will end, and that he is willing to do what it takes to do the Father's will despite having second thoughts toward the end (Mt 16:21, 26:38-42).[13] His woes against the Pharisees and the scribes portray zealous activism on behalf of God and provide a narrow window into what prompts Jesus to be so critical of them. He accuses them of being hypocritical because they fail to properly observe the Old Law, indeed, a serious charge; they prefer to honor themselves than to honor God; they impose a heavy burden upon the people that they themselves do not follow; he calls them *white-washed tombs, beautiful on the outside, but inside are full of dead men's bones and every kind of filth* and blames them for the death of previous prophets (Mt 23:13-35, Mk 12:38-39, Lk 11:37-52).

In the synoptics, Jesus acts like God's special prosecutor seeking to indict the religious authorities. Their offenses are not anything like we might suspect, murder, embezzlement, robbery, kidnapping, sexual assault, or other felonious crimes. Their crimes consist of disfiguring God in the eyes of the people through their hypocritical, ostentatious, egotistic, and demagogic behavior that in contemporary societies is regarded as customary among elected officials, and not illegal. In John's Gospel, on the other hand, there is only one charge, unbelief. Jesus's attacks are severe and include his characterization of the religious authorities as being children of the devil, by far the most venomous representation of Pharisaic Judaism (Jn 8:44).

This is a conflict between two sides that do not care to understand each other; they have become too polarized. The Pharisees and scribes strongly believe they are following the Law and consider Jesus an interloper who has no business telling them what to do. Jesus knows the Sanhedrin would not consider his charges. He realizes that his desire to eradicate them from their positions based on his rhetoric is at best a dead-end. He is incessant in his attacks, as if he truly seeks to be immortalized. The issue comes down to how God's Law is to be interpreted, and the religious establishment finds no credibility in his arguments or his deeds. Meanwhile, Jesus's denunciations are seriously undermining their authority before the people, which is why they consider him an existential threat that leaves them no room other than to pursue his death. But if his appeal to their shame is unable to convince them, is there anything else that might?

Jesus makes precisely that point in John's Gospel: *If I do not perform my Father's works, do not believe me; but if I perform them, even if you do not believe me, believe the works, so that you may realize [and understand] that the Father is in me and I am in the Father* (Jn 10:37-38). What does Jesus mean by works? He involves himself in two types of activities according to the texts, preaching about God's kingdom (repentance from sin, forgiveness, and love of neighbor); and performing miracles. Today, there is no lack of Christian preachers, and while their virtuous behavior and their rhetoric may qualify them as prominent personalities, no one believes any of them is divine. Hence, it all boils down to unnatural feats or miracles. If the texts account for over two dozen miracles, is it possible that the religious authorities did not witness any of them? In Matthew, the chief priests, scribes, and elders shout at the crucified Jesus, *let him come down from the cross now, and we will believe in him* (Mt 27:42). They keep asking for a sign; what kind of signs? It seems that curing the blind, the disabled, and the deaf without medical instruments and medications; resurrecting the dead; multiplying fishes and loaves of bread is not enough. In John, the Pharisees conduct an investigation about the blind man Jesus cures, since apparently, they did not witness the incident. They query the blind man and his parents and confirm that Jesus had returned his sight. Still, they refuse to believe them (Jn 9:18-34).

As skeptical as contemporary society is today (particularly when compared to Jesus's time), it is almost incomprehensible that humans would not respond to an unearthly feat. Statistically speaking, there will always be unbelievers, people whose instincts would tell them that Jesus is a magician, and magic as we know, involves skilled deception. Is this what the Pharisees and the scribes think of Jesus? Or is it possible that the religious establishment witnessed signs but preferred to ignore them and hold on to their status and authority rather than to recognize Jesus as being divine, or at least divinely inspired? How would contemporary non-Christians or atheists react if they were to witness true public miracles that defy scientific explanation? The answer to this question might hold the key to understanding the conflict.

Notes:

1. NEs' note, Mt 23:1-29.

2. Ibid., note on Mk 2:10. The editors say that the use of Jesus's moniker is one of many gratuitous insertions (similar to relying on poetic license) that Mark uses as a commentary to address people who already knew that Jesus was the Messiah.

3. Not meant to be scientifically, often I have asked relatives and acquaintances with a cultural Christian background if they understand the parable; the answer is always No. Chances of understanding some of these parables seem to increase among those who attend Bible classes. Nonetheless, one wonders, how would people know if Jesus seldom explains his parables publicly. Interestingly, Jesus seems to approve of fasting in Matthew as long as they do not seek to show others the sacrifice it takes to do so (Mt 6:16).

4. NEs point out that *the order of events in the gospel narratives is often determined by theological motives rather than by chronological data.* Note on Jn 2:14-22. While such may be the case, discretion by the authors of the Gospels certainly confuses the average reader, particularly wondering how it is possible that God's revelation can be rearranged to suit religious education without providing any explanation.

5. "Ancient Jewish History: Pharisees, Sadducees & Essenes," *Jewish Virtual Library, http://www.jewishvirtuallibrary.org/pharisees-sadducees-and-essenes,* (accessed 21 June 2018).

6. James F. Driscoll, "Pharisees," CE *Catholic Encyclopedia*, Vol. 11, 1911, http://www.newadvent.org/cathen/11789b.htm (accessed 21 June 2018).

7. Ibid.

8. Isidore Singer, M. Seligsohn, Wilhelm Bacher, Judah David Eisenstein, "Scribes," *Jewish Encyclopedia,* henceforth JE, *http://www.jewishencyclopedia.com/articles/13356-scribes (accessed* 2 July 2018).

9. James F. Driscoll, "Scribes," CE, Vol. 13, 1912, http://www.newadvent.org/cathen/13634a.htm (accessed 21 Jun. 2018).

10. Shira Schoenberg, "Ancient Jewish History: The Sanhedrin," *Jewish Virtual Library,* https://www.jewishvirtuallibrary.org/the-sanhedrin (accessed 26 June 2018).

11. "Elder," *Jewish Virtual Library, https://www.jewishvirtuallibrary.org/elder (accessed* 26 June 2018).

12. Flavius Josephus, *The Antiquities of the Jews,* (Book XIII, Chapter 10, 6. Project Gutenberg e-book, trans by William Whiston, last updated Aug 9, 2007. https://www.gutenberg.org/files/2848/2848-h/2848-h.htm#link132HCH0010 (accessed 27 June 2018).

13. In Martin Scorsese movie, *The Last Temptation of Christ,* (1988, Cineplex Odeon Films), based on a vividly imagined novel by the same name by Nikos Kazantzakis, Jesus rejects the temptation to become married, have children, and lead a safe life in order to fulfill the Father's will.

The Jewish People

This category examines how Jesus and the Jewish people interact with each other according to the Gospels. The content analysis results indicate that Christianity emerges as the outcome of a drama between two primary interlocutors, Jesus, and the Jewish people; everyone else seems inconsequential. It is conceivable that if Paul had not persuaded the disciples to reach out to Gentiles, Christianity might have remained a sect within Judaism. History, certainly, would have had to be written differently. Hence, it would have been reasonable to combine the religious authorities and the Jewish people into one category given their close relationship with Jesus throughout his public mission. Nonetheless, keeping them separate allows us to understand the Jewish people's sudden change of attitude toward Jesus as well as to scrutinize charges of anti-Semitism in the texts.

The findings of the Jewish People category indicate there was a love/hate-admiration/rejection relationship between both Jesus and the authors of the Gospels, and the Jewish people. This is different from results about the religious authorities' category that reveal mostly a negative relationship on both sides.

Surprisingly, given the high significance of both categories, the term 'Jewish' seldom appears in the texts. It shows only (7xt), pertaining mostly to feasts or customs, to a town, and the guards under the command of the religious authorities. The term 'Israeli(te)' shows up only (2xt), once by Matthew who mistakenly attributes a passage to Jeremiah,[1] and another by Jesus who calls Nathanael *a true Israelite* (Jn 1:47). The term *Israel* indicating the people, the land, or the nation is referenced (22xt), including (3xt) times as Jesus's title, *king of Israel.* The term *Judea*, equivalent to the land of Israel, appears (23xt). And, likely indicating its significance in Israeli history, the word *Jerusalem* appears (68xt).

The use of the terms *Jew(s), crowd,* and *people* in the texts, however, is controversial and often imprecise. The most telling is the term *Jew(s).* It appears (15xt) in the synoptics, mostly in the phrase 'king of the Jews' attributed to Jesus, and frequently in a mocking manner by the Romans and Pontius Pilate. In other instances, the term appears only (3xt), once in each of the synoptic texts (Mk 7:3, Lk 7:3, Mt 28:15). These low numbers in the synoptics stand in contrast with the use of the term in John's Gospel where it appears (58xt). The discrepancy is simply too obvious to ignore. The disproportionate use of the term in John's Gospel, not by Jesus, but by the authors of the text, sheds light on their motives.

The background against which the Gospels were written was characterized by deep polarization. Often, Jews who had adopted the Christian faith were harassed by the great majority of Jews who had remained culturally and religiously attached to the Old (Mosaic) Law. Accordingly, the constant use of the term *Jew*, particularly in John's Gospel, refers not to the time when Jesus was alive, but to the contempt the authors of the text likely felt decades later following their experiences at being expelled from the synagogues for displaying their faith in Jesus (Jn 9:22, 12:42, 16:1). Strong Jewish opposition toward Christian Jews engendered an anti-Jewish reaction that found its way primarily into John's Gospel.[2]

Content analysis sorted passages involving the interaction between the Jewish people and Jesus and tallied them (in terms of space or sp) according to positive/negative/neutral depictions. Passages in which Jewish crowds follow Jesus, listen to his teachings, or praise him, reflect well on Jewish people and are deemed to be positive; instances in which people refuse to listen to him, reject him, or seek his death are characterized as negative. Neutral depictions go either way; however, they tend to be too few to significantly alter the results. Although these are subjective evaluations, the wording in the texts makes the process straightforward.

Nonetheless, often, it becomes difficult to tell when the usage of the terms *Jews, crowd,* and *people* in the texts refer to ordinary Jewish people, the religious authorities, or both. It is reasonable to presume that crowds that are present when Jesus teaches and heal people are endeared to him, and acting on their own. However, the opposite would seem to be true; when these crowds oppose Jesus, for example, at the time of the crucifixion, the authorities are present, and likely leading them.

According to the results in Table 2, the positive/negative/neutral classification is well distributed among the synoptic texts. All three authors show slightly more positive than negative characterizations of the Jewish people. John's Gospel, nonetheless, is considerably lopsided with negative passages accounting for three times as many as positive ones. This has led over the years to the question of whether John's Gospel presents strong anti-Jewish sentiments. The findings suggest that, although a subtle prejudicial attitude may be noticed in all three synoptic texts, John's Gospel clearly projects an unfavorable view of the Jewish people. The evidence is seen in the indiscriminate use of the terms *Jews, people,* and *crowd* while referring to both ordinary Jews and the Jewish religious authorities, making it difficult at times to distinguish between the two. Whenever there is doubt about these passages, they are proportionately divided between the two groups in the results.

Jesus and the Jewish Crowds in the Synoptic Texts
How did the people of Israel interact with Jesus according to the synoptic texts? Prior to Jesus's birth, God is aware that his people are sinners in need of a *great light* (Mt 4:15-16). Thus, from the beginning, the Gospels indicate that a man that shall be named Jesus will come into the world to rule the people of Israel (Mt 2:6) as king of the Jews, king of Israel (Mt 2:1-2, Jn 1:49), Messiah, and Lord (Lk 2:10-11). He will be known as Son of the Most High (Lk 1:32) and will save God's people from their sins (Mt 1:21). Zechariah, Mary, Simeon, and Anna are told that Jesus is God's merciful answer to his promise to deliver the Israelites from its enemies (Lk 1:46-55, 1:68-79, 2:29-31, 2:38). He will be preceded by John the Baptist who *will turn many of the children of Israel to the Lord their God* (Lk 1:16).

King Herod is troubled by Jesus's birth, likely because he sees Jesus as a threat; however, *all Jerusalem* is concerned (Mt 2:3), although no explanation is given why the Israelites would feel uneasy (as opposed to joyful) since many were anticipating a Messiah. Divine intervention constantly keeps the child away from harm's way and eventually leads the family back to Israel (Mt 2:19-21).

Initially, people of the whole Judean countryside and all the inhabitants of Jerusalem welcome the Baptist and his message of repentance. He baptizes many who show up in the Jordan River to acknowledge their sins (Mk 1:5, Mt 3:5). Strangely, he calls these crowds *brood of vipers* (Lk 3:7); not a good choice of words for those who wish to repent. Matthew, however, addresses the epithet at the Pharisees (Mt 3:7), which is more credible, given the rivalry that was brewing with representatives of the religious authorities. Nonetheless, the difference between the two passages is substantial and is likely to confuse the reader.

From the moment he initiates his public mission, Jesus is attracted to the Jewish crowds as he performs wondrous deeds; *all were amazed ... his fame spread* throughout Galilee as he is praised while teaching at the synagogues (Mk 1:21-28, Lk 4:14-15, Mt 4:23-25). The more deeds he performs the more famous he becomes, as *people kept coming to him from everywhere ... And great crowds from Jerusalem, from Idumea, from beyond the Jordan, and from the neighborhood of Tyre and Sidon*, come to glorify God. So many people are present that at one point Jesus feels they would crush him (Mk 3:7-10).

While preaching inside a synagogue in Nazareth Jesus promises his people that he will liberate them from oppression, and those who hear him are *amazed at the gracious words that came from his mouth*. Following his talk at the synagogue, something happens, supposedly in Capernaum, whereby Jesus infuriates the people by condemning Jewish rejection of past prophets. In turn, they lead him *to the brow of the hill on which their town had been built, to hurl him down headlong* (Lk 4:24-29).

Able to escape the maddening crowd, Jesus continues to astonish people with his teaching and his charisma and power as he cures a demoniac. News of him spread everywhere in the region (Lk 4:37). Matthew states that his fame reaches Syria, and *great crowds from Galilee, the Decapolis, Jerusalem, and Judea, and from beyond the Jordan followed him* (Mt 4:23-25). The crowds follow him to a nearby elevation where he delivers his Sermon on the Mount. His teachings include the Beatitudes, the Lord's Prayer, and a series of moral directives through which he admonishes the crowds on sinful behavior, instructing them not to act hypocritically, to serve God, not mammon, to forgive others if they wish God to forgive them, to beware of false prophets, to become righteous, and to focus on doing God's will rather than merely to acknowledge his existence. This time the crowds react differently. Despite scolding them, they are *astonished at his teaching, for he taught them as one having authority, and not as their scribes* (Mt 5, 6, 7).

As a large crowd assembles by the sea and intently listens to him, he begins to speak through parables (Mk 4:1-34). Sick people are brought to him to be cured. He leaves for a deserted place, but the crowd goes looking for him, even preventing him from leaving them. He insists, however, that he must continue to proclaim the kingdom of God (Lk 4:42-44). Once again, the crowd welcomes him to the point of crushing him (Lk 8:40-42). Some people are uncertain of who he is. They ridicule him as he approaches a child that has died, but once he revives her, their feelings change; they are *utterly astounded,* and *news of this spread throughout all that land* (Mk 5:39-42, Mt 9:23-26). He cures a demoniac, and the crowds are amazed, remarking that *nothing like this has ever been seen in Israel* (Mt 9:32-33). He travels to his own town to teach at a synagogue, and those who hear him are *astonished* at his wisdom. But, upon finding out that he is a mere carpenter they reject him, and he leaves the area because of their lack of faith (Mk 6:1-6, Mt 13:54-57).

Despite experiencing rejection, Jesus instructs his disciples to start preaching the good news; however, he warns them not to go into pagan lands, or to visit Samaritans, their religious cousins. Instead, they are to pursue *the lost sheep of the house of Israel* ... proclaim the kingdom of God and *cure the sick, raise the dead, cleanse lepers,* and *drive out demons* (Mt 10:5-8). Afterward, he withdraws to Bethsaida to be alone with his disciples, but the crowds (about five thousand) learn about his whereabouts and go to him; he preaches to them and moved by pity he miraculously feeds them (Lk 9:11-16, Mt 14:13-21). He then travels to Gennesaret where people recognize him and bring the sick to him to be cured (Mt 14:35-36).

With the same ease that he responds to the many that pursue him, supposedly because they believe in his powers, Jesus turns his wrath upon people who refuse to believe. Following his return from a mountain, a large *crowd* is awaiting Jesus and greets him. A man brings his son to him because his disciples are not able to heal him. Irately, he speaks out by calling the crowd of Jews (that supposedly include his disciples), a *faithless and perverse generation,* wondering how long he would have to endure them (Mk 9:14-19, Lk 9:41). In another instance, he goes out of his way to cure the servant of a Roman centurion, and upon finding extraordinary faith in this non-Jew, he expresses misgivings about his people's disbelief. He issues one of several threats to take the kingdom of God away from them and promises to drive them *into the outer darkness* (Mt 8:10-12).

He blames *the people of this generation* for saying that the Baptist is possessed and for calling him a drunkard, a glutton, and a friend of sinners (Lk 7:31-32). He manifests that because of their disbelief he will not reveal to them the mysteries of God's kingdom, and instead will seek to confuse them by speaking in parables (Lk 8:9-10, Mt 13:13-15). This is an astonishing remark that keeps the reader wondering what Jesus could be preaching inside the synagogues and to the crowds.

Not everyone is persuaded by Jesus's charismatic personality, however, or by his teachings or even his miraculous deeds. People run him out of his own town again; he curses inhabitants in Chorazin, Bethsaida, Tyre, Sidon, and Capernaum (where previously they were astonished at his words) for their unbelief. He casts a wide net referring, again, to his generation as evil, possibly alluding to the religious authorities (Lk 11:27-29). He addresses another *crowd* about upcoming calamities and calls them hypocrites, without the reader knowing if he is referring to his people or the religious authorities (Lk 12:54-56). He warns people that they will physically perish if they do not repent (Lk 13:1-5). Nonetheless, he comes out in their defense by harshly criticizing the burden the religious authorities impose upon them (Lk 11:46). He reprimands leaders of the synagogue who become indignant because he cures a woman on the Sabbath, and, upon seeing his opponents humiliated, the crowd (supposedly ordinary Jews) rejoices at the *splendid deeds done by him* (Lk 13:14-17).

Leaving Jericho with a sizable crowd following him (Mk 10:46) he enters Jerusalem triumphantly. He finds that many people have spread their cloaks on the road, and others spread leafy branches that they had cut from the fields to welcome him by calling him king, and crying out, *Hosanna! Blessed is he who comes in the name of the Lord! Blessed is the kingdom of our father David that is to come!* (Mk 11:8-10, Lk 19:36-37, Mt 21:8-11). He has attained great fame, as he is now seen as God's sent Messiah and king.

Perhaps driving out the merchants from the temple is the latest affront that compels the Pharisees to put Jesus to death; but they cannot do it yet, because *all the people were hanging on his words* (Mk 14:1-2, Lk 19:47-48). Nevertheless, he continues teaching in the city, but his misgivings about the religious authorities and his own people become evident, and again he threatens through parables to take away God's kingdom from them if they do not repent (Lk 13:24, 14:15, Mt 22:1). He ridicules the Pharisees (Lk 20:25-26) who attempt to conspire against him, but they become fearful because the people are siding with him (Lk 22:1-2).

Nonetheless, events seem too fluid. Despite his show of popular support, Jerusalem deserts him, and he laments that the city will become desolate because of its unbelief (Lk 13:34-35, 21:20-24, Mt 23:37-38). A puzzling string of events brings about Jesus's crucifixion, and the crowds of Jewish people seem to be intricately involved. The temple authorities rule the city; they have their guards and their followers (it is impossible for leaders not to have followers), and they have recruited one of Jesus's disciples, Judas Iscariot, who has offered to lead them to arrest Jesus.

What has changed? What happened to those sizable crowds that followed Jesus and were continuously amazed by his teachings and grateful for siding with them against religious oppression from their own kind; where did all the gratefulness for his healings go? What prompted the religious authorities to finally move against Jesus? Only a while ago the chief priests did not dare to arrest Jesus because too many people sided with the one who had been welcomed as a hero into Jerusalem.

Once arrested, the chief priests summon *many false witnesses* to testify against Jesus (Mk 14:56, Mt 26:60). They gather a crowd to support their request to release Barabbas and instead press to crucify Jesus. There are other people too, passersby (likely Jews) who revile Jesus (Mk 15:29). Many women appear to support him (Mk 15:40-41), but his disciples are nowhere to be seen. The plan that Judas devises with the chief priests (taking guards to arrest Jesus in the open) is no plan at all; this scheme could have been implemented at any time, as Jesus was not hiding. Did the crowds that followed Jesus suddenly become so apathetic that they do not protest or put up any type of resistance? It seems that fear or indifference overcomes them. Yet, awkwardly, on the eve of his crucifixion, there is still *a large crowd* of Jewish people following him, resignedly lamenting what is about to happen (Lk 23:27, 48-49).

There are yet other explanations for how these events transpire. Three times Jesus has predicted his death, and he is aware that he will be betrayed by one of his own. According to Matthew and John, Jesus's death is unavoidable because it is predicated upon divine fatalism. Jesus chooses not to resist his arrest, indicating that God's will stands above everything else, thus it must be fulfilled (Mt 26:55, Jn 18:11, 12:27). The crowd that followed him and welcomed him as a temporal messiah now has deserted him. How were the religious authorities (who were afraid of the crowds) able to turn around the people's sentiments against Jesus? What did he do to alienate the people he came to help? The synoptics provide no explanations.

Jesus and the Jewish People-The Gospel of John
John's Gospel is less endearing of the Jewish people than the synoptics. Already in the first chapter John concludes that Jesus *came to what was his own, but his own people did not accept him* (Jn 1:11-13). The term *people* means just that: a group of ordinary human beings, in this case, Jewish people.[3] Moreover, in a veiled manner, John associates Jewish unbelief with belonging to the world (Jn 1:9-10) that, according to Jesus, is controlled by Satan.

Upon baptizing Jesus, the Baptist acknowledges that his mission is to announce him to Israel so the people would know him (Jn 1:31). Jesus begins to announce who he is through signs (his miracles) and many begin to believe in him and are baptized (Jn 3:23). Nonetheless, their faith seems questionable to Jesus. The text indicates that *Jesus would not trust himself to them because he knew them all* (Jn 2:23-25). Is this Gospel referring to the people Jesus is baptizing, realizing perhaps that eventually, they will turn against him? Is he affirming that he does not trust his own people? Account must be taken that while writing this text the authors of John's Gospel are working their way in history backward. In other words, they are aware of the ending, the death of Jesus. Hence, John's gospel begins with a negative viewpoint, and by chapter 3 the authors already know the conclusion: *And this is the verdict, that people preferred darkness to light, because their works were evil* (Jn 3:19). It just happens that those *people* that Jesus comes to save are the Israelites.

Nonetheless, straying away from his mission to minister only to the Jewish people, Jesus meets a Samaritan woman who is surprised that *a Jew* would dare to ask her for a drink (Jn 4:19) since Jews and Samaritans do not get along because of differences in belief. Jesus slights her telling her that she is wrong, because *salvation is from the Jews* (Jn 4:22), supposedly referring to God's chosen people. Somehow, he endears himself to the Samaritan woman; she likes him, calls him a prophet, and goes on to tell her people. She must have told them incredible things since they concluded that Jesus *is the savior of the world* (Jn 4:39-43).

He travels to Galilee where is welcomed by many who have seen his deeds in Jerusalem (Jn 4:45). Returning to Cana, where he performed his first miracle (according to John), he cures the son of a Roman official,[4] and remarks, *unless you people see signs and wonders, you will not believe* (Jn 4:46-48). Who is he addressing? It appears he is scolding a pagan, the royal official who asserts his belief in Jesus; this, however, would not make sense. But in Luke's and Matthew's version of the incident, the reference is clearly about Jews, whether ordinary Israelites or the religious authorities, who refuse to have faith unless they see signs (Mt 8:10 and Lk 7:9).[5]

The most problematic aspect of this gospel is the usage of the terms *Jews, crowd,* and *people,* which often refer to the Jewish people as well as to the religious authorities. It is known that John is a Jew; it is not known whether those responsible for writing or editing subsequent versions of the text were Jews too. Regardless, it may be observed that the authors of John's Gospel often place a certain distance between their ethnicity and religion, possibly because of their hostility toward the Jews who have expelled them from the synagogues for confessing their faith in Jesus.

For example, the authors write that Jesus travels to Jerusalem because there is *a feast of the Jews* (supposedly referring to all Jews, not only the religious authorities).[6] Upon seeing a man who has been ill for thirty-eight years Jesus decides to heal him. John's text points out that *the Jews* are upset because the healing has taken place during the Sabbath: *So the Jews said to the man who was cured, "It is the sabbath, and it is not lawful for you to carry your mat."* The man tells *the Jews that Jesus was the one who had made him well,* after which *the Jews began to persecute Jesus ...* and *the Jews tried all the more to kill him* (Jn 5:1:18). It is important to notice that in the texts' most virulent attacks, Mark, Luke, and Matthew do not refer to the authorities as *the Jews,* but as scribes, chief priests, and/or Pharisees (Mk 7:1,5, 8:31, 10:33; Lk 5:21,30, 6:7, 11:53; Mt 5:20, 9:3, 23:1-29, 27:41). Supposedly John is referring to the religious authorities (the guardians of the Law) as *the Jews.* Why would he generalize instead of making a distinction as the synoptics do?

John acknowledges that Jesus is stirring the people with his signs as large crowds begin to follow him. After the multiplication of the loaves, people call him a prophet and even want to make him king (Jn 6:1-15). Crowds continue to follow him (Jn 6:22, 24) and he enters into another confusing exchange in which the text conflates the crowds with the religious authorities asking for signs that would legitimize Jesus's role. Jesus then addresses *the crowd* (Jn 6:22, 24) saying that he is *the bread of life,* but they refuse to believe (Jn 6:35-36). Immediately thereafter, the text uses the term the Jews: *The Jews murmured about him because he said, I am the bread that came down from heaven* (Jn 6:41). Thus, who represents the crowds and the Jews, ordinary people, or the religious authorities? Would readers be able to tell the difference?

Additional passages are equally conflated. Although Jesus initially refuses to travel to Judea because *the Jews were trying to kill him* (Jn 7:1), he decides to attend the Feast of the Tabernacles, and immediately *the Jews* begin looking for him. However, there is *murmuring in the crowds;* some say he is a good man; others attest that he misleads the crowds, *but no one spoke openly about him because they were afraid of the Jews* (Jn 7:1-13). At the end of the feast, he begins to teach, and *the Jews were amazed and said, "How does he know scripture without having studied?* (Jn 7:14-15). Who are these Jews who now are so amazed, and who make up the crowds?

Ahead in the same chapter confusion ensues again. Jesus remarks, *why are you trying to kill me? The crowd answered, 'You are possessed.'* (Jn 7:19-20). There is even dissension within the crowd; some start to believe in him and others try to arrest him. Who constitutes this crowd? Nothing seems to indicate that it refers to the religious authorities alone. Any attempt at an explanation becomes complicated because at times the text makes a subtle distinction between crowd and Pharisees; for example, *but many of the crowd began to believe in him, and said, "When the Messiah comes, will he perform more signs than this man has done? The Pharisees heard the crowd murmuring about him to this effect, and the chief priests and the Pharisees sent guards to arrest him* (Jn 7:31-32). The distinction becomes evident as another division occurs among the crowd, some believing that Jesus is the Messiah while others do not. Some want to arrest him, but now even the guards seem to believe in Jesus. At this moment the Pharisees (the religious authorities) indicate that the guards are being deceived and *the crowd ... is accursed* (Jn 7:40-49).

Despite the conflict surrounding Jesus's words, the next day he appears in the temple area and once again people show up to listen to him (Jn 8:2). His words cause a quarrel because *many came to believe in him* (Jn 8:30). It does not stand to reason that *many* refer only to the religious authorities who dislike Jesus; in this passage, the word *many* likely refers to common Jews who are listening to Jesus. However, since the text does not make any distinction, everyone involved is identified as *Jews,*[7] and all end up being called children of the devil by Jesus (Jn 8:44).

While it is readily apparent that the term *Jews* in chapter nine refers to the religious authorities (Jn 9:18-35), the passage dealing with Lazarus's death and resurrection is more puzzling, unless we accept the unlikely view that many Pharisees are friends with Lazarus and his sisters and have a good relationship with Jesus. As Jesus arrives at Lazarus's house *many of the Jews had come to Martha and Mary to comfort them about their brother* (Jn 11:19). These Jews begin to express sympathy for Jesus when he becomes *perturbed ... and weeps,* although some of them express cynicism (Jn 11:33-37). He praises God saying, *Father, I thank you for hearing me. I know that you always hear me; but because of the crowd here I have said this, that they may believe that you sent me* (Jn 11:42, emphasis mine). Following his command to bring Lazarus back to life, *many of the Jews* begin to believe in him. The text adds that *some of them went to the Pharisees and told them what Jesus had done*, after which the religious authorities convene the Sanhedrin to plot against Jesus (Jn 11:43-53). In these verses, *the Jews* seem to be ordinary Jewish people who go to inform the religious authorities (Pharisees) about Jesus's feat. Even though there may be some Pharisees who are tracking Jesus's move, are we to assume that *the crowd* and *the Jews* in these verses are all members of the religious authorities; that there are no ordinary people among them? When the text reads, *Now the Passover of the Jews was near, and many went up from the country to Jerusalem before Passover to purify themselves* (Jn 11:55), does it mean that the Feast of the Passover refers only to the religious authorities; that the feast has no meaning for common Jews?

While in Bethany, there is a *large crowd of the Jews* who have come to see Jesus and Lazarus. It is then when the chief priests plot to kill Lazarus too *because many of the Jews were turning away and believing in Jesus because of him* (Jn 12:9-11). Who are these Jews who are beginning to believe in Jesus, common people, or the religious authorities?

The next day, a *great crowd* gathers in Jerusalem to welcome Jesus, chanting *Hosanna! Blessed is he who comes in the name of the Lord, [even] the king of Israel* (Jn 12:12-13). This *great crowd* cannot possibly mean the religious authorities, as it must include those who have been following Jesus and those who are awaiting his arrival. The term *the crowd* also becomes confusing toward the end of the chapter. Part of this *crowd* hears the voice of an angel from heaven speaking to Jesus; others believe it is just thunder. Jesus speaks up and the *crowd* answers him back rejecting him, so he leaves and hides from them (Jn 12:28-38). Are we supposed to believe that these crowds refer only to the religious authorities, the Pharisees; that there are no ordinary Jewish people among them?

John's text makes a distinction between Jewish Jews and those who by now have become followers of Jesus. When Jesus tells his disciples to go back to Judea, they reply, *Rabbi, the Jews were just trying to stone you, and you want to go back there?* (Jn 11:7-8). Why would the disciples (who are Jews) distance themselves from their ethnicity and religion by using a term (*the Jews*) that disparages their own people? Then, while speaking to his disciples Jesus says, *my children, I will be with you only a little while longer. You will look for me, and as I told the Jews, 'Where I go you cannot come,' so now I say it to you* (Jn 13:33). It now appears that even Jesus relies on his ethnic roots, i.e., his own people, his ancestors, Abraham, Moses, and the other prophets, by using the term *the Jews* with the same apparent hostility as John's text uses it. The narrative insinuates that Jesus no longer considers himself a Jew; there are Jews, and there is Jesus and his disciples. Furthermore, while conversing with Pilate, Jesus tells him, *my kingdom does not belong to this world. If my kingdom did belong to this world, my attendants [would] be fighting to keep me from being handed over to the Jews* (Jn 18:36). Again, is Jesus referring to the religious authorities or the people; and regardless, why call them Jews, as if he is not himself a Jew? We must remember that at no time do the authors in the synoptic texts, or Jesus, refer to the religious authorities as Jews; instead, when Jesus condemns their behavior, he refers to them as scribes, Pharisees, and Sadducees.

In chapter fifteen in John's Gospel, Jesus speaks of the world's hatred toward his disciples and him. What world is this? As far as we know, there is no expressed hatred in the Gospels from the Romans toward Jesus and his followers or from any other nation or ethnic group. So far, in all four Gospels hatred emanates mainly from

Herod, the Pharisaic religious establishment along with its followers, and ordinary Jewish people who at the last minute turn against him either because they are fearful or indifferent. The world, which is controlled by Satan, once again becomes associated with the Jewish people; John's Gospel reminds the reader that Jesus *came to what was his own, but his own people did not accept him* (Jn 1:11). Moreover, if there is still doubt about who partakes in Jesus's crucifixion, Pontius Pilate is asking Jesus, *what have you done? Your own nation and the chief priests handed you over to me* (Jn 18:35, emphasis mine). Who is Pilate referring to as a *nation?* A reasonable conclusion would be to assert that there was a large portion of the Jewish people who supported the religious authorities who in turn approved the temple aristocracy's desire to put Jesus to death. It would be foolish, however, to ascribe the primary responsibility for Jesus's death to the Jewish people or the religious authorities. Many people turn against Jesus; Herod, the Sanhedrin, the chief priests, the elders, all reject him (except two, Nicodemus and Joseph of Arimathea who liked Jesus). The religious authorities take the lead by accusing Jesus of making himself God; a blasphemy no less. But the greatest act of injustice that the Gospels overlook lies with Pontius Pilate, who could care less if one Jew would die since he considers Jews second-rate people that merit being subjugated. It is interesting, and awkward, that Jesus does not raise his voice in opposition to Pilate, suggesting that, in the end, Jesus does not seem to care for the temporal conditions of the Jewish people. His concerns are cosmic.

Anti-Jewishness and the Gospels
Negative characterizations regarding Jews are noticeable in all four Gospels, and it is understandable, as is too the reverse (anti-Jesus's followers). The texts record serious opposition by the Jewish people and the religious establishment against Jesus's followers (more frequently in The Acts of the Apostles). In Mark the degree of anti-Jewishness is subtle. There is an underhanded remark that the author attributes to Pilate during his exchange with Jesus in which Pilate places the blame for Jesus's arrest on the chief priests: *For he knew that it was out of envy that the chief priests had handed him over* (Mk 15:10). There is no characterization in Mark of Pilates's indifference to having Jesus scourged and handed over to be crucified merely to satisfy the crowd (Mk 15:15). Moreover, it is not only the religious establishment that is responsible for Jesus's crucifixion; *a crowd with swords and clubs who had come from the chief priests, the scribes, and the elders* (Mk 14:43), and the participation of *many* ordinary Jewish people that are gathered to falsely testify against Jesus (Mk 14:56, emphasis mine) assist in his arrest.

In Luke, a crowd that includes *chief priests, temple guards,* and *elders* accompany Judas Iscariot to apprehend Jesus (Lk 22:47-52). There are no false witnesses to testify against him, but there are crowds that have gathered along with the chief priests when he is taken before Pilate (Lk 23:4). The presence of ordinary citizens is evident as Pilate summons *the chief priests, the rulers, and the people* to discuss Jesus's case, and all end up calling for his crucifixion (Lk 23:13, emphasis mine). Pilate's indifference to what amounts to injustice is noted in Luke as he hands Jesus over to the religious authorities *to deal with as they wished* (Lk 23:25).

Reading Luke literally, the text implies that the religious authorities are the ones who oversee the planning of Jesus's crucifixion while there are no indications about the presence of Roman soldiers (Lk 23:26, 34-35). Meanwhile, in Mark, Matthew, and John it is the Roman soldiers who carry out the crucifixion (Mk 15:16-24, Mt 27:27-37, Jn 19:23). It is worth pointing out that negative characterizations against Jews abound in Luke's Acts of the Apostles (written about the same time as Luke's Gospel). The author describes what is now an open clash between *the Jews* and the new Christians in which *the Jews* are depicted as attempting to kill Paul (Acts 9:23); they support James's execution and seek to arrest Peter (Acts 12:2-3); they are jealous of Paul (Acts 13:45), and they poison the minds of Gentiles against Paul (Acts 14:2). Luke (likely a non-Jew) even quotes Paul (a Jew) saying that *the people of Jerusalem and their rulers* did not recognize Jesus, condemned him, and asked Pilate to execute him (Acts 13:27) while *I make my defense against all the accusations of the Jews* (Acts 26:2). In effect, accusatory charges against the Jews are depicting a well-marked ethnic and religious animosity between the new Christians and Jews that has prevailed until today.

Meanwhile, anti-Jewishness in Matthew is more perceptible. There is a crowd with swords and clubs that represent the religious establishment, the entire Sanhedrin, *and many false witnesses* (that) *came forward* (Mt 26:60, emphasis mine), although we do not know if they were being compelled or if they came willingly. The remark in Mark blaming the chief priests for Jesus's arrest points in the same direction (Mt 27:18). However, what might be of interest to the reader is a note by NABRE editors that points out: *this is an example of the tendency, found in varying degree in all the gospels, to present Pilate in a relatively favorable light and emphasize the hostility of the Jewish authorities and underline of the people.*[8] In Matthew, Pilate is so unmoved by the action he is about to take that he washes his hands in public and indicates that he has nothing to do with Jesus's death (Mt 27:24); in other words, it is all on the Jews. Matthew then adds a reply that came from *the whole people*: *His blood be upon us and upon our children* (Mt 27:25), meaning that those Jews who were present at Jesus's mock trial were willfully accepting the sentence as eagerly as those who favor the execution of a criminal. It is even more extraordinary that NABRE editors point out that the statement constitutes an admission of culpability *by the entire people of Israel.*[9] Seemingly to ensure that the story is recorded for posterity, Matthew narrates a passage in which the chief priests and the elders hand out *a large sum of money to the* (Roman) *soldiers* to explain the disappearance of Jesus's body from the tomb by saying *his disciples came by night and stole him while we were asleep*, adding that *this story has circulated among the Jews to the present [day]* (Mt 28:11-15). It is plausible that these two incidents may have happened. Nonetheless, what certainly has happened is that Christians have circulated Matthew's story for centuries.

The matter surrounding John's Gospel has to do with the extent to which this text, more than the others, accounts for inspiring anti-Jewishness from its very beginnings throughout the Middle Ages and up until today. The difference between John's Gospel and the synoptic texts in examining anti-Jewish sentiment is significant because of the indiscriminate instances that the term *Jews* is used, as indicated in the tally. In 2011 Pope Benedict XVI tackled the question of who was responsible for the death of Jesus. Scrutinizing the meaning of the term 'Jews' Benedict argues:

> *In John's Gospel, this word has a precise and clearly defined meaning: he is referring to the Temple aristocracy. So the circle of accusers who instigate Jesus' death is precisely indicated in the Fourth Gospel and clearly limited: it is the Temple aristocracy.*[10]

Benedict is correct in identifying the Temple aristocracy as instigating Jesus's death, provided that the term refers to the few who exercised religious authority at the time, namely the Pharisees, Sadducees, scribes, the chief priests, and the head priest. They were the ones who felt their authority threatened by Jesus, and the synoptics showed them conspiring against him early in the texts. Nonetheless, John's Gospel misconstrues the word *Jews* by not distinguishing between the religious authorities and ordinary Jewish people who follow the leadership, the outcome of which is to affirm anti-Jewishness sentiments, an aspect that Benedict omits.

Two events certainly have lasted until today that shed light on what transpired at the time: the rift that took place between Jews and the soon to become Christians that not only divided Judaism but left the majority of Jews (people and religious authorities) siding with Mosaic Law and against a Christian minority; and the charge of deicide leveled against Jews that gave rise to anti-Jewish sentiments that remain, although under a new label: anti-Semitism. After recognizing the consequences of the stigma that for centuries cultural and institutional Christianity had directed at Jews, the Catholic hierarchy (for one) has accepted responsibility for misconstruing Jewish behavior and exculpated the Jewish people of the charge of deicide.[11]

John's Gospel is written at a time when the new Christian Jews and the Jewish religious establishment that included a sizable majority of the Jewish people were engaged in clashes in which the former are being thrown out of the synagogues.[12] As a result, John's use of the term *the Jews* is charged with understandable hostility. The problem presents itself because John's Gospel uses the term indistinguishably while lacking (at the time) the significance of Pope Benedict's qualifications, presuming he is entirely correct. The absence of vital clarifications in the Gospels is precisely what leads to prejudicial generalizations over time. It is implausible to accept that the way John's Gospel uses the terms *people, crowd, nation,* or *Jews* refer only to a very restricted group. The citations that are shown above simply do not support this view.

For example, when the high priest questions Jesus about his doctrine, Jesus replies, *I have always taught in a synagogue or in the temple area where <u>all the Jews</u>*

gather, and in secret I said nothing (Jn 18:20, emphasis mine). Who is Jesus referring to by the term *the Jews*? It cannot possibly be only the Temple aristocracy since ordinary Jews would gather there too. Furthermore, John's statement that Jesus came to the world, *but his own people did not accept him* (Jn 1:10-11 emphasis mine), is no different in Matthew (in whom the Church sees the term as referring to the entire Israelite people) than in NABRE editors who point out that the term means *property/possession, his own people.* Even the Vatican declaration that exculpates the Jewish people contradicts Pope Benedict's statement; it reads, *True, the Jewish authorities and those who followed their lead pressed for the death of Christ.*[13]

Attempting to understand the phenomenon, it would have been nearly miraculous that, given the cultural and religious devotion among Jews at the time, a fierce split would not have occurred between the dominant religious culture in Judea (Judaism), and newcomers (Christians), who insisted (following the crucifixion of their leader) that they were the true and faithful worshippers of Yahweh.

Moreover, it is clear that anti-Jewishness did not originate out of nothingness. Since the printing press had not emerged, the few who were able to read the text decades and centuries later would interpret Jesus's crucifixion while being aware of the existing animus between the two religious groups. These few would instruct Christians by word of mouth who in turn would orally pass along beliefs already conditioned by negative characterizations found in the text; and herein lies the origins of Christian anti-Jewishness. This type of routine oral messaging throughout the centuries played a role in stressing an attitude and a belief that is found in the Gospels, particularly in John's Gospel. The anti-Jewish sentiment that emanated from the Gospels had become so toxic over the centuries that the Catholic hierarchy attempted to distance itself from the meme that anti-Jewishness has anything to do with the Gospels.[14]

Anti-Jewishness and the Fathers of the Church

As a likely consequence of this reading of the Gospels, the educated Christian elite passed along their anti-Jewish attitudes through their writings. Thus, we read how the Early Church Fathers (who set the tone of the theological discourse for centuries to come) contributed their share of condemnations against Jews.[15] A brief reading of passages from the writings of among the most renowned of them would allow us to realize the historical reasons that explain the evolution of anti-Jewishness.

Justin Martyr, one of the greatest apologists of the Christian faith, writes in his *Dialogue with Trypho* (a Jew)[16] only decades after the Gospels appear:

> - *it is demonstrated that the Jews deliberated about the Christ Himself, to crucify and put Him to death* (Ch 72).
> - *Circumcision given as a sign, that the Jews might be driven away for their evil deeds done to Christ and the Christians* (Ch 16).
> - *The Jews sent persons through the whole earth to spread calumnies on Christians* (Ch 17).

- The Jews, in rejecting Christ, rejected God who sent him (Ch 136).

John Chrysostom (fourth century), *generally considered the most prominent doctor of the Greek Church and the greatest preacher ever heard in a Christian pulpit,*[17] writes in *Against the Jews,* Homily 1:[18]

> *- But do not be surprised that I called the Jews pitiable. They really are pitiable and miserable. When so many blessings from heaven came into their hands, they thrust them aside and were at great pains to reject them.*
> *- But at any rate, the Jews say that they, too, adore God. God forbid that I say that. No Jew adores God! Who say so? The Son of God say so. For he said: "If you were to know my Father, you would also know me. But you neither know me nor do you know my Father." Could I produce a witness more trustworthy than the Son of God?*

Augustine (end of the fourth century to mid-fifth century), among the most influential of the Church Fathers on Christian theology and Western political philosophy, writes in "Treatise Against the Jews"[19] that the people of God are the Christians (ch 3), not the Jews (ch 7). Additionally,

> *- why do not the Jews realize that they have remained stationary in useless antiquity rather than hurl charges against us who hold fast to the new promises because we do not observe the old? (6);*
> *- Sion, however, and Jerusalem, although spiritually understood as the Church, is nevertheless a fitting witness against the Jews, because from that place where they crucified Christ the Law and the Word of God have proceeded to the Gentiles. (7, deicide?).*

Disputations over rites, customs, and personal sentiments along with invectives taking the form of theology sought to prove that the newly created religion was the only truthful one. This was taking place at a time when the Christian Church was triumphantly seeking to assert its identity while Jews were trying to preserve theirs. For centuries, anti-Jewishness spread throughout Europe through the perpetuation of social and religious stigma. A reading of the texts was giving way to a social and ordinary oral tradition pointing out that according to God's revelation found in the Gospels, the Jews had rejected and then killed Jesus, thus deserving the wrath and contempt of Christians. What remained throughout the centuries was not that some people who happened to be Jews at the time participated in the killing of Jesus, but that *the Jews*, i.e., a historical generalization about a religious and ethnic group of people, were to be tainted forever for the actions of a few. While these beliefs and behavior were seldom officially sanctioned by the Church, it seems to be no less true that the institution did not combat them with the same energy and force as when it dealt with heresies. This view accounts for an extraordinary public apology made by the head of the Catholic Church.[20]

Notes:

1. NEs' note, Mt 27:9-10 reads, *Matthew's attributing this text to Jeremiah is puzzling, for there is no such text in that book, and the thirty pieces of silver thrown by Judas "into the temple" (Mt 27:5) recall rather Zec 11:12–13.*

2. Ibid., note John 9:22.

3. Ibid., note Jn 1:11, editors point out that the phrase indicates *his own people (the Israelites).*

4. Ibid., note on Jn 4:46-54 suggests that this is likely a different version of the same deed in Matthew, where the sick person is a servant, and in Luke where he is a slave.

5. This is an awkward remark since Jesus, who claims to know human nature, realizes from the beginning of his mission that he must rely on signs, otherwise people would not believe.

6. The feast may refer either to Passover or Pentecost according to NEs' note, Jn 5:1. John makes references to 'a Jewish feast' three times and twice to *the Passover of the* Jews; in the synoptic, Pentecost is never mentioned, however, the Passover is mentioned sixteen times without the Jewish qualifier.

7. NEs' note indicates that verse 8:31 constitutes a rough editorial suture (sarcasm on the part of the author) since in Jn 8:37 they are described as trying to kill Jesus. However, there is no such indication about verse 8:30.

8. Ibid., note on Mt 27:18, emphasis mine.

9. Matthew sees in those who speak these words the entire people of Israel. NEs' note, Mt 27:24-25. This statement, however, seems to be quite different than Pope Benedict's explanation that Matthew's reference to blood, *does not cry out for vengeance and punishment; it brings reconciliation. It is not poured out 'against' anyone; it is poured out 'for' many.* Benedict adds that Matthew's statement has to be read *in the light of faith,* supposedly because otherwise it can be misunderstood (as it has). Pope Benedict XVI, *Jesus of Nazareth, Part Two,* (San Francisco: Ignatius Press, 2011), 187.

10. Pope Benedict XVI, 185. Benedict insists that the crowd who supported the release of Barabbas were only his supporters, suggesting that none of those who shouted *crucify him!* included ordinary Jews. 185. This supposition claims that all Jewish citizens in Jerusalem remained indifferent or fearful to take a stand and that in no way were persuaded to oppose Jesus. Is it plausible? In the end, most of the Jewish people did not side with Jesus or with his disciples; they remained with the religious establishment.

11. The declaration states, *What happened in His* (Jesus) *passion cannot be charged against all the Jews, without distinction, then alive, nor against the Jews of today.... the Church, mindful of the patrimony she shares with the Jews and moved not by political reasons but by the Gospel's spiritual love, decries hatred, persecutions, displays of anti-Semitism, directed against Jews at any time and by anyone. Although the Church is the new people of God, the Jews should not be presented as rejected or accursed by God, as if this followed from the Holy scriptures.* "Declaration on the Relation of the Church to Non-Christian Religions Nostra Aetate," (4), Vatican II, 28 October 1965, http://www.vatican.va/archive/hist_councils/ii_vatican_council/documents/vat-ii_decl_19651028_nostra-aetate_en.html (accessed June 8, 2018).

12. NEs' note, Jn 9:22 indicates: *Rejection/ex-communication from the synagogue of Jews who confessed Jesus as Messiah seems to have begun ca. A.D. 85, when the curse against the mînîm or heretics was introduced into the "Eighteen Benedictions."*

13. *Nostra Aetate* 4. Emphasis mine. How could Pope Benedict, who participated in the writings of Vatican II documents, have overlooked this statement?

14. *Although the Church is the new people of God, the Jews should not be presented as rejected or accursed by God, as if this followed from the Holy scriptures.* Nostra Aetate," (4),

15. Bernhard Blumenkranz, "Church Fathers," *Encyclopedia Judaica,* (accessed 12 June 2018).

16. Justin Martyr, *Dialogue with Trypho,* Translated by Marcus Dods and George Reith. From Ante-Nicene Fathers, Vol. 1. Edited by Alexander Roberts, James Donaldson, and A. Cleveland Coxe. (Buffalo, NY: Christian Literature Publishing Co., 1885.) Revised and edited for New Advent by Kevin Knight, http://www.newadvent.org/fathers/0128.htm (accessed 12 June 2018).

17. C. Baur, "St. John Chrysostom," *Catholic Encyclopedia,* 1910), http://www.newadvent.org/cathen/08452b.htm (accessed 13 June 2018).

18. John Chrysostom, "Against the Jews," Homily 1, *The Tertullian Project,* II & III, http://www.tertullian.org/fathers/chrysostom_adversus_judaeos_01_homily1.htm. Uploaded by Roger Pearse, Ipswich, UK, 2011, from a translation of unknown origin formerly hosted at the Medieval Sourcebook (accessed 12 June 2018).

19. "Augustine's 'Treatise Against the Jews,'" posted by Roger Pearse in his blog, *Thoughts on Antiquity, Patristic, Information Access, and More,* https://www.roger-pearse.com/weblog/2015/06/11/augustines-treatise-against-the-jews/comment-page-1/ (accessed 12 June 2018).

20. During his trip to Jerusalem in 2000 Pope John Paul II echoed such behavior as he followed a custom of inserting a note to God into the Western Wall. It read: *"We are deeply saddened by the behavior of those who in the course of history have caused these children of yours to suffer. And asking your forgiveness, we wish to commit ourselves to genuine brotherhood with the people of the covenant.* Deborah Sontag and Alessandra Stanley, "Ending Pilgrimage, the Pope Asks God for Brotherhood, *The New York Times,* March 27, 2000, https://www.nytimes.com/2000/03/27/world/ending-pilgrimage-the-pope-asks-god-for-brotherhood.html (accessed 23 June 2018).

Gentiles

Gentiles constitute a hidden element in the Gospels. While the texts are mostly about Jesus and the Jewish people, decades following Jesus's death, Gentiles comprise the primary source of what eventually becomes the Christian religion. From a Jewish viewpoint, and particularly during the Second Temple period, the term had acquired a pejorative connotation, because it referred to people who did not adhere to the Jewish faith; because of the abuse and injustices Jews had to endure at the hands of Gentiles; and, because of their substantially different moral conduct as opposed to strict Jewish observation of Mosaic Law.

Gentiles likely were aware of their designation by Jews, which is evident by the religious and political conflicts taking place at the time, particularly with the Romans. Once the Christian faith begins to nourish from Gentile populations, followers of the new faith refer to themselves as Christians.[1] Interestingly, the origin of the term Gentiles is neither Hebrew nor Greek, but Latin (on account of Roman Empire influence), and stands for being part of a common people, tribe, or nation that is non-Jewish. At times, even Jesus uses the term *pagan* pejoratively, to refer to Gentiles who worshipped a multitude of gods such as the Romans did. Although Jews would discriminate against Gentiles, e.g., prohibited marriages and social contacts, because they were considered insidious, their laws called for equitable treatment in some instances, and they willingly would reciprocate kindly treatment by them.[2] Today, the dictionary continues to define the term from the Jewish perspective.[3]

The term appears infrequently in the Gospels: 2xt in Mark, 6xt each in Luke and Matthew, and none in John. In John's Gospel references to Gentiles occur mostly through the term *world* that he uses extensively (78xt). Irrespective of the term itself, the category is ranked as significant, largely because of extensive narratives about Jesus's travels through Gentile territory, parables, miracles involving Gentiles, and passages related to his trial and execution at the hands of the Romans. To assess the Gospels' attitude toward Gentiles, all passages in this category were subjectively evaluated as being positive, negative, or neutral from the viewpoint of the authors' and Jesus's views. Table 2 shows that references to Gentiles in the Gospels were about equally divided in terms of allocated space (sp): 527 *sp* were positive, 562 *sp* were negative, and 86 *sp* were neutral.

Jesus and Gentiles – A Complicated Relationship
Jesus's association with Gentiles needs to be examined against four different settings: his statements in Matthew and John's words that he only comes to seek the lost sheep of Israel (Mt 10:6, 15:24, Jn 1:11); his specific instruction to his disciples not to go into pagan or Samaritan lands (Mt 10:5); the Jewish people's expectations (in both the Old and New Testaments) of a temporal Messiah that would address their religious and political oppression; and, the loving, merciful, and inclusive manner, in which Jesus (and God) is presented to the world today by mainstream Christianity.

Prior to Jesus's public mission, Luke reveals that Simeon, a righteous Jewish man awaiting the *consolation of Israel*, refers to Jesus as a *light for revelation to the Gentiles* (Lk 2:25-32). Simeon's prediction does not explain the phrase, although it suggests an early disconnect between God's plans in the Old Testament and Jesus's message. This split is observed as John the Baptist preaches throughout the Jordan quoting Isaiah that *all flesh*, i.e., including non-Jews, *shall see the salvation of God* (Lk 3:3-6). Furthermore, in Matthew, wise men (*magi*) from the east,[4] representing distant geographical areas populated by Gentiles, foretell a call about a *newborn king of the Jews* and travel to Jerusalem to pay homage to him. Following King Herod's suggestion, they go to Bethlehem, find the newborn, prostrate, and offer him gifts (Mt 2:1-12). This passage represents another clue regarding Jesus's ministry to Gentiles.

The Gospels clearly indicate that Gentiles are among the people Jesus ministers; he makes their acquaintance, heals, and preaches the kingdom of God to them. Nonetheless, there are incongruences in Jesus's behavior. He goes into Gentile territories despite saying that he comes only for the lost sheep of Israel and commands his disciples to do the same.[5] Moreover, having been raised in a faith that regards non-Jews as less than righteous people, Jesus's directive contradicts the presumed universality of his mission. Hence, it is difficult to understand why Jesus would make disparaging comments about people that he will include as part of God's salvation.

In the absence of explanations in the Gospels regarding Jesus's decision to go into gentile territories to preach the kingdom of God, his actions bring about mixed results. He seems to be well received at times by Gentiles, but his allure does not translate into an effective group of converts that would actively support him against his opponents. He goes into the land of the Gerasenes (Gadarenes in Matthew) where he drives out unclean spirits by having them entering a large herd of swine and leading them down a steep bank into the sea. In the process, he destroys the people's livelihood and alienates them; they become fearful and ask him to leave the area (Mk 5:1-20, Lk 8:26-39, Mt 8:28-34).

He travels to Tyre and Sidon, lands that were historically inhabited by the Canaanites, and conquered first by the Phoenicians and then by Alexander the Great. Many people from beyond the Jordan and from these territories hear of Jesus and come to listen to his teachings. He cures the sick and ousts unclean spirits (Mk 3:7-11,

Lk 6:17-19). At Tyre, he enters the house of a Greek woman, (Syrophoenician by birth), and heals her daughter who is possessed by a demon (Mk 7:24-30, Mt 15:21-28). At the Decapolis, a mixture of Hellenistic, Roman, and Semitic cultures, he cures a deaf man and is acclaimed by the people (Mk 7:31-37). His fame extends throughout Syria and beyond the Jordan River, a Gentile territory (Mt 4:24-25).

He travels to the region of Zebulun and Naphtali that has become largely inhabited by *people who sit in darkness,* and for whom Jesus represents *a great light in a land overshadowed by death.* He urges repentance, insisting that the kingdom of heaven is already present on earth (Mt 4:12-17). Preaching in his own town of Nazareth, he favorably alludes to the prophet Elijah after ministering to two Gentile persons; however, the remark angers his people who drive him out of town with the intention of killing him (Lk 4:24-29).

In another passage, Jesus praises a Gentile, a Roman centurion who is friendly with the Jewish people and asks him to cure his slave. His demeanor is humble; he believes that Jesus has healing powers. Impressed by the centurion's attitude, Jesus exclaims, *not even in Israel have I found such faith* (Lk 7:1-10, Mt 8:5-13, Jn 4:46-54), and he cures the centurion's slave. His praise of the centurion and the reception he receives at Tyre and Sidon are revealing, particularly when he condemns the Israelites' lack of trust in him following the rejection he encounters in his travels to Chorazim, Bethsaida, and Capernaum, three typically Jewish towns, whose people end up cursing and rejecting him. (Lk 10:13-15, Mt 11:20-24).

Along with his disciples, he journeys into Samarian territory, but the people, religious rivals of the Jews, would not let them go through. Two of his disciples are displeased and ask Jesus if they should pray for fire from heaven to consume them, illustrating not only hostility but that they have not yet incorporated Jesus's teachings on non-revenge. Not manifesting ill-will, he objects and proceeds to another village (Lk 9:51-56).

Notwithstanding how the Samaritans treated Jesus and his disciples, he encounters a self-righteous Jewish scribe who wants to know what he needs to do to attain eternal life. Jesus responds with a parable in which none other than a Samaritan becomes the righteous character (Lk 10:25-37). While in Samaria, he engages a Samaritan woman in one of the lengthiest exchanges in all the Gospels. The woman realizes that Jesus is a prophet and believing that he could be the awaited Messiah runs to tell the people in her town. In contrast with his first encounter with Samaritans, the people invite him to stay with them, and based on their conversation, somehow, they realize (*know*) that he is the savior of the world (Jn 4:4-42).

Yet, Jesus seems to have reservations about Gentiles. One day, he tells his disciples that he will be handed over to the Gentiles who will mock him, insult him, and kill him (Mk 10:32-34, Lk 18:31-33, Mt 20:17-19). Jesus does not explain why all this will happen. Nonetheless, amid his prophetic death, Mark and Matthew quote Jesus saying that before this is to happen *the gospel must first be preached to all nations* (Mk 13:9, Mt 24:14), suggesting that Gentiles are part of Jesus's plan of cosmic salvation. Whether Jesus's decision to include Gentiles in his plan is based on Israel's rejection of him (as suggested by some of his parables) or a later insertion by the authors once the disciples agree that they would seek to convert Gentiles, is difficult to tell; this instruction appears at the end of the synoptics, although it is absent in John's text (Mk 16:15-16, Lk 24:46-47, Mt. 24:14). Luke's narrative (Lk 21:1-28) is no kinder to Gentiles. Jesus seemingly combines the Parousia with the destruction of Jerusalem in which people will be slaughtered by Gentiles who will then govern Jerusalem for an indefinite period until his Second Coming. At this time, his judgment will include not only the Jewish people but all nations of the world, supposedly meaning that Gentiles too will be held accountable to his teachings. Jesus's insistence that he comes to judge humanity as a whole shows up in the lengthy passage on the judgment of nations in which he unmistakably indicates that on Judgment Day he will separate humans *as a shepherd separates the sheep from the goats* (Mt 25:31).

Despite his disparaging views toward Gentiles, Jesus's healings seem to attract many of them. Matthew attributes these deeds to the fulfillment of a prophecy by Isaiah in which God places his delight in his son Jesus to *proclaim justice to the Gentiles,* perhaps suggesting that, ultimately, the Gentiles will be won over by Jesus's meekness (Mt 12:15-21). Isaiah's passage (Is 42:1-4), however, may not necessarily refer to a person although this is the traditional Christian interpretation.[6] If Isaiah's passage were to refer to Jesus, then Matthew's use of Isaiah becomes incomprehensible, as it is in Matthew's Gospel that Jesus denigrates the same Gentiles he wishes to save. Not only does Jesus acknowledge that he has nothing to do with non-Jews; in the passage in which he addresses the Greek woman who asks him to cure her daughter, Jesus refers to her kind as dogs, which is an offensive term that Jews would use to refer to Gentiles (Mt 15:21-28, Mk 7:24-28).

Previously, while preaching to a crowd (likely of Jews) he counsels that, that which is holy (the scriptures), should not be given to Gentiles, whom he refers to as dogs and swine, since they would not appreciate its worth (Mt 7:6). While this passage may be a late insertion rather than Jesus's comment in reference to disobedient Christians,[7] the fact remains that, when the passage is read literally, it maligns Jesus and his relationship with people to whom he preaches the kingdom of God. This is not, however, the only passage that misconstrues Jesus's teachings. While instructing his disciples on how to deal with a rebellious follower, Jesus indicates that *if he refuses to listen even to the church, then treat him as you would a Gentile or a tax collector*; that is, as people not worthy of Jewish respect (Mt 18:15-17).

Moreover, on several occasions, Jesus contrasts the behavior he expects of his followers with that of *pagans*, a puzzling term (of Latin extraction) that Jesus uses to belittle the idolatrous behavior of non-Jews. In Matthew, Jesus does not want his disciples to be like pagans who love only those who love them; *babble* instead of praying properly; and do not place their dependence on the true God (Mt 5:43-48, 6:5-8, 31-34). He directs his disciples not to go into pagan territories or Samaritan towns (supposedly because it is not worth spending time with people who will treat his disciples with contempt). These instructions contradict his actions since he goes into those lands and preaches to these people (Mt 10:1, 5-6, 17-18). Such contemptuous language suggests that Jesus conducts himself in a parochial manner, not unlike Jews' attitudes toward Gentiles; and, that authors of the Gospels seem to have put together a disorganized collection of stories seeking to instruct others about the life of Jesus, without realizing how less credulous (and more methodical) future generations might react to these offensive remarks.

He instructs his disciples that the Gentiles are planning to mock him, spit upon him, scourge him, and put him to death. Nonetheless, these remarks do not trigger immediate hatred (or introspection) among Gentiles toward themselves, in the same manner as usage of the term *Jews* throughout the Gospels led Christians to the charge of Jewish deicide and anti-Semitism. Moreover, Jesus belittles Gentiles indicating that they act in a despotic fashion over the people. Instead, he offers himself as the role model saying that he comes not to be served but to serve and tells his disciples to do likewise (Mk 10:42-45, Lk 22:24-27, Mt 20:25-28).

Ironically, from a certain vantage point, Gentiles are given the opportunity to become part of God's salvation because of the Israelites' rejection of Jesus; otherwise, their future would have been uncertain at best. Certain parables indicate this view. The metaphor for entering through the narrow door suggests that simply because people *ate and drank in* Jesus's *company* does not mean they will be allowed into the kingdom; instead, others will be given the opportunity. (Lk 13:22-30, Mt 8:10-12). Similarly, in the Parable of the Great Feast, Gentiles are allowed to enter into the kingdom only because those who are first invited turn down the invitation (Lk 14:15-24, Mt 22:1-9). He addresses the Parable of the Tenants to the religious authorities in which the owner of the vineyard (God) threatens to put the tenants (the Jewish people) to death, take away the kingdom of God, and offer it instead to supposedly non-Jewish people (Mk 12:1-11, Lk 20:9-18, Mt 21:33-46).

At one point, he tells the religious authorities that he is the gatekeeper for those that follow him and the good shepherd who will give his life for his sheep. He reveals that he has *other* sheep *that do not belong to this fold,* presumably referring to Gentiles, that eventually he must lead, until *there will be one flock, one shepherd* (Jn 10:16). Interestingly, John's Gospel indicates that the chief priest, Caiaphas, has prophesized that Jesus is prepared to die not only for his nation but to gather into one *the dispersed children of God*, perhaps confirming Jesus's efforts to attract Gentiles to his flock. Caiaphas's remark caused consternation among the religious authorities, who *from that day on they planned to kill him* (Jn 11:49-53).

Jesus's ambivalence in dealing with Gentiles must have been puzzling to his followers. He is critical of them yet reaches out to them with the same vigor as when he meets with Jewish tax collectors. Jesus, however, refuses to act likewise toward the Jewish religious authorities. Interestingly, despite being pagans, Jesus legitimizes (at least by default) Gentile political authority when he allows payment of the census tax to Caesar (Mk 12:13-17, Lk 20:20-26, Mt 22:15-22). Whether it was his intention or not, his remark has left an indelible footprint in secular society.

The results of the *Jewish people* and *Jewish religious authorities'* categories suggest a noticeable predisposition in the Gospels against the Jewish people (far more evident in John's text) and the religious authorities in all four texts. Much of the negative space allocated to the Gentiles in the Gospels, on the other hand, is related to Jesus's trial and crucifixion by the Romans. These events, however, appear to have been relegated by history and Christian culture to an outcome in which the Jewish people alone appear to be responsible. Although the Jewish religious authorities act as instigators, largely because they see their authority threatened, it is Pilate who decides to carry on with his crucifixion without any justifiable grounds other than to ingratiate himself with the Jewish leadership (Mk 15:1-27, Lk 23:1-26, 32-37, Mt 27:1-2, 11-37, 45-54, 57-66, Jn 18:28-40, 19:1-34). There are two examples of Romans who behaved differently, the centurion (and the men with him) who immediately after Jesus dies, realizes that *truly this man was the Son of God!* (Mk 15:37-39, Lk 23:46-47, Mt 27:54), and the one who asks him to cure his servant. Within this context, Pilate's decision to hand over Jesus's body to Joseph of Arimathea (Mk 15:43-45, Lk 23:50-52) cannot be seen as a gesture of goodwill toward Jesus's followers, but rather as his desire to put Jesus's death behind him (Mt 27:65, Jn 19:21-22).

The Old Testament makes it abundantly clear that Jews are God's chosen people. God's choice seems whimsical, since there were other groups of people on earth who were as righteous and as sinful as the Israelites (Gen 10-12:1-3), and God had authority over all nations (Gen 22:18, Deut 15:6), indicating that he could have been impartial. Nonetheless, through suasion and wrath, God desires to make Israel the earth's center of power and govern the world through the Israelites. The Psalms, Isaiah, and Ezekiel are major exponents of this narrative (Ps 22:28-30, 46:11, 47:3-10, 82:8, 86:9, 96:7; Is 10:14, 13:1-22; 24:1-23; 30:28; 33:3; 34:1-2; 40:15-17; 41:1-2; 42:1-25; 60, 61, 62, 66:18; Ez 25, 32, 36).

What is noticeable in these passages is that God insists on attaining his objective, *all flesh shall come to worship before me, says the LORD* (Is 66:23), mostly by remaining loyal toward Israel, notwithstanding centuries of captivity he allowed them to endure. Within this context, Jesus's dealings with Gentiles are mystifying. His teachings and his deeds point toward the renewal of God's promises to the Israelites; promises that no longer appear to be temporal, but cosmic or supernatural. In contrast, Gentiles in the Old Testament are characterized as second-class citizens (perhaps, except for Cyrus, the Persian king). Paradoxically, history (so far) has turned this narrative upside down; Gentile-turned Christians are now the new followers of the Son of God, while, after centuries of propagating anti-Jewishness, Christianity today regards the Jewish people as *the root on to which the Gentiles would be grafted, once they came to believe.*[8]

Notes:
1. First records of the term *Christians* (followers of the resurrected Christ) appear in *Acts of the Apostles* 11:26 and 26:28. This is Luke's second volume (after the *Gospel According to Luke*) written between 70 CE, after the destruction of Jerusalem by the Romans, and 80-90 CE. These converts are scattered out of Jerusalem following the stoning of Stephen by a crowd of Jews and their religious authorities, angered by Stephen's belittling depiction of them (Acts 7:51-60). Some of these new Christians go to Antioch, near the modern city of Antakya in Turkey, where they establish a church. NEs, Introduction to Luke's Gospel. Also, a single use of the term appears in Josephus's Antiquities (near the end of the first century) where he describes Christians as a tribe; XVIII, 3, 3.
2. "Gentile," *Jewish Virtual Library, https://www.jewishvirtuallibrary.org/gentile* (accessed April 26, 2019); Francis Gigot, "Gentiles," *CE*, Vol. 6. http://www.newadvent.org/cathen/06422a.htm (accessed April 26, 2019).
3. *Merriam-Webster Dictionary, Oxford Dictionary, Cambridge Dictionary,* online s.v. "gentile, pagan."
4. A traditional and well-documented Catholic account indicates that these men belonged to the religious caste of the Medes in Persia, practiced Zoroastrianism, and were not kings. Interestingly, in Spanish culture, these men are known as magicians (festively referred to as *reyes magos*), likely because, at the time, magic and sorcery were traits identified with possessing wisdom. Walter Drum, "Magi." *CE,* Vol. 9. http://www.newadvent.org/cathen/09527a.htm (accessed April 30, 2019). Nonetheless, the Spanish Bible translation uses the term *magos* or magicians. Mateo 2:1-16. *Biblia Latinoamericana,* https://www.sanpablo.es/biblia-latinoamericana/la-biblia/nuevo-testamento/evangelio-segun-mateo/2 (accessed April 30, 2019).
5. Such a prohibition does not appear in Mark's or Luke's Gospels that, perhaps, not coincidentally were addressed to Gentiles. Hence, Jesus's instruction in Mark and Luke not to go into Gentile lands would have been awkward, i.e., it would signify that Jesus was not interested in converting Gentiles. NEs suggest that the absence of this prohibition, *indicate a certain adaptation to conditions in and outside of Palestine and suggest in Mark's account a later activity in the church.* However, once again, these issues raise legitimate questions concerning divine revelation, since there are numerous passages in the Gospels that were inserted after the initial texts were written. Hence, are such *adaptations* the authors', or is it God making corrections at a later time?
6. *Whether the servant is an individual or a collectivity is not clear* ...although *in the early Church and throughout Christian tradition, these poems have been applied to Christ.* NEs' note on Isaiah 42:1-4.
7. Ibid., note, Matthew 7:6: *Dogs and swine were Jewish terms of contempt for Gentiles. This saying may originally have derived from a Jewish Christian community opposed to preaching the gospel (what is holy, pearls) to Gentiles. In the light of Mt 28:19 that can hardly be Matthew's meaning. He may have taken the saying as applying to a Christian dealing with an obstinately impenitent fellow Christian.*
8. CCC 60.

Mosaic Law

Among the most puzzling sayings in the Gospels is Jesus's remark that he did not come to abolish Mosaic Law but to fulfill it. It is perplexing that by the time copies of the Gospels first appeared (just before or after 70 CE and 110 CE), Paul already had refuted Jesus's words, at times referring instead to the law of Christ (Rom 10:4, Gal 3:23-35, 6:2, 1 Cor 9:20). Interestingly the Old Law (as it is known today in Christianity) is of fundamental significance in the Gospels. Viewed comprehensively, it consists largely of a vast set of rules regulating the moral behavior of the Israelite people, including worshipping, socio-economic, political, and sexual practices. According to both Judaism and Christianity, the author of the Law is God (Yahweh) speaking through his spokesperson and presumable author, Moses.[1] Its purpose, *seems to be to make Israel a kingdom of priests and a holy nation.*[2] According to content analysis results, Mosaic Law scores relatively high although it does not appear among the highly significant categories.

Its relevance to the Gospels is shown in numerous passages denoting Jesus's conflict with the Pharisaic leadership regarding his interpretation of the Law. His proclamation that he does not come to abolish the law or the prophets but to fulfill it (Mt 5:17, Jn 15-25), provides the background to examine this category. To abolish a law means *to end its observance or effect of; to completely do away with; or to annul it.*[3] To fulfill the Law is more difficult to define, as it may imply several meanings. For purposes of this work, it signifies to *carry out a task, duty, or role as required, pledged, or expected.*[4] While the term *to abolish* indicates complete and absolute cessation of a law, *to fulfill* a law suggests that there is more than one manner to carry out a designated task. For example, new circumstances not previously contemplated may require that aspects of the law be replaced as a means to fulfill its initial intent.

The Gospels indicate that, regardless of definitions, Jesus amends Mosaic Law, at times substantially. Reading between the lines, he insinuates that the Law is no longer compatible with his teachings, arguing metaphorically that it does not make sense for the wedding guests to mourn while the bridegroom is with them, any more than new wine can be put into old wineskin (Mk 2:18-22, Lk 5:32-38, Mt 9:14-17).[5] His proclamation is awkward and transcendental. Why God would provide his people with moral laws that turned out not to be timeless? What deficiencies does Jesus find in Mosaic Law that requires overriding the Father?

Mosaic Law in the Gospels
Before Jesus, Mosaic Law guided the Israelite people. The Law sculpted their lives, giving them meaning and hope as they journeyed out of Egypt until settling down in Judea. The religious authorities' observance of the Law was their primary claim to power; they used the Law to police the lives of the Jewish people (Mk 2:24, Lk 11:46, Jn 5:10, 7:49-51, 18:31, 19:7). Their animosity toward Jesus begins when they question him about his non-compliance with the Law (Mk 10:2, 12:14, Lk 20:22, Mt 19:3). John the Baptist condemns Herod for adultery by relying on the law (Mk 6:17-18, Mt 14:3-4). The disciples find out about Jesus because of their knowledge about Moses and the Law (Jn 1:44-45). References to the *righteous* as those who comply with the Law abound in the texts, particularly in the synoptics; it is the *righteous* who will be resurrected and rewarded (Lk 14:13-14, Mt 5:6,10, 10:41, 13:43, 25:46).

Who are these righteous people? Zechariah and Elizabeth *were righteous in the eyes of God* because they observed his commandments *blamelessly* (Lk 1:5-6, 1:17, 1:68-75). Tax collectors who repent and *acknowledge the righteousness of God* (Lk 7:29, Mt 21:31-32), as well as Joseph of Arimathea, who is secretly awaiting the kingdom of God (Mk 15:43, Lk 23:50, Mt 27:57, 19:38), are also righteous. The Gospels consider Simeon and Anna as being righteous because they follow the law. Mary and Joseph are faithful observants of the Law too (Lk 1:28, Mt 1:19) (despite Luke's errors concerning certain aspects of it).[6]

The texts indicate that, initially, Jesus shows great respect for the Law. He goes into the synagogue on the Sabbath day, *according to his custom,* and complies with Jewish feasts (Mk 14:12, Lk 4:16, 22:7, Jn 7:2,10, 12:12, Mt 4:23). After he heals a leper, he tells him to offer for his healing what Moses prescribed (Mk 1:40-44, Lk 5:12-14, Mt 8:2-4). When asked how someone may attain eternal life Jesus points out to the Law, *follow the commandments,* he says (Mk 10:19 Lk 18:19, Mt 19:17).

Jesus shows great admiration for Moses (Jn 3:13). It is Moses who appears with Elijah and Jesus during the Transfiguration (Mk 2:2-4, Lk 9:28-36, Mt 17:1-4). He relies on Moses to warn people of their sins (Mk 7:10-11, Lk 16:29-31). In fact, Jesus does not dare to contradict Moses during an exchange with the Sadducees concerning marriage. Although the Sadducees seem to be correct in their citation of the Law (Deut 25:5), Jesus abruptly changes the subject insisting that they ignore the scriptures, Moses, and God (Mk 12:18-27, Lk 20:27-38, Mt 22:23-32).

He upholds the Law and supports Moses in his critique of the Pharisees who disregard God's commandment in favor of their human traditions (Mk 7:1-22, Mt 15:1-20). He defends him when the Pharisees corner him on the issue of divorce, suggesting that Moses had to take into account *the hardness of your hearts* to grant a bill of divorce;[7] subsequently, he establishes its prohibition (Mk 10:2-12, Mt 19:1-8). The passage is significant, as it suggests that Moses amends God's pronouncement and Jesus upholds the decision. Moreover, Jesus does not contradict Moses's commandment regarding the stoning of an adulteress (Lev 20:10, Deut 22:23-24). Instead, while seemingly defending the law, he appeals to the crowd's conscience to save the woman's life: *Let the one among you who is without sin be the first to throw a stone at her* (Jn 8:3-11).[8]

Changing the Law While Fulfilling It
The Gospels cite Jesus as noting that it is not the Law that needs to be changed, but its misrepresentation by the religious authorities that lead people to misbehave (Mk 8:15, 12:38-40, Lk 11:37-52, 12:1, Mt 16:6, 12, 23:1-39, Jn 5:45, 7:19). Although Jesus's harsh criticism of hypocrisy on the part of the religious authorities is amply cited in all four texts, Jesus first decides to strike at the heart of the commandments given to Moses by the Lord: the sabbath.[9] The Lord had ordained that the sabbath was to become *an everlasting covenant* throughout generations of Israelites (Ex 31:12, 16); the day when God rested following creation was to be kept holy (Ex 20:8). The sabbath was so sacred that no one could even light a fire on their dwellings on that day (Ex 35:3). Anyone defying this commandment would be put to death (Ex 31:14).

Jesus thinks and acts differently. His constant violations of the sabbath indicate his contempt for how this practice is observed. Conditioned by words coming from the Lord, however, the religious authorities' reaction to Jesus's behavior would seem proper. Whether picking grain on the sabbath because he and his disciples are hungry or healing a woman from her infirmity (Mk 2:23-24, 3:1-6, Lk 6:6-11, 13:10-16, Jn 5:8, 9:13-16), it would be difficult to suggest that the Pharisees and scribes misunderstand the Lord's commandment; not even a fire could be lit on that day, reads the law on the sabbath.[10] To their astonishment and rage, Jesus makes an extraordinary claim; in his capacity as Son of Man, he declares that he *is lord even of the sabbath* (Mk 2:23-28, Lk 6:1-5, Mt 12:1-8). He asserts that the Law is all about him (Lk 24:27, 44). Presumably, Jesus can do as he wishes because he claims to have authority over all people (Jn 17:2), and it is the Father who commands him what to say and speak (Jn 12:49, 14:10). The words he cites are not his *but that of the Father who sent me* (Jn 14:24), and who has given Jesus *all power in heaven and on earth* (Mt 28:16). Amending the sabbath law may suggest that God had not been too precise in its wording, a reason perhaps that led to the Law becoming legalistic and hypocritical (Lk 13:10-17, 14:5, Mt 12:11-12).

Christian church authorities have sought to enforce the Christian Sabbath throughout history, although results have been mixed. It appears, however, that Christians have taken to heart the words of Jesus about the Sabbath being made for man; the development of the industrial world, mercantilism, and postmodern capitalism could not have succeeded by observing the Christian Sabbath.

Jesus's behavior while amending the Law is inconsistent at times. Part of Mosaic Law deals with the practice of fasting, an act of penance that seeks God's compassion to avoid or bring an end to a calamity mandated in Leviticus 16:29 along with observance of the sabbath.[11] Jesus, however, fasts in the desert (Mt 4:1-3) and recommends that the practice be done with undue humility (Mt 6:16-18). His objection to the practice is that it is not necessary, particularly as an external ritual that overlooks its motive (MK 2:18-22, Lk 5:30-39, Mt 9:14-17). But then again, he says that fasting is essential (along with prayer) to nudge God's will in other instances, such as moving a mountain from one place to another (Mt 17:20-21).

The Tradition of the Elders, unlike fasting, was not dictated in the Law; however, it was a pious custom calling for Jews to *carefully wash their hands* before eating for purifying themselves, along with *cups and jugs and kettles, and beds*. The practice to present themselves pure in the eyes of God was an important tenet of the Pharisaic leadership; it was no different than Christian rituals instituted to please God today, such as reciting the rosary, personal use of holy water, holding holy processions, or fasting and abstinence. The Tradition of the Elders, however, did not arise in a vacuum; in Judaism, the term *tradition* refers to an unwritten code that was binding and had *the force of law,* which God gave to Moses on Mount Sinai.[12] Jesus does not necessarily regard the Tradition of the Elders as unholy. Instead, he objects to the hypocrisy of focusing on purifying the external parts of the body while not paying attention to what truly offends God: evil that comes from the heart, such as murder, adultery, unchastity, theft, false witness, and blasphemy (Mk 7:1-23, Mt 15:1-20).

Jesus chooses compassion over legality when he overlooks regulations in the Old Law that pertain to sexual uncleanness. The Law, for example, considers unclean a woman suffering from a flow of blood outside her menstrual period along with any physical object or person she touches (Lev 15:25-28). Nonetheless, Jesus allows a woman who is suffering from hemorrhages to touch his cloak believing that she will be cured. Indeed, she is healed, and Jesus blesses her for her faith (Mk 5:25-34, Lk 8:43-48, Mt 9:20-22).

He ignores the Pharisaic custom related to the laws of ritual impurity that prevent them from meeting with sinners, including tax collectors, and Samaritans (Mk 2:15, Lk 5:30, Mt 9:11, Jn 4:1, 40). In one of Jesus's harshest condemnations of theological legalism (that may be of great significance today), he not only tells the religious authorities that his mission is to persuade sinners (not the righteous) to end their ways; he insists that he prefers mercy to ritualistic sacrifice (Mt 9:9-13).

Having amended significant aspects of Mosaic Law, Jesus takes a different position when it comes to the issue of divorce laws and adultery. He admonishes the Pharisees, in effect, reversing Moses's permission to allow divorce because of the *hardness* of men's hearts (without explanation), relying instead on God's desire that what he *has joined together, no human being must separate* (Mk 10:2-12, Mt 19:1-9).

In one of the most significant changes that Jesus carries out, he reverses God's disposition to reward obedience to the Law with material wealth (Gen 24:34-35, 26:12-13, Deut 8:7-20, Josh 22:1-8, 1 Kings 3:13). In Mark, Jesus makes eternal salvation conditional to dispossessing of one's possessions (Mk 10:17-22). Mathew's version of this passage is different; it calls on those who only *wish to be perfect,* to give up their possessions (Mt 19:16-22). Since there have been no in-depth explanations on whether Mark's recollection of revelation is correct, Christianity (as viewed in its theology) has chosen Matthew's version as being the proper one. Nonetheless, through his teachings, Jesus transforms the religious expectations of the children of the kingdom as well as God's intentions.

Moreover, Jesus alters Mosaic Law as he opposes the system of justice that God had established regarding revenge. Whereas God allowed the death penalty as punishment for homicide, and the well-known *eye for an eye, tooth for a tooth* system of justice (Lev 24:17-20), Jesus now says *offer no resistance to one who is evil* (Mt 5:38-39). Regarding blasphemy, a serious offense meriting death (Lev 24:15-16), Jesus contravenes God's dictate, teaching that it may now be forgiven (except blaspheming the holy Spirit Mk 3:28-29, Lk 12:10 Mt 12:31). It is notable, however, that despite altering the commandment on blasphemy (even against the Son of Man) Jesus is unmovable regarding the laws of divorce.

He also legislates a new practice that has significant consequences regarding salvation, the institution of baptism as a ritual signifying repentance, the forgiveness of sins, and a new life from above. At the time, the Jewish people had (and still do) a similar practice that is found in other religions, *ablution,* an act to restore ritual purity done for religious and not hygienic purposes.[13] In Jesus, however, baptism becomes a supernatural requirement to enter the kingdom of God (Jn 3:5). Given its importance, the fact that God does not include baptism among the Ten Commandments (or anywhere else) seems a glaring omission on his part. On the other hand, it affirms Jesus's role as spokesperson for God, insofar as he can alter God's dictates.

Notwithstanding the way Jesus goes about in 'fulfilling' the Law, his most recognizable (and daring) act is to replace God's first commandment with his own, love of God and one's neighbor (including one's enemies (Mt 5:44), regardless of faith (Lk 10:25-37), and irrespective of ethnicity, gender, status, or nationality),[14] as the foundation of *the whole law and the prophets* (Mt 22:40).

The rule to love one's neighbor as oneself appears in Leviticus 19:18 although it is not part of the Ten Commandments. It extends to aliens, however, in Leviticus 19:33-34. Additional passages that may be part of the directive to love one's enemies appear in 2 Kings 6:22 and Proverbs 25:21. Nonetheless, the passage in Leviticus shows up among dozens of rules that are inconsequential in Christianity today such as forbidding clipping one's hair at the temples (Lev 19:27), cutting one's body for the dead, painting tattoos on oneself (Lev 19:28), or breeding domestic animals with others of different species. It prohibits sowing the same field with different kinds of seed and sewing a garment with different kinds of thread (Lev 19:19). The chapter also includes regulations about sexual relations with female slaves (Lev 19:20), and it prescribes the time when *uncircumcised* fruits may be eaten (Lev 19:23).

Hence, he seizes two obscure decrees from a pool of more than five hundred laws, instructions, and proclamations, and combines them into the two most important commandments, neither of which were originally set in stone. Moreover, far from ignoring the Ten Commandments, Jesus asserts their validity (Mk 10:17-31, Lk 18:18-30, Mt 19:1630). But when asked which is the first commandment, rather than quoting from the Decalogue (Ex 20:1-17, Deut 5:6-21), he exclaims, *Hear, O Israel! The LORD is our God, the LORD alone! Therefore, you shall love the LORD, your God, with your whole heart, and with your whole being, and with your whole strength* (Deut 6:4-5). And without being asked, he cites from Leviticus 19:18 and complements it with a second decree, *you shall love your neighbor as yourself*, adding afterward, *there is no other commandment greater than these* (Mk 12:28-34, Mt 22:34-40). Thus, Jesus couples these two commandments and places them atop everything else that God had stated in the Old Testament.

Interestingly, his instruction to love one's enemies does not show up in John. Instead, he issues his commandment, *to love one another,* several times, but only in conversations with his disciples (Jn 13:34, 35, 15:12). In John's Gospel, Jesus does not make public his most significant and recognizable commandment.

Although Jesus fails in his attempt to gain acceptance of his teachings among the Jewish people, he succeeds in establishing a new and more succinct version of Yahweh's laws among his initial followers; in effect, he overrides deficiencies in the Old Law that the Father had initially ordained. Did God err in enacting absurd laws and regulations that would apply only to a small segment of the world population? Jesus's affirmation that he can alter the Law as he wishes because the Father has given him the authority to do as he pleases has no significant foundation (only cryptic extrapolation) in the Old Testament. Moreover, although Jesus alters Mosaic Law substantially, it is Paul who claims explicitly that it was Christ (not the Jesus of the Gospels) who had ransomed humanity (Jews and Gentiles) from the curse of the law (Gal 3:3). It is awkward that Paul makes a substantial revelation that goes somewhat unnoticed in the Gospels.

On the other hand, it is not known the extent to which Paul's interpretation of Jesus's teachings was able to influence the Gospels. Paul's letters lack detailed accounts of Jesus or God personally speaking to him (akin to lengthy quotes by Jesus in the Gospels), other than at the time of his conversion when Jesus tells him to go to Damascus where he will be told what he must do (Act 9:4-6). He merely indicates that it is Jesus who reveals his views to him (Gal 1:12, 2:2, Eph 3:3). He then gets baptized and at once begins to proclaim that Jesus is the Son of God (Act 9:20). According to Acts, in a vision, Jesus had told a disciple named Ananias that Paul would become his *chosen instrument* to spread his teachings to Gentiles and Israelites and *will show him what he will have to suffer for my name* (Acts 9:10-16). Within this context, Paul's theology overshadows the Jesus in the Gospels, daring to interpret Jesus without the benefit of Jesus's words that would appear years later. It now seems as if there are three distinctive revelations, Mosaic Law, Paul's letters, and the Gospels, with questionable underpinnings binding them together.

Notes:

1. It is generally acknowledged that Moses could not have been the author of the entire five books that constitutes the Torah or Jewish Written Law, also known as the Pentateuch in the Old Testament. For a summary of the complexity surrounding its authorship please refer to NEs, Introduction to the Pentateuch (accessed February 8, 2019).

2. "Judaism: The Written Law – Torah," JVL, *Jewish Virtual Library.* www.jewishvirtuallibrary.org/the-written-law-torah (accessed February 8, 2019). Thomas à Kempis Reilly, "Mosaic Legislation," CE, Vol. 10, 1911, http://www.newadvent.org/cathen/10582c.htm (accessed February 8, 2019).

3. *Merriam-Webster Dictionary,* online, s.v. "abolish."

4. *Merriam-Webster Dictionary*; *Dictionary.com,* online, s.v. "fulfill.

5. NEs suggest that Jesus establishes a new law because the gospel cannot be contained *within the limits of Mosaic law.* Note on Matthew 9:16-17.

6. Luke (or Revelation?) states that Joseph and Mary completed their purification prior to presenting the newborn to the Lord *according to the law of Moses.* According to NEs, Mosaic Law does not mention purification of the husband; also, the woman who gives birth to a child is not allowed to enter the temple area until after forty days have passed; and there is no requirement that the child be presented to the Lord at the temple. Note on Lk 2:22.

7. The manner in which Deuteronomy 24:1-4 is worded indicates a slant that favors the man who, once he marries his wife, may become displeased with her *if he finds in her something indecent* and divorces her. The texts, however, do not explain what *hardness of the heart* means in the context of Jesus's exchange with the Pharisees.

8. For practical purposes Jesus amends the Law. Had there been someone without sin Jesus would have had to allow the woman to be stoned. On the other hand, since all humans are sinners, the law would carry no weight.

9. The Jewish custom calls the Sabbath the first day of the week; it begins on Saturday after sunset. Following the resurrection of Jesus, the apostolic community began to informally observe the Sabbath on a Sunday (Act 20:7). In 336 CE during the Synod of Laodicea, Christians were forbidden to *Judaize by resting on the Sabbath* (the Jewish Sabbath), after which the practice to observe the Sabbath on Sunday (the day Jesus was resurrected) officially began. "Synod of Laodicea," Translated by Henry Percival. From *Nicene and Post-Nicene Fathers,* Second Series, Vol. 14. Edited by Philip Schaff and

Henry Wace. (Buffalo, NY: Christian Literature Publishing Co., 1900.) Revised and edited for New Advent by Kevin Knight. http://www.newadvent.org/fathers/3806.htm (accessed February 13, 2019).
10. His followers keep observing the sabbath after his crucifixion (Mk 15:42-43, 16:1, Mt 28:1, Jn 19:31).
11. "Jewish Holidays: Fast and Fasting Days," JVL, *https://www.jewishvirtuallibrary.org/fasting-and-fast-days* (accessed February 11, 2009); James David O'Neill, "Abstinence," CE, Vol 1, http://www.newadvent.org/cathen/01067a.htm (accessed February 11, 2009).
12. "Tradition," JVL, *https://www.jewishvirtuallibrary.org/tradition* (accessed February 12, 2009).
13. "Ablution," JVL, *https://www.jewishvirtuallibrary.org/ablution* (accessed February 12, 2009).
14. Officially, the extent of the commandment in the Catholic hierarchy is limited because of its opposition to gay sexual behavior in marriage and gay adoptions (while it accepts gay tendencies and identification). On transgenderism, there has been no official pronouncement beyond Pope Francis's view that *the young need to be helped to accept their own body as it was created*, (not clear if it applies only to the physical aspect while excluding the psychological identity), and the official words of the U.S. bishops reflecting Vatican doctrine that *consistently affirms the inherent dignity of each and every human person and advocates for the wellbeing of all people, particularly the most vulnerable*. See "The Many Faces of Pope Francis: A Five-Year Timeline of His LGBT Record," *New Ways Ministry. https://www.newwaysministry.org/2018/03/13/many-faces-pope-francis-five-year-timeline-lgbt-record/* (accessed February 14, 2019). Other Christian denominations would seem to share mixed views regarding faith, ethnicity, gender, status, or nationality. When it comes to Christian believers' positions on love and each of these categories, however, it appears (through observation) that unrequited love is not extended to all, including one's enemies. See, for example, Christian Americans' view of Muslims in "U.S. Muslims Concerned About Their Place in Society, but Continue to Believe in the American Dream: Findings from Pew Research Center's 2017 survey of U.S. Muslims," Section 7, How the U.S. general public views Muslims and Islam. Pew Research Center *Religion and Public Life,* July 26, 2017, http://www.pewforum.org/2017/07/26/findings-from-pew-research-centers-2017-survey-of-us-muslims/ (accessed on February 14, 2019).

Reason

Often, being religious is associated with piety or foolish sentimentality; a bleeding-heart person that gets carried away by emotions; someone who tends to be weak-minded and would rather 'feel' than to think. There is some validity to this characterization. Christianity has an undeniable emotional component that concurs with being human. Without necessarily extending judgment, emotions (call it instinct, drive, need, reaction) often prompt many of our actions; they constitute the impulsive side, the accelerating pedal of human behavior.

There is, nonetheless, an element in the Christian faith that at times overrides emotions: our capacity to think, to rationally or logically question reality as it appears before us. At times, Jesus's teachings tend to be quite introspective; they compel the believer to ponder his or her choice of actions. As a human exercise, introspection requires a critical examination of the self, and the Christian message seems to constantly quiz the believer's motives, values, and goals that he or she pursues to ensure they are in line with the faith's core beliefs. This means that the cognitive or rational component plays a significant role in deciding among the myriad of values and choices that are showered daily upon the believer.[1] Content analysis results indicate that this category scored significantly high in Table 2, even when other legitimate terms were not included.[2]

Any communication written with the purpose of being disseminated as an educational manual (like the Gospels) requires that it be understood by those for whom it has been prepared. In the Introduction, I indicate that difficulties surrounding an accurate interpretation of God's message pose a serious problem to anyone seeking to understand God's plan for humanity. Such complications are responsible for divisions among Christians, for the creation of obstacles to the spreading of the faith, and for Christianity's need to remain relevant in a secular world. Humanly speaking, it is likely that God wishes his message to be clearly communicated and understood. But according to the texts, at times Jesus's message appears to be not easily grasped, including by his disciples. Other passages even indicate that Jesus himself creates impediments to understanding his message by resorting to mind riddles, confounding parables, or simply by refusing to dialogue with his opponents.

It would be difficult to deny the proposition that there was a serious attempt by the authors of the Gospels to provide as accurate and detailed descriptions as possible of what transpired at the time in a manner that could persuade newcomers to the faith. At the beginning of Luke's Gospel, we read:

> *Since many have undertaken to compile a narrative of the events that have been fulfilled among us, just as those who were eyewitnesses from the beginning and ministers of the word have handed them down to us, I too have decided, after investigating everything accurately anew, to write it down in an orderly sequence for you, most excellent Theophilus, so that you may realize the certainty of the teachings you have received (Lk 1:1-4).*

The passage suggests that many others already have sought to do what Luke is attempting: to gather information as part of a thorough investigation among eyewitnesses and those who were part of the oral tradition with the purpose in mind of providing accurate information regarding the *certainty* of what Jesus taught. Mark and Matthew follow a similar approach. Luke's passage, however, suggests a willful attempt to reasonably explain and help others understand Jesus's message. The words *many, compile, eyewitnesses, investigating, accurately, anew,* and *certainty* are elements of an undertaking comparable to current research techniques. It is unlikely that the authors were as rigorous as today's researchers since newer methods of historical or journalistic investigation had not yet evolved; nonetheless, they were trying to assemble as best they could a narrative of what they considered to be important episodes related to Jesus's public life in a manner that could be understood.

In various instances, Jesus's teachings appeal to reason to reach peoples' emotions. Through parables, he attempts to make believers aware of their actions while relying on fear and anxiety. He provides explanations about sin, salvation and condemnation, righteousness, faith, prayer, love, and other forms of behavior. He needs to make himself understood if humanity is to benefit from his mission. But that does not mean he always succeeds. Nonetheless, it is worth examining the rational approach within the Gospels, largely because it has been overlooked both in popular religiosity and in philosophical critiques of the texts.[3]

Words such as the verbs *know, think, believe,* and *feel,* indicating rationality or cognition, appear numerous times in the Gospels. These are not words that were whimsically translated from Greek. Instead, they rely on the idiomatic or common use of the language used in the texts at the time of Jesus. It is likely that Hellenistic influence, i.e., the need to explain, to understand, to know, to think wisely, or to acquire knowledge, exercised a significant role in the writing of the Gospels. For example, if defined in terms of truth, *to know* something to be true is the result of having empirical evidence; *to think* something is true means to rely on reason to arrive at a preliminary conclusion that may require more information; *to believe* something is true indicates coming to an uncertain conclusion based on unsubstantiated information, and *to feel* something is true suggests relying on instinct or stimuli from the senses. Nonetheless, today these words are used interchangeably without much consideration to the essence of their meanings. The use of these four verbs is different in the Gospels, suggesting that the evolution of language may affect its understanding.

In the four texts, the word *feel* appears only (1xt), used by Jesus. Nevertheless, relying on three different databanks, the word *feel* ranks very high today (higher than *know, think,* and *believe*) among the 100 commonest English words according to the Oxford English Corpus; also very high (though lower than *know* and *think,* but higher than *believe*) according to the Word Bank of 1200 High-Frequency Writing Words; and similarly high to the other terms, according to the Top 5000 words researched by Word Frequency Data.[4] (Caveat: there are more than 560 million words in the English language according to the Word Frequency Data). As we may recall, the word *believe* is well distributed in the synoptics, although their count is quite low compared with the disproportionately high count in John's Gospel. A tentative conclusion may be that the terms *think* and *know* were highly favored in the Gospels as well as today, while the word *feel* is far more prevalent nowadays than *believe.*

Truth and Reason in the Gospels
Truth has various seemingly disparate connotations; it indicates scientific accuracy, accordance with reality or with facts, genuineness, legitimacy, honesty, sincerity, and goodness (among others). That whatever is true cannot be false is evident; nevertheless, many things considered to be true for centuries today are being constantly questioned, thus making truth an elusive term. Nowhere does truth seems more questionable than in morality and ethics.

In the Gospels, Jesus not only appeals to the truth that he represents; he goes even further by saying that he is the truth (Jn 14:6). Jesus is not interested in scientific, journalistic, or any other type of factual truth. His concept of rational truth as it relates to humankind covers only four areas; the existence of an almighty, wise, omniscient, supernatural entity and creator of all things (the Father) whose recognition he seeks; his intimate relationship with the Father; the existence of an afterlife; and his teachings regarding moral behavior that he regards as true and necessary for salvation.

He describes himself as the personification of intelligibility (capable of being understood). Hence, it is reasonable to presume that given his interest in saving humankind through his teachings he would manage to overcome human deficiencies to make us understand his message. Among these deficiencies are our incapacity or unwillingness to use reason in most of our actions; our flawed yet seemingly existing level of free will or freedom of action; and the conditioning effects of our external environment upon our value choices that frequently 'make' us reject his teachings.

From the start of his public life Jesus knows, i.e., is aware, that he has the authority to assert his claims. He believes the Father has empowered him to carry out his mission to proclaim the existence of the kingdom of God and the way to become a part of it. This knowledge is internal, and in his mind, it is objective and absolute. The problem is how to translate that knowledge to unbelievers and to those who have not seen deeds like the ones he performed.

That Jesus is an insightful man who acts rationally and wisely is beyond dispute, according to passages in the texts. In Luke we read, *the child grew and became strong, filled with wisdom;* and *Jesus advanced [in] wisdom and age and favor before God and man* (Lk 2:40, 52). Defined as having the knowledge to distinguish between doing right and wrong and acting accordingly and at the appropriate moment, wisdom[5] relates to truth and rationality. Particularly in Luke's and John's Gospels, Jesus is wise beyond his years. At twelve years of age, Jesus is having discussions with rabbis in the temple! (Lk 2:46-47). According to the tally results, the texts indicate that (except for John's Gospel) people know him more as a Teacher (someone who imparts knowledge) than as Savior, and he acknowledges the title without hesitation (Table 1A). After forgiving the sins of a paralytic he reproves the religious authorities once he *knew in his mind what they were thinking to themselves.* He then proceeds to provide concrete evidence that he possesses God's authority by curing the disabled man (Mk 2:3-11, Lk 5:21-24, Mt 9:2-6). He replies cogently to their charges that he drives demons because he is empowered by the devil by pointing out that their argument is simply non-sensical; 'why would I want to do the work of my enemy?' he argues (Mk 3:23-26, Lk 11:15-20, Mt 12:24-27). He seems to realize that the Pharisees want to ensnare him, and he questions their sincerity (Mk 12:13-15, Lk 20:20-23, Mt 22:15-18). His discourse at the synagogue leaves the audience in wonder, *where did this man get all this? What kind of wisdom has been given him?* (Mk 6:2, Mt 13:54). His parables on the kingdom of God seem reasonable descriptions of a reality that he says it exists (Mk 4:26-32, 10:24-25, Lk 13:18-19, Mt 13:24-33, 13:44-50), and can be as truthful (believable) to the ears of common Jews as the detailed explanation of the cosmos that an astrophysicist may provide to a layperson.

His knowledge of Mosaic Law is vast; he knows what is needed to attain salvation (Lk 10:25-28), or to open the minds of two disconsolate disciples by explaining to them the scriptures (Lk 24:44-45). He is wiser than Solomon (Lk 11:31, Mt 12:42). He realizes that knowledge implies accountability; hence, he forgives those who crucify him because they do not seem to know what they are doing (Lk 23:34).[6] He knows who the false prophets are; *by their fruits you will know them.... A good tree cannot bear bad fruit, nor can a rotten tree bear good fruit,* he says with penetrating logic (Lk 6:43-44, Mt 7:15-18). He even teaches people about the spiritual features of the digestive system, reminding them that his teachings have nothing to do with the washing of hands and the intake of food but with actions that come out of the heart (Mt 15:10-20). Moreover, he corrects the religious authorities on issues they should know about, such as divorce, adultery, and the resurrection (Mt 19:1-9, 22:23-33). He explains the end of temporal existence and the coming of the kingdom of God in vivid detail (Lk 21:1-31, Mt 24:32-43). His disciples tell him that they understand his parables (Mt 13:51); people praise his teachings, supposedly because they understand them. But do they?

To Avoid Evil Means to Understand
Jesus's earthly mission entails imparting knowledge that may guide humanity to eternal salvation. His teachings consist of a concatenation of beliefs, values, ethos, and attitudes geared toward shaping individual and social moral behavior that is required to become righteous. At times, being righteous in the Old Testament and parts of the Gospels meant following Mosaic Law. The purpose of the law was to regulate behavior, and the first step in avoiding evil is to possess knowledge of good and evil. Moreover, while ignorance of the law does not exculpate the individual in civil society, in the eyes of God it does; only those with a clear understanding of right and wrong may be found guilty of wrongdoing. Incongruously, however, in Genesis, the snake's rationale for persuading the first humans to eat from the tree of knowledge of good and evil is that they will acquire this understanding (Gen 3:5). But in the Garden of Eden, God forbids Adam and Eve to acquire that which Jesus is seeking to provide, knowledge of right and wrong to distinguish between good and evil (Gen 2:16-17).

Indeed, while God may have had his reasons for issuing a regulation that seemingly contradicts Jesus's mission, it is reasonable for humankind to question God's decision. To show Adam and Eve that he is in charge, God simply could have said 'do not eat from this tree because its fruits are poisonous,' presuming they were; that would be in line with a rational God who knows how to communicate with his creatures. Humanity, realizing that God has their wellbeing in mind, would understand and abstain from disobeying him. Today, considering humans' rational capacity and the purpose of the Christian message, God's command to Adam and Eve would seem an unreasonable prohibition that places at risk eternal salvation. In their naiveté, Adam and Eve were paying attention to the snake, *the most cunning of all wild animals that the Lord God had made* (Gen 3:1), and disobeyed God possibly because they thought it was important for them to have this type of knowledge. Did God provide human beings with the ability to reason but did not expect they would use it?

Among the primary reasons why there has been so much discordance throughout history is because of moral and religious relativism based on the presumption that right and wrong are not absolutes (or cannot be expressed as absolutes). Temporally speaking, this presumption stems from a lack of universally well-known positivist standards of right and wrong that can be easily apprehended by the human mind. Given the difficulties in recognizing absolute values, the person has no other choice but to exercise his or her limited intellect, as mistaken as it may be proven to be. This does not mean that if objective knowledge were to exist it would necessarily prevent all evil behavior; only a predisposition to do good, a characteristic that would make us like angels, could do that, which in turn might have spared Jesus's life and made his mission unnecessary. This would suggest that Jesus's mission is to provide us with what we lack: understanding and wisdom about right and wrong.

In the Book of Job (written five to seven hundred years before Jesus) there is a chapter that deals with Wisdom (Jb 28:12-28). The chapter ends by saying that *avoiding evil is understanding*, i.e., *understanding* appears to be the key to righteous behavior. If we all can possess wisdom, hypothetically the world might be a better place. It seems, however, that wisdom is the private property of God. The Book of Wisdom, written about fifty years before Jesus's birth[7] (rather recent within the context of the Old Testament), tells us that God's wisdom lies in wishing humankind to rule the earth (Wis 9:1-2). In the same chapter, however, another passage indicates the downside of being human in terms of how temporal life affects our understanding:

> *For the corruptible body burdens the soul and the earthly tent weighs down the mind with its many concerns. Scarcely can we guess the things on earth, and only with difficulty grasp what is at hand; but things in heaven, who can search them out? Or who can know your counsel, unless you give Wisdom and send your holy spirit from on high?* (Wis 9:15-17).

In other words, humanity can only escape ignorance through the assistance of God.[8] This assertion poses a problem. We know that human intelligence and the application of reason have considerably reduced guessing while increasing our knowledge of life on earth. We do not know, however, the role that God has played in human progress. Moreover, we seem to be aware that regardless of the knowledge we have accumulated, it appears to be insignificant given what scientists claim we do not know.[9] Although it is likely that, barring a catastrophic ending of the world, humankind will continue to gain exponential knowledge about the physical world, it is doubtful that we can make rapid moral progress unless the human condition or external circumstances force humanity to change drastically.

Although many praise Jesus because of his wondrous deeds and teachings, we notice an inability among Jesus's disciples, to understand. If they, who are closest to Jesus fail to understand his teachings, what does it say about the crowds he comes to save? This lack of understanding resonates throughout the synoptics;[10] Is Jesus such an abysmal teacher? Could it be that his teachings were difficult to comprehend? Surprisingly, perhaps, religious experts conclude rather candidly that Wisdom *is beyond the attainment of creatures and known only to God.*[11] Their view reads like an echo of Genesis 2:16; if understanding is a prerequisite to avoiding evil, why do humans lack this understanding? Presuming the theologically accepted answer is Original Sin, a disease that still affects humanity, why has God chosen not to share the cure with humans so that avoiding evil would become less demanding?

Part of the problem lies with Jesus's method of imparting wisdom. While teaching by the sea Jesus narrates the Parable of the Sower to a crowd that includes his disciples. We do not know if the crowd understands what Jesus is saying, but we know that his disciples do not. Jesus becomes exasperated; *Do you not understand this parable? Then how will you understand any of the parables?* (Mk 4:13). His disciples too, fail to understand the miracle regarding the multiplication of the loaves as well as their fear when Jesus appears walking on the sea because, according to Mark, *their hearts were hardened* (Mk 6:49-52). Awkwardly, this phrase is of the same mindset as those who reject Jesus and plot his death.[12] This is a harsh rebuke, either by Mark or by Jesus. It seems that that the disciples (who are undergoing one surreal experience after another) are supposed to understand Jesus's signs from the moment they meet Jesus. Their inability to understand indicates they do not (or cannot) accept Jesus's teachings. Under these circumstances, what may we expect of a skeptical and critically-minded world attempting to understand and accept Jesus?

On another day, Jesus is severely critical of the Pharisees. They have inquired why his disciples do not follow the Tradition of the Elders, a daily ritual in which they carefully wash their hands before eating, purifying cups, jugs, their beds, even themselves. This tradition had been decreed (even if mistakenly) out of a sense of respect for Yahweh and is similar to compulsory practices dictated by various Christian denominations throughout history.[13] Jesus is clearly irritated that no one seems to understand his teachings. In private, he scolds his disciples, again, *are even you likewise without understanding?* He then explains to them what he meant initially (Mk 7:1-23 Mt 15:1-20). The texts do not indicate, however, whether he teaches the same explanation to the crowd, which would seem just as important.

Later, Jesus warns his disciples about the leaven of the Pharisees and the leaven of Herod, but once more they do not understand. By now Jesus probably thinks that the associates he has hired are not the brightest, and again he becomes truly exasperated:

> *Why do you conclude that it is because you have no bread? Do you not yet understand or comprehend? Are your hearts hardened? Do you have eyes and not see, ears and not hear? And do you not remember, when I broke the five loaves for the five thousand, how many wicker baskets full of fragments you picked up? ... Do you still not understand?* (Mk 8:14-21).

Once again, Jesus questions his disciples' commitment because their hearts are hardened. In Matthew, Jesus tells them that they lack faith (16:5-11). Today, exegetes are more charitable and suggest that the disciples are simply obtuse.[14]

According to the synoptics, Jesus tells his disciples that he will suffer greatly, be killed, and rise on the third day; 'simple stuff' that an emboldened Peter says he will prevent, as he does not want anything to happen to his Master. But Jesus brushes him aside and calls him Satan because he is thinking like human beings do, not like God (Mk 8:31-33, Mt. 16:21-23). Did Jesus expect his disciples to think like God?

For a second time, Jesus tells his disciples about his passion, crucifixion, and resurrection; but they still do not understand, and according to Mark they are intimidated and refrain from asking (Mk 9:30-32). Being uneducated simple people, perhaps they have reasons to feel intimidated by their self-assured leader who is constantly critical of their lack of understanding. In Matthew, the disciples are *overwhelmed with grief* when they hear Jesus say that he will be killed (Mt 17:23). However, in Luke the reason they do not understand is not because of their lack of cognitive skills; the reason is mysterious: the *meaning was hidden from them, purposefully, so that they should not understand it* (Lk 9:45). This remark may have been unnerving to the disciples who previously have been told that everything will be disclosed to them (Mk 4:11).

In another instance, Jesus warns his disciples that human life on earth one day will end with the same bang it may have begun. His garish details of the Parousia must have scared millions of people throughout history for it is inevitable; there is nothing humanity can do to change the outcome. Moreover, Jesus does not tell them when this will happen (or why), because not even the Son (the second person of the Trinity) knows, only the Father, suggesting that both are not too communicative about such an important event (Mk 13:14-36, Lk 21:20-36, Mt 24:15-36).

This lack of understanding on the part of the disciples is remarkably puzzling, given that in Luke, an angel tells Elizabeth that his son, John the Baptist, will *turn the hearts of fathers toward children and the disobedient to the understanding of the righteous* (Lk 1:17). John's father, Zechariah, foretells that his son *will go before the Lord ... to give his people knowledge of salvation through the forgiveness of their sins* (Lk 1:76-77). This is the vital information that humanity expects from God, but no sooner than news of Jesus's birth is known, the message becomes mysterious. Simeon, a righteous man who desperately wants to see the baby before dying, portends that Jesus will be *a light for revelation to the Gentiles, and glory for your people Israel*; that he is *destined for the fall and rise of many in Israel,* and will *be a sign that will be contradicted*; (Lk 2:29-35). Anna the prophetess then speaks about Jesus representing the redemption of Israel, an enigmatic phrase, since its temporal existence would not take place until thousands of years later (Lk 2:38). The problem with such pronouncements is that their vagueness gives way to a variety of interpretations and disputes that provide little knowledge about the salvation that is promised. Even evil spirits seem to know more about Jesus than his own disciples (Lk 4:33-34, 8:27-28).

Jesus's pedagogical method is somewhat different from contemporary approaches based on critical reasoning. As he imparts lessons on righteousness, at times he explains how and why we must behave accordingly while relying on logic. But in other instances, he simply dictates ordinances without much explanation, often issuing threats to facilitate learning. For example, he preaches that the kingdom of God is at hand, and he sends his disciples to spread the message. He gives them authority to heal, nonetheless, he reinforces his message by warning people that the destruction that took place in Sodom would be light compared to what awaits those who reject his message (Lk 10:12, 13:1-5, 24-30). The same happens in his relationship with the religious authorities. Much already has been said about Jesus's reluctance to sit down with them and explain why they are mistaken. Since we do not know about the origins of the dispute, it appears that by the time Jesus engages them he becomes so enraged he considers them not worthy of redemption and instead says that they will receive a severe condemnation (Mt 23:13-14).

After considerable time instructing his disciples, they still have not been able to grasp aspects of his message. Somehow, they interpret Jesus to be saying that *the kingdom of God would appear there immediately* (Lk 19:11), even though previously he has told the Pharisees (and supposedly his disciples had heard it too) that the kingdom of God is already present among them (Lk 17:21). He tells them the Parable of the Talents, seemingly to clarify their mistaken notion, except that the parable is the wrong segue; it has no direct relation to the issue at hand in either Luke or Matthew (Lk 19:11-27, Mt 25:14-30).

The two disciples Jesus encounters on the road to Emmaus also fail to understand Jesus, so he explains everything the scriptures say about him from Moses on (Lk 24:27). Neither do his other disciples understand what he has been saying repeatedly about his death. Following his crucifixion, they are in hiding because they do not realize that Jesus must resurrect before everything falls into place (Jn 20:9). Once resurrected, Jesus feels his disciples need a refreshing course, and once again *he opened their minds to understand the scriptures* by relying on a narrative that is nowhere to be found in the Old Testament (Lk 24:45-46).[15]

Even some of Jesus's parables are not easy to understand; they require a high level of abstract comprehension in addition to historical, archeological, linguistic, scientific, and religious assistance to reconstruct the context in which they are narrated. In one instance, he characterizes the people of his generation as *children who sit in the marketplace and call to one another, 'We played the flute for you, but you did not dance. We sang a dirge, but you did not weep'* (Lk 7:31-32, Mt 11:16-19). Many have sought to make sense of this passage, but it is still highly debated.[16] More important, at times it appears that Jesus is not interested in being transparent. Who, then, is responsible for the lack of clarity?[17]

The disciples and crowds are not the only ones who do not understand Jesus. The religious authorities cannot make sense of some of Jesus's teachings. The Gospels present this group as ardent opponents of Jesus. But at times it seems they want to engage Jesus: *show us a sign that we may understand*, they tell him. But they have seen signs; Jesus tells them not to believe him if they wish, but at least believe in his works (Jn 10:37-38)? They are supposed to understand, but they do not. He calls them hypocrites because they know how to forecast the weather but cannot understand *the sign of the times* (Mt 16:1-3), a reply that many scholars think is not an original part of Matthew's Gospel.[18] Is it reasonable to presume that the Pharisees keep asking for signs simply to pester Jesus? Are they as incredulous or as obtuse as his disciples who have witnessed his deeds and still fail to understand?

In John's Gospel, Jesus's attitude concerning his disciples is quite different from the synoptics; he does not rebuke them for their unbelief or not understanding. The disciples appear as docile students willing to accept his teachings despite not understanding; for example, the washing of their feet (Jn 13:7) or the significance of Lazarus' death (Jn 11:12-13).

The major theme in John's Gospel as it relates to the Reason category is the direct relationship between the terms *to believe* and *to know,* which at times are used interchangeably. We recall that the term *believe* appears (96xt) in John, eight to twelve times more than in each of the synoptics, in most instances referring to faith. The term *to know* shows up (113xt), in disproportion to the synoptics, and often related to belief/unbelief and acceptance/non-acceptance of Jesus. John's text suggests that the religious authorities are the only ones who are unwilling to understand. Quite possibly the Pharisees do not wish to understand because they are proud and find Jesus's challenge to their authority distasteful. He engages them (and their supporters) in 'back and forth' debates, but they find his supernatural explanations baffling (Jn 6:35, 6:52). Did Jesus expect that people would accept cosmic teachings at face value without understanding them?

Apparently yes. Despite the numerous times that John's Gospel relies on the term *to know* and the intellectual activity denoted by the term *the Word,* Jesus expects that his words be accepted without questioning because of his relationship with the Father. In the synoptics, the Pharisees refuse to understand because they are hypocrites, and his disciples cannot understand because they are either obtuse or heart-hardened. But in John Jesus goes even further. He tells a crowd of Jews (likely religious authorities and common people) that they refuse to (or cannot) understand because they do not love God; because their father is the devil (Jn 8:42-44, 8:46-47).

Then, there is Nicodemus, a Pharisee, and an educated member of the Sanhedrin who believes Jesus is an emissary from God. When Jesus explains to him that all people need to be *born from above* to partake in the kingdom of God, Nicodemus does not understand (although Jesus thinks he should), and he reproaches him (Jn 3:1-10).

Now, even the learned who believe in Jesus cannot comprehend him. Since those closest to him do not understand, are they children of the devil too?

There is in John's Gospel another way to uncover rationality. The first chapter provides vital information indicating the extent of Jesus's rational approach and his wisdom in a manner the synoptics do not:

> *In the beginning was the Word, and the Word was with God, and the Word was God. He was in the beginning with God ... And the Word became flesh and made his dwelling among us, and we saw his glory, the glory as of the Father's only Son, full of grace and truth (Jn 1:1-5, 14).*

Literally understood, it is difficult to know the identity of the Word. Only after we keep on reading and we ask experts, we may find that Jesus is the Word; that the Word stands for intelligibility or the capability of being understood as well as something that can only be apprehended by the intellect (reason).[19] The passage then adds that *the Word (Logos, i.e., intellectual activity) became flesh and made his dwelling among us*; that is, Jesus embodies the intellect; he is reason and wisdom incarnated. It is not known if John intended to provide evidence for this assertion or if it was accidental; however, its confirmation is astounding. Within the context of the few miracles through which John's Gospel seeks to persuade the reader of Jesus's divinity, the imposing figure of Jesus as the Word being human surfaces in a disguising manner through the *I* pronoun. When the pronoun *I,* meaning *self* is tallied, John's Gospel reads like a Jesus monologue. The term appears (413xt), and approximately (351xt) refers to Jesus; this is three to four times as many as in the synoptics. Although in some or many cases the excessive use of the **I** pronoun may indicate egotism, narcissism, depression, or even selfishness, Jesus's use in John's Gospel reads authoritatively, suggesting confidence or self-assurance in what he says.[20] The phrase *I know* conveys an image of certainty about his relationship with the Father and about his convictions that are highly persuasive to those with faith (Jn 5:32, 42, 7:29, 8:14, 37, 55, 10:14-15, 27, 11:22, 42, 12:50, 13:18, 17:25).

If Jesus is the incarnate *Logos,* he is supposed to be able to understand humankind; however, if we do not share the same capacity, it is extraordinarily difficult (if not impossible) to understand the person of Jesus in the manner that John reveals him other than through blind faith; a faith that certain passages suggest is not given to all or given in a lesser degree. The outcome is that there being vast differences in intellect between the teacher and his students, communicating and understanding the message becomes an arduous task. The relationship between Jesus and humans is akin (but much greater) to that between an insect and a human being. If most of the world's population does not believe or accept Jesus, and those who say they do are either divided or simply share a cultural faith, wherein lies the failure? Why is not Jesus able to grasp that humans lack the necessary intelligibility to understand him. That is, why would God send humanity a Word that is often incomprehensible?

The answer perhaps is found in some passages in all four Gospels. Again, the mark of an effectively good (human) teacher is to make himself/herself understood, otherwise, both the teacher and the students waste their time. The Gospels indicate that those who are closest to Jesus (the disciples), those whom he comes to save and teach (the people), those he condemns (the religious authorities), and the Nicodemuses of the Gospels have failed to understand him. Yet, he tells his disciples,

> *No one who lights a lamp conceals it with a vessel or sets it under a bed; rather, he places it on a lampstand so that those who enter may see the light. For there is nothing hidden that will not become visible, and nothing secret that will not be known and come to light (Lk 8:16-18, 12:2-3, Mt 10:26).*

His remarks appear to favor transparency. He sends his disciples to preach the kingdom of God to all parts of the world (Mk 16:15, Lk 24:47, Mt 28:19). We do not know, however, the content of what they preach to others, except what we read in the New Testament. But the conclusion of biblical experts (Chapter 2) and the myriad of interpretations about the Gospels indicate that human understanding of the Christian message is still not entirely clear. This brings us back to Jesus's pedagogical method; it relies on mystery, elitism, and purposeful obfuscation, and threats. Why?

His teaching in many instances is quite straightforward; Dos and Don'ts that, regardless of whether we agree with them or not, can be understood. Nonetheless, Jesus likes to remain mysterious; the crowd asks him who the Son of Man is, and his reply is tangential and cryptic: *The light will be among you only a little while. Walk while you have the light, so that darkness may not overcome you* (Jn 12:34-35). He relies on parables, approximately fifty-eight of them if we include metaphors and similes (Table 2), whose interpretations can be challenging to today's average layperson. Moreover, Jesus is aware of peoples' difficulties in understanding his symbolisms, but it does not seem to concern him: *With many such parables he spoke the word to them* (the crowds) *as they were able to understand it. Without parables he did not speak to them, but to his own disciples he explained everything in private* (Mk 4:33-34, emphasis mine). Thus, Jesus does not use parables because they are easier to understand; they are not, and the experts seem to agree. Parables are *figurative speech that demands reflection for understanding* i.e., reasoning. But reasoning is probably not the crowds' strong suit. As for his disciples, often they require private tutoring that he does not provide to others. The conclusion seems to be that understanding is a gift of God, not extended to crowds or future generations because God thinks or feels that humans are incapable of understanding, which begs the question: why then even try.[21]

In one of the most disconcerting passages in the Gospels, Jesus tells his disciples that he intends to reveal the kingdom of God to them, but not to others, i.e., the majority of the people, *in order that they may not be converted and be forgiven*

(Mk 411-12, Lk 8:10). Hence, if salvation depends on understanding the Word, but the Word remains hidden, how will people be saved? Jesus's attitude is more bewildering when he praises and gives thanks to God for hiding these things *from the wise and learned* (I am thinking of Nicodemus), but he includes prophets and righteous people too), and reveals them only to the *childlike*. Is this a disguised critique of reason, wisdom, learning, and understanding? Is it that the wise and learned tend to be arrogant and wish to emulate Adam's and Eve's desire to know right from wrong for which they are punished? Jesus goes even further to say that it is his prerogative to reveal the mysteries of the kingdom to whomever he wishes (Lk 10:21-24, Mt 11:25-27, 13:17). He organizes an exclusive group whose members are granted admission by God in a way he sees fit. Salvation now takes a new meaning; it is like winning a rigged lottery, in which God selects *a priori* the winners.

Matthew indicates that not understanding the Word is a curse placed by God upon those whose hearts are gross; but what about the righteous people that are not able to know about the kingdom or good Christians that cannot seem to understand unless they go to Bible school or become theologians? Matthew even seems to relish this curse, as it means that Isiah's prophecy is being fulfilled in Jesus, which he presents as historical evidence that he is God's envoy (Mt 13:14-15). John's passage is even more disturbing. The religious authorities appear to have witnessed Jesus's miracles, but they do not believe because of God's curse: *Although he had performed so many signs in their presence they did not believe in him, in order that the word which Isaiah the prophet spoke might be fulfilled* (Jn 12:37-39).

This is yet another conundrum; God is telling humans that they must believe despite not being allowed to fully understand. Among Christianity's greatest challenges will be whether it can reverse present trends toward non-religious and non-denominational generations, particularly Generation X, Millennials, Generation Z, and among educated populations in the most technologically and democratically based nations where Christianity is fast becoming a cultural status symbol or simply irrelevant to being a moral person. Thus, the question needs to be asked if postmodern societies can survive and prosper without a consensus on moral values that can deter the human abominations witnessed in the twentieth and twenty-first centuries.

Notes:
1. I realize that science tends to analyze the whole by breaking it down into specialized areas. Without getting involved in the argument of whether there exists something we refer to as *the mind* as an independent object where behavior is initiated (as opposed to simply there being a brain where all activity takes place), or how many parts coexist in the mind, I am simplifying matters by distinguishing only between reason or cognition and emotions or affections. Some have referred to a third part of the mind labeled *conation*, defined as *an inclination or impulse to act purposefully*. *Merriam-Webster Dictionary*, online, s.v. "conation." For purposes of this study, conation refers to the outcome of conscious or subconscious exchanges that take place between reason and emotions or between the cognitive and affective sources of human behavior.
2. Jesus's accusations against the religious authorities are not merely rants but constitute concrete charges that he considers to be evil. The term *word* is used 80xt in all four Gospels (37xt in John); it stands also for 'reasonable' explanations about the kingdom of God and God's plan of salvation. None of these are used in tallying this category except for *The Word* in Jn 1:1, 5 whereby it refers to Jesus, connoting

wisdom as *the ultimate intelligibility of reality* (*Hellenistic philosophy*) according to NEs' note, Jn 1:1. If Jesus's attacks and the term *word* had been used, the Rationality category would have increased its ranking, although it would not have affected the results radically; that is, no category would have shifted from Highly Significant to Insignificant, or vice-versa.

3. A rough comparison suggests that in proportion to their lengths, the New Testament emphasizes Reason and related words far more than the Old Testament. The Old Testament in the 21 Century King James Version is about 4 to 4.25 times longer than the New Testament; the NEs' Catholic version of the OT is longer, as it includes several books that the Protestant version chose not to include in its Bible: "How Many Pages Are There in the Bible," *WordCounter.net,* February 2016, https://wordcounter.net/blog/2016/02/21/101241_how-many-pages-are-there-in-the-bible.html (accessed March 15, 2020). The data extracted from both Bible versions are still similar enough to confirm the more 'Rational' nature of the NT. Thus, relying on data from BibleGateway.com, although the OT is 4xt longer than the NT, the number of times the word Reason shows in the OT and the NT are almost similar in both Bible versions; Know appears only 1 ½ to 2 xt more in the OT; Knowledge, 3xt more; Understand, equal to 2.5 xt more; Think, .5 to 1.5 xt more; Learn, equal to 2.5 xt more; Mind, equal to 2xt more; Explain, equal to .5xt more; Comprehend, almost equal in both versions. Only the term Wisdom shows great disparity, as it is used 5xt more in the OT than in the NT in the Catholic Bible, and only 3xt more in the Protestant version.

4. *Oxford English Corpus,* https://web.archive.org/web/20111226085859/http://oxforddictionaries.com/words/the-oec-facts-about-the-language (accessed July 22, 2018); *Word Bank of 1200 High-Frequency Writing Words,* http://www.achievementstrategies.org/2014/docs/ela/MostFrequentlyUsedWords.pdf (accessed July 22, 2018); *Word Frequency Data,* https://www.wordfrequency.info/free.asp?s=y (accessed July 22, 2018).

5. *The ability to make good judgments based on what you have learned from your experience, or the knowledge and understanding that give you this ability. Cambridge Dictionary,* online, s.v. "wisdom."

6. NEs' note, Lk 23:34 signal that *this portion of Lk 23:34 does not occur in the oldest papyrus manuscript of Luke and other early Greek manuscripts and ancient versions of wide geographical distribution.*

7. Ibid., *Book of Wisdom,* Introduction.

8. *The plight of humankind is clearly one of ignorance, unless the "holy spirit" is sent from God,* explain NEs. Ibid., note, Wis 9:15.

9. Caleb Scharf is the director of the multidisciplinary Columbia Astrobiology Center at Columbia University in New York. In his article, "This is What We Don't Know About the Universe," he suggests that *it's relatively easy to focus on what we know, yet to me the wonder of the cosmos, the awesomeness, is never greater than when we contemplate all that we don't know. Scientific American,* (2014), https://blogs.scientificamerican.com/life-unbounded/this-is-what-we-done28099t-know-about-the-universe/ (accessed July 21, 2018).

10. A search for the terms *understand* and *realize* throughout the Gospels indicates that often the disciples fail to understand Jesus, leading him to the point of becoming exasperated with them.

11. NEs' note, Job 28:1-28. A passage in this chapter in Job reads partially, *As for wisdom, where does she come from? Where is the place of understanding?.... Mortals do not know her path, nor is she to be found in the land of the living.... But God understands the way to her; it is he who knows her place. For he beholds the ends of the earth and sees all that is under the heavens....*

12. Ibid, note on Mk 6:52. Mark is the only one who provides this interpretation. In Matthew, once Jesus identifies himself, Peter doubts it is him and asks him to prove it by ordering him to walk on water; Peter becomes frightened and begins to sink. Jesus rescues him, and mildly chastises him, *O you of little faith, why did you doubt?* (Mt 14:25-31); in John, Jesus merely says, *it is I, don't be afraid* (Jn 6:16-21).

13. In Catholicism, the following were among various practices mandated: no meat (and preferably fish) had to be consumed during Lent on Fridays; communion could not be received in the hands, and those receiving it had to abstain from eating anything hours before.

14. NEs' note, Mt 16:12.

15. Ibid., *The idea of a suffering Messiah is not found in the Old Testament or other Jewish literature prior to the New Testament period, although the idea is hinted at in Mk 8:31–33.* NEs' note, Lk 24:24-26. That God somehow could misguide Luke is yet another of the many surprising human revelations found in the Gospels.

16. Ibid., note on Mt 11:16.

17. If the parables were so easy to understand, maybe Fr. John Meier, one of the foremost experts in Jesus, has wasted his time writing a 464 pages volume questioning many of them. John P. Meier, *A*

Marginal Jew: Rethinking the Historical Jesus, Volume V: Probing the Authenticity of the Parables, (New Haven: The Anchor Yale Bible Reference Library, 2016).
18. NEs' note, Mt 16:2.
19. *Merriam-Webster Dictionary,* online, s.v. "intelligibility."
20. There are simply too many uses of the 'I' pronoun in John's Gospel to illustrate the point. However, through BibleGateway.com the word 'I' is identified, and readers may be able to see for themselves the extent to which Jesus relies on 'I.'
21. NEs' note, Mt 13:11.1.

Faith

Faith in Jesus as a divine being holds a central position in Christianity, as it transforms teachings about morals and ethics from human philosophy into absolute supernatural truths. The basic definition of faith is to believe without having evidence; having *a priori* trust in someone or something because of various reasons, among them, competence, love and friendship, a proven record, daily experiences, necessity, and even fear. Fundamentally, faith is a human act that permeates our daily lives; for example, when we believe, i.e., take for granted, that the food we eat is as safe as the air we breathe and the water we drink. Religious faith in a supernatural entity[1] is no different, although it is somewhat more demanding.

In the Old Testament, the term faith occurs frequently, although it dispenses with the connotation observed in the Gospels in which evidence is not necessary to believe. In the old texts, faith means, above all, being faithful or loyal to a God the Israelites 'know,' or take for granted that it exists. Questions about doubt in God's existence as they abound today, or about Jesus's divinity rarely show up. The terms *righteous* and *sinner* find their proper meanings only when related to an ever-present God in the lives of the Israelites.

In examining the Faith category, we are guided by a central question whose answer is problematic. The faith Jesus is asking of his disciples and the Jewish people is faith in him because he is trustworthy; but is it faith in him only as God's emissary; or is he asking people to believe that he is a supernatural or divine Messiah, or even that he be accepted as the Son of God?

Today, the answer is far less complicated. The Christian faith already had been defined in the Nicene Creed (325 CE), then slightly modified and confirmed during the First Council of Constantinople (381 CE), affirming that Jesus was divine, the Son of God, and the third person of the Trinity, who died, was resurrected and shall come again to judge the living and the dead.[2] Once the New Testament was canonically anointed, faith in Jesus became easier to accept, although the Gospels and Acts suggest that faith in Jesus already had begun to spread slowly outside Jerusalem.

Nonetheless, at the time, it appears that faith in Jesus meant trust (at least for a time), similar to how we may feel toward our loved ones, our physician, the priest, pastor, or deacon in the local church. For the most part, the Gospels do not indicate that most people accepted Jesus as the Son of God. Following his death, most Israelites remained faithful to God through Mosaic Law, the Temple, and the synagogue. The data profile on Jesus indicates that the title Son of God attains significance only on account of the disproportionate references to Jesus's divinity in John's Gospel, suggesting a degree of skepticism in the synoptics among people.

The second part of the question is whether Jesus wanted people to have faith in him or God? In all four Gospels, the answer appears to be, in both, namely in John's Gospel that, as previously mentioned, seems to be a correction to the synoptics, either by God or by human hands. In most instances, when the terms *faith, believe,* and *accept* appear in the Gospels, they imply confidence; except that it is not clear that, despite Jesus's assertions, people's responses reflect anything other than a belief in a very important human being that God may have anointed. There is, however, a wider view in the texts that refers to a faith in the supernatural that is quite different than the human faith in Jesus. To compound the problem, Jesus is responsible for both teachings. This section will focus on the narrow definition of faith shown by the disciples and the few people that toward the end continued to believe in Jesus, with the understanding that adding other faith-oriented components, a different type of faith—one that transcends the temporal world--emerges. As the Afterlife, Prayer, Kingdom of God, God's Will, God as Everyone's Father, and the Resurrection of Jesus and Humans categories are added to this narrow view, all of which imply faith in God and in Jesus's claims of being divine, the Faith Plus category becomes the second most significant according to the rankings in Table 2.

Faith and Jesus's Miracles

Jesus's miracles would be secularly interpreted as his strategy designed to call attention to himself and to whom or what he represents. Without his miracles, Jesus would have been known as a preacher, another prophet, or a rebel opposed to the behavior of the Jewish religious authorities. Today, anyone capable of performing miraculous deeds is likely to be regarded as an extraterrestrial or a supernatural being. But at the time, people were more credulous; they believed that Jesus could heal the sick and feed the hungry, and judging from the texts' narratives people, indeed, were cured and fed. That is, they had human faith that he was someone special and with special powers. What is of interest to those who study the life of Jesus is that by the time he is arrested and crucified only a few of his followers come to support him. Where did all that human trust go, including the faith of his disciples? Even Jesus's resurrection was not able to persuade most Jewish people.

The examination of faith in the Gospels shows that in most instances when miracles are involved, faith expresses probably nothing more than a desire by numerous sick people who may have heard of Jesus's deeds and believe that he can cure them (Mk 1:39-45, 2:1-12, Lk 4:40-41, 6:17-19, Mt 4:23-24). Nonetheless, there is nothing in the narratives to suggest that people accepted that Jesus was divine. Their trust in him was similar to human expectations that sick people experience when they go to their trusted physicians to be cured. Other instances suggest that this type of trust goes beyond merely a desire, to indicate a profound (still human) belief in someone special that may transcend or not our temporal existence. This is the case of the Roman Centurion who believes that Jesus's word alone can heal his servant without his physical presence (Mt 8:5:13); the blind man who is healed and tells the religious authorities that only a man from God would be able to perform this deed (Jn 9:30-33); or the example of Martha, Lazarus's sister, who confesses her faith in Jesus as the Son of God while trusting that he can bring Lazarus back to life (Jn 11:25-27). None of these instances indicate that Jesus is divine, but only that these people may have believed it.

The type of faith Jesus preaches seems to be highly demanding. He asks people to believe in him with the same innocence as children depend on their parents (Mk 10:15). He preaches a faith that is not troubled about fulfilling basic needs in life since God will take care of these, insofar as people seek God's kingdom first (Lk 12:22-31, Mt 6:25-34). It is a faith so deep that, according to Jesus, it is capable of moving mountains and uprooting trees (Mk 11:20-24, Lk 17:5-6, Mt 17:20); so bizarre that it must accept that unless people consume Jesus's flesh and blood they will not be resurrected on the last days and live eternally (Jn 6:53-57). His words are as shocking as they are imposing, and he is not surprised or embarrassed that many of his followers will desert him after he voices these remarks (Jn 6:66). His teachings run against a human nature that is selfish and prone to hatred and violence, indicating instead that, to love and forgive one's enemies and care for the stranger, amounts to loving God (Mt 5:44, 22:34-40, Lk 10:30-37). These teachings would be regarded merely as philosophical ethical principles unless they would emanate from God.

Jesus seems aware that such a demanding faith will not be easily accepted, and he chooses to rely on supernatural powers to generate belief. He walks on water before the unbelieving eyes of his disciples, calms the seas, transfigures himself, his face shining like the sun, turns water into wine, heals a paralytic, cures the blind, and feeds thousands, hoping that deeds, unseen until now, would lead people to believe that he is whom he says he is: divine. But understanding Jesus does not come easily, even to his own disciples who fail to grasp the meaning of some of his teachings (Mt 15:16, 16:9). The ultimate test lies in his resurrection. Already, he has told them, three times, that he would be crucified but that he would rise on the third day (Mk 8:31, 9:31-32, 10:32-34), and that their faith would be shaken by his death ((Mk 14:27-31, Lk 22:31, Mt 26:31). Indeed, on the eve of his execution, his disciples disappear, Peter denies him, and when told that Jesus has risen, they all refuse to believe it (Mk 16:14, Mt 28:16-17); they need to see for themselves.

Jesus needs to provide them with empirical evidence so they will believe. Following the resurrection, he appears before them, and they feel they are seeing a ghost. A resurrected Jesus tells them, *touch me and see* that I am real (Lk 24:36-43). He issues Thomas a mild rebuke for insisting on seeing before believing (Jn 20:24-29). Their unbelief appears to be forgiven perhaps because Jesus appears to understand human nature's weaknesses.

But this is not the case with others. Prior to his ascension to heaven, he tells his disciples to proclaim the gospel throughout the world, and *whoever does not believe will be condemned* (Mk 15:16).[3] Hence, Jesus forgives his disciples, yet he refuses to reprieve others for their unbelief. He had forewarned people, threatening towns for rejecting him (Lk 10:10-15). Faith in him, he said, would require perseverance, even during persecutions, in order to be saved (Mk 13:9-13, Lk 21:16-19, Mt 10:16-22). Does it mean that those who succumb to fear will be condemned? On the other hand, when out of desperation or fear a criminal who has nothing to lose insinuates belief in him at the last minute, Jesus does not hesitate in allowing him to enter Paradise (Lk 23:39-43). Jesus's teachings are convoluted, a reason why critically-minded people have problems understanding them.

Judging by the small size of the original community that surged following Jesus's death and resurrection, and despite the many miracles he performed before thousands of witnesses, unbelief prevailed not only among the religious authorities but among most Jewish people. Empirical evidence, it seems, had not been enough to call attention to the person of Jesus. Somehow, like the mustard seed that grows by itself becoming *the largest of plants* (Mt 13:31-33), the kingdom of God begins to expand. Those who were present during Jesus's lifetime doubted, but later affirmed their faith, likely aided by the belief in the miracle of his resurrection. Word of mouth, however, seems to have been the necessary yeast that allowed other people who had not seen the resurrected Jesus to believe; until then, they only had heard of the Jesus story. Was this story so appealing, or was the desire for eternal salvation coupled with the fear of condemnation for unbelief that motivated people to have faith? What causes some people to turn to Jesus? What about billions of others who have not been raised under a Christian environment or chosen not to believe because of credibility issues; can we say that they have rejected the grace God extended to them?

In John's Gospel, Jesus insists that without faith in him no good deed is possible (Jn 15:1-5). Is he suggesting that God does not recognize good works being done today by humanists and non-Christians because they lack correct belief? Or is it possible that Jesus may be implying that only those works that replicate his teachings are truly Christian and that it is he who inspires all good works, regardless of belief? A central question for Christianity and the world it now faces is whether Jesus would consider the equivalent of Christian-like deeds meritorious when done simply out of compassion, humanity, and love of neighbor. The future of the Christian faith and its influence in postmodern society may hinge on the answer to this question.

Ironically, at a time when a culture of credulity surrounded by sorcery and magical incantations prevailed, Jesus had to rely on empirical proof, e.g., his miracles, to persuade his disciples and others to believe in him. It suggests that today's skeptical and secularized world is the greatest obstacle to the Christian faith.

Examining the tally on the narrow view of the Faith category reveals interesting patterns. The words that were searched show no great variation throughout the four

Gospels, with one exception: John's use of the term *believe* is notoriously high. While Mark uses the word 18xt, and Luke and Matthew 8xt respectively, in John's Gospel the term appears 96xt. John seldom uses the term *faith* (2xt) while the other authors use it more frequently. It seems that the sole purpose of John's Gospel is to stress belief as its main theme; belief in Jesus, and belief that God the Father and Jesus are one. In John's text, belief becomes active behavior, similar to loving one's neighbor, forgiving one's enemy, assisting the needy, or abstaining from committing adultery or theft in the synoptics, except that it is not active behavior; it is only belief. The results suggest that in John's Gospel faith is the most significant means to attain eternal salvation (even more so than love). It is an end to itself, while in the synoptics, faith or trust in Jesus is a first step in doing God's will.

Hence, John's Gospel has far-reaching consequences. In the synoptics, doing God's will is defined as acting out Jesus's teachings, which he emphasizes frequently, presumably perceiving that faith in him will lead believers to carry out his instructions. But in John, Jesus's teachings become secondary. Jesus tells his *disciples if you love me you will keep my commandments*; except that he does not teach these commandments to the crowds; all he says to his disciples is to love one another.

In John, the truth that sets free is the belief that Jesus is divine. While engaged in a dialogue with a *crowd* who refuses to believe him, they ask him what they can do to fulfill God's works, and Jesus replies, *this is the work of God, that you believe in the one he sent.* The skeptic group asks for a sign, but this time Jesus does not dismiss them as an unfaithful generation as he does in the synoptics. Instead, he tells them that he is the sign: *I am the bread of life .... This is the will of my Father, that everyone who sees the Son and believes in him may have eternal life* (Jn 6:22-40). Moreover, Jesus insists that the consequences of unbelief are serious:

> - *Whoever disobeys the Son will not see life, but the wrath of God remains upon him* (Jn 3:36).
> - *Whoever rejects me and does not accept my words has something to judge him: the word that I spoke, it will condemn him on the last day* (Jn 12:48).
> - *Anyone who does not remain in me will be thrown out like a branch and wither; people will gather them and throw them into a fire, and they will be burned* (Jn 15:1-10).

In these passages, Jesus's words lead to admissions of faith due to fear, similar to what victims of the Inquisition faced throughout the Middle Ages and into the eighteenth century. To learn that unbelief would lead to eternal condemnation would leave people little choice but to believe in Jesus. Fear of condemnation, then, becomes a persuasive mechanism to ensure compliance with human and divine authority. If enforced, this approach would be reminiscent of totalitarian systems whereby people had to feign loyalty to a higher authority to survive. These passages might not enthrall secular-minded people and non-Christians who might prefer to forego such beliefs, even if their own afterlives were to be at risk.

The act of believing in John's Gospel becomes a highly individualistic behavior based on self-preservation; that is, faith becomes an egotistical act that negates Jesus's teachings on Judgment Day (Mt 25:31). Today, surveys are conducted worldwide inquiring about the number of people who believe in God, supposedly under the assumption that simply having faith in God might be a positive element in postmodern society. These surveys seldom, if ever, ask how people manifest their faith.

Acting out Jesus's words is not a central feature in John, whereas in Luke and Matthew Jesus dismisses those who cry out *Lord, Lord* but ignore his teachings, comparing them to fools who build their houses on sand (Mt 7:21-27, Lk 6:46-49). Behaving according to God's will is so important that Jesus honors *those who hear the word of God and observe it,* over praises to his own mother (Lk 11:27-28).

In today's post-modern world, the Christian faith may create false expectations that can lead to disappointment because of Jesus's seemingly hyperbolic remarks. He says that if someone without a doubt in his heart says to a mountain, *be lifted up and thrown into the sea,* it will happen (Mk 11:23). If such a feat has not happened, does it mean that no one has been capable of this type of faith? How do people who live in abject poverty would react to his words in which he explicitly says that they should not worry about what to eat, drink, or wear since God will provide these needs once they seek first the kingdom of God? (Mt 6:25-33). Non-Christians who hear these words likely would discard them as nonsense.

It may be dispiriting too, to read in Mark's Gospel that signs will accompany those who believe: *in my name they will drive out demons, they will speak new languages. They will pick up serpents [with their hands], and if they drink any deadly thing, it will not harm them* (Mk 16:15-18). Setting aside the question of whether any type of rational communication exists among those who speak 'new languages' they have not previously learned, or the efficacy of exorcism, the handling of venomous snakes as a sign of faith or drinking poisonous substances would seem to border on foolish credulity once the experiment fails.[4] Along these lines, any religious faith that leads to unwarranted beliefs may prove to be its own worst enemy.

Another critique of the Christian faith as defined by Jesus is found in the Parable of the Sower (Mk 4:1-20, Lk 8:4-15, Mt 13:18-23)[5] in which he remarks that some people will not believe because they cannot understand the words of the kingdom, so *the evil one comes and steals away what was sown in his heart* (Mt 13:19). Should these people be blamed for not understanding?[6] Moreover, many who abandon their faith because they are unable to live a life without care (as Jesus recommends) may be anxious because they are unemployed and unable to support their families; will they be condemned too? Or the many who are conditioned by a culture of greed into becoming wealthy and leave the faith by the wayside; are they fully aware that they are being subconsciously seduced by external structures that entice this behavior?

Faith in Jesus becomes even more difficult in a secularized world where it must compete with human philosophies. Today's politics offer an empirical example of the problem. Nowadays, there are elected public officials in democratic systems that belong to the same Christian faith who nonetheless oppose each other on policies that directly relate to Jesus's teachings. Aware of the possibility, Jesus confronted the problem of competing philosophies and warned about it (Mk 13:22, Mt 24:24). The question is how do Christians identify false prophets when they cannot even seem to identify those that roam within their faith? Under such circumstances, it must be difficult for the non-believer and the non-Christian who witness these conditions to accept Jesus as the Son of God. Thus, Christianity faces a conundrum; faith without evidence weakens faith, while if enough evidence were to become available faith would no longer be required. Today, scholars, both Christians, and non-Christians, are questioning the evidence upon which faith is based, and so far, the answers are lacking. Without answers, Christianity is asking believers merely to have faith in faith.

Ultimately, it may be asked if the Christian faith can be a temporal asset. Some have claimed that all religions are morally and socially nefarious, damaging of the individual psyche, or enemies of progress and peace.[7] Without denying instances in which religion has led to unnecessary conflict or even spiritual suffocation, those who hold this view have focused on the negative aspects of the Christian religion while ignoring the injurious attitudes and behavior of non-religious people, and while overlooking positive contributions that religion has provided throughout history. That is not to say that many of their criticisms are unenlightening; they highlight the challenges the Christian faith confronts today, namely inexplicable behavior on the part of God in the scriptures that would probably alienate even a devoted newcomer.[8]

Moreover, if non-Christians could see in the behavior of Christians a positive reflection of their faith their views might be swayed. Nonetheless, insofar as divisions, selfishness, violence, discrimination, and inequality reflect the Christian faith, it is more likely that non-Christians would look somewhere else, in which case God's kingdom would begin to shrink, as it is happening today.

Notes:
1. The term supernatural, as used in this work, indicates the existence of a reality that transcends human phenomena or is beyond scientific explanations and usually associated with divine beings (including satanic entities). It does not include the possible existence of non-divine extra-terrestrial beings.
2. Line by line comparison of the original Nicene Creed in 325 and changes made at the First Council of Constantinople in 381, at New World Encyclopedia Contributors, "Nicene Creed," *New World Encyclopedia,* 8 January 2015,
 http://www.newworldencyclopedia.org/entry/Nicene_Creed#The_original_Nicene_Creed_of_325 (accessed 18 December 2016).
3. The longer ending of Mark's text 16:9-19 appears to have been written during the second century but was accepted as part of the gospel centuries later at the Council of Trent. NEs' note, Mark 16:9:20.
4. Snake handlers have died while wishing to prove to others that the passage in Mark ought to be taken literally as a sign of faith in God. Accordingly, the response is that if the snake handler dies it is because God wished it or because he/she did not have enough faith, a poor example of sophistry. For evidence

that God may have wished some to die or that they lacked faith see: Lisa Alther, 'They shall take up serpents,' *The New York Times,* 6 June 1976, www.nytimes.com/1976/06/06/archives/they-shall-take-up-serpents-serpents.html (accessed July 8, 2018); Ashley Fantz, "Reality show snake-handling preacher dies -- of snakebite," *CNN,* 18 February 2014, www.cnn.com/2014/02/16/us/snake-salvation-pastor-bite/index.html (accessed July 8, 2018); Robert Winston, "Why do we believe in God?" extracts from his book *The Story of God,* published in *The Guardian,* 13 October 2005, www.theguardian.com/world/2005/oct/13/religion.scienceandnature (accessed July 8, 2018).

5. NEs' note in Mt 13:18 explain that scholars question the veracity of Jesus's words in this parable.

6. Ibid., editors indicate that Satan steals away their faith because they are people who *never accept the word of the kingdom.* This is quite different than having their faith taken away because they do not understand it. Note, Mt 13:19.

7. A similar view prevailed during the French Enlightenment among individuals with a strong Christian background, largely because the Catholic Church supported despotic French monarchs, its intolerance regarding non-Catholic denominations, and strong opposition to individual human rights. Among them stand out Jean Jacques Rousseau (*The Social Contract*) and Voltaire (*Treatise on Tolerance on the Occasion of the Death of Jean Calas, Questions on Miracles*). In the nineteenth century, Friedrich Nietzsche (*Beyond Good and Evil, The Anti-*Christ) and Karl Marx (*A Contribution to the Critique of Hegel's Philosophy of Right*) are among the most notable representatives of this view. Today this view has been propounded by Daniel Dennett, *Breaking the Spell,* (London: Penguin Books, 2007); Christopher Hitchens, *god is not Great*: *How Religion Poisons Everything,* (New York: Twelve, 2009); Sam Harris, *The End of Faith: Religion, Terror, and the Future of Reason*; (New York: W.W. Norton, 2005); Richard Dawkins, *The God Delusion,* (New York: Mariner Books, 2008).

8. Dawkins describes the God of the Old Testament as *arguably the most unpleasant character in all fiction: jealous and proud of it; petty, unjust, unforgiving control-freak; a vindictive, bloodthirsty ethnic cleanser; a misogynistic, homophobic, racist, infanticidal, genocidal, filicidal, pestilential, megalomaniac, sado-masochistic, capriciously malevolent bully.* It is difficult to object to his characterization after reading passages in the Old Testament that may leave the reader wondering what type of Maker we are likely to meet. Dawkins, *The God Delusion,* 51.

Prayer

The act of praying, including music and singing, fasting, reading the scriptures, or church services, presumes belief in God's existence, belief that God is listening, and belief in an active providence, i.e., that God responds to prayer. This practice is not new with Jesus; it existed among the Israelites too,[1] and passages in the Gospels confirm this belief (Lk 1:13, Jn 9:31, 11:22). It may be said that Jesus enters his public life already imbued by this view, which then becomes an essential part of his life and his teachings.

An interesting, yet largely unnoticed, aspect of Jesus's life is that, other than during the Transfiguration and the voice of God that is heard from the clouds, there is no communication (or personal revelations) between God and Jesus. This type of interaction occurred throughout the Old Testament; God was then a personal God that talked to his prophets and close friends. In the Gospels, the Son is often alone praying, at times conversing with the Father, at other times praising him.

Prayer appears to provide hope, solace, and emotional reassurance amid the uncertainties that life brings. Prayer allows the believer to penetrate the mystery of the afterlife and its creator, offering a sense of spiritual and emotional security that many people seek. Although in popular religiosity *prayer* is the equivalent of asking God to fulfill needs or wishes (largely because that is what Jesus teaches), Christian spirituality suggests that *prayer* is, above all, an act of humility that reminds the believer of one's dependence on God (Lk 18:9-14). Sincerity, i.e., religious gravitas, is another element of prayer, suggesting that hypocrisy or ritualistic praying is abominable in the eyes of God (Mk 7:7, 12:40, Lk 20:47, Mt 6:5-8, 15:8-9, 23:14).

In the content analysis results, *Prayer* ranks among the less significant categories. This is not in accordance with the importance Christianity ascribes to it, since it is the most intimate expression of communication with God. The results, nonetheless, indicate that prayer is important to Jesus and to those he teaches. Jesus prays constantly (Mk 1:35, 6:46, 14:32, Lk 3:21, 5:16, 6:12, 9:18, 9:28, 11:1, 22:41, Mt 19:13, 26:36, Jn 17:1), and praises God frequently (Mk 6:41, 8:7, 14:22, Lk 9:16, 22:19, 24:30, Mt 14:18, 15:35-37). Throughout his mission, he seeks to glorify God, indeed, a form of prayer (Jn 4:23-24,7:18, 11:4, 13:31-32, 21:19). He asks for God's blessings for those whom he identifies as being righteous (Mk 10:14-16, Lk 6:20-22, 11:28, Mt 5:1-12, 11:6, 24:46, Jn 13:16-17, 20:29). Prayer is central in Jesus's life, to the point that he even considers the temple surroundings a sacred place in which no commercial activity ought to take place (Mk 11:15, Lk 19:46, Mt 21:12, Jn 2:13).

The main issue that confronts prayer in the postmodern world is that, in the Gospels, Jesus heightens human expectations regarding its significance and necessity as well as its results. The following passages characterize Jesus's views on indicating that God listens to and answers everyone's prayers:

> - *I say to you, whoever says to this mountain, 'Be lifted up and thrown into the sea,' and does not doubt in his heart but believes that what he says will happen, it shall be done for him. Therefore, I tell you, all that you ask for in prayer, believe that you will receive it and it shall be yours (Mk 11:23-24, Lk 17:6, Mt 17:20-21).*
> - *And I tell you, ask and you will receive; seek and you will find; knock and the door will be opened to you. For everyone who asks, receives; and the one who seeks, finds; and to the one who knocks, the door will be opened. What father among you would hand his son a snake when he asks for a fish? Or hand him a scorpion when he asks for an egg? If you then, who are wicked, know how to give good gifts to your children, how much more will the Father in heaven give the holy Spirit to those who ask him? (Lk 11:9-13, Mt 7:7-11).*[2]

In Luke, there is one example that supports the claim that prayers are answered: the angel tells Zechariah, an old man whose wife Elizabeth is unable to have children, *your prayer has been heard. Your wife Elizabeth will bear you a son* (Lk 1:13). Other passages that indicate similar outcomes such as Mary's and Zechariah's Canticles (Lk 1:46-55, 67-79), and Simeon's and the prophetess Anna's belief that their prayers for the liberation of Israel have been answered (Lk 2:29, 38), are enigmatic and likely pious remarks.

We do not know if Jesus's teachings on prayer are meant to be taken literally or hyperbolically. Jesus's reassurances have no limits; whatever we ask it shall be granted, he says. These guarantees exacerbate one of the most serious issues confronting Christianity: whether the content of the Gospels is credible. Jesus had to realize that if his assertions fail to occur in daily life his credibility would be fatally weakened. By now, believers and leaders of the various Christian denominations and non-Christians, know (or should know) that there is no historical or empirical evidence to suggest that Jesus's characterizations of prayer manifest themselves as stated. It is conspicuously real that there has been enough praying throughout the centuries by many good men and women for there to be peace, less suffering, and a world more akin to God's wishes. The historical reality, however, has been quite different. May we attribute these failures to a lack of faith on the part of Christians? The human reaction to this rude awakening does not mean that believers will stop praying any time soon. Prayer fills a human void, and Jesus still has a significant number of followers, although Christian officials are aware that with each passing year the faith keeps losing adherents by the millions, as polls indicate.[3]

If prayer were to work in the manner Jesus indicates there might not be any reason for him to predict that human conditions on earth will continue to deteriorate, to warn of apocalyptic disasters (Lk 21:26), or millions of his followers being hated by all nations. Many, he predicts, will be led into sin; fathers will turn against sons, and love will grow cold (Mt 24:7-13). It appears that no amount of prayer will avert these events or that righteous people will succeed in preventing the weeds from taking over the kingdom of heaven.

There are numerous inconsistencies in the Gospels regarding the use of prayer. Jesus indicates that prayer may be used to fend off unpleasant situations (Mk 13:18, Mt 24:20) and to request joyful conditions (Lk 11:1-4, Mt 6:9-15); and he is adamant that whatever is asked in his name will be granted. History, however, points to a different reality; sometimes dreadful things befall good people while good things happen to evil people. Hence, prayer is not a panacea. People may not realize that reciting the Lord's Prayer is not a cure for being delivered from evil or to avoid falling into temptation; these occurrences still happen despite praying.

Gradually, events in life are motivating believers to reappraise the role of prayer in the Gospels. In Nigeria, terrorism has become such an ordeal that one of its Catholic bishops has concluded that *prayers won't eradicate Boko Haram, education will.*[4] Following another mass shooting, this one in Texas, USA, its governor remarked that people *need to do more than just pray for the victims and their families.*[5] Moreover, we are reminded that Pope Paul VI became *the first pope to all but rebuke God in public* when he complained to the Almighty following the execution of his good friend, Italian Prime Minister Aldo Moro saying, *You did not grant our plea for the safety of Aldo Moro ... who was my friend.*[6]

It seems that, from a historical and empirical reasoning perspective, the presumed power of prayer is not sustainable. This is not to say that prayer does not work or that it may not elicit a response from God; if it does, certainly humans do not know, and it is important that we know, if only for the sake of Jesus's credibility. What the historical record and any well-prepared empirical study would indicate is that the outcome of prayer does not function in the precise manner that Jesus claims in the Gospels. In other words, there is no reliable evidence to believe that there might be a causal relationship between petitioning praying and its desired result.

Perhaps, the best examples of the outcome of prayer are found in the synoptics. Jesus prays to the Father that the faith of his disciples does not falter (Jn 17:1-26, Lk 22:31-32), yet one of them denies him three times and another betrays him. During Jesus's agonizing moments in the Garden of Gethsemane, he does not ask the Father for emotional and spiritual strength to overcome fear; he asks not to be crucified, but above all, he wants to fulfill God's will; (Mk 14:36, Lk 22:42, Mt 26:39). His prayer is partially dismissed. God does not grant him his wish to escape death while conceding Jesus the second part of the prayer, *but not what I will but what you will.* This passage may likely be largely responsible for the pious remark that many Christians remark when prayer fails and horrific events take place; that whatever happens in one's life, 'it is God who wills it.'

Beyond being an act of piety, the phrase 'God wills it,' or 'may God's will be done' became, for centuries, a rationalization for willful misdeeds as well as an act of resignation amid a calamity. The sentiment suggests that any physical tragedy or personal misfortune that takes place finds a suitable (if unreasonable) explanation in God's will. Furthermore, a cynical skeptic might wonder why despite spending time praying the believer concedes that God has abandoned him (Lk 23:46). Or why, despite Jesus's prayer, his disciples desert him.

Among the most interesting questions that have gone unanswered is why Jesus needs to pray. Despite being God or closely associated with God, and given the powers at his disposal, Jesus resorts to constant prayer. What could the Son of God possibly ask God that he cannot have or do for himself? Does he need to pray to God to prevent falling into temptation, as he appears to do when he retreats into the desert (Lk 4:1-13)? Why would he praise God for hearing his petition to resurrect Lazarus, suggesting that he would not have been able to do it without God's assistance (Jn 11:41-42)? Why does he pray for the spiritual or physical wellbeing of his disciples if God knows what they will need to fulfill Jesus's mission? Why would he not pray for the world that needs God's assistance more than his disciples (Jn 17:1-26)? Or why would he praise the Father for revealing the mysteries of the kingdom to his disciples, suggesting that God opens the minds of some people (but not others) to allow them to understand his teachings (Lk 10:21-22, Mt 11:25-26, 16:17)?

If Jesus is not aware of his divinity or is not divine, it is reasonable to think that he needs to pray in the same manner as any believer would do to seek divine assistance. But this is not the view that Jesus projects when he rebukes an evil spirit who has taken hold of a child because his disciples are not able to do it. He says that these matters require prayer. Nonetheless, while he establishes the theological basis for the church to conduct acts of exorcism, the texts do not indicate that he needs to pray; he exorcises the demon relying on his own powers (Mk 9:14-29, Mt 17:14-21).

Jesus suggests that prayer helps believers to overcome temptations to do evil; it assists them in living righteously, and he teaches that praying for one's enemies is an act of love. But is Jesus truly expecting a positive outcome? Again, history indicates that no matter how much we pray, more often than not, people will fall into temptation; circumstances may transform the righteous into a non-believer; and people likely will not be delivered from their enemies, particularly if their enemies have similar requests (Jn 16:2).

Nonetheless, that does not stop Jesus from teaching that believers must be persistent in their prayers. In fact, Jesus indicates that God loves to be begged (Lk 18:1-8). Characterization of a god who enjoys being implored might not convey nowadays an adequate image of a loving God. If we transpose Jesus's teachings on prayer into everyday life on earth, the impression of loving parents enjoying or demanding their children to constantly beg them is likely undesirable. Likewise, why would God need or want to be implored to grant people health, peace, happiness, or to be beseeched to deliver them from evil or to prevent them from falling into temptation if God is aware of people's needs (Lk 12:29-31)?

Jesus's incongruences on prayer may contribute more to the demise of the faith than any other teaching. People tend to pray out of desperation, when life's events extend beyond their control, to ask for menial things, believing (or wanting to believe) that their prayers will be granted. When prayer is not replied to in kind, disappointment seeps in. Some abandon the faith; others become cynical; and still, others continue to pray because they 'have nothing to lose' by doing what human impotence demands at the moment. These conditions suggest there is a need for a realistic understanding of prayer if Christianity is to remain an influential voice in a secular society.

Notes:

1. It is interesting to observe how closely related are Jewish and Christian views on prayer. In Judaism, prayer is based on the conviction that God exists, hears, and answers (Ps. 65:3; cf. 115:3–7); that He is a personal deity. *In a sense, it is a corollary of the biblical concept that man was created "in the image of God" (Gen. 1:26–27), which implies, inter alia, fellowship with God. Although prayer has an intellectual base, it is essentially emotional in character. It is an expression of man's quest for the Divine and his longing to unburden his soul before God (Ps. 42:2–3 [1–2]; 62:9[8]). Hence prayer takes many forms: petition, expostulation, confession, meditation, recollection (anamnesis), thanksgiving, praise, adoration, and intercession.* "Prayer," JVL, *https://www.jewishvirtuallibrary.org/prayer* (accessed February 28, 2019).

2. *Similar passages appear throughout the texts:*
  - *I say to you, if two of you agree on earth about anything for which they are to pray, it shall be granted to them by my heavenly Father* (Mt 18:19).
  - *Whatever you ask for in prayer with faith, you will receive* (Mt 21:22).
  - *I say to you, whoever believes in me will do the works that I do, and will do greater ones than these because I am going to the Father. And whatever you ask in my name, I will do, so that the Father may be glorified in the Son. If you ask anything of me in my name, I will do it* (Jn 14:12-14).
  - *If you remain in me and my words remain in you, ask for whatever you want and it will be done for you* (Jn 15:7).
  - *Whatever you ask the Father in my name he may give you* (Jn 15:16).

- Amen, amen, I say to you, whatever you ask the Father in my name he will give you (Jn 16:23).
3. Pew Research Center, "Religious Belief and National Belonging in Central and Eastern Europe," May 2017, http://www.pewforum.org/2017/05/10/religious-beliefs/ (accessed 9 September 2017); Stoyan Zaimov, "Most Western Europeans No Longer Believe in Heaven and Hell, Survey Finds," Christian Post, Dec. 2017, https://www.christianpost.com/news/most-western-europeans-no-longer-believe-heaven-hell-survey-209270/ (accessed 9 September 2017). Pew Research Center, "Being Christian in Western Europe," May 2018, http://www.pewforum.org/2018/05/29/being-christian-in-western-europe/ (accessed 30 May 2018); Conrad Hackett, David McClendon, "Christians remain world's largest religious group, but they are declining in Europe," Pew Research Center, 5 April 2017. http://www.pewresearch.org/fact-tank/2017/04/05/christians-remain-worlds-largest-religious-group-but-they-are-declining-in-europe/ (accessed August 14, 2018); PBS, "World Religions Map," https://florida.pbslearningmedia.org/resource/sj14-soc-religmap/world-religions-map/ (accessed August 14, 2018); Pew Research Center, "Global Christianity – A Report on the Size and Distribution of the World's Christian Population," 19 December 2011, http://www.pewforum.org/2011/12/19/global-christianity-exec/ (accessed August 14, 2018); Becka A. Alper, "Why America's 'nones' don't identify with a religion," Pew Research Center, August 8, 2018, http://www.pewresearch.org/fact-tank/2018/08/08/why-americas-nones-dont-identify-with-a-religion/ (accessed August 17, 2018); Already in 2015, Millennials in the United States (ages 22 to 37 in 2018) regarded Christmas as more cultural than a religious holiday, (forty percent of Millennials saw Christmas as a religious holiday compared with fifty-six percent for Baby Boomers): Michael Lipka, "Many Millennials see Christmas as more cultural than a religious holiday," Pew Research Center, December 18, 2015. http://www.pewresearch.org/fact-tank/2015/12/18/many-millennials-see-christmas-as-more-cultural-than-religious-holiday/ (accessed on December 13, 2018). Another Pew poll's title is indicative of this trend: "Americans Say Religious Aspects of Christmas Are Declining in Public Life," December 12, 2017. http://www.pewforum.org/2017/12/12/americans-say-religious-aspects-of-christmas-are-declining-in-public-life/?utm_source=Pew+Research+Center&utm_campaign=acf747a218-EMAIL_CAMPAIGN_2018_12_11_07_10&utm_medium=email&utm_term=0_3e953b9b70-acf747a218-399935645 (accessed December 13, 2018); Lydia Saad, "Record Few Americans Believe Bible Is Literal Word of God," Gallup, 3-7 May 2017, http://news.gallup.com/poll/210704/record-few-americans-believe-bible-literal-word-god.aspx (accessed 9 September 2017).
4. Ngala Killian Chimtom, "Prayers won't eradicate Boko Haram, education will, says Nigerian bishop," Crux, October 21, 2017, https://cruxnow.com/global-church/2017/10/prayers-wont-eradicate-boko-haram-education-will-says-nigerian-bishop/ (accessed October 27, 2017).
5. *Clare Foran, "*Texas governor calls for action after shooting to 'make sure this tragedy is never repeated,'" CNN Politics, May 18, 2018. https://www.cnn.com/2018/05/18/politics/texas-school-shooting-governor-greg-abbott/index.html *(accessed May 18, 2018).*
6. *The question he left hanging, unstated but clear to everyone present, was, "Why didn't you help?"* John L. Allen Jr., "Celebrating one of history's most refined, and recognizably human, popes," Crux, October 12, 2018, https://cruxnow.com/news-analysis/2018/10/celebrating-one-of-historys-most-refined-and-recognizably-human-popes/ (accessed October 15, 2018).

Church

In Christianity, the term *church* denotes an organized religious institution embodying and projecting a set of beliefs, moral codes of behavior, laws, rules, and ritual practices, created to carry on the commandments that Jesus gives to his disciples (Mk 16:15, Lk 24:46-47, Mt 28:18-20, Jn 21:15-17). In a divided Christian faith, each denomination is made up of, a) the clergy, men and/or women that are ordained, i.e., invested with religious authority to conduct religious services and lead the institution in accordance with rules agreed to by its leaders; and b) the laity or non-ordained members that constitute the majority within the church that usually tends to have a more passive role in decision-making. Although all denominations share a common set of beliefs, each one is responsible for developing its own doctrine. Furthermore, there is a distinction within the hierarchy, which refers to the various levels of authority within the clergy, and the laity that is subordinated to hierarchical authority in all matters that pertain to the faith and morals.

Given the significance of the term within Christianity, one would think that Jesus considers it important; he does, but not in the manner that may be expected today. The word *church* only appears 3xt in the Gospels, referring to an assembly or community of believers; once when Jesus, supposedly referring to Peter, says *you are Peter, and upon this rock I will build my church,* in effect giving him authority to make decisions that shall be respected in heaven (Mt 16:18-19).[1] Nonetheless, on another occasion in which Jesus is teaching his disciples on how to deal with recalcitrant sinners within the assembly, Matthew inserts the passage on binding and loosening in which Jesus appears to delegate the disciples with a similar authority that previously had been given only to Peter (Mt 18:18). Jesus uses the term twice again while addressing his disciples, but in a manner that denigrates Gentiles and tax collectors (Mt 18:15-17).[2]

In the Gospels, the use of the term *church* about a gathering or assembly of worshippers sharing common beliefs is awkward. It is doubtful that Jesus used the term since at the time it does not appear that he had yet created an organized house of worship different from the synagogue that Jews normally attended. That the term is mentioned only three times in all four Gospels might suggest that Jesus's plan to set up a *church* (as opposed to a synagogue) is less significant to him or the Gospel's authors. Indeed, other than the above passages, the commandment Jesus gives to his disciples before departing this earth differs noticeably in all four Gospels, none of them clearly indicating the well-defined purpose that Jesus conveys to Peter in Matthew 16:18.

In Mark, Jesus gives his disciples a simple and broad mission along with a predetermined outcome: to go into the world and proclaim the gospel to every creature (Mk 16:15-16). In Luke, Jesus does not assign his disciples with a mission; instead, the task of preaching the good news is to be realized through the fulfillment of scriptures, but without identifying who is to carry on specific assignments: *Thus, it is written that ... repentance, for the forgiveness of sins, would be preached in his name to all the nations, beginning from Jerusalem* (Lk 24:46-47).

In Matthew, Jesus communicates his disciples the authority to convert hearts and minds and to *make disciples of all nations, baptizing them in the name of the Father, and of the Son, and of the holy Spirit, teaching them to observe all that I have commanded you* (Mt 28:18-20). In John, Jesus does not assign his disciples with a mission; he only speaks to Peter, cryptically suggesting through his questions and Peter's replies that he is delegating on Peter the responsibility to care for and oversee his followers (Jn 21:15-17). These passages suggest that Jesus wishes his disciples to continue with his mission; however, he does not tell them how to do it.

The awkward significance of the term *church* lies in that it appears extensively in Paul's letters (written prior to the Gospels) and yet its authors do not use the term in the Gospels. In Christianity, the term is specifically used to distinguish it from the Jewish synagogue. However, not knowing if Jesus had an Aramaic word in mind,[3] his use of the term *church,* derived from the Greek *ekklēsia,* referring to the assembly of believers he wants his disciples to institute, is unusual. This does not mean that Jesus does not wish to establish a unique institution. Although it seems he does, it must be noted that this action would have formalized a complete rupture with Judaism. Moreover, regardless of Jesus's intentions to establish a church, his disciples would have had only three choices: take over the synagogues by force, continue to preach Jesus's teachings while attempting to persuade the Jewish community to change its beliefs, or go their separate way and organize a distinctive community of worshippers.

Interestingly, following Jesus's death and resurrection, the apostles are *continually in the temple praising God* (Lk 24:57). The Acts of the Apostles further indicate that after Pentecost (seven weeks after Jesus ascends into heaven) they establish a community of their own, but they still attend the temple, suggesting that they are not entirely aware of how to carry out Jesus's mandate.[4] Although Christians believe that their church(es) is a divinely-established institution, its historical and sociological human origins cannot be disregarded.

Despite the term *church* is not widely used in the texts, this category scores relatively high once other words that relate to worshipping are identified. Activities dealing with Jesus's ministry, e.g., teaching, healing, prayer, and rituals, take place in different locations like the temple, synagogues, houses, and open areas. Paradoxically perhaps, a review of the passages indicates that, notwithstanding the numerous mentions of these terms, Jesus's concern with establishing a physical worshipping place is considerably downplayed in the texts.

Jesus's church may be traced back to God's successful efforts to liberate the Israelite people from Egyptian enslavement, and to his wishes to sign a covenant with them in return for his desire to be worshipped as the only god. Passages in Exodus indicate that God is the originator of Jewish worshipping. He makes a covenant with the Jewish people: *You will be to me a kingdom of priests, a holy nation* (Ex 19:3-6); he seals his covenant by giving Moses his commandments, and then orders him to make an altar where burnt offerings and animal sacrifices are to be used as part of worshipping rites (Ex 20:24-26); gives Moses laborious details of how his worshipping is to be conducted; provides the design for the Ark of the Covenant, the location where God's covenant will be placed, and the area where God will meet with Moses to tell *you all that I command you regarding the Israelites* (Ex 25:10-22).

God provides details concerning the design of various religious objects such as the menorah (Ex 25:23-40), and a design of the Tabernacle where the Ark of the Covenant would rest (Ex 26). He specifies all aspects of the altar and the court of the Tabernacle, including oil for the lamps, veils, priestly vestments, rules for the consecration of the priests and sacrifice of animals, taxes to be paid as a reward for liberating the Israelites as an insurance policy so that no plague may come upon them for being enrolled in God's census of the Israelites (Ex 30:12), a basin to wash hands and feet before entering the Tabernacle (otherwise they would die), and types of anointing oil and incense (Ex 29-30). God even chooses the architect and his assistants to build the tabernacle, the ark, and other accessories for worshipping and reminds them about the importance of keeping the Sabbath rule (Ex 31). When Moses finished all the work, a cloud covered the tent, *and the glory of the Lord filled the tabernacle* (Ex 40:34).

Although the Ark of the Covenant is less significant among Jews today, it became at the time *the manifestation of God's physical presence on earth (Shekhinah)*[5] through which God would communicate his wishes to his people, a rare combination of the Christian Eucharist and the Holy Spirit. Along with the Tabernacle, they served as God's signals to the Israelites while they traveled to the Promised Land; *whenever the cloud rose from the tabernacle, the Israelites would set out on their journey. But if the cloud did not lift, they would not go forward* (Ex 40:36-37). It is believed that King David transported the Tabernacle to Jerusalem, where Solomon, King David's son, fulfills his father's wishes to build the First Temple as a permanent house of worship. The Temple, built during Solomon's reign in 10 BCE, was as elaborate as anything God would have proposed (1 Kings 6-7). It is not merely an act of grandeur, but a symbol of human worship to the greatness of God (1 Kings 8:13, 8:63). Twenty-two thousand oxen and one hundred twenty thousand sheep were offered in sacrifice during its inauguration (1 Kings 8:63).

The destruction of the First Temple in 586 BCE by the Babylonian king Nebuchadnezzar led to a forced decentralization in the Israelites' worship of God. Although it is not known when the first synagogues begin to appear, some basic community gatherings may have been formed as precursors to the synagogues that existed at the time of Jesus. By then, the synagogue becomes a significant institution among the Jewish people.[6]

It is the Second Temple, initially built in 537 BCE and rebuilt by Herod the Great beginning around 19 BCE, that lies at the heart of the Jewish faith during Jesus's lifetime. As in Solomon's Temple, it included the menorah and the most sacred of places, the holy of holies, which could only be accessed by the High Priest once a year during the Day of Atonement (Yom Kippur). Citing the Second Temple period and rabbinic sources, Jewish scholar Lawrence Schiffman indicates that *the Jews believed that the temple was the place from which divine powers emanated to the world; it endowed sanctity to the entire city of Jerusalem and the land of Israel beyond it.*[7] According to Josephus, the Second Temple was larger than Solomon's Temple; a combination of a religious place of worship and a military fortress.[8] Its splendor led a Franciscan missionary to write that it rivaled *the most beautiful buildings of antiquity and far surpassed even that of Solomon.*[9]

Among Jews who believe that God dwells in the Temple is Jesus. He regards the Temple so hallowed that even the Court of the Gentiles (an outer court where non-Jews are permitted to enter, as they are not allowed to go into the Temple) is sacred to him. Considering commercial activities that were taking place outside the Temple a desecration, he throws merchants and money-changers out, telling them, *it is written: 'My house shall be a house of prayer,' but you are making it a den of thieves* (Mt 21:12-13). This passage, which appears in all four Gospels, indicates how significant Jesus considers the place where worshipping occurs.[10]

Since worshipping activities, e.g., prayer, teaching, and providing social services, may take place anywhere, at any place, and any hour, what is the justification for the Temple, the synagogue, the Christian basilica, or the local church? From the standpoint of Judaism, the answer appears to be that the Lord tells the Jewish people in explicit terms to set up a place of worship that they would attend to perform a series of activities mandated to keep them united in the faith and obediently respectful of his wishes. Christians might be able to provide a similar answer except that the justification for building a church is less precise, and perhaps, inadvertently ambiguous in contrast with God's directives in the Old Testament. Jesus's perspective on his church may be sought in the Gospels by examining the relationship between his actions and words representing this category (*temple, synagogue, assembly house, room*, and deserted or open areas) where Jesus conducts his ministry. The usage of these terms according to each author indicates that Luke and Matthew focus more on church-like activities, followed by Mark. John's Gospel is conspicuously silent on this issue (Table 2 online).

Jesus's Attachment to the Temple
In accordance with Mosaic Law, Jesus is raised by parents who teach him high devotion to the Temple. Early after his birth, he is presented to the Lord and the appropriate animal sacrifice is offered. Inside the Temple, Simeon, a righteous man, and Anna, a prophetess, portend that Jesus will become a significant figure for Gentiles and the people of Israel (Lk 2:22-38). At the age of twelve, while the family attends the feast of Passover, the precocious child disappears from his parents' side and is found three days later in the Temple, *sitting in the midst of the teachers, listening to them and asking them questions.* Apparently not remorseful, he tells his parents that he must be in his Father's house (Lk 2:41-49). Prior to the beginning of his public mission, in the desert the devil leads him to the Temple and induces him to jump from the parapet to see if God's angels would save him. Jesus refuses, arguing that God is not to be tempted for vanity's sake (Lk 4:9-12, Mt 4:5-7).

Jesus habitually goes to the Temple area to teach. Interesting events occur there. He observes the poor widow's offering at the Temple and contrasts it with the rich's offerings, making a point about the detachment of material wealth (Mk 12:41-44, Lk 21:1-3). He forgives the adulteress woman in the Temple area, teaching the religious authorities a lesson in humility and forgiveness (Jn 8:2-9). And it is in the Temple area where on one occasion he acknowledges being the Father's Son (Jn 8:18-20).

Soon, the Temple becomes a site of contention for discussing religious matters with the Jewish leadership (Mk 12:35-37, 14:49, Lk 21:37-38, 22:53, Mt 26:55, Jn 5:13-14, 7:14-31, 10:22-26). Jesus vehemently argues with them regarding his authority and antagonizes them further after he addresses them the Parable of the Tenant Farmers (Mk 11:27-33 12:1-12, Lk 20:1-19, Mt 21:23-27). In Matthew, Jesus's most virulent attack against the religious authorities appears to take place in the temple area (Mt 23:1-39);[11] in Luke, this passage takes place inside the home of a Pharisee (Lk 11:37-54). In the temple area people praise Jesus when he cures the blind and the lame, angering the religious authorities to the point that they even try to stone him (Mt 21:14-15, Jn 8:52-59). He also challenges the legitimacy of the religious authorities when he throws out the merchants and money changers (Mk 1:11, 15-17, Lk 19:45-48, Mt 21:10-13, Jn 2:13-22).

He charges his generation with rejecting all the prophets *since the foundation of the world*, who died between the altar and the temple building (Lk 11:49-51, Mt 23:34-35). Jesus even predicts the destruction of the Temple (Mk 13:1-3, Lk 21:5-7, Mt 24:1-3). His disciples do not ask him why this calamity would take place. Matthew's text suggests that its destruction would come as punishment for the Israelites' rejection of Jesus (Mt 23:37-39). Nonetheless, it is highly unlikely that the Temple's destruction by the Romans on account of the Jews' revolt against the empire in 70 CE could have been averted if the Jewish people had accepted Jesus; the two events are unrelated. Eventually, the Temple becomes the site of the conspiracy between Judas and the religious authorities. Temple guards are part of the contingent that arrests Jesus (Lk 22:1-6, 52, Mt 27:3-6), and it is inside the Temple that members of the Sanhedrin charge him with blasphemy and condemn him to die after admitting he is the Messiah and the Son of God (Mk 14:55-64, Lk 22:66-71, Mt 26:57-66).

But, as great as the Temple may be, Jesus minimizes its significance, suggesting that he and his teachings are greater than the structure itself (Mt 12:6). He violates the rule of the Sabbath recalling when David goes into the house of God (mobile temple) to take food for him and his companions (Mk 2:23-26, Lk 6:1-5, Mt 12:1-8), teaching that human needs precede temple rules and regulations. Notwithstanding his devotion to the Temple and what it stands for, the texts do not show Jesus offering sacrifices or praying, two of the most important activities in Jewish religious life at the time. He signals that he does not even recognize the Temple as part of the kingdom of God when he considers that it is not important to pay the temple tax as the Old Law requires. He complies with the tax only in order not to offend (Mt 17:24-27).[12]

Jesus and the Synagogue
After departing the desert, Jesus begins to teach in the synagogues (Lk 4:16, Mt 4:23). His primary mission is to teach about the kingdom of God: it is *for this purpose I have been sent* (Lk 4:43-44). He speaks publicly in the Temple and the synagogues,

indicating that he is not engaged in worldly conspiracies (Jn 18:12-14, 19-24).[13] His teachings are as daring as they are jarring. He alludes to the Eucharistic service while preaching in a synagogue in Capernaum stating, *I say to you, unless you eat the flesh of the Son of Man and drink his blood, you do not have life within you.* His words drive many of his followers away (Jn 6:53-66).

At the synagogue he ousts unclean spirits, heals the sick, maintains good relations with some synagogue officials (cures the daughter of an official), and is praised by his people; yet he also antagonizes the religious authorities for violating the Sabbath (Mk 1:21-28, 1:39, 3:1-6, 5:21-43, Lk 4:31-37, 6:6-11, 8:40-56, 13:10-17, Mt 4:23, 9:35, 12:9-14). At one point he goes into the synagogue in his town, Nazareth, and reads from the prophet Isaiah indicating that the role of proclaiming liberty to captives and bringing good news to the poor is fulfilled in him (Lk 4:16-21). Other teachings, however, anger his own people who try to drive him out and hurl him from the top of a hill (Mk 6:1-6, Mt 13:54-58, Lk 4:24-30).

He is critical of the false honor the religious authorities occupy in the synagogues (Mk 12:38-40, Lk 11:42-44, 20:45-46, Mt 23:1-7). His teachings cause consternation among the people who are fearful of acknowledging him as Messiah for fear of being expelled from the synagogue (Jn 9:18-23, 12:42). Jesus is aware of the dilemma, yet he continues to teach, realizing that his followers will be persecuted, arrested, and beaten at the synagogues on account of his name (Mk 13:9, Lk 12:11-12, Mt 10:16-18, Jn 16:1-4). Throughout his time with his disciples, Jesus does not appear to recommend setting up different worshipping locations or provide instructions to establish an alternative to the Temple or the synagogue. He does not ask his disciples to keep copious notes of his teachings to pass them on to potential followers. The Gospels (and Paul's letters) are the first attempt to instruct Jesus's followers in the faith, and the first step in creating small assemblies of believers. The *Didache,* a brief treatise on the faith written possibly late in 1 CE, is yet another tool used to educate the new Christians.[14]

Following his death, his disciples continue to go back to the Temple to praise God (Lk 24:51-53). Moreover, for decades, Jesus's followers (mostly Jewish Christians) [15] attend the synagogues, seemingly not aware that a house of worship would need to be instituted at some point. Furthermore, Pentecost is of no help to them in establishing a church; there are no plans at this time, because political circumstances would not allow it. It takes years before anything resembling an overarching congregation with the mission of spreading the good news is established. Smaller congregations are founded as Christians become dispersed prior to the Roman onslaught in Jerusalem in 70 CE, but it takes centuries and political intervention in the fourth century before a full-fledged church acquires temporal legitimacy. Whether Jesus intended for his church to become a theocracy (Christendom) by attaining political power is a reasonable question. The answer is, perhaps; but only if it was to be organized voluntarily. Today, this possibility seems unrealistic.

Jesus Conducts His Ministry in Private Homes

Although Jesus tells his disciples to obey what the scribes and the Pharisees tell them (though not what they do, Mt 23:3), he conducts much of his ministry outside the Temple and the synagogue. He teaches about God's kingdom going from village to village (Mk 6:6) and summons his disciples to proclaim the kingdom of God (not to set up a church), going from house to house while healing the sick (Mk 6:7-13, Lk 9:1-6, Lk 10:1-11).

He ministers the sick, including Gentiles, at private houses, and the houses of religious authorities (Mk 1:29, 5:21-43, 7:24-30, Lk 7:1-6, 8:41-56, Mt 8:5-13, 9:18-26, 15:24-28, Jn 4:46-54). He even strays off his mission to look only after the *lost sheep of Israel,* and to heal a Gentile woman (Mk 7:24-30, Mt 15:24-28). He preaches to people and cures a paralytic at his home (Mk 2:1-5, Lk 5:17-25). He doesn't discourage attending the synagogue, but he teaches his followers to pray in private in their *inner room* (Mt 6:1-8). He meets with sinners and tax collectors in eating places to teach them about the kingdom of God, and he argues contentiously with religious authorities at Levi's house (Mk 2:14-17, Lk 5:27-39, Mt 9:9-17). He celebrates the Last Supper, the basis for the Mass and the Eucharist among Catholics and some Protestant denominations, and symbolically the seed of the first Christian church, inside a guest room in a private house (Mk 14:12-24, Lk 22:7-20, Mt 26:17-19). His prayer to the Father for his disciples also takes place at this house (Jn 17:1-26).

And in Open Areas

Jesus does not need to go to the temple area or the synagogue to fulfill his mission. Many of his parables, including his private tutoring of the disciples, take place in open areas. He teaches and heals people by the sea or on open and deserted plains. This is where he tells the crowds the Parable of the Sower, the Beatitudes, and the lengthy set of rules of moral conduct we find in Matthew (Mk 4:1-9, Lk 5:1, 6:17-49, 8:4-8, Mt 5, 6, 7). It is in these open areas where he teaches people to pray the Lord's Prayer (Lk 11:1, Mt 6:9), and where after teaching them he feeds thousands (Mk 6:34-36, 8:1-9, Lk 9:11-17, Mt 14:13-21, 15:32-39, Jn 6:1-15). Jesus's other most significant activity, praying, does not take place in the Temple or the synagogue. He prays at deserted places (Mk 1:35, Lk 5:15, 6:12, 9:18, 9:28). His last and most agonizing prayer, before being arrested, is at Gethsemane, a garden on the Mt of Olives close to Jerusalem (Mk 14:32-42, Lk 22:39-46, Mt 26:36-46).

The Gospels indicate that Jesus has no strategy (or possibility) to wrest authority from the religious leaders given the opposition he encounters at the end. Nonetheless, it is likely that because of those circumstances he indicates in a few ambiguous passages the need either for his disciples to continue his mission to win over Jewish people until faith in him supersedes Pharisaic Judaism or to conceive a different institution. The Acts of the Apostles do not recall Jesus' words to Peter, nor is Peter recognized as head of the church immediately following Jesus's death (although there is more deference to him by his peers than to any other disciple). Matthew's and

John's passages on Peter's primacy suggest an idea that, had it been more important at the time, would have been considered more fully; however, it would take many decades for this view to be accepted. At the time, the recognition that an institution requires someone to guide it was simply lacking.

Within these parameters, it is significant to examine a few other passages that in Jesus's mind may apply to his idea of a church. His parable regarding Satan driving out Satan concerns an assembly of followers that, if divided, it will not stand (Mk 3:23-27, Lk 11:17-22, Mt 12:25-29). This passage is significant for its indirect appeal for unity among his followers. His simile about the house built on solid foundations follows the same train of thought suggesting that infighting over beliefs weakens the overall structure. This is, perhaps, why Jesus insists that listening to his words and acting upon them is *like a wise man who built his house on rock, the rain fell, the floods came, and the winds blew and buffeted the house. But it did not collapse* (Mt 7:24-27). Three additional references to the term *house* indicate that Jesus deems *the house of Israel* not only as an ethnic people but as an extension on earth of the house of God (Mt 10:6, 15:24, 23:38).

Hence, it is rather clear that Jesus does not establish a physical church or spends time trying to organize it; at least in the manner in which human beings formulate plans and create institutions. Nonetheless, through his teachings and deeds, he delineates the activities that he wishes his disciples to undertake on his behalf. His church is not limited to a physical place of worship but extends to anything that any of his followers do on his behalf. Authority over the institution is as important as the authority he believes he has over the rulers of the world; it is essential. This, he seems to have left up to his followers, and to the Holy Spirit.

He promises special protection to his church. How accurate are Jesus's words depends on how we interpret the phrase, *the gates of the netherworld shall not prevail against it*. After two thousand years, the religious institution that follows the teachings of Jesus still stands; however, it is divided and battered by evil (as well as having done much good). Despite an increase in the world's population, its numbers are declining in areas where it attained preeminence. The faith and the institution still provide solace at the personal and community levels. Nonetheless, beset by divisiveness over moral issues (culture wars among and within Catholics and Protestants throughout the world), institutional corruption, the child abuse scandal, failure by the laity to abide by Jesus's teachings, and the insecurity of a rigid faith amid an increasingly secular world, Christianity's moral influence in the world's cultural, political, and social arenas has declined considerably. Given its history, it is difficult to accept at face value the premise that evil shall not prevail over the Christian Church. At best, the struggle appears to be a pyrrhic victory, except that it is not clear who the victor is.

Notes:
1. Although the Protestant version is identical to its Catholic counterpart (a few may use congregation or assembly), it differs regarding the type of authority that Jesus gives to Peter; a crucial issue in the existing rift within Christianity.

2. According to NEs, the offensive words appear to be a reflection of the conflict between Jews and early Jesus's followers in a local Matthean church and may not have been said by Jesus at all. If this is the case, it is Matthew who ascribes such words to Jesus in reference to Gentiles and tax collectors. NEs' note, Matthew 18:15-17. Once again, we must ask if such insertions are part of God's revelation or gratuitous insults that Matthew attributes to Jesus.

3. Ibid., note on Mt 16:18. NEs only suggest that there might be *several possibilities for an Aramaic original.*

4. Ibid., note on Acts 2:4-6. According to NEs, *in this initial stage there was little or no thought of any dividing line between Christianity and Judaism.* Also, it must be noted that nearly all of Jesus's followers at the time were Jewish Christians. Non-Jewish Christians (Gentiles) begin to appear largely through the work of Paul, and the numbers increase following Peter and James's decision in 50 CE at the so-called Council of Jerusalem that allows Gentiles not to follow Mosaic Law (with some exceptions) as a prerequisite to conversion. Florentine Bechtel, "Judaizers," CE. Vol. 8. newadvent.org/cathen/08537a.htm (accessed April 19, 2019).

5. "Ancient Jewish History: The Ark of the Covenant," *JVL, https://www.jewishvirtuallibrary.org/the-ark-of-the-convenant (accessed* April 11, 2019).

6. Although Jews use the synagogue for community prayer services, they can pray anywhere except for certain prayers that require the presence of ten adult men. The synagogue can be used as well as a center of study, education, social hall, and charitable activities (quite similar to Christian churches today). "The Synagogue: Background and Review," *JVL,* https://www.jewishvirtuallibrary.org/synagogue-background-and-overview (accessed April 11, 2019).

7. Lawrence H. Schiffman, "The Second Temple," *Bible Odysee,* www.bibleodyssey.org/places/main-articles/second-temple (accessed April 12, 2019). According to Schiffman, *sacrificial offerings and prayers were performed twice daily, in the morning and late afternoon, with additional rites on Sabbaths and festival days. Offerings were tendered for forgiveness of sin, purification from contact with the dead and other ritual impurities, and expressions of gratitude to God. These and other offerings involved pure (kosher) animals such as cows, sheep, goats, and birds, grain offerings, or the first fruits of each season.*

8. Josephus, Book XV, Chapter 11, 3.

9. Barnabas Meistermann, "Temple of Jerusalem," CE, Vol. 14, www.newadvent.org/cathen/14499a.htm (accessed April 12, 2019).

10. The religious authorities' view of the sacredness of the Temple is different; it is based mostly on Mosaic Law and human tradition. An example of the rigidity of following the Law occurs when Judas returns the thirty pieces of silver he was paid for handing Jesus to the chief priest and the elders; they refuse to accept it because, i*t is not lawful to deposit this in the temple treasury, for it is the price of blood.* So, they use it to buy a burial plot for foreigners (Mt 27:3-6).

11. It is possible that part or much of Jesus's critique of the religious authorities, although well-founded according to NEs, is conditioned (and perhaps even misattributed to Jesus) because of the existing conflict between Pharisaic Judaism and the Matthean church. NEs' note, Matthew 23:1-39.

12. Ibid., NEs' note, Matthew 17:24-27. The editors indicate that the accuracy of this account is questionable, as it is heavily influenced by conditions prevailing within the Matthean church that at this time is made up mostly of Jewish Christians.

13. It may be accurate to say that, according to the Gospels, Jesus is not involved in conspiracies; his attacks against the religious authorities and his people for rejecting his teachings are visibly public. On the other hand, the texts indicate that Jesus spends an inordinate amount of time with his disciples to teach them about the mission they will embark on once he is no longer around. A quick search for the phrase *his disciples* indicates how often Jesus is alone with his disciples. The phrase appears 120 times in all four Gospels. In a few instances, the phrase does not apply to this point; it is, however, in almost 100xt. During these private moments, he tells his disciples that they get to know more about God's kingdom than the rest of the people who are taught through parables, some of which are less enlightening (even meant to confuse) than what his disciples get to learn (See section on Parables).

14. [John Chapman, "Didache," CE, http://www.newadvent.org/cathen/04779a.htm (accessed April 18, 2019).

15. Theologian Alister McGrath suggests that the early Christians were, for a time, following Jewish law; [they] *seemed to regard Christianity as an affirmation of every aspect of contemporary Judaism, with the addition of one extra belief, that Jesus was the Messiah.* The qualifying phrase *every aspect* might be an overstatement given that McGrath makes this assertion within the context of the practice of circumcision that some of the disciples sought to impose on converts. Jesus, however, had taught his disciples that the law was meant to serve human beings, not the other way around. Thus, likely these Jewish Christians

were, indeed, following some but not all of the Old Law. Alister E. McGrath, *Christianity: An Introduction.* (Hoboken, NJ: Blackwell Publishing 2006), pp172-175; Adrian Fortescue, "Jerusalem (A.D. 71-1099)." CE, *Vol. 8,* http://www.newadvent.org/cathen/08355a.htm (accessed April 18, 2019).

Divine Providence

Divine Providence is perhaps the most elusive term explored in this work. It does not show up in any English translation of the Gospels and only three times in the Old Testament (Job 10:12, Wis 14:3, 17:2).[1] Yet, despite being imperceptible to the casual reader the term is noticeable in the texts. Since no specific words can be searched in the Gospels, I rummaged through the texts seeking to identify passages that relate to divine providence. The results in Table 2 indicate that, despite its extraordinary theological and religious significance, the term does not rank high in the texts.

What is Divine Providence

The secular meaning of the term appears to be universally accepted. It refers to divine guidance, conceived as the power sustaining and guiding human destiny; an influence that is not human in origin and is thought to control people's lives; or the protective care of God.[2] These definitions may be subsumed under an even more generic description: divine providence refers to the belief that God is not disconnected from, but rather actively participates, in human affairs. Under this definition, the term now becomes apparent in the Old Testament throughout numerous instances of interaction between God and humans.

The Old Testament itself is a lengthy narrative about God's active involvement in the affairs of his people, the Israelites, and his concern for their wellbeing. He converses with their leaders and spokespersons (Noah, Abraham, Moses, Isaiah), issues his commandments, and establishes worshipping rituals and rules of conduct through them. He accompanies the Jewish people in their journey to the promised land; he punishes them when they transgress his will and saves them from peril time and time again.

In the Gospels, the term *divine providence* (used here as expressing God's activity) acquires relevance and becomes more visible as Jesus himself indicates its certainty through his teachings and actions; they are the source of what eventually becomes an integral part of the Christian faith. The purpose of this section is to explore passages in the Gospels that provided the Fathers of the Church with the groundwork to frame a concept that, because of its vagueness, is difficult to decipher.

None of the mainstream Christian denominations reject God's intervention in human affairs.[3] Yet, mindful of existing differences among the Catholic and Protestant (even Jewish) views, I rely on the Catholic usage of the term for purposes of expediency. The Catholic Encyclopedia describes divine providence as the act through which God, not only creates the universe but *orders all events,* including evil and sin itself, to the end for which it was created. That end is that all creatures should acknowledge God's creation, and *that man should glorify Him, recognizing in nature the work of His hand, serving Him in obedience and love.*[4]

In this portrayal, God is shown as a powerful being that directs the activities of human beings toward the sole purpose of manifesting his own glory and relish in their worshipping of him. This would seem to be an egocentric characterization of a God that enjoys looking at himself in the mirror to see the reflection of his magnificence. Although it may be God's prerogative, in parents we might be able to recognize a degree of pomposity and self-indulgence if they were to procreate children for similar purposes. Since according to Christian theology God is an absolute being that does not need admiration or self-glorification, the above description (which mirrors medieval theology) would seem to demean the greatness of God. If God were to emulate human parents, he would beget his creatures, nurture them, and enjoy time with them. This, however, is not what happens on account of sinfulness, according to Genesis. It appears that sin interrupted God's initial beneficent end of creation. Nonetheless, although the presence of evil in the form of human action and natural calamities has plagued humanity since its creation, Christianity still holds that God's action continues undeterred toward his end, the establishment of his kingdom on earth.

Spending time discussing the question of why God allows evil on earth would be a fool's errand, something that post-modern theology seems to recognize. Nonetheless, Christianity seems to have no other alternative but to stand by the concept of a good and loving God that does not abandon its creatures once created; that, as in the Old Testament, the Divine continues to exert its influence or its will on earth seeking to manage human conduct, including sinful misfortunes, toward the good of humanity. Using the human metaphor once again, this behavior would be similar to parents purposefully allowing their children to suffer while they grow up, often for no reason at all.

Post-modern Christianity refers to divine providence as the *dispositions by which God guides all his creatures with wisdom and love to their ultimate end,* calling them throughout to a personal relationship with him.[5] This definition differs in some degree from the one that appears in the Catholic Encyclopedia over one hundred years earlier. The proposition that God guides his creatures with wisdom and love indicates that Christianity would not allow a conception of God as being less than perfect and loving, who cannot be the willful cause of evil. Hence, the only possible alternative is to believe, and to hope, that this loving God would know how to overcome human obstacles and derive good from evil.

A contemporary Christian interpretation has been refined in a manner that dovetails with evolutionary theory. It points out that creation has its own goodness and proper perfection, but it did not spring forth completely from the hands of the Creator. The universe was created *in a state of journeying* toward an ultimate perfection yet to be attained, to which God has destined it. It calls divine providence *the dispositions by which God guides his creation toward this perfection.*[6] Accordingly, creation emanates from a perfect being and awaits its perfect consummation sometime in the future: *With physical good, there exists also physical evil as long as creation has not reached perfection.... Only at the end, when our partial knowledge ceases, will we fully know the ways by which God has guided his creation.*[7] Since we will not know about God's plan until the end, this clarification gives God the benefit of the doubt.

Meanwhile, rather than oscillating between accepting a degree of randomness in the universe and allowing the divine to predetermine human existence to the point of denying free will, theology and religion maintain a paradigm that is otherwise incomprehensible to the human mind. This point is stressed as God's plan takes evil into account, characterizing it as a terrible mystery to which no quick answer will suffice.[8] This explanation still fails to clarify its rationale. In general, Christian understanding of divine providence has sought to veer toward the view that God allows evil to happen even though it does not ordain it. This view, however, is contradicted when God orders plagues upon innocent human beings to free his people from subjugation (Ex 7-11). Moreover, if evil and suffering play a positive role in God's actions, it might be worth asking if there are reasons to prevent them since we might be countering God's disposition.

The concept's insistence that God sustains the universe and guides humanity toward his end would seem to reassure that humanity will not disappear from the face of the earth. That, despite death afflicting the individual, the course of humanity will continue, meaning that it will not be obliterated by natural disasters, such as the earth being hit by an asteroid or human beings being sickened by a deadly pandemic that could eradicate human life. Divine providence would seem to prevent that sinfulness would not lead to catastrophic events, such as a nuclear war that would completely devastate life on earth. It suggests that any of these scenarios would deny Jesus the opportunity of his Second Coming and God's plan to guide creation toward its perfection. Not fully trusting divine providence, or perhaps making use of their responsibility to rely on reason as a problem-solving element, the possibility of any of these potentially devastating events are seriously considered by scientists, political leaders, and all religious hierarchies.

Divine Providence in the Gospels
Although vague and mysterious, the Christian description of divine providence finds corroboration in the Gospels. The texts provide several instances in which God becomes intimately involved in the early years of Jesus's life. The angel of the Lord, for example, communicates directly with Zechariah to inform him about the child his wife Elizabeth will bear and the role the child will have preceding Jesus (Lk 1:10-17). The angel then tells Mary that she will conceive the Son of God (Lk 1:26-35). Both Mary and Zechariah eulogize God's providence indicating all the great things he has done for their people (Lk 1:46-55, 67-79). In Matthew, the angel of the Lord appears to Joseph in a dream to urge him to take Mary into his home as his wife, for she will bear a son who *will save his people from their sins* (Mt 1:18-24).

Supposedly, it is God who provides magi from the east with a sign where Jesus will be born to render him homage (Mt 2:1-2). When the child is born the angel of the Lord again appears, this time before shepherds, to announce to them that *in the city of David a savior has been born for you who is Messiah and Lord* (Lk 2:8-18). Not aware of the threat Herod poses to the baby, the angel warns the new family urging them to flee to Egypt (Mt 2:13-14, 19-22). Later, when presenting the child in the Temple, God reveals to the righteous the expectations he has placed on Jesus (Lk 2:27-32, 36-38). Then, once Jesus is set to begin his public mission, God's voice is heard saying that he is well pleased in Jesus, his beloved son (Mk 1:10-11, Lk 3:21-22, Mt 3:16-17).

When Jesus is *led by the Spirit* into the desert to be tempted by the devil, angels are present to comfort him (Mt 4:1, 11). At the time he is brought before Pontius Pilate, Jesus tells him that he could ask God to provide him with twelve legions of angels to save him from being executed (Mt 26:52-54). Thus, God's actions taking the utmost care of his son resembles his involvement in the Old Testament.

Considering these events, Jesus's crucifixion appears as a devastating jolt to human understanding. Despite praying to the Father to spare him from the ordeal that awaits him (Mk 14:36, Lk 22:42, Mt 26:39-42), God suddenly seems to abandon him; at least that is how Jesus felt (Lk 23:46). Attempts to render plausible human explanations fail. Skeptics might think that none of the above ever takes place since they are all mythical supernatural events used by the authors to color the life of Jesus. Believers, however, would not find a contradiction in this narrative, believing that it gives credence to the mission God assigns Jesus. which includes his death. It is Jesus, however, who prophesizes his own death. Nowhere does it show in the Gospels that God or the angel of the Lord suggests that Jesus would be or ought to be crucified.

It is Jesus, nonetheless, who provides the strongest arguments supporting the existence of divine providence. The first indication that God is not an alien god, but instead is truly engaged with his creatures, is Jesus's insistence on the efficacy of prayer. After all, why teach his followers to pray to God unless he knows that God will listen and reply in kind? Jesus's most powerful statement in this regard is found in all four Gospels: *all that you ask for in prayer, believe that you will receive it* (Lk 11:5-13, Mk 11:24, Mt 7:7-11, Jn 16:23).

To make his point, Jesus seems to exaggerate when he says, whoever says to this mountain, *'Be lifted up and thrown into the sea,' and does not doubt in his heart but believes that what he says will happen, it shall be done for him* (Mk 11:23, Mt 17:20-21, 21:21). Jesus leaves no room for doubt; a good father will not hand his child a scorpion when he asks for an egg. His belief in prayer seems absolute.

He instructs his followers to pray to God for his kingdom to come, for their daily bread, to forgive their sins, for protection against the final test, for one's enemies, and for those that persecute them (Lk 11:1-3, 6:28, Mt 6:9-13, 5:44). They are to pray to have the strength *to escape the tribulations that are imminent* (Lk

21:36). He prays to the Father to keep his disciples united and away from the evil one, and for unity among all that will believe in him (Jn 17:11-26). He promises that hell will not triumph over his church (Mt 16:18). Nonetheless, despite Jesus's reassurances, an extended examination of history may easily suggest that divine providence does not operate in the manner Jesus described it. Today, his church is divided; the kingdom of God lacks credibility in the eyes of the world; enemies are not being forgiven; persecutions continue; tribulations are daily occurrences; moral relativism has set in, and many still lack bread.

The texts are ambiguous regarding how providence operates. Jesus tells the crowd not to be afraid of being killed; instead, they should be concerned about the one that can cast them into hell (the devil). Since in the eyes of God human beings are worth more than many sparrows, Jesus suggests that God will shield them from harm, although the texts do not explain what God means by *harm* (Lk 12:4-9, Mt 10:28-31).

Another indication of divine providence looking after all people (or only after those that believe) is that a loving God knows our needs and is delighted to satisfy them. Thus, in an extensive passage, Jesus tells the crowds that God loves them more than the birds in the sky or flowers and grasses in the field. Hence, they ought not to worry about what to eat or drink but merely seek his kingdom and their needs will be fulfilled (Lk 12:22-34, Mt 6:25-34). Even the smallest things, he says, are beyond our control (Lk 12:26), in which case there is no need to be concerned. He tells the crowd why *work for food that perishes* when instead we ought to focus on *the food that endures for eternal life, which the Son of Man will give you* (Jn 6:27)?

The Catechism maintains that God *does not abandon his creatures to themselves… but gives them being and existence, and at every moment, he upholds and sustains them in being, enables them to act, and brings them to their final end.*[9] The proposition that regardless of whatever evil may happen to humans God will not abandon them, requires, at least, a redefinition of the term abandonment. If the term implies that no matter the state of disarray in the world, and what humanity has had to go through in past centuries, God will be waiting at the end to ensure a joyful ending following the resurrection, then it might be possible to consider that God does not abandon his creatures. As for the wisdom through which God operates on earth, we may say that human reason (a reflection of God) cannot even attempt to understand it.

Jesus's Parables and Divine Providence
Some of Jesus's parables provide conflicting views on divine providence. Supposedly, God operates through the kingdom that Jesus initiates. This kingdom is like a mustard seed that once sown, *it springs up and becomes the largest of plants and puts forth large branches* (Mk 4:30-32). The Parable of the Growing Seed is even more explicit. According to this parable, God's kingdom works its way without human intervention. Once God scatters the seed, it sprouts and grows *of its own accord.* (Mk 4:26-29). Relying on contemporary phrasing, the kingdom of God is like a sailing vessel with a Global Positioning System (GPS) that operates according to the commands that God

has uploaded into its central processing unit (CPU). Theoretically, if anything alters God's course on account of free will and sin, the GPS will correct itself allowing the vessel to continue to its established end. Since God has properly programmed the GPS, there ought to be no need to pray, even during a hurricane. Placing extraordinary trust in God, the believer will not act like the fearful disciples who feel they are going to capsize but instead will remain calm and enjoy the journey.

Nonetheless, there will be persecutions, and Jesus tells his disciples not to worry about their defense since the Holy Spirit will be present to protect them (Mk 13:9-11, Lk 12:11-12, 21:12-15, Mt 10:16-20), *and not a hair will be destroyed* (Lk 21:18). He will send the Spirit of truth to guide them and prevent misunderstandings (Jn 16:12-13). The historical record, filled with wars, persecutions, greed, famine, and confusing shades of truth that have arisen, suggests either that humanity has not been cognizant of the Spirit or that the Spirit has not made its presence strongly felt.

The Parable of the Weed among the Wheat provides a different aspect of divine providence (Mt 13:24-30). In this parable Jesus seems to suggest that divine providence has only a single function, to sustain the land while a variety of malevolent occurrences take place. This reasoning is similar to the definition provided above by the Catholic Catechism that God provides his creatures only with *being and existence*. Prayer might be useful although its efficacy may be questioned; the Spirit is present, but it will not succor those in need or become more involved in human affairs; good and evil will continue to coexist until God determines he has seen enough of his experiment and decides to take more active participation in human affairs.

There is one difficulty with interpreting this parable as a manifestation of divine providence. Who or what is Jesus referring to as the weed? Likely, it has to do with human sin. According to Jesus, there is evil in the world, e.g., greed, coldness of heart, and selfishness, because humanity has been unwilling (or not able) to adopt God's way. The problem is that God's way, even under the best of circumstances and good intentions, appears on earth in a variety of colors; there are different religious faiths, different moral philosophies as well as a wide assortment of Christian beliefs, all vying for credible primacy. Thus, the combination of evil and sin and the inevitability of religious pluralism and moral relativism that surge from flawed human understanding (even among the wisest of beings), creates a pernicious type of weed that cannot (and probably will not) be easily eradicated barring the manifestation of objective, i.e., supernatural, phenomena.

In the Parable of the Sower (Mk 4:3-20, Lk 8:4-14, Mt 13:3-23), Jesus explains that God's action in the world is limited to spreading the word while it is up to each person to respond. There is in this parable, however, a degree of unpredictability in human activity that goes beyond free will, thereby questioning a basic premise in the Christian concept of divine providence. None of the first three groups of people are evil; they become evil because their soil, i.e., their psychological make-up is weak or disinterested in God's teachings. The fourth group is fortunate to have rich soil, so the word of God leads to a fruitful outcome. But what accounts for the personality differences in these groups? Are there random acts, or does God dispenses his grace unequally? How does God order things to work toward his beneficent end in these cases? Only by accepting divine providence as a mystery may humans understand (or not) its meaning.

God Works in Mysterious Ways

Christian theology suggests that it is God's purview to ordain humanity toward a benevolent end, including his prerogative to hide things *from the wise and the learned* while revealing them to the childlike (Lk 10:21-22, Mt 11:25-27). The remark suggests that Jesus's teachings will bear fruit only among the naïve and the credulous, i.e., those that do not rely on critical thinking. Since moral truth is at stake in a convoluted world full of pretentious messiahs, encouraging this type of behavior might not be the best antidote to combat falsehood.

Additionally, Jesus favors granting some people the mysteries of the kingdom while denying them to others, so they will *look but not see and hear but not understand.* Jesus is probably referring to people exemplifying a combination of fatuousness, stubbornness, and pride; people who believe they have attained moral perfection and even thank God for it (Lk 18:9-14). But if their attitude is sinful, there are likely psychological elements that might explain their behavior, most likely insecurity, fear, and a grotesque sense of pride. These are people who would seem to need God the most. Hence, why would God deny them (in advance) the opportunity to become rich soil? Does Jesus not say that he comes for the sick instead of those who are healthy? How much more affected can these people be?

Jesus remarks that only by remaining in him will humankind be able to do good, *because without me you can do nothing* (Jn 15:1-7). He seems to indicate that providence can only work through him, a view that appears to contradict God's love for all his creatures. His remark poses the question of whether Jesus (and Christians) would recognize Christian-like deeds done by a secularized world, despite having been raised in non-Christian faiths or having no faith, or if they *will be thrown out like a branch and wither* into a fire where they will burn (Jn 15:6). At a time of religious conflicts and ecumenical efforts to create a common (universal) core of values and attitudes, this question becomes highly relevant.

Limitations to Understanding Divine Providence

Given that humanity must coexist with good and evil until the end of time, it appears that God is unwilling to go beyond upholding and sustaining it. It suggests that the combination of the Parables of the Growing Seed, the Mustard Seed, the Weed among the Wheat, and the Sower, offers a more realistic vision of how divine providence operates. Divine providence appears as a religious attempt to provide a modicum of understanding regarding two inimical forces, *good* and *evil* that are in contention with each other, in which God is never wrong regardless of how dreadful conditions on earth become.

Neither the physical nor the social sciences have advanced enough to provide a cause-effect explanation about a conflict that has characterized humans probably since they first appeared on earth. The vagueness of the term *divine providence* satisfies the senses of the religious-minded because of its mysterious simplicity, and because it eases the difficulty of conceiving human existence arising out of nothingness.

Jesus states that God's kingdom grows through divine providence without human intervention, suggesting that growth will continue until it reaches its perfection. Nonetheless, do the Gospels offer concrete indicators both of its growth and its realization? We may surmise that the most visible sign would be the eventual overpowering of evil; good being defined in terms of lasting peace, happiness, material and spiritual fulfillment through caring, compassion, and understanding, and the acknowledgment that eternal salvation comes through Jesus as the Son of God.

If these signs are accepted, it may be safely assumed that the end is not imminent; not until the Divine takes more forceful action in human affairs to remedy earthly ills without having to punish the innocent. In the meantime, life on earth, permeated by the good/evil conflict, will continue its unknown path affected by a mixture of human passion, rationality, technological and scientific development, and fractured religious beliefs. Otherwise, asking believers to accept a vague concept that is simply irreconcilable with the historical record might be too much to ask of empirically minded non-Christians. Christianity, meanwhile, has no alternative but to encapsulate the concept in mystery because it refuses to accept randomness in the universe, a view that would deny God a part of his absolute jurisdiction. However, for the non-Christian and the non-believer, it might be easier to accept a God that expresses regret at making human creatures and constantly alters courses depending on human action, as it occurs in the Old Testament.

Notes:
1. Although the same passages in other Bible versions do not use the term *providence,* their substance is similar. (Job 10:12 in NEs and New King James Version). The Book of Wisdom does not appear in Protestant versions of the Bible as it is considered of dubious origin, or likely not being divinely inspired. The term *Providence,* however, may appear as a title or subtitle to a particular chapter throughout the Bible, but it is not tallied because it is not part of the original passage. Contrast Psalm 33:1 in NEs and NKJV in BibleGateway.com.
2. *Merriam-Webster Dictionary, Cambridge Dictionary, Oxford Dictionary,* online, s.v. "providence."
3. Throughout history, even pagan religions have accepted some form of divine providence. Leslie Walker, "Divine Providence." *Catholic Encyclopedia,* Vol. 12. www.newadvent.org/cathen/12510a.htm (accessed July 16, 2019).
4. Ibid.
5. CCC 321.
6. Ibid., 302. The Catechism quotes from Vatican Council I, *Dei Filius* 1: DS 3003: *By his providence God protects and governs all things which he has made, "reaching mightily from one end of the earth to the other, and ordering all things well".* Empirical reasoning would require clarification regarding the phrase *ordering all things well.*
7. Ibid., 309-314.
8. There have been Christian religious and political leaders that, relying on the Old Testament, accept the premise that God punishes humans for their iniquities, including the innocent. Warren J, Blumenfeld,

"God and Natural Disasters: It's the Gays Fault?" *Huffpost.com.* February 2, 2016. https://www.huffpost.com/entry/god-and-natural-disasters-its-the-gays-fault_b_2068817 (accessed July 18, 2019); John Gallagher, Chris Bull, *Perfect Enemies: The Religious Right, the Gay Movement, and the Politics of the 1990s,* Chapter 1, *The Washington Post,* 1996. https://www.washingtonpost.com/wp-srv/style/longterm/books/chap1/perfectenemies.htm?noredirect=on (accessed July 18, 2019). The view that natural disasters, such as the fourteenth-century Black Death plague, constitute God's punishment for human sin has prevailed throughout Christian history, even though this notion has been rejected by the Church's hierarchy.

9. CCC 299-301.

Predestination

Did Jesus's redemptive death open the gates of heaven for all, for many, or did he die only for the few that may have been predestined to be saved? The question is pertinent to Christianity's claim about the universality of its mission. Unfortunately, the answer is ambiguous, and it depends not only on what each denomination decrees but on the words of Jesus himself, according to the authors of the Gospels.

Content analysis results indicate that the Gospels have little to say about *Predestination.* The category does not rank high; it is among the least significant as well as among the most controversial terms in the scriptures. Christian denominations have originated on account of this word, even though it only appears twice in the Bible (Rom 8:29-30).[1] There are, however, other words that show up in the texts conveying its general meaning. The term is intriguing because of its close association with philosophical terms, such as predeterminism, determinism, indeterminism, free will, and freedom, all of which add to its interest in political philosophy, psychology, and theology, among other branches of knowledge.

In this section, predestination is defined in broad terms to suggest various connotations that the casual reader of the scriptures may notice. Generally, it refers to actions that, according to Jesus, God has taken toward specific people that affect their salvation. This section, however, does not deal with the fulfillment of prophecies in the Bible as examples of predeterminism. The focus is on human salvation; the main questions leading the examination of this term being, whether God preordains or predestines who shall be saved and who shall be condemned, on account or irrespective of their actions, sins, and beliefs.

What does Jesus mean when he speaks about *the chosen* and *the elect*? If God predestines some humans but not others, is there anything anyone can do to alter God's decisions? Do passages in the Bible point to the possibility of human free will (regardless of whether it exists or not).

According to the *Catholic Encyclopedia,* predestination refers to the process by which *owing to His infallible prescience of the future, [God] has appointed and ordained from eternity all events occurring in time, especially those which directly proceed from, or at least are influenced by man's free will.*[2] This definition is more specific than anything provided by the *Catholic Catechism.*[3] Its puzzling feature is that it affirms human free will without contradicting God's predetermined actions.

The belief in predestination arises, not only from certain passages in the Gospels and Paul, but also because of the *a priori* theological belief in a God that, representing absolute perfection, e. g., omnipotence, and omniscience, cannot entertain the possibility of changing his mind or not being able to anticipate the future. The scriptures, however, are filled with examples indicating that God is not concerned with anticipating the future. He changes his mind constantly, depending on the outcome of his plans. In Genesis, God regrets making human beings and decides to wipe out the human race from the earth (6:6-7); then, he changes his mind and promises to himself not to curse his creatures or *strike down every living being as I have done* (8:21). Moreover, throughout the Old Testament, he makes promises to the Israelites but alters them according with their behavior.

The terms *chosen* and *the elect*, both of which provide credence to predestination in the New Testament, are used differently in the Old Testament. In both cases, the words suggest a form of divine nepotism; an omnipotent right that is, nevertheless, highly disliked in secular society, possibly even by believers. In the Old Testament, the term *chosen* implies temporality or worldliness and supposes human free will. God chooses the Israelites as his people, not knowing whether they will obey him or not, and allows them the opportunity to repent (Deut 7:6, 14:2). He chooses Abram to lead his people (Gen 12:1), then Moses (Ex 3:7-22), David (I Kings 8:16), Jacob (Is 44:1), King Cyrus, a non-Jew (Isa 45:1), all for temporal tasks, some of whom make enormous misdeeds and are still hailed as righteous. Eventually, God chooses Jesus to install his kingdom on earth (Mt 12:18) and makes Jerusalem the center of the promised land (1 Kings 11:32). Even in Psalms, God holds people accountable for their wickedness, thus presupposing their free will (Psalm 92.8).

In the New Testament, the term *chosen* acquires a supernatural dimension, as it relates to eternal salvation (Lk 18:7, Mt 22:14, Romans 8:33). It expresses a new form of divine predilection; this time not toward the Israelites, but to those whom God (*who is the immediate cause of the new spiritual life*)[4] has chosen to believe in him (Jn 1:12-13); even though the light Jesus represents is supposed to enlighten everyone (Jn 1:9). That God may now seem to favor some over others is implied in Paul too, when he says that God chooses those who would believe in Jesus *before the foundation of the world* (Ephes 1:3-5); although, perhaps, he is trying to say that God knew ahead of time who would accept or reject God's grace. Somehow, in philosophy and theology, it appears that God's omniscience leads inexorably to some form of predestination.

At times, the Gospels convey the impression that God predetermines human events. If indeed, this is the case, the human drama is nothing more than God's scripted film of inevitable events produced and directed by a divine sovereign for his enjoyment. There would be no mystery regarding the ending (except for human beings); for God, it would be like watching the premiere of his movie.

Whether God's predeterminism negates free will or not may not present a social and behavioral problem. Even if there is no free will, and human freedom is no more than an illusion, it is to the credit of humankind to have created the concept as necessary to hold people accountable for transgressing laws and norms without which civilized society might not be possible. The presence of free will, on the other hand, would not contradict God's omniscience. Omniscience would allow him to realize who will freely respond to his love and who will reject it. In other words, the term does not necessarily lead to predestination.

Nonetheless, the term had been confusing for a long time, finding among its supporters St Augustine because he used the term *predestination* in his writings.[5] It was only a matter of time that the view that God preordains human life would lead to particular interpretations that would run afoul of the Catholic hierarchy. At the time of the Reformation, the Catholic hierarchy chose (or perhaps it was predetermined by God) to articulate a simplistic end to the philosophical and theological morass the term *predestination* created by referring to it as a *divine secret mystery* at the Council of Trent in the sixteenth century.[6]

Although Martin Luther and Ulrich Zwingli are among the forerunners of the Protestant version of predestination, it is John Calvin who takes the term to a most extreme form. He concludes that if God knows even the number of hairs in one's head (Mt 10:30), he must certainly know everything else (which seems logical). Calvin then makes an enormous leap while relying on the Gospels. Nothing happens, he says, that God not only knows but also has *willingly decreed.*[7] Hence, everything in heaven and earth is *so governed as to move exactly in the course which he has destined.*[8] Predestination according to Calvin refers to,

> the eternal decree of God, by which he determined with himself whatever he wished to happen with regard to every man. All are not created on equal terms, but some are preordained to eternal life, others to eternal damnation; and, accordingly, as each has been created for one or other of these ends, we say that he has been predestinated to life or to death.[9]

Although Calvin relies on St Augustine for his views on predestination,[10] whether he misinterprets Augustine (as the Catholic hierarchy has maintained),[11] is irrelevant for purposes of this examination. Augustine deals with the term, perhaps without fully knowing its profound impact at the time, although there are clues that free will prevails in his thoughts. On his part, Augustine leans on Paul who himself uses similar language in some of his letters, but without adding clarity to the term.[12] In what might be Paul's best exposition of the term, he says in his Letter to the Romans:

> We know that all things work for good for those who love God who are called according to his purpose. For those he foreknew he also predestined to be conformed to the image of his Son, so that he might be the firstborn among many brothers. And those he predestined he also called; and those he called he also justified; and those he justified he also glorified (Rom 8:28-30).

Paul uses the words *chose us in him before the foundation of the world; in love he destined us for adoption and those he predestined.* It is unclear whether those whom Paul addresses refer to humanity or only to those that God knows would respond to his grace since the beginning; at first glance, it appears that it is the latter. Thus, if God can choose, ordain before time, or preordain that some people receive his love and his grace, logically others do not, which means that there are *elected* people who will be saved and *non-elected* people that will not. Paul finds support for this view in Isaiah through whom God says,

> *At the beginning I declare the outcome; from of old, things not yet done. I say that my plan shall stand, I accomplish my every desire. I summon from the east a bird of prey, from a distant land, one to carry out my plan. Yes, I have spoken, I will accomplish it; I have planned it, and I will do it (Is 46:10-11).*

To minimize or eradicate confusion and the stigma arising from thinking that God willfully preordains some people to be condemned, the Catholic hierarchy since Trent has utilized the term *predestination* selectively to refer to those whom God has chosen to inherit his kingdom (the elect), and the word *reprobation*, to refer to those who (through their own fault according to the hierarchy) are predestined to be damned. [13] Nonetheless, since reprobation is part of God's foreordained plan, it follows that God has predestined some people to be condemned, although supposedly through their fault.

Predestination in the Gospels
What do the Gospels, and namely Jesus, say about predestination? In terms of predestining the salvation or condemnation of humans, the record in the Gospels is filled with incongruities; some passages or words suggest that the elect (or chosen) are foreordained while in other instances it is the opposite. For example, the elect are those (whoever they may be) that will be saved. But from the standpoint of the Old Testament, it is clear that the Israelites are God's chosen people, at least from the beginning of time. Whether symbolically or literally interpreted, even some Christian denominations admit that God promises Abraham to be the *father of a great people* (the Israelites) that eventually will include Gentiles. [14]

Hence, it is to be expected that if the gathering of the Israelites as the people of God is preordained, they will be saved. The Old Testament, however, indicates that God's people consistently sin and show their unfaithfulness against him, suggesting that their actions work against God's plans. Thus, there appears to be free will in these instances and, if so, God's people stand to be condemned. But despite their actions, the Catholic hierarchy affirms that God never stops saving the Israelite people and pardoning them; his love *will be victorious over even the worst infidelities.* [15] These words render the impression that God predetermines initial events even if events do not go as planned, Somehow, God will upset free will and prevail in order to make

Gentiles his other chosen people. All this is supposed to have been preordained; and yes, it is that confusing.

The first signs of predestination or divine predeterminism in the Gospels may be seen in John's Gospel. At the beginning of time, Jesus is already with God; God preordains that all things come through Jesus and that nothing shall occur without him (Jn 1:1-4, 17:24). All who accept Jesus become children of God *not by natural generation nor by human choice nor by a man's decision but of God* (Jn 1:12-13). Jesus confirms John's narrative as he preaches to a crowd of Jews telling them, *No one can come to me unless the Father who sent me draws him* (Jn 6:44, 65 emphasis mine), suggesting that it is God who gives faith to whomever he wishes. He reiterates this view to a group of Jewish religious authorities that gather in the temple area in Jerusalem (Jn 10:29), and in his prayer to the Father in which he gives thanks for those followers the Father gives to him (Jn 17:2, 6, 11).

Jesus begins to predict his death (and resurrection), suggesting that it has been preordained by God (Mk 14:35-36, Lk 22:40-42, Mt 26:42, Jn 18:11), so that scriptures may be fulfilled (Mk 14:49, Lk 18:31, Mt 26:54-56); and that his suffering and death are necessary (Lk 24:26-27) as a ransom for many (Mt 20:28). If these passages are broadly interpreted, we might conclude that Jesus may lack free will to act differently. On its part, the Catholic Catechism does not shy away from using the term *predestination* to signify that, as part of his plan, God preordains undesirable outcomes to happen (Jesus's crucifixion) to fulfill a positive end.[16]

There are passages in the Gospels that relate to the predestination of human beings, namely some of Jesus's parables describing the kingdom of God. In Mark, Jesus suggests that God's kingdom is like a seed that grows of itself after the man scatters it throughout the land. The next day the seed somehow sprouts and grows, and *of its own accord* (without human intervention)[17] *the land yields fruit* (Mk 4:26-29). Jesus then follows with a similar parable suggesting that the kingdom of God grows on its own, like a mustard seed (Mk 4:30-32, Lk 13:18-19, Mt 13:31-32). In another instance, he likens the kingdom of God to yeast that, when mixed with wheat, leavens the dough (Lk 13:20-21, Mt 13:33). In the parable of the Weeds Among the Wheat Jesus suggests that the kingdom of God operates according to its own laws, only requiring passive human action until harvest time (Mt 13:24-30). Within the context of the eschatological kingdom of God, everything seems to have been pre-planned; humans do not appear to have much control (if any) in their destinies.

Responding to two of his disciples, the sons of the Zebedee, who would like first row seats in paradise, Jesus indicates that such decisions are not his to make but is *for those for whom it has been prepared by my Father* (Mt 20:23, Mk 10:35-40). On another occasion, while discussing future tribulations, Jesus refers to *the elect* twice as being those that the Lord (God) has chosen. Immediately following, he indicates that on his second coming, it is he who will ask his angels *to gather* [God's] *elect from the four winds, from the end of the earth to the end of the sky* (Mk 13:14-27, Mt 24:15-

31). In another passage, Jesus suggests that God will promptly secure *the rights of his chosen ones* (Lk 18:1-8). He seems to affirm predeterminism when he tells his disciples not to worry about any aspect of their lives since *even the smallest things are beyond* [their] *control.* (Lk 12:24-28). The above passages suggest that human destiny already has been pre-arranged, as has been Jesus's incarnation, death, and resurrection. Taken literally (as God's revelation) these passages indicate that human events are predetermined to the point that the divine controls human conduct, thus rendering free will unsustainable. The impression left on the reader is that God elects or chooses some people to be saved but not others, without providing any explanation other than his desire. These passages, despite how logically unpleasant and bizarre they seem, represent an attempt to solve a dilemma that Jesus's words appear to have created: the need to reconcile the idea of free will and predestination with the concepts of a sovereign and omniscient God.

Is There Free Will in the Gospels?
The term free will does not appear in the Gospels, and Jesus never mentions it; or does he? If predestination of humans is accepted, indicating that the elect and the non-elect already have been chosen, Jesus's duty to spread God's message is superfluous. That is, why would God send his son on a mission to save the world in which he would spend countless days and nights teaching repentance, praying, forgiveness, and love, all of which indicate free will, if it would not alter human behavior?

Why would Jesus say that he *did not come to call the righteous but sinners* (Mk 2:17, Lk 5:32) if it were not for sinners to repent, i.e., to change their behavior? Why would he teach about the importance of prayer to avoid temptation? Is it not part of Jesus's mission to redeem? Is not that the reason he must die? Predestination suggests that Jesus's crucifixion is in vain since he dies for those that God has already predestined to be saved. Yet, despite Jesus being the main protagonist in God's film, his actions are to save people that otherwise would not be saved. Accordingly, any type of appeal he makes to others to change their behavior presupposes that a modicum of free will exists in humans even if a degree of spiritual coercion is present.

If we were to include the Repentance, Prayer, Baptism, Forgiveness, and Love categories (all of which suggest behavioral change) into a new category, it would undermine the concept of predestination. Telling the crowds that all they ask for in prayer and with faith shall be granted (Mk 11:24, Mt 21:22), suggests that it is possible to change God's attitude; a*sk and you will receive; seek and you will find; knock and the door will be opened to you* (Lk 11:9-13, Mt 7:7-11). But why should the non-elect ask or knock if nothing will be given to them and the door will not be opened? Besides, how do the non-elect know that they are not among the chosen? The concept contradicts the Lord's Prayer that asks God that which is not yet foreordained.

Jesus's parables indicating that there is more joy in heaven over one sinner who repents than over ninety-nine righteous people who do not need repentance (Lk 15:7, 10) makes sense only if salvation is not predestined. Going into the world proclaiming the gospel to every creature (Mk 16:15-16) knowing that it would not lead to a productive outcome constitutes Christianity's greatest misuse of time and resources.

The terms *repentance* and *praying* also would seem to contradict predestination; they suggest that change is possible. Repentance entails the willful change of behavior in real-time. If God already knows who is going to repent, what is the use in asking his son to teach conversion of heart? When Jesus asks the crowd to pray to the Father, is there a possibility that God may alter his preordained plan?

Passages in which John the Baptist appears in the desert yelling, *prepare the way of the Lord, make straight his paths*, proclaim the need to repent and ask for forgiveness (Mk 1:2-4, Mt 3:1-3). What is John's purpose in paving the way for Jesus? Isaiah's prophecy that *all flesh shall see the salvation of God* (Lk 3:3-6) seems meaningless given predestination. Jesus's teaching on Judgment Day would be anti-climactic, an absurd parade unrelated to the content of the passage that deals with a choice of behavior. Predestination would be nothing more than a project illustrating God's whimsical majesty rather than an act of justice and mercy.

And Then There is Satan

There is still the question of how does Satan fit with God's plan? Is the devil a predestined anomaly? According to Christian theology, the devil enjoyed sufficient free will to reject God. If the devil is predestined to do evil, Jesus cannot claim to have defeated him. Moreover, it seems that it is God who allows the devil to tempt humans. In such cases, God determines how narrow the gate is through which we must enter, and how many will be chosen (Mt 22:14). From this perspective, predestination is the concept that most closely resembles an exclusive country club since most humans seem to be preordained to follow Satan.

Notes:

1. Some non-Catholic versions include two additional instances, (Eph 1:5, 11) while others do not include any. *BibleGateway.com.*
2. Joseph Pohle, "Predestination," CE Vol. 12. http://www.newadvent.org/cathen/12378a.htm (accessed June 13, 2019).
3. The *Catechism* pays negligible attention to this concept. It states that God *establishes his eternal plan of predestination"* with his plan of salvation (a confusing definition); CCC 600. The catechism also quotes Rom 8:28-30, CCC 2012.
4. NEs' note, John 1:13.
5. Says Augustine: *But that what was hidden may come to light, and what was unpleasant may be made agreeable, is of the grace of God which helps the wills of men; and that they are not helped by it, has its cause likewise in themselves, not in God, whether they be predestinated to condemnation, on account of the iniquity of their pride or whether they are to be judged and disciplined contrary to their very pride if they are children of mercy.... Now this same Lord of ours has never yet refused, at any period of the human race, nor to the last judgment will He ever refuse, this His healing to those whom, in His most sure foreknowledge and future loving-kindness, He has predestinated to reign with Himself to life eternal.* Augustine of Hippo, *On Merit and the Forgiveness of Sins, and the Baptism of Infants,* Trans. Peter Holmes and Robert Ernest Wallis, and revised by Benjamin B. Warfield. Book II, Chapter 26, 47. Nicene and Post-Nicene Fathers, First Series, Vol. 5. Edited by Philip Schaff. (Buffalo, NY: Christian Literature Publishing Co., 1887). http://www.newadvent.org/fathers/1501.htm (accessed June 12, 2019). Emphasis mine.
6. *The Council of Trent,* Chapter XII. http://www.thecounciloftrent.com/ch6.htm (accessed June 18, 2019).

7. John Calvin, *The Institutes of the Christian Religion,* (1509-1564) trans. Henry Beveridge (Grand Rapids, MI: Christian Classics Ethereal Library, 1845). Book First, Chapter 16, par. 3. http://www.ccel.org/ccel/calvin/institutes.pdf?url= (accessed June 12, 2019).

8. Ibid., Book First, Chapter 16, p. 8.

9. Ibid., Book Third, Chapter 21, p. 5.

10. Ibid., Book First, Chapter 16, par. 8.

11. Pohle.

12. *Paul, an apostle of Christ Jesus by the will of God* (Col 1:1); *giving thanks to the Father, who has made you* (Colossian disciples) fit *to share in the inheritance of the holy ones in light* (Col 1:12); *But now it has been manifested to his holy ones, to whom <u>God chose</u> to make known the riches of the glory of this mystery among the Gentiles* (Col 1:26-27); *Blessed be the God and Father of our Lord Jesus Christ, who has blessed us in Christ with every spiritual blessing in the heavens, as <u>he chose us in him</u>, before the foundation of the world, to be holy and without blemish before him. In love <u>he destined us</u> for adoption to himself through Jesus Christ, in accord with the favor of his will* (Eph 1:3-6)... Emphasis mine.

Moreover, it is interesting that NEs use the phrase *destined us for adoption*; all other 27 English translations show either *predestined, foreordained, had already decided,* or *in advance.* https://biblehub.com/ephesians/1-5.htm. The Jerusalem Bible translates the phrase as *determining that we should become his adopted son.*

13. Pohle, Par. "Notion of Predestination."

14. *The remote preparation for this gathering together of the People of God begins when* [God] *calls Abraham and promises that he will become the father of a great people. Its immediate preparation begins with Israel's election as the People of God.... They would be the root on to which the Gentiles would be grafted, once they came to believe.* CCC 762, 64.

15. Ibid., 218, 219.

16. Ibid., 599, 600. Furthermore, when the Catechism states that God has *adopted us as his children* (2782), it suggests that *us* means humanity (redemption), although it may be referring only to those who have accepted Jesus in faith.

17. NEs' note, Mark 4:26-29.

Repentance

In Christianity, repentance is the first step on the path to eternal salvation. *There will be rejoicing among the angels of God over one sinner who repents,* Jesus tells the crowd (Lk 15:10). In the Gospels, John the Baptist and Jesus begin their public mission with a call for repentance for the forgiveness of sins (Lk 3:3, Mt 4:17). In the content analysis results, *repentance* scores slightly lower than the significant categories, appearing 23xt in the four Gospels. Luke uses it more often (13xt) than Matthew (7xt) and Mark (3xt), although in all three synoptics the term distinctively signifies acknowledgment of sin and a call for change in behavior.

On the other hand, there is no reference to repentance in John's Gospel, although some passages allude to the action. For example, the Baptist makes a call to straighten one's life in accordance with Mosaic Law (Jn 1:22-23); Jesus stresses the need to be reborn from above by accepting him (Jn 3:3-18); baptism, along with consuming Jesus's flesh and blood, become the external symbols of rebirth (Jn 3:22-24, 6:53-59).

Repentance in the Old Testament

As significant as repentance is in the Christian faith, it does not appear to be as relevant in the Hebrew Bible as it is in the New Testament. The term shows up fewer times relative to the size of the texts, and readings of passages suggest that God did not require the Jewish people to repent of their sins. It was the priest who asked for forgiveness on behalf of the person or the community, although people's offerings at the Temple were symbolic of atonement for their sins. More often, it is God who repents from punishing his people by establishing new covenants or by being gracious toward the Israelites despite their transgressions (Deut 30:1-10). Their prophets and leaders, whether Abraham, Moses, Joshua, or Solomon repented on behalf of their people by praying for forgiveness (e.g., Num 21:17, Deut 9:25-27). In David's case, he repented for his misdeeds by asking God for forgiveness (e.g., Psalm 51:1).

Repentance in the Gospels
In the Gospels, repentance signifies recognition of individual wrongdoing and the willingness to become openly righteous. Christian repentance is similar to its temporal or secular meaning: *to feel regret or contrition for misdeeds to the point whereby the person decides to turn around his or her life.*[1] Only through repentance God forgives the believer. It is then that faith acquires its true meaning (Lk 3:8-9). Without sincere repentance, Jesus would find expressions of love of God and forgiveness of others to be wanting or even hypocritical.

As his teachings indicate that eternal life is a reward for good behavior (Mk 1:4, 1:14-15, 6:12, 16:15-16, Lk 1:17, 3:3, 24:47, Mt 3:1-3, 4:17, Jn 1:22-23), there can be no salvation without repentance. Jesus's insistence (and the Baptist's) on repentance presumes that all humanity is sinful, hence in need of individual repentance from their sins. However, if Jesus maintains that he comes to call on sinners, not on the righteous (Mk 2:13-17, Lk 5:32, Mt 9:13), who then is righteous? Noticing that he seeks primarily the company of sinners, e.g., tax collectors and prostitutes, among others, it may be assumed that those who follow Mosaic Law are among the righteous. Yet he is critical of the religious authorities for strictly following (albeit hypocritically) the Law. Moreover, Jesus soon begins to change Mosaic Law, despite the Jewish people had been observing it for thousands of years. We may surmise that the real sinners are those who willfully reject Jesus, as indicated by his reproach of unbelieving towns (Lk 10:101-6, Mt 11:20-24). What the Gospels do not explain is the extent to which these people refuse to repent precisely because of Jesus's radical modifications of the Law.

As Jesus preaches to the crowd about God's joy when sinners repent (Lk 15:1-7, Mt 18:12-14), we come to an intriguing passage: there will be more joy in heaven over one sinner who repents than over ninety-nine righteous people who do not need repentance. It suggests that the number of righteous people in the world surpasses sinners (in which case the gate is not so narrow).[2] He reiterates the same teaching in the Parable of the Lost Coin (Lk 15:8-10) and the Parable of the Lost Son (Lk 15:11-32). The Gospels do not indicate how many people Jesus converted, but judging by the sizable crowds that were baptized, many heeded the call (Mk 1:5, Lk 3:7, 10-12, 7:29-30, Mt 3:5-6, Jn 3:22).

Interestingly, repentance indicates that humanity has in its hands the possibility of being forgiven (once they repent); that it is not only up to God to grant salvation

(Mt 19:25-26), but up to humans too. That is, if God issues the call for salvation through repentance, he is obliged to follow through on his word if people reply to his call. This view would seem to leave out the *chosen* that the Gospels refer to on occasions.

At times, however, Jesus's teachings lack clarity. Jesus's assertion (particularly in John) that only those who accept him and/or are baptized (a minority of humanity) will be saved, seems to indicate that the number of people who will enjoy eternal life might be much less than God desires; again, this would indicate that the gate is much narrower than initially thought. Hence, it would be up to God's mercy to override human limitations if more people are to be saved. However, once Jesus tells his disciples to spread his message, he marginalizes ninety-nine percent of humanity when he tells them not to go into pagan territory or Samaritan towns, but *to the lost sheep of the house of Israel* (Mt 10:5-6). Thus, insofar as the word is not being preached to non-Jews, how could they possibly repent?[3] His remark becomes even more puzzling once we read that Jesus derides non-Jews: *If a church brother refuses to acknowledge his wrongdoing, then treat him as you would a Gentile* (Mt 18:17), suggesting an uninterested attitude on his part to save those that constitute most of the world's population at the time.[4] This is surprising since Jesus ministers to non-Jews, such as a Roman centurion, a Canaanite woman, and a Samaritan adulteress (Lk 7:1-10, Mt 15:21-28, Jn 4:4-26) among others.

Additionally, for many people, repentance can be a restless and unpleasant experience since it is not a one-time deed. Since people will likely sin again, they must remain constantly vigilant since death may catch up with them (Mt- 24:42-51, Lk 12:35-47). Having to live with the uncertainty of when we might die without being allowed to repent generates high levels of emotional and mental anxiety. As a result, many Christians might desist living like the faithful servant or like the five virgins whose clumsiness kept them from entering the kingdom (Lk 12:35-47, Mt 25:1-13). Furthermore, God says that he will not wait forever for individuals to repent or grant us too many opportunities, because the door will not remain open indefinitely.[5]

Adding to the stress is the concern that those who refuse to listen to the word of God and repent will be severely punished. Passages abound in the Gospels, both directly (in the synoptics) and indirectly (in John) that the threat of condemnation is all too real; *Every tree that does not bear good fruit will be cut down and thrown into the fire.* (Lk 3:9, Mt 3:8-10). The Parables of the Tenants (Mk 12:1-11, Lk 20:9-19, Mt 21:33-43), the Ten Gold Coins (Lk 19:11-12, 27), and The Great Feast (Mt 22:1-4), among others, convey the same message. In the Parable of the Rich Man and Lazarus, Jesus even indicates that no additional warnings will be provided to those who are still alive (Lk 16:27-31). In Matthew, Jesus warns *it will be more tolerable for the land of Sodom and Gomorrah on the day of judgment* than for those who will not listen to his words (Mt 10:14-15). Inconceivably, Jesus even appears to threaten some people that they might perish, in the same manner as Galileans who were killed by Pilate, if they fail to repent (Lk 13:1-5); it is difficult to understand, however, how repentance would have prevented their deaths. Moreover, being accepted as Messiah or Son of God is so important that he forewarns that Jerusalem will be destroyed for its refusal to acknowledge him (Lk 13:34-35, Mt 23:37-38).

Overall, Jesus's message of repentance is based more on fear and the threat of eternal punishment than on the positive aspect of salvation. This is in contrast with postmodern Christian theology that emphasizes God's compassion and forgiveness. The implication is not that people may sin knowing that eventually, God will forgive them. Perhaps, God's understanding of his creatures leads him to understand that threats would be more effective to persuade them to live according to his teachings. Interestingly, this is not unlike the temporal world that relies on punishment to keep its citizens leading lawful lives.

Culturally, it appears that repentance can become quite complex. Because of prevailing religious pluralism and moral relativism, believers may have no reason to acknowledge misbehavior they believe is righteous. Jesus was likely aware that his message would confront such hurdles, as there were competing beliefs at the time. Despite this obstacle, it is inexplicable why Jesus would purposefully want to blur God's way to those that need it the most by hiding the mystery of the kingdom of God from them (Mk 4:11, Lk 8:9-10, Mt 13:10-15). The Parable of the Sower provides among the best explanations about the complexity involving repentance. In this parable Jesus conveys his knowledge of how humans interrelate in society, ultimately indicating that many people that are not necessarily evil will be condemned because sinful cultural and socio-political structures are conditioning their lives (Mk 4:2-20, Lk 8:4-15, Mt 13:3-23).

Repentance has another limitation that is psychologically dubious; *blasphemies against the holy Spirit will not be forgiven,* says Jesus (Mk 3:28-29, Lk 12:10, Mt 12:31-32), indicating that, once done, it is impossible to repent.[6] The statement presumes that blasphemy is a deliberate act in which there is free will and full understanding of the act, elements that are difficult to find in imperfect human beings. Hence, is it possible that an emotionally stable person acting in a rightful state of mind might not be concerned with eternal damnation after realizing what it entails? The question is mostly rhetorical, as it lacks reasonable explanations in the Gospels. It is doubtful, however, that unless God resorts to extraordinary measures that can be empirically attributed to him, his attempts to instill fear is likely to fail (perhaps to the detriment of humanity).

Although repentance is highly regarded within Christianity, the act has been denigrated in secular society. Publicly repenting for misdeeds, issuing an apology, or admitting a mistake is seen often as a sign of weakness, despite being a teaching that children learn from their parents and in school early in life. Nowhere, it would seem, is acknowledging mistakes more important than in politics. It not only sets a notable example before citizens, but it demonstrates courage and honor as part of the character of a nation.[7]

Notes:
1. While Merriam-Webster Dictionary emphasizes internal conversion or change of attitude, Cambridge Dictionary stresses only a sense of regret or sorrow for one's misdeeds. *Merriam-Webster Dictionary,* online; *Cambridge Dictionary,* online, s.v. "repent."

2. A pious explanation by a modern-day apologist would insist that *the gates of a father's house are never too narrow for his children, no matter how obese they get. There have always been more good people than bad ones, and not all who have done wrong are ill intentioned.*

3. The decision to extend the Christian faith outside Judaism is the result of Paul's discussions with Peter and James at the so-called Council of Jerusalem in 50 CE (Acts 15:1-33). The Gospels offer no adequate explanation for the sudden and similar endings at the end of the synoptics in which Jesus urges his disciples that his teachings be spread to all nations of the world rather than only to the Jewish people (Mk 16:15-20, Lk 24:47, Mt 28:18-20). Although Jesus threatens the Israelites to take away salvation if they do not accept his version of God's message, there is no explanation why he opens the path to salvation to all humanity.

4. According to NEs, *the harsh language about Gentile and tax collector probably reflects a stage of the Matthean church when it was principally composed of Jewish Christians.* If so, this is not Jesus's teaching, and instead reflects an early Christian form of derogatory comments toward Gentiles and sinners, the bulk of Christianity's base.

5. This is NEs conclusion; note, Lk 13:22-30.

6. It is interesting that on the issue of blasphemy Thomas Aquinas begs to differ from Jesus as he concludes that, *considered in itself this sin* (blasphemy against the Holy Spirit) *is unpardonable, although God can pardon it.* Aquinas's conclusion would make sense since God supposedly can do anything he wishes, including forgiving the unforgiven, out of mercy, or because of his understanding of human nature. Thomas Aquinas, "Question 14 - Of Blasphemy Against The Holy Ghost, Article. 3 - Whether the sin against the Holy Ghost can be forgiven?" *Summa Theologica,* II/II, p 2778 in pdf format. http://www.ccel.org/a/aquinas/summa/cache/summa.pdf (accessed online September 25, 2018).

7. Among the most notable politicians in the United States that glorify not having to apologize on behalf of the nation are George H. W. Bush, Mitt Romney, and Donald Trump. Bush is known for his remark following the United States accidentally shooting down an Iranian commercial airline saying, *I will never apologize for the United States of America, ever. I don't care what the facts are.* CSpanClassics, December 20, 2010, Courtesy the C-Span Archives, August 1988, https://www.youtube.com/watch?v=10qatUWwIeg. Mitt Romney in his book *No Apology: The Case for American Greatness,* chastised Barack Obama for his admissions of America's misdeeds overseas, (New York: St. Martin's Press, 2010). Donald Trump, feeling that America is the greatest fighting force, told U.S. Naval Academy graduates that *we are not going to apologize for America. We are going to stand up for America. No more apologies.* Mel Leonor, "Trump proclaims 'we are not going to apologize for America'," *Politico,* May 25, 2018, https://www.politico.com/story/2018/05/25/trump-no-apologies-america-608713 (accessed online September 10, 2018). On the opposite end stands Richard Nixon, who despite colluding with North Vietnam to get himself elected to the US presidency, did apologize for his Watergate misdeeds. John A. Farrell, "When a Candidate Conspired With a Foreign Power to Win An Election," *Politico Magazine,* August 6, 2017, www.politico.com/magazine/story/2017/08/06/nixon-vietnam-candidate-conspired-with-foreign-power-win-election-215461 (accessed March 2, 2020). Nixon apologized for Watergate during an interview with David Frost in 1977, Brian Stelter, "David Frost, Interviewer Who Got Nixon to Apologize for Watergate, Dies at 74," *The New York Times,* September 1, 2013, https://www.nytimes.com/2013/09/02/world/europe/david-frost-known-for-nixon-interview-dead-at-74.html (accessed March 2, 2020). John McCain admitted mistakes for his involvement in the Keating 5 financial scandal and for not condemning the Confederate Flag during his run for the presidency in 2000. Lauren Gambino, "John McCain: 10 moments that will shape the senator's legacy," *The Guardian,* August 25, 2018, https://www.theguardian.com/us-news/2018/aug/25/john-mccain-death-moments-life-shape-legacy (accessed March 2, 2020). Barack Obama acknowledged US misconduct throughout history toward Europe and the Arab and Muslim worlds. Affan Chowdhry, "Fact or fiction: Is Obama the 'apologist' president?" *The Globe and Mail,* May 8, 2018, www.theglobeandmail.com/news/world/us-politics/us-election-blog/fact-or-fiction-is-obama-the-apologist-president/article4542089/ (accessed March 2, 2020). Pope John Paul II issued an apology in 2000 for errors committed by the Catholic Church throughout its 2000 years of history, including religious intolerance and injustice toward

Jews, women, indigenous peoples, immigrants, the poor, the unborn, and persecution of Catholics by other faiths. Alessandra Stanley, "Pope Asks Forgiveness for Errors of the Church Over 2,000 Years," *The New York Times,* March 13, 2000, https://www.nytimes.com/2000/03/13/world/pope-asks-forgiveness-for-errors-of-the-church-over-2000-years.html (accessed March 2, 2020).

Forgiveness

Forgiveness is another central element in Jesus's teachings. Realizing that he is preaching to flawed human beings, he expects conflict. So, following the Lord's Prayer, he warns the crowd, *if you forgive others their transgressions, your heavenly Father will forgive you. But if you do not forgive others, neither will your Father forgive your transgressions* (Mt 6:14). Nonetheless, Table 2 indicates that in the Gospels *forgiveness* is not among the significant categories. The word itself is mostly used in the synoptics (Mk 10xt, Lk 21xt, Mt 16xt) as a teaching to be followed; a measure of divine justice; a show of Jesus's mercy; an indication of his authority to forgive sins; and, as a directive to seek personal repentance to attain redemption. The term appears only 2xt in John's Gospel; not as a teaching principle but to indicate the authority that Jesus delegates to his disciples to forgive or retain sin (Jn 20:23). The tally, however, includes passages that imply forgiveness, such as when Jesus forgives the woman accused of adultery (Jn 8:10-11)

Forgiveness and Conflict Resolution
It may be reasonable to presume that from a humanist standpoint forgiveness would play a crucial role in modern-day instances of conflict resolution. Nonetheless, unwillingness to forgive is often viewed as a symbol of weakness or as an emotional need to preserve self-esteem (one's ego), in addition to genuine personal and social difficulties in overcoming deep-rooted anger. Such an unwillingness or inability occurs despite a cost-benefit analysis that may show the detrimental consequences of unforgiveness throughout all levels of society.

While considering the obstacles in overcoming unforgiveness, both Christianity and secularized society may be shown to bear responsibility for this trait. Seemingly casting Jesus's teachings aside, Christian laity (and the clergy) appear to have failed throughout history at implanting the commandment to forgive into their minds. Even today, many conflicts in democratic societies occur among Christians themselves. Moreover, unwillingness to forgive (and its counterpart, revenge) is often perceived as a worthy individual and social value, as may be observed in movies, music, and politics.[1] Secular democratic societies (often ruled and populated by Christians), however, rarely will reflect on these consequences and act.

Nonetheless, perhaps a most interesting feature happening today, is that concerned social scientists in post-modern secularized societies have begun to realize the significance of forgiveness by exploring its benefits while studying conflict resolution. In the fields of psychology, sociology, management, and international affairs, researchers are conducting studies indicating that forgiveness plays a major role in ending conflicts, whether at the interpersonal or national domestic and international levels. This recognition, after two thousand years, merits attention.[2] Still at incipient stages, the knowledge being derived from these studies has not yet attained the status of a social vaccine that could minimize conflict by changing hearts and minds. As culture progresses, it may be expected that younger generations might be more amenable to the value of forgiveness.

Forgiveness in the Old Testament

Forgiveness offers another example in which Jesus's teachings differ from God's in the Old Testament. In Mosaic Law, forgiveness was mostly about rituals and animal sacrifices (LEV 4:20, 26, 31, 35, 5:10, 13). The priest was instructed to atone on behalf of the offender if a person or the community would inadvertently commit an offense against God (Lev 4, 5, Num 15). If the person, on the other hand, acted defiantly and reviled God there would be no forgiveness (Num 15:30-36). In addition to there not being directives to forgive others for their offenses, messaging is mixed in the Old Testament. God is merciful and forgiving in temporal life, although largely (if not only) toward his people. God is *slow to anger,* yet his punishment extends not only to the guilty but even *to children and children's children to the third and fourth generation* (Ex 34:6-7).

Joshua indicates that God will not forgive anyone serving strange gods; *he will then do evil to you and destroy you (*Josh 24:19-20, Lam 3). In Jeremiah, there is even a prayer to God for vengeance against enemies (Jer 18:19-23). Moreover, God threatens to punish his people to remind them to return to him and be forgiven of their sins (Jer 36:2-3). It is Solomon who sees the need to pray to God, asking him to forgive his peoples' sins (1 Kings 8:22-61, 2 Chr 6). Ben Sira (2 BCE),[3] also acknowledges that God forgives sins and is merciful to those who return to him and accept his discipline (Sir 17:29, 18:11-12, 14), but suggests that people should not be overconfident because *his wrath will come forth and at the time of vengeance, you will perish* (Sir 5:5, 7). He is one of the few who calls for forgiving one's neighbor for *the wrong done to you,* otherwise, we should not expect God to forgive us (Sir 28:2-4).

Forgiveness in the Gospels

There is, nonetheless, a marked difference in Jesus's teachings on forgiveness. In many instances, he appears to override God, as in the case of the sabbath whose violation God punishes the offender with death (Num 15:32-36) while Jesus violates the sabbath at will because he claims to be lord of the sabbath. In Jesus, the forgiveness of others is an overt act of love. His teachings suggest that not to forgive implies holding grudges, harboring resentment, and possibly even seeking revenge, all sinful behavior that attempts against the commandment to love one's neighbor, including one's enemies (Mt 5:44-47). Forgiveness is so important that Jesus considers it a prerequisite to seeking forgiveness from God (Mk 11:25, Lk 6:37, Mt 6:12-15), commanding that people forgive each other *not seven times but seventy-*

seven times (Mt 18:22). Moreover, although he is forgiving in temporal life, he is very unforgiving in the afterlife, resembling God in the Old Testament whereby he constantly threatens (through his parables) people who sin with eternal condemnation.

Jesus's message appears to be rather simple: humans are prone to sin, and if they care to be forgiven by God to attain eternal salvation, they need to begin by forgiving each other (Mk 11:25, Lk 6:37, 11:4, Mt 18:21-35). According to Jesus, the love commandment cannot be realized genuinely unless there is forgiveness. He teaches that God will forgive in the same measure as we forgive others. He makes this point quite explicit in Matthew's Parable of the Unforgiving Servant, telling his disciples that God will not forgive *unless each of you forgives his brother from his heart* (Mt 18:21-35).

Since Jesus claims to have the authority to forgive (and to retain) sins, he delegates it to his disciples (Jn 20:22-23). This is an implicit signal of his intention to organize an institution to spread his message. In John, his intention becomes explicit as he commands them to teach a baptism of *repentance, for the forgiveness of sins ... to all the nations* (Lk 24:47). Jesus also uses forgiveness supernaturally during the Last Supper to indicate that his death will serve to redeem humankind (or part of it) from its state of sinfulness (Mt 26:27-28).[4]

The Gospels provide various examples of Jesus's forgiveness. He forgives a woman with *many sins* who shows repentance through her expressions of *great love* for him (Lk 7:44-48); he saves an adulterous woman from being stoned and refuses to condemn her, telling her not to sin again (Jn 8:1-11); he cures a paralytic man once he forgives his sins (Mk 2:1-11, Lk 5:17-25, Mt 9:1-6); supposedly he forgives a blind man when he cures his blindness, although the man has not requested to be healed;[5] and he forgives those who execute him (Lk 23:34) as well as one of the criminals being crucified next to him after he repents (Lk 23:39-43).

Perhaps the most discernible pattern exhibited in the Gospels regarding forgiveness is how Jesus teaches forgiveness. Much of the space in the Gospels dealing with forgiveness is about the perils of non-forgiveness. His message is that forgiveness needs to take place throughout one's life on earth. The Parable of the Unforgiving Servant and the Parable of the Rich Man and Lazarus make it clear that God refuses to forgive in the afterlife (Mt 18:21-35, Lk 16:19-31). These teachings appear to contradict God's most significant attribute, his mercy, which would take place precisely upon the person's death.

Jesus's message about entering the kingdom of God through the narrow gate, suggesting that only a minority of humans will be saved (Lk 13:23-30, Mt 7:13-14), shows that God's forgiveness is not easy to attain. Other passages in the Gospels point to Jesus's seemingly unyielding attitude:

- *Whoever blasphemes against the holy Spirit will never have forgiveness, but is guilty of an everlasting sin* (Mk 3:28-29, Lk 12:10, Mt 12:31-32).

- *To those outside everything comes in parables, so that they may look and see but not perceive, and hear and listen but not understand, so that they may not be converted and be forgiven* (Mk 4:10 Mt 13:10).
- In the Parable of the Tenants, *He* (God) *will come, put the tenants to death, and give the vineyard to others* (Mk 12:1-9, Mt 21:33-41).
- The Parable of the Wedding Feast ends by reinforcing the view stated in the passage referencing the narrow gate: *Many are invited, but few are chosen* (Mt 22:1-14).
- In the Parable of the Unfaithful Servant, God will come *on an unexpected day ... and will punish him severely and assign him a place with the hypocrites, where there will be wailing and grinding of teeth* (Mt 24:45-51).
- In the Parable of the Ten Virgins, five of them are locked out of the wedding feast (salvation) because of their clumsiness. *I say to you, I do not know you*, God tells them (Mt 25:1-13).
- In the Parable of the Ten Gold Coins, one of the servants hesitates in following the master's directives and purportedly loses his job; as for those who refuse to accept his authority, God regards them as enemies and asks his servants to slay them before him (Lk 19:11-27, Mt 25:14-30).
- It is not enough to *do mighty deeds* in Jesus's name; if we falter and fail to do God's will, Jesus will tell us, *I never knew you. Depart from me, you evildoers* (Mt 7:21-23).

It appears that God is not likely to apply Jesus's teaching to forgive seventy times seven. It seems that Jesus would not allow anyone to take advantage of his generosity, in which case we need to forgive often because, being imperfect, he expects misdeeds from humankind. The question is, should God not have the same expectations at the time of judgment? If the outcome of Original Sin or evolution is sinfulness, should God be more understanding of human nature's shortcomings and the existential pressures humans face throughout their lives that predispose their behavior toward evil?

Despite the dogmatic belief (among many Christians) that humans cannot earn salvation through their own efforts (only through God's grace and mercy), quite often Jesus appears to indicate that he will not be so lenient during Judgment Day; despite claiming that he has the authority to forgive sins (Mk 2:10, Lk 5:24). Given his earnest desire to save the world (as revealed in various passages in John), it appears, nonetheless, as if God is either bent on making it difficult for humans to be saved or not doing enough to mitigate human evil.

Jesus's most telling example of how he (or God) will forgive relates to his forgiveness of Peter. If the chronology of events is correct, Jesus has conferred upon Peter the keys to the kingdom knowing that, out of fear for his life, Peter will deny him three times publicly at a later time (Mk 14:66-72, Lk 22:54-62, Mt 26:69-75, Jn 13:38). He forgives Peter, perhaps knowing that Peter would repent, which he does.

On the other hand, Jesus's attitude toward Judas Iscariot is quite different. Although Judas goes a step further than Peter and conspires to put Jesus to death (out of greed or for political reasons), he regrets his conduct, returns the thirty pieces of silver he was paid to hand Jesus over to the chief priest, and hangs himself (Mt 27:1-5). This is, indeed, an extraordinary act of remorse. Nonetheless, Judas is excoriated in all four Gospels; Jesus even calls him a traitor (Mk 14:21, Mt 26:24).

Why It Is Difficult to Forgive

Forgiving others is emotionally difficult; it entails a struggle between Jesus's teachings and an infuriated inner self.[6] Too often we find it challenging to forgive strangers who have done nothing to us other than to uphold beliefs and look different than we do. As humans, we tend to like our own kind; we find security in likeness, whether it be race, ethnicity, religion, gender, or nationality. Those who are not like us are often regarded as outsiders or aliens. Without wishing to admit it to ourselves, this attitude of exclusiveness seems to distort Jesus's message. Neither religion nor science has been able to persuade humanity that hatred is self-destructive (hubris); that it impedes peaceful and constructive relations among relatives and friends, in the neighborhood, and among peoples at the international level.

Hatred emerges too, as the by-product of socio-political ideologies and the action values they disseminate. Once resentment is given free rein, the behavior is rationalized to the point that it dehumanizes one's opponents. It then becomes much easier to label our opponents as being evil. Once this happens it becomes easier to morally justify our behavior, because, since God hates evil, we pretend to be on God's side. Christians are not exempted from this behavior, having weaponized hatred to become more effective at war.[7]

Another important consideration is that forgiveness could bring about perverse consequences. If I forgive my offenders two, three, or seven times, am I not enabling them to persist in their behavior? Would it not be more effective to physically bring them into submission, isolate them, take them to court, or deter them by engaging in the same behavior? The case here is not that forgiving others is tantamount to being weak but that in some circumstances it becomes ineffective. For example, Jesus's teaching about forgiving others for their trespasses presumes the existence of moral conscience, such as those who want to stone the adulterous woman but realize that it would not be proper to do it given their sins. In other instances, however, he sets aside the goodness in humans focusing instead on the need to threaten those who fail to forgive despite possibly knowing that human forgiveness may be ineffectual at times. Moreover, it must be remembered that Jesus did not forgive (but condemned) the Pharisees (Mt 23:13-14).

Who are Christians Supposed to Forgive?

Are Christians supposed to follow Jesus's example and forgive those that conspire against the kingdom of God, including Jihadists, white supremacists, drug pushers, slave traders, and greedy Christian politicians looking after their own self-interests? A non-Christian, Mahatma Gandhi, once said that *the weak can never forgive, as forgiveness is an attribute of the strong.*[8] Hence, it must have taken a great deal of strength for Jesus to forgive his executioners, possibly including Pilate (perhaps even the Jewish religious authorities), for failing to recognize him. In modern times, Pope John Paul II forgave the man who attempted against his life,[9] an action that resonated culturally at the time, although its echo did not seem to last long.

There is a religious explanation for the human inability to forgive. Insofar as people's belief in God and eternal life declines (largely happening in secularized societies) the incentive to forgive others diminishes. The only recourse left is to limit hatred and revenge by relying on punishment. Thus, a vastly secularized world perhaps lacks the necessary answer to this problem because it cannot find consensus on a predominant set of beliefs other than punishment to offset human desire for hatred and revenge. This state of affairs ought to make us realize that Jesus's teachings are far from becoming universal, which in turn raise questions about significant aspects of the Christian faith, such as providence, grace, prayer, God's understanding of human nature, the concept of a merciful God, and the power of evil.

Notes:

1. The belief that forgiveness is only up to God seems to have become a meme in secular culture. The phrase 'may God forgive you because I won't,' has been used in films equating un-forgiveness with toughness: *God Forgives, I Don't,* dir. by Giuseppe Colizzi (1967, Italy, Produzioni Atlas Consorziate (P.A.C.); in the film *Man on Fire,* dir. by Tony Scott, (2004, 20th Century Fox, USA), there is a line uttered by Denzel Washington that reads, *Forgiveness is between them and God, my job is to arrange the meeting; Only God Forgives,* dir. by Nicolas Winding Refn, (2013, Radius-TWC, Denmark). In music, Rick Ross, *God Forgives, I Don't* (2012; Maybach . Slip-n-Slide . Def Jam, 2012). Ross, an American rapper, sends a cryptic religious message through the songs in the album. In one of the songs, "Pray for Us," the lyrics ask for forgiveness for the sins they (African Americans) will commit in the future as a result of how they are currently being treated. https://genius.com/rick-ross-pray-for-us-lyrics (accessed online September 12, 2018). The meme has surfaced in politics too. Snopes.com reports that variations of the phrase "to forgive the terrorists is up to god, but to send them to him is up to me" have been circulating for several years. In 2001, the quote was incorrectly attributed to General Norman Schwarzkopf. *While we haven't been able to pinpoint the exact origins of the phrase, we previously noted that the phrase could be a misremembering of a message commonly told to soldiers in ROTC training in the 1980s: Your enemy's duty is to die in defense of his country. Your duty is to see that your enemy does his duty.* Dan Evon, "The Last Putin Hero," *Snopes.com,* 19 November 2015, https://www.snopes.com/fact-check/putin-forgive-terrorists-quote/, (accessed online September 10, 2018). Additionally, many of today's action movies and television programs portray revenge as daring, exciting, courageous, and necessary.

2. A few examples may suffice to learn about the inroads into studying forgiveness: "Using Conflict Resolution Skills: Trying to Forgive and Move Forward," Program on Negotiation, Harvard Law School, June 25, 2020, https://www.pon.harvard.edu/daily/conflict-resolution/trying-to-forgive-and-move-forward/ (accessed September 11, 2020); Frank D. Fincham, Steven R. H. Beach, Joanne Davila, "Forgiveness and Conflict Resolution in Marriage," *Journal of Family Psychology,* Vol. 18, No, 72-81, 2004, American Psychological Association, Inc. 2004, Vol. 18, No. 1, 72–81, http://www.fincham.info/measures/jfp-for%26ineff-2004.pdf (accessed September 11, 2020); Ellen F. Kandell, "Managing Conflict Through Forgiveness," November 2, 2012, https://www.alternativeresolutions.net/2012/11/02/november-2012-newsletter/ (accessed September 11, 2020); Deborah S. Butler, Fran Mullis, Butler, D. S., & Mullis, F. (2001). Forgiveness: A conflict resolution strategy in the workplace. The Journal of Individual Psychology, *2001,* 57(3), 259–272, https://psycnet.apa.org/record/2001-18877-004 (accessed September 11, 2020); Nava Löwenheim, "A haunted past: Requesting forgiveness for wrongdoing in International Relations," *Review of International*

Studies, July 2009, 35(3), 531-555; Yehudith Auerbach, "Conflict Resolution, Forgiveness, and Reconciliation in Material Identity Conflicts," *Humboldt Journal of Social Relations*, vol. 29, no. 2, 2005, pp. 41–80. *JSTOR*, www.jstor.org/stable/23262796 (accessed 11 Sept. 2020).

3. These writings are not part of the Hebrew Bible or accepted by Protestants. They are, however, regarded as canonical by the Catholic church. NEs' note, "Introduction," *Sirach*.

4. This view is controversial. It alludes to Jesus's role as savior and redeemer, except that it is not known who he is supposed to save: he sheds his blood for many (Mk 14:24), or *for you* (Lk 22:20); gives up his life as *ransom for many* (Mk 10:45); comes into the world *to seek and to save what was lost* (Lk 19:10); *saves his people from their sins,* without knowing whether it refers to the Israelites or humankind (Mt 1:21); offers himself as the sacrificial Lamb of God (Jn 1:29), his *flesh for the life of the world* (Jn 6:51), and gives his life for the sheep (Jn 10:15), i.e., the Jewish people, his disciples, or others.

5. The question of whether Jesus equates physical illness with sinfulness is provocative. Particularly in modern times, it has given way to Christian preachers blaming human sinfulness for natural and human disasters, which would seem a perversity on God's part to victimize the innocent along with the guilty, although God resorts to such punishment in the Old Testament. There are passages in the Old Testament that suggest a direct relationship between illness and sinfulness (Ez 18:18-20); and in John, Jesus's disciples seemingly believe it too, when they ask him whether the blind man or his parents' sins were responsible for his disability. In this instance, Jesus replies that the man's blindness is providential, *neither he nor his parents sinned; it is so that the works of God might be made visible through him* (Jn 9:1-3). Other instances appear to lend support to the view that the opposite may be true. For example, in John's Gospel, he cures a crippled man and later tells him, *Look, you are well; do not sin anymore, so that nothing worse may happen to you* (Jn 5:14). Possibly, Jesus may be telling the man that sinning (doing evil) may lead to him being jailed or killed, as opposed to being victimized by God. In Luke, there is a telling passage in which Jesus is made aware of atrocities committed by Pontius Pilate. Jesus relates such calamities to sinfulness and warns the crowd (twice), *But I tell you, if you do not repent, you will all perish as they did!* (Lk 13:1-5). On the other hand, he tells the crowd that the great peril of sinning is not that it may bring about physical death. Instead, people ought to be afraid of the devil that has the power to send them into eternal condemnation; *I tell you, be afraid of that one,* he tells them (Lk 12:4-5).

6. Forgiving also means having to overcome the contempt we feel toward relatives and friends to tolerate values we enormously abhor. I include myself in this category, often having to explain (to myself) the choices I face: either I tolerate alien values among those I love or isolate myself from them. It is likely as agonizing to me as it is probably to them.

7. An interesting article by psychiatrist Anna Fels cites historian Rick Atkinson illustrating how during WWII hatred was used by the Allies as *the emotional engine needed to drive troops into battle for that "just war." Allied officers were constantly fretting that the troops' hate levels weren't high enough. A memorandum urged commanders to "teach the men to hate the enemy — to want to kill them by any means." George Patton's aide praised him as "a great hate builder." Dwight Eisenhower bragged, "I am not one who finds it difficult to hate my enemies."* Anna Fels, "The Point of Hate," *The New York Times,* April 14, 2017. https://www.nytimes.com/2017/04/14/opinion/the-point-of-hate.html (accessed online 8 September 2018).

8. "Mahatma Gandhi Forgiveness Quotes," *Success Story,* www.successstory.com/inspiration/mahatma-gandhi-forgiveness-quotes *(accessed* online September 12, 2018).

9. Alessandra Stanley, "Pope Asks Forgiveness for Errors of the Church Over 2,000 Years," *The New York Times,* March 13, 2000.

Kingdom of God

References to Jesus's undertaking on earth preaching about the Kingdom of God abound in the texts. Content analysis results rank this category as significant. Most (if not all) Christian denominations would consider that announcing the coming of this kingdom is Jesus's most important temporal and eschatological mission.

The Kingdom of God in the Old Testament

Despite its relevance in the Gospels, the Old Testament provides scant information about Jesus's version of this kingdom. This is yet another example of the discontinuity between God's designs as narrated in the Hebrew Bible and the Gospels. Temporally, the term *kingdom of God* or *kingdom of heaven* gives the impression that it is a place set off by boundaries, inhabited by people, and ruled by a king. Throughout the time in which the Old Testament is written (1500 to 50 BCE),[1] two major titles for rulers were known: *pharaohs*, the rulers in ancient Egypt, and *kings*, those who ruled the many kingdoms that existed at the time in and around Mesopotamia and the Eastern Mediterranean or the Levant.[2] In the Old Testament, the title used to refer to God as a ruler is *Lord,* although in a few cases there are references to God being king.[3]

The Kingdom of God in the Gospels
A ghostly kingdom emerges on earth with the birth of Jesus according to an announcement by the angel Gabriel to Mary:

> *Behold, you will conceive in your womb and bear a son, and you shall name him Jesus. He will be great and will be called Son of the Most High, and the Lord God will give him the throne of David his father, and he will rule over the house of Jacob forever, and of his kingdom there will be no end* (Lk 1:31-33).

This kingdom is related to God's promises to the Israelite people, and it is clear in the Gospels that Jesus will head it. Nonetheless, this is an earthly Israelite kingdom, not a kingdom of all people, entrusted with power and authority from heaven (Mt 6:9-14) to bring salvation from Israel's enemies (Lk 1:71). There follows a cryptic phrase suggesting that salvation (whatever it meant at the time to the Jewish people) would come about through the forgiveness of their sins (Lk 1:77) that may (or may not) refer to supernatural salvation.

That the nature and objectives of this kingdom pertain to the Israelite people is soon noted when Jesus tells his disciples not to preach the kingdom of heaven throughout the world, but to *go rather to the lost sheep of the house of Israel* (Mt 10:5-6). Jesus, however, does not follow his own directive, as he decides to go into pagan territory and teach among pagan peoples (Mk 3:8, 5:1, Lk 6:17, 8:26, Mt 4:24-25, 8:24).

Why would Jesus override God's mission and inexplicably extend this kingdom beyond the Jewish people? It appears that he follows through with his veiled threats in some of his parables (Lk 14:15-24, 20:9-19, Mt 21:33-44, 22:1-14), suggesting that the kingdom may be taken away from the Israelites and offered to others if they continue to reject him. Adding to the confusion, the text in Luke suggests, not only that this kingdom will serve as a *revelation to the Gentiles* too (Lk 2:32), but citing Isaiah 40:5, the author hints that *all flesh* (not only Jews) *shall see the salvation of God* (Lk 3:6). Moreover, the synoptics ends with a proclamation that the kingdom of God is opened to everyone (Mk 13:10, Lk 24:47, Mt 28:19), and *people will come from the east and the west and from the north and the south and will recline at table in the kingdom of God* (Lk 13:29, Mt 8:11).

Upon learning that John the Baptist has been arrested, Jesus begins his public ministry announcing that the promises God has made to his people are about to be realized: *The kingdom of God is at hand*, he proclaims; *repent, and believe in the gospel* (Mk 1:14-15, Mt 4:2-17). The call to repent, however, changes the nature of the mission. What does repent from one's sins have to do with being liberated from one's enemies? This is Old Testament talk; God intervening in earthly affairs seeking to protect his people insofar as they obey him.

Continuing with his mission, Jesus stands before worshippers at the synagogue in Nazareth and tells them that he brings good news to the poor; that he will proclaim liberty to the captives and let the oppressed go free (Lk 4:16-19). This is a depiction of what the Israelite people are awaiting, including Joseph and Mary, Zechariah and Elizabeth, the righteous Simeon, the prophetess Anna, and even Joseph of Arimathea (Lk 23:51). It thus appears that the kingdom of God has a contradictory agenda; the kingdom the Israelites await is temporal, yet the type of liberation Jesus promises refers to a supernatural reality that has little if anything to do with temporal liberation.

Jesus's actions do not necessarily mean that there is not an earthly component to his mission to establish the kingdom of God. His confrontation with the religious authorities shows that he is leading a religious/political movement to undermine their authority and establish his own interpretation of God's rules. The texts indicate that the power struggle with the religious authorities already has begun by the time they accuse him of working on behalf of the devil. (Mk 3:23-27, Lk 11:14-20, Mt 12:22-28). Unless Jesus is predisposed to die to comply with God's redemption of humankind or to fulfill a prophecy, we might think that Jesus would have preferred to accomplish his mission without dying. His actions, however, lead to a different outcome.

Access to the Kingdom of God
Various passages in the texts allow us to think about the nature of the kingdom that Jesus preaches. Interestingly, while the angel refers to this kingdom as being led by Jesus, it is Jesus who calls it the kingdom of God. Is he referring to God the Father or is he calling himself God?

He appoints his disciples to assist him in establishing his kingdom as a non-profit institution whose objective is to do good deeds (Mt 10:7-10, Lk 10:1-7) while preaching about the afterlife. Work is not necessarily enjoyable, as there will be persecutions (Mt 5:10-11); his followers must abide by strict rules (Lk 9:59-62); and dependence on God for physical subsistence is required (Lk 12:29-31, Mt 6:31-33). The second part of Jesus's instructions is more troubling. His disciples are to wish peace wherever they go, but if they are rejected, they are to rebuff its residents, warning them that their fate would be worse than what Sodom and Gomorrah experienced (Lk 10:11-12, Mt 10:14-15), i.e., their condemnation would almost be certain. These examples of fire and brimstone threats, however, might have worked at the time (although they did not), and it is less likely to prove effective today when the credibility of the message is declining throughout secular society.

Through his parables, Jesus compares the kingdom of heaven to a mustard seed and yeast, predicting that in time it will expand considerably (Mt 13:31-33). Surprisingly, somehow amidst sinfulness, the kingdom has grown through time. Moreover, despite the prevalence of patriarchal structures at the time, Jesus calls upon women to accompany him, among them, Mary Magdalene, Joanna, the wife of Herod's steward Chuza, Susanna, *and many others who provided for them out of their resources* (Lk 8:2-3). Furthermore, decrying insurmountable barriers according to different faiths, Jesus is willing to accept assistance in expanding his kingdom from others who might not necessarily be among his followers, insofar as they share his objectives (Lk 9:49-50, 10:30-37), suggesting interdenominational efforts that cut across the various beliefs.

Jesus tells the crowd that, as important as John the Baptist is, the most insignificant person in the kingdom of heaven would be *greater than he* (Lk 7:28, Mt 11:11), alluding that being part of the kingdom is a *privilege*,[4] not an act of kindness and mercy on God's part, as Christian preachers are telling their followers today. Jesus provides a tenuous explanation for regarding salvation as a perk. The kingdom, it appears, is very discriminating and not everyone will be able to enter it; it is like a fishing net that collects all sorts of fishes, although some (or many) will be thrown away into a *fiery furnace, where there will be wailing and grinding of teeth* (Mt 13:44-48). He realizes that only a few people will support him wholeheartedly to the end. The rest will not pay attention, either because Satan will not allow it (and there seems to be nothing God can do), or because world anxieties will consume people's lives (Mk 4:1-20, Lk 8:4-8, Mt 13:1-8). Inexplicably, Jesus suggests that many people will not be able to enter the kingdom because of circumstances beyond their control.[5]

Who then are these privileged people who are admitted to this kingdom of God? As opposed to being wealthy or enjoying a solid reputation in the community, God's kingdom focuses on very different people: the poor in spirit, those who mourn, the meek, those who desire righteousness, the merciful, the clean of heart, the peacemakers, those who are persecuted and insulted in his name (Mt 5:1-12). God's kingdom allows tax collectors (loan sharks) and prostitutes to enter, supposedly if they repent and change their behavior (Mt 21:31); moreover, those who care for the forgotten and the needy will be invited (Mt 25:31-46).

Significantly, as much emphasis as John's Gospel makes on faith as the key to entering into *life*, Jesus reminds the crowd that calling out *Lord, Lord* will not be enough; only those who do the will of God will be admitted, making behavior an integral component for admission into the kingdom (Mt 7:21, 16:27). Looking at these qualifications, the ruthless, the selfish, the arrogant, the unmerciful, and those who are indifferent to suffering or refuse to welcome and care for the stranger will be excluded from his kingdom.

An issue with this behavioral typology is that the poor and the meek can become ruthless following continued disappointments in life; those asking for justice can despair and become unmerciful, and peacemakers may resort to violence to end violence. This is to say that attitudes are not cemented; they are fluid. Given that human nature is flawed and complex, for Jesus to tell the crowd that they need to enter the kingdom through the narrow door and that many are simply not strong enough (Lk 13:24, Mt 7:13-14) seems extraordinarily harsh and typical of someone who at times does not seem to understand earthlings.[6] This view of human reality is likely at odds with younger generations that, while devoid of faith, wish that Jesus would provide people with the same opportunity he accords to the criminal who enters the kingdom at the last minute. This, he does, seemingly contradicting himself in the Parable of the Workers in the Vineyard in which late-coming workers receive the same wages as those who had been working longer hours (Mt 20:1-16).

In the Parable of the Great Feast (Lk 14:15), the Parable of the Ten Gold Coins/Talents (Lk 19:11, Mt 25:14), the Parable of the Ten Virgins (Mt 25:1-13), the Parable of the Unforgiving Servant (Mt 18:23-35) and similar ones, the reader may wonder what makes once innocent children become terrorists, robbers, selfish, insensitive, or greedy people, who according to Jesus, are not likely to enter the kingdom. Moreover, despite his expressions of joy, and his wish that all be saved, as seen in in the Lost Sheep (Lk 15:3), the Lost Coin (Lk 15:8), or the Lost Son (Lk 15:11), it appears that this type of salvation happens randomly. These examples raise the question, what is God doing to increase the probabilities of people being saved?

The view stemming from the Gospels is that humans are endowed with free will and with a full understanding of their actions, to the point that everyone can be held accountable for their decisions. The emphasis on the difficulties to enter the kingdom, however, questions this premise. Jesus suggests that humanity is so senseless it would reject a treasure of fine pearls worth millions, when perhaps in many instances what it simply lacks is the necessary willpower to resist temptation; the same temptation that Jesus overcomes in the desert through divine assistance.

For example, Jesus teaches that *whoever does not accept the kingdom of God like a child will not enter it* (Mk 10:13-16, Lk 18:15-17). Now, childhood stands for two characteristics, innocence or inability to distinguish between good and evil; and dependence or trust in adults for survival, which does not happen in parts of the world where children are left to their own ability to survive. Innocence is unavoidably lost when children reach adolescence. By the time they acquire an understanding of good and evil, they begin to experience the freedom to exercise choices, most of which have moral overtones. The influence of external factors, however, can easily derail goodness in a child. Doing evil, in other words, is not always a matter of choice; and since Christianity teaches that proclivity toward evil exists in all human beings (postmodern psychology likely would agree), wrongdoing becomes even easier than doing good, particularly if it is socially learned. Thus, under these circumstances how do adults maintain enough innocence to enter the kingdom of God while being surrounded by all sorts of external temptations?

The other characteristic is dependence on God or humility (Mt 18:4), i.e., trust in a superior being whom we cannot see to govern our conduct. Although adults place blind trust in others in all phases of life, it becomes difficult to trust God to provide health, employment, food, and shelter, historically the most anxiety-producing human needs. What humans may realistically expect is to rely on the emotional and psychological strength that faith and hope provide. This attitude, whether on the part of the believer or non-believer, leads to a *grin and bear it* theology (or in today's lexicon, *deal with it*) in which humankind, trying to solve its problems, ultimately resigns itself to the circumstances that life presents. Nonetheless, whether humans divest themselves of possessions and practice charity and forgiveness, which according to Jesus is enough to be considered for admission into the (final) kingdom (Lk 19:8-9), it might not suffice since, ultimately, it is God who heads admission into the kingdom regardless of his teachings (Lk 18:26-30).

In John's Gospel Jesus injects more confusion into the nature of the kingdom by adding to its supernatural component: *I say to you, no one can see the kingdom of God without being born from above ... without being born of water and Spirit* (Jn 3:3-5). Nicodemus, a teacher of Israel, is perplexed by those words; he simply does not understand them because he has never heard this viewpoint. In John, belief is almost everything, including ensuring admission into *eternal life* (Jn 3:16, 4:14, 5:24, 6:27, 6:47, 20:30-31). Alluding to the Eucharist, Jesus claims that whoever eats his flesh and drinks his blood will have eternal life and will be welcomed into the kingdom. The religious authorities and many of Jesus's disciples are disconcerted by those words (Jn 6:52-60). The issue is not that people are not interested in eternal life, but that they do not believe because they do not understand while others (who may be saved) believe without understanding.

There is an even more enigmatic description of the kingdom that, according to Jesus, it is like a field in which the seeds the farmer spreads *sprout and grow* without external assistance (Mk 4:26-29). His disciples accept Jesus's explanation and do not question him despite this parable is among the most disheartening words that Christians could hear. If the kingdom of God grows on its own, without human intervention, why does the field need laborers to work the soil and gather the harvest?[7]

Another puzzling narrative concerns the true ruler of the kingdom of God. Jesus refers to this kingdom as being his (Jn 18:36), insisting that he is *the way and the truth and the life*. No one enters the kingdom unless it is through him (Jn 14:6). Having received authority from the Father *over all people* (Jn 17:2), he is the one who will preside Judgment Day from his throne (Mt 25: 31-46). On the other hand, Jesus admits that it is not his prerogative to judge what status or privileges each person is likely to have in the kingdom; the Father will make those decisions, suggesting two different types of authority in the kingdom (Mt 20:20-28).

Conceptualizing the Kingdom of God

According to the texts, God's kingdom is portrayed as the ultimate reality beyond temporal life that, nonetheless, has its roots on earth, hence, its eschatological feature. That the nature of the kingdom of God is eschatological, i.e., it exists on earth and is destined to end at the end of time, then manifest itself physically somewhere, is suggested in Matthew when Jesus gives Peter the keys to the kingdom of heaven, seemingly a blank check that Jesus might have regretted doing since then. He tells the Pharisees that *the coming of the kingdom of God cannot be observed*, as it is already among them (Lk 17:20-21), suggesting that both the temporal and supernatural reality is personified in him. But in another passage, Jesus relies on the metaphor of the fig tree to indicate that *the kingdom of God is near*, hinting that it has not arrived (Lk 21:29-33). Then, during the Passover meal prior to his death Jesus says that *from this time on I shall not drink of the fruit of the vine until the kingdom of God comes* (Lk 22:14-18), suggesting that the kingdom is not present yet.

As if the above passages are not confusing enough to the average reader, during the same meal Jesus tells his disciples, *I confer a kingdom on you, just as my Father has conferred one on me ... and you will sit on thrones judging the twelve tribes of Israel* (Lk 22:29-30). There now seems to be two, perhaps three, kingdoms whose boundaries are difficult to delineate. At least, it may be confirmed that the kingdom of God is not a temporal but an alien (supposedly supernatural) kingdom; that much Jesus tells Pontius Pilate (Jn 18:36).

How this kingdom is to be governed on earth elicits disturbing questions. Jesus's Parable of the Weeds Among the Wheat conveys the image of a temporal kingdom that eventually leads possibly to its demise. The king (either Jesus or God) allows good and evil to coexist, telling the righteous not to uproot evil. Instead, he will wait until the end of time when he will collect the weeds (evil people) and burn them, then gather the wheat (the righteous) into his barn (Mt 13:24-30). Is Jesus aware that if the righteous do not combat evil, his own kingdom will be destroyed? Scholars interpret the parable literally indicating that the righteous must accept the present state of affairs until Judgment Day with patience and while preaching repentance.[8]

As a teaching device, the significance of this parable, suggesting what amounts to a 'do-nothing' policy amid violence would appear to be temporally unsustainable. If the teaching were to be applied to the agricultural sector alone it would lead to famine, suffering, and death as the weed would effectively kill the food supply.[9] If applied to civil society, results would be much worse, since good people would continuously be at the mercy of wicked forces that, according to the teaching, ought not to be confronted. A policy of patience and the preaching of repentance while wicked people are scorching the earth would inevitably lead to the destruction of human civilization along with foundations to the kingdom of God.

Notes:
1. There is no consensus of the exact dates of the various books in the Bible. In this work, the approximate chronology of the books of the Bible is taken from NABRE's introductions to "The

Pentateuch," "Genesis," and "the Book of Wisdom." See also Jonathan Petersen, "When was Each Book of the Bible Written? *BibleGateway.com,* February 1, 2016, biblegateway.com/blog/2016/02/when-was-each-book-of-the-bible-written/ (accessed March 1, 2019).

2. Alexander the Great was given the title Lord of Asia following his victorious invasion of the Persian Empire (331BCE). The title emperor acquires significance following the creation of the Roman Empire in 27 BCE, and thus it was not known at the time. Also, the Seleucid Empire (312 BCE to 63 BCE) that had dominion over territories conquered by Alexander the Great is initially governed by a king. Franz Schühlein, "Seleucids," CE, Vol. 13, newadvent.org/cathen/13690a.htm (accessed February 17, 2019).

3. In Exodus, the Lord suggests to Moses that he is establishing something resembling a kingdom on earth occupied by his people (the Israelites): *You will be to me a kingdom of priests, a holy nation. That is what you must tell the Israelites* (Ex 19:6). In Isaiah, Hezekiah, one of Judah's kings, intimates that God is the supreme ruler of the universe: *You alone are God over all the kingdoms of the earth,* and *it is you who made the heavens and the earth* (Is 37:16). In the Book of Wisdom (50 BCE), there is a verse that reads, *They shall judge nations and rule over peoples, and the LORD shall be their King forever* (Wis 3:8); and another one, in which Wisdom, i.e., God, shows Jacob *the kingdom of God and gave him knowledge of holy things* (Wis 10:10). In the Books of Samuel (6-5 BCE), *The LORD said: Listen to whatever the people say. You are not the one they are rejecting. They are rejecting me as their king* (1 Sam 8:7). In the Book of Daniel (2 BCE), there are two references: a vision by the author revealed to King Nebuchadnezzar of Babylon indicating that God will set a kingdom on earth that shall never be destroyed or delivered up to another people (Dan 2:44), and someone calling himself the Son of Man reigning over a kingdom that will include *all peoples* (Dan 7:13-14). The Book of Wisdom is rejected by the Protestant King James Bible and it is not part of the Jewish canon. The Book of Daniel is accepted as part of the Hebrew Bible.

4. This is the interpretation given by NEs note on Mt 11:11.

5. Somehow, NEs see this outcome as indicating that despite initial opposition the coming of the kingdom will have enormous success. Note on Mat 13:3-8.

6. Luke *stresses there is an urgency to accept the present opportunity to enter because the narrow door will not remain open indefinitely.* Ibid., note, Lk 13:22-30.

7. Ibid., NEs point out that the passage suggests that the seed grows mysteriously and without human intervention. Note on Mk 4:26-29.

8. Ibid., note on Mt 13:24-30.

9. The harmful effects of not controlling weeds are probably not well-known except to farmers and governments. For quickly shortening the learning curve the reader may go to the following sites: Dwight D. Ligenfelter, "Introduction to Weeds: What are Weeds and Why do we Care?" Department of Agronomy, Penn State University. December 2009. https://extension.psu.edu/introduction-to-weeds-what-are-weeds-and-why-do-we-care (accessed on February 26, 2019); "Weeds in Australia - Impact of Weeds," Australian Government. www.environment.gov.au/biodiversity/invasive/weeds/weeds/why/impact.html (accessed on February 26, 2019); H.R. Cates, "The Weed Problem in American Agriculture," US Department of Agriculture. https://naldc.nal.usda.gov/download/IND43843083/PDF (accessed on February 26, 2019).

Jesus's Mission

Although preaching the kingdom of God appears to be Jesus's primary mission, the Gospels allude to other motives that may have inspired his actions. This category ranks as being among the least significant. Its purpose serves only to seek additional explanations about the mystery surrounding the public Jesus. There are keywords and discernible passages in the texts that distinctively relate to Jesus's mission that, when interpreted literally, allows us to notice serious incongruences in the authors' attempt to communicate God's message to humanity.

Jesus's words indicate there are several reasons for coming into the world and he seems to ascribe equal value to each one. Ideally, the communication of a strategy would unveil one overarching end while other reasons would constitute the means toward achieving that ultimate end. Herein lies the difficulty with the Gospels. The first indication of Jesus's mission appears in Matthew when the angel tells Joseph that Mary will bear a son whose name will be Jesus *because he will save his people from their sins* (Mt 1:21). In this passage, Jesus is supposed to be some sort of supernatural (not temporal) savior, namely because the phrase 'salvation from their sins' would have been eschatologically inconsistent with Jewish beliefs at the time.

Secondly, it may be deduced that the passage indicates that Jesus's mission relates only to the Jewish people. Nonetheless, since the term *salvation* has also a strong temporal connotation in the Old Testament as well as in parts of the New Testament, it is not clear whether Jesus is to serve as God's emissary, continuing the Lord's lengthy trajectory of sending prophets and rulers to 'save' the Jewish people from their earthly predicaments. Moreover, the angel does not specify which sins the Jewish people have committed this time. What is known is that the Israelites are living under Roman oppression, which is why they are expecting a God-sent messiah that would liberate them as God had done during the Egyptian and Babylonian captivities.

According to Mark's and Matthew's texts, God sends John the Baptist as a messenger to *prepare the way of the Lord by proclaiming a baptism of repentance for the forgiveness of sins* (Mk 1:2-4, Mt 3:1-3), suggesting a possible eschatological motive.[1] Luke indicates that John's mission is somewhat different: to *turn many of the children of Israel to the Lord*. John's Gospel says that the Baptist would pave the way for Jesus to come *to what was his own people*, the Israelites (Lk 1:11-17, Jn 1:11) without there being a clear reason.[2] God's voice from the heavens, *you are my beloved Son; with you I am well pleased,* confirms Jesus's prophetic mission to turn the Israelites into righteous people.

Nothing in these passages denote references to eternal salvation, a notion that, despite not being an essential part of the Jewish faith, remained as a logical possibility.[3] The angel's announcement to Mary in Luke's Gospel that she will bear a son, emphasizes that Jesus *will be called Son of the Most High,* will rule the house of Jacob, i.e., Israel (Gen 32:29), and his kingdom (supposedly temporal) will have no end (Lk 1:30-33). Additionally, Mary's and Zechariah's Canticles (Lk 1:46-55, 67-68) offer a preview of God's temporal intentions indicating that some type of salvation will come through the forgiveness of their sins, suggesting perhaps that if they repent and straighten their lives, they will enjoy God's previous promises of material abundance, liberation from oppression, and political and economic power (Gen 15:13-14, Deut 15:6, Is 60, 61, 62). These passages appear to conflict with today's understanding of Jesus's eschatological mission.[4]

People view Jesus's mission through different prisms: *the consolation of Israel,* God's salvation, *a light for revelation to the Gentiles*, glory for the people of Israel, and the redemption of Jerusalem (Lk 2:10-11, 2:25-32, 2:36-38), none of which necessarily points to eternal salvation. In Matthew, Jesus is referred to as *king of the Jews,* the Messiah, and a ruler who is to shepherd the Israelite people (Mt 2:1-6), all of which suggest an earthly political and religious mission. In John's Gospel, the Baptist identifies Jesus as the Lamb of God, alluding to a sacrificial lamb that assumes upon himself the sinfulness of his people (Jn 1:29); clearly a non-temporal mission, as it pertains to a cosmic redemption whose final effects humanity still awaits.

Jesus begins his mission as a preacher focusing on repentance and teaching at synagogues that *the kingdom of God is at hand* (Mk 1:14-15). But this mission attains a socio-political character that has less to do with repentance. The objectives are purely temporal: *to proclaim liberty to captives and recovery of sight to the blind, to let the oppressed go free, and to proclaim a year acceptable to the Lord* (Lk 4:15-21). That Jesus spends much of his time attacking the religious authorities (Mk 12:38-40, Lk 11:37-54, Mt 23:1-39), suggests that he considers them a serious obstacle to the realization of God's kingdom on earth. Hence, part of his mission is to legitimize his authority through his teachings and his miraculous deeds.

He recruits his disciples to become *fishers of men* (Mk 1:16-20, Lk 5:10, Mt 4:12-23). Does this mean that he pretends to create a new religion or a religious socio-political movement? He spends time praying, which means that his mission has a spiritual component. He acknowledges that he needs to preach at the synagogues because *for this purpose have I come* (Mk 1:35-39, Lk 4:42-44), i.e., to be a teacher. Nonetheless, contrary to established Jewish tradition, his students are not virtuous people; instead, he comes to call on sinners (Mk 2:16-17, Lk 5:30-32, Mt 9:11-13). His role may have to do with turning people's lives around; activities that are similar to what a social worker, a community police officer, or a religious official might do today in crime-infested neighborhoods. His emphasis is not to eliminate delinquent behavior (a temporal offense), but on eradicating sin (an offense against God). The behavior is the same, but his intention assumes eschatological characteristics. Additionally, Jesus indicates, rather authoritatively, that one of his functions is to forgive sins, something only God can do (Mk 5:1-11, Lk 5:18-26, Mt 9:2-8, Jn 8:2-11). With his departure from the world, his sin-forgiving activities would cease, so he delegates this authority to his disciples, signaling a continuation of his mission. In these passages, the kingdom of God seems to play, at best, a modest role.

He then asks his twelve disciples to begin to proclaim the kingdom of God and to heal the sick (Mk 6:6-13, Lk 9:1-6). He adds seventy-two more companions (Lk 10:1-16) assigning them similar duties and reminding them that they are not to go into pagan territory, but only to retrieve the *lost sheep of the house of Israel* (Mt 10:5-6) because that is what God tells him (Mt 15:24, Lk 24:21, Jn 1:31). Incongruously, in Mark, there appear to be no restrictions as to where they can go. Meanwhile, Matthew indicates that Jesus fulfills a prophecy from Isaiah indicating that he is to proclaim justice and bring hope to the Gentiles (Mt 12:15-21), which he does by going into Gentile lands (Mk 7:24-30, Mt 15:21-28, Jn 4:4-42). Jesus's action to override the Father's is among the most striking oddities in the New Testament. Once Jesus (or the authors) decides upon a new course of action, the synoptics include the same phraseology toward their endings to go *into the whole world* (Mk 16:15), preach *repentance ... and make disciples of all nations* (Lk 24:47, Mt 28:19).

Another aspect of his mission is to fulfill a most sacred Mosaic Law (Mt 5:17-19). Jesus, however, makes substantial changes to the law itself, something that no other prophet likely would have dared to do. At the same time, his mission entails resistance to wickedness through non-violent means (Mk 14:43-50, Lk 22:47-53, Mt 26:50-56, Jn 18:7-11); nonetheless, his intentions, as depicted through some of his parables suggest the opposite (Lk 12:49-53, Mt 10:34-36).

As a teacher, Jesus's mission is to educate the world about good and evil, a subject matter that God had denied to Adam and Eve in the Garden of Eden. By becoming *the true light, which enlightens everyone* (Jn 1:9), his mission changes noticeably in John's Gospel (as opposed to the synoptics), as he focuses on becoming the eschatological savior of the world. In John's text, salvation has less to do with temporal liberation from oppression. Instead, claiming to be the son of the Father, he is to exercise judgment, not only upon the Israelites but upon all humankind at the end of time (Jn 5:21-27). Belief in Jesus is the trademark in John's Gospel; repentance, although presumed, does not even appear in the text (Jn 3:16-18, 5:23-24, 6:28-33, 39-40, 12:44-50).

He teaches his disciples that his mission entails great suffering and rejection, and eventually will lead him to be killed, but he does not explain to them why it must happen; and his disciples do not inquire (Mk 8:31-32; 9-31-32, 10:32-34, Lk 9:22, 9:43-45, 18:31-34). The answer shows up at Gethsemane. Presumably, one of his disciples overhears Jesus praying to the Father (Peter and the two sons of the Zebedee are with him) that it is God's will that he should accept his destiny (Mk 14:32-36, Lk 22:4-42, Mt 26:36-39), even though he gives no reason for such a tragic ending. In John's Gospel, however, he indicates he is following the Father's command to lay down his life for the sheep (Jn 10:14-18), but again, no motive is given.

To complicate our understanding of Jesus's mission even further, other citations in the synoptics indicate that Jesus's death takes place, not because he freely accepts his destiny or because the Father wills it, but only to fulfill the scriptures (Mk 14:48-49, Lk 24:25-27, 44-47, Mt 26:53-56). Since this explanation does not appear anywhere in the Old Testament, why does it show up in the Gospels?[5] Does it make human sense that God uses his son merely to legitimize someone else's words, without additional explanation?

Jesus's mission as savior or redeemer (examined in Jesus's Database Profile) is problematic because the term *savior/salvation* in the Gospels has temporal and eschatological connotations. Additionally, as a title, the term is noteworthy only because it is overstressed in John's Gospels; otherwise, it would have been among the least significant of Jesus's titles. He indicates that his mission is to give up his life as a ransom for many for the forgiveness of sins (Mk 10:45, 14:24-24, Lk 22:20, Mt 20:28, 26:27-28). This aspect of his mission is reinforced by his metaphorical remark to the sons of Zebedee regarding the cup that God gives to each representing one's destiny; in the case of Jesus, it signifies his resignation to the destiny that God assigns to him, a redeemer (Mk 10:39, Mt 20:22-23, Jn 18:11).[6] These passages provide a similar interpretation to the motive for Jesus's death (the forgiveness of sin), although they do not provide an explanation why Jesus's mission as the Messiah changes from temporal to cosmic; or why he is entrusted with the responsibility to assume the sins of others.

Jesus's mission entails acknowledging his role as the Jewish Messiah (Mk 8:27-30, 14:61-62, Lk 7:18-22, 9:18-21, 22:66-70 23:1-5, Mt 11:2-5, 16:13-20, 26:63-64). But what kind of a messiah is he? According to Jewish tradition, the Messiah is God's chosen (anointed) envoy to the Israelites. He is to be a descendant of King David who would secure the land of Israel, enabling all Jews to worship God in accordance with the laws in the Torah, as a result of which there would be peace throughout the world.[7] For this to happen, however, Judaism (or the teachings in the Torah) would have to extend throughout all four corners of the earth.

But the Jewish Messiah seems to have a dual personality. Although there may be theological insinuations to a temporal messiah in the Old Testament, the eschatological characteristics of this person begin to appear only at the time of the Second Temple. During this time, however, Jesus is not the only one who claims to be the Messiah; others, including Judas the Galilean, the founder of the Zealot movement, and Simon bar Kokhba, who leads a revolt against the Roman Empire, assert messianic leadership. While being human, (whether king or priest), the Jewish Messiah could embody supernatural qualities (as Roman emperors did); yet according to other interpretations, the Jewish Messiah is *never a savior in the Christian meaning*.[8] In the words of still another interpreter, the Messiah is *to be prophet, warrior, judge, king, and teacher of Torah*.[9]

When Jesus travels to Jerusalem he is welcomed and acclaimed as the king of Israel who comes in the name of God, the son of David, and a prophet. The term *Messiah* does not show up in these passages in the Gospels, although the attributes he receives (and he accepts) partially qualify him for the designation (Mk 11:8-10, Lk 19:36-40, Mt 21:8-11, Jn 12:12-15). In the eyes of the Israelites, is Jesus the temporal king who comes to liberate Israel from oppression as God has promised, or is he a different type of messiah? His insistence on going after sinners, and the joy he says there is in heaven *over one sinner who repents than over ninety-nine righteous people who have no need of repentance,* suggest that Jesus's mission is not what the Jewish people expect (Lk 15:1-7, 8-10, 11-31, 19:9-10); unless successfully persuading Jewish sinners to repent might bring about a cosmic deed through which God will liberate them from oppression. Since the Jewish people do not repent, Jesus's role takes a different turn; his mission now becomes universal and eschatological.

Jesus's mission cannot be judged entirely by his victorious entrance into Jerusalem. Days after, Jesus is crucified, thereby dampening the expectations of the Jewish people that, in his capacity as a prophet, he would redeem Israel (Lk 24:13-21) from oppression. The Gospels indicate that Jesus chooses not to confront Roman oppression, notwithstanding his promise (Lk 4: 16:21).[10] Instead, he remains passive amid Roman crimes (Lk 13:1-5). These disappointments weigh heavily today as reasons why the Jewish people fail to accept Jesus as the Messiah.[11] Could God have been aware that his promise of a Jewish Messiah would fail, thereby being obliged to change his mind? Other than the Parable of the Tenants in which Jesus threatens to take away God's kingdom from his people (Mt 21:33-46, Mk, 12:1-12),[12] there are no plausible explanations in the Gospels about Jesus's reasons for altering his mission.

Is his mission successful or is it a failure? As noted above, by Jewish criteria Jesus fails to deliver on God's and his own promises. It is far more difficult, however, to evaluate Jesus's mission from a Christian vantage point. Passages in the Gospels coincide with the Jewish people's expectation of a temporal messiah; other passages suggest eschatological objectives. Much incongruence is observed throughout the texts that make it difficult to extend a fair conclusion.

A Yet to Unfold Epilogue

Jesus's mission is to look after the lost sheep of Israel, but he goes after others too, including sheep that do not belong to the fold that he expects to lead until there is one flock and one shepherd (Jn 10:16). He is the *consolation of Israel,* God's salvation, *a light for revelation to the Gentiles*, glory for the people of Israel, redeemer of Jerusalem, and the Lamb of God. He says he will preach freedom from oppression and liberation of the captives but focuses instead on repentance. His claim that he has defeated Satan by defying death may be true, but his feat has yet to translate into eradicating evil on earth. Many of his teachings focus on the end of time, which means that his work is still unfinished. Moreover, any mission that ends in death does not necessarily imply failure by temporal accounts; if that were the case, the millions that have suffered heroic deaths saving others may be said to have died in vain.

Jesus's greatest success (for purposes of the faith) lies in the resurrection event, a topic that will be examined in the section on miracles; his teachings, as contradictory as sometimes they appear to be; and generating human hope, without which life for many would become unbearable. Ultimately, Jesus becomes, not the Jewish but the Christian Messiah, ushering completely different expectations; largely, the hope that through his teachings the righteous would rise into eternal life, and that through God's mercy the less righteous might be afforded a similar opportunity. His mission, indeed, was complex, hence difficult to comprehend.

Notes:

1. Mark misattributes the prophecy. According to NEs, the attribution of the prophecy to Isaiah refers to *a combination of Mal 3:1; Is 40:3; Ex 23:20.* Note on Mark 1:2-3.

2. Ibid., NEs' note, John 1:11 suggests that the term *what was his own* indicates property or possession, probably referring to Israel, while *his own people* refer to the Israelites. NEs indicate that Jesus *will create a new people of God.* The words *new people* suggest that God is renewing his bonds with his children, the Israelites. Note, Mark 1:8-9.

3. The Torah has little to say about the afterlife. Nonetheless, *in Judaism the belief in afterlife is less a leap of faith than a logical outgrowth of other Jewish beliefs. If one believes in a God who is all-powerful*

and all-just, one cannot believe that this world, in which evil far too often triumphs, is the only arena in which human life exists. Telushkin, "Jewish Concepts: Afterlife," reprinted in JVL, https://www.jewishvirtuallibrary.org/afterlife-in-judaism (accessed May 8, 2020).

4. NEs interpret Mark's opening sentence, *The beginning of the gospel of Jesus Christ [the Son of God]* to signify the *"good news" of salvation in and through Jesus, crucified and risen, acknowledged by the Christian community as Messiah (Mk 8:29; 14:61–62) and Son of God (Mk 1:11; 9:7; 15:39),* note Mk 1:1. This definition of Jesus's mission does not stem from the Old Testament in any clear fashion; it is at best a post-resurrection interpretation in which the term salvation implies a supernatural event. Moreover, the name *Christ* next to Jesus suggests a latter insertion after the initial manuscript is written. (See Chapter 3, Profile Database on Jesus, sub-section Christ – The Missing Title).

5. NEs indicate that *the idea of a suffering Messiah is not found in the Old Testament or in other Jewish literature prior to the New Testament period.* Note, Luke 24:26. This annotation is significant because it casts doubt on the role of Jesus as Messiah as well as on the role of divine revelation.

6. NEs' note, Mark 10:38-40 suggests that *in Jesus' case this involves divine judgment on sin that Jesus the innocent one is to expiate on behalf of the guilty (Mk 14:24; Is 53:5). His baptism is to be his crucifixion and death for the salvation of the human race; cf. Lk 12:50.*

7. Telushkin, "Jewish Concepts: The Messiah," 1991, reprinted in the JVL by permission of the author, https://www.jewishvirtuallibrary.org/the-messiah (accessed April 22, 2019).

8. David Flusser, "Messiah," in JVL, https://jewishvirtuallibrary.org/messiah *(accessed* April 22, 2019).

9. Gerald J. Blidstein, "Messiah," in JVL, *jewishvirtuallibrary.org/messiah (accessed* April 22, 2019).

10. NEs awkwardly contend that Jesus's sermon, according to Luke, not only *inaugurates the time of fulfillment of Old Testament prophecy*; Jesus's ministry fulfills *Old Testament hopes and expectations.* Note, Luke 4:21.

11. Telushkin, "The Messiah." *The most basic reason for the Jewish denial of the messianic claims made on Jesus's behalf is that he did not usher in world peace, as Isaiah had prophesied: "And nation shall not lift up sword against nation, neither shall they learn war anymore" (Isaiah 2:4). In addition, Jesus did not help bring about Jewish political sovereignty for the Jews or protection from their enemies.*

12. *Because of that heavy allegorizing, some scholars think that* (this parable) *does not in any way go back to Jesus, but represents the theology of the later church. That judgment applies to the Marcan parallel as well, although the allegorizing has gone farther in Matthew. There are others who believe that while many of the allegorical elements are due to church sources, they have been added to a basic parable spoken by Jesus. This view is now supported by the Gospel of Thomas 65, where a less allegorized and probably more primitive form of the parable is found.* NEs' note, Matthew 21:33-46.

Jesus's Conflicting Personality

The chapter on Jesus's profile provides a glimpse of his public life. Nevertheless, approaching the Gospels from different angles, as this book has attempted to do, might provide dispassionate readers with an opportunity to deepen their knowledge of Jesus. Whether the real Jesus is the same as the Jesus of the Gospels is difficult to answer. As we know, the texts do not tell the full story of the public Jesus (Jn 21:25); only what its authors were able to gather from human oral tradition or what God chose to reveal to them. Account must be taken that the Jesus of the Gospels is not like a photograph; the texts, instead, constitute the authors' rendering of a portrait, a subjective collage of events designed to portray Jesus through his public life and his teachings. If all sayings and teachings that the Gospels attribute to Jesus are accepted, there are serious inconsistencies and inaccuracies that defy clarification.

It is universally accepted that the Gospels were not written to explain the Jesus phenomenon. The writers intended to create an educational tool (a catechism) that would depict their truth (or God's) about Jesus as a person that embodied all qualities of human perfection to the point of being considered divine. What followed was the defense of this belief by apologists, men of deep faith whose task was to interpret

Jesus while defending him and his teachings. There are passages in the Gospels that conform with an amiable and merciful image of Jesus whose actions and teachings were worthy of being emulated. Concentrating on these passages, however, would distort the Jesus of the Gospels, diminishing rather than enhancing his personality.

The *Jesus's Conflicting Personality* category does not pretend to be an in-depth psychological examination of Jesus. Instead, it attempts to juxtapose a view of the apologetic Jesus with other passages from the Gospels in which Jesus's behavior and teachings differ from the apologetic view.

Christianity's View of Jesus

This brief presentation of the apologetic view merely centers on those traits that make Jesus an endearing person worthy of being worshipped. Thus, it would not be difficult for our dispassionate readers to infer that the Jesus of the Gospels is fearless. He defends what he claims to be God's truths while denouncing the behavior of powerful opposition, despite not having a strong following at the beginning of his public life or an army to guard him. Part of his mission entails making claims about his relationship with God that are so outrageous to the ears of his opponents that they begin to conspire against him. Jesus, nonetheless, continues his denunciations realizing that his actions might result in his death. Throughout his appearances before members of the Sanhedrin and Pontius Pilate, he accepts his fate by admitting to the charge of who he is, and by abstaining from defending himself against allegations he does not consider worthy of refuting (Mk 14:55-62, 15:1-5, Lk 22:66-71, Mt 26:57-66, Jn 18:19-37).

The Gospels portray a Jesus with a charismatic personality; *he taught them as one having authority and not as the scribes* (Mk 1:22). His magnetism prompts his disciples to drop everything to follow him. A search for the word *crowd* in the Gospels indicates that Jesus attracts a considerable following. It is conceivable, no doubt, that beyond his charisma, his healing deeds heighten the crowds' curiosity and the interest of the sick in being cured. His fame becomes evident by his triumphant entrance into Jerusalem (Mt 21:8-9).

Amid his claims of grandeur and his recognition as king, or as God's envoy, his imposing personality stands in contrast with his humility. His prominence does not require occupying a regal throne or boasting about his unique set of skills. He counters John the Baptist's admission that he must allow Jesus's stature to increase, by instead crediting the Father for his accomplishments (Mt 11:26-27). He declines offers of wealth, power, and glory (Lk 4:6-8); his greatest desire being to faithfully execute the Father's will (Mk 14:36).

His actions and his teachings revolve around love, compassion, and forgiveness. He is merciful toward sinners; at least toward some of them. He heals the sick, feeds the hungry, and gives hope to the hopeless. He welcomes children into his fold and is gentle toward them (Lk 18:15-17). Though passionate and strict about his mission, he is tolerant of others with similar goals (Lk 9:49-50). Given his powers, he is reluctant to use violence to attain his objectives (perhaps to the chagrin of many of his followers), so he accepts an undeserving and humiliating death on the cross; an act that evokes sadness, disgust, and heroic love, since according to him, he is shedding his blood to ransom others. He loathes hypocrisy, selfishness, meanness, and dishonesty. Perhaps, his most virtuous deed occurs at the moment of his death, as he forgives a bandit who dies with him as well as his executioners. Today, Jesus is loved and worshipped because a partial portrait emanates from the Gospels depicting him as someone who only wanted to do good and to save the world (Jn 12:47).

The Other Jesus

Along with the lovable Jesus stands the same Jesus but with a seemingly violent disposition; someone who at times appears self-righteous and insensitive toward people, becomes easily irritated and vengeful, unhelpful, and unforgiving. Some passages depict him as being unnecessarily unpleasant and with a fearful autocratic streak, and although he is sociable and playful with his friends, at times he is offensive. Hiding behind his divine claims lie uncertainty and fear at the time of his death, traits that would lead to disappointment among his trusted disciples. This other Jesus not so much contradicts the apologists' Jesus as it raises questions about the veracity of both views.

An Angry Jesus

Some people may regard anger as an unchristian disposition. Anger, however, is a universal emotion occurring usually when events or human behavior fail to line up with the individual's expectations. Given numerous and diverse situations taking place daily, there might be proper or rightful and improper or wrongful anger. People might become angry (even curse) if their candidate's opponent for office is elected or if their soccer team is defeated. But is their anger justified (or at least understandable) if the elected official stands for values that Jesus would find objectionable, for example, nativism, fear, and hatred as means to divide people, hoping that these views would resonate within the electorate? Would losers' anger be justified if the opponent wins the World Series through dishonesty? Is it improper to be angry at those who do not care about the well-being of others?

It seems that anger in these cases follows the same definition of justice; it depends on the values the angry person upholds. For example, according to Jesus, healing the sick is far more important than observing the Sabbath, thus looking at the religious authorities *with anger and grieved at their hardness of heart* he decides to cure the man with the withered hand, thereby infuriating them because they believe his action is in opposition to God's commandment on the Sabbath (Mk 3:1-6, Lk 6:6-11, Mt 12:9-14). Is Jesus's anger morally justifiable in this case? Since he claims to represent absolute truth, it seems to be.

There are passages in the Gospels that depict a type of Jesus that many Christian apologists set aside, or else they provide a different angle that in their eyes justifies Jesus's behavior. Readers of the Bible may need to be reminded that the Jesus phenomenon takes place at a time when there are questions about who he is and what he does, as noticed through his various titles. Additional questions may even be raised regarding his mission. Why does he become incarnate? Why does he say he will become a temporal leader but refuses to engage those who oppress his people? Why does he malign pagans and then instruct his disciples to go after them? These passages might upset the faithful, despite being the word of God.

The Pharisees demand to see a sign from Jesus that would authenticate his mission (Mk 8:11-12, Lk 11:29-32, Mt 12:38-42). What kind of a sign do they want? Is not restoring sight to a blind person a sign? Perhaps moving a mountain would have quieted the opposition, in which case, why not do it? Jesus becomes angry at these requests and calls them evil because they demand too much. Nonetheless, in today's age of disbelief people demand even more, and concrete signs would go a long way to restoring a faith that has been weakened by reason, empiricism, and science, ironically, elements that according to the Christian faith have been divinely provided to humans to build the earth.

At one point, Jesus becomes irate when either his disciples or others are unable to cure a child that is likely suffering from epilepsy. He refers to them as a *faithless generation,* impatiently wondering how long he will have to endure them (Mk 9:4-19, Mt 17:14-18). Is it proper for Jesus to insult seemingly unpretentious and meek people who simply want to heal a sick boy? On another day, while on the road in the company of his disciples, Jesus becomes hungry, and in an apparent fit of anger, he curses[1] at a fig tree because there were no fruits while knowing (according to the text) that it was not the time for figs yet. *May no one ever eat of your fruit again* (Mk 11:12-14), he says, thereby depriving others of being nourished at a later time.[2] Today, people likely would have found this behavior to be contemptible. Not Peter, however; when they find the fig tree again, all he does is acknowledge that the plant Jesus cursed had withered (Mk 11:20-21).

In Jerusalem, Jesus overthrows the tables of moneychangers and merchants in the court of the Gentiles, outside the temple area, claiming that they were making God's house a den of thieves. John's Gospel indicates that Jesus makes a whip and forcefully drives them out (an unusual streak of violence) indicating that his father's house is not a marketplace (Mt 21:12-13, Jn 2:13-17). He must have known that these people were engaged in activities directly related to worshipping God, and yet, his zealousness affected their livelihood. One explanation is that Jesus is claiming his legitimate authority by defying the Pharisees.[3] But, is this burst of anger and violence justified? It is not as if these merchants are selling indulgences. Moreover, does it mean that similar activities taking place in churches and basilicas around the world, including St Peter's, are morally wrong?

He calls the crowds *hypocrites* simply because they are unable or unwilling to interpret the sign of the times (Lk 12:54-56). He must have been quite upset, as this action follows an outburst in which he says that he comes to set the earth on fire and to divide family members among themselves (Lk 12:49-53). There may be reasonably obscure explanations for this behavior; nonetheless, even at the time, his words would have contradicted other parts of his teachings.[4]

His temperament when addressing the Pharisees, today would lead to divisiveness and possibly violence. His rhetoric is inflammatory to the point of hurling insults at them. His vituperations (no other way to qualify them) seem to go beyond righteousness as he attacks the Jewish authorities (Mk 7:6, Lk 11:37-52, (Mt 12:34-37, Mt 15:7-9, Mt 23:1-39). In Jesus, the behavior of the religious authorities becomes personal; it is not only their actions he dislikes; he dislikes them, calling them *brood of vipers* and *whitewashed tombs*. Given that Christians are supposed to emulate Jesus, would his behavior toward the religious authorities today be considered an exemplary way to treat one's opponents? Although he teaches not to judge so that they may not be judged in return (Mt 7:1-2), Jesus refers to Judas Iscariot as a devil for betraying him (Jn 6:70-71, Mt 27:1-5), presumably not realizing that Judas would repent most unequivocally prior to his crucifixion.

Hiding the Truth

Part of Jesus's mission is to help people understand the kingdom of God. But by his own account, he seems to do the opposite by being secretively selective in revealing God's mysteries despite his call for transparency. He reveals mysteries of the kingdom of God to his disciples while hiding them from other people, either because he does not consider them worthy or faithful enough to understand his teachings. Bewilderingly, he is aware that the consequences of his actions entail the possibility *that 'they may look and see but not perceive, and hear and listen but not understand, in order that they may not be converted and be forgiven* (Mk 4:1-20, Lk 8:4-15, Mt 13:1-15, Jn 12:37-41). He even acknowledges that he comes into the world *so that those who do not see might see, and those who do see might become blind* (Jn 9:39). Keeping the truth from unbelievers so they may not be converted is disconcerting. It appears as if Jesus is punishing people's unbelief by making it even more difficult for them to believe.[5] Jesus's motives for approaching unbelief in this manner would seem to work at cross-purposes with his mission. His method seems vindictive, particularly given the many times that his own disciples fail to understand his teachings and desert him prior to his crucifixion.

As part of his teachings, Jesus says, *to the one who has, more will be given; from the one who has not, even what he has will be taken away* (Mk 4:24-25, Mt 25:14-30). Since the Gospels did not include footnotes, it probably took some time to realize that Jesus was not referring to an innovative economic concept whereby resources are taken away from the poor to stimulate them to work harder.[6] Exegetes, on the other hand, may have arrived at a reasonable supposition; Jesus is insinuating that God will provide an understanding of the kingdom to those who choose to believe while preventing those who reject Jesus from acquiring it, thereby making it more difficult for skeptics to believe.[7] Jesus even praises the Father for hiding the mysteries of the kingdom from *the wise and the learned* (Mt 11:25).

After two thousand years, it is still difficult to understand Jesus's pedagogical approach to teach unbelievers. In the Parable of the Talents, Jesus uses the above citation as a punitive measure, this time against a lazy servant, who in addition to being deprived of his belongings ends up *where there will be wailing and grinding of teeth* (Mt 25:26-30). As if understanding God is already not difficult enough, Jesus seems more interested in punishing unbelievers than in understanding their unbelief. His unwillingness to keep the narrow door open indefinitely (Lk 13:23-30, Mt 7:13-14)[8] is matched by his reluctance to understand human behavior. His recalcitrance turns into offensive behavior as he instructs his disciples to join him to spread the good news about the kingdom of God. They are to go into towns and villages and wish peace upon each household. If, however, members of the household are unwilling to receive them, they are to *go outside that house or town and shake the dust from your feet*, in effect, disassociating themselves from them (Mt 10:14),[9] predicting that they will suffer more than people in Sodom and Gomorrah. He reproaches people who have not repented declaring that they will end up in hell for not accepting the kingdom of God (Lk 10:13-15, Mt 11:20-24).

Disparaging his Disciples

Jesus rebukes his disciples because of their observation that a costly perfumed oil a woman pours over Jesus's head could have been sold and the money given to the poor (Mk 14:3-8, Mt 26:6-13, Jn 12:1-8). His rebuke must have startled them; after all, it is he who has taught them that assistance to the poor is among his most important teachings. Although Jesus probably has reasons for not rejecting an act of love from a repentant woman, his decision may have ensued confusion after telling them that they will always have the poor with them to practice their charity. It appears as if the poor exist as a means for benefactors to attain salvation.

The Parable of the Servant's Attitude is most enigmatic. Literally understood, Jesus praises the attitude of the master, who is not only demanding of his servant; he is ungracious despite the hard work the servant does. Would not an employee deserve kind words from his supervisor, if only to reinforce his diligence? Would God not feel proud that his children obey his commandments? Would they not wish to hear words of encouragement from God? Interpreters of this parable suggest that *the Christian disciples can make no claim on God's graciousness* since they are only doing their duty (Lk 17:7-10).[10] The passage suggests that Jesus's followers should not seek solace in God for the deprivations they endure for the sake of the kingdom.

In another passage, Jesus chastises Peter for objecting to allowing his teacher to die. Jesus refers to Peter as Satan because he thinks like humans and not like God (Mt 16:21-23, Mk 8:31-33). Why would Jesus expect a human being to think like God? Is it not somewhat unreasonable, particularly since Peter does not yet understand Jesus's mission? Then, before his ascension, Jesus replies to Peter's question in a hostile manner (Jn 21:21-22). The Gospels do not indicate Peter's reaction, although it must have felt disappointing for Peter to be reprimanded by his teacher after expressing concern for his wellbeing or inquiring about another disciple.

As Well as his Friends and Strangers
As Jesus journeys into a village, Martha and Mary welcome him to share a meal at their house. Mary decides to sit down with Jesus and leaves Martha alone to do the cooking. As Martha complains to Jesus, he reprimands her telling her, *you are anxious and worried about many things.... Mary has chosen the better part and it will not be taken from her* (Lk 10:38-42). Martha must have felt dejected since she was as interested as her sister in being with Jesus. His rebuke to Martha that listening to him is far more important than anxiously preparing a meal for him, may be considered unnecessarily unpleasant and conceited.

When a Greek (non-Jewish) woman appeals to Jesus to heal her daughter that is possessed by a demon, Jesus initially indicates he is willing to help, but he acts condescendingly, telling her that being a Gentile makes her inferior to Jews, and thus not entitled to his assistance. He says to her, *Let the children* (Jews) *be fed first. For it is not right to take the food of the children and throw it to the dogs* (Gentiles). The woman's love for her daughter enables her to overcome Jesus's disparaging remark (which apologists and exegetes see as a test of the woman's faith), and she tells him she is willing to wait if it means that her daughter would be cured. Jesus sees in her words remarkable faith and decides to heal her daughter (Mk 7:24-30, Mt 15:21-28).

Whether Jesus is referring to home puppies or stray dogs would not make a difference since, at the time, the term *dogs* was considered a sign of Jewish contempt for Gentiles. According to the texts, Jesus would refer to Gentiles derisively calling them dogs and swine (Mt 7:3-6), an old Jewish custom that was later incorporated into the early Jewish Christian community in which Gentiles were treated as inferior and sinful people (Mt 18:15-17).[11] Today's secular readers likely would regard Jesus's remark as unbecoming, a *faux pas* that would generate headlines if said by a religious or a political leader.

The Gospels point out Jesus's bizarre attitude toward Gentiles when he travels to the territory of the Gerasenes and cleanses a man (two men in Matthew) possessed by demons. He allows the demons to enter a herd of swine belonging to the people residing in the area. The herd rushes down a steep bank into a lake and drown. Jesus saves the man while destroying the livelihood of these people. They, in turn, are seized with fear and ask him to leave the town (Mk 5:1-17, Lk 8:26-39, Mt 8:28-34). Since Jewish regulations forbade eating pig meat (Lev 11:7), there was no reason for Jesus to be concerned with Gentile sensitivities. Today, however, causing damage to other people's property on account of one's faith would be regarded as objectionable and possibly unlawful behavior. Interestingly, it is Paul who reverses the Old Law on eating habits (1 Tim 4:4).

In another instance, Jesus addresses a crowd telling them, *whoever is ashamed of me and of my words in this faithless and sinful generation, the Son of Man will be ashamed of when he comes in his Father's glory with the holy angels* (Mk 8:38, Lk 9:26, Mt 10:32-33). Understandably, everyone likes to be accepted and loved. Nonetheless, shame is often a cultural by-product conveying emotional insecurity. In John's Gospel, people do not acknowledge Jesus because of fear the Pharisees would expel them from the synagogues (Jn 9:22). Would Jesus take fear into account when judging these people? Presuming the saying is accurate, his behavior is akin to an emotional reaction by a person who feels scorned. Although Jesus's sentiment is suitably human, is it proper of a loving Messiah who teaches forgiveness and regards himself as the Son of God?

Apologists like to remind the faithful of a friendly Jesus who is *meek and humble of heart,* and whose yoke is easy and his burden light. This Jesus, however, calls on people to follow him without granting them time to bury their relatives or to say farewell to their families (Lk 9:59-62, Mt 8:21-22). His attitude calls for his followers to reject their families (a Christian value); to hate their fathers, mothers, wives, children, brothers, and sisters, to be worthy of him (Lk 14:25-26, Mt 10:37). In words that can be easily distorted (depending on what they originally meant), Jesus suggests that people must hate their temporal lives to attain eternal bliss (Jn 12:25). In another passage, while addressing God, he excludes the world from his prayers to the Father, indicating that he only prays *for the ones you have given me* (Jn 17:9).

And Mary, His Mother
Among Jesus's traits, none is perhaps so disconcerting as his behavior toward Mary, his mother. When she asks him to remedy the situation at a wedding in which the hosts run out of wine, Jesus replies to her, *Woman, how does your concern affect me?* (Jn 2:1-5). He not only expresses indifference to his mother's thoughtful request (an atypical yet human mannerism); he uses a phrase that in Hebrew constitutes an expression of hostility. Referring to his mother as *woman* is highly unusual; and although polite, it was not regarded as the proper way to refer to one's mother.[12] This would not be the only instance in which Jesus disparages his mother. Being told that Mary, along with brothers, and sisters have come to visit him, he ignores her presence and their blood relations and instead points to those sitting around him to indicate that his real mother and brothers are those who do the will of God (Mk 3:31-35, Lk 8:19-21, Mt 12:46-50). Was it necessary for Jesus to belittle his mother to express God's priorities? It appears that Mary is too humble and understanding of God's mission to become affected by her son's slight, an act that would have saddened most mothers. Mary (and generations of Christians) may have been troubled too, by Jesus's failure to visit his mother following his resurrection (according to the texts). Given Mary's place in Christianity, particularly among Catholics and a few Protestant groups, this omission, if indeed it happened, seems to diminish her significance greatly.[13]

Jesus and Eternal Punishment

Jesus's teachings on eternal punishment present the greatest dilemma concerning his personality. Although there is precise teaching in the Old Testament indicating that temporal punishment must fit the crime (Deut 25:2), there is little consolation in having to read that God is a jealous and angry God capable of inflicting punishment against the wicked as well as the innocent (Ex 12:12-29, 20:5). In the Gospels, namely in John, anyone not willing to believe in Jesus will face *the wrath of God* and be eternally condemned (Jn 3:35-36, 3:16-18, 5:21-29, 6:40, 47, 54, 10:27), even though Jesus's mission is not to condemn the world but to save it. Those who wish to be eternally saved must accept him, Otherwise, *whoever rejects [him] and does not accept [his] words has something to judge him: the word that [he] spoke, it will condemn him on the last day* (Jn 12:47-48).

Although the doctrine of eternal punishment is not the central theme of the Old Testament, it appears in full bloom with Jesus. In the Old Testament, eternal punishment seldom shows up, more often than not in emotionally cryptic language.[14] It is possible that, as he appears to have done in the Gospels, Jesus reveals new things or stress realities that for some reason God chooses not to inform the Jewish people through his prophets. The doctrine of eternal punishment has been defended by the Fathers of the Church, namely by Augustine, and by Thomas Aquinas. They sought to validate Jesus's pronouncements as an essential constituent of divine justice based on the supposition that sinful behavior committed by a flawed temporal human being against an infinite being is of such proportions that it can render God susceptible to being eternally vindictive. The image of a temperamental God who shows his wrath along with his love and forgiveness would appear to be theologically inconsistent with the attributes that theologians accord to him. This image seems more akin to how a resentful human being would react under similar circumstances.

Reason and science, however, appear to have advanced throughout the centuries to provide a more accurate notion of human behavior beyond the interpretations of Augustine or Aquinas. It is reasonable and humane to accept that no sentence imposed by the sternest judge on earth, whether life imprisonment in solitary confinement or death, can compare with eternal suffering. Thus, in the case of eternal punishment, particularly based on Jesus's teachings in the Gospels, sentencing imperfect beings with a predisposition for sinning (that by definition would imply having a limited and inadequate sense of moral knowledge and free will) would appear to be a miscarriage of divine justice. Given the way human nature has evolved, it is difficult to conceptualize that anyone (or at least most people) meriting eternal punishment in accordance with Jesus's teachings could possibly have acted with complete and perfect realization of their evil deeds and the unrestricted use of their faculties (the Christian definition of mortal sin). Despite cosmic or supernatural arguments advanced by theologians, the concept of eternal punishment is equivalent, in temporal terms, to finding a medically certified insane person guilty of a crime of which he or she has little understanding and insufficient free will to reject the action, and still execute the person.

Many Christians may take great pride in God's sense of justice, to the point of desiring a just God over a merciful and understanding God. The Christian rationale tends to be that anyone who merits eternal punishment acts with full volition. But how do we know that this is the case in every instance, particularly if it is said that only God knows the human heart? It may be argued that if the guilty escapes punishment it would make a mockery of divine justice. This rationale favors a cleansing stage (purgatory) in which the wicked is confronted with their evil deeds and receive afterward fair or more equitable sentences. Hence, are Jesus's threats of eternal punishment serious or merely hyperbolic? If the latter, it would seriously weaken his image (and that of the Gospels).

Unfortunately, we cannot depend on the Gospels to provide an adequate answer since the texts show remarkable inconsistencies. Jesus promises to eternally convict the truly wicked. They include the scribes and Pharisees (Mt 23:14); the unmerciful servant (Mt 18:21-35); murderers (Lk 20:9:19, Mt 21:33-45, 22:1-14); both the Rich Fool and the Rich Man (Lk 12:13-21, 16:29-31); and those that meet his Judgment Day criteria for punishment (Mt 25:31-46). Nonetheless, he also condemns eternally those who are guilty of what we might refer to as misdemeanors, such as people who become distracted and become inattentive to the Lord's coming (Mt 25:1-13); lazy servants who are insecure and ill-prepared to become Wall Street brokers (Lk 19:2-27. Mt 25:14-30); those who find excuses for not accepting his invitation to a banquet, i.e., his teachings (Lk 14:15-24); and rowdy servants who become drunk and mistreat others (Mt 24:45-51). Additionally, according to the Parable of the Sower, he would convict those whose beliefs are weak or stolen from them by Satan or by external circumstances; and those depicted at the end of Mark's Gospel (and most of John's text), who exercise their religious freedoms (non-believers and non-Christians) and that, accordingly, would not accept Jesus. Reasonable speculation would tell us that most of the world's population matches these characteristics.

But while part of the Gospels' dual image of Jesus is similar to a present-day avenging Terminator, he indicates that he would eagerly leave ninety-nine of his sheep unattended to go searching for a lost one (Lk 15:3-7, Mt 18:12-14); or leave the door ajar for those who repent at the last minute (Mt 20:1-16). Moreover, the core of Jesus's teachings includes love, caring, and forgiveness of enemies. He forgives sinners who do not ask for forgiveness or may have not shown repentance (Mk 2:1-5, 3:28, Lk 5:17-21, 7:47-48, 12:10, Mt 9:1-2, 12:31, 26:28, Jn 8:3-11). He follows through in his teachings with his last deed on earth, as he forgives those who are responsible for his crucifixion despite not showing repentance (Lk 23:34).[15] Although in Mark's text Jesus indicates that those who do not believe will be condemned (Mk 16:15-17), in Luke, Jesus is not condemning; he shows his disciples his resurrected body, reasons with them, teaches them about the scriptures, and asks them to preach repentance (Lk 24:39-47). In Matthew, Jesus appears more mellow, telling them to make disciples of all nations and to teach them all he has commanded them (Mt 28:19-20). At the end of John's text, despite his continuous teachings that salvation is based on belief, Jesus does not appear vindictive (Jn 20:29).

A reading of the Gospels tells us that there are two basic competing traits in God: his justice and his mercy depicting the harsh and just Father and the loving God. The Fathers and Doctors of the Church have incorporated this dualism in their Christology; dispassionate intellect and emotional realism seeking to validate the stern and uncompromising Son of God while commingling it with a merciful Jesus; the horrific rational explanations that prevailed in earlier centuries as opposed to the understanding heart of a merciful God that is in vogue nowadays. Ironically, today the image of a vindictive Jesus prevails among many people who would relish knowing that ruthless historical figures, as well as their opponents, will pay their dues eternally.

Paradoxically, the term *mercy* signifies understanding, compassion, leniency, and forgiveness. Hence, why would Jesus teach these types of behavior unless they were meant to be applied to a sinful nature? After all, only the guilty facing eternal punishment, not the innocent, requires mercy.

Notes:
1. According to the dictionary the definition of cursing includes, *to execrate and imprecate, utter profanity, and blaspheme. Merriam-Webster Dictionary,* online, s.v. "cursing."
2. The theological explanation deserves attention even though it does not seem to exculpate Jesus's behavior. NEs' note, Mk 11:12-14.
3. *The activities going on in the temple area were not secular but connected with the temple worship. Thus Jesus' attack on those so engaged and his charge that they were making God's house of prayer a den of thieves constituted a claim to authority over the religious practices of Israel and were a challenge to the priestly authorities.* NEs' note, Mt 21:12-17.
4. Jesus expects that his teachings would be a divisive element; perhaps remarkably similar to the political and cultural polarization being experienced today in many parts of the world, except that it is happening among Christians themselves, even within the same denomination.
5. To unbelievers the kingdom is presented in parables to hide the truth. NEs' note, Mk 4:11-12.
6. The saying has been interpreted in ways that have nothing to do with Jesus. Robert K. Merton, "The Matthew Effect in Science," reprinted from *Science,* January 5, 1968, Vol. 159, pp 56-63, http://www.garfield.library.upenn.edu/merton/matthew1.pdf (accessed April 29, 2020); Alexander M. Petersen, Woo-Sung Jung, Woo-Sung; Jae-Suk Yang, Eugene H. Stanley, "Quantitative and empirical demonstration of the Matthew effect in a study of career longevity," *Proceedings of the National Academy of Sciences of the United States of America,* January 4, 2011, vol. 108,1 (2011): 18-23. doi:10.1073/pnas.1016733108, ncbi.nlm.nih.gov/pmc/articles/PMC3017158/ (accessed April 29, 2020).
7. NEs' note, Mt 13:12.
8. Ibid., note, Luke 13:23-30.
9. Ibid., note, Matthew 10:14.
10. Ibid., note, Lk 17:7-10. The passage seems to counter Jesus's proclamation in Matthew 19:29: *And everyone who has given up houses or brothers or sisters or father or mother or children or lands for the sake of my name will receive a hundred times more, and will inherit eternal life.*
11. Jews would use the terms *dogs* and *swine* to make insulting remarks about Gentiles. Ibid., note, Mt 7:6. Nonetheless, NEs question whether Jesus made these remarks. This attitude prevailed within the early Matthean Church, and even in Paul. Ibid., note Mt 18:17. This is still another issue that raises questions regarding the true nature of God's revelation.
12. *A normal, polite form of address, but unattested in reference to one's mother.* Ibid., Jn 2:4.
13. Apologists could not overlook this image without expressing 'human certainty' (not the same as Revelation, but merely a supposition that makes sense) that *Christian tradition is confident that Jesus appeared first to his Mother after rising from the tomb, as a reward for Mary's faith and suffering.*

Somehow, the author of this pious document attests that as Jesus bids farewell to his disciples, *with them was the Mother of Jesus.* J. A. Loarte, "Life of Mary (XVII): Christ's Resurrection and Ascension," *Opus Dei,* March 17, 2014, https://opusdei.org/en-us/article/life-of-mary-xvii-christs-resurrection-and-ascension/ (accessed March 27, 2019).

14. There are (at least) two passages related to the concept of eternal punishment succinctly: Isaiah 66:24 and Daniel 12:2.

15. Interestingly, this passage may have been added much later into Luke's text, since the phrase *does not occur in the oldest papyrus manuscript of Luke and in other early Greek manuscripts and ancient versions of wide geographical distribution.* NEs' note, Luke 23:34.

Hell

Most Christian denominations accept the existence of hell as a place or state of being where humans suffer physically, mentally, or both for all eternity as a central element in Christianity.[1] This section examines Jesus's views on hell according to the Gospels.

The NABRE Bible does not use the term *hell*, instead choosing 'netherworld' and 'Gehenna.' Meanwhile, the King James Bible and other Protestant versions (as well as older Catholic translations) utilize the term hell. Examining the uses of this term is challenging because of the numerous incongruences in the texts. In this section, the term *hell* is used generically to signify a place where the wicked are destined to go after death, regardless of whether it is a temporary or permanent location, or whether the dead sense their punishment or merely face complete annihilation of their existence. Given that Jesus uses terminology that may be interpreted ambiguously, words and threatening phrases alluding to a punishing place are tallied in this category. Relying on these terms, phrases, and its synonyms show there are 85 references to hell in the Gospels, 144xt less than references to Satan. The results indicate that Jesus's references to hell were insignificant in contrast with other terms despite his teachings on eternal condemnation.[2]

Having been raised under Old Testament Judaism, it is likely that Jesus's views on *hell* reflected his religious education. References to an everlasting life following the resurrection of the dead are negligible and/or inconclusive in the Old Testament, suggesting that Judaism did not look forward to an afterlife punishment (whether temporary or permanent) associated with hell. Only traces of hope show up that God will deliver the righteous from death and into eternal life (Psalm 16:10), along with a desire for eternity coupled with a sense of despair that God will *destroy the hope of mortals* (Job 14:19).

Instead, Judaism held various views regarding where people went following their death. The dead would go *down into the underworld* and *live there a colorless existence;* or into *Sheol,* an underground pit deep into the earth, where all (or only the wicked) would go and disappear. Sheol is described as *a horrible, dreary, dark, disorderly land*; *the appointed house for all the living,* from which no one was expected to return, and where the dead exist in silence *without knowledge or feeling.* Gehenna, a term Jesus used, refers to a valley south of Jerusalem where children were sacrificed to the Canaanite god Moloch in the seventh century BCE; it became known as a place where the wicked would go once dead. Passages in the Old Testament describe Gehenna as filled with a smell of sulfur and immense masses of fire that never dies down, likely the reason it was known as the *fiery furnace*. Still, another view held that God created hell when he created fire at the time of creation.[3] These views raise an elusive question that offers no reasonable explanations; why the wicked would end up in a horrible place filled with fire if they would not be able to sense punishment. Conversely, there are cryptic passages in the Old Testament suggesting punishment (though not necessarily in the afterlife), in the Book of Judith (Jdt 16:17), the Book of Enoch (Chapter XCVIII. 3), and Isaiah (Isa 33:10-12) among others.

Jewish views on the resurrection of the dead, however, change prior to Jesus's birth, as Jews begin to hope that God somehow would reward them for their loyalty by resurrecting the righteous while punishing the wicked in the afterlife. The Book of Daniel, for example, alludes to a resurrection when *those who sleep in the dust of the earth shall awake; some to everlasting life, others to reproach and everlasting disgrace* (Dan 11:33-35). Moreover, in 2 Maccabees (around 124 BCE), as a Jewish mother and her seven children are about to be executed rather than to renounce their faith, the brothers say to their killer, *you are depriving us of this present life, but the King of the universe will raise us up to live again forever;* and, *it is my choice to die at the hands of mortals with the hope that God will restore me to life; but for you, there will be no resurrection to life* (2 Macc 7:9-14). The Book of Enoch, not considered canonical, i.e., valid, by Judaism (other than Ethiopian Jews) or by most Christian denominations, includes references to the immortality of the soul for the righteous while the wicked would go down into Sheol where they would dwell forever amid darkness and fire.[4]

While considering Jesus's teachings on hell, it may be helpful to understand Jewish views on the soul at the time. As it tends to be accepted today, the soul is the immaterial or invisible part of human beings, as opposed to the body, which is its visible counterpart. No one knows whether the soul can or may survive after death, or whether it will be resurrected or not with the body, presuming there is an afterlife. The view held by ancient Judaism was that the soul was not immortal; it was destroyed along with the body upon death. This view held that the soul could not become separate from the body and be resurrected independently.[5] Other experts in ancient Judaism sustain that *the belief that the soul continues its existence after the dissolution of the body is a matter of philosophical or theological speculation rather than of simple faith, and is, accordingly, nowhere expressly taught in Holy scripture.*[6] In Christianity, there is an array of beliefs regarding the soul.[7]

In this context, there are at least two passages in the texts in which Jesus suggests the possibility of the body existing independently of the soul. Just before his death, Jesus tells one of the men being crucified with him, *today you will be with me in Paradise* (Lk 23:43), suggesting that, either the soul or the body and the soul, will exist in a different dimension while awaiting the resurrection. Moreover, Jesus tells his disciples, *do not be afraid of those who kill the body but cannot kill the soul;*

rather, be afraid of the one who can destroy both soul and body in Gehenna (Mt 10:28, Lk 12:4-5). He indicates that one should be afraid of having both body and soul thrown into Gehenna because at the time of the resurrection these people would not be among those living eternally. This is significant. If Gehenna is not related to the afterlife in Jesus's teachings and is only a dead-end place on earth, the being (the person) simply would become dust or enter into a permanent stage of no consciousness and no feelings, in which case there would be no real punishment. If Gehenna is a living site for the wicked, then there would be actual punishment, whether physically or mentally, or both.

The questions to be considered in this section include the extent to which ancient Judaism may have influenced Jesus's views on hell; and, whether Jesus taught the belief that the wicked could be punished eternally. Jesus is known to have frequently departed from Old Testament views, upending in the process essential aspects of Mosaic Law. Hence, it might be foreseen that content analysis results would indicate that among the central tenets of his mission, none is more important than the affirmation of the existence of an afterlife and the resurrection of the dead; views that do not show up explicitly in the Old Testament.

In the Gospels, Jesus points to the existence of a place similar to our understanding of hell, i.e., *the eternal fire prepared for the devil and his angels* (Mt 25:41), where the wicked will be cast on Judgment Day. He does not, however, explain who created it (God or Satan), or when or why, as he makes no reference to Original Sin. The imagery that Jesus depicts of hell in the synoptics is terrifying. There is *unquenchable fire* (Mk 9:43); a place *where the worm does not die,* (Mk 9:48); more fateful than Sodom (Lk 10:12); where people are *thrown into eternal fire* (Mt 18:8); where *there will be wailing and grinding of teeth* (Lk 13:28). There is *fiery Gehenna* (Mt 5:22), a state of *outer darkness* (Mt 8:12), and *eternal fire* (Mt 18:8) where *the whole body will be thrown* (Mt 5:29) and the wicked will *go off to eternal punishment.* Passages in John's Gospel are chilling. Jesus indicates that the condemned *will be thrown out like a branch and wither into a fire, and they will be burned* (Jn 15:6); that *whoever disobeys the Son will not see life, but the wrath of God remains upon him* (Jn 3:35); and that *those who have done wicked deeds* (go) *to the resurrection of condemnation* (Jn 5:29).

Jesus's words in describing punishment for those he will condemn are troublesome. The phraseology used in the texts is typical of the plight sentient beings will feel. If Jesus is not prepared to condemn anyone to face these conditions, why would he rely on frightening words such as *eternal fire* and *the resurrection of condemnation* to indicate that humans will experience either of these outcomes?

Jesus uses the term *condemn/condemnation* to express disagreement with specific conduct, and to dictate a punishable sentence or conviction in the afterlife. Within this context, his remark that the scribes will receive *a very severe condemnation* (Mk 12:38-40) seems awkward. It suggests that it will take place in the afterlife; however, is there a less severe condemnation than eternal punishment? Could he be referring to purgatory where punishment is supposed to be temporary?

In his parables, he condemns the wicked to an immediate death or be thrown into the fire where *there will be wailing and grinding of teeth.* But what does Jesus refer to when he says that, for those who cause the innocent to sin, *it would be better for him if a great millstone were put around his neck and he were thrown into the sea* (Mk 9:42, Lk 17:2, Mt 18:6)? The only condition worse than drowning would be to continuously feel the sensation of drowning eternally. Is Jesus merely relying on hyperbole when he asserts that conditions in hell are so horrific that it is better to cut off a hand or a foot or pluck out an eye than to risk going into Gehenna and its unquenchable fire (Mk 9:42-48, Mt 5:29-30)? Is he merely referring to a punishment of non-existence in which the wicked will not feel anything, whether fire or despair?

Anger and hurling insults at one another would land the offender in *fiery Gehenna* (Mt 5:21-22); adultery would too (Mt 5:28). People will even be held accountable for *every careless word they speak.* Those who fail to wear the proper attire to a wedding (simile for not being righteous) will have their hands and feet bind, then be thrown *into the darkness outside* (Mt 22:12-13). Could hypocrites, liars and cheaters, murderers, and selfish people be *thrown into the fire* in which people would not suffer but merely cease to exist? The Parable of the Rich Man and Lazarus indicates that the rich man will continue to suffer forever (Lk 16:19-31). Is Jesus suggesting that people ought to regard the parable as hyperbole? In John's Gospel, Jesus makes belief in him necessary for eternal life while condemning those who reject him. Why would he condemn unbelief if condemnation only signifies the disappearance of one's existence?

Historically, the above passages gave way to depictions of people consumed by fire and desolation that were used throughout the Middle Ages to religiously educate a vastly illiterate population. The purpose of this type of imagery, which has lasted into contemporary times, was to check immoral behavior by instilling fear and obedience to God. As literacy increased, so did writings about hell. The concept was immortalized during the early Renaissance period with Dante's vivid description of his Inferno in The Divine Comedy.

If Jesus's words are credible, it seems as if hell will be overpopulated. By issuing constant threats (they are not merely warnings), Jesus seeks to regulate belief and behavior to save lives, one of his primary objectives; *God did not send his Son into the world to condemn the world,* Jesus says, *but that the world might be saved through him* (Jn 3:17). Whether his threats are effective may depend on whether people believe him or not. It is noteworthy, however, that behavioral experiments have found a correlation between criminal conduct and belief in hell, suggesting *that people who don't believe in the possibility of punishment in the afterlife feel like they can get away with unethical behavior,* which contributes to increasing criminal conduct.[8]

Jesus's insistence on intimidating people to radically alter their ways suggests that he is engaging in warfare with a supernatural force (Satan) that lures good people to carry out wicked deeds that would bring eternal condemnation. Since no one in his right mind wants to be eternally condemned, there will be instances in which people will feel bound to act Christian-like despite their beliefs to prevent eternal damnation.

The affirmation of hell in religion, together with Jesus's threats, tends to elicit two initial and possible negative effects. It conveys a message of fear of divine retribution by an unreasonable and merciless God whose punishment—by human standards--would not seem to fit crimes committed. Moreover, while disregarding other aspects of human behavior (as well as the after-effects of Original Sin), the threat of hell leads to a cavalier attitude on the part of Christian authorities who hold the human person fully accountable for his/her actions, based on *a final, deliberate, irrevocable decision* (by the sinner) *to reject any notion, any response, any willingness to be open to God,* even though enough information is available to suggest that meeting these requirements while retaining free will is difficult at best.[9]

Most human behavior appears to be conditioned by the circumstances and places where people are raised; their reactions to incidents and the choices they make according to their personal experiences throughout their lives; to their fears and desires; and to what they see, hear, and believe. This means that it would seem more likely that if a merciful Supreme Being were to take into account human flaws, responsibility for evil deeds may be considerably minimized in his eyes. If that were the case, the gate to heaven would no longer be so narrow, and there would be even more joy in heaven since more of God's children will be saved. Granted, many of the wicked would bypass the stage of repentance, and the righteous would find themselves living together with the undesirable. Eventually, some 'respectable' believers might wish to head to heavenly suburbs to lead a more refined life away from those they did not like while on earth.

In civil society, both the law and civic education serve as important elements in ensuring proper behavior. It appears that it is no different in Christianity. If Jesus's teachings on hell are not hyperbolic, but accurate depictions of what may happen in the afterlife, they may be useful as a moral deterrent. Otherwise, an important element within Christianity fails. If, on the other hand, a consensus emerges that Jesus's teachings on hell are being misinterpreted or they indicate that there is no divine retribution, and the texts are not actualized, divine revelation, an article of faith in Christianity, becomes irrelevant. For now, secularism and religious pluralism seem to be slowly eroding the belief in hell, while civic education has largely disappeared, being replaced by political ideologies dictating norms of conduct. Nonetheless, it becomes apparent that the so-called culture wars going on in many countries are based on what people value individually. To hold people accountable to his values, Jesus relied on eternal reward as well as on divine retribution, i.e., eternal condemnation. If his values are being delegitimized by religious pluralism and a divided Christianity, what else could fill the vacuum? The answer might lie in attaining secular consensus among Christians, humanists, and other faiths backed by civil laws. Whether such a consensus will become permanent is anyone's guess.

Notes

1. In March 2018, a press release by an atheist friend of Pope Francis indicated that according to his recollection of an unrecorded chat in which no written notes were kept by either side, Pope Francis indicated he did not believe in the existence of hell. John L. Allen, "Ferment over pope's supposed Hell bombshell mounts in Italy," *Crux,* Apr 5, 2018, https://cruxnow.com/global-church/2018/04/ferment-over-popes-supposed-hell-bombshell-mounts-in-italy/ (accessed 8 April 2018). Days later, following media headlines that shook many around the world, the pope issued a document that, although it did not pertain to the question at heart, insisted that the devil does exist: *we should not think of the devil as a myth, a representation, a symbol, a figure of speech or an idea. This mistake would lead us to let down our guard, to grow careless and end up more vulnerable. Apostolic Exhortation Gaudete Et Exsultate of the Holy Father Francis On The Call to Holiness in Today's World*, Libreria Editrice Vaticana, March 19, 2018, 161, http://w2.vatican.va/content/francesco/en/apost_exhortations/documents/papa-francesco_esortazione-ap_20180319_gaudete-et-exsultate.html (accessed 8 April 2018). The media reacted as if Francis had dealt with the initial question and gave the pontiff a pass. Nonetheless, a review of the document indicates that Francis did not refer specifically to the question of whether hell exists or not. The term *evil* appears 40xt; *Devil* shows up 15xt; but the term *hell* appears only 1xt, referring indirectly to the place where the eternally damned go. We may contrast Pope Francis' usage of the term hell with that of Pope John Paul II. While briefly speaking to a General Audience in 1999, John Paul II's talk totaled 888 words. He mentioned hell 8xt and damnation 5xt as specific terms. https://w2.vatican.va/content/john-paul-ii/en/audiences/1999/documents/hf_jp-ii_aud_28071999.html (accessed 8 April 2018). Francis's document, meanwhile, was 19,750 words long, and no references were made explicitly to the existence of hell. This in no way means that Francis does not believe in the existence of hell; only that he chose—consciously or subconsciously—not to deal with the subject.

2. The tally according to each author: Mark: 12xt/4p/28sp: hell 0xt; Wailing and grinding of teeth 0xt; Condemnation (when related to eternal damnation) 2xt; fire (pertaining to hell) 2xt; Gehenna 3xt; save his life or forfeit his life 3xt.

Luke: 15xt/11p/112sp: hell 0xt, Wailing and grinding of teeth 1xt; Condemnation (when related to eternal damnation) 2xt; eternal punishment 1xt (punish); fire (pertaining to hell) 2xt; Gehenna 1xt, netherworld 2xt; save his life or forfeit his life 5xt; more tolerable for Sodom 1xt.

Matthew: 36xt/18p/266sp: hell 0xt, Wailing and grinding of teeth 6xt; Condemnation (when related to eternal damnation) 2xt; eternal fire or eternal punishment or fire (pertaining to hell) 5xt; fiery furnace 2xt, Gehenna 7xt, netherworld 2xt, outer darkness 3xt, save his life or forfeit his life 4xt.

John: 22xt/13p/60sp: hell 0xt; Condemnation (related to eternal damnation) 9xt; eternal life 12xt, fire (related to hell) 1xt.

3. Executive Committee of the Editorial Board., George A. Barton, Kaufman Kohler, "Resurrection," *JE,* http://www.jewishencyclopedia.com/articles/12697-resurrection (accessed May 15, 2020); Emil G. Hirsch, "Sheol," *JE,* http://www.jewishencyclopedia.com/articles/13563-sheol (accessed May 15, 2020); Kaufman Kohler, Ludwig Blau, "Gehenna," *JE,* http://www.jewishencyclopedia.com/articles/6558-gehenna (accessed May 15, 2020); Solomon Schechter, Emil G. Hirsch, "Fire," *JE,* http://www.jewishencyclopedia.com/articles/6132-fire (accessed May 15, 2020).

4. *The Book of Henoch* (Ethiopic), 1907, CE, http://www.newadvent.org/cathen/01602a.htm (accessed 10 February 2018). The date is subject to a great deal of speculation ranging from the second to first century BCE. It was highly regarded by the early Fathers; it is quoted in the Epistle of St Jude in the New Testament and is disregarded after the ninth century.

5. James Tabor, "What the Bible says about Death, Afterlife, and the Future," *The Jewish Roman World of Jesus*, https://pages.uncc.edu/james-tabor/ancient-judaism/death-afterlife-future/ (accessed December 14, 2013); Bart D. Ehrman, "What Jesus Really Said About Heaven and Hell," *Time,* May 8, 2020, https://time.com/5822598/jesus-really-said-heaven-hell/ (accessed May 16, 2020).

6. Kaufman Kohler, "Immortality of the Soul," *JE,* http://www.jewishencyclopedia.com/contribs/563 (accessed May 16, 2020).

7. Some mainstream Christian denominations believe that the soul separates from the body and continues to exist 'alive' upon death; others hold that the soul remains in deep slumber until Jesus's Second

Coming. Still, other denominations believe that body and soul remain together until the resurrection of the dead.

8. The University of Oregon, "Belief in hell, according to international data, is associated with reduced crime," *Science Daily,* June 19, 2012, www.sciencedaily.com/releases/2012/06/120619093217.htm (accessed May 17, 2020).

9. A Catholic Cardinal in the United Kingdom rejects the image of the fiery furnace as having been simply the product of the Church's iconography and not part of its official teaching. Affirming the existence of hell, the prelate indicates that it would be up to a person who by making *a final, deliberate, irrevocable decision to reject any notion, any response, any willingness to be open to God,* would separate himself/herself from God. "Cardinal says Church teaching doesn't put any specific person in hell," *Crux,* Mar 31, 2018. https://cruxnow.com/church-in-uk-and-ireland/2018/03/cardinal-says-church-teaching-doesnt-put-any-specific-person-in-hell/ (accessed 8 April 2018).

Devil

The origin of the Devil in Christianity finds its roots in the Bible through the term *evil.* In the Old Testament, the word *evil* appears 537xt, invariably denoting wicked, sinful, or immoral behavior; an inclination or predisposition toward wickedness; and an impediment to righteousness.[1] Throughout these passages, there are hardly any explanations regarding its cause. Not only do humans commit evil; it appears that God does something similar, although he would call it divine retribution. Nonetheless, it entailed delivering evil deeds against his people, the Israelites, and to others who defy his teachings (Gen 3:16-19, 6:1-11, 19:1-27, Ex 7, 8, 9, 10, 11, 32:30-35, 2 Sam 12:11, 1 Kings 9:9, 14:10, Job 42:11, Ezek 14:21).

In the Garden of Eden evil assumes an entity, a snake, the most cunning of all wild animals that God had created. According to the narrative, the snake commits what is probably the most atrocious offense in human history, the corruption of human nature. Nonetheless, God punishes the snake rather lightly while still allowing it to roam freely on earth (Gen 3, 14-15).[2]

Once their nature becomes corrupted on account of someone else's action, humans now must assume responsibility for their wickedness, despite an independent entity that will continue to tempt them all the time.[3] There are very few instances in the Old Testament in which evil is personalized other than as an inclination toward wickedness or a snake; instead, it appears as *an evil spirit from the Lord* (1 Sam 16:14-16, 23, 18:10, 19:9), *a lying spirit* (2 Chron 18:20-21), and an *evil spirit* (Tob 6:8), or *the satan* in the Book of Job.

In the New Testament, this entity acquires significance when Jesus recognizes it as Satan, whom he asserts is the ruler of the world. Jesus and the Gospels' authors use the names 36xt, often interchangeably, as an individual being. Interestingly, the term *the devil* shows up only once in the Old Testament, and seemingly in relation with Original Sin: *by the envy of the devil death enters the world* (Wisd 2:24). Content analysis results classify this category as more significant than *hell.*

Given its standing in the New Testament, it may be surmised that the terms *Satan/the devil* have deep roots in Judaism and the Old Testament, thus Jesus may well have been influenced by its views. Ancient Judaism considered the devil as an obstacle to righteousness, a tempter, or *an antagonist who puts obstacles in the way* (Num 22:32),[4] a view similar to the entity in the Gospels. In the Book of Job (7-5 BCE) *the satan* appears as an agent of God that roams the earth and patrols it, under God's authority no less. Although not a historical—but a literary--manuscript, the book presents this *satan* as cunning as the snake in Genesis and even seems to outwit God into allowing calamities to befall on a righteous Job just to prove Job's fealty to God (Job 1:7-12).[5] The Book of Zechariah (6 BCE) briefly refers to Satan, not by its name, but as God's *adversary* (Zech. 3:1), a view that coincides with the Hebrew interpretation. The notion of evil spirits being related to the devil is found in Jewish literature that is mostly regarded as non-authoritative or divinely inspired in Judaism and Christianity. In the Book of Enoch (2-1 BCE), for example, *evil spirits roam on earth.*[6] The Book of Jubilees (2 BCE) also refers to Satan and to malignant spirits *created in order to destroy ...* under the authority of its chief *Mastêmâ.*[7]

Jesus and the Devil

Jesus magnifies teachings about the devil found in the Old Testament. He assigns it a proper name (Satan) and provides a description that goes beyond *the satan's* role in the Book of Job. In the Gospels, God purposefully leads Jesus into the desert to be tempted--as it happens with Job (Lk 4:1, Mt 4:1). This episode is puzzling because, in the Lord's Prayer, Jesus regards the devil as a nefarious being with powers of its own that acts independently from and against God, which is why it asks to be delivered from *the evil one* (Mt 6:13). Today, the prayer asks God to be delivered from all afflictions, including physical calamities, diseases, or war.[8]

Although Jesus rebuffs the devil's requests—with help from angels (Mt 4:11), there is no reasonable explanation why God leads his son into the desert to be tempted. It is doubtful that religious institutions would recommend seminarians or the laity to be tempted as an exercise prior to entering religious life or marriage.

Jesus appears to know about the existence of the devil and does not seem to be surprised when he confronts it. He describes it as an angel that goes rogue from the beginning, and as a murderer, for which it would suffer eternally (Mt 25:41, John 8:44). On the other hand, he makes no reference to the devil's action leading to Original Sin, despite it is among the most important events in Christian biblical history, as it prompts God to send Jesus on a mission to redeem humanity.

In the Gospels, the devil's role is to counter God's creation on earth by seducing people to behave in ways that generate confusion and chaos. Somehow, at one point the devil wrests control of life on earth from God, and God allows it (Lk 13:16).[9] On three occasions, Jesus acknowledges that the devil is a formidable creature, even admitting that it rules over God's creation (Jn 12:31, 14:30, 16:11). Confident, however, that he can easily overcome Satan, he engages in what appears as an epic cosmological battle between good and evil taking place on a small planet, conveying the image that only humans inhabit the vast universe.[10]

The devil is not alone doing its work; it influences others to become its agents (Mt 12:43 Lk 11:24); as in the case of Judas who is tempted to betray Jesus (Lk 22:3). The devil dwells in other people's lives as unclean spirits that are responsible for physical and mental afflictions. Some of these spirits recognize Jesus and display their fear and anger at him (Mk 1:23, 5:1-15, 9:17, Lk 4:33, 8:27, 13:11, Mt 8:28). Jesus is not impressed. He engages in conversation with these demons; shows command over them, and crushes them during every encounter, regardless of peoples' faith, gender, or ethnicity (Mk 1:23, 3:11, 5:1, Lk 4:33, Mt 8:27, 15:21). He gives his disciples authority to cure the sick and drive out demons (Mk 6:13, Lk 9:1, Mt 10:1). Rather than interpreting driving out demons as a generous act, some people, including the religious authorities, accuse Jesus of working on behalf of the devil itself. Jesus counters the explanation by noting that Satan cannot drive out Satan, for that would be *the end of him.* Instead, he tells them that his power to drive out demons signifies that *the kingdom of God has come upon you* (Mk 3:20, Lk 11:14, Mt 12:22).[11]

Although he acknowledges the devil as ruler of the world, Jesus indicates that Satan has no power over him (Jn 14:30), and through his death and resurrection it will be driven out (Jn 12:31). He remarks that he has *observed Satan fall like lightning from the sky* (Lk 10-18), suggesting that, through his actions, evil is being defeated and Satan's control over humanity is at an end. Jesus's dominion over Satan, however, appears to involve only him, as he does not take any action to destroy Satan's rule over the world.[12] Instead, he alerts his disciples that Satan will weaken their faith (Lk 22:31), pointing out the need to pray continuously to the Father for help in keeping *the evil one* away from them (Jn 17:15). This attitude, reflected throughout the Gospels, indicates that God is not willing to curtail Satan's actions on earth. For example, Jesus tells people that the devil is to be feared not because it inflicts suffering, even physical death, but because being seduced into disobeying God can lead them to eternal condemnation (Mk 9:43-48, Lk 12:4-5, Mt 10:28). Furthermore, in the Parable of the Weed Among the Wheat, the master's decision not to pull up the weed for fear of uprooting the wheat (Mt 13:24) reinforces the view that Jesus allows the devil to operate freely until Judgment Day. This view is similar to the notion in the Book of Enoch (16:1) and the Book of Jubilees (10:7-10).

Whether the devil is a supernatural being or not, it is empirically evident that evil exists in the world. Although the definition of evil lies in the beholder's values and beliefs, most human beings likely agree that certain behavior is malevolent or morally wrong and ought to be deterred or personally avoided. This means that it is possible to agree on types of behavior and the circumstances that lead people to do evil. On the other hand, Christianity's explanation about the devil to an ever more secularized world presents problems. So far, there is no scientific or logical explanation (only the scriptures) to deny or to assert the possible existence of a supernatural force that whispers on one's ear seeking to lead humanity astray.

From a Christian standpoint, however, the concept of Original Sin and passages in the Gospel minimize—rather than heighten--the influence of the devil as the main cause of evil. The side-effects of Original Sin on human nature suggest that the unsettling of human moral faculties take place with or without the active participation of the devil. The view of the devil constantly harassing an already weakened human nature would seem to supplement, but not alter significantly, the explanation of evil. This theological view dovetails with evolutionary theory that suggests that evil may be the product of flawed humanity that, since its origins, has been relying upon itself while gradually advancing in a quest toward higher stages of moral truth through a process of social, physical, and psychological evolution that may bring about awareness and enlightenment.

There are other problems in the Gospels concerning the devil. By curing the possessed, Jesus demonstrates that it can defeat Satan. Still, he allows the power of darkness to continue to roam the earth and ascends into heaven leaving an almost defenseless and weakened humanity behind. The Spirit that Jesus sends to earth supposedly has an unspecified role in human affairs, but it does not appear to be strong enough to prevent even good people from committing evil deeds. Not persuaded by this explanation, or having to accept such a harsh reality, a secular mind has no alternative but to seek other motives to the causes of human evil.

Dealing with evil at a personal level requires awareness of right and wrong. Many good people, however, seem to have this awareness and still commit evil. The reason, according to Jesus, is that humans cannot deal adequately with temptation because they do not pray enough. This is psychologically possible. Going beyond a simplistic definition of asking God for help, prayer signifies a form of educating the senses by creating an *awareness* of the divine. Although living in God's presence may not altogether prevent evil, it may, however, reduce it.

Social science studies also suggest that prayer leads to increased self-control; helps to calm down emotions when feeling angry; and helps to reduce depression and anxiety, all of which contribute to lessening the possibilities of allowing temptation to gain the upper hand.[13] Although Jesus might not object to prayer as a means to enhance the emotional wellbeing of the person, its primary objective is to establish a relationship with God that in turn may inhibit evil behavior. However, how does religion persuade people who do not believe to pray for their own wellbeing?

The issue at large is not resisting temptation for its own sake, but wanting to avoid doing evil, for which struggling with temptation becomes crucial. Unfortunately, neither institutionalized religion nor secular societies consider the threats these societies face regarding evil as having its human origins (to an extent) in external stimuli, i.e., cultural ideologies and structures, each with a diverse set of values that condition human behavior. This observation would call for an examination of structural sinfulness in society. However, both Christianity and secularism view attempts to transform social structures as a means to improve the quality of life negatively. Christian authorities believe that focusing on sinful structures devalues free will and the change of hearts and minds approach that lies at the center of repentance and rebirth, despite its accepted truism that aligning social structures with Jesus's teachings might help in subconsciously promoting good behavior. Meanwhile, secularism is distrustful of this approach because it views it as social engineering, preferring to rely instead on individual and social freedom to engender solutions to social ills, rather than to upset social structures that favor the ruling classes.

Unwilling to rely on prayer, secularized society has been unable to find the means (yet) to overcome evil other than through punishment (including warfare), largely because there is still no consensus on what is right and wrong. Additionally, finding consensus in societies that emphasize individual freedom and personal rights is a never-ending task, regardless of the existence or non-existence of the devil. It appears that a flawed humanity has been left to its own resources to eradicate evil in the world.

Lastly, there is another type of evil in which neither God nor Jesus have chosen to intervene: natural disasters. The Gospels do not attribute responsibility for these tragedies to Satan, and the Old Testament indicates that natural disasters are God's doing. Nevertheless, ironically, Jesus has indicated, unequivocally, that he will be personally responsible for the most terrible natural disaster, his Second Coming, which entails the destruction of God's creation (Mk 13:24-28, Lk 21:25-27, Mt 24:29-31).

Notes:

1. *BibleGateway.com.*
2. God forces the snake to move on its belly and henceforth will be considered the most cursed and repulsive of all creatures. Additionally, the passage suggests that humanity will mortally oppose it. NEs' note, Gen 3:15: Christian tradition understood the passage *as the first promise of a redeemer for fallen humankind, the protoevangelium.* Nonetheless, in Christianity, the Fathers' tradition does not carry the same weight as divine revelation. The enormous consequences of the snake's act would have called for more than simple poetic symbolism so that it would be clearly understood by human beings. In the absence of more clarity, the Fathers' tradition becomes an apologetic extrapolation.
3. According to Christian belief, *the unsettling of human moral faculties* is a disease caused by Original Sin (CCC) 2515. Nonetheless, God's punishment to Adam and Eve, as described in Genesis 3, does not indicate that humans will develop a propensity toward wickedness (only death, pain, and hard labor), even though wickedness begins to happen. A general description of this tenet shared by other Christian denominations is found in (CCC) 390-406.
4. Joseph Jacobs, Ludwig Blau, "Satan," *JewishEncyclopedia.com,* http://www.jewishencyclopedia.com/articles/13219-satan (accessed May 29, 2020).
5. Job remains loyal to God despite the calamities that befall him because he is unaware that God is behind the plot with the satan. Also, it is surprising that Christians do not regard the idea that the satan can outwit God as being preposterous.
6. *Book of Enoch,* trans. M. Knibb, Introduction and Notes by Andy McCracken, 15:8-16:1, http://scriptural-truth.com/images/BookOfEnoch.pdf (accessed 9 February 2018). In its Introduction, Presbyterian Pastor Andy McCracken points out, *it is clear that this book was well known and studied in many countries well before the time of Jesus.* The date is subject to speculation ranging from the second to the first century BCE. It was highly regarded by the early Fathers and it is quoted in the Epistle of St Jude in the New Testament and is disregarded after the ninth century. *The Book of Henoch* (Ethiopic), 1907, CE, http://www.newadvent.org/cathen/01602a.htm (accessed 10 February 2018).
7. *The Book of Jubilees,* trans. by R. H. Charles, (London: Society for Promoting Christian Knowledge, London, 1917), Scanned and Edited by Joshua Williams, Northwest Nazarene College, www.sacred-

texts.com/bib/jub/jub24.htm (accessed 10 February 2018). Charles dates the book to the second century in his Introduction.

8. In Matthew, the verse reads, *and do not subject us to the final test, but deliver us from the evil one.* Although exegetes have not been able to decipher the true meaning of the "final test," to be subjected to temptation by God, has no reasonable spiritual or temporal objective.

9. NEs' note, Lk 13:16. Jesus's claim that a woman who had been crippled for eighteen years by an evil spirit signifies that *affliction and infirmity are taken as evidence of Satan's hold on humanity.*

10. In John, Jesus indicates he has *other sheep that do not belong to this fold* that he will lead until all come together into one flock under one shepherd (Jn 10:16). NEs' note, Jn 10:16 speculates that it may refer to Gentiles, *the dispersed children of God* in Jn 11:52, or to *"apostolic Christians" at odds with the community of the beloved disciple.* However, a former Vatican chief astronomer has offered interesting remarks suggesting that intelligent life at peace with God—thus not requiring redemption--may exist in the universe, in which case Jesus may have been referring to other beings as the lost sheep in need of a pastor; "Vatican astronomer cites possibility of extraterrestrial 'brothers'," *New York Times,* May 14, 2008, www.nytimes.com/2008/05/14/world/europe/14iht-vat.4.12885393.html (accessed 14 May 2018).

11. NEs' note, Lk 13:16: *The healing ministry of Jesus reveals the gradual wresting from Satan of control over humanity and the establishment of God's kingdom.*

12. NEs' note, Lk 10:18, indicating that *the dominion of Satan over humanity is at an end,* seems inexplicable given the continued power of evil on earth.

13. Julia Logan, LCPC, "The Psychological Power of Prayer," *MindandSpirit.com,* June 20, 2017, http://mindspirit.com/psychological-power-prayer/ (accessed May 30, 2020). References to studies in this article are the following: on prayer providing the individual with *the cognitive resources necessary to avoid temptation*: Piercarlo Valdesolo, "Scientists Find One Source of Prayer's Power," *Scientific American,* December 24, 2013, *https://www.scientificamerican.com/article/scientists-find-one-source-of-prayers-power/* (accessed May 30, 2020); on reducing anger: C. Munsey, "Prayer takes the edge off, a new study suggests," *American Psychological Association,* June 2011, Vol 42, No. 6, *https://www.apa.org/monitor/2011/06/prayer* (accessed May 30, 2020); on religious people being *less prone to depression and anxiety.* This study suggests that, given religious divisions in society, it might be possible to replace *religion with secular communities built on a common moral foundation....*although *such societies will still need many of the components of religion, including a belief that we're all part of the same moral community and, therefore, should make sacrifices that benefit the greater good*: Beth Azar, "A reason to believe," *American Psychological Association,* December 2010, Vol 41, No. 11, https://www.apa.org/monitor/2010/12/believe (accessed May 30, 2020).

Truth

I am the way and the truth and the life, Jesus tells his disciples (Jn 14:6). The terms *way, truth,* and *life* seem to be directly connected; Jesus believes (or knows) that his teachings emanate from God, thus they are truthful and constitute the only path to eternal life. This uncompromising assertion has deep-rooted temporal implications. Since it is claimed that he is addressing humanity (Jn 1:4), Jesus indicates that there is no moral truth outside of him. Even at the time (more so today in a relativistic social and religious culture), his remark sounded uncompromising. He is defiant in defending his teachings before the Jewish religious authorities because he believes that he is right.

But is Jesus a petulant religious fanatic, or is it that he is only acting according to whom he believes he is? Today, most people would frown upon Jesus's manner of expressing the truth. Although a dose of impulsivity tends to characterize Jesus at times, his zeal is offset by his forgiveness, his righteousness, his willingness to do good and follow through with his convictions by giving his life for his sheep rather than to engage in violence with his opponents (at least on earth).

In the Gospels, the word *truth* (including its synonyms) is devalued despite its profound meaning in Christianity. What stands out the most is the low use of the word in the synoptics relative to John's Gospel. The terms *truth* and *light* in John appear 66xt. In Luke, *truth* does not show up although he uses *light* 10xt and *dishonesty* 7xt. In Mark, *truth* appears only 3xt while *falsehood* appears 5xt. In Matthew, *truth* figures only 2xt, although *light* and *falsehood* appear 12xt and 10xt respectively. Hypocrisy, implying a deception of truth, is included in the category; Matthew uses the term the most, 14xt.

According to content analysis results, the category ranks as a less significant term. This does not necessarily mean that truth is unimportant in the Gospels (just relative to other categories). Jesus condemns falsehood and lying multiple times (Mk 10:17-19, 13:21-22, Lk 3:14, 18:18-20, Mt 5:11, 33, 7:15, 19:18). Truth, he says, needs to be exposed (*come to light*) and be transparent in one's behavior (Mk 4:21-22, Lk 8:16-18, Mt 5:14-16, Jn 3:19-21). Truth ought to guide one's conduct as a lamp guides the eye through darkness; otherwise, falsehood will drive the person's behavior. (Lk 11:33-36, Mt 6:22-23). All four texts acknowledge that Jesus is *the way* to God (Mk 1:3, Lk 3:4-5, 7:26, Mt 3:1-3, Jn 1:23); even the Pharisees sarcastically admit it (Mk 12:14, Lk 20:21, Mt 22:15-16). Nonetheless, he discloses that the children of light (presumably Jesus followers) are less earnest in their desire to attain eternal life than the children of the world are with managing their temporal affairs, going as far as to suggest that the children of light stand to learn from the children of the world (Lk 16:1-12).

He contrasts a dishonest tax collector who humbly accepts his sinfulness and is welcomed into the kingdom with a self-righteous Pharisee whose pride condemns him (Lk 18:9-14). In an interesting passage in Luke, Simeon appears to cite Isaiah 42:6 to indicate that Jesus will represent a light (truth) *for revelation to the Gentiles* and glory for the people of Israel (Lk 2:32). However, while the former assertion has been suitably proven, the latter prediction has not.

Perhaps Jesus's best example of living in truth is his admission before the Sanhedrin (cryptically in Luke and Matthew) that he is the Son of God; a confession that proves fatal as he is immediately accused of blasphemy and sent to Pontius Pilate to be crucified (Mk 14:60-64, Lk 22:66-71, Mt 26:59-66). He becomes more enigmatic, however, in a passage whose interpretation requires great imagination. He teaches his disciples, *there is nothing concealed that will not be revealed, nor secret that will not be known. Therefore, whatever you have said in the darkness will be heard in the light, and what you have whispered behind closed doors will be proclaimed on the housetops* (Mk 4:22, Lk 12:2-3, Mt 10:26-28).

The saying appears in all three synoptics although not in the same context. It seems to indicate that in the end truth will become self-evident to the point that it will not be questioned. On the other hand, some scholars think that he is *exhorting his followers to acknowledge him and his mission fearlessly* as he sends them out to preach the kingdom of God while *assuring them of God's protection even in times of persecution.*[1] Jesus, however, does not indicate what kind of protection God guarantees under these circumstances. Since there was no physical protection (and still there is none) when Christians were persecuted for their faith, the passage suggests that God will help his followers to avoid committing apostasy when being mistreated; not necessarily the greatest of sin when it occurs under duress.

John's Gospel indicates that Jesus represents the light that *shines in the darkness, and darkness has not overcome it* (Jn 1:5). What exactly this means is difficult to ascertain because two chapters later John's text reads that *the light came into the world, but people preferred darkness to light, because their works were evil* (Jn 3:19); that is, seemingly, truth did not overcome darkness.[2] That truth and darkness continue to conflict with each other suggests an enduring temporal struggle between Jesus's truth and his opponents'; in his view, a battle between good and evil. Yet, Jesus is emphatic in his assertions:

- Conversing with a Samaritan woman, Jesus tells her that he represents the type of true worshipping that God desires of people (Jn 4:23-24).
- He states that *my teaching is not my own but is from the one who sent me* (God); therefore, it must be credible (Jn 7:18).
- He proclaims, *I am the light of the world. Whoever follows me will not walk in darkness but will have the light of life* (Jn 8:12).
- He sounds unequivocal in saying to the religious authorities, *you know me and also know where I am from. Yet I did not come on my own, but the one who sent me, whom you do not know, is true. I know him, because I am from him, and he sent me* (Jn 7:28-29).

What basis is there that might legitimize Jesus's remarks? From the standpoint of the religious authorities, there is none. His assertions stand by themselves, although it may be surmised that they are supported by his miraculous deeds.

There is another challenging issue, particularly to those who believe that God reveals his mysteries to humanity through stages. Jesus tells his disciples that when the Advocate comes, *he will guide you to all truth. He will not speak on his own, but he will speak what he hears, and will declare to you the things that are coming* (Jn 16:12-13). But how are we to recognize the Advocate if false prophets will appear in his name? Moreover, since there are now dozens of Christian denominations, how will honest non-Christians be able to identify the true entity of the Advocate and the criteria it relies on for truth?

The above statements can be accepted only through an insubstantial type of faith. Jesus wishes to be believed because he believes it: *I speak the truth, (but) you do not believe me. ... If I am telling the truth, why do you not believe me? Whoever belongs to God hears the words of God; for this reason you do not listen, because you do not belong to God* (Jn 8:45-47). He presents a circular definition of truth; those who belong to God would believe in Jesus because if they believe in God they would believe in Jesus; conversely, those who do not believe in Jesus do not belong to God.

The statement condemns many people, leaving out of the kingdom those who believe in God but do not believe in Jesus, or those who might believe in the wrong Jesuses within the various Christian denominations. If Christianity asserts that faith is a gift, and Jesus is the savior of the world, may we not conclude that not everyone has received the 'same' gift of truth? Or are we to accept that God has given the gift of truth, i.e., Jesus, to everyone, but the majority has opted to reject it? The consequences are horrific. Since Jesus adds that he represents the truth, those who do not remain in him will be thrown into the fire and will be burned (Jn 15:1-6) regardless of the circumstances that lead people to not believe in him.

The Problem with Moral Truth
Perhaps, no other term in philosophy is as controversial as *truth* when moral behavior is concerned. Empirically, truth in morality stands for that which is objectively and demonstrably good as distinguished from what is self-evidently evil. In law, philosophy, religion, politics, and nowadays in science, most human conflicts and dissension revolve around the concept of moral truth. The Gospels make remarkable bold statements about Jesus: he is *the light of the human race* (Jn 1:4, 9); *truth came through Jesus Christ* (Jn 1:17); Jesus's flesh and blood are *true food* and *true drink* (Jn 6:55). There is also Jesus's astonishing comment contrasting himself as the true prophet while regarding others as deceivers (Mk 13:22 Mt 7:15). If these statements were authentic (they may be), why has most of the world's population throughout history not accepted them? Conceivably, there would be less acrimony and increased peace and joy on earth if objective moral truth could be identified and accepted. The problem is that, despite Jesus's assertion that he comes into the world to testify to the truth (Jn 18:37-38), the answer to Pontius Pilate's question, *what is truth?* still seems to elude humankind.[3]

Addressing the issue of *Truth in Trouble,* philosopher Dallas Willard acknowledges the crux of the problem: *no one has ever made a proposition true by believing,*[4] he says in reference to objective truth. But, from a religious (or ideological) perspective the opposite is true; beliefs can be accepted as truth so intensely that believers' convictions can change the cultural landscape when acted upon. Certainly, it would be best if human beings could easily detect objective truth; but we cannot. Hence dealing with the elusive nature of the term[5] has become among the most problematic issues of our times. Truth requires evidence if we are to minimize conflict and dissension. However, socially speaking, and in the absence of authoritarian imposition, truth, particularly moral truth, will continue to be subjected to relativism. Jesus's remark that he is the way, the truth, and the life, may be true for all who wish to believe it. What happens, however, to those who in good conscience cannot uphold such beliefs? How would Jesus judge these people?

The observation made in other sections merits being repeated. Although Jesus rebukes Thomas for wanting to see in order to believe, he is still willing to adjust his views by telling him, *put your finger here and see my hands, and bring your hand and put it into my side* (Jn 20:24-27). The proposition that, ideally, truth requires empirical evidence finds support in Jesus. In effect, Jesus provides empirical evidence so that Thomas may believe. This is not out of character with Jesus. The Gospels contain numerous passages indicating that people begin to believe in Jesus largely because of his supernatural deeds. Even Paul, who never meets the resurrected Jesus, accepts him by using a distinct form of empirical proof, 'faith-based substantiation,' to assert that if Jesus had not been resurrected the Christian faith would have been empty and vain (1 Cor 15:14-17).

John's text makes clear that, following Jesus's miracle at Cana, *his disciples began to believe in him* (Jn 2:11). Furthermore, Jesus sets his deeds as evidence that they are necessary for people to believe in him when he remarks, *these works that I perform testify on my behalf that the Father has sent me* (Jn 5:36). The message behind Jesus's deeds is to teach that we ought to be concerned with those who suffer. Nonetheless, he pursues a parallel, and maybe even more important purpose, to provide reliable evidence to people that would authenticate his mission and who he says he is.

Not that everyone will believe; it appears that, despite his deeds, at the time many remained unconvinced. This type of behavior, i.e., that people are willing to reject empirical evidence, preferring instead to follow their instincts, would seem to be a difficult proposition to accept even today. Nonetheless, there are people (including scientists) that likely would not concede to accepting a supernatural deed even if they were to witness it; many probably would insist that something else is being hidden from them or that there is a logical or scientific explanation for the miracle that has yet to be uncovered. This lack of evidence will keep Christianity a limited and divided religion, and eventually, through its involuntary confrontations with secularized society, barring an earth-shattering (supernatural?) event, it will lose its wonder and sense of awe.

Notes:
1. NEs' note, Luke 12:2-9.
2. Ibid., they suggest that *comprehend* may be another translation for *overcome*. Note on John 1:5.
3. There seems to be some interest in the topic. Although not a reliable metric, despite forty-four percent of the world's population not having access to the internet, and presuming that interest in the topic is found among people above 15 years of age (about 4.6 billion in the world), in 2019 there were over one billion searches in Google related to truth and nearly one billion searches related to the question "What is truth?" "Current World Population," *Worldometers,* www.worldometers.info/world-population/ (accessed June 8, 2019); "Internet Users in the World," *Internet World Stats,* www.internetworldstats.com/stats.htm (accessed June 8, 2019); "Population ages 15-64, male (% of total)," *The World Bank,* https://data.worldbank.org/indicator/SP.POP.1564.MA.ZS?view=chart (accessed June 8, 2019); Google search, "Truth," and "What is Truth?"
4. Dallas Willard, "Truth in Trouble," *The Veritas Forum,* December 7, 2003, www.veritas.org/what-is-truth/ (accessed June 8, 2019).
5. Michael Glanzberg, "Truth," *The Stanford Encyclopedia of Philosophy,* (Fall 2018 Edition), Edward N. Zalta (ed.), https://plato.stanford.edu/archives/fall2018/entries/truth/ (accessed May 31, 2020).

The Heart

In the process of identifying unique categories for this study I did a search for the word *heart* and found that it shows up 58xt in the Gospels;[1] about half the times being uttered by Jesus and the rest mostly by the authors of the texts. Intrigued, I sought to probe how Jesus uses the term, seeking to inquire whether he might have a behavioral theory of the heart, or if its usage in the texts is more conditioned by the cultural practice of the word at the time. This category does not rank highly in Table 2; yet, as it happens with other categories, its relevance ought not to be diminished because of the unusual way the term *heart* is characterized in the texts.

The human heart has been among the few organs that are necessary to sustain human life. Other organs include the liver that is responsible for performing hundreds of vital functions;[2] the lungs, which allow us to breathe air from the atmosphere, passing oxygen into the bloodstream, and releasing carbon dioxide waste back into the atmosphere.[3] The brain stem, which regulates the interaction between the brain and the body as well as performs basic body functions (breathing, swallowing, heart rate, blood pressure, consciousness) is also a vital human organ. It is possible to live with a damaged or severely defective brain if the brain stem functions properly. However, if the brain is removed from the body or is considered to be *dead*, i.e., lacks cognitive functions and brain waves, physical life may continue with the assistance of life-supporting devices, although rational or intelligent life (supposedly) is not possible.[4]

Is the Heart a Simple Organ?
The biological functions of the heart are extraordinarily simple. Through its pumping, it maintains a circular flow of oxygenated blood throughout the body without which the brain could not function, and then disposes of carbon dioxide being emitted from the lungs.[5] But the heart is more than a biological organ. Culturally speaking, the term *heart* stands for *feeling* as opposed to *thinking*; it connotes love, compassion, sincerity, courage, selflessness. To speak from the heart means to speak honestly about one's feelings; thus, the heart stands for truth and goodness. Used idiomatically, it may symbolize negative behavior, e.g., insensitivity (hardened heart) or wickedness (evil heart), or it may be used disparagingly, for example, when callous people refer to those who express a caring attitude toward others as 'bleeding hearts,' based on the belief that this attitude manifests human weakness.

In the Gospels, the heart is a vital organ too, yet it is anything but simple. Its role in human life is complex even though none of its biological functions are highlighted. The texts indicate that the heart has multiple functions; it feels, it thinks; it is the repository of God's word, and it is capable of instigating and nourishing both good and evil attitudes. Hence, the heart can become whimsical and mislead the believer, or even God. In Genesis, we read that the Lord soon notices that the thoughts of the human heart are inclined toward evil *all the time* (Gen 6:5). He reveals simultaneous changes of heart, first regretting having created humans and then expressing sorrow for having punished them (Gen 6:6, 8:21). Moreover, despite being closely associated with individual (and supposedly free) behavior, the heart remains under God's control, hardening it as he deems fit, thereby depriving the person of his/her freedom (Ex 4:21, 7:3, Lev 26:36-39).

Faculties of the Heart According to the Gospels
A breakdown of faculties attributed to the heart will indicate the multiplicity of its functions in the Gospels. In Luke, Simeon, a righteous Jewish man, metaphorically predicts that a sword will afflict Mary *so that the thoughts of many hearts may be revealed* (Lk 2:35), suggesting there are thoughts stored in the human heart. Moreover, in an interesting use of terms, early in his public mission Jesus knows in his mind what the scribes are thinking in their hearts, alluding to a direct cognitive relation between the mind and the heart (Mk 2:8, Lk 5:22). He seems to recognize intentions in others (Lk 9:47). Since intentions presuppose conscious awareness of a potential action associated with the brain, Jesus's words allude to the presence of cognition in the heart. That God too can read intentions in the hearts of humans (Lk 16:14-15) means that these reside in the heart.

According to Jesus, the heart is capable of reflection (Lk 2:17-19) and houses memory capabilities (Lk 2:49-51), indicating that the heart is an intelligent organ. It can register external stimuli and react to them. In this sense, it can express doubt and, in the process, weaken faith or increase it under different conditions (Mk 11:22-23, 16:12-14, Lk 24:25, 24:32). Moreover, Jesus suggests that the heart stores personality traits and may have a role in originating them (Mt 11:28-30, 12:33-35). Undoubtedly, Jesus treats the heart as an extraordinarily vital organ. Symbolically, he assigns it a prime location when he points out that his deceased body will reside for three days and three nights *in the heart of the earth* (Mt 12:40). Nonetheless, although the heart's most important function according to Jesus is to act as the repository of God's word, God's word is not even secured in the heart, since the devil may penetrate it and rob the word (Lk 8:1-15, Mt 13:18-23, 19:7-9).

According to passages in the texts, the heart processes external sensations and responds to them (Mt 15:8-9, 15:32-35, Jn 16:6, 16:22) by guiding these sensations in either a righteous or evil manner. Jesus is explicit when he states that evil behavior, including hypocrisy, unchastity, theft, murder, adultery, greed, malice, deceit, licentiousness, envy, blasphemy, arrogance, and folly emanate from the heart. Nonetheless, good and righteousness too originate in the heart (Mk 3:1-6, 6:3-4, 6:49-52, 7:21-23, 8:1-3, 8:14-21, 12:28-34; Lk 1:51, 6:45, 10:25-28, 21:34, Mt 5:8, 5:27-29, 9:35-36, 14:13-14, Mt 15:7-8, 15:18-20). Presuming that behavior (good or evil) is dictated by internal desires that in turn are generated by activity in the outside world, e.g., biological, social, or individual needs seeking to be satisfied, something must govern the actions of the heart to act rightfully or maliciously. This suggests that the heart is a malleable and unreliable device to tell right from wrong.

He teaches that the heart can be educated into behaving righteously (Lk 1:17), sometimes requiring harsh methods to accomplish it (Mt 18:32-35). Realizing the significance and value of things in life, the heart can then act upon them (Lk 1:66, 2:15-19, 3:15, 12:33-34, 24:32). Although at times Jesus refers to people as being naturally righteous or having a clean heart, in some instances he indicates that the believer needs to train the heart to love God *with all his heart* (Mt 22:34-39) as well as to not allow the heart to be troubled (Jn 14:1, 14:27).

There seems, however, to be an unfilled gap in Jesus's usage of the term. Since evil resides in the heart and is to be avoided, there must be an unnamed higher organ that can subdue the heart into doing right and avoiding wrong. Jesus does not explain in detail how the heart may be tamed to behave righteously. It may be surmised that the only way to train the heart is through prayer and sheer willpower (Mt 6:9-15, Mk 14:38, Lk 11:2-4). Nonetheless, given the lack of reliability of prayer (and the weakness of the flesh Mt 26:41) throughout history, it appears that evil will continue to exert pressure on the heart to do evil.

Issues with the Gospels' View of the Heart

Because the heart is not mentioned in the texts as a biological organ, its authors use the term to point to something they consider useful to convey specific aspects of the reality they experience. Today, we would refer to the cultural usage of the term as an idiomatic expression; however, it seems that in the Bible it is far more than that. Lacking basic scientific investigation, the authors of the Gospels use the word *heart* as a concept, a theoretical construct that they feel, believe, and think stands for something concrete that nonetheless confounds the senses. Hence, the heart is a source of strength and weakness, and good and evil; it feels, it plans and reflects, it stores information, and it responds to external emotions and events. Unaware (as they probably were) of what might be responsible for human behavior, the term *heart* encompasses everything human, quite distinctive from what non-human animals are capable of achieving.

Interestingly, nearly four centuries before Jesus's birth, the Greeks were engaged in studying the heart more scientifically, as a biological organ. Nonetheless, the functions they accorded to the heart were quite similar to those characterized in the scriptures. Among the most renowned students was Aristotle, who writes extensively about his observations of the heart in animals, declaring it as the place where sensations happen and as *the principle of life and the source of all motion and sensation.* He goes further than Jesus in discussing other vital organs that are deemed to be responsible for intelligence, such as the brain, and the liver, and their interconnected role with the heart in human behavior. He delves into the soul and the mind, terms that are rarely used in the Gospels, and identifies them as immaterial components; the soul residing in plants, animals, and humans, and the mind as the part that is responsible for thinking and exercising judgment. Without necessarily expressing causality, he attributes life, including perception and thought processes, to the soul; however, it is the heart that (biologically) sustains the soul.[6]

In a passage in Luke and Matthew, Jesus appears to diminish the role of the heart, as he asserts that *the lamp of the body is your eye* (Lk 11:34-36, Mt 6:22-23). Read literally, the eye, which in other instances may be responsible for sinfulness (Mt 5:28, 18:9), competes with the heart as guiding behavior. But if according to Jesus the heart is the center that registers and responds to external stimuli, Jesus may be referring to a heart that has been educated by his teachings and thus able to control whatever the eye sees. A different passage attests to this possibility. *Blessed are your eyes, because they see, and your ears, because they hear*, he tells his disciples, suggesting that they have grasped the essence of his teachings through their eyes and ears, and thus can understand while others cannot (Mt 13:16-17).

Hence, to Jesus, the heart is the most vital organ in the body. The heart is the equivalent of functions that are being attributed today to the brain. Thus, if according to Jesus the heart is the repository of God's word, i.e., natural law or his teachings, its equivalent location today might be the brain. I say *might* because as advanced as the natural sciences are today, we are still unable to make a precise judgment indicating that there is no intellectual/sensorial connection whatsoever between the heart and the brain. In no way is this statement suggesting that knowledge that so far has been developed making the brain the fount of human intelligence, is to be discarded. The issue is not whether the heart can think but whether it can do more than just pump blood; can it feel, to the point that both hatred and compassion stem from the heart, or do these behaviors originate in the brain? Until proven differently, I must abide by what science is telling us, that the brain registers, processes, and generates emotions, intentions, and reflection; that having a change of heart does not mean that the heart is responsible for the change. However, although emotions and intentions seem to be routed through (and involve) the brain, how they are triggered is far from being scientifically settled.[7]

Jesus, for example, attributes evil intentions to a hard heart, by which he means the inability or unwillingness to be like a child; to trust him. His disciples as well as the religious authorities are guilty of it. The instances in which he refers to others as being hardhearted, however, seem somewhat incomprehensible, as humans are conditioned into being distrustful of things that are beyond their own experiences. The religious authorities' opposition to Jesus; the fear and lack of trust that his disciples feel aboard a boat that is about to capsize; people's reluctance to accept God's laws on divorce; the disciples' expressions of doubt about his resurrection; or peoples' refusal to be persuaded by Jesus's miracles, all are caused by their hardheartedness (Mk 3:5, 6-52, 8:17, 10:5 16:14, Jn 12:39-40). Unfortunately, Jesus does not explain what is responsible for possessing a hard heart, how to heal it, or even what causes a clean heart. Are some people born with these traits? Are they God-instilled? Or does the devil play a role in their dispositions?

Intuition, for example, occurs when we devise a course of action that considers obstacles, means to ends, or alternative paths. It refers to information or knowledge (that can be right or wrong) that springs into awareness without having to rely on outside assistance or lengthy reasoning processes. When intuition is at work, sensations and past learning from previous experiences can result in specific dispositions, red or green flags, or immediate courses of action that are to be taken. It is similar to having a gut reaction, insofar as it refers to feelings that suggest solutions to a problem. Often, intuition provides instant true or false answers; secure or insecure paths to follow. Hence, is intuition a function of the heart or the brain? When we sense danger; when we readily act with compassion or selfishly without having to think, who or what is responsible for our behavior; is it God, the devil, conditioned responses, the values we cherish, peer pressure, or the heart? So far, we are limited by the lack of scientifically peer-reviewed studies unveiling concrete indications that the heart is responsible for cognition or that it houses the human senses.[8]

According to Jesus and the Gospels, God knows his creatures, i.e., whether they are good or evil, by their hearts. Interestingly, some years ago, a study suggested that the heart may reveal personality traits by measuring its electrical activity. So-called heart signatures may indicate negative traits, such as anxiety, depression, cold-heartedness, apathy, and others. The study did not indicate that the heart is responsible for personality traits, but rather that it physiologically registers emotions that can be noticed through wave patterns.[9] This means that (until new evidence is uncovered) the Gospels' theory of the heart is a unique (although unreliable) method of explaining moral behavior.

While science sorts these questions, Christianity faces a challenging issue in the decades to come. As the Bible will continue to be read without being actualized, what would be the impact of the continuous progress in science and technology upon believers as well as on the secular world? If the heart is the repository of God's word, the organ where good and evil seem to originate, and responsible for our uniqueness (or divine fingerprint), how would a real change of heart in the form of a heart transplant affect our understanding of Jesus's teachings or their credibility? Seemingly a heart transplant ought to radically affect (as in confusing) one's personality, emotions, and thinking patterns. So far, no study has revealed profound personality changes among those who have undergone the process. Does this mean that the Gospels need to be taken with a grain of salt? How are we to understand the texts once science can permanently replace a human heart with a mechanical device that performs the same physical functions?[10] How much credence are we then supposed to lend to Gospel truths? Would Christianity not be regarded as an archaic historical event whose validity eventually will be eroded? The various Christian leaderships have not given adequate answers to these questions as they seem content with apologizing for the written text and its tradition.

Notes

1. There are slight variations in the numbers according to Bibles translated into English, Spanish, French, or Italian. These differences occur when the term *compassion* or similar words are used instead of *heart,* or when the translators choose to add the term *heart.* Nonetheless, neither the differences in number nor in the usage of the term alter the overall results or its explanation. The following compares several translations in terms of the number of times the word *heart* appears in NEs, Mk 14xt, Lk 20xt, Mt 18xt, Jn 6xt; in 21st Century KJV, Mk 15xt, Lk 22xt, Mt 17xt, Jn 6xt; in the American Standard Version, Mk 13xt, Lk 21xt, Mt 16xt, Jn 6xt; in the Evangelical Heritage Version, Mk 13xt, Lk 21xt, Mt 16xt, Jn 6xt; in the New Living Translation, Mk 12xt, Lk 15xt, Mt 17xt, Jn 9xt. "Topical Index," *BibleGateway.co,*
 https://www.biblegateway.com/quicksearch/?quicksearch=%s&qs_version=31 (accessed July 26, 2019).

2. Donna Christiano, "Can You Live Without a Liver?" (reviewed by Saurabh Sethi, MD, MPH), *Healthline.com,* November 30, 2018. www.healthline.com/health/can-you-live-without-liver (accessed on July 23, 2019).

3. Stacy Sampson, DO, "What do the lungs do, and how do they function?" *MedicalNewsToday.com,* June 27, 2018, https://www.medicalnewstoday.com/articles/305190.php (accessed July 23, 2019). Although it is feasible to live with only one lung, it is not (yet) possible to survive beyond days without both lungs. John P. Cunha, DO, FACOEP, "Can You Live Without Both of Your Lungs," *eMedicinehealth.com,* emedicinehealth.com/ask_can_you_live_without_both_of_your_lungs/article_em.htm (accessed July 23, 2019).

4. Tim Verstynen Ph.D., "Do We Really Need a Brain," *PsychologyToday.com,* March 26, 2013,
 https://www.psychologytoday.com/us/blog/white-matter-matters/201303/do-we-really-need-brain
(accessed July 23, 2019); Joe Schwarcz, Ph.D., "Can You Live Without a Brain?" *McGill Office for Science and Society*, March 20, 2017, https://www.mcgill.ca/oss/article/health-you-asked/it-true-you-can-live-without-brain (accessed July 23, 2017).

5. Debra Sullivan, Ph.D., MSN, RN, CNE, COI, "The Heart: All You Need to Know," *MedicalNewsToday.com,* January 10, 2018, www.medicalnewstoday.com/articles/320565.php (accessed July 23, 2019).

6. Aristotle, *On the Parts of Animals,* trans William Ogle, Classics Archive, Book II, Part 10, Book III, Parts 3 & 4, http://classics.mit.edu/index.html (accessed July 28, 2019); Aristotle, *De anima,* Book I, Part 5, Book II, Part 4, Book III, Parts 3, 8 trans J.A. Smith, Classics Archive,
 http://classics.mit.edu/Aristotle/soul.html (accessed July 28, 2019).

7. Among some students of this matter, intentions are the by-product of the brain: Rick Hanson, Ph.D., "Wholesome Intentions," 2007, https://media.rickhanson.net/home/files/WholesomeIntentions.pdf (accessed July 30, 2019); others seem to be less certain: John J. Medina, Ph.D., "The Neurobiology of Conscious Intent," *Psychiatric Times,* February 10, 2011, psychiatrictimes.com/addiction/neurobiology-conscious-intent (accessed July 30, 2019).

8. HeartMath Institute, "Science of the Heart: Vol 1 (1993-2001) Exploring the Role of the Heart in Human Performance," www.heartmath.org/resources/downloads/science-of-the-heart/?submenuheader=3 (accessed August 1, 2019). This institution claims that the heart is capable of thinking: *Our research and that of others indicate that the heart is far more than a simple pump. The heart is, in fact, a highly complex, self-organized information-processing center with its own functional "brain" that communicates with and influences the cranial brain via the nervous system, hormonal system, and other pathways.* Whether these conclusions would hold following strict scientific peer-reviewed evaluations remains to be seen. The method appears to be based on some type of biofeedback that may or may not work depending on the individual's diligence. This is different from concluding that the heart can think.

9. Rachael Rettner, "Heartbeats Hint at Personality Traits," *Live Science,* March 8, 2012,
 https://www.livescience.com/18944-heartbeat-signatures-personality-traits.html (accessed July 27, 2019); another study suggests *that our personalities develop around basic needs* along with *accumulated experiences ... and is not simply about traits we're born with.*
 https://www.sciencedaily.com/releases/2018/02/180214150202.htm;
American Psychological Association, "Personality: Where does it come from and how does it work?" *Science Daily,* www.sciencedaily.com/releases/2018/02/180214150202.htm (accessed July 28, 2019); two studies suggest that the individual's personality originates in the frontoparietal network in the brain that generates its unique matrix similar to having unique sets of fingerprints. Susan Scutti, "Where Does Personality Reside In The Brain? The Frontoparietal Network Makes You Who You Are," *Medical Daily,* April 18, 2016. https://www.medicaldaily.com/brain-personality-frontoparietal-network-who-you-are-382142, (accessed August 1, 2019).

10. Emily Mullin, "A Simple Artificial Heart Could Permanently Replace a Failing Human One," *MIT Technology Review*, March 16, 2018. https://www.technologyreview.com/s/610462/a-simple-artificial-heart-could-permanently-replace-a-failing-human-one/ (accessed July 23, 2019).

Power

The study of *power* in the Gospels may bewilder the reader. Nonetheless, despite its mundane connotation, the Gospels have much to say about power. It is highly ranked in the content analysis results (Table 2). Dispensing with formal characterizations, power implies the ability of an actor, e.g., person, group, or nation, to do as it pleases, regardless of effort, and commensurate with its objectives. Ultimately, power means the ability to overcome whichever obstacles the actor may confront in order to attain its ultimate end(s).

The Power category owes much of its space to the inclusion of passages dealing with miracles. A miracle (the term is never used in the Gospels), is by definition *an extraordinary event manifesting divine intervention in human affairs.*[1] Consisting of the interruption of natural (physical) laws, humans tend to attribute these deeds to a divine being or someone or something possessing far more power than human beings. Whether Jesus possesses these powers, or the miracles were done on his behalf or through him, they were his doing according to the Gospels. The texts indicate that Jesus is acting freely when he heals a blind person, calms the sea and walks on water, multiplies loaves and fishes, transforms water into wine, or resurrects Lazarus. These actions suggest that Jesus is endowed with exceptional, i.e., supernatural[2], powers that he utilizes to attain specific purposes. His selective use of this capability may shed light on how humans ought to use power in accordance with Jesus's teachings.

How Powerful is Jesus?

Jesus commands no temporal armies; is not wealthy; has no legitimate temporal political or religious authority, and his assistants are not among the most competent. He indicates following his resurrection that, *all power in heaven and on earth has been given to me* (Mt 28:18), including the spiritual power for those who believe in him to *become children of God* (Jn 1:12-13). Additionally, Jesus says he possesses two extraordinary powers he has received from the Father: to exercise final judgment upon humanity, and the power over life and death (Jn 5:24-27). His words point to a higher dimension whose understanding humankind has not been able to grasp except through faith in a divine being. Nonetheless, his temporal powers are interconnected with the supernatural dimension. They are the means through which Jesus attempts to establish his credibility.

It appears that Jesus knows that without miracles he would not be believed. By healing the sick, feeding the hungry, and calming the seas, Jesus seeks to astonish people, call attention to him, and in this manner generate faith and gain believers. His powers provide him legitimacy regarding his claims. These supernatural deeds separate him from mere human beings.

The Jewish people, however, should not have been surprised by Jesus's deeds. The miracles that the Old Testament attributes to Moses are as extraordinary as Jesus's. Nonetheless, the difference lies in that the Bible clearly indicates that God is the author of these incredible feats; in the Gospels, it is Jesus, not God, who performs the miracles. At the time, no one had seen so much power in the hands of one man, a reason (that according to the texts) people begin to think that he is God's envoy on earth.

Jesus's Leadership Style
Leadership is a significant element of power; good leaders gain followers that in turn become a source of additional power. As Jesus gains influence through his teachings and his deeds, the religious leaders begin to perceive him as a threat to their authority, to their status, and a menace to the beliefs of the Jewish people. Searching the word *follow* allows us to identify the many instances in which people decide to initially accept Jesus, whether to be cured, to listen to his teachings, to make him king, or because he has become a famous teacher and a prophet. The word shows up 67xt, a rather significant number for a common word that is indicative of leadership. Thus, he calls on a group of fishermen to follow him and they drop their nets and go after him (Mk 1:16-20, Lk 5:10-11, Mt 4:18-22, Jn 1:37-49). He dares to invite Matthew, a distasteful tax collector, to follow him; he does (Mk 2:13-15, Lk 5:27-28, Mt 9:9-10). His disciples obey his commands (Mk 10:28, Lk 5:5, 18:28, Mt 19:27). Crowds regard him as a hero, a king, the Son of David, and the Messiah.[3] Even during his funeral procession *a large crowd of people followed Jesus* (Lk 23:27, Mt 27:57).

Although he claims to be doing the Father's will, his words carry an independently authoritative tone that sets him apart from other prophets. His personality is alluring. People are astonished at his teachings (Mk 17:22, Lk 4:31-37, Mt 7:28) and that he commands evil spirits and drives them out (Mk 1:27, 1:39, 3:15, 3:22, 7:26-30, 9:25, Lk 4:36, 8:29, 11:14, Mt 8:31-32, 12:24-28, 17:18). Thus, his fame spreads throughout Galilee (Mk 1:28). His disciples are bewildered that a human being has power over the winds and the seas (Lk 8:25).

Jesus's style is powerful. His commands are to be obeyed. Burying the dead or saying farewell first to the family are not sufficient reasons for not joining him immediately (Lk 9:61, Mt 8:18-22). His sayings are also intimidating, typical of someone that can stand behind his words.

The Gospels, however, suggest that Jesus makes promises that he is unable to keep and claims that are difficult to understand.[4] Nowadays, this behavior would be referred to as demagoguery that, if it becomes too apparent, tarnishes the leader's reputation and diminishes his credibility. At times his behavior seems arrogant and narcissistic: *whoever loves father or mother more than me is not worthy of me*, he says, *and whoever loves son or daughter more than me is not worthy of me* (Mt 10:37-38). Moreover, he argues that whoever does not support him is against him (Lk 11:23, Mt 12:30). These remarks, however, become problematic in multi-cultural and multidenominational societies because of their autocratic and exclusionary nature. They suggest an 'us versus them' mindset that prevailed in previous centuries and led to the Crusades, the Inquisition, and following the Reformation, to wars among Christians.

How Jesus Uses his Powers

Jesus's guiding principle on the uses of power would seem to be novel. Gentile rulers, he tells his disciples, tend to treat the ruled as pawns. Instead, he teaches that power is to be used in the service of others: *whoever wishes to be great among you will be your servant,* and *whoever wishes to be first among you will be the slave of all* (Mk 10:42-44, Lk 22:24-27, Mt 20:25-28). This principle might be useful today as a means to end polarization. To that effect, Jesus offers himself as a role model saying that he comes not to be served but to serve others.

Power ought to be used in the service of others because, as he tells Pontius Pilate, all power emanates from God (Jn 19:11) and delegated to humans for the wellbeing of all humanity, adding that rulers will be held accountable to a supreme power for their misdeeds. He provides his disciples with a tangible example as he humbles himself by washing their feet telling them, *I have given you a model to follow, so that as I have done for you, you should also do* (Jn 13:15). Jesus's gesture is counterintuitive, given that temporal power relishes domination, pomposity, and egocentric behavior. On the other hand, how is the reader to interpret another passage in which he says that to serve others first they must serve him unconditionally: *whoever serves me must follow me; the Father will honor whoever serves me* (Jn 12:26). The problem lies with his dual and confusing use of the term *to serve*; in some passages it means to be of service to others while in others it signifies to follow his teachings. In effect, Jesus is asking others to follow him by being of service to others.

Most of the miracles Jesus performs are related to the physical, mental, and spiritual wellbeing of those in need, particularly healing the sick. Nonetheless, one of the most intriguing characteristics of his powers is that he realizes that his authority on earth shall not be coercive; instead, he wants to persuade believers through reason, rewards, and fear. Despite his ability to heal the sick, he refuses to use his powers to apply physical punishment. Although supposedly capable of permanently changing the human condition (since he came to save the world), he tells people that they will be judged at the end of time (Mt 25:31-46). Within this context, Jesus's lament for Jerusalem in which he presages its destruction is puzzling. It suggests that Jewish failure to accept him will result in the city's destruction (Lk 19:41-44).[5] The statement seems inexplicable since even if Jerusalem had accepted Jesus, it would have found itself under Roman domination, which he failed to denounce. Jesus would have had to initiate acts of civil disobedience that Pontius Pilate likely would have opposed fiercely. Thus, Jesus's powers (given the objectives he sets for himself) are limited because he will not coerce others or use violence to dislodge the religious authorities.

Against this backdrop, it is difficult to understand Jesus's temporal threats in his use of power. Since ultimately, he seeks to persuade others, his desire *to set the earth on fire,* and his remark that he does not come *to establish peace on the earth ... but rather division,* (Lk 12:49-53, Mt 10:34-36), pose an incongruous image toward his cause today. In the absence of further explanations, his authoritarian and divisive words may be perceived as a discordant chord in many Western countries already deeply polarized over moral values. As an example to be emulated, listening to religious or political leaders expressing themselves in this manner probably would repel instead of attracting followers.

Interestingly, despite his perceived authoritarianism, Jesus sets an example that stems from the Old Testament. He refuses to keep all power in his hands. Instead, he delegates authority to his disciples to spread the Good News and provides them with powers to drive out demons and cure the sick. He says that they will be able to speak new languages, pick up serpents, and drink deadly drinks as evidence to others of their faith (Mk 16:17-18, Lk 9:1-2, 10:17-19, Mt 10:5-8). Nowadays, these sayings seem ludicrous and more likely to lead to a loss of credibility toward the faith, particularly if the acts fail.

A Struggle for Power

It long has been held that power constitutes the most important aspect in the world of politics as well as its most significant feature for understanding it.[6] Since then, political philosophers have sought to uncover inexorable laws that supposedly exist in the social sciences among humans. In the middle of the twentieth century, the claim was issued that politics is *governed by objective laws that have their roots in human nature* that consequentially lead actors to behave in accordance with these laws. Thus, politics on earth has been defined as a constant *struggle for power.*[7] Regarded as an axiom in the study of politics, this definition is not a social law based on realist observation. Eventually, this behavior becomes a normative value, as it attempts to persuade politicians that they *ought* to behave accordingly, lest they are willing to risk their power. Nonetheless, despite its quasi-scientific dimension, there is a grain of truth that in politics power becomes an essential instrument to attain specific ends. Highlighting the power struggle recorded in the Gospels may further our understanding of the public Jesus.

There is no denying that, as soon as he emerges on the public scene, Jesus is involved in a serious conflict with the religious authorities. Jesus's message about salvation, condemnation, and God's kingdom takes place amidst a constant struggle for power between the two main actors in the Gospels, Jesus and the Pharisaic leadership that controls the religious and political authority in Israel; Pontius Pilate, the ultimate holder of power, plays a secondary role. Jesus's objective does not appear to include assuming control of the Sanhedrin. He is not even interested in becoming a member of the ruling class. His mission (among others) is to denounce the falsehood he observes in how God's commandments are being implemented; that is, to delegitimize the authority of the Pharisees and the scribes (Lk 11:37-54, Mt 23:13-39). Ultimately, Jesus seeks to announce the arrival of God's kingdom and to establish its powers and authority that, although planted in the temporal world, is rooted outside of it. It is no coincidence that content analysis results indicate that the *Afterlife, Sinfulness, Love, Faith,* and *Jewish Religious Authorities* categories (all significant components of his message) emerge as among the highest ranked in the texts. In effect, Jesus's teachings (the source of his powers) attempt to radically alter the culture of the nation without gaining political power. His teachings constitute a type of moral ideology that seeks to change hearts and minds.

He confronts the religious authorities at every opportunity he gets. He claims to have the authority to forgive sins, which the authorities regard as blasphemous and worthy of the death penalty (Mk 21:1-12, Lk 5:17-25, Mt 9:1-7). On several occasions he purposefully violates the rule of the Sabbath (Mk 22:23-26, Lk 6:6-11, Mt 12:9-14), again enraging the Pharisees and scribes. In another instance, he waives the tradition of the elders, a ritual they have established that compels all Jews to purify themselves prior to touching food. He condemns the Pharisees' understanding of divorce, changing even that which Moses had commanded (Mk 10:1-12, Mt 19:3-9). He feels contempt toward them. Jesus is not only harshly critical of the religious authorities; at times he taunts them. They ask for a sign (a miraculous deed) that could legitimize his authority, and he tells them that none will be given; instead, he says that he, the Son of Man, is the sign (Mk 8:11-12, Lk 11:16, 11:29, Mt 12:38, 16:1). Through parables, he tells them (and the Israelite people) that the kingdom, i.e., salvation, will be taken away from them and given to others.

When the Pharisees ask him by what authority he acts, Jesus corners them with a question they fear answering because it would force them to acknowledge that his mission (and that of John the Baptist) is from heaven (Mk 11:27-33, Lk 20:1-7, Mt 21:23-27). Moreover, in one of the most provocative confrontations with the religious authorities, Jesus goes into the temple area and drives out merchants and money changers. His action irritates the Pharisees who feel their authority is being usurped by an itinerant preacher who has gained many followers and has a big mouth (Mk 11:15-18, Lk 19:45-48, Mt 21:12-13, Jn 2:13-17).

Disregarding his own safety, he insults the religious authorities and threatens them with eternal condemnation (Mk 12:1-9, Lk 19:12-27, 20:9-18, Mt 23:13-36). He belittles the Sadducees too, indicating they are ignorant about the scriptures and God's power (Mk 12:24). Lastly, he instructs his disciples to remain distrustful of their teachings (Mk 8:14, Lk 12:1, Mt 16:5).

The Limitations of Jesus' Powers
There is, however, ambiguity in the texts in their use of Jesus's powers. At times Jesus seems to be aware that the power to heal resides with his person and he does not have to ask God to intercede; people simply come to him to touch him *because power came forth from him and healed them all* (Lk 6:19). A woman suffering from hemorrhages is cured simply by touching him while Jesus notices that *power has gone out from* him (Mk 5:30, Lk 8:42-48, Mt 9:20-22). Conversely, in another instance he feels that *the*

power of the Lord is with him for healing, suggesting that God (not he) is the source of his powers (Lk 5:17).

In Nazareth, his birthplace, an interesting incident takes place. Jesus is only able to perform a few miracles because of their lack of faith (Mk 6:1-6, Mt 13:54-58). This passage suggests that faith is required for the miracle to happen, something that does not occur in other passages. Moreover, it appears that people turn down Jesus's offer to cure them, inconceivably suggesting that they would rather remain ill.

Notwithstanding his manifestations of supernatural power, Jesus refuses to defend himself during his trial, despite claiming that he has access to *twelve legions of angels* that would deliver him from his execution (Mt 26:53). He indicates that his crucifixion is necessary, not to redeem humanity of its sins (a view that only appears, although less clearly, in John's Gospel), but to fulfill the scriptures (Mt 26:53-54). From the standpoint of his earthly objectives, his public ministry seems to be a complete failure. Despite the good he attempts to do, and the many that initially follow him, his teachings antagonize the Jewish people, and his followers desert him. He fails throughout Israel; in Nazareth, Chorazin, Bethsaida, Capernaum, Jerusalem, and even Gentile lands in Tyre and Sidon (Lk 10:13-15, 13:34, Mt 11:21-23, 23:37). He wins a few Jewish adepts but loses the heart of the lost sheep of Israel that he came to lead. God's kingdom in the form of Christianity grows after his death, but only because of Paul's idea of opening the faith to the Gentiles, and because of the Roman Emperor's forceful political decision, centuries later, to impose the faith as the official religion of the empire.

Jesus's power struggle with the devil also does not end well, at least temporally. Initially, he rebuffs (with assistance from above) the glory and power the devil promises him. He claims he has defeated the devil, saying he has *observed Satan fall like lightning* Lk 10:18). Experts contend that the meaning of this passage suggests that, *as the kingdom of God is gradually being established, evil in all its forms is being defeated,* and *the dominion of Satan over humanity is at an end.*[8] It appears they are referring to a type of spiritual or cosmic struggle that humans on earth do not seem to recognize since evil continues to roam the earth. This is not surprising since Jesus claims that Satan rules the world (Jn 12:31, 14:30, 16:11).

Nonetheless, many of his teachings and the belief in his person have passed the test of time. His followers have increased throughout the centuries, suggesting that his power is based on the aura that surrounds his personality and his teachings; the courage of his convictions, and the content of his message relative to its recipients' needs, i.e., desire for eternal salvation and fear of hell. The belief that his miraculous deeds (his powers) are evidence of Jesus's divinity lies at the center of his aura.

Jesus's claim that all power emanates from God has left a discernible mark in politics. Along with passages in Paul's letters, this statement served as the Church hierarchy's justification of its moral and political authority over temporal monarchs, as popes pronounced themselves (and were initially perceived) as being the recipients of God's powers on earth. Later, monarchs themselves disputed temporal power with church authorities while accepting the proposition that all power, including theirs, originates in God. As it still stands today, the criteria for the legitimate use of power according to Christian political philosophy and theology is that power must be used in accordance with Jesus's teachings.

Power in John's Gospel

Power in John's Gospel is mostly manifested through two terms: the author's allusions to the ruling authorities or 'Jews,' as he refers to them (58xt), ten times more than in any other Gospel; and his use of the term *signs*, meaning Jesus's mighty deeds that appear (21xt), twice as many times as in the other Gospels. In John, Jesus's power struggle with the religious authorities and their followers is similar to the synoptics, although Jesus appears less hostile in this Gospel. In his role as prophet and loyal son, he indicates that God is commanding him to say the things he says (Jn 12:49-50). Hence, he denounces unbelief as sinful behavior and stresses belief in his person as a condition for eternal life. To this end, he needs to persuade the religious rulers to accept him as the Son of God based on the signs he performs. Nonetheless, Jesus rejects providing them with a sign, even though it might be sensible to provide them with the evidence. In John's Gospel, the argument about signs is sidetracked by Jesus's remark about the bread that comes from heaven. The passage seems bizarre since instead of providing a sign, Jesus merely insists that he is *the bread of life,* in effect asking the religious authorities to believe in him simply because he is the sign. Then, he rebukes them for not believing (Jn 6:30-36).

The point in John's narrative lies in Jesus's insistence that people ought to believe without signs. *Blessed are those who have not seen and have believed* (Jn 20:29), he tells his disciples, notwithstanding that the text concretely indicates that people become believers because they see signs.[9] Some of Jesus's miraculous deeds, e.g., as a fish finder, calming the seas, and walking on water, have nothing to do with healing the sick or feeding the hungry. His purpose is to create faith. The same occurs with Lazarus, whose illness and death Jesus uses for the glory of God (Jn 11:4) as he resurrects his friend so that others may believe: *Lazarus has died. And I am glad for you that I was not there, that you may believe* (Jn 1:14-15).

Still, despite his show of power, people do not know with precision who is Jesus. Once they witness the multiplication of loaves and fishes they exclaim, *this is truly the Prophet, the one who is to come into the world,* referring probably to Moses and Elijah.[10] These people consider Jesus simply a man, albeit an important one, who seems to be announcing the coming of the Messiah (Jn 7:31).

Jesus's contention that people should believe in him because he decrees it, is somewhat pretentious nowadays. Living during times of reasonable incredulity, it does not appear sensible or realistic to demand that which is difficult for humans to do, particularly when Jesus says that there will be false messiahs and prophets who can and will perform signs to deceive (Mt 24:4,5,11,24).

In John's text, it appears that it is Jesus's powers, more than the religious authorities' charge of blasphemy, that leads him to his death. True, the Pharisees conspire to kill Jesus because he violates their authority by breaking the Sabbath and calling *God his own father, making himself equal to God* (Jn 5:18). But along with his blasphemous remarks, public talk of his powers divides them (Jn 9:16), forcing the chief priests and the Pharisees to convene the Sanhedrin. They begin to argue among themselves: *What are we going to do? This man is performing many signs. If we leave him alone, all will believe in him, and the Romans will come and take away both our land and our nation* (Jn 11:46-48). Consequently, fear and self-interest prevail, and from that day on they conspire to kill Jesus (Jn 11:53).

Jesus's powers fail to convince the Israelites even though *he had performed so many signs in their presence.* Their unbelief may be due to their obstinate attitude, fear, or Jesus's irritating attitude. However, God seems to have a role in their unbelief as he blinds their eyes and hardens their heart *so that they might not see with their eyes and understand with their heart and be converted* (Jn 12:37-40).[11] Hence, if God is responsible for blinding their eyes and harden their hearts, can these people still be held accountable for not believing?

There is in John another source of power that is absent in the synoptics, the Holy Spirit or Paraclete that Jesus calls the *Advocate,* and whose role is to assist in the defense of righteousness. Its power appears to be strictly supernatural; *he will convict the world in regard to sin and righteousness and condemnation* because people do not believe in him (Jn 16:7-11). What exactly does that mean? Whatever concrete results the Advocate has shown throughout history does not seem to have been enough to mitigate evil. It is not clear that Jesus's condemnation of Satan really matters if the ruler of the world continues to induce people to engage in wrongdoing. Jesus's triumph over evil seems to be a personal event that may have benefited those who have faith in Jesus; for billions that do not believe in him through no fault of their own, Jesus becomes irrelevant.

Jesus's Accomplishments

Jesus's use of his powers left a profound legacy; it led to the establishment of a major religion that, notwithstanding its falling numbers in the areas where it originated, still accounts for 2.3 billion (supposed) followers or thirty-one percent of the world's population.[12] Nonetheless, empirical observation suggests that in the world, and in countries with a sizable Christian population, Jesus's values have failed to accomplish his objectives. His legacy questions the inability of his followers to manifest their faith, reflecting negatively upon Jesus's ability to use his powers effectively.

Does Jesus bear some responsibility for these conditions given the magnitude of his powers? Since humans do not operate in complete freedom, our flawed nature lacks the strength (or understanding of the faith) to overcome tendencies that are destructive of the type of kingdom Jesus sought to initiate. If we accept that reason is God's-given tool to humanity to build the earth, it has proven to be as impressive as it is limited. According to the Gospels, the essence of building God's kingdom lies in understanding, i.e., knowing, its moral truths and having the will to adhere to it. Known within the faith as the Son of God, was Jesus aware of the difficulties his way entailed? Did he not say that his yoke was easy and his burden light (Mt 11:30)? Did he not say that he came to save the world (Jn 12:47), and indeed that he had conquered the world (Jn 16:33)?

Building God's kingdom would seem to entail a personal contract between divine grace or providence, human reason, and willpower. Nonetheless, the coalescing of these elements has proven inadequate to advance moral behavior. Under present secular conditions, it would be difficult, if not impossible, for Christianity to exert increased influence in society. Present circumstances seem to call more for a universal set of values that might bridge the multiplicity of beliefs and ideologies that conspire against each other.

Jesus's powers left humanity with an unverifiable sense of righteousness that most of the world is incapable and/or unwilling to accept because there is no certainty surrounding its tenets, despite some of them seem to conform with positive personal and social outcomes. Reasonably speaking, other than to agree to be governed by a world entity with a coherent set of laws, absolute executive powers to police behavior, and fairly adjudicated laws, humanity needs to acquire and internalize the knowledge between right and wrong that God denied Adam and Eve for fear they would become divine. As a result, humankind has been left to its own devices, instinct, emotions, the inability to distinguish between good and evil, and a sense of rationality that is more capable of conquering the physical universe than building a moral world order.

The only way for Jesus to have left a more hospitable and caring world would have required the use of his powers to reverse the human condition that resulted from Original Sin. His redemption was supposed to enhance the human condition, but it seems that its outcome did not go far enough.

Given the manner he used his power, Jesus seems to indicate that he purposefully will allow the physical, human, and eschatological evolution of his kingdom to proceed within the setting of a defective physical world and a flawed human nature. Within these parameters, human existence is best portrayed by Jesus's Parable of the Weed Among the Wheat; good and evil shall continue to coexist until the end of time when the harvester comes and ties the weed in bundles for burning and gather the wheat into his barn (Mt 13:24-30).

Notes:
1. *Merriam-Webster Dictionary,* online, s.v. "miracle."
2. The term "supernatural" is most commonly used to characterize a miracle. This use presupposes at least two realms of existence, the natural or physical, and the supernatural. At least one modern philosopher, Baruch Spinoza, rejected the traditional interpretation of miracles as described in the Gospels, mainly because for him there is no realm other than the natural; everything, including God, exists in this realm. Writing in his own convoluted style, Spinoza would argue that Jesus's miracles and those that appear in the Old Testament may have taken place within the confines of nature, except that knowledge of how they took place continues to elude human reason and scientific inquiry. For Christians, the tendency is to believe in miracles, and for non-Christians to be skeptical or to reject them as

superstition. Baruch Spinoza, *A Theological-Political Treatise,* Part 2, Chapter VI, "Of Miracles." The Project Gutenberg EBook, http://www.gutenberg.org/files/990/990-h/990-h.htm (accessed January 18, 2019).

3. (Mk 3:7, 5:24, 11:9, Lk 5:15, 7:9, 9:11, 11:8-10, 18:42, 19:37 Mt 4:25, 8:1, 12:15, 14:13, 19:2, 20:29, 34, 21:9, Jn 6:2).

4. Inside a synagogue in Nazareth he claims that he has the Spirit of the Lord upon him and will seek the liberty of captives and the oppressed to go free (Lk 4:16-21). For unknown reasons, he abstains from attaining what are perhaps the most political or revolutionary aspects of his agenda, except perhaps in the spiritual sense. Furthermore, he claims that Satan will be driven out (of the world?) through his resurrection (Jn 12:31-32) and will no longer have power over him (Jn 14:30). These claims are difficult to interpret given the continued existence of evil in the world.

5. The lament on Jerusalem appears only in Luke. NEs' note, Lk 19:41-44.

6. The view that the drive for power as means to attain specific ends (and as an end in itself) is inherent in human nature, and is crucial in understanding the world of politics, is generally attributed to Niccolò Machiavelli. His views appear in the concise but well-known treatise, *The Prince,* and in a more elaborate work, *The Discourses of Levy,* both published posthumously in 1532 and 1531 respectively.

7. Hans J. Morgenthau, *Politics Among Nations,* (New York: Alfred A. Knopf, 1973), Fifth Edition, p. 4, p. 29. As a pioneer in this area, initially he had written *Scientific Man versus Power Politics,* (Chicago: University of Chicago Press, 1946).

8. NEs' note, Lk 10:18. In another note, Lk 13:16, NEs once again suggest that *affliction and infirmity are taken as evidence of Satan's hold on humanity. The healing ministry of Jesus reveals the gradual wresting from Satan of control over humanity and the establishment of God's kingdom.* A similar passage appears in John where Jesus is quoted as saying, *Now is the time of judgment on this world; now the ruler of this world will be driven out* (Jn 12:31). What exactly are the temporal (historical) implications of this viewpoint is not clear.

9. - Nathanael believes once Jesus foretells his character (Jn 1:45-49);
   - John insists that the disciples begin to believe following his first miracle at Cana (Jn 2:11);
   - In Jerusalem, *many began to believe in his name when they saw the signs he was doing* (Jn 2:23);
   - Nicodemus acknowledges that Jesus must come from God, *for no one can do these signs that you are doing unless God is with him* (Jn 3:1-2);
   - Jesus himself realizes that people will not believe unless they see signs (Jn 4:48);
   - Although a royal official who asks Jesus to save his child initially accepts without proof that the child will live, *he and his whole household came to believe* after they saw it with their own eyes (Jn 4:53);
   - The crowds also follow him because they see signs he is performing on the sick (Jn 6:12, 10:41-42);
   - Toward the end of the text, John acknowledges that although Jesus did many other signs the ones recorded in the text have a single purpose: *that you may [come to] believe that Jesus is the Messiah, the Son of God, and that through this belief you may have life in his name* (Jn 20:30-31).

10. NEs' note, Jn 6:14.

11. Isaiah's prophecy occurs in Matthew and John, however, within different contexts and/or motives. Although NEs provide examples in John to indicate that there is *no negation of freedom* in the fulfillment of the prophecy (Jn 3:20, 12:42), the wording itself suggests the opposite.

12. Estimate is based on a 2015 study. Conrad Hackett, David McClendon, "Christians remain world's largest religious group, but they are declining in Europe," Pew Research Center, https://www.pewresearch.org/fact-tank/2017/04/05/christians-remain-worlds-largest-religious-group-but-they-are-declining-in-europe/ (accessed March 24, 2020).

On Justice and Divine Retribution

After thousands of years of philosophical and religious argumentation, justice remains an elusive term, to the point that there is no adequate description that may objectively characterize it.[1] It may be generally agreed that justice encompasses certain areas among which are, what is fair and who decides it; how resources are distributed; how laws are enacted and adjudicated; who enjoys which rights, and which rights are considered just; and whether impartiality is a requirement of justice.

There being no consensus on the meaning of what is just, we may conclude that its philosophical, legal, and political definition depends on who controls political power. For example, Roman society had its own set of values that ultimately dictated its conception of justice. Christendom, however, demanded allegiance to a different and unique higher authority and its temporal institutions. Marxist justice is different from Sharia law and from traditional Jewish concept that combines beliefs set in the Torah and the Talmud. Moreover, despite their affinities, the secular administration of justice and the way resources are allocated in Western societies often reflect partisan political and economic values that differ among themselves and in contrast to nations where different religions, such as Hinduism and Buddhism, prevail.

Justice in the Gospels

At first glance, the reader may wonder if Jesus avoids dealing with temporal justice. The terms *just or justice* appear only 11xt in Luke, Matthew, and John; none in Mark. This is a significant and bewildering departure from the Old Testament in which the term *justice* shows up over 200xt, nearly all in reference to its temporal dimension; half the numbers appear in Psalms and Isiah alone.[2] Jesus, who according to the Gospels speaks on God's behalf, provides an interesting insight; he tells the crowds to be like *your heavenly Father, for he makes his sun rise on the bad and the good, and causes rain to fall on the just and the unjust* (Mt 5:45), suggesting that even those who do evil are entitled to the same God's gifts as the righteous. On the other hand, Jesus also shows preferential treatment for those who suffer the most, the sick, the hungry, and the oppressed, hardly an even-handed approach to equality under justice.

In another passage, Jesus foregoes a teaching moment when he is asked to intervene on behalf of a man whose brother refuses to share an inheritance with him. Although sharing possessions would appear to be a Christian value, Jesus responds rather rudely, *Friend, who appointed me as your judge and arbitrator?* Immediately thereafter, as if having second thoughts, he warns the crowd not to be greedy *as one's life does not consist of possessions* (Lk 12:15). In another instance, he becomes angry at the crowd for their inability to judge for themselves what is right. He opposes lawsuits, suggesting that conflicts be settled prior to going to court (Lk 12:57-59, Mt 5:25-27); today, this practice would signify the end of the legal industry whose members make much of their living by arguing matters of justice before magistrates. Another passage, seemingly dealing with a metaphor involving judges, has more to do with the necessity to pray (Lk 18:1-8).

At the time of his arrest, Jesus says, *have you come out as against a robber, with swords and clubs to seize me? Day after day I sat teaching in the temple area, yet you did not arrest me.* He realizes that he is being treated unfairly, indicating that he must have been quite sensitive to the concept of justice.

Some of Jesus's parables deal with afterlife justice, better known as his administration of divine retribution and rewards for human conduct on earth. Although his examples are described in a temporal setting, e.g., the owner of a vineyard, a king, or a wealthy master, the teachings are meant to show how God (or Jesus) would handle divine justice. Thus, Jesus sets rules of behavior that he expects the Israelites (and humanity thereafter) to follow, insisting that he will then judge according to those rules. This means that, for Jesus, justice is an eschatological term. But will God's justice be implemented in the same severe temporal manner Jesus suggests through the parables, or will he render a merciful justice that considers God's understanding of human frailty? For example, would God take into account past experiences that may have led a person into sinfulness; the lack of mercy and the killing instinct that condition a Roman soldier who was raised under a different set of values; or the insensitive upper caste person who was snobbishly educated into despising those he or she regards as insignificant people; or the cruelty depicted by Christian inquisitions on account of the self-righteous attitudes that developed from the understanding of Jesus's teachings at the time? The simple answer is that we do not know because the Gospels are rather ambivalent on this matter.

A reading of the Old Testament brings out two basic themes concerning justice (there are others). First, since the beginning, and for unknown reasons, God is partial to the Israelite people (hardly the Christian view of a Father who treats all its creatures equally). Divine nepotism requires God to protect those he loves the most from their enemies. Hence, he establishes rules of conduct that reflect his values and supposedly would result in the Israelite nation being able to lead a prosperous and fulfilling life.

The second theme is that, despite turning their back on him several times, whether out of unrequited love or divine persistence, God does not abandon the Israelite people. He pesters them with medicinal punishment to remind them of their moral obligations. He arranges with loyal friends (prophets) to convey his wishes to his people and their rulers, thereby engaging in a most crucial function: to deliver messages that deal primarily with temporal matters, at the center of which is justice.[3]

Although prophetic proclamations speak of salvation, it is difficult to know what is meant by the term. Denunciations about corruption and abuse that prophets address to the Jewish people and their rulers, at times seem to apply to nations other than Israel, suggesting that God's rule extends to all human creatures and nations. In the Gospels, these Old Testament references to temporal justice are largely absent, despite words about the temporal liberation of the poor and the oppressed for which Mary and Zechariah give credit to God (Lk 1:46-55, 67:75). Jesus proclaims that he favors the same type of temporal liberation (Lk 4:17-21), but he never fulfills this role as he becomes sidetracked by the conflict with the religious authorities.

Moreover, he chooses not to hold the Romans accountable for the oppression of his own people, and inexplicably uses examples of Roman repression to encourage repentance among sinners (Lk 13:1-5). By refraining from criticizing Roman conduct, Jesus gives them free rein to exercise their cruelty. His reluctance to become involved in matters of Roman taxation (Mk 12:17, Lk 20:25, Mt 22:21) further suggests that Jesus's mission is different from that of Old Testament prophets.

Jesus on Justice on Earth

Understanding temporal justice in the Gospels is complex as there are various scenarios, at times contradicting each other. According to the synoptics, earthly justice might be possible if people were to internalize and propagate Jesus's teachings, i.e., extend the kingdom of God on earth. There is, nonetheless, the proviso that justice will be hindered by the ruler of the world, Satan. Despite having driven out Satan through his cosmic victory over death, Satan (or evil) continues to exert control on earth. Moreover, Jesus suggests that any social progress on justice will entail a constant struggle against sinful behavior, both at the personal and social levels.

In the synoptics, Jesus focuses on earthly justice as a by-product of righteous behavior, which he teaches constantly, through the forgiveness of sin, and by radically altering the Old Law. Accordingly, the foundation of God's kingdom lies in the greatest commandment(s) upon which Mosaic Law and the pronouncements of all prophets are based, *love the Lord your God with all your heart, with all your soul, with all your mind, and with all your strength*, and *love your neighbor as yourself* (Mk 12:28-34, Lk 10:25-28, Mt 22:34-40). This means that, in principle, any type of justice, whether temporal or supernatural, emanates from this commandment. Supposedly, there can be no contradiction between the two components of the commandment; to love God requires, in addition to acknowledging his existence through prayer and rituals, caring for the wellbeing of other people. Insofar as they do this, they comply with loving God.

Examples of the synoptics' approach to the realization of justice on earth abound. People all over the Judean countryside are repenting their sins and being baptized (Mk 1:1-5, Lk 3:1-17, Mt 3-5-6). Jesus befriends tax collectors seeking to change their ways so they would stop their fraudulent activities (Mk 2:15-17, Lk 5:27-32, Mt 9:9-13). Justice advances, Jesus would claim, to the extent the unjust repent and mend their behavior (Lk 18:9-14, 19:1-10). A change of hearts and minds allows the believer to act justly, i.e., in accordance with Jesus's teachings.

On several occasions, he sets the example by purposefully violating the Sabbath to indicate that legalistic rituals can become oppressive and prevent people from doing good (Mk 2:23-28, 3:1-5, Lk 6:1-10, 13:10-16, 14:1-6, Mt 12:1-14). His criticism of the religious authorities is severe because of the unjust social and religious burden they place upon their people (Lk 11:37-44, Mt 23:1-39). He teaches that righteous behavior should not remain hidden but ought to be made public, suggesting that his values need to permeate social structures (Mk 4:21-22, Lk 8:16-17, Mt 5:15-16). Presumably, if Christians had emulated these practices, much divisiveness, e.g., schisms, poverty, and wars, might have been prevented. The multiplicity of denominations within Christianity, hardly what Jesus may have wanted, suggests that self-righteousness became embedded within Christianity.

On Inclusiveness

Jesus does not mind that activists with similar intentions could participate in his endeavors, despite not sharing his views entirely, indicating that intolerance could unnecessarily hinder his mission (Mk 9:38-41). The passage in Luke is even more explicit as Jesus adds, *whoever is not against you is for you* (Lk 9:49-50), suggesting that, as long as the person or group does not oppose Jesus, they might as well be considered allies. Its significance ought not to be overlooked. At first glance, Jesus does not seem to make distinctions regarding who is for him or against him based on religious creed (Mt 10:40-42). In the passage on Judgment Day, Jesus adds to his definition of justice by establishing the criteria that lead to salvation, and says, *whatever you did for one of these least brothers of mine, you did for me* (Mt 25:31-46). If this teaching were to be applied today, it appears that Jesus would invite well-intentioned people regardless of religious or political ideologies to partake in his kingdom. Hence, tolerance would become the new expression of charity and the foundation of a system of justice that is based on his teachings rather than on what people are, how they look, think, feel, or believe. Tolerance, nonetheless, would have its limits. In another passage, Jesus clearly indicates that he will consider anyone who does not side with him as an opponent (Lk 11:23). This is the embodiment of absolute truth; if there is to be justice, it will be on his terms.

Jesus's view that Christians cannot remain neutral in their opposition to his version of evil, however, may lead to conflict in a pluralistic society. Not only will his teachings have to prevail over different moral interpretations arising out of various non-Christian religions and philosophies; in a divided Christianity these denominations must compete among themselves, a situation that undermines Christian morality. Hence, it is likely that secular society will not condone embracing Jesus's absolutism into its system of jurisprudence, no matter how much Christians desire it, lest it may provoke the types of unjust ideological discrimination that Jesus seems to oppose.

On Material Possessions

In his teachings, Jesus encourages accepting a most difficult commitment that strikes at the heart of injustice: detaching oneself from material possessions and leading a simple life (Mk 10:17-21, Lk 10:18-23, Mt 19:16:22). This is yet another hurdle, courtesy of the materialistic and covetous impulses, often conditioned by social structures and secularized values that are subtly validated by some apologists of the Christian faith. The following data highlights Jesus's point on seeking justice in today's world: the average size of a new house in the United States increased by more than 1,000 sq ft since 1973 (1,600 sq ft to 2,687 sq ft) while the number of people living in these houses has declined considerably (3.01 to 2.54 persons per household), leading to doubling the average amount of living space per person in forty-two years in 2016.[4] These increases in living space are extolled as an indication of rising living standards, begging the question of how much living space and comfort is needed vis-à-vis housing conditions throughout the poor regions of the world.

While Jesus is critical of material affluence, he does not explicitly advocate for the redistribution of resources to aid the underprivileged since his preferential option for the poor implies such policies. He warns of the danger of greed and people's unbridled desires for material possessions because it detracts from his teachings. His warning points to a real struggle that takes place within each person between God and mammon (Mk 10:23-29, Lk 16:13, Mt 6:24). In his most severe critique against trickle-down-driven inequality, Jesus is unforgiving about the rich man's insensitive behavior toward poor Lazarus (Lk 16:19-31).

Detachment from material possessions, which does not imply having to endure poverty (Lk 14:25-32), would drive the believer to the realization that there are less fortunate people who are in need and who might benefit from the abundance of others. Individual sharing of wealth would be a sensible decision. But, what about if the rich are unwilling to share their resources with the poor? There is nothing in Jesus's teachings that forbid his followers from grouping together with others with similar values to oppose selfishness and greed. Jesus's metaphor of the lamp that is to be placed on a lampstand so that it gives light rather than under a bed, appears to suggest this approach (Mk 4:21-22, Lk 8:16-17, Mt 5:14-16). Moreover, those unwilling to share their resources would have to face him personally on Judgment Day, the consequences of which are not pleasant (Lk 6:20-26, Mt 25:31:46).

On (the Apparent) Separation of Church and State
The episode in which the Pharisees and the Herodians seek to pin down Jesus regarding the question of paying taxes to the Roman Emperor applies to the category of justice too. Jesus's reply deals more with the hypocrisy of his inquisitors (Mk 12:13-17, Lk 20:20-25, Mt 22:15-21) since they already are doing it. At the same time, he evades the question of whether those taxes are just, perhaps not wishing to confront the Roman authorities because it is not part of his mission. Today, however, the question is highly relevant (as it has been throughout history) since taxes are perceived by many people as a burden instead of being part of a social contract between the state and its citizens (since no state can afford to pay its expenditures without tax revenues). Jesus's decision to dodge the issue suggests two important considerations about justice: a) he is not opposed to the idea of separation of church and state, which medieval Europe conveniently forgets once Christianity becomes the dominant creed in Europe; and b), Jesus does not seem to be inimical to the concept of religious freedom, defined as the injustice of a state theocracy that tramples on the individual rights (and conscience) of different beliefs.

Other Immoral Behavior
Realizing that in many instances wicked people entice others to commit injustice, Jesus delivers one of his most serious pronouncements against these people, indicating

that *it would be better for [them] if a great millstone were put around [their] neck and be thrown into the sea* rather than cause others to sin. (Mk 9:42-48, Lk 17:1-2, Mt 18:6-7).[5] This saying has greater implications today upon the realization that evil is being caused by sinful human structures that condition people to generate injustice. Since injustice and other evils are intensified by the unwillingness to forgive, Jesus insists on forgiveness (Mk 11:25, Lk 6:37, Mt 6:14-15, 18:21-35).

Hypocrisy among public and religious officials blinded by temporal ideologies tends to support oppressive conditions, yet these officials *like to go around in long robes and accept greetings in the marketplaces, seats of honor in synagogues, and places of honor at banquets.* Jesus is highly critical of them: *they will receive a very severe condemnation* (Mk 12:38-40, Lk 20:45-47, Mt 23:13-14). He teaches that hypocrisy is among the primary reasons for the prevalence of unjust practices; thus, he reminds us that *the measure with which you measure will in return be measured out to you* (Lk 6:37-38, Mt 7:1-6). It is all about behavior; if the tree does not bear fruit it will be cut down and thrown into the fire (Lk 3:9, Mt 7:23). His Parable of the Tenants, although it appears to concern the Israelite people's rejection of Jesus, condemns cruelty and greed that prompts the crimes perpetrated upon the employees and the son of the vineyard's owner (Mk 12:1-9, Lk 20:9-19, Mt 21:33-42).

On Hatred and Injustice
It is an incontestable sociological and political reality that hatred is a major contributor to injustice on earth. Although unjust conditions may often be the result of cultural values that are kept alive through social conditioning until confronted by other values, hatred is both a causing agent and a by-product of injustice. Other than the biblical explanation, however, the cause(s) of hatred (as well as of love) is not well-known. Nonetheless, the proposition that people who love and care for others are less prone to engage in unjust and criminal behavior than those who habitually loath people, is empirically verifiable.

People that willfully care for others would seem less likely to support unjust conditions than those who are mostly concerned with their personal interests and needs at the expense of the rest. Hence, it might be sensible to conclude that Jesus's core teachings on love and its other manifestations, i.e., caring, compassion, mercy, forgiveness, might just be among the best antidotes to injustice. Nonetheless, it appears that the response from the laity has placed the faith in an embarrassing situation. As a member of a non-governmental organization involved in Africa who is critical of Christians said to me, 'your people don't give much of a damn and are too self-absorbed to strenuously oppose those who stand in the way of justice.'

Perhaps the most challenging way that Jesus teaches to address injustice requires, at the same time, the most incomprehensible and counterintuitive means. Seeking to change the behavior of the unjust person, Jesus calls to do good to one's enemies (Lk 6:27-36, Mt 5:38-48). Without attributing innovative theories of social psychology to Jesus, he is suggesting that changing the attitudes of those who support unjust conditions at times require radical measures that may lead to cognitive dissonance; the shock-effect that may be accomplished by doing good to those we dislike. Often, these acts make unjust people question themselves, leading them to a change in their attitudes. Doing good to one's enemies (which does not imply dismissing their injustices) is often described as a romanticized view of religion that becomes useless in practice. Believers and non-believers, however, fail to realize that this approach can pierce the hatred vicious cycle that otherwise would lead to worsening conditions.

Inexplicably, Jesus does not appear to follow his own teaching. His conflict with the religious authorities prevents him from overcoming his animosity (some call it zealousness) toward them. Moreover, as his disciples are about to go into unbelieving territories, he seems judgmental as he tells them that they should disassociate themselves from whoever rejects them, followed by a curse against those towns (Lk 10:8-16, Mt 10:11-15, 11:21-24). Jesus further recommends a harsh treatment for sinful followers who fail to heed his friends' advice: *treat him as you would a Gentile or a tax* collector; that is, as lesser beings (Mt 18:17).

An Insurmountable Contradiction

For the most part, it appears that despite seemingly conflicting views, Jesus's teachings could lead to increased justice on earth. But no discussion about his conception of justice is possible without reviewing (once again) his Parable of the Weeds among the Wheat (Mt 13:24-30, 36-43). Taken literally, this parable suggests that Jesus does not favor an earthly system of justice that would uproot evil from society. Instead, because the authorities run the risk of injuring or killing the righteous in the process of eliminating the wicked, the only alternative is to preach repentance and wait patiently until Judgment Day.[6] This parable invalidates major efforts at eliminating wickedness from the face of the earth while it creates millions of people that are blessed by Jesus in the Beatitudes. Meanwhile, it would be futile to attempt to establish God's kingdom on earth, as it would be constantly beseeched and taken over by evil; all it would take for the weeds (the wicked) to take over a wheat field (God's kingdom) is for the gardener to sit still and do nothing. The absurdity of the parable seems inescapable.

Divine Retribution

Perhaps God's creatures stand a better chance in the afterlife. I say perhaps because the concept of divine retribution is difficult to understand. Jesus's criteria for judgment are unconventional. Those who are righteous, i.e., who endure injury and injustice with patience and without resentment (meekness), the merciful, the clean of heart, those who seek justice and peace, are rewarded in the afterlife. The poor, the hungry, those who weep, and those who are hated, insulted, and persecuted for being his followers, they too shall receive their reward in heaven. These criteria may seem reasonably fair as the result of a loving and merciful God (Lk 6:20-26, Mt 5:2-12), even though they are the outcome of Jesus's Parable of the Weeds Among the Wheat.

What seems paradoxical, however, is that while Jesus insists on love, mercy, compassion, and forgiveness on earth (including of one's enemies), his standards of divine justice are so severe that in some cases the punishment exceeds the crime. Supposedly, the reason Jesus insists on forgiveness, compassion, and mercy is that he realizes that the flesh is weak; that human nature has a proclivity toward sin that often is inadvertent and/or conditioned by multiple factors that are difficult to manage. Human imperfection deters anyone (except the most arrogant) from casting the first stone, which is why it becomes difficult to understand Jesus's sense of retribution when taken literally. His sense of mercy and understanding seems to be absent in the Parable of the Sower, as some people may stand to be eternally condemned for circumstances beyond their control. In other cases, he seeks or allows people to be confused by speaking in parables so that they *may not be converted and be forgiven* (Mk 4:3-20, Lk 8:4-15, Mt 13:1-13). This attitude seems awkward, as no righteous person would ever attempt to deceive others. Moreover, he warns that people will be judged by every careless word they speak (Mt 12:36). A literal reading of this passage and others, such as his Parable of the Faithful and Unfaithful Servants and the Parable of the Ten Virgins, indicate that hell would be overpopulated by people guilty of misdemeanor offenses (Lk 12:35-47, Mt 24:45-51).

The Gospels portray a Jesus with a Jekyll and Hyde personality. At times, the texts depict a kind Jesus who asks the owner of a fig orchard to be patient and abstain from cutting down one of the trees that has failed to provide fruit (Lk 13:6-9).[7] But no sooner than he forgives and heals sinners, he becomes intolerant, insisting that people should seek to enter God's kingdom through the narrow door, or they will end up where there *will be wailing and grinding of teeth* (Lk 13:23-30, Mt 7:13-14).

He chastises his own disciples for not understanding his parables, seemingly demonstrating little patience (Mk 8:15-21, Mt 16:5-12). He demands complete loyalty to the point of becoming more absolutist, suggesting that whoever does not share his views works against God's kingdom (Mk 8:38, Lk 11:23, 12:8-9, Mt 10:32-33). He tells his disciples that at times of persecution only those who keep the faith will be saved (Mk 13:13, Lk 21:19, Mt 24:13). But what would happen to those who, like Peter, are not initially that strong? In Mark, Jesus instructs his disciples that those who choose not to believe or be baptized (perhaps because they were reared under a different faith) will be condemned (Mk 16:15-16). These standards of judgment seem unjust and contrary to other aspects of Jesus's teachings, which is why the religious unaffiliated or agnostics might not choose to seek him as savior and redeemer.

On the one hand, some parables depict a caring God who goes after one lost sheep (Lk 15:1-9); a God that rejoices over *one sinner who repents* (Lk 15:8-10); and a father who celebrates the return of his sinful son (Lk 15:11-32). Yet this God is quick to anger and becomes vindictive when people excuse themselves from attending his feast; when an employee fails to act with due diligence to secure his interests; or when they refuse to accept his kingship (Lk 14:15-24, 19:11-27, Mt 22:2-10).

Jesus's concept of divine retribution, however, includes mercy too. He is willing to forgive those who change their minds (Mt 21:28-32); or those who repent at the last minute, as suggested in the Parable of the Workers in the Vineyard and by his forgiveness of the criminal on the cross (Lk 23:39-43, Mt 20:1-16). He realizes that many who sin have little idea of their behavior; that they could be conditioned to sin by their surroundings, so he asks the Father to forgive those who crucify him even without having to repent (Lk 23:33-34). This would seem to be the Jesus that postmodern secularized society longs for, reflecting humanity's need for someone to be more understanding of their flaws.

There are likely millions of people that may be impervious to Jesus's teachings. An innate sense of good and evil is not easy to acquire (particularly when dissimilar definitions abound). Christianity believes in the existence of a *natural law* that is said to be 'imprinted' in people's hearts and thus accessible to all. Nonetheless, its lack of accessibility or ignorance of this law seems to suggest otherwise.

Jesus offers a behavioral model that is not easy to absorb. Its basis is that of an adult with a child-like demeanor suggesting *total dependence upon and obedience to God* (Mk 10:15, Lk 2:22-31, Mt 18:3, 6:30-33).[8] Righteousness, although possible, faces serious obstacles today, among them, the assortment of distractions that secularized societies provide, and the lack of harmony that exists among the various Christian denominations.

John's Gospel on Justice

John's Gospel's view on justice appears to be substantially different from the synoptics. Its relevance to temporal justice is marginal at best. John's disproportioned use of the term *belief/believe* (96xt), as opposed to Mark (18xt), and to Luke and Matthew respectively (8xt), provides a litmus test in its definition of divine retribution on Judgment Day. In John, justice is equated with belief, thus the person is more encouraged to believe correctly than to behave appropriately (Jn 3:14, 6: 40, 44, 54, 8:51, 9:39, 10:7-9, 12:44-48, 15:6, 20:31). For the most part, if the person accepts belief in Jesus as savior and as Son of God he or she is not punished; if the person chooses not to believe in Jesus or is not schooled into believing in Jesus, the person is condemned (Jn 3:36). Since non-Christians are considered second-class citizens, may we even begin to imagine a system of justice with such foundations in contemporary secular society? Freedom of religion would have to be abolished or radically curtailed. Other constitutional rights may be declared to be invalid as it applies to non-Christians. For practical purposes, secular society would become a neo-theocracy.

There is at least one passage indicating that Jesus's judgment will be based on people's acceptance of his teachings (Jn 5:29), although these teachings are not identified anywhere in the text other than to tell his disciples to love one another. Still, he practices his own type of temporal justice when he contravenes the Old Law by violating the sabbath law to heal the sick (Jn 7:21-24). Supposedly, his greatest accomplishment in terms of temporal justice would have been the annihilation of evil. Nonetheless, although he condemns Satan and declares victory over him (Jn 12:31, 16:11), the ramifications of these actions fail to eradicate evil. Awkwardly, relating infirmity to sinfulness, Jesus warns (or threatens) a paralytic he has healed not to sin again so that nothing worse may happen to him (Jn 5:10-14).

John's Gospel suggests the possibility that non-believers (through no fault of their own) might not be saved since salvation is based on belief in Jesus alone. Although this issue raises a serious predicament about justice in the afterlife, theologically (and canonically), some Christian denominations appear to have solved this issue by pushing back on John's text to indicate that there may be salvation to those who through no fault of their own have not been able to learn about Jesus.[9]

There is yet another incongruent passage in John. Despite their intellectual limitations, Jesus believes that humans are innately able to *just justly*; that applied common sense (or natural law) somehow will result in establishing justice on earth (Jn 7:21-24). Nonetheless, the veracity or accuracy of this Old Testament teaching (Lev 19:15, Is 11:3-4) can be seriously questioned given the inconsistencies that exist today on issues related to justice and morality.

The Ultimate Passage

Although it would be difficult for the casual reader not to conclude that John's Gospel is primarily about belief, there is one passage that undermines some of Jesus's own teachings on temporal justice. As the religious authorities ask Jesus to pass judgment on a woman accused of committing adultery, they know that the law is quite explicit; according to the Old Testament adultery is unlawful (Ex 20:14, Lev 18:20, Deut 5:18), and punishable by death by stoning (Lev 20:10, Deut 22:22, 24). Today, this law would be equivalent to an adulterer being charged with first-degree murder, thus warranting execution.

Intriguingly, Jesus renders his judgment not based on the law; instead, he rules the law null and void through an act that has to do with mercy as much as on the equal sinfulness of humanity: *Let the one among you who is without sin be the first to throw a stone at her*, he tells the scribes and the Pharisees (Jn 8:1-11). Once again, Jesus overrides God's dictates, as if telling the Father that he went too far with his initial laws. Even more incongruent, if this principle were to be adopted in earthly jurisprudence, it would invalidate all systems of adjudicating laws on wrongdoing since no jury (or judge) could find the accused guilty of their crimes since they themselves are sinners. Remarkably, this act of fairness, by today's standards, is absent in the synoptics.

What may be gathered from Jesus's teachings is that whatever role justice might serve on earth would be the outcome of following his first two commandments and all that they entail. The few examples he provides rely on compassion, mercy, understanding, and forgiveness. Temporal justice in the Gospels is not meant to serve as immediate deterrence to wrongdoing, given that it takes time for people to adopt his teachings. Perhaps to ensure their rapid acceptance, he relies on his commandments as well as on the threat of eternal condemnation. What seems to be absent is the compassion and understanding he shows toward the adulterer and the criminal he forgives on the cross. It is this type of understanding that newer generations wish to see in God.

Notes:
1. Dictionaries do not offer much assistance. *Cambridge Dictionary* defines justice as fairness in the way people are dealt with. But fairness is a subjective term that responds to a specific set of values, beliefs, and norms that may vary from one society to another. *Merriam-Webster* defines it as the impartial administration of what is just; except that *what is just,* again may depend upon a society's sets of values, beliefs, and norms. *Oxford Dictionary* defines it as *the quality of being fair and reasonable,* and as the process of administering law and authority. *Cambridge Dictionary,* online; *Merriam-Webster Dictionary, Oxford Dictionary,* online, s.v. "justice."
2. *BibleGateway.com,* "justice," in NABRE Bible.
3. NEs' preface to *The Prophetic Books*: *They focus on public morality, the treatment of the poor and disadvantaged, and the abuse of power, especially of the judicial system. They pass judgment in the strongest terms on the moral conduct of rulers and the ruling class, in the belief that a society that does not practice justice and righteousness will not survive.*
4. Mark J. Perry, "New US homes today are 1,000 square feet larger than in 1973 and living space per person has nearly doubled," *Carpe Diem Blog,* June 5, 2016. http://www.aei.org/publication/new-us-homes-today-are-1000-square-feet-larger-than-in-1973-and-living-space-per-person-has-nearly-doubled/ (accessed March 12, 2019). Emphasis mine.
5. The term *little ones* does not necessarily refer to children; it may also refer to good, trusting people that are enticed by others (or by social structures and institutions) to commit all sorts of crimes. See NEs' note, Mt 18:6. Also refer to Jesus's list of sins in the Sinfulness category, most of which deal with social injustice.
6. Ibid., note, Mt 13:24-30.
7. In Mark 11:12-14 and Matthew 21:19-20 Jesus does not appear to be kind; instead, he curses the fig tree.
8. NEs' note, Mk 10:15.
9. *Lumen Gentium,* Chapter 1, 16.

Poverty and Wealth

Jesus's teachings on poverty and wealth/riches are among the highly ranked categories. Content analysis results indicate that Jesus has a strong predisposition toward the poor, the sick, the hungry, and those who endure persecutions. However, he assists wealthy people (including pagans) and keeps their company. The qualitative narrative indicates there are no specific instances of negative remarks about poor or sick individuals, although it must be taken into account that Jesus's condemnation of greed, selfishness, or pride would apply to anyone regardless of their economic or social status.

On a separate note, the ranking of this category includes all miracles that Jesus does for those who are sick and hungry. Being at liberty to do as he wishes, most of his miraculous deeds are undertaken on behalf of those in need. In acting in this manner Jesus seems to propose a model of action (noted in the category dealing with *power*) indicating that those with more resources shall be held accountable for not helping the needy.

Jesus's teachings and deeds concerning the poor go hand in hand with extensive discussions about material possessions. He praises the poor (without necessarily preaching misery) while issuing a dire warning and projecting a sense of contempt for the rich and those who enjoy earthly esteem (Lk 6:20-26, Mt 5:1-12). We may surmise that Jesus favors those who hurt most because he feels compassion for them and abhors suffering, a reason for which he stresses *love of neighbor* as part of the First Commandment (Lk 10:27, Mt 22:37-40).[1] He instructs a scholar of the law on what is meant to love one's neighbor in the Parable of the Good Samaritan, suggesting that anyone in need is one's neighbor. His contempt for riches is because it blinds people from the path God has set for eternal salvation.

God's teachings are not without incongruences. In the Old Testament, being wealthy and accumulating material goods were indications that God favored these individuals.[2] Christopher Wright, an Anglican clergyman and scholar, presents the view that Jesus is not advocating the life of a pauper (much to the contrary of passages in the Gospels), but how the rich practice justice toward the poor.[3] Both views show up in the texts.

In the Old Testament, the Almighty sides with the lowly and against the powerful (Lk 1:51-53). In the desert, Jesus refuses temporal greatness favoring instead worshipping God (Lk 4:6-8, Mt 4:8-10). On the other hand, it must be noted that Jesus never says that all rich people will be condemned or that every poor person will be welcomed into God's kingdom. His denunciations of greed, avarice, theft, false witnesses, or fraud seem to apply to every person, rich or poor (Mk 7:20-23, Mt 15:19-20). However, the contrast lies in his actions and his words.

It is historically accepted that Jesus's birth in a manger (or similar type of humble abode) is symbolic of God's siding with the poor, despite it may have been a simple occurrence *because there was no room for them in the inn* (Lk 2:7). Additionally, as the texts suggest, given the possibility of selecting highly intellectual men with strong religious knowledge as disciples and future heads of his church, he focuses on men that, given their trades (as fishermen), today would be the equivalent of blue-collar workers belonging to a low-middle socio-economic class. It may be safe to assume that since some of them were running a simple business operation (Mk 1:16-20), they probably had writing, reading, and basic arithmetic skills. More than likely they were able to make ends meet, perhaps except for Matthew, who may have been better off since he was a tax collector. Otherwise, little is known about most of the apostles' socio-economic backgrounds other than hypothetical assumptions. Nothing in the texts, however, suggests they were homeless and unemployed.[4] Moreover, we may surmise that being the son of a carpenter, he learns the trade that at the time was considered an honorable way to make a living. However, nothing in the texts suggests that Jesus led an extravagant life.

His selection of a group of common workers to lead his mission may be considered managerially awkward today. The exception is Paul (not one of the twelve) who has a respectable resume and likely would have stood out intellectually among the twelve.[5] Hence, it appears that Jesus's hiring of modest men and a sinner is a purposeful act and not the type of decision most mainstream Christian denominations would make today. The typical ecclesiastic in Christian churches (of all denominations) nowadays are for the most part college-educated (many cardinals in the Catholic Church hold doctorate degrees). Among Christian ecclesiastics, their socio-economic status ranges from imposed poverty (religious orders) to the equivalent of the low middle class to multimillionaires.[6]

Jesus's selection of Matthew is unique; he is well-off and a sinner, the prototype of people he seeks to save as part of his mission (Mk 5:32, Lk 5:27-29, Mt 9:9-13). The way the texts read these passages, it appears that Jesus must have seen something radically different in Matthew, who in turn seems captivated by Jesus's audacity to call on someone whose profession is despised by the Jewish people. Matthew immediately drops his financially prosperous (if otherwise sinful) position to follow someone teaching detachment from material wealth. Others follow in his path. In Luke and Matthew, tax collectors are depicted, not as being hateful persons, but sensitive to the callings of John the Baptist and Jesus (Lk 3:12-13, 7:29, 15:1, 19:1, Mt 9:10, 21:31). Within this context, Jesus's disparaging remark to his disciples in which he refers to tax collectors with contempt seems disconcerting (Mt 18:17).

In the synoptics, Jesus violates the sabbath regulation by picking heads of grain from the field because he and his disciples are hungry. When the Pharisees become critical of him, he replies that norms may be broken if there is a critical need. If his words in Matthew, *I desire mercy, not sacrifice* (12:1-7), were to be applied today, he would be saying that the earth's resources are meant for all of God's creatures and that showing mercy toward those in need is more important than religious sacrifices.

Clearly, Jesus places eternal life ahead of temporal gains, for which self-denial is necessary (Mk 8:34-36, Lk 9:23-25, Mt 16:24-26). It is not clear, however, who is Jesus addressing; is it only his disciples, believers at large, or everyone? The question is relevant because it appears that righteousness seems to count only when it is done in his name, suggesting that outside of the Christian faith there is no merit for good behavior. He tells the crowd that anyone who does not *renounce all his possessions* cannot be his disciples (Lk 14:33). This far-reaching proposition seems to be addressed to today's religious orders, as it appears to be unattainable by the common believer. Stressing this point again, he indicates that it is not enough to follow the commandments to gain eternal life; additionally, it is necessary to *sell what you have, and give to [the] poor ... then come, follow me* (Mk 10:17-22, Lk 18:18-23). In Matthew, Jesus seems to clarify his teaching by indicating that following the commandments will be enough to attain salvation, and only if he wishes to be perfect should he dispose himself of his possessions and follow him (Mt 19:16-21).

Seeking social status is the equivalent of pursuing wealth, which is why he tells James and John (the sons of Zebedee) that they should follow his example to be of service to others rather than to be served (Mk 10:35-45. Mt 20:20-28). It is not only a matter of being detached from riches that Jesus teaches his followers. He praises humility, modesty, unpretentiousness; words that are in contrast with pagan values extolled by the Greeks, the Romans, modern worldly philosophers who attacked a so-called slave-mentality that comes down from the Old Testament, as well as with postmodern societies that emphasize wealth acquisition as a primary value.[7]

Poverty of spirit is the type of attitude that Jesus seeks in his followers. It is the tax collector who becomes aware of his wickedness and asks for forgiveness, and not the Pharisee who praises himself and looks down upon sinners. His teachings refer to those who find themselves without possessions, yet they are not greedy; they accept their condition in life while placing their dependence on God. This is the lesson Jesus teaches his disciples as he sends them to preach God's kingdom. Although they might encounter peril and deprivation, they are not to carry food, money, a sack, or sandals (in Luke he allows them to wear sandals); their existence depends on whatever others might provide them to eat or drink (Mk 6:7-9, Lk 10:3-4,7, Mt 10:8-10). A more ample definition of poverty of spirit might include those who suffer unjust persecution and those (regardless of socio-economic background) who are sensitive enough to the plight of others and feed the hungry, assist the stranger, clothe the naked, care for the sick, and visit those in prison (Mt 25:33-40). Interestingly, in this passage, as in the Parable of the Good Samaritan, Jesus does not seem to require that such actions be done strictly in his name; doing them *for one of these least brothers of mine,* amounts to doing them for him (Mt 25:31-46).

In one of the many examples Jesus cites of material detachment, he points to a poor widow who deposits a few pennies in the collection box that represented her whole income while others contribute from their surplus wealth (Mk 12:41-44, Lk 21:1-4). That the poor can be more generous than the rich shows up in studies in social psychology and economics today, incongruously suggesting that the poor have paid more attention to his teachings than the rich. In the last decades, the social sciences have uncovered a behavior pattern that while the wealthy *donate more money overall* ... proportionally, *many of them give less than those with far less wealth.*[8] Research showing *that just eight men own the same wealth as the poorest half of the world,*[9] suggest that billionaires in the Philippines, India, Swaziland, Georgia, Indonesia, Colombia, Brazil, Peru, and China could *completely eradicate extreme poverty in their respective countries.*[10]

Jesus's example of the poor widow, however, requires attention. If read literally, this passage suggests that she was extraordinarily generous. But is it wise or reasonable to act in such a manner? Today, the poor widow would be completely destitute with no choice but to be on welfare. While the poor enjoy God's blessing (Lk 6:20, Mt 5:3), receive *glad tidings* from Jesus (Lk 4:18, Mt 11:5), and are at the end of almsgiving (that Jesus certainly favors) (Mt 6:1-4), is Jesus truly interested in assisting the poor to eradicate poverty or is it simply a matter of individualistic behavior to show compassion and earn salvation?

In one of the most intriguing passages in three of the Gospels, Jesus maintains that *the poor you will always have with you, and whenever you wish you can do good to them* (Mk 14:7, Mt 26:11, Jn 12:8). The passage reads as if the poor were objects that can be taken care of in one's spare time. We may surmise that many people (including governmental and non-governmental agencies) assist the poor out of compassion (and good public relations), under the assumption that their actions will ameliorate poverty and one day eventually eradicate it. The above passage, however, indicates the opposite; and its reading could lead to disparate results as it may dishearten compassionate people to contribute less assistance to the poor. The devout may take Jesus at his word and continue to practice charity, but their behavior would lose empathy if done out of self-interest to earn eternal life. On the other hand, the Parable of the Good Samaritan highlights compassion as the end action of loving one's neighbor; Jesus, a Jew, chooses a Samaritan, strongly disliked by the Jewish people, as an example of true love of neighbor.

We then come to another passage that adds to what Jesus means by material detachment. He tells his disciples only (in Luke) and the crowds (in Matthew) not to worry about material life, what to wear, or what food to eat, since God will provide the necessities of life insofar as they first seek God's kingdom (Lk 12:22-34, Mt 6:25-34). Jesus's words seem poetic and idealistic, since, historically speaking, they have been proven to be untrue in many instances. Reality suggests that there is a difference between attachment to material possessions and indifference to material necessities; the former can be moderated, perhaps even averted. Being indifferent to material necessities while expecting God to provide for one's sustenance, on the other hand, is humanly unrealistic. With the exception of the mendicant orders, e.g., Dominicans, Franciscans, Augustinians, and Servites, that preached God's word while depending on people's goodwill for their basic needs, today, inside the most rigid monasteries and abbeys monks work within their walls to provide necessities for themselves.

Those who are called to an ecclesiastic life, both Catholic and Protestant, can afford to be completely disinterested in material things since these are provided by the institution. Although some sacrifices are required, namely celibacy, non-luxurious living standards, and a rather regimented lifestyle, members of religious orders and even diocesan priests (in good standing) have all their needs covered, including permanent employment, health care, vacation time, and a modest stipend. Protestant clergy enjoy certain amenities, such as marriage, having children, and some, even dancing. It is the laity (poor and middle class) that has become real mendicants, having to depend on socio-economic and political systems that do not have their wellbeing as their top priority. Even people in the more developed countries suffer the anxieties of being sick, unemployed, and unable to afford the necessities of life for themselves. Under these circumstances, it is quite difficult to achieve a balance between highly desiring material possession, accumulation of riches, and power, and living in complete destitution. What are people to do if Jesus's promise fails to take place? It took a more practical Paul to undo Jesus's unrealistic idealism by concluding that, in life, anyone who is unwilling to work neither should he eat (2 Thess. 3:10).

Still, Jesus's words could disrupt even the most amiable feast for the sake of the poor. When invited to eat at the house of a leading Pharisee during the Sabbath, he makes the invitees feel uncomfortable by discussing religion. He asks if it is allowed to heal on the Sabbath (knowing well what their answer would be). Rather than waiting for a reply, he heals a disabled man and follows by issuing a critical diatribe for not inviting the poor, the crippled, the lame, and the blind to the feast (Lk 14:1-14). His parable would send shocking waves today among middle and upper-class Christians who would rather socialize with members of their own socio-economic and political backgrounds.

Moreover, he recommends not to invite relatives, friends, or wealthy neighbors to a party but the poor (Lk 14:12-14). Does that mean that Christians are to forsake family members and friends both of which are crucial Christian values? Incongruously, immediately following the above passage, Jesus seems to contradict himself in the Parable of the Great Feast. Considering that the main character in most of Jesus's parables is God, this wealthy man gives a lavish party, but he is snubbed by those he invites. He then decides to bring in *the poor and the crippled, the blind and the lame* that were not among the initial invitees. Afterward, he takes revenge and decides that those that did not show up will not be saved (Lk 14:15-24).

Jesus's partiality toward the poor is seen in his deeds. A breakdown of his miracles suggests that, in today's world, Jesus's safety net might have favored universal health care and food assistance programs. For unknown reasons, he does not provide unemployment compensation. His view might have been that if people are healthy and well-fed, they ought to be able to work, assuming their respective socio-economic and political systems can provide them with jobs.

Although Jesus prioritizes attention to the poor, he is not against wealthy people or opposed to any activity that might involve profit-making, provided that the means to acquire possessions are honest and tempered by his warnings, and that the economic activity takes into account the 'mandate' to assist the poor. For example, he socializes with people of religious and social stature. There is Joseph of Arimathea, a distinguished member of the Sanhedrin and a disciple of Jesus (Mk 15:42-43, Lk 23:50, Mt 28:57); his good friends Lazarus and his sisters, Mary and Martha, who host a dinner for him (Jn 12:1-2); Nicodemus, a Pharisee *and ruler of the Jews* (Jn 3:1, 19:39); and the family that presides a wedding at Cana (Jn 2:1-11). Even Jesus's burial site cannot be said to be that of a poor man; he was buried in Joseph's *new tomb that he had hewn in the rock*, the body wrapped in linen *in a mixture of myrrh and aloes weighing about one hundred pounds;* altogether, an expensive proposition (Mt 28:57-60, Jn 19:38-40).

Jesus likes to sit at the table with tax collectors (Mk 2:15, Lk 7:34, Mt 9:10); in fact, Matthew hosts *a great banquet ... in his house* for Jesus that is attended by *a large crowd of tax collectors and others* (Lk 5:27-29). There is Zacchaeus, a chief tax collector and a wealthy man, whom Jesus decides to visit and stay at his house (Lk 19:1-10). Extrapolating this image through time it might be interesting to see how Jesus's followers would react today if he were to be seen having a pleasant dinner with shady loan sharks.

In some of his parables, the rich are the "good guys," such as the tax collector who humbles himself before Jesus (Lk 18:9-14); the nobleman in the Parable of the Ten Gold Coins (Lk 19:12); the owner of a vineyard in the Parable of the Tenants (Lk 20:15, Mt 21:33); a king in the Parable of the Unforgiving Servant (Mt 18:23); a landowner in the Parable of the Workers in the Vineyard (Mt 20:1); and a wealthy man in the Parable of the Talents (Mt 25:14). Some of the commercial activities and the lifestyles that take place in these parables are undertaken by upright individuals. Jesus uses these stories to distinguish between illicit and immoral behavior that he condemns, and behavior he praises. The message that comes across, however, is transparent: *take care to guard against all greed, for though one may be rich, one's life does not consist of possessions* (Lk 12:13-15).

Jesus rejects wealth, power, and merit as the means to enter God's kingdom, supposedly because they *generate false security.*[11] But, if this were the case, why would God reward good people with wealth and material possessions as an indication of their righteousness in the Old Testament? Once again, Jesus appears to amend another of God's teachings. He seems to show contempt, not only for ill-gained wealth while praising the poor; his disdain for a luxurious living is palpable. Referring to John the Baptist, who was preaching repentance in the desert *clothed in camel's hair* and feeding on locusts and wild honey, Jesus utters sardonically to the crowd, *what did you go out to the desert to see ... Someone dressed in fine garments? Those who dress luxuriously and live sumptuously are found in royal palaces* (Lk 7:24-28). Nonetheless, in seeming contradiction to his words and deeds Jesus is contented to receive an expensive jar of perfumed oil for his burial that instead could have been sold and the money be given to the poor (Mk 14:3-9, Mt 26:6-13, Jn 12:1-8).

In one of the best-known passages on poverty that succinctly defines his teachings, Jesus says, *how hard it is for those who have wealth to enter the kingdom of God! ... It is easier for a camel to pass through [the] eye of [a] needle than for one who is rich to enter the kingdom of God.* (Mk 10:23-30, Lk 18:24-26, Mt 19:23-24).[12] Probably, Jesus is seeking to illustrate how wealth and accumulation of possessions make it more difficult to listen attentively to the word of God; worldly anxiety, the lure of riches, and the craving for other things prevent his teachings to bear fruit (Mk 4:19, Lk 8:14, Mt 13:1-22), and material possessions may impede access to eternal life (Mk 10:17-22, Lk 18:18-23, Mt 19:16-21).

Perhaps the most chilling of all stories related to poverty and wealth is the Parable of the Rich Man and Lazarus. There are no nuances in the story; the rich man, *dressed in purple garments and fine linen, dined sumptuously each day* while Lazarus lives off breadcrumbs falling from the table of the rich man. The rich man is insensitive to Lazarus's plight. Upon their death, the rich man joins those who end up suffering in hell. Not being able to tolerate the suffering, the rich man asks Abraham for a reprieve, but he is denied. He then asks Abraham to send a warning to his family, and that is denied too, under the assumption that if they did not believe Moses and the prophets neither will they believe someone rising from the dead (Lk 16:19-31).

Jesus does not mind addressing commercial transactions approvingly, except when people become greedy. In the Parable of the Tenants, avarice on the part of the tenants disrupts the financial contract with the owner of the vineyard resulting in murder and retribution (Mk 12:1-9, Lk 20:9-16, Mt 21:33-41). Likewise, in the Parable of the Unforgiving Servant, the lending of money is illustrated. A merciful king shows compassion to his debtor who then refuses to be compassionate toward others. Angered by his debtor's behavior the king sends him to the torture chambers (Mt 18:21-35).

In the Parable of the Rich Fool, Jesus teaches that making wealth as a temporal end is unwise, as no one knows when they are going to die without being able to enjoy their wealth (Lk 12:16-21). In another well-known passage, Jesus insists that one cannot serve two masters, God and wealth (Mt 6:24); instead, he suggests not to *store up treasures on earth* (Mt 6:19-24). In a secularized society, these passages run counter to the type of financial prudence showered through advertising upon the average person today to ensure financial security through savings and buying stocks with the expectation of high returns. Meanwhile, Jesus teaches (only in Luke) to *sell your belongings and give alms* (Lk 12:33), seemingly believing that it is impossible to live modestly and still donate plenty to charity.

Interestingly, the Parable of the Ten Gold Coins/the Talents deals with the stock market, suggesting that Jesus does not oppose this type of trade activity. Nonetheless, the victim of Jesus's rage is not a thief, but a cautious and fearful man who, rather than to risk losing what has been entrusted to him, fails to engage in trading, not even thinking of putting the funds in the bank so they would earn interest. The employer's reaction is swift; he condemns the employee and throws him into *the darkness outside, where there will be wailing and grinding of teeth* for being useless (Lk 19:11-27, Mt 25:14-30). It may be gathered from this parable that wealth acquired in the stock exchange is appropriate and favored, although it does not say what would have happened if the other traders had lost the employer's funds while engaging in higher return stock. Another question is, why is the nobleman interested in making more money if he is already wealthy? Is he not involved in the kind of acquisition of wealth that Jesus condemns?

The Parable of the Workers in the Vineyard is unusual for its compassion. The owner of the vineyard needs laborers. As he begins to recruit workers, he decides that he will pay everyone the same wages regardless of the number of hours they work. The laborers who worked more hours complained. The owner tells them that they had agreed to their initial agreement, so they could not protest or be envious but be thankful they have work. Although the parable focuses on the evil of envy, it lends itself to displeasure if some who work hard for the sake of the kingdom would be paid less than those who work fewer hours. Jesus indicates that God wishes to be generous regarding salvation, even if implementing the practice in temporal life might be perceived as favoritism, and grossly unfair toward the rest.

One of the most disconcerting parables relating to poverty and wealth occurs in Luke in which Jesus counsels to make *friends for yourselves with dishonest wealth.* Supposedly, he is suggesting that his followers ought to take lessons from the children of darkness and apply them to their desire to attain eternal salvation (Lk 16:1-15). Without further explanation, it is problematic to accept Jesus's teaching at face value. Bearing in mind that in the Parable of the Talents the wealthy investor condemns one of his employees simply for being overly cautious, in this parable Jesus admires the cunning talent of his employee. Nowadays, having dishonest persons as one's financial advisors, aside from raising eyebrows among friends and family, might be the quickest way to find oneself in prison.

One last passage worth mentioning is Jesus's raid against money changers and those selling and buying sacrificial animals in the Temple area. Jesus perceives that such commercial activities are making the temple *a den of thieves* (Mk 11:15-17, Lk 19:45-48, Mt 21:12-13, Jn 2:14:22). These merchants, however, are engaged in permissible activities since they relate to temple worshipping, something that Jesus probably must know well; thus, there is no reason for him to engage in a violent outburst (Jn 2:15-16). The apologetic explanation is that his behavior has more to do with questioning the religious authorities' legitimacy than in opposing commerce.[13] A literal reading of the texts, particularly John's, *his disciples recalled the words of scripture, "Zeal for your house will consume me"* (Jn 2:17), suggests that the explanation is questionable given that it is the only type of violent behavior known to Jesus against a practice that is still preserved in Christian churches.

In these parables and the above examples, Jesus provides a glimpse of a war of values that has filtered down through the ages; selfishness, greed, avarice versus just compensation, honest work, compassion, and aid to the poor. Poverty in its temporal dimension confronts the Christian faith with a formidable challenge that, until now, it has not been able to meet. Although the wealthy are not exempted from eternal life and the poor can commit the same offenses as any other human being, content analysis results and the usage of the terms in the texts indicate that Jesus does favor the poor (not poverty for its own sake) over the wealthy, simplicity and modest living over a lavish lifestyle, and compassion and justice over selfishness.

Does Jesus Support a Class Struggle?

In the first chapter of the *Communist Manifesto,* Karl Marx affirms that *the history of all hitherto existing society is the history of class struggles.*[14] As a Marxist term, the concept of class struggle expresses the reality of opposing socio-economic classes throughout history. For Marx, the term served various purposes. It was a vehicle for political action used to raise awareness among the proletariat of their conditions and to energize them as a political movement. It was used as a political strategy (praxis) to emancipate the working class by overthrowing the dominant class and create a classless society. The term served too, as an explanatory tool to describe the deteriorating conditions of the proletariat (the poor) at the hands of the dominant bourgeois class (the rich), because of existing economic and political structures.

The term *class struggle* is not inherently imbued with violent action, although Marx realized that the dominant class would not surrender its control willingly, thus requiring revolutionary action to free the workers of their conditions. He ends his *Poverty of Philosophy* manuscript by borrowing a quote from a French novel (*Jean Siska*) by a socialist writer that reads: *Combat or Death: bloody struggle or extinction. It is thus that the question is inexorably put.*[15] Marx's concept of class struggle was reenergized by Lenin, Stalin, and other communist revolutionaries. It entailed the active promotion of class-consciousness, hatred, and violence among the poor as a political tool against the dominant rich class.

Despite Jesus's preference for the poor and his disdain for the accumulation of wealth, he does not pit one group against the other over issues of riches; nor does he wish to intentionally create hatred among the people to drive the Pharisees from power; loving one's neighbor and one's enemy distinguishes him from other reformers. His severe critique of the rulers, however, exposes the oppressor, and although his denunciations are religiously driven, they have inseparable political ramifications in a theocracy. Hence, there is in Jesus's teachings an element of class awareness. Nonetheless, somewhat inconsistently (since in Luke he promises he would liberate the captive from oppression), Jesus chooses not to take on the other center of political oppression, the Romans, despite his people have been long waiting for redemption. The texts do not indicate (nor does any other writing at the time) that his words were related to the Zealot movement that rebelled against the Romans decades later and led to the downfall of Jerusalem and the destruction of the Temple.[16]

Jesus's ideal of material detachment presumes the continued existence of the poor, even though his rhetoric and his deeds favor them. His teachings about wealth being an impediment to entering the kingdom of God represent a critique of the misuse of wealth and selfishness. The passage involving his disciples' complaint of the woman who pours a costly perfumed oil over Jesus's head and his reply, *the poor you will always have with you* (Mk 14:7, Mt 26:11, Jn 12:8), as bewildering as it may seem, suggest that Jesus did not want poverty to become the basis for social conflict. Instead, it appears that poverty should be mitigated, or even politically combatted, through the conversion of peoples' hearts and minds rather than through violent uprisings. However, he does not indicate what ought to ensue if hearts and minds are not converted. The Parable of the Weeds Among the Wheat runs in opposition to the Parable of the Tenants (Lk 20:19, Mt 21:33-45) and the Parable of the Wedding Feast (Mt 22:1-14) in terms of policy directions; the former focuses on repentance and patience until Judgment Day; the latter emphasizes violence to eradicate evil.

Hence, although Jesus does not explicitly point to violent revolutionary action on behalf of the oppressed, his words and action have not exempted others, including popes,[17] from using Jesus's words to create awareness about the plight of the poor. In this sense, Jesus's teachings may have contributed to the creation of a class consciousness that easily leads to class struggle; he favors the poor, opposes greed and wealth as an end, and condemns and punishes sinful wealth.

In Western capitalism, the concept of class struggle is anathema, mainly because the upper classes tend to accuse leaders of the working class of unlawful violence while disregarding that class struggles operate in two directions, from the base to the top, as grassroots efforts seek to gain benefits for the working class, and from the top down in the form of regressive laws and structures that favor the rich. These are the main elements of class struggle in postmodern societies. People may forget that the American Revolution entailed a political and socio-economic class struggle permeated by a dosage of religious convictions between more or less well-to-do colonists (only males property owners or tax-paying male citizens were allowed to vote) seeking to dismantle the yoke of monarchical despotism set up by the English Crown.

Notes:
1. For some reason, in Mark and Matthew the commandment is broken into two commandments: *The first is this: 'Hear, O Israel! The Lord our God is Lord alone! You shall love the Lord your God with all your heart, with all your soul, with all your mind, and with all your strength.' The second is this: 'You shall love your neighbor as yourself.' There is no other commandment greater than these.* Matthew's version is similar, including the ending: *The whole law and the prophets depend on these two commandments* (Mk 12:28-31, Mt 22:35-40). In Luke, Jesus presents one commandment made up of two parts: *You shall love the Lord, your God, with all your heart, with all your being, with all your strength, and with all your mind, and your neighbor as yourself* (Lk 10:25-28).
2. God considered Job a righteous man, and God allowed him to be quite wealthy by Old Testament standards: *he had seven thousand sheep, three thousand camels, five hundred yokes of oxen, five hundred she-donkeys, and a very large household so that he was greater than anyone in the East* (Job 1:3, 2:3); Psalm 128:2 suggests that those who fear the Lord will prosper and will enjoy the fruit of their labor; Isaiah 3:10 seems to predict that good fortune awaits the just. Incidentally, neither passage has proven to be historically correct.
3. Christopher J. H. Wright, "'The Righteous Rich' In The Old Testament," *The Other Journal – An Intersection of Theology and Culture,* The Seattle School of Theology and Psychology, August 5, 2010, https://theotherjournal.com/2010/08/05/the-righteous-rich-in-the-old-testament/ (accessed January 10, 2019).
4. It is accepted, that at least four of the apostles, Peter, Andrew, James, and John (sons of Zebedee) were fishermen, the latter two seemingly better off economically than Peter and Andrew, given that their fishing enterprise included hired men. The odd figure among the twelve is Matthew, also known as Levi, who happens to be a tax collector, a profession the Pharisees (and Jesus) considered sinful. Jewish people despised tax collectors for their unjust demands for taxes and their deceptive practices of keeping a portion of the revenue. About tax collectors or publicans, see James F. Driscoll, "Publican," CE. Vol. 12, http://www.newadvent.org/cathen/12553d.htm (accessed January 10, 2019). Biographical data (what little

there is) for each apostle also appears in CE. Also, modern scholarship cannot produce much reliable information beyond plausible conjectures.

5. A Jew and Roman citizen (in itself a temporal honor), Paul had a trade as a tentmaker and attended the school of Gamaliel, a member of the Sanhedrin and a doctor of Jewish Law. Ferdinand Prat, "St Paul," CE, http://www.newadvent.org/cathen/11567b.htm (accessed January 10, 2019).

6. A few Catholic bishops in Europe, Latin America, and the United States reside in stately homes typical of well-to-do-families; some lead a lavish lifestyle. Of the thirty-four active Catholic archbishops in the United States, in 2018 ten lived in houses worth over $1 million. Most Catholic and Protestant clergypersons in developed countries earn anywhere between $35,000 and $45,000 per annum. The median salary for Catholic priests in the United States is between $21,000 and $26,095; for Protestant pastors, it is $31,234 (in 2012-2014). Megachurch pastors are in a different category earning over $100,000 per year and some have a net worth in the millions of dollars. Daniel Burke, "The lavish homes of American archbishops," CNN, www.cnn.com/interactive/2014/08/us/american-archbishops-lavish-homes/index.html (accessed January 11, 2019); "Pastor Salaries in the United States," *Indeed.com.* https://www.indeed.com/salaries/Pastor-Salaries (accessed January 11, 2019); Brian Palmer, "What Type of Clergy Get the Highest Salaries?" *Slate,* January 12, 2012. https://slate.com/news-and-politics/2012/01/how-much-do-rabbis-priests-pastors-and-imams-earn.html (accessed January 11, 2019); "Fast Facts about American Religion," *Hartford Institute for Religious Research,* http://hirr.hartsem.edu/research/fastfacts/fast_facts.html (accessed January 11, 2019); Karen Bennet, "The Shocking Net Worth of These 10 Richest Pastors Will Blow Your Mind," *CheatSheet.com,* June 4, 2018. https://www.cheatsheet.com/money-career/net-worth-richest-pastors-will-blow-your-mind.html/ (accessed January 11, 2019). Nuns, although not considered part of the clergy, devote their time to the Church, and may earn much less since, not only do they take a vow of poverty, but usually they also turn their earnings over to their religious orders. Mary Nestor-Harper, "Catholic Nun Salary," *Career Trend,* September 16, 2017, https://careertrend.com/catholic-nun-salary-13660707.html (accessed April 6, 2020).

7. Says Nietzsche: *This Jesus of Nazareth, the incarnate gospel of love, this "Redeemer" bringing salvation and victory to the poor, the sick, the sinful—was he not really temptation in its most sinister and irresistible form, temptation to take the tortuous path to those very Jewish values and those very Jewish ideals?* Friedrich Wilhelm Nietzsche, *The Genealogy of Morals,* trans. by Horace B. Samuels, M.A., (Edinburgh and London: T.N. Foulis, 1913), Project Gutenberg. www.gutenberg.org/files/52319/52319-h/52319-h.htm (accessed January 12, 2019).
In *The Antichrist,* he continues with his argument: *What is good?—Whatever augments the feeling of power, the will to power, power itself, in man. What is evil?—Whatever springs from weakness. What is happiness?—The feeling that power increases—that resistance is overcome.... What is more harmful than any vice?—Practical sympathy for the botched and the weak—Christianity....* (p. 43). *Christianity has taken the part of all the weak, the low, the botched; it has made an ideal out of antagonism to all the self-preservative instincts of sound life; it has corrupted even the faculties of those natures that are intellectually most vigorous, by representing the highest intellectual values as sinful, as misleading, as full of temptation.* (p. 45). *The Antichrist,* trans. by H.L. Mencken, (New York: Alfred A. Knopf, 1918), Project Gutenberg. https://www.gutenberg.org/files/19322/19322-h/19322-h.htm (accessed January 12, 2019). Favoring pagan values, Nietzsche accused Jesus (correctly in my view) and the Jews of *transvaluation,* i.e., turning Nietzsche's superman's values upside down. Such a transvaluation must not have lasted long, as postmodern socio-economics and political culture largely has transvalued, i.e., upended, Jesus's teachings.

8. Helaine Olen, "Why Don't America's Rich Give More to Charity?" *The Atlantic,* December 16, 2017, https://www.theatlantic.com/business/archive/2017/12/why-dont-rich-give-more-charity/548537/ (accessed January 14, 2019). In this article, Olen adds that, according to The Philanthropy Roundtable (an organization of philanthropic groups), proportionately, people with fewer earnings would donate more money to charity than wealthier people. She adds: *A survey by The Chronicle of Philanthropy released in 2014 reached a similar finding: Those earning $200,000 or more per year reduced their giving during the Great Recession and its aftermath by 4.6 percent, while those bringing home less than $100,000 upped their donations by very nearly as much—4.5 percent, to be specific.* In fairness, even people within the $50-$100,000 bracket are not poor by world standards; just less wealthy.
Nonetheless, another study in 2010 by Paul K. Piff and Michael W. Kraus provided an even more significant conclusion: lower-income people were not only *more generous, charitable, trusting, and helpful to others than were those with more wealth,* but that their empathy and compassion diminished as they become wealthier. The study added that wealthy people could be "educated" to become more compassionate: if they *were instructed to imagine themselves as a lower class ... If they were primed by,*

say, watching a sympathy-eliciting video, they became more helpful to others — so much so, in fact, that the difference between their behavior and that of the low-income subjects disappeared. Judith Warner, "The Charitable-Giving Divide," *The New York Times Magazine,* August 20, 2010, https://www.nytimes.com/2010/08/22/magazine/22FOB-wwln-t.html (accessed January 14, 2019). Still, another article surveying various studies point out their conclusions as follows:
- The rich tend to be more self-centered: they *rationalize their advantage, and believe that they deserved it. They pursue their self-interest and moralize greed easily.*
- The poor are more characterized by their empathy: *Poorer people are more likely to notice, engage with, pay attention to and empathize with other humans, compared to the rich.*
- The rich seem to view the external environment quite differently: they *are not very good at reading emotions of the others and lack empathy and compassion. This deficit stems primarily from their lack of dependence on others.*
- The rich appear to possess a sense of entitlement: *A study of the attitude of car owners showed that more expensive cars were more likely to block and cross other cars, and less likely to yield to pedestrians who had the right of way. The rich paid lower taxes and were more prone to evade taxes and hide their wealth; the rich were more likely to adopt questionable accounting and business practices and sidestep ethical practices; and the rich were more likely to use their powers to perpetuate illegal and unlawful activities.* Uma Shashikant, "Why poor people tend to be more generous than the rich," *Economic Times, July 23, 2018, https://economictimes.indiatimes.com/wealth/save/why-poor-people-tend-to-be-more-generous-than-the-rich/articleshow/65078320.cms (accessed* January 14, 2019).
9. Deborah Hardoon, "An economy for the 99%," *Oxfam International,* January 16, 2017, https://www.oxfam.org/en/research/economy-99 (accessed January 14, 2019).
10. Andrew Soergel, "An Antidote to Extreme Poverty: Generous Billionaires," *U.S. News and World Report,* January 22, 2016, https://www.usnews.com/news/articles/2016-01-22/billionaires-could-eradicate-extreme-poverty-report-says (accessed January 14, 2019).
11. NEs' note, Mark 10:23-27.
12. There are various interpretations to the meaning of the term "eye of a needle" whose discussion might be of little help in understanding Jesus. All interpretations point toward something very difficult to attain, in this case, salvation for those who are greedy and selfish. The passage that follows (in Mark 10:23), however, appears to be unintelligible in and of itself, and as a segue to the previous one: *Jesus said, "Amen, I say to you, there is no one who has given up house or brothers or sisters or mother or father or children or lands for my sake and for the sake of the gospel who will not receive a hundred times more now in this present age: houses and brothers and sisters and mothers and children and lands, with persecutions, and eternal life in the age to come.* It is not clear what those who practice self-denial will receive *now in this present age,* other than eternal life. In Matthew 19:30 the passage reads more clearly. Both passages are in line with Mary's praise of God stemming from Old Testament temporal promises that God makes: *He has thrown down the rulers from their thrones but lifted up the lowly. The hungry he has filled with good things; the rich he has sent away empty.* (Luke 1:52).
13. NEs' note, Mt 21:12-17.
14. Karl Marx, *Manifesto of the Communist Party,* 1848, trans. by Samuel Moore and Frederick Engels in 1888. Chapter 1. (Moscow: Progress Publishers, 1969), www.marxists.org/archive/marx/works/1848/communist-manifesto/ (accessed January 27, 2019).
15. Marx, *The Poverty of Philosophy,* 1847, trans. from the French by the Institute of Marxism Leninism, 1955, Chapter 2, Part 5, www.marxists.org/archive/marx/works/1847/poverty-philosophy/index.htm (accessed January 27, 2019).
16. "Ancient Jewish History: The Great Revolt (66-70 CE)," *JVL,* www.jewishvirtuallibrary.org/the-great-revolt-66-70-ce (accessed March 22, 2020). Josephus does not relate the movement to Jewish Christians, Book XVIII, Chapter 1.
17. Since the inception of Catholic social doctrine by Pope Leo XIII in his encyclical *Rerum Novarum* in 1891, other popes have followed with teachings reinforcing and advancing Jesus's preference for the poor. Notable among these are, Pope Paul VI's *Populorum Progressio* in 1967 with his emphasis on justice as the road to peace; in Pope John Paul II's *Laborem Exercens* in 1981 and *Centesimus Annum* in 1991, he uses terminology that may be interpreted as having been taken from Marx's works.

Mary and Pilate

Placing together Mary, the mother of Jesus, and Pontius Pilate in this study begs the question: what could they possibly have in common? Plenty, from a content analysis evaluation whose results are quite revealing. In Catholicism as well as in Orthodox Christianity, Mary enjoys a privileged place. If Jesus is revered by billions, it is reasonable to assume that his mother ought to be an endearing figure. Thus, the institutional church and popular religious piety (particularly in the Catholic and Eastern Orthodox churches) have fostered a cult of the Virgin Mary that places her as a loving historical person second only to Jesus.[1] This devotion—in addition to theological reflections--likely has sensible human roots. Humanly speaking, the mother of any person is someone significant simply because that person owes his or her existence to her. It becomes noteworthy if her pregnancy, the caring, and the raising of the child is not accidental but willfully wanted. Mary's role as a mother stands for life, a personally valuable 'commodity' desired by nearly all human beings.

Within Protestantism the historical record is mixed. A Catholic theologian points out that since the Reformation, *devotion to Mary was often seen as a form of idolatry, a view which continued to unfold throughout the centuries.*[2] This Protestant view would reject Mary's intercession on one's behalf as unnecessary, despite it is an endearing human sentiment to solicit favors off the son by petitioning the mother. Karl Barth (among the most famous Protestant theologians of the twentieth century and widely admired by Catholic thinkers) accepts Mary's motherhood as a biological fact, and her virginity as a sign of God's predominant role in the process of salvation and redemption. Nevertheless, he rallies against the excessive devotion shown by Catholicism, indicating that it is heretical and may lead to idolatry.[3]

Mary, however, continues to be the subject of interesting developments. Popes have taken Marian piety to heart. Pope Francis, for example, indicates that *devotion to Mary is not spiritual etiquette,* <u>but</u> *an exigency of Christian life.*[4] Nonetheless, lately there seems to be a Protestant revival of Marian devotion. Theologian Scot McKnight favors an Evangelical recovery of the devotion to Mary. He presents Mary as a *subversive* and *dangerous* religious version of the postmodern feminist political activist who issues *a call to subvert unjust leaders* in her *Magnificat.*[5]

These theological elaborations and conflicts seem excessive in view that the texts indicate that Mary plays a modest—and almost passive--role in Jesus's public life, raising the question, why? We must remember that the authors of the Gospel had to decide on the most significant aspects of Jesus's life, whether received from oral tradition or directly from Revelation and include them in the texts. In this regard, what the texts reveal is somewhat disconcerting. Content analysis results in Table 2, show that the Mary category ranks as less significant. She is referenced in the texts more than Mary of Magdala, although the latter outshines Mary in unique situations. Mary is mentioned only once in the Acts (1:14), and her disappearance in Paul's letters is nothing short of astonishing. Mary had to wait until 431 CE to be officially proclaimed as the Mother of God at the Council of Ephesus.[6]

This is not to say that her actions prior to Jesus's birth and through his adolescence are insignificant. Aside from any religious connotations, we know of the physical and emotional sacrifices many parents endure to make possible the careers of their children. Mary's travails, from the moment she recognizes the responsibility she is to assume throughout Jesus's childhood and youth are comparable to conditions that millions of parents experience today in war-torn and ecologically devastated lands throughout the world.

In Luke, Mary's virtues, complying with God's will, and her motherly love and understanding of Jesus, are amply displayed. Being told that she will bear a child that *will be called holy,* and *the Son of God,* she appears dismayed and confused, leading her to question the angel Gabriel, the bearer of the news. She accepts her mission and in joy praises God through her *Magnificat,* a canticle filled with socio-political expectations that Luke inserts as fitting Mary's response (Lk 1:26-56). Luke writes what must have been an arduous journey while expecting; the birth of the child and her caring for him, and her presentation of the child to God in the Temple according to Mosaic Law (Lk 2:1-7, 2:15-20, 2:22-24). Soon thereafter, Mary meets Simeon, a righteous Jewish man, and an old prophetess, Anna, both of whom tell her cryptically what her son will mean for Israel and maybe others, as well as the suffering she will have to endure as the mother of Jesus (Lk 2:25-39).

Luke continues his narrative with an account of a precocious twelve-year-old who aware of or captivated by the responsibility he believes he has toward the Father disappears from his parents' eyes. They find him in the Temple in Jerusalem listening to the teachers and asking questions. Luke tells us that his worrisome mother asks him, *Son, why have you done this to us?* Jesus shows surprising indifference toward his mother's feelings and replies, *why were you looking for me? Did you not know that I must be in my Father's house?* (Lk 2:41-51). This passage, at such an early age, is one of Jesus's most extraordinary verbalizations of his belief that he is the Son of God. Intriguingly, it appears that Jesus recognizes that he has made a mistake since the passage tells us that (supposedly afterward) he was *obedient to them.* Mary, instead of feeling hurt by her son's reply, accepts her subordinate role and keeps the experience *in her heart.* Perhaps today we may understand this type of behavior as typical of a child who at times may disobey his parents. Nonetheless, the Gospels (and supposedly God) justify the child's indifference toward the woman that God chose to be the mother of the Son of God.[7]

Such detachment from his mother by a now adult and public Jesus becomes more glaring in a passage all three authors of the synoptic texts deem important enough to record. When told that his mother, brothers, and sisters are asking for him, Jesus appears to ignore their presence to make the point that, *whoever does the will of God is my brother and sister and mother* (Mk 3:31-35, Lk 8:19-20, Mt 12:46-50). The authors seemingly want to stress that one's parents are unimportant when it comes to the divine, a view Jesus makes abundantly clear even while appearing to contradict himself, as we shall see ahead. Whichever reason, today's standards likely would find Jesus's attitude as nothing short of offensive, particularly since he is aware of how caring his mother had been throughout his life. This brings another question to mind; at a time when Christianity emphasizes family values, is this event an example that Christians should follow in their daily lives?

Luke ends his narrative about Mary with the above passage. Mark barely mentions Mary other than in the above example, and in an instance in which others identify a shrewd Jesus as being merely the son of Mary (Mk 6:2-3). In Matthew, Mary is scarcely present. Joseph is told by the angel about Mary's forthcoming conception, and later he is constantly alerted about the danger to the baby's life. Matthew also records a brief visit by the Magi to mother and child and includes the same two passages that appear in Mark (Mt 1:20-21, 2:13-15, 2:19-23, 2:9-10, 12:46-50, 13:54-55).

Inexplicably, none of the synoptics show the mother of Jesus present at the crucifixion, nor does she go to the burial site or appear with Jesus after the resurrection. These are unique situations where one would presume a mother would be present; instead, it is Mary of Magdala who shows up at the crucifixion (Mt 27:55-56), then goes to the burial tomb (Mk 15:46-47, Mt 27:61), and appears at the resurrection site the next day eagerly searching for the body of Jesus (Mk 16:1-11, Lk 24:1-11, Mt 28:1-10). It is Mary of Magdala who first sees the resurrected Jesus (Jn 20:11-18). Moreover, none of the texts mention whether Jesus sees his mother before he ascends into heaven. Human piety would think he does. John's Gospel limits itself to saying that following the crucifixion he (John) takes Mary into his home (Jn 19:27). Since Jesus meets with his disciples following his resurrection, it is reasonable to assume that Mary sees her son too, but we do not know. However, it is puzzling that the texts do not record such instances. It appears that the authors of the Gospels do not consider it significant to point them out, indicating that, overall, Mary does not play a role that is commensurate with her position in Christianity today.

In John's Gospel, Mary persuades Jesus to perform the miracle at the wedding in Cana, showing her gracious sensitivity toward the hosts who had run out of wine. Jesus obliges, but once again, his reply to his mother—at the time and by today's standards—leaves much to be desired: *Woman,* he says, *how does your concern affect me? My hour has not yet come* (Jn 2:1-5). To their credit, exegetes' explanations of the passage are blunt to the point of being disturbing.[8] Again, by today's standards, Jesus's reply to his mother, and John's recording of this passage, present an adverse public image of Jesus in light of Christianity's promotion of family values. Interestingly, the passage at the wedding is the only one in all four Gospels that indicates that Mary is aware of her son's supernatural power since it is at Cana where *he revealed his glory,* giving a reason to his disciples *to believe in him* (Jn 2:11-12).

In John's Gospel, John, Mary, and Mary of Magdala appear at the site of the crucifixion, and Jesus seems to be aware of his mother's presence. While being crucified he appears to symbolically confer upon Mary the role of mother of those who will follow him and vice-versa (Jn 19:25-27). This brief passage is telling, as it would support her role within the Christian Church.

Regarding Mary's socio-political activism, a superficial reading of the Magnificat suggests that its temporal objectives regarding Roman and/or Jewish oppression are never fulfilled in Mary or Jesus. There is a total disconnect between the expectations the Magnificat creates of a temporal Messiah and Jesus's transformation of his role from a temporal into a supernatural messiah.

The Role of Mary in a Secularized Society
We may want to examine Mary's relevance in a postmodern world by asking the extent to which she may represent a role model for women today. Four social roles stand out in Mary as the Gospels present her: her unconditional faith in God; her virginity and fidelity in sexual relations; her example as a caring mother; and her nearly passive or submissive role in public life. If Mary's significance stems from being the mother of Jesus, who is recognized as the Son of God, is it reasonable to assume that religious faith ought to instruct believers to uphold these values?

Since the so-called sexual revolution in the 1960s in most countries in the Western world, virginity as a religious value has declined despite its continued official teaching by various Christian denominations. This is not done for the sake of purity as some may believe, but, at least in the Catholic Church, it is practiced as a virtue, if called upon for the *sake of the Kingdom of heaven*.[9] Mainstream Protestantism presents a substantial divide between a more liberal view that focuses on sexual restraint and a conservative (mostly Evangelical) advocacy in favor of virginity.[10] Among Muslim women, virginity is viewed differently; it represents purity and is still so important that in Europe some women seek to physically 'restore' their virginity prior to marriage.[11] Meanwhile, as seen in Table 2, in the Gospels, virginity as a category is practically insignificant and rarely mentioned. Ironically, virginity has acquired heightened attention today, not only as a virtue but as a practical matter involving sexual responsibility once the negative consequences that may arise out of early and/or careless sexual activity are realized.

Nonetheless, the burden of socially and religiously created taboos, and our apparent fixation with sexuality have yet to provide solutions regarding what the proper role of sexual activity ought to be. As a result, the terms themselves— virginity/purity--seem arcane and the subject of ridicule. In this regard, neither religion nor secular views have yet been able to strike a happy medium between celibacy and complete sexual freedom.

Fidelity in a relationship, however, is still highly desirable, at least in principle. Unfaithfulness continues to be regarded as the equivalent of disloyalty in any relationship, which is why it usually takes place secretively. The tide in secular societies toward adultery is rather strong, particularly in countries where sexual freedom is highly valued. Its consequences are willfully ignored because of the complexities found in today's societies where relationships are often not highly valued beyond the necessity of not being alone.[12] Adultery being a primary cause for the termination of relationships all over the world, suggests that it might be more prudent to safeguard new types of unions by insisting more on the significance of love and commitment in a relationship than on imposing penalties for sinful acts. Perhaps society needs to become more aware of the negative social effects of family break-ups, including emotional and mental problems on parents and children, adverse effects at the worksite, crime, and government expenditures to deal with these problems. Under these circumstances, the example set by Mary and Joseph--mutual devotion-- may be regarded as a social value worth being encouraged even by secular governments. It is unlikely, however, that governments, NGOs, and the private sector would be willing to experiment with social messaging in favor of enduring relationships, despite secular values created to deal with social ills, such as obesity, smoking, drinking, texting, and drugs.

Motherhood stands for nurturing and caring or setting oneself aside in favor of the child's wellbeing. Mary's role as a mother is no different than how ordinary women can act under adverse conditions. It appears that she fulfills her duties as a mother exceptionally well. Nonetheless, today motherhood appears to be threatened by the secular desire of the postmodern assertive woman who wants 'to have it all' or by generational changes that seem to be undermining the institution of the family. All despite there being nothing passive or non-assertive in a woman who takes an active role in the rearing of their children. At the same time, women's desires to go beyond motherhood seem sensible--even healthy and socially valuable—without being necessarily anti-religious, provided that the 'all' is attained in stages and shared equally by supportive husbands and fathers. Consciously or not, traditional values are questioning the desire to deny women their self-fulfillment, insisting on keeping men as hunters and breadwinners because they might be unwilling—or feel uncomfortable—with sharing the 'burden' (as opposed to happiness) of being fathers.

Furthermore, there is nothing that would make us think that Mary could not have been assertive in public life. Probably, patriarchal values at the time hindered her behavior. Despite there being examples in the Gospels, the Acts, and in Paul's letters of various women whose significant collaboration with the nascent church was relished, we do not know if Mary ever becomes the woman in the Magnificat; it does not appear to be the case. But, if that was her choice, there are no reasons why that option ought not to be respected.

Overall, Jesus's teachings, other than his limited view on marriage and divorce, and his incidental mention of licentiousness as sinful, do not seem to provide significant ethical considerations that would support Mary's attributions.

Pontius Pilate

Mary's exposure in the Gospels becomes more telling when we notice that a despotic Pontius Pilate receives slightly more attention in the Gospels. It is reasonable to think that the authors of the Gospels want to underline Pilate's mock trial of Jesus to make the reader aware of the injustice that is being perpetrated. However, all four authors moderate those passages leading to a prejudicial view of events throughout history.

According to the Gospels, Pilate is fully in charge in Judea, his authority outranking that of the Jewish religious authorities who fear him because of his repressive ruling over the Israelites. He is the one who ultimately decides Jesus's fate, not Herod or the chief priest, elders, and scribes. Yet, all four Gospels portray the ruthless governor as strenuously opposing Jesus's crucifixion, insisting that he finds no guilt in him (Mk 15:13-15, Lk 23:14, 23:22, Mt 27:22-23, Jn 18:40). Pilate's view seems reasonable since Jesus had not conspired against the Roman Empire; all he did was admit he is king, to which Pilate pays little attention. Nonetheless, all four texts portray the religious authorities and the mob they have organized as demanding Jesus's execution, claiming that he is guilty of blasphemy, opposing payment of the census tax to the Roman Empire, making himself king, and saying he is the Son of God (Mk 15:1-15, 42-45, Lk 23:1-25, Mt 27:11-26, Jn 18:28-40, 19:1-22). Nonetheless, these passages treat Pilate's actions less harshly than the Jewish authorities, because *of the tendency, found in varying degrees in all the gospels, to present Pilate in a relatively favorable light and emphasize the hostility of the Jewish authorities and eventually of the people.*[13] In other words, the texts are partial, an act that was either consciously perpetrated by the authors, or as the result of a faulty oral tradition process. These prejudicial sentiments on the part of the authors of the Gospel may be explained too, because of the ensuing conflict between the Jewish religious authorities and their followers (most of Israel, as it turned out) and those who ardently followed Jesus.

The written text is the product of what the authors deem to be important; what God reveals to them; or what comes to them through oral tradition. Therefore, it is difficult for any sensible human being not to judge Pilate's actions as a heinous crime. To calmly wash his hands of the action he is about to commit seems akin to absolving a judge who willfully sentences an innocent man to death in the name of political and military expediency. Many Christians continue to misread the texts by placing a higher degree of accountability on the Jewish accusers who despise Jesus because they feel their authority threatened, possibly because of their own understanding or misunderstanding of Mosaic Law. The Law fostered in them an excessively legalistic attitude (ironically taught by God according to the Pentateuch) leading to hypocrisy and to emphasizing the law while overlooking the spirit of the law. This attitude had been questioned by prophets and later by Jesus. On the other hand, Christians may not understand that lessening Pilate's responsibility for his miscarriage of justice is a stain in the Gospels for which, I presume, God's revelation cannot be blamed.

Notes

1. Although Catholic devotion to Mary has a long history, recent popes have stressed Mary's role in the redemptive process. Pope John Paul II's motto *totus tuus* (completely yours) is reflected in his 1997 encyclical "Redemptoris Mater," vatican.va/content/john-paul-ii/en/encyclicals/documents/hf_jp-ii_enc_25031987_redemptoris-mater.html. For the role of Mary in Orthodox Christianity see Archbishop Dmitri (Royster), "The Veneration of the Virgin Mary in the Orthodox Church, January 2, 2013, *Orthodox Christianity*, taken from *The Dawn*, Newspaper of the Diocese of the South Orthodox Church in America, http://orthochristian.com/58526.html, (accessed 22 January 2018).

2. *They believed Christians should pray to the God revealed in Jesus Christ. Mary was a historical person upon whom God's favor shined, and she should be admired and perhaps imitated. But anything more is a serious problem.* Kevin P. Considine, "What do Protestants Think of Mary," *U.S. Catholic*, May 2016, (Vol. 81, No. 5, 49), www.uscatholic.org/articles/201604/what-do-protestants-think-mary-30627 (accessed 22 January 2018).
Protestants and Catholics are half right and half wrong in their views, I think. Protestants deny a considerate and proper veneration of Mary while the Catholic Church continues to allow a religious frenzy over Mary's supposed mysterious apparitions—over thirty throughout history--because it creates religious piety it deems healthy. Perhaps, it is Jesus who ought to be blamed; one wonders why is not Jesus the one who appears, and why does he not do it publicly?

3. Jayson Byassee, "What About Mary?" *The Christian Century,* December 14, 2004, https://www.christiancentury.org/article/what-about-mary (accessed July 27, 2020). This article also provides the Protestant perspective, including changes undergoing in the veneration of Mary.

4. Quote by Pope Francis in John Allen's, "Pope on New Year's: If you want peace, start with Mary and the crib," *Crux*, January 2018, https://cruxnow.com/vatican/2018/01/pope-new-years-want-peace-start-mary-crib/ (accessed 22 January 2018). A new feast declaring Mary as the "Mother of the Church" was instituted by Pope Francis in March 2018. It will be celebrated on the Monday after Pentecost. John Allen, "Pope Francis establishes new feast of Mary as 'Mother of the Church,'" Crux, March 3, 2018, https://cruxnow.com/vatican/2018/03/pope-francis-establishes-new-feast-mary-mother-church/ (accessed 3 March 2018).

5. Scot McKnight, "The Mary We Never Knew - Why the mother of Jesus was more revolutionary than we've been led to believe," *Christianity Today*, November 2006. Article is adapted from *The Real Mary: Why Evangelical Christians Can Embrace the Mother of Jesus,* (Brewster: Paraclete, 2006), http://www.christianitytoday.com/ct/2006/december/8.26.html (accessed 22 January 2018). NEs, however, note that Mary was not the author of the *Magnificat,* citing that it *may have been a Jewish Christian hymn that Luke found appropriate at this point in his story. The editors add that the loose connection between the hymn and the context is further seen in the fact that a few Old Latin manuscripts identify the speaker of the hymn as Elizabeth, even though the overwhelming textual evidence makes Mary the speaker.* NEs' note, Luke, 1:46-55. See also, Tim Perry, Mary for evangelicals: toward an understanding of the mother of our lord, (Westmont: Intervarsity, 2006).

6. A synthesis of the council's proclamation is well detailed in Pope John Paul II's talk published in *L'Osservatore Romano*, December 1996, https://www.ewtn.com/library/papaldoc/jp2bvm37.htm (accessed 22 January 2018). "Council of Ephesus – 431 A.D.," Papal Encyclical Online, https://www.papalencyclicals.net/councils/ecum03.htm (accessed 22 January 2018)

7. NEs justify Jesus's behavior and his reply to his mother, indicating that obedience to God is far more important than family ties. NEs' note, Lk 2:49. While perhaps true, humanly speaking Jesus's action suggests an uncharacteristic youthful insensitivity toward his mother.

8. According to NEs' note, Jn 2:4, the term *woman* is *a normal, polite form of address, but unattested in reference to one's mother.* As for the phrase *how does your concern affect me*, NEs indicate that taken literally, it constitutes *a Hebrew expression of either hostility or denial of common interest,* found in passages in the Old Testament (Jgs 11:12; 2 Chr 35:21; 1 Kgs 17:18 Hos 14:9; 2 Kgs 3:13), *and used by demons to Jesus* (Mk 1:24; 5:7)

9. CCC, 922, 1618, 1619.

10. For an ample view of the struggle within Evangelicalism over the issue of virginity see: Abigail Rine, "Why Some Evangelicals Are Trying to Stop Obsessing Over Pre-Marital Sex," *The Atlantic*, 23 May 2013, www.theatlantic.com/sexes/archive/2013/05/why-some-evangelicals-are-trying-to-stop-obsessing-over-pre-marital-sex/276185/ (accessed 23 January 2018); Sara J. Moslener, "Evangelicals' obsession with "sexual purity" has nothing to do with sex," *Salon*, 8 July 2015, https://www.salon.com/2015/07/08/evangelicals_obsession_with_sexual_purity_has_nothing_to_do_with_sex/, (article originally appeared on Religion Dispatches) (accessed 23 January 2018); Brandi Miller, "The Evangelical Social

Construction of Virginity," *The Salt Collective*, http://thesaltcollective.org/evangelicals-social-construction-virginity/ (accessed 23 January 2018).

11. "In Europe, debate over Islam and virginity," *The New York Times*, June 11, 2008, http://www.nytimes.com/2008/06/11/world/europe/11virgin.html (accessed 23 January 2018).

12. Harriet Marsden and Narjas Zatat, "These are the most adulterous countries in the world," *Indy 100*, https://www.indy100.com/article/most-adulterous-countries-world-map-affairs-cheat-unfaithful-french-survey-7424631 (accessed 23 January 2018). Also, Clifford N. Lazarus, Ph.D., "Is Everything We Think We Know About Adultery Wrong. *Psychology Today*, Jul 17, 2013, https://www.psychologytoday.com/blog/think-well/201307/is-everything-we-think-we-know-about-adultery-wrong (accessed 23 January 2018).

13. Such is the astonishing admission by NABRE Editors that led initially to anti-Semitism, even though it runs contrary to the popular opinion of the Christian world. NEs' note, Mt 27;18. In their note on Lk 23:1-5, they state that *twice Jesus is brought before Pilate in Luke's account, and each time Pilate explicitly declares Jesus innocent of any wrongdoing (Lk 23:4, 14, 22). This stress on the innocence of Jesus before the Roman authorities is also characteristic of John's gospel (Jn 18:38; 19:4, 6). Luke presents the Jerusalem Jewish leaders as the ones who force the hand of the Roman authorities (Lk 23:1–2, 5, 10, 13, 18, 21, 23–25).*

Joy

The term *gospel*, from the Greek *euangelion*, means good news. Despite being filled with disappointment, rejection, and suffering, reading the Gospels supposedly ought to radiate a sense of joy, happiness, or satisfaction. After all, the good news is about the announcement that a savior is born that promises eternal life to those who accept his teachings and/or choose to believe in him. This joy emanates primarily from the person of Jesus, who as God's messenger is given the task of announcing that *the kingdom of God is at hand* (Mk 1-15, Mt 4:17). This category deals with questions such as, are there instances of joy in the Gospels; is Jesus a joyful person; does he possess a charming or delightful personality that compels people to follow him and to be like him? There is an even more pertinent issue; do readers derive enjoyment or pleasure from reading the Gospels; if so, what kind of enjoyment would they feel?

Determining the extent of *joy* in the Gospels requires agreeing on a generic definition of the term and contrasting it with one of its most used synonyms, *happiness.* The effort is like getting lost in a linguistic labyrinth. Some writers, psychologists, and intellectual observers find a distinction, arguing (almost invariably) that joy is getting to know and loving God (Christian authors add Jesus) and/or feeling empathy and compassion toward others; that while happiness is good, joy is even better because joy lasts while happiness is temporary. One Christian pastor goes as far as to suggest that since happiness depends on one's circumstances, and joy *is the ability to experience peace and contentment day in and day out, regardless of the circumstances*, we should stop trying to be happy and focus on joy. A Christian ministry organization suggests that happiness happens to us (not a choice) while joy is a willful action. Based on his experiences, a historian writes that *joy is a deeper, richer experience than happiness.* Overall, the tendency among these authors is to slightly devalue happiness in favor of joy.[1]

On the other hand, others would regard happiness more meaningfully, suggesting that it requires a *sense of meaning and deep satisfaction.*[2] Another author appears to equate happiness and joy suggesting that in happiness we may be able to *experience a deep peace or joy even while our world seems to be falling apart.*[3] Still, others, taking a more traditional theological tack, emphasize happiness even while indicating joy.[4] Additionally, a more scientific approach in the field of psychology and emotions (Positive Psychology) indicates that despite disagreements among researchers on the definition and scope of happiness, this field of study provides a generic but sensible definition: *happiness is a state characterized by contentment and general satisfaction with one's current situation.*[5] Additionally, in contrast with previous views diminishing happiness, it seems that in dealing with emotions, both joy and happiness are similarly valued in this field.[6]

The dictionaries, however, which account for the daily use of language, beg to differ from the many notions of joy and happiness that prevail nowadays. Oxford and Cambridge dictionaries associate joy with happiness[7] while Merriam-Webster dictionary defines joy as *the emotion evoked by well-being, success, or good fortune or by the prospect of possessing what one desires,*[8] a definition that psychology today ascribes to happiness, and whose roots in European languages indicate *good fortune, good chance, good happening.*[9]

Where exactly is this linguistic labyrinth taking us? It appears that outside of professional circles, joy and happiness might be often interchangeable. Still, *joy* is ranked 2840 among the 5000 most used words in the English language; *happiness* is even lower at 3907. Nonetheless, *happy* seems more familiar, and is highly ranked at 748.[10] Google searches, however, indicate that *joy* had nearly 1.3 billion hits; *happiness* 977 million (as of May 2020). Academically, the numbers change drastically. The Stanford Encyclopedia of Philosophy recorded 409 documents that deal (at least partially) with *happiness,* and 175 documents with *joy.*[11] Meanwhile, biblically, joy seems to be a more religious term than happiness; the former shows up (192xt in both the New King James Version and NABRE while the latter only appears 4xt and 16xt respectively in both English translations of the Bible); happiness does not even show up in the New Testament.[12]

Simply searching for the words *joy* and *rejoice* would indicate that cheerfulness in the Gospels is a scarce commodity. Nonetheless, other words and passages that suggest a feeling similar to joy were used to rank this category. Content analysis results still rank the Joy category as less significant.

In the Gospels, the terms *joy* and *rejoice* are mostly oriented toward situations that Jesus values: repentance, belief, acceptance of the kingdom of God and its teachings, and conversion as well as instances related to God. Although not stated in the texts, there is no reason that Jesus might have been opposed to earthly joy, e.g., one's team winning a championship, dancing, or the celebration of a birthday. The texts indicate that Jesus enjoys moments of joy; he attends a wedding; gladly receives children; and, he is seemingly joyful when he heals the sick and provides food to the hungry. Nonetheless, the message in the Gospels, as shown in its content analysis results, is that earthly joy (as important as it is emotionally and psychologically for human beings) is secondary in God's eyes. As depressing as this statement may sound to postmodern generations, it is vintage Jesus and well within the logic of salvation; his remark, *do not be afraid of those who kill the body but cannot kill the soul; rather, be afraid of the one who can destroy both soul and body in Gehenna* (Mt 10:28), succinctly conveys his view on the issue.

This category focuses on terms and passages indicating joy, rejoice, happiness, cheerfulness, laughter, pleasure, pleasing, satisfaction, blessed, and others that convey a feeling of *hope* and of inner *peace* that are manifestations of joy.[13] Table 2 includes a breakdown of this category, in one instance adding Jesus's miracles, presuming that there is joy when people are healed of their infirmities, and excluding them altogether in the other while focusing only on the temporal use of the term. When miracles are added to this second subcategory (*Joy added to miracles*), Table 2 indicates that *joy* is ranked among the significant categories in the Gospels.

An interesting term that was included in this category is *blessedness*. It is highly used in the Gospels, although awkwardly from an earthly standpoint, as it refers to a feeling of joy that God finds in people who accept their deprivations, humiliations, and persecutions with meekness, in the hope of an eternal reward in heaven. Although Jesus teaches that people experiencing these conditions ought to be joyful because they are blessed in God's eyes (Lk 6:20-23, Mt 5:1-12), it may be doubtful that many rejoice in this type of existence. Moreover, the use of the term is not always positive. In some instances, Jesus uses the words *laugh, rejoice,* and *peace* as undesirable behavior (Lk 6:23, Jn 16:20-24, Mt 10:34, Lk 12:51).

Joy in the Gospels
There are instances of joy in the Gospels, although they do not refer to people's temporal yearnings on earth, indicating that Jesus is teaching a new and more difficult way of life that runs contrary to human desires:

- God is pleased with his son (Mk 1:11, Lk 3:21-22);
- those who hear God's word receive it with joy (Mk 4:16, Lk 8:13);
- acting in accordance with Jesus's teachings bring about inner peace (Mk 9:50, Lk 7:50);
- Jesus welcomes and praises children, telling his disciples that becoming child-like leads to the kingdom (Mk 10:13-16, Lk 18:15-17);
- hoping (*awaiting*) for the kingdom of God is a positive, i.e., joyful attitude (Mk 15:43, Lk 23:50-51);
- Gentiles will hope in Jesus (Mt 12:21);
- there is joy when Elizabeth bears her son, John the Baptist (Lk 1:14);
- Mary is blessed because she will give birth to Jesus, and rejoices that God is her savior (Lk 1:39-55);

- people are rejoiced when John the Baptist is born because he is Jesus's messenger (Lk 1:57-58), and he rejoices when he meets Jesus (Jn 3:27-30);
- Jesus's birth is a joyful event (Lk 2:8-11, 13-14, Mt 2:9-10);
- God favors (blesses) the poor, the hungry, and those who weep and are persecuted (Lk 6:20-23, Mt 5:1-12);
- presumably, being fed when hungry makes people feel *satisfied* (Mk 6:41-42, Lk 9:16-17, Mt 14:19-20, 15:33).
- peace among those who accept God's word is a cause for joy (Lk 10:5-6, Mt 10:12-13);
- seeking God's kingdom rather than material possessions leads to joy, according to Jesus (Lk 12:30-32, Mt 13:18-21, 13:44);
- people rejoice at Jesus's wondrous deeds (Lk 13:16-17);
- there is joy in heaven when sinners repent (Lk 15:1-32, Mt 18:12-14);
- people are joyful when they see Jesus (Mk 11:7-9, Lk 19:1-6, 36-38, Mt 21:8-9, Jn 12:12);
- the disciples will be joyful that Jesus will be reunited with them in the future (Jn 14:19-20);
- Jesus rejoices to be doing the Father's will (Jn 4:34-38);
- Jesus and others are contented with John the Baptist's work (Jn 5:34-35);
- Abraham is rejoiced that God kept his promise (Jn 8:54-56);
- Jesus says that God rejoices at those who faithfully serve him (Mt 24:46, 25:21-23);
- Jesus is joyful of his work with his disciples (Jn 15:11-13);
- there is joy when Jesus wishes his disciples inner peace, and they are joyful to see the resurrected Jesus parting to heaven (Lk 24:36-41, 52, Mt 25:8, Jn 14:27-28, Jn 20:20);
- Jesus rejoices that he is going back to his Father (Jn 17:12-13);
- Jesus indicates that it pleases God that people believe without seeing (Jn 20:29).

The type of joy observed in the above passages is mostly characterized by its relationship with the supernatural; the passages refer to an eschatological joy that is interwoven with Jesus and the kingdom of God. There is almost nothing worldly about them. Nevertheless, although the texts do not convey an explicit image of an amused Jesus enjoying a heartened laughter, he engages in playful antics or mischievous acts with his disciples. He scares them by appearing unannounced walking on the sea while they are fishing (Mt 14:24-26). Following his resurrection, he engages two of them in a conversation without being recognized and decides to play hide and seek with them (Lk 24:13-31, Mk 16:12). He appears before a weeping Mary Magdalene who thinks he is a gardener (Jn 20:11-17). Seemingly enjoying himself, he shows up again before the other disciples who think they are seeing a ghost, and suddenly they are incredulously filled with joy (Lk 24:36-41). He relishes coming in through locked doors to surprise them (Jn 20:19, 26). Eventually, his disciples renew their regular fishing activities (oblivious to the extraordinary event that has taken place during the previous days) and the resurrected Jesus appears to them from the shore, unannounced, this time in his role as a fish finder (Jn 21:1-12). This is behavior that projects lightheartedness on Jesus's part.

Ironically, Mark's rendition of the resurrection is dispirited. Acting more like a killjoy, Jesus rebukes his disciples for not believing that he has risen from the dead (Mk 16:14). It is puzzling too, that, once resurrected, Jesus does not spend all the time with his disciples. At times he seems to disappear, and the texts do not provide information on Jesus's whereabouts; including whether he ever visits his mother.

It may be understandable that, prior to the resurrection, Jesus's expressions of joy would be different. He seems not to have much time for enjoyment as he spends time preaching and struggling with unrepentant towns, the religious authorities, and with his inability to get through to his disciples. Moreover, he is concerned knowing that his actions eventually will cost him his life. He is aware that his mission might be a disappointment, and he appeals to God from the cross: *my God, why have you forsaken me?* (Mk 15:34). Amid these feelings, he reveals to his disciples that his greatest joy is doing the Father's will, no matter the outcome (Jn 4:34-38, 17:13, Mk 14:36).

Jesus must have enjoyed knowing that the Father is pleased with him (Mk 1:9-11). He must have felt gratified (at least temporarily) that crowds followed him and listened to him. He was probably soberly ecstatic when he is raised from the dead. His joy, however, is puzzling; it stems from someone who carries an enormous burden that he is willing to accept.

Nonetheless, not everything is joyful according to the Gospels. John the Baptist tells soldiers that they must be satisfied with their wages (Mk 3:14), supposedly because they were not. There is no joy when Jesus and his disciples are rebuffed by unrepentant towns, threatening them instead with condemnation (Lk 10:12-16, Mt 10:15). Even to those who seem to enjoy their lives on earth knowing that others suffer, Jesus promises that they will grieve and weep afterward (Lk 6:25). Moreover, if there is joy in heaven for every sinner that repents, presumably there must be sadness when someone forfeits his or her life because of sin.

Having established that there is in the Gospels a sensation of joy in Jesus and among others that befriend him, there is still the issue of whether believers derive any joy from reading the Gospels. This question takes us into a second category, *Joy added to miracles*. The Gospels illustrate a series of dramatic events with an extraordinary joyful ending. Moreover, although the Bible has been highly read throughout history, it is difficult to ascertain the exact motive(s). Its attraction among its followers probably lies in at least three significant elements that evoke joy, peace, love, and hope: the existence of a noble person with supernatural powers who has defied and triumphed over evil and death, whose interest is the wellbeing of others, and who is willing to give his life for that ideal; the joy (hope) that humans derive from the possibility of attaining everlasting happiness; and, powerful sentimental accounts that appeal to people such as love, forgiveness, compassion, wonder, fear of hell, a loving yet frightening God, and a day of reckoning at the end of time.

Nonetheless, what links these themes together creating a lively interaction between the texts and readers are faith and hope. Humanly speaking, faith by itself is a dead-end. It is only when it nourishes hope, that faith would seem to attain a practical and eschatological value by transforming belief into the expectation that life might become better in the future. Faith compels the person to hope, and hoping (amid work, sleep, and entertainment), is all that humans can do while on earth. Biblically, human life amounts to awaiting while believing and acting righteously. Without hope (including temporal hope) that life somehow will become better, human beings would despair. In the Gospels, the joy of hope stems from Jesus's works, including his resurrection. Thus, if we are to gauge more accurately the extent of joy that people may derive from the texts today, it would be reasonable to include all of Jesus's miracles into account, since from that moment on the faithful believes he/she is in a relationship with the divine.

Paraphrasing Paul, and without getting into any kind of theological mysticism, it is worth acknowledging that without the miracle of the resurrection (and Jesus's other deeds), there would be no hope among believers and no reason to read the Gospels, other than as a treatise in moral philosophy and the struggle for power between a rebel and the authorities. This means that the greatest joy that believers find in the Gospels is probably the hope that proceeds from miracle narratives, regardless of whether they are factual or not. Accounts of Jesus's miracles evoke majesty, kindness, and joy, emotions that humanity has yearned for throughout history.

Notes:
1. Dr. Cheryl A. MacDonald, "Is there a Relationship between Happiness and Joy?" *Health Psychology Center*, https://healthpsychology.org/is-there-a-relationship-between-happiness-and-joy/; "What is the difference between joy and happiness?," *Compellingtruth.org*, https://www.compellingtruth.org/joy-happiness.html; David Brooks, "The Difference Between Happiness and Joy," *New York Times*, May 7, 2019, https://www.nytimes.com/2019/05/07/opinion/happiness-joy-emotion.html;
Rev. Dr. Christopher Benek, "God can be found in difference between happiness and joy," *The Island Packet*, October 7, 2014, https://www.islandpacket.com/living/religion/article33609807.html (accessed May 29, 2019); Sandra L. Brown M.A., "Joy-vs- Happiness," *Psychology Today*, December 18, 2012, https://www.psychologytoday.com/us/blog/pathological-relationships/201212/joy-vs-happiness;
Lawrence Samuel Ph.D., "Happiness Versus Joy," *Psychology Today*, October 2, 2018, https://www.psychologytoday.com/us/blog/psychology-yesterday/201810/happiness-versus-joy (all accessed May 29, 2019).
2. "What is happiness," *Psychology Today*, www.psychologytoday.com/us/basics/happiness (accessed May 29, 2019).
3. Gary Zimak, "The Secret to Happiness," *Catholic Digest*, September 12, 2017, http://www.catholicdigest.com/wellness/body-soul/the-secret-to-happiness/ (accessed May 30, 2019).
4. Catholic theologian Charles Camosy cites his colleague Bill Mattison suggesting that both St. Augustine and Thomas Aquinas understood that happiness lies in the love of God and love of neighbor: Charles Camosy, "What is Happiness," *Catholic Moral Theology*, March 27, 2011, https://catholicmoraltheology.com/what-is-happiness/ (accessed May 30, 2019).
Michael Maher, "Happiness," CE, Vol. 7, http://www.newadvent.org/cathen/07131b.htm (accessed May 30, 2019). Its entry on Joy consists of citing Thomas Aquinas's disputation: Thomas Aquinas, "Joy,"

Question 28, Article 1, *Summa Theologica*, in *CE*, http://www.newadvent.org/summa/3028.htm (accessed May 30, 2019).

5. Courtney Ackerman, "What is Happiness and Why is it Important," *Positive Psychology Program,* February 16, 2019. https://positivepsychologyprogram.com/what-is-happiness/ (accessed May 29, 2019).

6. The Handbook of Positive Psychology states: *the field of positive psychology at the subjective level is about positive subjective experience: well-being and satisfaction (past); flow, joy, the sensual pleasures, and happiness (present); and constructive cognitions about the future—optimism, hope, and faith.* Martin E. P. Seligman, "Positive Psychology, Positive Prevention, and Positive Therapy," p. 3, http://www.positiveculture.org/uploads/7/4/0/7/7407777/seligrman_intro.pdf (accessed May 30, 2019); Barbara L. Fredrickson, "The Value of Positive Emotions: The emerging science of positive psychology is coming to understand why it's good to feel good," *American Scientist,* Vol 91, No. 4 (July-August 2003), pp 330-335, https://www.americanscientist.org/sites/americanscientist.org/files/20058214332_306.pdf (accessed May 30, 2019).

7. *Cambridge Dictionary*, *Oxford Dictionary*, online, s.v. "joy."

8. *Merriam-Webster Dictionary,* online, s.v. "joy."

9. Maher, "Happiness."

10. "Word Frequency Data," *Corpus of Contemporary American English,* https://www.wordfrequency.info/free.asp?s=y (accessed May 30, 2019).

11. "Happiness," *Stanford Encyclopedia of Philosophy*, https://plato.stanford.edu/search/search?query=happiness (accessed May 30, 2019); "Joy," *Ibid,* https://plato.stanford.edu/search/search?query=joy (accessed May 30, 2019).

12. *BibleGateway.com.*

13. Quite often there is joy among people in loving and forgiving one's enemies, and in being merciful and compassionate toward people we dislike. Nonetheless, these terms are not included because they would unnecessarily dilute the category. Miracles, however, are included because they generate hope and faith among believers.

Holy Spirit

In mainstream Christianity, the Holy Spirit refers to a supernatural being that is independent of God the Father and Jesus, and that together make up the Trinity; three divine persons sharing the same substance or nature.[1] In the synoptics the term appears numerous times as *holy Spirit* (lower case h) or *Spirit.* Only in John's Gospel does Jesus refer to the holy Spirit as the *Advocate,* still a separate being but with significant supernatural callings. It is beyond the scope of this work to explain how Christianity conceptualizes the Trinity, except to note that only in one instance does Jesus group the three persons together into what has become a trademark of the Christian faith, the sign of the cross (Mt 28:18-20).

The *holy Spirit* is far more mysterious than God. As the term appears in the Old Testament, it is difficult to say if there is any relation to the holy Spirit in the Gospels.[2] The term itself is not to be confused with the Hebrew word *ruah* that ordinarily means air, wind, or breath. In the Gospels, when used in lower case (spirit), the word appears numerous times and it stands for the innermost part of the human person, i.e., life (Mk 8:12, 14:38, Lk 1:46, 23:46, Mt 5:3, 27:50). References to the Spirit in Old Testament versions in Christian Bibles indicate that the term is different from the way Jesus (or Christian theology) presents the holy Spirit; otherwise, the concept of the Trinity would have become known before his lifetime.[3] Once again, the Gospels indicate the extent to which Jesus differs from other personalities in the Hebrew Bible.

The tally in Table 2 ranks this category as less significant, indicating that it is not commensurate with the significance that Christian theology attributes to the Holy Spirit; given that Jesus has left the temporal world, according to Christianity the Holy Spirit is all they have to instruct them. A review of other mainstream Bibles does not indicate that there is much difference in the tally if other versions had been used, other than to note, for example, that the King James version relies on the term *Holy Ghost* instead of holy Spirit.[4]

Who is the Holy Spirit and What it Does
When grouped, the information about the holy Spirit in the Gospels allows at least a glimpse of this puzzling entity. We know that it dwells on several righteous people and speaks through them. For example, Elizabeth is said to be filled with the Spirit, as well as is her husband Zechariah, through whom the Spirit prophesizes (Lk 1:41, 67-79). Their son, John the Baptist, is aided by the holy Spirit to turn people toward God (Lk 11:13-16). The righteous and devoted believer, Simeon, prophesizes about Jesus and Mary while filled with the Spirit (Lk 2:25-32). The Spirit inspires David too to distinguish between himself and God (Ps 110), thus allowing Jesus to astutely suggest to the religious authorities that he, and not David, is the Messiah.[5]

The initial narratives about the Spirit in the synoptics contain a series of odd remarks. The Spirit makes its first appearance when it accompanies God during Jesus's baptism and assumes the physical body of a dove (Mk 1:10, Lk 3:21-22, Mt 3:16). It is an awkward image for a supernatural being, although perhaps it is symbolic of its special role in guiding Noah and his family to dry land during the flood (Gen 8:8-12). John the Baptist emphasizes the significance of the holy Spirit when he attests that his baptisms on the Jordan River are not as meaningful as Jesus's who is baptizing with the holy Spirit (Mk 1:8, Lk 3:15-16, Mt 3:11, Jn 1:33). The Spirit escorts Jesus to the desert to be subjected to Satan's temptations. Throughout, the Spirit supposedly protects him and enables him to overcome temptation (Mk 1:12-13, Lk 4:1-13, Mt 4:1-11). This, however, is an awkward passage; if Jesus is the Son of God, should he not be able to reject temptation by himself? Is he not divine at the time? Jesus's temptations in the desert are one of many significant passages that find no reasonable explanation from a human viewpoint.

The holy Spirit, once again, accompanies Jesus as he walks into a synagogue and assumes the role of prophet anointed by God to proclaim God's kingdom to the people (Lk 4:14-21). Moreover, the Spirit assists Jesus in driving demons (Mt 12:28), even though at times it appears that he can do it by himself. Furthermore, alluding to its role as a defender, Jesus tells his followers that they should not worry if they endure persecution, since when they are tried before the courts, *it will not be you who are speaking but the holy Spirit* (Mk 13:11, Lk 12:10-12, Mt 10:17-20). Jesus, however, does not explain how the Spirit will manifest itself during those instances.

Perhaps one of the holy Spirit's most unusual roles is that of spiritual progenitor akin to physical *in vitro* fertilization that creates pregnancies outside of sexual intercourse. Two passages narrate how the holy Spirit becomes responsible for Elizabeth's and Mary's pregnancies (Lk 1:35-37, Mt 1:20); in the case of Elizabeth because she is infertile, and in Mary's case, it may be surmised that God wishes to signal Mary and Joseph the significance of Jesus's birth. Similar miracles are narrated in the Old Testament. For example, Hagar becomes pregnant when Abram is eighty-six years old (Gen 16:16), and an old and *worn-out* Sarah (Gen 18:11) when she is in her nineties by him too when he is one hundred years old (Gen 21:1-5). Nothing in the narratives, however, indicates that the holy Spirit is responsible for these pregnancies.

Another passage in the synoptics is vexing to the extent that it raises questions about God's mercy. Jesus indicates that *all sins and blasphemies that people utter* (including those against the Son of Man) *will be forgiven; but whoever blasphemes against the holy Spirit will never have forgiveness, but is guilty of an everlasting sin* (Mk 3:28-30, Lk 12:10, Mt 12:31-32). In this passage Jesus assigns the holy Spirit a status greater than himself, as he does not explain why blaspheming against the holy Spirit should be considered more sinful than others insulting him. Supposedly, the sin of blaspheming against the Spirit lies in *attributing to Satan what is the work of the Spirit of God,*[6] an unflattering accusation. But can such a blasphemy be worse than someone being responsible for the execution of the Son of God, an act that Jesus himself forgives? The Catholic hierarchy provides an alternative explanation, indicating that blasphemy against the holy Spirit consists of one's refusal to accept the salvation that is offered through the holy Spirit; in effect, rejecting redemption.[7]

The Holy Spirit in John's Gospel
In John's Gospel, Jesus provides information that does not appear in the synoptics. The Spirit, it seems, has a notable role in salvation and the revelation of truth. In this Gospel, Jesus indicates that there are two types of births in Christianity: first, people are born as God's creatures, but this birth does not appear to make them God's children, a more esteemed status. Jesus argues that once born, anyone who wishes to enter the kingdom of God needs to be *born of water and Spirit* (Jn 3:5). How the process works is somewhat obscure. Supposedly, Jesus's redemption already had paved the way to salvation, subject to individual response. This response would then constitute a second or *new birth from above,*[8] provided that the person the Spirit calls upon accepts believing in Jesus. According to Jesus, this new birth seems to be conditional, arbitrary, and mysterious, as it depends on whom the Spirit decides to call. This Spirit, he says, *blows where it wills, and you can hear the sound it makes, but you do not know where it comes from or where it goes* (Jn 3:8). This remark confuses Nicodemus, and probably many others, particularly when Jesus adds that salvation requires being born of *water and Spirit* (Jn 3:5). Is Jesus alluding to the Spirit of God i.e., a special gift, or is he referring to the third person of the Trinity? Moreover, in Luke, Jesus indicates (in contradiction to earlier remarks) that the Spirit will assist anyone who asks for it, not those it wills (Lk 11:13).

This lack of clarity appears in another passage in which the Spirit is a feature that God possesses, e.g., his omnipotence. In this passage, Jesus refers to the Samaritan people in a manner that would not be acceptable today. While speaking with a Samaritan woman he says,

> *you people worship what you do not understand; we worship what we understand, because salvation is from the Jews. But the hour is coming, and is now here, when true worshipers will worship the Father in Spirit and truth; and indeed the Father seeks such people to worship him. God is Spirit, and those who worship him must worship in Spirit and truth (Jn 4:22-25).*

It is difficult to view the Spirit in this passage as an entity different from God. John's Gospel presents the Spirit as someone distinctive from the Father and the Son. Although Jesus refers to him as the *Advocate,* he is a combination of mediator, accuser, and judge who will appear on earth only following Jesus's resurrection (Jn 7:39, Jn 16:5-7). Nonetheless, it is Jesus who will ask the Father to replace him on earth to speak the truth (Jn 14:15-17); to *teach you everything and remind you of all that [I] told you* (Jn 14:26, 15:26). This *Advocate* will convict those that do not believe in Jesus (Jn 16:8-10), guide his disciples *to all truth ...* and will tell them *the things that are coming* (Jn 16:12-15).

What exactly Jesus is saying might be difficult to interpret. How will the Advocate remind his followers of Jesus's teachings, guide them to the truth, and declare what is to come? Presuming that there will not be further public revelations or apparitions, Jesus indicates that the Spirit will work through his disciples and through the community that Jesus establishes; a community with authority to forgive and to retain sin (Jn 20:21-23). Allegedly, the holy Spirit will manifest itself *in the forum of the disciples' conscience* [through which] *he prosecutes the world* by leading *believers* **to see** *(a) that the basic sin was and is refusal to believe in Jesus; (b) that, although Jesus was found guilty and apparently died in disgrace, in reality righteousness has triumphed, for Jesus has returned to his Father; (c) finally, that it is the ruler of this world, Satan, who has been condemned through Jesus' death.*[9]

It might be difficult, even for believers, to understand that Jesus perceives events in the opposite manner of how people may interpret them. Jesus sees his death not as a defeat but as a triumph, and, although he condemns Satan, nothing indicates that his condemnation was significant since Satan (according to Jesus) still rules the world. An even greater problem confronting Jesus's expectations is that his community of followers has, since his death, splintered into dozens of denominations with opposing beliefs and moral ideologies. In this case, it may be argued that the Spirit's prosecution has had little effect if any, or that Jesus's followers lack a forum in their consciences.

Today's secularized world likely will resist manifestations of a Spirit they cannot detect through the senses, even by those with faith. As a result, multiple generations across the world stand to be condemned by the Spirit, raising the question of how it will succeed in its mission if its works are being denied because they cannot be verified.

Notes

1. Although not being privy to this mystery, the concept of the Trinity is not difficult to imagine if we were to light up three matches and join them together to form one flame. Nonetheless, other Christian denominations do not believe in the Trinity, among them Jehovah's Witnesses, The Church of Jesus Christ of Latter-day Saints (Mormon Church), Christian Scientists, and other Unitarian churches. Furthermore, some mainstream Protestant denominations, while accepting the Trinity, differ from Catholic beliefs regarding its precise meaning.

2. It is difficult to tell if citations in the Old Testament refer to an individual entity with personal characteristics or to God's spirit (as in something that is an integral part of God: a) *Or who can know your counsel, unless you give Wisdom and send your holy spirit from on high?* (Wisdom 9:17); b) *But they rebelled and grieved his holy spirit* (Isaiah 63:10); c) *Do not drive me from before your face, nor take from me your holy spirit* (Psalm 51:13); d) *Could we find another like him," Pharaoh asked his servants, "a man so endowed with the spirit of God?* (Genesis 41:38); e) *When Balaam looked up and saw Israel encamped, tribe by tribe, the spirit of God came upon him* (Numbers 24:2); f) *As he listened to this report, the spirit of God rushed upon him and he became very angry* (1 Samuel 11:6); g) *Then the spirit of God clothed Zechariah, son of Jehoiada the priest* (2 Chronicles 24:20). In the above examples only (a) appears to refer to a separate entity.

3. An entry in the *JewishEncyclopedia.com* indicates that, although distinct from God, the Holy Spirit is created by God, thus different than Jesus's holy Spirit: *although the Holy Spirit is often named instead of God (e.g., in Sifre, Deut. 31 [ed. Friedmann, p. 72]), yet it was conceived as being something distinct. The Spirit was among the ten things that were created on the first day (Ḥag. 12a, b). Though the nature of the Holy Spirit is really nowhere described, the name indicates that it was conceived as a kind of wind that became manifest through noise and light.* Joseph Jacobs, Ludwig Blau, "Holy Spirit," *The Jewish Encyclopedia.com,* http://jewishencyclopedia.com/articles/7833-holy-spirit#2294 (accessed September 25, 2019).

4. *BibleGateway.com,*

5. NEs' note, Matthew 22:41-46 and 42-44.

6. Ibid., note, Matthew 12:31.

7. Pope John Paul II, *Dominum et Vivificantem - On the Holy Spirit in the Life of the Church and the World,"* St. Peter's, Rome, May 18, 1986, http://w2.vatican.va/content/john-paul-ii/en/encyclicals/documents/hf_jp-ii_enc_18051986_dominum-et-vivificantem.html (accessed September 26, 2019). The explanation, however, would seem to apply to any sin in which the sinner does not wish to repent, which in principle could be forgiven if God is prepared to override the sinner's sentiment for reasons he alone would know.

8. NEs' note, John 3:1-21.

9. Ibid., note, John 16:8-11.

Baptism

According to most Christian denominations, *baptism* (often termed *regeneration)* is not the mere religious ceremony of sprinkling water or immersing a person in the water. It is an act that carries supernatural effects, including the washing away of sin and the subsequent incorporation of believers in Jesus into the Christian community. It implies a spiritual restoration to the state of grace existing before Original Sin through which God adopts his creatures as his children, a belief indicative of the significance of baptism within mainstream Christianity.[1] Content analysis results in Table 2 indicate that, according to the Gospels, Jesus did not have much to say about this practice; it ranked among the less significant categories.

In Mark's Gospel, Jesus indicates that baptism is necessary toward attaining salvation, although the passage reveals some ambivalence on the topic. Indeed, Jesus instructs his disciples to proclaim the gospel throughout the world (a radical change from his initial mission to come only for the Jews), indicating that *whoever believes and is baptized will be saved* and *whoever does not believe will be condemned* (Mk 16:15-16). Nonetheless, he does not say if believers that are not baptized cannot be saved. In Matthew, Jesus is less compelling, as he tells his disciples to *make disciples of all nations, baptizing them in the name of the Father, and of the Son, and of the holy Spirit, teaching them to observe all that I have commanded you* (Mt 28:19-20). In this passage, Jesus does not link baptism with salvation. These distinctions have led to various practices and beliefs within Christianity regarding the necessity of baptism for salvation, such as whether partial or total immersion or water trickling over the head, might be sufficient to be saved from eternal damnation. Even a Catholic politician has charged that the baptism of children constitutes a violation of human rights.[2]

Jesus's discussion with Nicodemus in John's Gospel seems to provide revealing details regarding baptism. Jesus tells him, *I say to you, no one can see the kingdom of God without being born from above... No one can enter the kingdom of God without being born of water and Spirit* (Jn 3:3, 5). His words confuse Nicodemus, who is supposed to be well learned in God's matters. Throughout his revelations in the Gospels, could God have forgotten to include such a significant practice in the Old Testament? Other than imaginative extrapolations,[3] there are no references to baptism in the biblical texts. Once again, Jesus resorts to creating a new teaching that is alien to the Israelites and which by now has become the trademark of Christianity.

If baptism is required for salvation, Jesus's teachings imply that God had been withholding salvation from the Israelites (and the rest of humanity) for thousands of years. Nothing in God's covenant with Abraham suggests that the righteous could ever live eternally. God does not tell Abraham that he would deprive his people (and humanity) of something that would atone for Adam and Eve's Original Sin. Jesus's teachings do not indicate that his mission is to become the new Adam. This theology is the outcome of Paul's musing about Jesus. At the time, the outcome of baptism must have been an unexpected teaching. Since Jesus does not say says that baptism is necessary to erase the effects of Original Sin, why would he institute a supernatural practice, similar to the Eucharist, without providing more explicit explanations than that provided to Nicodemus?

While the term *baptism* does not show up in the Old Testament, there are certain words and phrases, such as cleansing, purification, and atonement, that reference the existence of human sinfulness, repentance, and God's kindness in expunging the sins of the Israelites (Ex 30-10, Lev 4 & 5, Num 6, 7, 8, Jos 22:17, Neh 13:18-22, Job 35:2-3, Psalms 19:12, 51:2, Prov 20:30, Jer 4:14, 33:8, Ezek 36:33, 37:23). None of these passages, however, seem to carry the cosmic connotation that Jesus ascribes to baptism in the Gospels. The term, *ablution*, i.e., immersion of the body into water, is an ancient tradition of the Jewish people that relates to a spiritual act of cleansing impurities (sin). Ablution applied to the act of cleaning that which was soiled, whether religious vessels, the priest, or a menstruating or postpartum woman, but also implied a type of rebirth.

Ezekiel, writing in the sixth century BCE, points to the relationship between water and the removal of a sinful nature that is said to be a type of pre-baptism at the time:

> *I will sprinkle clean water over you to make you clean; from all your impurities and from all your idols I will cleanse you. I will give you a new heart, and a new spirit I will put within you. I will remove the heart of stone from your flesh and give you a heart of flesh. I will put my spirit within you so that you walk in my statutes, observe my ordinances, and keep them (Ezek 36:25-26).[4]*

However, Ezekiel was not referring to a requirement that God deemed necessary for eternal salvation; the passage is about God's promise to regenerate his people. i.e., making them righteous. Nonetheless, the religious authorities never institutionalized the practice as a ritual to enter the kingdom of God. The Gospels indicate that the Israelites continued to adhere to the revered Mosaic Law prior to Jesus, until one day when God's angel appears to Zechariah to announce that John the Baptist has been assigned by God *to turn the hearts of fathers toward children and the disobedient to the understanding of the righteous, to prepare a people fit for the Lord* (Lk 1:13-17). The type of baptism John would conduct emphasizes repentance of one's sins (Lk 3:3-5); similar to Jesus's baptism in that regard, but lacking the presence of the holy Spirit, the mysterious supernatural entity that is included in Jesus's baptisms (Mk 1:7-8, Lk 3:16, Mt 3:11-12, Jn 1:26-27).

People, nonetheless, respond to John the Baptist's call. They begin to come from different regions and repent from their sins (Mk 1:5, Lk 3:10-14, Mt 3:5-6). In one instance, John becomes incensed at the sight of Pharisees and Sadducees who are present to witness the ceremony (Mt 3:7-10). Possibly, they were mere observers of a practice that until then was unknown and perhaps uncalled for since John lacked the authority to conduct religious ceremonies. Likely, given his insults, this passage suggests that John's confrontation (and probably Jesus's) with the religious authorities must have originated in the past, prior to Jesus's public mission.

Although John the Baptist's baptisms are of lesser value than the one Jesus conducts, it is baffling that Jesus asks to be baptized by John. After all, Jesus did not need to repent of any sin. Instead, he does it *to fulfill all righteousness* (Mt 3:15), a puzzling statement, since baptism was not part of Mosaic Law. Incidentally, the Gospels also indicate a lack of familiarity between John the Baptist and Jesus. Although they are supposed to be close relatives, according to Luke, they behave like strangers to one another during their encounter in the waters of the Jordan River. This estrangement continues, according to John's Gospel, as noticed in a dispute between John and *a Jew* (perhaps Jesus) over the ceremonial washings taking place (Jn 3:25-

26).[5] Nonetheless, it appears that God is pleased with the practice of baptism and with Jesus's role in it, hazily manifesting his satisfaction (Mk 1:10-11, Lk 3:21-22, Mt 3:16-17).

Is Baptism Overvalued?

The term *baptism,* as it appears in the Gospels, seems to carry several connotations, suggesting that the ranking of this category is artificially magnified. In Mark, for example, Jesus refers to his baptism as the way he is going to die, not to the institution of the practice (Mk 10:35-45).[6] Additionally, Jesus's discussion with the religious authorities about John's baptisms constitutes an awkward segue to Jesus's claim to authority (Mk 11:27-33, Lk 20:1-8, Mt 21:23-27). The Gospels do not explain his unwillingness to discuss the origins of baptism; it does, however, indicate Jesus's reluctance to enter into any form of dialogue with the religious authorities. Moreover, a passage in Luke indicates that those who listened to the Baptist, including tax collectors, are baptized, but the Pharisees and scholars of the law are not, because they *rejected the plan of God for themselves* (Lk 7:28-30). This would appear to be a subjective judgment on Luke's part, given that the religious authorities may have been rejecting an unorthodox practice by a man dressed in bizarre clothing who insults them and does not consult with those who are in charge of rituals.

In another passage, Jesus conflates his baptism by death with his desire *to set the earth on fire* and bring division into the world (Lk 12:49-51), a statement that fails to provide an adequate explanation of the significance of baptism. In John's Gospel, other than the aforementioned passages, nothing else written in the Gospels is relevant to the practice of baptism. Altogether, there are 56 references to baptism in the Gospels in seventeen passages. Nonetheless, in only nine passages does the word baptism relate more or less directly to its practice (Mk 1:2-11, 16:14-18, Lk 1:13-17, 3:1-18, 21-22, Mt 3:1-17, 28:16-20, Jn 1:22-34, 3:3, 5-7); in the other passages, the term is inconsequential.

Given that the practice of baptism extended among the first community of believers (as portrayed in the Acts of the Apostles), it is likely that there was more discussion about its significance at the time that the oral tradition failed to detect. It suggests that people simply were led into baptism by John's and Jesus's charisma, or they accepted being baptized as a type of life insurance policy.

Baptism's distinctive features are its emphasis on repentance of one's sins, a desire to belong to the newly established kingdom of God through a physical and spiritual sense of community, and the disposition to follow the teachings of Jesus. Although not explicitly stated in the texts, Jesus initially means to institute the practice for the Jewish people, since they are the ones for whom he came. Moreover, there are no references in the texts in which non-Jews are being baptized, although it likely began to happen after Paul met with the Apostles in Jerusalem in 50 CE. But why did Jesus believe that baptism was necessary? In Judaism, the concepts of *atonement* and *ablution* imply human reconciliation with God through repentance of sins that include sacrificial rites, prayer, suffering, fasting, and death.[7] Thus, the institution of baptism seems to lack a religious rationale, other than God's decision (after thousands of years) to ask Jesus to do it for unspecified reasons.

The idea that through baptism some of the effects of Original Sin are forgiven and regeneration of the self takes place is not based on the Gospels. This view is based on Pauline theology (or revelation as Paul insists, Gal 1:4, 12) since the Gospels do not indicate that there was any communication between Jesus and Paul concerning this view. On the other hand, not much of Paul's views on the effects of baptism have been proven historically accurate. History has shown that there is an abyss between what baptism is supposed to accomplish within the believer and its reality. Despite signifying a rebirth, except this time conjoined with God, the overall social effects of baptism on human beings seem to be no different than what may have been accomplished without it. The supposed grace that comes with it does not necessarily guarantee righteousness; people who are baptized go on to sin years after.

Secular eyes look upon baptism as an anachronism devoid of (substantial historical, i.e., empirical) value. Part of the reason that the rite of baptism is fading is that a secularized world has abandoned the traditional sense of what is sacred, e.g., the mysteries concerning God's human incarnation; belief in the death and resurrection of Jesus; the sense of awe and fear that God once represented; the evil that sinfulness signifies; and the expectation of the afterlife. Religious sacredness is being replaced with symbols of secular sacredness, some of which are quite worthy, such as dignified respect for human life; human rights; an awakening sensitivity toward the ecology that makes life on earth possible; and the value of reason and science.

Far from being an antidote to sin, baptism has become a cultural rite of passage, and a symbol of social acceptance.[8] Although good intentions may prevail on the part of the baptized child or adult, or the parents or godparents, experience indicates that the effects of Original Sin (or flawed evolution) continue to predispose the destiny of human beings toward evil.

Notes:
1. In 1439 Pope Eugene IV declared in *Exsultate Deo* at the Council of Florence that, *Holy Baptism holds the first place among the sacraments, because it is the door of the spiritual life; for by it we are made members of Christ and incorporated with the Church. And since through the first man death entered into all, unless we be born again of water and the Holy Ghost, we cannot enter into the kingdom of Heaven, as Truth Himself has told us.* William Fanning, "Baptism," *CE*, Vol. 2, www.newadvent.org/cathen/02258b. htm (accessed on October 22, 2019). Writing in his *Small Catechism* in 1529 Martin Luther shows similar views: *Baptism is not just plain water, but it is the water included in God's command and combined with God's word... The Small Catechism of Martin Luther, Part Four: Holy Baptism, Tran by Robert E. Smith, June 10, 1994,* www.christian.net/pub/resources/text/wittenberg/luther/little.book/book-4.txt *(accessed October 22, 2019).*
2. Some fundamentalist denominations tend to reject the necessity of baptism indicating that to insist on its necessity suggests *that Jesus' death on the cross was not sufficient to purchase our salvation.* "Is baptism necessary for salvation?" *GotQuestions.Org.,* http://www.gotquestions.org/baptism-salvation.html, (accessed January 20, 2018). The views of the Christian Apologetics and Research Ministry, a conservative Christian ministry with Calvinist tendencies, are similar, although they go further in declaring that neither water nor a ceremony is necessary for salvation since *we are justified by faith*; Matt Slick, "Is baptism necessary for salvation?" *CARM,* Nov 22, 2008, https://carm.org/is-baptism-necessary-salvation, (accessed January 20, 2018). Some internet entities have conducted their

own research on the practices of baptism, and they tend to conform to one another, with some exceptions: "Compare Religions: Baptism," *ReligionResourcesOnline.org.*
http://www.religionresourcesonline.org/different-types-of-religion/compare/baptism.php, (accessed October 24, 2019); Beverly Beyer, "Which Religions Practice Baptism? Which Do Not?," (updated July 29, 2019), *Owlcation.com.* https://owlcation.com/humanities/Which-Religions-Practice-Baptism-Which-Do-Not, (accessed October 24, 2019). Regarding the statement that baptizing children violates human rights and amounts to *creating infant conscripts* (a most inane statement in my personal view) by a former Catholic President of Ireland, see Charles Collins, "Ex-president of Ireland says baptism creates "infant conscripts,"" *Crux,* June 23, 2018, https://cruxnow.com/church-in-uk-and-ireland/2018/06/ex-president-of-ireland-says-baptism-creates-infant-conscripts/ (accessed June 30, 2018).
3. Brian Pizzalato, "Baptism foreshadowed in Old Testament," *Catholic News Agency,*
 https://www.catholicnewsagency.com/resources/sacraments/baptism/baptism-foreshadowed-in-old-testament (accessed July 13, 2020).
4. Circumcision, although it is the sign of God's covenant with the Jewish people, only applies to men. Nonetheless, its significance lies in that God regarded the uncircumcised as having their soul cut off from his people (Gen 17:7-14).
5. NEs' note, John 3:25.
6. The passage appears in Matthew too; however, the term baptism does not appear.
7. "Atonement," *Encyclopedia Judaica,* Jewish Virtual Library, www.jewishvirtuallibrary.org/atonement, (Accessed October 23, 2019).
8. Jesuit priest James Martin refers to baptism *as the most familiar but misunderstood sacrament.... It's become a rite of passage for the family rather than what it really means -- an incorporation into the Christian community. So, some parents don't realize why it takes place during a Mass or why godparents should be Catholics. They are surprised that preparation is involved.* Cathy Lynn Grossman, "Baptism rates slide despite high-profile boosts," *National Catholic Reporter,* Oct 24, 2013, https://www.ncronline.org/news/parish/baptism-rates-slide-despite-high-profile-boosts (accessed October 24, 2017).

Sexual Behavior in the Gospels

It is important to note that the Gospels have extraordinarily little to say about matters of sexuality. Hence, there is no narrative for this category, only its overall tally that appears in Table 2, and its breakdown by author in Table 3. Sexual Behavior in the Gospels is an aggregate of all Righteous and Sinful Sexual Behavior categories, each of which is dealt with separately. Discussion of Righteous Sexual Behavior deals with *marriage, celibacy*, *chastity*, and *virginity*, and appears below while Sinful Sexual Behavior shows under the Sinfulness category.

(See Method Note on Sexual Behavior for additional explanation on each of these categories)

Righteous Sexual Behavior - Marriage

The act of marriage may be seen as comprising two distinctive elements: the humanly sacred commitment entailing love and companionship, and its sacred yet profane aspects, referring to the biological reproduction of the species and the sexual drive that leads to physical intercourse, a drive humans share with animals. Interestingly, the Bible deals with all types of human sexual acts, both righteous and sinful, at times depicted in a rather imaginative language. Even some acts that today appear sinful and illegal in many countries are allowed by God in the Bible such as de facto bigamy, sexual intercourse outside of marriage, or out-of-wedlock pregnancies at an early age.

It appears that realizing how volatile sexuality would become, God soon begins to enact legislation to curb human sexual relations.[1] It does not take long for Christian church hierarchies to establish codes of ethics to regulate sexual behavior and provide the nations' cultures with a sense of morality. Christian denominations have altered some of these regulations throughout time, by allowing divorce and annulment, considering sexual love as an end in marriage, and approving same-sex unions. In most of these cases, the laity along with profane culture appears to have taken the lead in inducing these changes, perhaps responding to a reading of the sign of the times.

Where this understanding of sexuality and marital relations comes from remains a mystery since in the Gospels Jesus has little to offer in this regard. Content analysis results rank *marriage* as among the least significant categories. The results are quite telling. It means that Jesus's teachings about the goodness of marriage are rare, except within the context of divorce and/or adultery. For example, there are 93xt references to *marriage* in the texts, though only 50xt deal directly with the term *marriage,* and most of them are immaterial to Jesus's teachings on marriage; the other 43xt relate to marriage indirectly through the terms *divorce* and *adultery.*[2] Viewed from a different perspective, of 28p passages dealing with *marriage*, only 12p relate directly to marriage, and they are inconsequential to marriage as a sacred institution:

> - in the synoptics Jesus tells the Sadducees that in heaven there are no marriages and the resurrected will be like *angels in heaven*, suggesting the absence of sexuality (Mk 12:19-25, Lk 20:27-36, Mt 22:23-30).
> - a brief depiction of the righteous marriage between Elizabeth and Zechariah (Lk 1:5-6).
> - Mary's engagement to Joseph on account of her pregnancy (Lk 1:26-35, 2:1-7), and his effort to avoid shaming her because she becomes pregnant before becoming married (Mt 1:18-25).
> -a brief notation of the righteous prophetess Anna whose marriage lasted seven years before she becomes a widow (Lk 2:36-37).
> - a man who excuses himself from following Jesus because he has just become married (Lk 14:20).
> - Jesus's description about people frivolously getting married during Noah's time (Lk 17:27, Mt 24:36).
> - Jesus attending a wedding ceremony in Cana where he performs a miracle (Jn 2:1).

Jesus does not formulate any teachings on marriage beyond God's mandate as stipulated in Genesis. He defends Moses who (per God's commandment) has permitted the Israelites to file a bill of divorce. In this passage, Jesus indicates that *from the beginning of creation, God made them male and female. For this reason, a man shall leave his father and mother [and be joined to his wife], and the two shall become one flesh.* In the same passage, however, Jesus goes beyond God's revelation in Genesis, saying, *what God has joined together, no human being must separate*; in effect, he forbids divorce.

He tells his disciples that if a man or a woman divorces his/her spouse and marries another they commit adultery (Mk 10:2-12, Mt 19:3-12). Matthew, however, inserts the phrase *unless it* (marriage) is *unlawful,* referring to grounds that would make divorce possible. In Jesus, marriage simply becomes an edict from God that cannot be questioned. Although Jesus has probed other significant aspects of Mosaic Law, he does not provide a human rationale or teachings about a most important religious and social institution. This task was taken over by the Fathers of the Church and by church denominations. It is significant that the institution of marriage is not even among the Ten Commandments, except in a negative (or protective) manner, e.g., *thy shall not commit adultery,* and *thy shall not covet your neighbor's wife.* The remaining passages address *marriage* only when they relate to divorce and adultery:

- John the Baptist warns Herod that he should not marry Herodias because he would be committing adultery (Mk 6:17-18, Lk 3:19, Mt 14:3-4).
- Jesus names adultery as an evil that comes from the heart that would violate the Commandments (Mk 7:20-23, 10:19, Lk 18:20, Mt 15:18-19, Mt 19:16-18).
- Jesus warns that anyone who divorces their spouses and marries another commits adultery (Mk 10:11, Lk 16:18).
- Jesus condemns a Pharisee who praises himself in the eyes of God for not being adulterous (Lk 18:11).
- Jesus's teaching that anyone who looks at a woman with lust commits adultery with her in his heart (Mt 5:27-28).
- Jesus's teaching in which he seems to allow room for a divorce if the marriage is unlawful, and if it is preceded by presenting the wife with a bill of divorce; it is not clear, however, if the wife enjoys the same prerogative as the husband. This clause, however, does not appear in either Mark or Luke (Mt 5:31-32).

The marriage-related passages in the Gospels indicate that Jesus is more interested in teaching about the evil of adultery (as a means to safeguard God's law on marriage) than in promoting marriage as a positive blessing ordained by God as a religious institution. He provides no teachings about the undesirability of divorce itself, such as the impact on children and the spouses, the emotional traumas that each member of the family experiences, and their lasting emotional, psychological, and social consequences. Jesus views divorce as risky (not hurtful), because it may lead to adultery and a violation of God's commandment, rather than separating what God has joined together. Moreover, passages in Mark and Matthew present marriage as an inviolable contract, i.e., a divine ordinance, without saying anything about love and commitment, the personal and social worthiness of having children, or the value of the family.

Ironically, given that Jesus appears to be concerned with divorce and adultery as a transgression of God's commandments, it is interesting to read that in the only two instances in which he confronts adulterous women, he does not condemn them (Jn

4:16-18, 8:3-5). In one case, Jesus seems to forgive the Samaritan woman who appears remorseful as she admits that she has been married five times. In the other (and most dramatic) case he openly forgives the woman who is on the verge of being stoned to death for committing adultery. While these passages seem to devalue adultery, it appears that Jesus focuses on forgiving human transgressions, suggesting that, understanding the human condition, forgiveness ought to trump the rigidity of the law in many circumstances. Forgiving human flaws, however, does not lead to an understanding of the complexity and consequences of marriage, divorce, and adultery. Rather, Jesus's views on marriage seem insignificant when compared with Christianity's teachings on the issue today.

Notes
1. Leviticus, chapters 15, 18, 20; Deuteronomy, chapter 22.
2. See data online at www.RicardoPlanas.com/notes.

Celibacy, Virginity, and Chastity

These terms suggest either abstention or limitations on sexual activity. Added together, the three terms are among the least significant categories in Table 2. Incongruently, some Christian groups have heightened their importance today, which in turn have become divisive issues in culture wars.

Celibacy

Celibacy or the abstention of marriage and sexual relations seems to be important to the clergy in Catholicism, less so to the Eastern Orthodox Church, and even less among Protestant denominations. It appears that Jesus's celibate status may have influenced Catholic views on priesthood celibacy. Certainly, there does not seem to be any links in the Old Testament suggesting that celibacy ought to enjoy a higher or more sacred status in life. Moreover, Jesus speaks of no prohibition by the Father regarding his marital status.

There is, however, a brief and indirect note in Matthew in which Jesus's disciples ask him if it is better not to marry. He replies that celibacy is meant only for *those to whom that is granted* (Mt 19:10-12), supposedly by God. Jesus, however, does not explain if this status might be the outcome of a subjective internal call. He adds that some renounce marriage *for the sake of the kingdom of heaven* (Mt 19:10-12), which possibly may be the reason Jesus chose not to marry. Indeed, Jesus remains celibate throughout his life, even though God does not impose this state of life on him, nor does he compel his disciples to accept this condition in their lives.

Virginity

The term refers to someone that has never had sexual intercourse. This behavior is indirectly commended in the Gospels, likely to limit licentiousness, and possibly to confirm the religious significance of marriage, at which point it ends. Supposedly, virginity too may be adopted as a way of life as an offering of love to God. It is similar to celibacy, except that virginity only applies up to the time the person has sexual intercourse. For example, we know from his *Confessions* that St. Augustine was not celibate during his youth,[1] which would not have made him a virgin. However, once he acquired faith, he became celibate and abstained from sexual relations by foregoing marriage. According to the Gospels, Jesus remains a virgin (celibate and chaste) during his lifetime. However, the most illustrious case of virginity, which interestingly has had gender consequences throughout history, is that of Jesus's mother, Mary. Although the Gospels attest that Mary gives birth to Jesus without having sexual intercourse, a passage in Mathew leaves it to the imagination as to whether Mary may have had intercourse with Joseph following Jesus's birth. The passage reads that Joseph *had no relations with her until she bore a son* (Mt 1:25). The word *until* translated from Greek does not attest to sexual intercourse in marriage, nor does it exclude it.[2] Nonetheless, it is Mary's virginity that is highlighted in Christianity, and the term has been traditionally lauded in Christian culture as a trait to be emulated mostly by women, leading to double standard critiques by feminists.

Notes:
1. Augustine of Hippo, *Confessions,* trans by E.B. Pusey, Books 2, 3, 8, Project Gutenberg, online https://www.gutenberg.org/files/3296/3296-h/3296-h.htm (accessed November 8, 2019).
2. NEs' note, Matthew 1:25.

Chastity

This term is similar to the previous ones in that it signifies the absence of sexual relations. Nonetheless, the difference lies in that chastity is a call to single and married persons (both men and women). In the case of single individuals, chastity proscribes sexual intercourse outside of marriage while spouses are supposed to remain faithful to each other by refraining from sexual intercourse outside of their marriages. Chastity also appears to be a regulation to limit licentiousness as well as adultery, but perhaps more important as a means to underline the spouses loving commitment to each other. Given the increasing incidence of divorce, out-of-wedlock pregnancies, and sexually transmissible diseases, chastity might be the most virtuous and socially necessary (as well as most difficult) call to accept in today's highly sexed culture.

There is, nonetheless, in Jesus a code of sexuality that is closely related to the above terms. In condemning adultery, he is indirectly calling for a chaste life among the spouses. In referring to licentiousness and lust as sinful behavior, he is indicating moderation if not complete abstinence, supposedly until after marriage, although he does not discuss the issue.

Both chastity and virginity (until marriage) might be thought of as anachronistic behavior in times when human sexuality is publicly discussed, and pornography has become mainstream. Their significance, nonetheless, might not be well understood. The terms stand for commitment, love, faithfulness, and sacrifice; behavior that is not easily accepted in secularized and hedonistic societies that subliminally encourage casual sexual activity.

Hope

Hope is a subconscious reflex that humans rely on for emotional, psychological, and/or physical survival. The essential characteristic of hope is that it aims toward a positive or good outcome; it is an expectation of good things to happen, even if the expectation is for one's enemy to suffer, die, or be defeated. Regardless of whether it is a drive or an instinct, or whether it is infused by God or acquired through evolution, it is part of how humankind is constituted. Hope arises when we confront difficult situations whose outcome we fear, e.g., the desire to regain health during a serious illness or to find employment, or the expectation that a relationship may endure prior to marriage or following a crisis. It also applies to mere temporal desires, e.g., wishing a favorable result after being promised something good, such as a promotion, or acquiring wealth by winning the lottery. Hope is not only inherently individualistic; it may have significant social overtones, for example, hoping for the ending of warfare; the passage of legislation that benefits the wellbeing of many; or that a cure may be found for pandemics.

The emotional and psychological power of hope may best be seen among people facing dire existential conditions, such as persecution, war, hunger, disease, enslavement, family disruptions who, nevertheless, cling to the belief or feeling that their situations will improve in the future. Generally, hope is the antidote to despair, disillusionment, or suicide as well as a strong feeling that keeps alive human drives toward positive goals.[1]

Without necessarily objecting to its human aspect, Christian theology takes the definition of hope further, centering it on the yearning that God places in humans to desire the kingdom of heaven; it is supposed to be the outcome of faith in God and Jesus. Thus, hope is subject to the same questions that beleaguer faith and love: does God grant these virtues equally to all human beings or only to some? Do non-Christians and atheists experience this type of hope or only its human dimension?[2]

Despite its theological significance within Christianity, the term *hope* is largely ignored in the Gospels; it shows up only twice, once by Matthew while quoting Isaiah (Mt 12:15-21), and the other one, expressed negatively by Jesus when referring to the hope the religious authorities had placed in Moses (Jn 5:45). Content analysis results in Table 2 indicate that the texts have far more to say about faith and love than about hope. Nonetheless, religious/theological hope is closely related to faith, since Jesus's teachings are meant to induce people to hope what their faith tells them is possible to attain. Hence, the term's ranking is not high probably because Jesus assumes that there can be no hope without faith, even though he does not emphasize the act of hope. Hence, to have faith in the kingdom of God without the hope to attain it would be like a cruel joke or a fool's errand. Accordingly, Jesus's teachings about eternal life in God's kingdom would make sense only if people believe and hope in the possibility of reaching the kingdom.

Christian doctrine defines hope as the expectation that the promises made by Jesus will be realized, although in the afterlife, not on earth. The Christian connotation as read in the Gospels, however, constitutes a departure from how the term is used in the Old Testament, where it relates (mostly) to Jewish expectations of positive outcomes on earth. As they battle their enemies, the Israelites would express the hope that God would be on their side to defend them. Jewish hope takes the form of pleas and praises to God to be delivered in this life from the ills brought about by their enemies. This is to say that the Old Testament does not stress a type of hope that aims at the afterlife. Glimpses of hope in the afterlife appear in 2 Maccabees 7, Job 14, Wisdom 3, Ben Sira 11, and Isaiah 51; but these instances are not as concrete as the manner in which Paul elaborated the term following the death of Jesus. It is he who uses the term extensively, over 50xt, to indicate not only its temporal but its eschatological connotation too.[3] This means that although the Gospels appear much later than Paul's letters, they ignore such teachings by Jesus himself. Moreover, it suggests that these topics were not discussed at the time when Paul meets with Jesus's disciples in Jerusalem in 50 CE or later. This is yet another example in which Paul's letters seem to diminish the significance of the Gospels.

Since the term seldom appears in the Gospels, content analysis search focused on other words that closely suggest similar connotations, such as *promise, await, reward, and longing,* regardless of whether their intent is temporal or eschatological. The results indicate a combination of temporal and eschatological hope:

- Jesus promises that whoever loses his life because of him will be saved (Mk 8:35).
- Anything one does for his disciples will be rewarded, likely in the afterlife (Mk 9:41, Mt 10:40, Jn 13:20).
- Joseph of Arimathea awaits the kingdom of God, a temporal expectation (Mk 15:43, Lk 23:51).
- God's promises to his people, Abraham, and his descendants to disperse the arrogant of mind and heart; throw down the rulers from their thrones and lift up the lowly; fill the hungry with good things and send the rich away empty, a temporal promise (Lk 1:49:55).
- God's temporal promises to his people of salvation from their enemies and from those who hate them; to show mercy to their fathers and to rescue them from the hand of enemies (Lk 1:67).
- Awaiting the consolation of Israel (Lk 2:25-26), and the redemption of Jerusalem (Lk 2:38).
- Jesus promises to fulfill temporal expectations as the anointed one (Lk 4:16-21).
- Jesus makes promises (Beatitudes) that will find their reward in the afterlife (Lk 6:23-20, Mt 5:1-12).
- The disciples on the road to Emmaus hope for the redemption of Israel (Lk 24:21).
- The Father will reward those who do good deeds in private (Mt 6:1-7).
- Ask and you will receive; both temporal and eschatological connotations (Mt 7:7-8).

- An enigmatic insertion in Matthew of a passage in Isaiah suggesting that God would send his servant in whom the Gentiles *will hope* (Mt 12:15-21).
- Jesus tells his disciples they are being witnesses to see things that *many prophets and righteous people longed to see* (Mt 13:15-17).
- Jesus tells the religious authorities that Moses will accuse them of placing their hope in him and then refusing to believe in Jesus, about whom he had written (Jn 5:45-47).
- The Parable of the Faithful Servant awaiting the return of the master has a temporal connotation (Lk 12:35-48, Mt 24:45).
- Jesus's promise to send the Holy Spirit to earth creates a hopeful expectation (Lk 24:49).

The glaring omission of such an important word suggests that the use of the term in the Gospels is similar to its temporal meaning in the Old Testament. On the other hand, if hope is intertwined with faith, as it appears to be in Christianity, it would be reasonable to search for passages that evoke the anticipation of promises that entice believers to hope in that which Jesus teaches.[4] For instance, a rough count of the construct *Hope Plus* (not shown in Table 2) would include Jesus's constant *preaching* about eternal salvation as the ultimate prize; the numerous times and descriptions of the term *kingdom of God* that Jesus promises; the number of times *faith* and *believe* are mentioned as the vehicles that lead to the kingdom; his vivid accounts of the Parousia and Judgment Day; the miracles he performs so that people would believe; and passages concerning the resurrection of humans, probably humanity's greatest longing. Through these teachings Jesus is manifesting that which can be attained in the afterlife, thereby inducing people to hope for it on earth. If these terms were to be accounted for in a single category (*Hope Plus*), hope would rank as the most significant category in the Gospels except for righteousness.

Confusion, however, seems inevitable because of the term's double meaning. There is hope that God will fulfill temporal expectations, but Jesus transforms temporal hope into its current eschatological meaning, quite different from the term's connotation in the Old Testament.

Hope as a Gift

Although hope expresses a desire for the kingdom of heaven and eternal life (CCC 1817), according to Christian theology humans cannot respond to God's call through their own powers; they must depend on God. This view is problematic, for it presents a God that is physically remote and inaccessible to many people. It suggests a god that enigmatically offers human beings eternal happiness knowing they cannot respond on their own if they are non-Christians. This scenario is akin to a father that displays candy before his creatures but denies them the possibility to fetch it. An empirical look at history suggests that God's ability to communicate hope to humankind falls short. Since most people have not been properly exposed or educated in any of the various Christian denominations, could God's message be meant only for a few?

The use of the term hope is mostly a post-Jesus theological construct that is broadly implied in the Gospels. Although Jesus does not use the term as it is being used today, its implication is embedded in the texts to the extent that their reading radiates a sense of hope. It may be argued that since all of Jesus's sayings appear in the Gospels, his promise of eternal life must be considered valid. After all, who else would promise to deliver something extraordinary that cannot be attained unless he is an impostor, a demagogue, or delusional?

The Jesus that emerges from the Gospels can hardly be said to be an impostor or a demagogue; these traits are typical of a willfully deceiving person. The third characterization, that Jesus is delusional, seems more reasonable if we presume he is not who he says he is. Delusion is considered a mental illness characterized by persecutory, referential, and grandiose beliefs,[5] all of which fit Jesus's behavior and personality. Nonetheless, not everyone who experiences these feelings is necessarily delusional if the person's beliefs are based on real circumstances. Jesus realizes that he is going to be persecuted and killed, the possibility of which is supported by his constant accusatory remarks against the religious authorities that threaten their authority. His personality reveals self-referential behavior, i.e., Jesus and the Gospels are about him; he constantly refers to himself, who he is, why he comes into the world, and what he will accomplish. His personality exudes grandiosity; this is unavoidable given the attention he receives from the crowds and the miraculous deeds he performs. Nonetheless, he does not appear to be irrational, but rather the opposite; he is cogent in his teachings and his debates with the religious authorities.[6]

It would be difficult to diagnose Jesus based on the Gospels alone, particularly since modern medicine acknowledges that the delusional personality can appear and behave like a normal person (aside from his/her delusion). There is also the possibility that teachings attributed to Jesus are not his own (which is yet to be established) but were inserted by those who participated in the writing of the texts. Hence, the verdict is still out; Jesus said he was the Son of God, and he acted as if he was, but the only evidence lies in the Gospels that, as this work has attempted to show, presents serious problems concerning their validity as the word of God or as being divinely inspired.

Literally interpreted, the expectation of Jesus's promises is the definition of hope insofar as they create hope. Such a desire for an afterlife is cherished by other religions, and it is doubtful (although possible) that even agnostics and atheists would decline the opportunity if offered to them. However, the validity of an eschatological hope declines in proportion to a decline in the belief in Jesus as the Son of God and the extent to which his teachings are dismissed in a postmodern society that is not well suited for supernatural beliefs; at least not unless dread seizes the senses, in which case desperation leads to human hope.

Notes
1. Two views on the human aspect of hope: *Hope is not just a feel-good emotion, but a dynamic cognitive motivational system. Under this conceptualization of hope, emotions follow cognitions, not the other way around. Hope allows people to approach problems with a mindset and strategy-set suitable to success,*

thereby increasing the chances they will actually accomplish their goals. Scott Barry Kaufman, "The Will and Ways of Hope," *Psychology Today,* December 26, 2011, https://www.psychologytoday.com/us/blog/beautiful-minds/201112/the-will-and-ways-hope (accessed November 28, 2019).

A different view: *If I could find a way to package and dispense hope, I would have a pill more powerful than any antidepressant on the market. Hope is often the only thing between man and the abyss. As long as a patient, individual or victim has hope, they can recover from anything and everything. However, if they lose hope, unless you can help them get it back, all is lost. One thing I can tell you is that hope is an emotion that springs from the heart, not the brain. Hope lays dormant until its amazing strength is beckoned, supplying a sheer belief that you will overcome, you will persevere and you will endure anything and everything that comes your way.* Dale Archer M.D., "The Power of Hope," *Psychology Today,* July 31, 2013, https://www.psychologytoday.com/us/blog/reading-between-the-headlines/201307/the-power-hope (accessed November 28, 2019).

2. Hope *keeps man from discouragement* and *sustains him during times of abandonment,* CCC 1818.

3. *BibleGateway.com.*

4. According to CE, distinctions arose during the Reformation regarding the scope of hope. Both Luther and Calvin believed that to hope for an afterlife reward, or to hope out of fear of being condemned was not considered pure and selfless behavior, a reason both opposed the Catholic version. Joseph Delany, "Hope," CE, Vol. 7, http://www.newadvent.org/cathen/07465b.htm (accessed November 28, 2019).

5. James A. Bourgeois, MD, OD, MPA, "Delusional Disorder," Overview, *Medscape,* November 14, 2017, https://emedicine.medscape.com/article/292991-overview#a1 (accessed December 10, 2020).

6. Much has been debated about the trilemma apologetic argument attributed to C S Lewis in which he combatively concludes that Jesus is the Son of God since he cannot be either a lunatic or the devil. C.S. Lewis, *Mere Christianity,* Book 2, 4, https://www.dacc.edu/assets/pdfs/PCM/merechristianitylewis.pdf (accessed December 10, 2020). Lewis not only left out the possibility that Jesus could have been delusional, a different type of mental illness than being a lunatic, but also that the texts may have been altered to make him look and sound as being divine.

7. Bourgeois, Clinical Features.

Prophecy

The *prophecy/prophet* category ranks significantly according to content analysis results. The synoptic texts relied heavily on prophets of the Old Testament and the fulfillment of prophecies to bolster Jesus's claim to religious authority and lay the foundation that Jesus is a prophet as well as divine. There are fifty-four instances in which Old Testament prophecies are said to be fulfilled in Jesus. The breakdown of the words searched in this category according to each author is extensive.[1]

Prophets always had played a significant role in Judaism. Their primary role was to guide the Jewish people and their leaders through a righteous path by denouncing wickedness, voicing threats of punishment for disobeying God, and encouraging obedience to the law.[2] Today, however, Judaism minimizes the significance of prophecies being fulfilled in Jesus, largely because their acceptance would necessarily lead to a reinterpretation of the Jewish faith.

In Christianity, the prophet's role is similar to Judaism. However, it also tends to highlight the foretelling of events that may take place in the future,[3] a feature that raises its religious significance. The knowledge that is foretold in a prophecy is supposed to be supernatural, and it is dispensed by God through supernatural beings (angels, devils) or human beings of all kinds (men, women, children, heathens, Gentiles, even wicked people, e.g., Balaam). Moreover, the purpose of the prophecy is to serve the well-being of people. Since its content is not accessible by human reason, the prophecy needs to be announced and manifested by words or signs.[4]

Interestingly, Jesus refers to John the Baptist as the greatest of all prophets (Lk 7:28). Accordingly, he is the most quoted prophet in the Gospels (four to five times more than anyone else), although his duties are not comparable to those who foretold events hundreds of years before they happened. John the Baptist appears to be a prophet in the old Judaic tradition that denounces earthly wickedness and preaches repentance. He does not, however, issue prophecies that would be fulfilled in the distant future. Instead, he announces the immediate coming of Jesus and the kingdom of God (Lk 7:18-23, Jn 1:30-33).

How Relevant is Prophecy Today?
The fulfillment of various prophecies spanning hundreds or thousands of years in Jesus, if true, renders empirical and historical credibility to Jesus being the anointed messiah. But what exactly constitutes fulfillment of prophecies in Jesus is important. For example, in Matthew's Gospel, regarded as the most significant one in Christianity, several of the author's attestations concerning the realization of prophecies are imprecise. He suggests that a prophecy indicating that a virgin will bear a son and name him Emmanuel (Mt 1:23) relates to Isaiah, 7:14; it does, except that in Isaiah, the prophecy is a sign God provides to Ahaz, king of Judea, who needs God's reassurance immediately to deter his enemies. Nonetheless, the sign Matthew refers to is Jesus, and the prophecy is manifested hundreds of years later. May we speak in this case of a prophecy being fulfilled in Jesus?

Matthew claims that Jesus's acts of driving demons out and curing the sick of their physical infirmities (MT 8:16-17) relate to Isaiah's pronouncement, *yet it was our pain that he bore, our sufferings he endured. We thought of him as stricken, struck down by God and afflicted* (Is 53:4). It appears, however, that Isaiah was referring to afflictions as sins while Matthew instead refers to physical infirmities.[5]

Something similar occurs when Matthew writes, *and you, Bethlehem, land of Judah ... from you shall come a ruler, who is to shepherd my people Israel* (Mt 2:6). Matthew attributes fulfillment of this pronouncement to Micah referring to someone who will become Israel's ruler (Mi 5:1). Although Micah's passage coincides with Jesus's birthplace (Bethlehem), Jesus never becomes a ruler in Israel.

In Jeremiah 31:15, written about six hundred years before Jesus's birth, God says he hears sobbing in the town of Ramah because Rachel's children are being murdered. Matthew attributes this passage to Herod's massacre of two-year-old children that occurs when Jesus is supposed to be of the same age.[6] How could something that already happened centuries before be fulfilled in Jesus?

Moreover, Matthew misattributes the fulfillment of Hosea 11:1 that references the Jewish exodus from Egypt to Jesus's return from Egypt (Mt 2:15).[7] He incorrectly assigns the passage regarding the thirty pieces of silver paid to Judas being used to purchase a potter's field (Mt 27:9-10) to Jeremiah when the passage seems to be from

Zechariah (11:12-13).[8] Furthermore, his attribution to a nameless prophet of a prophecy being fulfilled (Mt 13:34-35) is mistakenly taken from Psalm 78:2.[9]

Additionally, Matthew mixes two passages from different Old Testament prophets leading to what amounts to a laughable confusion suggesting that Jesus was sitting on two different animals at the same time as he enters Jerusalem (Mt 21:4-5).[10] Perhaps an even more blatant distortion occurs as Matthew suggests that Jesus goes to the town of Nazareth because the words of anonymous prophets are being fulfilled claiming that *he went and dwelt in a town called Nazareth, so that what had been spoken through the prophets might be fulfilled, "He shall be called a Nazorean."* The issue in this case is that the town of Nazareth does not appear in the Old Testament, hence, this prophecy does not exist.[11] NABRE editors seem to belittle Matthews' interpretations of the Old Testament indicating that, *for him, any Old Testament text that could be seen as fulfilled in Jesus was prophetic.*[12]

Likewise, how is the reader to understand Jesus's warning of false prophets rising to deceive believers (Mk 13:22, Mt 24:11)? Pope Benedict XIV (1740-1758), *one of the most erudite men of his time* [with] *the distinction of being perhaps the greatest scholar among the popes,*[13] writes that moral goodness is not among the requirements to be chosen by God to be a prophet, adding that even God can make use of the Devil for purposes of prophecy.[14] Hence, given the diversity of Christian denominations existing today, and the number of scientists, theologians, politicians, and moral philosophers emitting ominous warning, how is humanity to distinguish between a false prophet and a true one?[15]

To say these issues do not pose a credibility question on Christian Revelation would be an understatement. Anyone approaching the Gospels today for the type of reassurances the texts seek to provide regarding the truthfulness of Old Testament prophecies being realized may feel sensibly disillusioned.

Jesus as Prophet

The Profile on Jesus (Table 1A) indicates that Jesus identifies himself at times as being a prophet, and he is aware that others regard him as a prophet. He does not seem to downplay this role when he compares himself to a prophet (Mk 6:4, Lk 4:16-21, Mt 5:17-18, Jn 3:14-18), or when he considers himself greater than them, including John the Baptist and Abraham (Mt 12:38-40, Jn 5:33-36, 8:51-58).

There is in John's text a brief passage that, taken literally, is puzzling. As Jesus compares himself to a shepherd, he says that he is the gate for the sheep, *all who came [before me] are thieves and robbers, but the sheep did not listen to them.* He characterizes these people as *hired* men who work for pay and have no concern for the sheep, in contrast with him who is the real shepherd that gives his life for his sheep. Who is Jesus referring to as *all* who came before him? He seems to allude to past prophets; they are the ones who come before him, but they cannot possibly be impostors, or thieves and robbers if it is God who sends them. Since Jesus would be maligning these prophets (which would not make sense to apologists), a reasonable explanation is that he is referring to men who falsely claim to be the messiah, although he never identifies these men.[16]

Furthermore, Jesus is not shy about pointing to himself as being closely associated with God. He is mindful that some prophecies apply to him and others will be fulfilled in him (Mk 14:18-21, 14:27, Lk 4:16-21, Mt 15:7-9, 26:54-56, Jn 13:18, 15:24, 17:12). At times, his words are bewildering, for they seem to express a predisposition to act in accordance with the scriptures. Hence, the question surfaces whether prophecies are fulfilled in Jesus or if he or the texts' authors are purposefully attempting to fashion Jesus's behavior according to prophecies to validate who he says he is. For example, Jesus not only realizes that he will be persecuted; he insists that he does not mind being persecuted so that the scriptures be fulfilled: *For I tell you that this scripture must be fulfilled in me, namely, 'He was counted among the wicked,' and indeed what is written about me is coming to fulfillment* (Lk 22:37). In Luke, Jesus claims that he (the Messiah) *should suffer* according to scriptures (Lk 24:36), except that the view of a suffering Messiah does not appear in the Old Testament or any other Jewish literature until the time of the New Testament.[17]

In Matthew, while being arrested, Jesus claims that he could call upon God to send twelve legions of angels to save him. He chooses to bypass this option, again, so that the scriptures would be fulfilled (Mt 26:54). In another instance, Jesus walks into a synagogue, reads a passage from Isaiah regarding God's promise about the coming of a temporal messiah (Lk 4:16-27), then claims that the prophecy is fulfilled in him. Jesus's behavior in the Gospels, however, indicates that he does not become the temporal messiah mentioned in Isaiah.

Unfortunately, certain prophecies lack sufficient explanations regarding why they must happen. The most important ones refer to Jesus's passion, death, and resurrection that he predicts three times, and why the end of time must occur in such a horrific manner. These sayings are certainly important for humanity to understand, yet all Jesus says about them is that they will happen because they need to happen.

That several of the prophecies are exceedingly unclear in terms of historical timing, geography, literary errors, or that some prophecies simply do not show up in the Old Testament, may suggest the possibility that aspects of the public life of Jesus were purposefully added to coincide with fulfillment of prophecies in him, or that public enthusiasm for the person of Jesus led to interesting (if loose) oral narratives that the authors incorporated into their texts. If this were the case, could the authors have written the Gospels to deceive, to create a religious movement antithetical to the existing Jewish faith? Although this question is as valid as any other critical inquiry, given the degree of imprecision, contradictions, and other errors observed in the Gospels, the effort does not amount to a well-elaborated conspiracy. The authors may have been well-intentioned, and yet careless in their efforts to provide newcomers to the faith with an uncritical patchwork of sayings about the public Jesus that they gathered decades after his death. Although these views may question the role of divine revelation, it is possible to accept that the texts are, if not objectively reliable, at least subjectively honest.

Once again, prophecies are important to Christianity if it can be established beyond a reasonable doubt that they have been realized. For example, Jesus prophesizes that Jerusalem will be abandoned (Lk 13:35, 21:20) and its Temple destroyed (Mk 13:1-2, Lk 21:5-6, Mt 24:1-2). The Temple, indeed, was destroyed in 70 CE, however, his words may have been prophetic (or not) depending on the date on which Mark's Gospel was written, just before or after 70 CE. Jesus's other prophecies await the passing of time since they have not taken place yet. Nonetheless, he is adamant that his prophecies will be realized: *heaven and earth will pass away, but my words will not pass away ... until all things have taken place* (Lk 21:33, Mt 5:17-18).

This brings us to Jesus's most ominous prophecy, the Parousia and Judgment Day (Mk 13:7-36, Lk 21:9-36, Mt 24:6-44, 25:31-46). There is a significant difference between this account in the synoptics and John's Gospel. In John, there are no lengthy prophetic descriptions of the calamities that will befall humankind at the end of time. The author simply points out that there will be a *last day*, after which humans that have died will be resurrected into eternal life or into eternal condemnation depending on whether they believe in Jesus at the time of their death (Jn 3:17-18, 3:36, 5:28-29, 6:40). In the synoptics, Jesus's prophecy is about destruction and death, e.g., wars, earthquakes, parents and children betraying each other, all of which already have happened throughout history. He goes further and says, *that stars will fall from the sky and the powers of heaven will be shaken ... and they will see the Son of Man coming upon the clouds of heaven with power and great glory* (Mt 24:29-30). Human hands cannot possibly initiate this type of event; it seems that it will be the work of a supernatural power. Being the most chilling of prophecies in the Gospels, descriptions of the Parousia are incorporated in all three synoptics, suggesting that it was an important belief that needed to be taught to early Christians. The question, nonetheless, is that, although John's Gospel addresses a different audience, how is it possible that such graphic descriptions are omitted?

Jesus tells his disciples that toward the end of time many will be led into sin; they will betray and hate one another ... false prophets will arise and deceive many; and because of the increase of evildoing, the love of many will grow cold (Mt 24:12). Who is he referring to, the Jewish people whom he comes to address, the Romans, or peoples in other parts of the world that he does not even acknowledge exist?

Much of Jesus's account of the Parousia resembles part of Isaiah's chapter 13 referencing God's overthrow of Babylon that may have been mistakenly attributed to Isaiah;[18] Ezekiel's Chapter 32 concerning God's plan toward Egypt's Pharaoh; and Joel's prophecy in Chapter 2 regarding the potential destruction of Jerusalem. All were written centuries before Jesus's birth, but they do not address the end of time. Instead, they refer to specific enemies of God. Hence, it appears as if the authors of the Gospels (or Jesus?) appropriate temporal events from the Old Testament and use them toward an apocalyptic/eschatological ending of time.

Some of Jesus's parables (as well as his cursing of unbelievers) are meant to intimidate the religious authorities and the Jewish people into believing. Jesus, however, chooses not to disclose the frightening end of time to the crowds. Only the disciples are made aware of this ending. Is there a reasonable explanation for Jesus to hide this prophecy from others? His tone is alarmist; nowadays believers may require anxiety-reducing medications to absorb the message: *for we must all not be caught sleeping. What I say to you, I say to all: 'Watch!* This prophecy has resonated throughout the world for over twenty centuries, and all indicators that Jesus provides of the end of time already have happened to the point, perhaps, that most people likely will continue to go about their lives without losing sleep over it; otherwise, it becomes too emotionally stressful since it is psychologically difficult if not impossible to remain watchful every day. Hence, his greatest prophecy may not achieve its intended effect, despite not knowing that this event may still happen.

Notes:

1. *Prophet or prophecy*: 7xt in Mark; 29xt in Luke; 33xt in Matthew; 13xt in John. *Fulfillment*, including *as written* and *scriptures*: 10xt in Mark; 12xt in Luke; 19xt in Matthew; 13xt in John. *John the Baptist*: 35xt in Mark; 37xt in Lk; 47xt in Matthew; 53xt in John. *Moses*: 9xt in Mark; 10xt in Lk; 7xt in Matthew; 14xt in John. *Abraham*: 1xt in Mark; 16xt in Luke; 3xt in Matthew; 11xt in John. *Elijah*: 10xt in Mark; 7xt in Lk; 11xt in Matthew; 2xt in John. *Isaiah*: 2xt in Mark; 2xt in Lk; 6xt in Matthew; 4xt in John. *Jesus*: 2xt in Mark; 3xt in Luke; 4xt in Matthew; 5xt in John (although understated since there are numerous times in which Jesus prophesizes that whoever believes in him will be saved). *Simeon*: 8xt in Luke. *Isaac*: 1xt in Mark; 3xt in Luke; 2xt in Matthew. *Jonah*: 4xt in Luke; 2xt in Matthew. *Anna*: 4xt in Luke. *Jeremiah*: 3xt in Matthew. *Angel Gabriel*: 2xt in Luke. *Micah, Hosea, Daniel,* and *Zechariah*: 1xt each in Matthew. *Elisha*: 1xt in Luke.

2. "Jewish Concepts: Prophets," *JVL, https://www.jewishvirtuallibrary.org/prophets (accessed* March 3, 2019).

3. The prophet *was the interpreter and supernaturally enlightened herald sent by Yahweh to communicate His will and designs to Israel. His mission consisted in preaching as well as in foretelling. He had to maintain and develop the knowledge of the Old Law among the Chosen People, lead them back when they strayed, and gradually prepare the way for the new kingdom of God, which the messiah was to establish on earth.* Jean Marie Calès, "Prophecy, Prophet, and Prophetess." CE, Vol. 12, http://www.newadvent.org/cathen/12477a.htm (accessed March 3, 2019).

4. Arthur Devine, "Prophecy," CE, Vol. 12, http://www.newadvent.org/cathen/12473a.htm (accessed March 3, 2019).

5. NEs' note, Mt 8:17 indicates that *this fulfillment citation from Is 53:4 follows the MT, not the LXX. The prophet speaks of the Servant of the Lord who suffers vicariously for the sins ("infirmities") of others; Matthew takes the infirmities as physical afflictions.*

6. Rachel is the wife of Jacob whom Judaism regards as a matriarchal figure embodying Israel. Yishai Chasidah, "Rachel," *Encyclopedia of Biblical Personalities.* (Brooklyn: Shaar press, 1994), in "Rachel," *JVL, https://www.jewishvirtuallibrary.org/rachel (accessed* March 4, 2019).

7. NEs' note, Hosea 11:1: *Hosea dates the real beginning of Israel from the time of the exodus. Mt 2:15 applies this text to the return of Jesus from Egypt.*

8. Ibid., note on Mt 27:9-10: *Matthew's attributing this text to Jeremiah is puzzling, for there is no such text in that book, and the thirty pieces of silver thrown by Judas "into the temple" (Mt 27:5) recall rather Zec 11:12–13.*

9. Ibid., note on Mt 13:35: *The quotation is actually from Ps 78:2; the first line corresponds to the LXX text of the psalm. The psalm's title ascribes it to Asaph, the founder of one of the guilds of temple musicians. He is called "the prophet" (NAB "the seer") in 2 Chr 29:30, but it is doubtful that Matthew averted to that.*

10. Ibid., note on Mt 21:7.

10. Matthew's verse reads, *They brought the ass and the colt and laid their cloaks over them, and he sat upon them.* NEs conclude that sitting on two animals presents *an awkward picture resulting from Matthew's misunderstanding of the prophecy.* NEs note on Matthew 21:4-5.

11. Ibid., note Mt 2:23.

12. Ibid., Mt. 13:35.

13. Patrick Healy, "Pope Benedict XIV." CE, Vol. 2, http://www.newadvent.org/cathen/02432a.htm (accessed March 5, 2019).

14. Devine.

15. Ibid. In his article, the author seems to contradict himself arguing that one indication of a true prophet is that *the recipient of the gift of prophecy should, as a rule, be good and virtuous, for all mystical writers agree that for the most part this gift is granted by God to holy persons.* But he adds, *the disposition or temperament of the person should also be considered, as well as the state of health and the brain.* The problem with this indicator is that anyone prophesizing today that the sky will fall will have his mental sanity seriously questioned, which would include Jesus himself. Another indicator is that *the prophecy must be conformable to Christian truth and piety because if it proposes anything against faith or morals it cannot proceed from the Spirit of Truth.* This indicator also presents problems because the Catholic Church would want to authenticate the prophecy, and Protestants, or even many Catholics, may not agree with papal pronouncements.

16. Charles Ellicott, a nineteenth-century Christian theologian, offers such a traditional explanation in his commentaries to the Gospels. Charles Ellicott, "John 10:8," *Ellicott's Commentaries for English Readers,* BibleHub.com. https://biblehub.com/john/10-8.htm (accessed April 5, 2019). John Gill, an eighteenth-century Baptist pastor, offers a similar account, saying that this passage must *be understood with some restrictions.* John Gill, "John 10:8," *John Gill's Exposition of the Bible,* BibleStudyTools.com. https://www.biblestudytools.com/commentaries/gills-exposition-of-the-bible/john-10-8.html (accessed April 5, 2019). NEs limit themselves to indicating that the words "before me" *are omitted in many good early manuscripts and versions*; a factual statement that still leaves the reader guessing about what to believe the passage means. NEs' note, John 10:8.

17. NEs' note, Lk 24:26.

18. Ibid., note, Isaiah 13:1-22: *Although attributed to Isaiah (v. 1), this oracle does not reflect conditions of Isaiah's time.*

God's Will

Despite its enormous importance to Christianity, content analysis results in Table 2 indicate that the God's Will category does not rank high relative to other categories. This section seeks to identify what Jesus means by God's will, examples of doing God's will, Jesus's relation with it, and the consequences of abiding by or rejecting it.

The Significance of Doing God's Will

Abiding by God's will is at the center of the Christian faith. The Gospels present it as the path that Jesus proposes to those who wish to be saved. *Not everyone who says Lord, Lord, will enter the kingdom of heaven, but only the one who does the will of my Father in heaven,* he tells the crowds and his disciples (Mt 7:21). Depending on whether salvation is extended to every human being or only to the chosen ones, Jesus's affirmation begs the question of whether non-believers and those who do not follow Jesus because they abide by another faith are under the obligation of complying with Jesus's interpretation of God's will. Presuming that most people would want to be saved if given the opportunity, how could non-Christians be saved? In other words, is there salvation outside the Christian faith? If we take Jesus's words as written in the Gospels the answer is a clear-cut No. Today some Christian denominations have amended Jesus's words (while seeking to prevent Christian relativism) to indicate that under certain circumstances non-Christians may be saved. Within mainstream Protestantism, interpretations vary according to each denomination.[1]

In John's Gospel, Jesus underscores the point that his teachings are not his own but rather God's, at times becoming repetitive, as if he wishes to avoid being perceived as the originator of what he teaches.[2] To leave no doubt that he speaks on God's behalf, Jesus intimately connects his teachings to God's will by warning that *whoever does not honor the Son does not honor the Father who sent him* (Jn 5:23). Indeed, from the moment God proclaims that Jesus is his most beloved son and is pleased in him (Mk 1:9-11, Lk 1:21-22, Mt 3:13-17), Jesus becomes God's main envoy (the Messiah) to transmit his will. Throughout his public life, he remains loyal to the Father's command until the end of his life. He insists that the most important part of his mission is to do the Father's will: *My food is to do the will of the one who sent me and to finish his work,* he says (Jn 4:34). Offering his own testimony, he rejects Satan's offerings of power and wealth emphatically in favor of God's will (Lk 4:1-13, Mt 4:1-11).[3] He proclaims that he lays down his life because it is the command he receives from the Father (Jn 10:17-18), despite his reluctance to accept his death: *Abba, Father, all things are possible to you. Take this cup away from me, but not what I will but what you will* (Mk 14:35-36, Lk 22:41-42, Mt 26:36-39).

On the other hand, somewhat incongruently, Jesus indicates that he chooses not to defend himself against his adversaries, not because it is God's will, but so that scriptures may be fulfilled (Mk 14:49, Mt 26:53-56). This attitude on Jesus's part creates uncertainty regarding the question of why he chooses to die; is it to ransom and redeem others or to validate prophecies?

In its most basic form, God's will derives from Mosaic Law. As interpreted by Jesus, he replies to a scholar of the law who asks what he ought to do to attain eternal life by saying, *you shall love the Lord, your God, with all your heart, with all your being, with all your strength, and with all your mind, and your neighbor as yourself* (Lk 10:25-28).[4] Jesus, however, goes further and illustrates the content of God's will in detail. It comprises the Beatitudes that teach having to accept a less than desirable life on earth while awaiting one's reward in heaven (Lk 6:20-23, Mt 5:1-12) as well as several parables, and Matthew's passage on Judgment Day (Mt 25:31-46), all of which indicate the type of behavior that is to be expected of his followers.

He teaches that one cannot serve two masters, God and mammon, i.e., the desire for wealth (Lk 16:13, Mt 6:24) (or Satan). He counsels not to worry about physical necessities, but instead to seek God's kingdom trusting that God will provide everything else (Lk 12:22-34). He demands that those who wish to be his disciples must bear their own cross (Lk 14:25-33), probably alluding to the suffering and burden that life sometimes brings. Moreover, Jesus explains God's will through other parables that focus on punishment in the afterlife if certain types of sins are committed, such as greed, murder, or indifference to God's call (Mk 12:1-11, Lk 14:15-24, Mt 22:1-14, Lk 19:11-27, Mt 25:14-30 Lk 20:9-18, Mt 21:33-44). In John's

Gospel, Jesus is unequivocal about the repercussions for not doing his will: *whoever disobeys the son will not see life, but the wrath of God remains upon him* (Jn 3:36); *whoever rejects me and does not accept my words has something to judge him: the word that I spoke, it will condemn him on the last day* (Jn 12:48).

Luke portrays Mary's humble attitude (responding to the angel's announcement that she will bear the Son of God) as being the model for accepting the Lord's will (Lk 1:26-35). God's will is so important to Jesus that he awkwardly belittles his relation to his mother in favor of God's will by not acknowledging her presence when she and his brothers come to visit him. Instead, he indicates that those who do God's will are his real brother and sister and mother (Mk 3:31-35, Lk 8:19-21, Mt 12:46-50). In another instance, someone praises Mary's womb for carrying Jesus and her breasts for nursing him, but he sets the comment aside replying, *rather, blessed are those who hear the word of God and observe it* (Lk 11:27-28).[5]

Abiding by Jesus's teachings are symbolic of one's love for him: *whoever has my commandments and observes them is the one who loves me* (Lk 10-16, Jn 14:15, 21, 23-24), indicating that *you are my friends if you do what I command you* (Jn 15:14). This amounts to loving both God and Jesus; the one cannot exist without the other: *If you keep my commandments, you will remain in my love, just as I have kept my Father's commandments and remain in his love* (Jn 15:10). Openly displaying a reward and punishment approach that parents use toward their children, he acknowledges that, *if you remain in me and my words remain in you, ask for whatever you want and it will be done for you; otherwise, anyone who does not remain in me will be thrown out like a branch and wither; people will gather them and throw them into a fire and they will be burned* (Jn 15:6-7).

Humanity cannot be blamed for wanting to know what it stands to gain by complying with God's will. To the question *what is in it for me?* Jesus makes it abundantly clear that he is only the messenger; that it is God who makes the rules. Hence, he limits himself to saying that there will be a reward in heaven for those who accept to do what God tells them: everlasting life. But Jesus does not appeal to a sense of moral obligation that might be persuasive. As the creator, God expects his creatures to obey his rules, particularly if these rules are established for their wellbeing. This rationale would be no different than someone who is given employment with full benefits; hence he feels obliged to fulfill his part of the contract by abiding by the CEO's rules that are meant to ensure the company's success.

Nonetheless, numerous people on earth decline to do God's will, suggesting that they do not acknowledge God as their creator. It is possible these people feel they were not allowed to choose being born, or because their conditions on earth are not as good as they envisaged, or because they believe they can be better off by themselves or by following other lifestyle options. Facing such circumstances, Jesus limits himself to offering a simile for listening and accepting his teachings that is mystifying:

Everyone who listens to these words of mine and acts on them will be like a wise man who built his house on rock. The rain fell, the floods came, and the winds blew and buffeted the house. But it did not collapse; it had been set solidly on rock. And everyone who listens to these words of mine but does not act on them will be like a fool who built his house on sand. The rain fell, the floods came, and the winds blew and buffeted the house. And it collapsed and was completely ruined (Mt 7:24-27, Lk 6:46-49).

Although it is reasonable to comprehend that building a house on a solid foundation is safer than building it on the sand, nowhere in the texts does Jesus explain why or how his teachings are more valid than the wisdom that may be found in other philosophies. The believer is being asked to trust Jesus because of his close relationship to God, perhaps upon the basis of his miracles. As God's envoy, Jesus sets God's rules for humanity on a 'take it or leave it' basis. He seldom elucidates why humans must love their creator or why loving one another is better than selfishness.

The teachings in some of his parables appear to be self-evident, e.g., if I treat you well, why should you not be kind to others? Most parables are simply rules of behavior God expects from his creatures because he is God. At face value, it may be observed that Jesus does not force anyone to do God's will; rather, he teaches his followers to pray for God's will to manifest itself on earth as in heaven (Mt 6:9-15). Readers, however, must be aware that these rules carry a heavy price (in the afterlife) when ignored (Lk 14:25-33, Mt 22:1-14, 25:31-46).

Penalties are not the only difficulty in grasping and complying with God's will. The Parable of the Sower (Mk 4:1-20, Lk 8:4-15, Mt 13:10-23) indicates the obstacles human beings face in assenting to God's rules. Whether it is the devil that steals God's word, or deplorable living conditions that force people to focus on their problems, or distractions in the temporal world that tempt them, only a few seem to have the wherewithal to understand God. Jesus candidly suggests that God has a hand in those who abide by his will. He tells his disciples that *every plant that my heavenly Father has not planted will be uprooted* (Mt 15:13), inexplicably suggesting that God is responsible for creating only part of humanity, the chosen ones. This view would seem to conflict with God being everyone's Father. Considering Jesus's remark that even prostitutes and tax collectors can change their attitudes and enter the kingdom of heaven (Mt 21:28-32), the above assertion in which God disavows responsibility for the salvation of some people is puzzling.

Jesus is candidly transparent in telling his disciples (and now humanity) that God hides the mysteries of the kingdom from the wise and the learned (Lk 10:21-22, Mt 11:25-27), and from others that profess different faiths. Taken literally, it means that billions of people throughout history have not received the opportunity given only to a select group. Within this context, apprehending God's will may be a far more difficult endeavor than even Jesus might have thought.

Notes:

1. The Roman Church had maintained that there was no salvation outside the Church. Catholicism continues to insist on this view, although it makes room for those who are *inculpably ignorant of the Gospel* to be saved. *Ad Gentes – on the Mission Activity of the Church, Vatican II Council,* 1.7, December 7, 1965
 http://www.vatican.va/archive/hist_councils/ii_vatican_council/documents/vat-ii_decree_19651207_ad-gentes_en.html (accessed July 9, 2020);
Dogmatic Constitution *Lumen Gentium, Vatican II Council,* 16, December 7, 1965, https://www.vatican.va/archive/hist_councils/ii_vatican_council/documents/vat-ii_const_19641121_lumen-gentium_en.html (accessed July 9, 2020); Protestantism agrees with this view once it redefined the Church as those who believe in Jesus Christ without having to recognize papal authority. "A sermon by Martin Luther from his Wartburg Church Postil, 1521-1522," 27, http://reverendluther.org/pdfs2/Luther.Christmas.Sermon.1521.pdf (accessed July 9, 2020).

2. The following are examples of Jesus not taking credit for his teachings:
    - *I do not seek my own will but the will of the one who sent me* (Jn 5:30);
    - *I came down from heaven not to do my own will but the will of the one who sent me* (J 6:38);
    - *My teaching is not my own but is from the one who sent me* (Jn 7:16);
    - *I say only what the Father taught me* (Jn 8:29);
    - [I know the Father] *and I keep his word* (Jn 8:55);
    - *I did not speak on my own, but the Father who sent me commanded me what to say and speak*
    - *So what I say, I say as the Father told me* (Jn 12:49-50);
    - *I do as the Father has commanded me* (Jn 14:31);
    - *I glorified you on earth* [Father] *by accomplishing the work that you gave me to do* (Jn 17:4).

3. It is revealing that passages on the temptations of Jesus do not appear in John. And in Mark, angels are said to minister to Jesus and supposedly help him with Satan's temptations (Mark 1:12-13). If so, such assistance likely would be welcomed by humans, who often seem to be on their own.

4. In Mark's and Matthews's texts the issue becomes more complicated. Jesus advises that he should follow basic commandments (*You shall not kill; you shall not commit adultery; you shall not steal; you shall not bear false witness; you shall not defraud; honor your father and your mother*). However, according to Mark, he does not include the greatest of all commandments in the passage (which appears in 12:28-31). Instead, Jesus inserts an addendum telling the scholar that he lacks one thing, *Go, sell what you have, and give to [the] poor and you will have treasure in heaven; then come, follow me* (Mk 10:21). As previously discussed, relating God's will with having to renounce one's possessions places an unrealistic burden on most human beings; something that has never become an integral part of the Christian dogma on salvation. In Matthew, Jesus does include love of neighbor, but simply as one of several commandments and without embracing love of God (that appears in 22:34-40). Then, he adds an addendum similar to Mark's in which renouncing one's possessions becomes only an ideal and not a prerequisite for salvation (Matthew 19:16-21).

5. NEs acknowledge (rather harshly) that Mary's natural kinship *with Jesus counts for nothing; only one who does the will of his heavenly Father belongs to his true family* (Matthew 12:46-50).

Christianity as the Opium of the People

Religion, writes Karl Marx, *is the opium of the people.* His indictment refers mostly to Christianity, as it was the prevailing religion in Europe during his lifetime. In Marx's view, religion provides *illusory happiness* that consoles humanity. Hence, if humanity wishes to attain its real happiness it must begin by abolishing religion.[1] Marx's use of this powerful metaphor is meant to expose the type of false consciousness that protected and legitimized political power throughout Europe during previous centuries. Although Jesus would have disagreed with Marx's phrase, it needs to be asked, is such a view present in the Gospels?

This category is a construct that may assist in explaining Marx's metaphor. Its basis lies in searched passages (*p*) and space (*sp*) in the texts. That the category does not rank highly in content analysis results does not mean it is irrelevant given certain passages in the Gospels that seem to render Marx's remarks credible.

To recreate Marx's use of his metaphor it might be important to briefly describe what opium is and what it does to anyone that consumes it. Opium, from which morphine, heroin, and other opiate drugs are produced, is a substance derived from a type of opium poppy, a flower that is among the oldest plants recorded in history (5,000 BCE).[2] The technical word used to describe it, *somniferum,* indicates its soporific effects, i.e., it causes sleep and dulls awareness, among other effects.[3] When absorbed, the substance attaches to (and stimulates) opioid receptors in areas in the brain that control human feelings of pain and pleasure. Among its immediate effects in human behavior are sedation and sleep, reducing anxiety and stress by creating an artificial state of euphoria, and ecstasy or pleasure that gives way *to a feeling of supreme tranquility that can last for hours.* Additionally, its properties are highly effective in blocking the feeling of pain.[4]

Karl Marx's Case Against Religion
The purpose of this section is to set Marx and Jesus side by side, to examine whether the former's critique about religion[5] constitutes (or not) a mischaracterization of Jesus's teachings. By labeling it the opium of the people, Marx is suggesting that, rather than motivate people to change conditions that will improve their wellbeing, religion acts as an expression of their pain, *the sigh of the oppressed creature, the heart of a heartless world, and the soul of soulless conditions.* Thus, religion, i.e., Christianity, anesthetizes the pain people feel by persuading them to accept their wretched conditions in exchange for a treasure in heaven.

The way Marx explains the term *opium* suggests that he must have read some passages from the Gospels from which he develops his view of religion. The term *opium* has distinctive connotations (even during his time). There are, indeed, numerous passages in the Gospels that line up with Marx's viewpoint. The most significant passage is, perhaps, Jesus's Sermon on the Mount where he outlines the Beatitudes. These are distinctive types of behavior (the poor, those who mourn, the meek, those who seek righteousness, the merciful, and those who are persecuted) that find favor in God's eyes, which is why their *reward will be great in heaven* (Mt 5:1-12, Lk 6:20-24). In other passages Jesus teaches not to resist evil behavior; not to strike back when someone strikes us; not to take legal action over contested possessions, but to grant them what they want. When compelled to do something, comply; give to those who ask and do not turn down anyone who wants to borrow; and lastly, love *your* enemy and pray for those who persecute you (Mt 5:38-48, Lk 6:27-37).

While Jesus asks the crowds to rejoice on account of their unpleasant conditions, Marx is reading that Jesus is not only indicating that it is proper to accept their imposed fate but to do it with joy.[6] Jesus, Marx would say, is teaching people to compromise with (or temporarily accept) the evil structures that oppress them;

conditions that even Jesus would regard as sinful. No matter how the above passages are read, there seems to be no room for Jesus being misinterpreted; love thy enemy, accept mourning and poverty,[7] do not mind being persecuted or insulted means exactly what the words say. Marx believes that Jesus's teachings create a false reality that will perpetuate people's deplorable conditions. Getting rid of that false reality is necessary according to Marx, so that humankind may regain their senses and fashion their own reality; *so that* [man] *will move around himself as his own true Sun.* Hence, Marx argues that *the abolition of religion as the illusory happiness of the people is the demand for their real happiness.* Since there was a symbiotic relationship of support between the state and religion throughout much of the nineteenth century, following Marx's logic, the criticism of religion and theology become necessary to divert humanity's attention toward the earth, the laws, and the politics that are responsible for existing dismal conditions.[8]

The terminology Jesus uses in some of his teachings would contribute to Marx's critique of Christianity. Jesus indicates that the Gentile world (the temporal world) operates through authority by the powerful over the rest. But that is not what Jesus teaches his disciples; *rather, whoever wishes to be great among you will be your servant; whoever wishes to be first among you will be the slave of all* (Mk 10:43-44, Lk 22;24-27, Mt 20:25-28). In his teachings with his disciples, Jesus utilizes the terms *servant* and *slave* continuously to illustrate that God's high regard for humble behavior overpowers, arrogance, or pride. Marx, however, believes that God's existence is irrelevant when it comes to changing social conditions.

Washing his disciples' feet may have been Jesus's most noble gesture to symbolize humility. He asks them to follow the same model in being of service to others. (Jn 13:15). Since words are descriptive of reality, Marx would argue that a servile mindset is averse to addressing human poverty. He would add that in the struggle with selfishness and greed, Jesus's teachings (as well as his use of the words *slave* and *servant*) serve no purpose since workers cannot provide a leadership role by acting submissively.[9]

Nor will Jesus's advice to the man who wants to inherit eternal life suffice. Telling him *go, sell what you have, and give to [the] poor and you will have treasure in heaven* (Mk 10:21, Lk 18:18-25, Mt 19:16-21), will not solve the problem, Marx would argue since it would lead to the creation of a destitute class. Besides, Marx's objective (and that of non-Marxist progressive Christian believers) is not to briefly aid the poor, but to change conditions that may permanently eradicate poverty on earth. Jesus's remark to his disciples that poverty will continue to exist on earth (Mk 14:7, Mt 26:11, Jn 12:8) suggests that the poor are a means to practice charity. The passage, Marx would say, shows that Christianity is not only an obstacle to eliminate poverty, but it treats the poor as religious pawns for the benefit of others.

Likewise, Marx would question Jesus's remark about a poor widow who contributed *all she had, her whole livelihood,* to assist others (Mk 12:41-44, Lk 21:1-

4) as an example of righteousness. No one has to be a Marxist to realize (unless Jesus is being hyperbolic) that, as noble a gesture as the widow's behavior may be in God's eyes, no religion or political system ought to encourage a person to become destitute and a burden to society in order to help others. Moreover, Marxists would indicate that psychological studies suggest that the attitude of rich people perpetuates unjust structures, thereby giving credence to Marx's views.[10] On the other hand, Marx may have favored Jesus's attitude in driving out the merchants and money changers from the temple area if they were acting usuriously, but Marx would have blamed religion for conditioning people to accept needs created by religion, e.g., purification, forgiveness of sins, and giving alms.

Marx would have agreed with Jesus if he had acted as the temporal messiah the Israelites were hoping for in accordance with God's promises. It must be remembered that since Exodus, God's promise to his people entailed material abundance (*land of milk and honey*) and freedom from oppression (Ex 3:7-9, 3:16-17, 13:4-6, Lk 1:46-55, 67-75). Jesus indicates that he intends to assume that role when he walks into a synagogue in Nazareth and reads a scroll from the prophet Isaiah suggesting that God has anointed him *to bring glad tidings to the poor*; *proclaim liberty to captives and recovery of sight to the blind,* and *to let the oppressed go free.* The Gospels do not explain why Jesus chooses not to fulfill this task (Lk 4:16-22).

Instead, Jesus becomes an eschatological messiah whose teachings carry supernatural overtones. He emphasizes salvation from the slavery of sin rather than physical slavery, while his mission minimizes the significance of improving material conditions. Jesus shows more interest in correcting the teachings of the Jewish authorities than in being critical of Jewish oppression at the hands of Herod and Pilate. And, although Jesus proclaims that the blind regain their sight, the lame walk, lepers are cleansed, the deaf hear, and the dead are raised, all the poor receive is the good news about rewards in heaven (Lk 7:18-22, Mt 11:2-5).

Jesus tells the crowds not to be afraid of losing their lives if persecuted, but rather to be afraid of the devil that has the power to cast people into Gehenna (Lk 12:4-7, Mt 10:28-31). Marx might agree that giving one's life for a revolution that would improve the condition of humanity would be a worthy death. Nonetheless, it is Jesus's apparent indifference toward life on earth in general that would be a concern to Marx, for whom material conditions are everything. To Marx, Jesus's teaching that there should be total dependence on God would create a mental picture of humanity staring at the heavens expecting food, shelter, clothing, and employment to come from God (Lk 12:22-31, Mt 6:25-33). This would be the type of false consciousness and unrealistic expectations that religion would offer humanity according to Marx.

Jesus's words sound alarmingly unrealistic, considering that they may lead to an overall indifference about human progress, including the eradication of sinful structures that perpetuate the conditions of the poor. He calls upon all his disciples (including Christians today) to renounce all their possessions, otherwise, he would not accept them as followers (Mk 10:17-22, Lk 18:18-25, Mt 19:16-22). Marx would argue that it would be wiser to encourage the rich to use their resources unselfishly. Jesus, however, urges the crowds not to work *for food that perishes but for the food that endures for eternal life* (Jn 6:24-27); Marx would frown upon such remarks after noticing that even Paul found the idea unsettling (2 Thes 3:10).

Nonetheless, setting aside that Christians are far from complying *en masse* with their teacher's wishes, according to Marx, Jesus's teachings could be detrimental to society. If Christians were to renounce their possessions, where would these go today; to charities, NGOs, the government? In which case, how would these people live? How would they support their families? These believers would become an intolerable burden to a government that would not be able to support their messianic hope. Could Jesus possibly be referring to a radical reorganization of society's economic and financial structures? The advice he presents in his Parable of the Talents/Ten Gold Coins contradicts this view. In this parable, a wealthy man goes on a journey and entrusts his fortune to his servants with instructions to engage in trade (Wall Street style) for a profit. Upon his return, the man praises those who have gained a profit by trading with his talents while berating and punishing the useless servant that chooses not to heed the master's instruction. (Mt. 25:14-30, Lk 19:11-24). Ironically, Jesus's teaching did not involve asking the wealthy man to renounce his possessions, but rather to try to profit by engaging in trade. Marx would agree with the actions of the industrious employees that would result in better conditions and higher wages for them, and who in turn could contribute to charitable institutions while providing better living conditions for their families.

It might prove difficult, even for believers, to discard Marx's observations about Christianity. Jesus's words appear to give credence to Marx's thesis that Christianity is indifferent to human progress and the eradication of poverty. This is seen clearly in the Parable of the Weeds Among the Wheat whereby he suggests that Christians ought to take no action against evil, as he will take on this role at the end of the harvest, i.e., the Parousia (Mt 13:24-30, 36-43, 25:31-46).

Paradoxically, the specter of Marxism in the nineteenth century played a significant role in the Catholic hierarchy's decision to make a systematic turn toward the temporal world, as it sought to establish a balance between eternal salvation and improvement of the human condition on earth. Against the backdrop of social upheavals in the European continent in 1848, urban and rural workers' dissatisfaction with their conditions, the threat of liberalism to the Church's doctrine on freedom, the publication of the Communist Manifesto, and the events surrounding the Paris Commune (among others), Pope Leo XIII published his encyclical *Rerum Novarum* on Capital and Labor in 1891. It established the church's opposition to unfettered capitalism and Marxist socialism. Since then, the Catholic hierarchy and several mainstream Protestant denominations have formulated a social justice agenda that relies on Jesus's teachings; in effect, overriding some of his sayings.

Jesus's Case Against Marx

Marx's critique rests upon his view that religion numbs the senses of the poor by making them feel contented with their condition. Cynically, Marxists could favor a religion that desensitizes the wealthy who in turn would aid the poor. Nonetheless, content analysis results corroborate a conclusive emphasis on the supernatural dimension of the Gospels at the expense of the temporal world. The results concede to Marx the view that improvement of the human condition is secondary in Jesus's teachings. This inference ought not to be surprising; after all, Jesus's mission is not to create a land of milk and honey on earth but to deliver a message of eternal salvation to humanity.

Although Jesus's emphasis on humility and his indifference to material necessities leads Marx to say that religion is the opium of the people, results in Table 2 suggest that the Gospels present an alternative view. The categories Power, Love, Religious Authorities, and Poverty and Wealth are highly ranked too, and they indicate Jesus's concern with the material/physical plight of humanity. The Miracles and the Poverty and Wealth categories also prioritize assistance to the poor. Although Jesus's miracles do not include providing money, education, or employment to the poor, most passages indicate his concern with the sick and with feeding the hungry; two significant endeavors that continue to fail humanity throughout history.

Nonetheless, the most encompassing category of all, upon which Jesus makes his case, lies in the two commandments that are greater than any other, love of God and love of neighbor (Mk 12:28-34). Supposedly, his teachings about love, caring, and forgiveness suggest that if Christians were to comply with these commandments, poverty might be alleviated or eradicated, albeit in opposition to Jesus's view. His conception about the uses of power and divine justice are oriented toward the wellbeing of all, and in aiding and comforting the poor. Moreover, an aspect of Jesus's mission that contributes to his death is the various acts of defiance of the Sabbath to cure the sick (Mk 1:21-28, 2:23-27, 3:1-6, Lk 6:1-15, 6:6-11, 12:9-14, 13:10-17, 14:1-6, Jn 5:1-18, 9:1-17). Through his actions, he affirms that it is lawful *to do good on the Sabbath rather than to do evil, to save a life rather than to destroy it* (Mk 3:4).

Perhaps Jesus's idealistic view on depending on God reflects indifference toward material necessities. However, his powerful critique about selfishness and greed, and the peril of damnation on account of attachment to material possessions (Lk 16:19-31, Mt 25:31-46) make his teachings more relevant today, as they address the opium of our time, a materialistic, self-indulgent, and highly individualistic life-style that technological progress has given rise to in the more developed countries. Marx certainly would approve of Jesus's critique. In many instances, material comfort and the *good life* tend to insulate people from the ugliness created by misery and despair. To the extent that Jesus's teachings put forth such a vision, it would negate Marx's proposition that religion does not contribute to the wellbeing of society.

Does it mean then that Marx's assessment of the [Christian] religion is wrong? Not necessarily. Perhaps the reason for Marx's observation is that he accepts those aspects of the Gospels that relate closely with his views while ignoring those that oppose them. Moreover, he uses Christianity's views outside their proper context, a valid approach because the Gospels, being timeless, had not been actualized. Besides, Jesus's Beatitudes and the importance he ascribes to humility and meekness cannot simply be erased by other teachings that oppose them; they stand next to each other as seeming inconsistencies that Christians need to sort out.

Marx's position is better understood when we observe that Jesus's teachings regarding the poor have been traditionally interpreted merely as relief of their conditions, and not oriented toward their eradication. The term that usually stands out as Christian assistance to the poor is *charity,* a benevolent act of pity (or self-guilt) by those who have toward those that have little. However, the type of charity that would truly reflect love of neighbor would, by definition, lead to a restructuring of society's standard of living, so that those who have little (while working as hard as others) may have a chance at a decent life. This operational definition of charity would require a political leadership that is more sensitive to the poor without obliterating a private sector that works responsibly toward the common good.

A major difference that might be reflected in Marx's and Jesus's views is that Marx places more emphasis on the social level, i.e., structures, while Jesus emphasizes the person. Marxism proposed to assist humanity as a whole; Jesus sought to do it one person at a time. Marx wanted to upend existing social structures in the hope that new ones would eventually lead to an image of a new man that is free and in control of his own creative forces. Whether his utopian view could have emerged through class envy and hatred is no longer questionable; it did not work. Jesus, on the other hand, stressed personal conversion of individual hearts and minds.

Both shared the image of human sinfulness (Marx would call it injustice). There are differences, however. Marxist-Leninism and similar theories lead ultimately to repression unless each individual and society freely accepts its imposition by a minority that claims to understand the needs of the people. Conversely, the implementation of Jesus's teachings, insofar as they are freely accepted, does not call for social or political repression because it is not based on authoritarianism. At the same time, there is nothing in Jesus's teachings that prevent Christians from establishing the types of social, economic, and political structures that will enable individual and social behavior to function along the lines of his principles and values.

Today, Christianity faces a critical dilemma: how to balance the Beatitudes, humility, and meekness, as read in the Gospels, with a realistic attitude aimed at improving the conditions of the poor and other neglected groups. If the wealthy and powerful (including middle and upper classes) refuse to become humble, the *forgotten ones* shall remain forgotten, although they will enjoy God's blessing.

Notes:

1. Karl Marx, *Critique of Hegel's Philosophy of Right,* (1843), Introduction, trans. Joseph O. Malley, (Oxford: Oxford University Press, 1970), www.marxists.org/archive/marx/works/download/Marx_Critique_of_Hegels_Philosophy_of_Right.pdf (accessed June 28, 2019).

2. Helen Askitopoulou, Ioanna A Ramoutsaki, Eleni Konsolaki, "Archaeological evidence on the use of opium in the Minoan world," (Abstract). International Congress Series, Vol 1242, Elsevier, December 2002, https://www.sciencedirect.com/science/article/pii/S0531513102007690?via%3Dihub (accessed June 30, 2019); S. Norn, PR Kruse, E Kruse, "History of opium poppy and morphine," (Abstract), 2005, National Center for Biotechnology Information, https://www.ncbi.nlm.nih.gov/pubmed/17152761 (accessed June 30, 2019).

3. *Merriam-Webster Dictionary,* online, s.v. "somniferous."

4. "Opium," *Alcohol and Drug Foundation,* June 26, 2019, https://adf.org.au/drug-facts/opium/ (accessed June 28, 2019). A list of additional effects appears in Bronwen Jean Bryant, Kathleen Mary Knights *Pharmacology for Health Professionals*, 3rd ed (Sydney: Mosby Elsevier, 2011) 290-91, books.google.com/books?id=TQV6sLzYsOYC&pg=PA290#v=onepage&q&f=false (accessed June 30, 2019).

5. Although Marx refers to religion in a few of his writings, he never writes a specific treatise about it. His early life experiences and studies, however, are likely to have influenced his attitude. Having been born Jewish, his family converts to Protestantism to escape Christian-induced anti-Semitism. Living under a divided and contentious Christian conglomeration of German political states also gives him some notion of the side-effects of religion. His dictum is ultimately a product of the materialist views of human life he developed, and his (quasi-scientific) reaction to Georg W F Hegel's philosophy of idealism.

6. Arguing in favor of the Beatitudes, Fr. Jeffrey Kirby echoes Pope Francis's belief that the Beatitudes can lead to man's inherent happiness because of their universality among *people of goodwill* presuming they *possess a poor spirit, sorrow over loss or evil, meekness, a keen desire for righteousness, mercy, purity of heart, working for peace, and a willingness to suffer persecution for what is right and just*. While agreeing with Fr. Kirby, there are problems in defining *people of goodwill* by relying on Christian criteria. If the term includes atheists and members of other religions, who is responsible for putting these values in their hearts and minds? Can *people of goodwill* disagree with the Beatitudes? Are the Beatitudes the only measure of *people of goodwill*?

7. While Matthew emphasizes the poor in spirit (suggesting spiritual poverty), Luke (who is more concerned with real deprivation) simply writes *Blessed are you who are poor, for the kingdom of God is yours* (Lk 6:20).

8. Marx, *Critique.*

9. It is perhaps ironic that in Marxism-Leninism, the party is supposed to pursue the interest of all workers and society thus making the party the servant of the people. In Leninism, once in power, the party demands absolute obedience, thus turning the people into servants. However, the concept of attaining political power to alter socio-economic and political structures is not necessarily alien to Christian political thought in its pursuit of a just society.

10. A study in 2010 by Paul K. Piff and Michael W. Kraus provided a significant conclusion: despite lower-income people being *more generous, charitable, trusting and helpful to others than were those with more wealth,* their empathy and compassion diminished as they become wealthier. Judith Warner, "The Charitable-Giving Divide," *The New York Times Magazine,* August 20, 2010, https://www.nytimes.com/2010/08/22/magazine/22FOB-wwln-t.html (accessed January 14, 2019). Another article surveying various studies indicate that,

- The rich tend to be more self-centered: they *rationalize their advantage, and believe that they deserved it. They pursue their self-interest and moralize greed easily.*
- The rich seem to view the external environment quite differently: they *are not very good at reading emotions of the others and lack empathy and compassion. This deficit stems primarily from their lack of dependence on others.*
- The rich appear to possess a sense of entitlement: *A study of the attitude of car owners showed that more expensive cars were more likely to block and cross other cars, and less likely to yield to pedestrians who had the right of way. The rich paid lower taxes and were more prone to evade taxes and hide their wealth; the rich were more likely to adopt questionable accounting and business practices and sidestep ethical practices, and the rich were more likely to use their powers to perpetuate illegal and unlawful activities.* Uma Shashikant, "Why poor people tend to be more generous than the rich," *Economic Times, July 23, 2018,*

https://economictimes.indiatimes.com/wealth/save/why-poor-people-tend-to-be-more-generous-than-the-rich/articleshow/65078320.cms (accessed January 14, 2019).

Violence and Non-Violence in Jesus

The fact that Christians have engaged in violence throughout history raises important considerations. What accounts for violence among Christians and by Christians? Is Jesus prone to violence; is he peaceful, or is he a pacifist? And, could his teachings foster violence? Passages related to violence and non-violence in the Gospels were added together in tallying this category; ideally, they ought to provide enough information to answer the above questions. Table 2 ranks this category as significant.

What Do We understand by Violence Today?
The dictionary defines *violence* as *the use of physical force so as to injure, abuse, damage, or destroy.*[1] This definition, however, is extraordinarily narrow by today's standards. Its central point stresses mostly physical force; it excludes domestic and international law, norms and regulations in the private sector and education, and worldwide cultural discussions indicating that emotional violence (as suggested by various forms of bullying, mockery, intimidation, and harassment) is an integral component of violence. This heightened awareness suggests that continuous verbal and graphic attacks to demean and humiliate can be as harmful to the psyche of individuals and groups as physical violence. Accordingly, threats or incitement to violence (conveyed verbally and/or physically) that target the physical body or the individual and social psyche as well as particular groups of people because of their race, gender, religion, or political affiliation, may have to be included in the definition of violence. Continuous social agitations and demonstrations along these lines may also constitute violence, if they create a disposition to threaten people, thereby generating a state of physical or emotional insecurity.

There is another element missing in the definition; it does not include the harm done to people on account of the negligence or insensitivity by developed nations and by the governments and elites of poorer nations resulting in the suffering of millions who undergo hunger, sickness, persecutions, trafficking, and other social and legal injustices. Violence is also inflicted upon the physical environment if humans abuse, damage, or destroy natural resources upon which the survivability of the planet depends; or when human conduct willfully abstains or conspires to undermine policies and behavior that mitigate or oppose efforts to reverse the causes of climate change, regardless of whether they are naturally or humanly created. Furthermore, the terms *injure, abuse, damage, or destroy* do not only apply only to personal or individual action; they pertain to humanly-created cultural, social, political, and economic structures that not only prevent fair and balanced individual and social progress, but increase the likelihood of military conflict, and perpetuate corruption, criminal activity, and prolonged impoverishment.

The above definitions of violence stand in contrast to violent outbursts, i.e., occasional emotional displays of anger that humans are prone to in specific circumstances. This behavior may not be categorized as violent insofar as it does not lead to physical confrontation or does not become a recurring pattern that may be considered intimidating to others, particularly if they are followed by acts of apology or contrition.

The Case for a Violent Jesus

The sections on *Jesus's Conflicting Personality* and *Justice* suggest that there is an element of violence in Jesus's behavior that accords with the broad definition of the term. Despite his self-professed assertion of gentleness, *I am meek and humble of heart* (Mt 11:29), and apologetic claims of kindness, Jesus is shown in the Gospels to be aggressive, tempestuous, and downright lethal,[2] specifically in his conflict with the religious authorities, with people in towns that reject his teachings, and throughout his teachings in some of the parables.

Jesus's reliance on violence is portrayed in the Gospels, not through actual physical abuse, but in terms of warnings that he issues in the course of his teachings. These warnings are seen in John the Baptist as he preaches repentance, presaging that if people do not change their conduct, they will be eternally condemned (Lk 3:7-9, Mt 3:10-12). He indicates that the one who comes after him, i.e., Jesus, will collect the wheat (righteous people) and burn the chaff (sinners) *with unquenchable fire* (Lk 3:16-17, Mt 3:10-12). Jesus's public mission is a continuation of John's preaching, threatening people with eternal damnation if they act sinfully.

His parables are about human incidents in which a master or a king threatens to inflict gruesome punishment upon those who dare to defy him. Although the parables signal punishment in the afterlife, the tone is quite earthly, suggesting what he would do to sinners on earth:

- the master puts the vineyard tenants to death for murdering his servants and his son (Mk 12:1-9, Lk 20:9-16, Mt 21:33-41);
- those who store material treasures on earth will be condemned (Lk 12:16-21);
- the master will punish severely those who become intoxicated and beat his servants; he is more considerate of those who proceed out of ignorance, in which case they will be *beaten only lightly* (Lk 12:45-48, Mt 24:45-51);
- an angry host coerces strangers to come to his dinner after being rebuffed by others, and bars his initial guests from his feast, i.e., they will not be allowed into God's kingdom (Lk 14:15-24, Mt 22:1-14);
- a slighted king slays those who are unwilling to accept his authority and condemns the servant who is negligent with his fortune (Lk 19:17-27, Mt 25:14-30);
- the wicked will be eternally condemned (Mt 13:47-50, 18:21-35);

- a lazy servant is condemned to eternal damnation for ignoring his master's instructions on investing his resources (Mt 25:14:30);
- five young women who act foolishly are barred from eternity (Mt 25:1-13).

It should be noted that in a few instances, severe punishment is inflicted upon those who commit serious crimes; however, in most of the examples above, the penalties, at least by today's human standards, are harsh and typical of an autocrat. It may be asked if Jesus is being hyperbolic or if he intends to follow through with the punishments he outlines in these parables.

Additionally, Jesus promises earthly suffering, such as the destruction of the Jerusalem Temple (Mk 13:1-3, Lk 21:5-6, Mt 24:1-2); and earthly tribulations, wars, earthquakes, persecutions, famines, and desolation (Mk 13:3-24, Lk 21:7-36, Mt 24:3-31) that will precede the *Parousia* or Second Coming, supposedly affecting the innocent as well as the guilty. He describes these events as terrible catastrophes (Lk 17:26-36, 21:25-27, Mt 24:29-31), denoting unimaginable levels of destruction.

Although punishment for wicked acts takes place in all societies, there are some differences. Eternal punishment means just that; it is for eternity, thus in disproportion to the mental state or mindset of the guilty party. Moreover, anger seems to drive the master or king, i.e., God, when he is disobeyed.

Jesus's only documented instance of relying on physical violence occurs in one passage in which he *made a whip out of chords and drove* money changers and merchants from the outskirts of the Temple (Jn 2:13-17). The passage shows up in all four Gospels, but only in John does Jesus use a whip, although the passage does not indicate whether he uses it to strike people physically or only to disperse the offenders. It suggests that Jesus does not regard anger and violence as evil in some instances; sometimes, it may even be morally mandated. Moreover, in the Parable of the Tenants, in which men injure and kill the master's servants, including his son, the master decides to *put those wretched men to a wretched death* (Mt 21:33-41). If transposed into an earthly incident, this parable indicates that violence may be necessary as a recourse to evil.

There is also behavior in Jesus that, although not as transparent as the one in the Temple, suggests a tendency toward violence. For example, throughout his public mission, Jesus is unwilling to be critical of the oppression his people are suffering at the hands of Pontius Pilate and his associate, King Herod. He reneges on his promise to proclaim liberty to the captives and freedom from oppression, as he said he would do (Lk 4:18-19). At one point, he even abstains from denouncing Pilate's massacre of Galileans and instead tells the people that, if they do not repent, they will also perish (Lk 13:1-5).[3]

When Jesus is welcomed into Jerusalem, the crowds proclaim him to be God's sent king of Israel. Fearing that Pontius Pilate might perceive this demonstration as a threat to his authority and respond with force, some Pharisees make Jesus aware of the situation and ask him to *rebuke* his disciples who are part of the festive parade. Given the political circumstances at the time, the possibility of a violent uprising could not have been ruled out. Nonetheless, Jesus opts not to silence the crowds, telling the Pharisees, *if they keep silent, the stones will cry out!* thereby indicating the unfairness of the Pharisees' request (Lk 19:36-40). The passage suggests that Jesus is either oblivious to the possibility of violence erupting or that he would not mind if it occurs.

In another passage, according to Luke, Jesus indicates that since the moment John the Baptist proclaims the kingdom of God, *everyone who enters does so with violence* (Lk 16;16). Matthew cites a similar saying, indicating that *the kingdom of heaven suffers violence, and the violent are taking it by force* (Mt 11:12). Both passages (though slightly different from each other) attest to numerous interpretations that relate to violence: 1) people who begin to follow Jesus are experiencing forms of violence from opponents; 2) Jesus's followers are countering the opposition violently; 3) Jesus's followers are staging a social and religious coup to take control over the religious authorities; 4) Jesus's teachings are encountering opposition leading to social, religious, and political unrest. The passage may also refer to emotional or spiritual violence within the self, as it occurs in repentance and conversion, both of which entail confronting regrets and sin in one's life.[4]

A more inexplicable incident occurs when Jesus tells his disciples that the hour has come to arm themselves with swords, suggesting that public attacks against him have begun to expand and he and his disciples might need to defend themselves. Intriguingly, when his disciples produce two swords, he abruptly changes his mind shouting, *it is enough!* and nothing else is said (Lk 22:35-38). Taken literally, the passage may suggest that two swords are enough to forestall an attack, meaning that they are not well-armed. It is also possible that Jesus realizes that nothing can be done to forestall his arrest, so he resigns himself to the circumstances.[5]

Perhaps the most extraordinary saying related to Jesus's support for violence occurs when he proclaims in Luke that he wants to set the earth on fire, adding that *from now on* there will be division rather than peace, and family members will oppose each other (Lk 12:49-53). In Matthew he is more explicit, stating that it is not his intention to bring peace upon earth, *but the sword* (Mt 10:34). The saying may suggest that Jesus is a social and religious revolutionary who seeks violence as a means to attain the changes he desires. However, it also suggests the possibility that Jesus realizes that his teachings are in opposition with worldly behavior and are likely to cause division that in turn may generate social upheavals or even wars. Ultimately, he does not seem to mind, *how I wish it were already blazing!* he says. Presuming these sayings are not metaphorical, they suggest that Jesus supports religious and social change through violence. If so, they contradict Jesus's otherwise peaceful disposition. Nonetheless, although he attests that his offering of peace to his disciples is different from the peace the world offers (Jn 14:27, 20:19-21), he does not explain what earthly peace consists of.[6] How do readers begin to make sense of these passages? One way is to examine them from a historical perspective and the events that occurred (or not) at the time.

The Case for a Non-violent Jesus

The term *non-violence* suggests various interpretations. It may refer to someone who either by temperament or conviction prefers not to engage in any form of violence; however, conditions may arise that morally compel the person to engage in various methods of violence, e.g., physically intervening, financially contributing, or publicly engaging in defending one's family, people in need, or one's nation if attacked. If these conditions are not present the person opts for non-violence. There is also 'peaceful behavior' that is similar to non-violence in its distaste for violence. The individual actively pursues behavior and policies related to conciliation, minimizes or prevents escalation of conditions that may lead to conflict, and in the end chooses preemptive (as opposed to preventive) violence as a last defensive resort.[7] The non-violent and peaceful personalities are neither belligerents nor appeasers. By contrast, a pacifist is someone who (usually) by ideological or religious conviction believes that there is no justification for violence of any type, although there may be shades of gray even among pacifists; some prefer to die or would not mind the death of others rather than defending life, while others may even engage in violence to prevent violence.

There are exceptional passages in the Gospels that point to a non-violent, peaceful, and even pacifist Jesus, some in open contradiction to passages illustrating violent behavior. Following a literal reading of the texts, Jesus's conflicting personality emerges once again leaving many questions unanswered.

In one instance the disciples are critical of the woman who pours costly perfumed oil over Jesus's head because the oil could have been sold, and the proceeds given to the poor. Nonetheless, Jesus asks them not to make trouble for her, as she is doing a good deed for him, while there will always be poor people in the world (Mk 14:3-9, Mt 26:6-13, Jn 12;1-8). Extrapolating Jesus's behavior into the world of politics suggests that aiding the poor ought not to become a source of violent conflicts.

Jesus's Sermon on the Mount offers a broader insight into his apparent distaste for violent social upheaval. Although he announces that he comes to liberate the captive and bring good news to the poor, the focus on the mount is not to revolt, but to patiently and meekly bear the evil to which people are being subjected. The poverty, grief, and hatred they endure along with their thirst for justice and peace, transform them into blessed people in the eyes of God. They shall receive their reward in the afterlife, he tells the crowd (Lk 6:20-26, Mt 5:1-12). Hence, the Beatitudes may be seen as Jesus's example to his followers to abstain from violence despite the violence that is being forced upon them.

His teachings on anger, also underscore his partiality toward non-violence. Whoever is angry with his brother or insults him will be liable to judgment and possibly face eternal condemnation. Bringing one's gift to the altar is not a substitute for enmity; rather one ought to reconcile with his brother, then offer the gift (Mt 5:21-

24). Jesus does not like legal disputes; these are to be settled outside the courts (Mt 5:25-26, Lk 12:57-59). He teaches not to resist evil; not to strike back if attacked; walk the extra mile with those who ask; assist those in need; *love your enemies and pray for those who persecute you;* be merciful (Mt 5:38-48, Lk 6:27-36); do not judge others for their evil ways since we all have our own faults; forgive others so that God may forgive us (Mt 6:1-5, Lk 6:37-42). Could these sayings be the teachings of a violent man, his threats of physical violence in the parables and eternal condemnation notwithstanding? It might be challenging for the reader to answer this question, namely because the Gospels portray Jesus being engaged in a human/temporal and a divine/eschatological role at the same time, which makes it challenging at times to distinguish between the two.

His parables concerning upright behavior center on compassion and caring for others. In the Parable of the Good Samaritan, the righteous is not he who practices orthodoxy but the one who acts with compassion. Stepping away from his religious roots, Jesus chooses someone who is despised by the Jewish people and sets him as a role model worthy of his praise (Lk 10:25-37). In another instance, Jesus and his companions decide to enter Samaritan territory, but they are not welcomed. James and John become enraged and (incongruently) ask Jesus if they should *call down fire from heaven to consume them.* Jesus, however, rebukes their hostility and they resume their journey (Lk 9:51-56).

Another example of Jesus's non-violent disposition occurs when the scribes and the Pharisees bring a woman to him that has been accused of adultery, and which according to Moses Law ought to be stoned to death. Rather than complying with the Law, Jesus seizes the moment to save a life rather than to justify a violent act. On another occasion, the religious authorities attempt to stone him. Instead of defending himself physically, Jesus argues with them, retreats, and eludes his opponents (Jn 10:31-33, 39). He refuses to engage in combat with his adversaries; as a good shepherd, he insists that he would rather give his life for his sheep without recourse to violence (Jn 10:14-18).

His entrance into Jerusalem is enlightening. As the leader of a theocratic religious/political movement Jesus is welcomed as a hero, as God's messenger, and as a king. Nonetheless, he shows up not on a warhorse leading a contingent of armed men, but rather riding on an ass' colt, a gentler animal symbolic of peace. Then, at the time of his arrest, his disciples appear to be armed with swords. This time one of Jesus's followers (Peter in John's text) attacks the high priest's servant cutting off his ear. Nonetheless, in Luke's version of the incident Jesus appears to react angrily to the attack and orders them to stop; *no more of this!* he tells them. Seeking to reduce tensions he touches the servant's ear and heals him. He tells his captors that he has been preaching for some time out in the open without protection. Matthew's text provides a slight variation; Jesus tells his armed companion to stand down, *for all who take the sword will perish by the sword,* adding that while he could call on God to send twelve legions of angels to protect him, he chooses not to do it (Mt 26:53). Subsequently, rather than to provoke a slaughter by confronting his opponents he tells them that he will comply with their orders to arrest him while asking them not to detain his companions.

During his trial in the Sanhedrin, and later before Pontius Pilate, he fearlessly admits who he is, mindful that it may cost him his life. He even tells Pilate that he is a king (Jn 18:33-37). He denies being the leader of a conspiracy calling on others to revolt (Mk 14:56-62, Lk 22:66-71, 23:3 Mt 26:62-68, 27:11, Jn 18:19-23), admitting that he has spoken openly to the world in the synagogue and the temple area, *and in secret I have said nothing* (Jn 18:19-23). Finally, on the cross, he forgives those who take part in his crucifixion (Lk 23:34). These passages accentuate Jesus's non-violent and pacifist behavior. Albeit his motives are partially cosmic; he chooses not to contest his arrest so that scriptures may be fulfilled, although in John's text his motive is to do God's will (Mk 14:43-49, Lk 22:47-51, Mt 26:47-54, Jn 18:7-11).

How Violent is Jesus?
Having established the cases for a violent and a non-violent Jesus, how do the above passages stack up against each other? Content analysis results indicate that in terms of *xt, p,* and *sp,* the count for a violent Jesus is twice as high (66xt/66p/898sp) as for a non-violent Jesus (31xt/31p/420sp, data online). The reason is that a violent Jesus scores higher mostly because of his parables dealing with punishment in the afterlife; the numbers on the non-violent Jesus stem mostly from his behavior and teachings while on earth; other than expelling the merchants from the temple area, the texts do not record any other instance in which Jesus becomes physically forceful, although his words at times suggest division and conflict.

His relentless attacks against the religious authorities could have coalesced into a violent political movement akin to the Zealots and the Sicarii. These movements become prominent because of their violent opposition to the Roman Empire and even participate (the Sicarii) in the killing of Jews who oppose them. It is intriguing, however, that while opposition movements originate at the time of the Roman occupation of Israel in 63 BCE and slowly expand throughout Jesus's public life, history does not record any relations between the Zealots and the Sicarii and Jesus.[8] Furthermore, there is no documentation that acts of hostility are committed in the name of Jesus when this movement begins its offensive against the Roman Empire in 66 CE. Although the Zealots seem to co-opt followers of the Pharisees into revolting, no symbiotic relationship occurs with followers of Jesus.[9] Moreover, there are no records that Jesus's preaching on the kingdom of heaven arises to the level of public demonstrations, other than gatherings for public baptisms, crowds converging at sites where Jesus speaks about the kingdom, and his welcoming into Jerusalem. Jesus's verbal attacks seem to occur at specific sites (Lk 11:37-54, Mt 11:20-24, 23:1-39) where crowds gather, but they do not result in violence on his part. Instead, his rhetoric leads to plots by the religious authorities against him.

Whether Jesus's wish to set the earth on fire and establish division has borne true historically is open to question. His teachings established a moral code of behavior and a set of beliefs that have divided Christian households and Christian nations. Indeed, there have been persecutions of Christians throughout history; some are taking place today (along with other faiths), although their causes may have more to do with prejudice and nativist fear of proselytism than overt opposition to Jesus's teachings. Other earthly conflicts, including large-scale warfare, find their roots in sinful behavior that Jesus opposed, e.g., selfish domination of others, greed, wanton murder, revenge, sheer hatred, and others. This is to say that nothing in the Gospels indicates that Jesus commanded his followers to convert others through force. Instead, it appears that misguided interpretations or zeal lie at the center of the Crusades, the Inquisitions, and the religious wars. Moreover, throughout history, so-called Christian politicians have been responsible for legitimizing economic and military dominance and wars into the twenty-first century.

Contributing to the image of an extreme pacifist is Jesus's teaching in the Parable of the Weeds Among the Wheat. A literal application of this parable to domestic and international affairs indicates that Jesus forbids a government to take any action against evil for fear of making matters worse for the righteous. It is difficult to say if Jesus was cognizant or not that lack of action to stop the spreading of the weed could destroy the entire crop, i.e., civil society and the kingdom of God on earth.[10] Inexplicably, exegetes accept the moral implications of Jesus's teaching.[11]

On the other hand, an opposite reaction is no less worrisome in a relativistic world in which a sinner is seen as a righteous person. Today, the lines between good and evil appear to have been blurred almost beyond recognition. Morality is being dictated more in terms of survival and ideologies, both domestically and internationally. We can no longer ascertain whether nations may be able to distinguish between the weed and the wheat, in which case wars will continue.

Jesus's teachings, and his own conduct on earth, suggest that on matters related to the world he is peaceful, forgiving, non-violent, and likely a pacifist; he is a most severe and violent adjudicator of human deeds, however, in the afterlife, as indicated by numerous passages in the Gospels. His constant threats of eternal punishment against those who would disobey God's commands, or against those that reject him or refuse to believe in him suggest that he intends to deter evil behavior by instilling fear among believers. In that sense, it appears that he is not concerned with being feared instead of being loved; a Machiavellian trait. Whether this approach is effective depends on the credibility of the Gospels, i.e., whether he is regarded as a social and religious philosopher or as divine.

Without additional divine corroboration, Jesus's pacifism may prove insufficient to guide people of goodwill seeking to implement his teachings in a complex world characterized by a flawed human nature. On the other hand, it is possible that the Gospels may have been purposefully distorted to make Jesus appear as a pacifist in an attempt by an incipient religious group of Christians to be viewed as non-violent before the eyes of Roman emperors. Accordingly, these new Christians would have wanted to avoid the types of persecutions that decimated much of the Jewish population in Israel on account of their violent opposition to Rome.[12] Nonetheless, the fact that these early Christians were unarmed while in Rome gives credence to Jesus's teachings. Overall, the preponderance of the evidence in the Gospels points instead to a non-violent or pacifist Jesus.

Notes:

1. *Merriam-Webster Dictionary,* online, s.v. "violence." Both Cambridge and Oxford dictionaries offer similar definitions.

2. These are synonyms of violent behavior that appear online. *Merriam-Webster Dictionary*, online, s.v. "violent."

3. NEs assert that this event is not known historically outside of Luke's Gospel. Notes on Luke 13:1 and 13:4. In the same passage, Jesus also relies on an accident that kills several people to warn that the same fate awaits those who do not repent.

4. Ibid., note, Mt 11:12. NABRE exegetes characterize the meaning of these sayings as *difficult,* suggesting that *probably the opponents of Jesus are trying to prevent people from accepting the kingdom and to snatch it away from those who have received it.*

5. Ibid., Jesus was probably using *figurative language about being prepared to face the world's hostility,* note, Lk 22:38.

6. Ibid., the peace Jesus offers is the peace that comes through salvation, according to NEs' note, John 14:27. What exactly this means is uncertain; if salvation is attained in the afterlife, it means that only then may believers find peace.

7. Today, in many parts of the world the term *preemptive* action has been adulterated to signify support for *preventive* measures that traditionally and by international norms and laws are morally and legally unjustifiable. Many governments, including the United States, have pursued policies that are more predisposed toward violence as a first course of action by calling them preemptive action.

8. The historical rumor that Judas Iscariot may have been a secretive Zealot who becomes disappointed that Jesus has no intention of opposing the Romans carries less weight when he returns the thirty pieces of silver and is overridden by guilt commits suicide (Mt 27:3-4).

9. Josephus, Book XVIII, Chapter 1, 1. & 6. Although Josephus uses the terms *zeal* and *zealous* numerous times (74xt and 48xt respectively), he never refers to these people as Zealots. He writes about the founder of the movement (a philosophy, he calls it), *Judas, a Gaulonite, of a city whose name was Gamala who, taking with him Sadduc, a Pharisee, became zealous to draw them* (the Jewish people) *to a revolt.* He charges them with sedition and murder of their own people and famine, and ultimately blames them for the destruction of the Temple by the Romans. See also, Joseph Telushkin, *Jewish Literacy*, (NY: William Morrow and Co., 1991), in "Ancient Jewish History: The Great Revolt (66-70 CE)," JVL, https://www.jewishvirtuallibrary.org/the-great-revolt-66-70-ce (accessed April 6, 2019).

10. The type of weed referenced in Matthew is said to be darnel, *a poisonous weed that in its first stage of growth resembles wheat.* NEs' note, Matthew 13:25. It is possible (though doubtful) that farmers at the time might not have had enough information about this weed. Today it is acknowledged that *even a few grains of this plant will adversely affect crop quality. Its seeds are poisonous to people and livestock. It is very difficult to separate the seeds of L. temulentum* (darnel) *from those of wheat and other small grain crops as they are similar in size and weight. L. temulentum can be a host to a variety of crop pests and diseases. The best form of invasive species management is prevention. If prevention is no longer possible, it is best to treat the weed infestations when they are small to prevent them from establishing (early detection and rapid response).* BioNET-EAFRINET, "Lolium temulentum (Darnel Ryegrass)," https://keys.lucidcentral.org/keys/v3/eafrinet/weeds/key/weeds/Media/Html/Lolium_temulentum_(Darnel_Ryegrass).htm (accessed April 7, 2019).

11. NEs' note, Matthew 13:24-30: *The refusal of the householder to allow his slaves to separate the wheat from the weeds while they are still growing is a warning to the disciples not to attempt to anticipate the final judgment of God by a definitive exclusion of sinners from the kingdom. In its present stage, it is composed of the good and the bad. The judgment of God alone will eliminate the sinful. Until then there must be patience and the preaching of repentance.*

12. The Romans begin to retaliate against Jewish uprisings by 66 CE; in the year 70 CE they destroy Jerusalem, and it is estimated that up to one million Jews are killed. Telushkin, "The Great Revolt."

Humility

In the Gospels, Jesus exhorts his followers to learn from him, who is *meek and humble of heart* (Mt 11:29). Although these two words show up only 11xt in the texts, he relies on other terms, such as *slave, servant, children,* and *poverty,* to express his views on humility. His teachings on the subject are found through his critique of behavior like *arrogance, pride, hypocrisy,* and *wealth* that he considers inimical to being humble. Table 2 indicates this category as being significant.

While loving and forgiving refer to actions the believer is asked to observe toward others, the call to be humble points straight at the believer. It would be difficult (perhaps impossible) to love and forgive others (or oneself) without being humble.

There is a rich tradition in the Old Testament regarding humility, although with a nuance. The term presupposes the recognition of a superior being to whom the Israelites owe respect and deference. God dislikes haughtiness (Isa 26.5); it brings humiliation upon the arrogant while the humble of spirit is exalted (Psalm 18:28, 25:9, Prov 29:23). Humility finds mercy in the eyes of God (Sir 3:18). Being humble was the required Israelite behavior toward God and oneself. At the time, however, the term had not expanded to denote a sense of dignity that would entitle humans to equal respect and treatment among others and before the law; in its own way, it may be said that Christianity facilitated the foundation for these views.

Secularly, however, humility has other meanings, some of which are similar to the Christian definition while others are different. To be humble, both in the Christian and secular versions, means not being proud, haughty, or arrogant. Thus since no one is perfect, feelings of superiority are regarded as sheer vanity, attitudes that Jesus despises. Nonetheless, humility also carries uncomplimentary negative social connotations, such as being unassertive, unambitious, weak, insignificant, poor, or of low social status, or having a low estimate of one's importance,[1] temporal traits that Jesus esteems. Secularly, the term is related to the word and action verb *humiliation/to humiliate* that, when viewed from the perspective of the person being humiliated, means *to* [be reduced] *to a lower position in one's own eyes or others' eyes;* to be made to feel *ashamed or embarrassed,* or to have one's dignity and pride injured by someone's action or remarks.[2] Such behavior would be contrary to Jesus's teachings as well as uncalled for by people irrespective of beliefs.

The term, *meekness,* on account of showing up in three significant passages in Matthew, relates to humility too. *Meekness* is secularly defined as *enduring injury with patience and without resentment,* i.e., similar to the Christian view; although it is seen disapprovingly, as being *deficient in spirit and courage, submissive, not violent or strong, quiet, unwilling to disagree or fight or to strongly support personal ideas and opinions.*[3] Except for enduring injury with patience, Jesus probably would disagree with the other interpretations as they applied to him.

Following Jesus's teachings to be humble would not appear to be an easy task given the incongruences found in the Gospels. From the above definitions, we may gather that, to Jesus, humility is an amalgamation of seemingly contradictory personal attributes; a way of being in relation to God that is more in line with the Old Testament, but without necessarily negating its positive modern social conclusions. Jesus believes that *the lure of riches and craving for things* and greed present a risk to salvation (Mk 4:3-19, 10:23-25, 12:6-9, Lk 8:7-14, 12:13-15, 12:16-21, 20:9-16, Mt 13:22), to the point where he insinuates that donating one's possessions might be necessary to inherit eternal life (Mk 10:17-22, Lk 12:33-34, 14:33, 18:18-25, Mt 19:16-24). Hence, humility, i.e., being unpretentious, is a form of neutralizing emotional attachment to material possessions that Jesus considers false treasures. Instead, he calls for dependence on God on all aspects of life (Lk 12:22-34, Mt 6:19-21, 6:25-33), an attitude that might prove unworkable for most people. Humility calls for enduring humiliation and poverty; and yet, those who suffer and are hated and insulted are among Jesus's most *blessed*. His words convey having to freely accept submissiveness, an attitude that likely is abhorred nowadays:

> *[O]ffer no resistance to one who is evil. When someone strikes you on [your] right cheek, turn the other one to him as well. If anyone wants to go to law with you over your tunic, hand him your cloak as well. Should anyone press you into service for one mile, go with him for two miles. Give to the one who asks of you, and do not turn your back on one who wants to borrow (Mt 5:39-42).*

In contrast with these sayings, and despite his remarks about wealth and his preference for the poor, Jesus is not necessarily opposed to rich people; he relates well with the wealthy, including tax collectors (Lk 19:1-9). Instead, he feels contempt for ostentatious behavior (Lk 7:24-25, Mt 11:7-8) because it projects a deceptive sense of grandeur in the person that leads to a false feeling of superiority over others. Thus, he teaches abnegation to counteract those desires (Mk 7:22, 8:34, 12:38-40, Lk 9:23-24, Mt 16:24-25).

His praise of the poor widow who gives everything in her possession as opposed to the rich who contribute from their surplus wealth (Mk 12:41:44, Lk 4:16-21, 6:20-23, 21:1-4) is in line with his condemnation of greed and his judgment against human insensitivity (Mk 12:6-9, Lk 16:19-31, Mt 18:23-35, 25:31-46). Jesus insists that his followers ought to be modest (regardless if they are rich). His disciples are of humble origin rather than magnates of the fishing or financial sectors (Mk 1:16-20, Lk 5:9-10, Mt 4:18-22, 9:9-13). He tells them to set an example by taking nothing on their journeys to preach the good news but a walking stick and sandals (Mk 6:7-9, Lk 10:3-4, Mt 10:8-10). He prefers to meet with sinners that are rejected by the religious upper crust, because they are the ones in need of repentance (Mk, 2:13-17, Lk 5:27-32, Mt 11:19), despite the religious authorities are among the greatest sinners.

In Jesus's teachings, humility is an attitude that leads to visibly distinctive behavior. He stresses this attitude in the Parable about the Conduct of the Invited Guests in which he sternly warns that *everyone who exalts himself will be humbled, but the one who humbles himself will be exalted* (Lk 14:7-14). A superficial reading of the passage might suggest that the parable leads to a false sense of humility; that is, to pretend to be humble only to be exalted by others. Jesus, however, is referring to persons who regard themselves as important and believe they are entitled to occupy the front seats to be noticed and envied by others.

His type of humility is critical of hypocrites and self-righteous people that place prestige, power, and tradition ahead of caring for the sick, and of those who would point out the mistakes in others while ignoring their own (Mk 3:1-6, Lk 6:6-11, 6:39-42, 10:30-37, 11:37-52, 13:10-17, 14:1-6, 20:45-47, Mt 7:1-5, 12:22-24, 13:10-17, 15:1-9, 23:1-36). He teaches the crowds to become modest and unassuming, whether when giving alms, praying, or fasting (Mt 6:1-6, 16-18).

Jesus brings out the conflict between self-righteousness and humility in his Parable of the Pharisee and the Tax Collector. The Pharisee regards himself as righteous and gives thanks to God for being a better person than the rest of humanity. He is not greedy, dishonest, or adulterous, and he fasts twice and pays tithes on his income. Nonetheless, he despises everyone else who is not like him, because he considers them to be beneath him. The tax collector, on the other hand, acknowledges that he is a sinner and instead asks God for mercy. Unequivocally, Jesus says that the tax collector will be exalted in heaven while the self-righteous Pharisee will be humbled, i.e., punished in God's presence (Lk 18:9-14).

He teaches values and attitudes that are almost in direct opposition to earthly ways. He tells his disciples that, just as he came to serve and not to be served, they need to do the same by becoming servants and slaves to one another (Mt 20:25-27). Nonetheless, seemingly contradicting himself, Jesus calls on his followers to serve him (Jn 12:26). Today, this behavior would be perceived as arrogant. People usually dislike being told to be subservient to others; unless the term refers to honorable/respectable domestic work at a house, e.g., maid or butler, or being employed by the government as a civil servant.

At the time (including throughout the Old Testament), the terms *slave and servant* were symbolic of humility (Lk 1:54, 69, 2:29, Mt 12:18). By asking his followers to become slaves and servants, Jesus is telling them not to regard themselves as being more important than others, since in the eyes of God all people enjoy the same dignity. Thus, in the Gospels, these terms mean (other than when referring to a servant) obeying Jesus's teachings as slaves and servants obey their masters (Mk 9:33-37, 10:35-45, Lk 1:69, 2:29, 22:24-27, Mt 20:20-28). He utilizes the image of children as the archetype of those who will inherit the kingdom of God, for which it will be necessary that each of his followers sees himself as *servant* and *slave of all* (Mk 10:13-16, Lk 18:15-17).

Although Jesus enjoys greater status than his disciples (Messiah, Son of Man, Son of God), humility in him signifies equivalence of outcome. Since no slave is greater than his master, whatever he (the master) will suffer his disciples will suffer too (Jn 15:20). Today, the terminology Jesus uses is no doubt outdated, and likely would not be well received by a postmodern mentality. This lack of actualization of the scriptures probably presents the biggest obstacle in accepting Jesus's teachings.

Is Jesus Humble?
Viewed from a secularized viewpoint, and in contrast with the secular definitions of humility and meekness (attitudes he approves), Jesus appears to be far from being humble. He refers to himself as *the way, the truth, and the life*; calls himself king, Son of Man, and Son of God; and claims to have been given the power to judge humanity; these are features that could easily lead to arrogance.

There is one definition of true humility, however, that is not mentioned in the dictionaries: to realize and accept one's place in life. If Jesus is everything he claims to be, there is no reason to become conceited or haughty. Hence, he acknowledges that he is subservient to the Father, admitting that the words he teaches are not his' but the Father's. He admits not even knowing when he would come back again, as only the Father knows when that time will come. Despite his supernatural prominence, Jesus does not lead a lavish lifestyle, even rejecting the devil's offer to receive earthly power and glory in exchange for worshipping him (Lk 4:6-8).

Notwithstanding his remark that he is meek, he dares to verbally criticize the religious authorities, chastising them for their hypocrisy and self-righteousness. In return, they accuse him of sedition and blasphemy, charges that lead to his execution. He accepts his death fearlessly, hardly an example of being deficient in spirit and courage as today's definition of humility states.

Probably, Jesus's most memorable display of humility (given his self-described status), is washing the feet of his disciples. The practice of washing another's feet as a symbol of graciousness and service appears to be common among the Israelites prior to Jesus's lifetime. In most instances, however, a host would provide water to the guest to wash his feet (Gen 18:4 and 19:2, 24:32, 43:24, Judg 19:21, 2 Sam 11:8), or someone of lesser status would wash the guest's feet, even if that someone is to become one of David's several wives (1 Sam 25:41). Nonetheless, within the context of how Jesus sees himself and how others regard him (teacher, prophet, Son of God, king, savior), this action was unheard of at that time.

The washing of the feet has become a Christian ritual performed on Holy Thursdays. However, when read against the backdrop of all four Gospels, it appears that Jesus's intention goes further than a mere symbol: *You call me 'teacher' and 'master,' and rightly so, for indeed I am. If I, therefore, the master and teacher, have washed your feet, you ought to wash one another's feet. I have given you a model to follow, so that as I have done for you, you should also do* (Jn 13:1-17). His teaching on humility becomes a model that he asks his followers to replicate in life. This teaching, seemingly an act of subservience, becomes symbolic of their obligation to be of service to others. In secular terms, it is akin to the French term *noblesse oblige*, i.e., *the idea that someone with power and influence should use their social position to help other people.*[4]

Jesus's meekness manifests itself in the humiliations that he willingly endures without altering his forgiving disposition. Despite thinking of himself as the Son of God, he is called a servant of the devil (Mk 3:20-22, Lk 11:15-16, Mt 10:24-25); he is rejected by his people in his native place (Mk 6:3-6, Lk 4:22-30, Mt 13:54-58) and suffers betrayal at the hands of one of his disciples; he is arrested as if he were a robber (Mk 14:48, Lk 22:52, Mt 26:55), mocked, beaten, spat on, and charged to die an excruciating death on a cross while a thief (or revolutionary) is set free in his place (Mk 15:1-37, Lk 23:1-37, Mt 26:47-27:1-50, Jn 19:1-30).[5] Once hanging from the cross, he forgives the criminal who repents at the last minute (Lk 23:39-43) as well as his executioners (Lk 23:34). In Jesus, meekness does not seem to be a personality flaw, but an incongruous sign of strength and character that he uses to upset temporal values based on egotism, power, material possessions, and social status.

There are, nonetheless, two passages that appear to contradict Jesus's humility. He allows a sinful woman to bathe his feet with a jar of *costly perfumed oil*. His disciples become indignant, not because it might be improper for a man who claims to be humble to believe that he deserves the costly oil or to be the recipient of a servile act. They complain because Jesus is not showing concern for the poor (something they learned from him). Jesus, nevertheless, objects and tells them that, since there will always be poor people (Mk 14:7, Mt 26:11, Jn 12:8), it is he who now deserves attention, because he is about to die. The scene, as depicted in Mark, Matthew, and John, probably would generate a negative public reaction today, as it appears that Jesus is focusing on his personal needs (as appropriate as they may be).

The narrative in Luke, however, adds a different dimension; it indicates that through her action the sinful woman is showing repentance and great love toward him. Realizing her motive, Jesus promptly forgives her sins (Mk 14:3-9, Lk 7:36-50, Mt 26:6-13, Jn 12:3-8). Although the passage may create a negative image, e.g., lack of concern for the poor or self-preferential treatment, there is in Jesus a certain graciousness in accepting the woman's kindness; an act of gratitude that casual readers may overlook. Today, a humble person may react with humility by graciously accepting gifts or praises that he thinks are not required or deserved.

The other passage is more puzzling because it projects features that defy postmodern secular explanations, or even Christian values. While instructing his disciples on the mission they are about to carry out, Jesus makes them aware that anyone who *loves father or mother more than me is not worthy of me, and whoever loves son or daughter more than me is not worthy of me* (Mt 10:37). The phrase *not being worthy of me* suggests that the person believes that he is more important than others and deserves more consideration. Jesus's saying that he is superior to others by birth or position (which might be true), denotes arrogance and haughtiness.[6] The passage in Luke has even a more revolting feeling that is difficult to associate with Jesus. In this instance, he tells the crowds, *if anyone comes to me without hating his father and mother, wife and children, brothers and sisters, and even his own life, he cannot be my disciple.* (Lk 14:26). Having to hate one's family as a condition to follow Jesus seems indicative of a repugnant display of power and tyrannical behavior; today's definitions of being lordly and overbearing.[7]

Only if Jesus is, or believes, he is divine, could we possibly understand his words, since he says that he is more important than humans and worthy of more consideration. Moreover, it would be his prerogative as God to dictate how people ought to treat him while expecting retribution if they reject him. Nonetheless, thrusting those words into people's ears sounds more intimidating and repulsive than being affectionate or compassionate. Although in some of his teachings Jesus's deeds are marked by compassion and forgiveness, in other passages and parables he displays features that do not reflect Christianity's image of him today.

His teachings, nonetheless, contradict today's secularized world. He calls upon his followers to be like him (*humble and meek*), except that he is not shy, fearful, or insignificant. He is gratified to receive the accolades of people who welcome him as a leader. Moreover, given his imposing personality and the titles he claims to represent, he rejects positions of power. He reminds his disciples to be of service to others, even if it calls for divesting themselves of their possessions to live modestly.

Humility is probably not the kindest attribute most people would choose today unless they are forced to be humiliated or to live in abject poverty. Today's secularized cultural values and desires are inimical to being humble, despite the fact that, in general, people dislike others' boastfulness and arrogance (there are exceptions, as seen in politics). The need to be noticed, become self-righteous and egotistic, and acquire wealth as an end or means to that end, appear to be values conditioned by a culture that, ironically, is filled with Christians. These values dictate that unpretentiousness is the equivalent of being insignificant, a feature no one seems to relish. Hence, the setting is present for contemporary psychology and sociology to examine the results of diverse types of behaviors to find out if humanity might best be served by false pride, pretentiousness, and self-centeredness than by being modest, respectful, gentler, and unpretentious. Meanwhile, inconsistencies will continue. While it might be difficult to find humility among prevailing ethos today, there is no lack of unwanted and undeserved humiliation, such as the type of behavior that the powerful forces upon the weak. It appears that Jesus's teaching on siding with the weak has eluded much of Christianity.

Notes:
1. *Merriam-Webster Dictionary, Cambridge Dictionary, Lexico/Oxford,* online, s.v. "humble," "humility."
2. *Merriam-Webster Dictionary, Cambridge Dictionary, Lexico/Oxford,* online, s.v. "humiliate," "humiliation."

3. *Merriam-Webster Dictionary, Cambridge Dictionary, Lexico/Oxford,* online, s.v. "meekness." The passage in Mt 11:29 is variously translated into English as *gentle, lowly, peaceful,* as well as *meek.* BibleHub.com, https://www.biblehub.com/matthew/11-29.htm (accessed June 21, 2009).
4. *Cambridge Dictionary,* online, s.v. "noblesse oblige."
5. Content analysis results indicate that space accorded to the crucifixion in the Gospels ranks higher than 52 other categories (Table 2, Table 3)
6. *Merriam-Webster Dictionary,* online, s.v. "arrogant, haughty."
7. *Merriam-Webster Dictionary,* online, s.v. "lordly, overbearing."

War and Peace

Warfare has been a constant aspect of human life since prehistoric times.[1] While deadly events, such as plagues, volcanic eruptions, floods, and earthquakes, have occurred, and still do, the major difference is that in warfare human behavior is responsible for the devastation that these conflicts create. The killing and maiming that occur in armed conflicts are horrific, denoting the dispensation of the value of human life. Additionally, the havoc it causes to the morals and ethics of the international system and the political and social fabric of nations; the continued existential threats of a nuclear apocalypse; and the lingering residue of hatred it leaves among peoples, often for generations, may qualify warfare as a willfully caused human pestilence. Table 2 indicates that Jesus speaks at length about war and peace. Nonetheless, his use of these terms does not constitute a treatise in political theory or international relations, and incongruences within his teachings make their understanding difficult.

Jesus is Surrounded by Political Conflict

Luke writes in his Gospel that Jesus is a precocious young boy; he eludes his parents for days and goes into a synagogue, sits among the teachers to listen to them and ask questions, *and all who heard him were astounded at his understanding and his answers* (Lk 2:46-47). Nothing has surfaced (yet) that would tell us how Jesus spends his years from that time on into adulthood. However, the Gospels indicate that Jesus acquires a great deal of knowledge about the Jewish religion and the circumstances confronting the Jewish people. The Gospels portray Jesus at the age of thirty years as an exceptionally intelligent person who seems well aware of his purpose in life. The way he quotes Mosaic Law and confronts the sinful behavior of the religious authorities, his rhetorical skills and charismatic attitude that attracts him, not only to his disciples but to the many who follow and pursue him to learn about God, and ultimately, the wondrous deeds that cast him as a prophet, a teacher, the Messiah, a savior, Israel's redeemer, and the Son of God.

Although it appears that he does not travel extensively outside his native region, he likely learns about other nearby cultures, including the Hellenistic period and Alexander's warring conquests. Just by reading the Jewish Bible, he would have understood the history of Israel's wars with numerous enemies that sought its destruction; among them, the Egyptians, the Amalekites, the Edomites, the Amorites, the Canaanites, the Syrians, the Moabites, the Arameans, the Ammonites, the

Philistines, the Assyrians, the Babylonians, and the Persians.[2] Jesus also would have noticed that in the Old Testament God is a warrior, and the peace he promises his people comes through the annihilation of their enemies (Lev 26:6-8, Deut 20:10-12). Jesus could not have been uninformed of the expansion and domination of the Roman Empire under which he lived most of his life. Indeed, he could not have ignored the specter of political violence, the result of Roman and Jewish oppression from which the Jewish people hoped to see themselves freed.

Numerous passages in the Gospels denote the profound desire for earthly peace the Israelites had always wished for, largely because of the promises God makes to Abraham. God fiercely combats the high and mighty, dethrones evil rulers, lifts the low, and fills the hungry while sending the rich empty as he saves Israel from its enemies and guides its people toward peace (Lk 1:49-54, 68-79). When Jesus is born, a multitude in heaven praises God and wishes peace on earth *to those on whom his favor rests*, awkwardly suggesting that peace is a gift that God might not provide to everyone (Lk 2:10-14). Moreover, the righteous see in Jesus the much-awaited temporal redeemer of Israel and Jerusalem (Lk 2:29-30, 36-38, 24:21, Mk 15:43, Lk 23:51), although the Gospels do not indicate the precise means Jesus is going to utilize to attain the peace that has eluded the Jewish people for generations.

Jesus's life and death, nonetheless, would prove to be a disappointment to the Jewish people. As Satan rules the world (Jn 12:31, 14:30, 16:11), Jesus's condemnation and personal victory over the evil one would not be enough to bring an end to the sinful effects of warfare. He leaves the earth very much in the same conditions as when he was alive. Far from advancing peace, Jesus tells his disciples that they will find *trouble in the world,* and somehow, they will have to face it (Jn 16:32-33). He even issues an enigmatic prediction musing over the destruction that awaits Jerusalem, the Jewish people, and possibly his followers too. The blame, however, lies not with him, he would say, but with those who refuse to recognize him as someone who truly wishes peace. A passage in Luke reveals Jesus's cause-effect relation on war:

> *If this day you only knew what makes for peace—but now it is hidden from your eyes. For the days are coming upon you when your enemies will raise a palisade against you; they will encircle you and hem you in on all sides. They will smash you to the ground and your children within you, and they will not leave one stone upon another within you because you did not recognize the time of your visitation (Lk 19:41-44).*

At the time, these words were meant only for the Israelites. Since then, and given the supposed timeless nature of the Gospels, they likely remain valid today. Whether his teachings are sufficient to create an era of peace is a different question.

Jesus's Peace

The type of peace Jesus offers is not the equivalent of modern-day social and political conflict resolution, diplomacy, balances of power through strategic alliances, or adherence to international laws.[3] The peace he offers relies on the acceptance of his teachings and belief in him. This peace consists of an internal serenity based on the certainty that the Father is present so that no matter what happens in this life, Jesus's followers can seek solace because he will be with them *until the end of the age* (Mt 28:20). He speaks about wars among nations in a casual manner as events he expects will happen and tells his disciples no to be alarmed (Lk 21:9, Mt 24:6). Thus, his words seem to be inconsequential to the eradication of warfare.

There are attestations throughout the texts that indicate that Jesus is a peaceful man. He constantly wishes peace to his disciples when he greets them (Lk 24:36, Jn 20:19-21, 20:26), and he sends them into the world to teach others about the kingdom of God with instructions to wish peace to the households they visit (Lk 10:4-5, Mt 10:12-13). The only time he exhibits a mild degree of violence occurs when he harasses the merchants and money changers on the outskirts of the temple, perhaps because he believes that the house of God is off-limits to commercial activity.[4] However, he surrenders to his captors and rejects violence against them, even averting a cosmic war between his celestial attendants and the Romans (Jn 18:36).

The terms *peace, consolation,* or *redemption,* whenever they appear associated with Jesus in the Gospels, suggest a sincere wish for personal tranquility or serenity, a life freed from inner turmoil (Jn 14:27) along with physical security, all amid social conflicts, persecutions, and wars. He associates peace with the forgiveness of sins and the absence of physical or emotional affliction. Jesus, however, does not assume the role of a politician or a diplomat who seeks to mediate conflicts; on the contrary, he contributes to divisiveness (Mt 10:34-38). His role is to teach his followers how to remain calm and live the faith in a hostile environment permeated by oppression, warfare, and injustice.

The peace he offers is no mere greeting. The equivalent Jewish term for peace, *shalom,* is used as a simple *hello* as well as a form to wish others well. In Jesus, however, the term seems to have a special connotation. As he wishes peace to his disciples, he says that it is *his* peace that he is offering (*my peace I give to you*), and he adds, *not as the world gives, do I give it to you.* He does not say how his peace offer is different from our understanding of the term, but when he continues saying, *do not let your hearts be troubled or afraid* (Jn 14:27), it may be inferred that his peace includes a supernatural element; a comforting acceptance to human events similar to how he consents to his crucifixion. He seems to be saying, 'I have accomplished what I came to do; I am not alone, and now I am returning to the Father' (Jn 14:1-4, 12, 16:5, 10, 17, 16:28-32). That he believes his peace is special may be seen in the condemnation he issues to the ungrateful who refuse it: his disciples are to *go outside that house or town and shake the dust from your feet*, adding that horrific punishment would befall these towns (Lk 10:1-12, Mt 10:12-15).

Jesus's peace projects an active self-resignation to events. That is, this peace entails his followers' acceptance of his commandment to love one another. However, it has little, if anything to do with peace as the absence of warfare. He considers peace a supernatural gift that might or might not be extended to everyone. Additionally, it is interesting that when Jesus enters triumphantly into Jerusalem, he is welcomed by the crowds chanting *blessed is the king who comes in the name of the Lord; peace in heaven and glory in the highest* (Lk 19:36-38). While the chant may or may not allude to a supernatural messiah, this time it does not proclaim peace on earth. His peace appears even more puzzling in a metaphor in Mark in which Jesus suggests to his disciples to keep salt in themselves to have peace with one another. Salt is known as a cleansing and healing agent, and *being salted with fire,* as Jesus recommends (Mk 9:49-50), is similar to pouring it over an open wound to heal it; not a pleasurable feeling, although perhaps it alludes to the sacrificial cost of his type of peace.

Is Jesus the Prince of Peace?

Throughout his teachings, Jesus is aware of the social, religious, and political conditions that surround him. He refers to warfare, insurrections, and persecutions as a reality that is most destructive and likely inimical to the kingdom of God. Yet he is resigned that these acts will continue to happen (Lk 19:43-44, 21:8-11, Mt 5:1-12, 24:5-11). He approaches socio-political conflict indirectly, at best, by focusing on repentance for one's sins and renewal or rebirth of the heart and the mind. His formula, exhorting love of neighbor and praying for one's enemy is the best antidote to human conflict, provided it works.

Jesus's teachings, however, are unable to dissuade either the Israelites or future Christian generations from relying on military power. Once Christians are given religious, political, and military recognition by Emperor Constantine and his successors, they choose to retain the tools of power that accompany this recognition, including waging warfare.[5]

Jesus's approach to peace, preceded by John the Baptist, is based on repentance and rebirth and is meant to serve primarily as the path to the believer's eternal salvation (Lk 1:15-17); peace on earth, defined as the absence of socio-political conflict, is secondary and supposedly comes as the result of the world's recognition of his teachings and belief in him. Indeed, not only does Jesus expect his followers will face socio-political and religious conflict; he will be a major source of it.

Focusing only on personal conversion (as significant as it may be) lessens the importance to confront warfare at the social and political levels, particularly if people refuse to repent and convert. The Gospels' use of the terms *war* and *peace*, and Jesus's seeming indifference to political conflict, tend to support this view, given that he does not denounce or mediate Roman or Jewish oppression of his people. Moreover, his literal test of personal loyalty to hate mother, father, wife, children, brothers, and sisters to be worthy of him (Lk 14:26); his remark that his mission is not to establish peace on the earth, but division; and his desire to set the world on fire, wishing it were already blazing (Lk 12:49-53), regardless of what he meant at the time, would be reminiscent of Al-Qaeda or ISIS leaders, and not the Jesus that is preached in the churches. Ironically, the man who wishes to divide and set the world on fire eventually becomes known as the Prince of Peace.

Another of Jesus's enigmatic sayings point to his views on conflict: *from the days of John the Baptist until now, the kingdom of heaven suffers violence, and the violent are taking it by force* (Mt 11:12, Lk 16-16). The passage has been the subject of various interpretations, as it may be understood both as a desire for conflict or to its inevitability.[6] He refers to wars and insurrections as expected calamities for which people ought not to be alarmed, *for such things must happen first* (Mk 13:5-13, Lk 21:8-10, Mt 24:4-14). Presenting himself as the embodiment of truth, it seems inevitable that Jesus's words would ruffle the world's feathers.

The Beatitudes, perhaps Jesus's most concise example of Christian behavior, provide a mixture of consistency and incongruency. He praises the meek, those that hunger for justice, the poor, and those who are persecuted. Nonetheless, by indicating they shall receive their rewards in heaven, he is acquiescing to crucial root causes of war, such as poverty, hunger, and injustice. At the same time, he praises the merciful, the righteous, and the peacemakers, whom he calls *children of God* (Mt 5:1-12, Lk 6:20-23). It is relevant to ask, if Jesus intends to set the world on fire and bring about division, in addition to the evil that the Satan and his followers create, is it possible for peacemakers to truly make a difference in the world? Or is peacemaking a personal exercise in futility that, nonetheless, will be rewarded in heaven? It appears as if his teaching maxim may well have been, *have faith in me, apply my teachings, and seek peace through division.*

Jesus indicates that for his peace to be attained it is essential to forgive one's enemies. Forgiveness of enemies, however, requires a different explanation; one that Jesus does not provide. Jesus may be referring to the type of forgiveness that is possible once evildoers recognize their wrongdoing, otherwise forgiveness becomes a form of appeasement that leads to further aggression. Whether this is what Jesus implies is difficult to say. His Parable of the Weeds Among the Wheat strongly suggests that, until Judgment Day, the righteous have to tolerate social and political conflict for fear that innocent lives may perish while confronting evil (Mt 13:24-30).[7] This proposition is undeniably suicidal and conducive to the end of God's creation. Additionally, Jesus's literal version of forgiveness of enemies is a complete reversal of God's actions. The Old Testament indicates that God averts the destruction of Israel through warfare against its enemies. Hence, either Jesus once again contradicts the Father, or he is given *carte blanche* to amend God's past behavior.

Does Jesus Tolerate Killing?

It cannot be said, however, that Jesus stands for wanton killing. According to content analysis results, murder ranks among the highest of sins he outlines in his teachings. What then are non-Christians, or even Christians themselves, supposed to learn in the Gospels about war and peace? If Jesus realizes that warfare seems inevitable, does he provide a clear path toward a Christian code of ethics on peace and warfare? A literal understanding of the texts suggests that Jesus's followers are to be merciful, compassionate, just toward others, and bring about peace on earth to the best of their abilities. His teachings point to two variants, interpersonal peace, e.g., having good relationships with others in proximity as the product of love and forgiveness (interpersonal peace), and a serene and blissful life amidst the world being on fire (internal peace).

There are additional incongruences in the type of peace Jesus wishes. The commandment to love one's neighbor presumably entails the moral responsibility to defend those who are being maliciously attacked and murdered, including loved ones. This is not, however, what Jesus recommends. Thus, Jesus's apparent indifference to temporal warfare (since his mission relates primarily to eternal salvation), along with the realization that killing is incompatible with God's kingdom, led his followers hundreds of years later to distance themselves from his teachings and establish norms that would justify warfare. Writing during the fourth century, Ambrose, one of the Fathers of the Church, paraphrased Jesus's commandment saying, *he who does not keep harm off a friend, if he can, is as much in fault as he who causes it.*[8] Eventually, the writings of the Fathers of the Church were codified into what is known today as the Doctrine of Just War. Whether the doctrine has been or not effective lies in the eyes of the beholder. It may be surmised that Christianity's influence on the issue has been disappointing given the excesses seen throughout history. On the other hand, it is difficult to know how much destruction has been averted because of it; these Christian roots are embodied today in international laws in the United Nations Charter; their purpose being to minimize warfare.[9]

If it is accepted that the Just doctrine on warfare is valid, it suggests that Christians may have saved the temporal world from oblivion (at least for the time being) first by ignoring then reformulating Jesus's teachings. His views on war and peace evoked a dilemma that Christianity has not been able to solve, as a clever observer wrote one century ago:

> *If we accept the spirit of Jesus's utterances as final, as orthodox Christianity has always proposed to do, then the ethical sanctions for war that have been built up within historical Christianity are false and should be repudiated. On the other hand, if it be granted that institutionalized Christianity's moral sanctions for war are valid and meet the approval of the best men of every age, including the hosts of Christian men who are enlisting in the present great crusade to make the world safer for democracy, then we must be honest with*

ourselves and say that the moral ideal cherished by Jesus and his immediate followers, an ideal in which ... war had no place, cannot be considered binding upon the consciences of men under all conditions and under every age.[10]

The predicament Christians must confront today suggest that they must choose between the word of God as divine revelation and its human interpretations. The historical consequences are portentous. This is not to say that Jesus's teachings on war and peace are clear or that they do not conflict with his love of neighbor commandment. Nonetheless, his attitude denotes a preference for non-involvement in warfare, in which case his teachings would not only seem to justify the atrocities that humans have committed toward each other throughout history; they would suggest too, that proper Christian morals call for an internal and serene resignation to conflict on earth while awaiting real peace that can only be found in heaven.[11]

Notes:

1. Whether warfare occurred prior to recorded history seems to be open-ended; archeological findings point to physical conflicts going as far back as nine to ten thousand years ago. Bret Stetka, "Prehistoric Carnage Site Is Evidence of Earliest Warfare," *Scientific American,* January 22, 2016, https://www.scientificamerican.com/article/prehistoric-carnage-site-is-evidence-of-earliest-warfare/ (accessed July 25, 2020).

2. *BibleGateway.com.* www.biblegateway.com/resources/dictionary-of-bible-themes/8728-enemies-Israel-Judah (accessed December 9, 2019).

3. Interestingly, Jesus is no stranger to military strategy. While preaching on the wisdom of following his teachings, he relies on a metaphor about a king who would not dare march into battle without first knowing if he has enough troops to face the enemy (Lk 14:28-32).

4. The activities of both merchants and money changers were legitimate since they supplied the material resources (animals and currency exchange) that worshippers needed in their sacrifices and offerings. It is also said that the reason Jesus undertakes this action was to question the authority of the religious leaders. NEs' note, Matthew 21:12-17. The zeal depicted in the texts suggests (at least to me) that Jesus was angered by actions that desecrated the Temple.

5. It may be said too, that religious-political responsibilities emanating from Paul's view of political authority, and existential matters, e.g. the physical security of the Church, compel the papacy to accept military power.

6. The saying is typical of Jesus's mystifying personality that unnecessarily allows for several interpretations. NEs note that its meaning is difficult to decipher, suggesting that *opponents of Jesus are trying to prevent people from accepting the kingdom and to snatch it away from those who have received it.* Matthew 11:12. On the other hand, the *Evangelical Heritage Version* translates the saying as *the kingdom of heaven has been advancing forcefully and forceful people are seizing it,* suggesting a clash between a Jesus's brigade and others that oppose it. Nonetheless, the historical record does not indicate that Jesus proposes any type of religious or political uprising. If anything, his peaceful surrender to the religious authorities is evidence of the opposite.

7. NEs' note, Mt 13:24-30.

8. Ambrose of Milan, *On the Duties of the Clergy,* Book 1, chapter 36, par 179, http://www.documentacatholicaomnia.eu/03d/0339-0397,_Ambrosius,_De_Officiis_Ministrorum_Libri_Tres_[Schaff],_EN.pdf (accessed December 18, 2019).

9. Main contributors to the Just War Doctrine include Ambrose, and Augustine in the fourth century, Aquinas in the thirteenth century, Vitoria and Suárez in the sixteenth century, and Protestant philosophers Grotius and Pufendorf in the seventeenth century.

10. John M. Mecklin, "The War and the Dilemma of the Christian Ethic." *The American Journal of Theology,* vol. 23, no. 1, 1919, pp. 14–40. *JSTOR,* www.jstor.org/stable/3155383 (accessed on December 12, 2019).

11. Pope Francis's encyclical, *Fratelli Tutti – On Fraternity and Social Friendship,* questions the long-standing Just War Doctrine as originally formulated by St Augustine. Franciscus, *Fratelli Tutti – On Fraternity and Social Friendship,* 258, (Assisi: October 3, 2020), http://www.vatican.va/content/francesco/en/encyclicals/documents/papa-francesco_20201003_enciclica-fratelli-tutti.html (accessed October 6, 2020). It is not clear whether his words amount to complete rejection. If Francis is suggesting a rejection of the doctrine without replacing or refining it, it may be taken as his fervent desire to avoid warfare. He is correct in his critique of the Just War Doctrine—that nations are disguising their intentions by hiding behind moral rationalizations to go to war and calling them *just.* Nonetheless, historically, the most fervent desires and prayers have failed to eradicate warfare, and there is nothing on the horizon that may be expected to change this panorama. Given that there is certain soundness to the doctrine, insisting on its criteria along with zealous opposition to those that disingenuously seek to disguise evil may be a rational alternative. This approach would be no different than what Christian churches rely on today to educate their followers on sinfulness. Nonetheless, since there is no unity among Christians, much less on issues of warfare, Christian churches have been reluctant to openly condemn governments that violate the doctrine and to organize an energetic opposition to illegal and immoral warfare. At the same time, it is to be observed that even Catholic prelates continue to demonstrate ignorance of their own teachings. In their almost silent critique of the American invasion of Iraq in 2003, the American bishops referred to the planned actions of the US Government as being preemptive, despite sound reasons that would have characterized the actions that were going to be taken as a preventive attack, i.e., an immoral and illegal war. United States Conference of Catholic Bishops, "Statement on Iraq, 2002," November 13, 2002, (2nd par), https://www.usccb.org/resources/statement-iraq-2002 (accessed October 6, 2020).

Unity

Calling himself in John's Gospel *the light of the world* (Jn 8:12); *the resurrection and the life* (Jn 11:25); *the way and the truth and the life* (Jn 14:6); and *the true vine* (Jn 15:1), Jesus portrays himself as the embodiment of absolute truth. In the synoptics, he does not characterize himself that boldly, yet his teachings are no less authoritative. There are no shades of gray in his sayings; everything seems to be black and white. His teachings on morals and his actions reveal that there can be no other truths besides his own. He indicates he is God's messenger transmitting to the world simply what the Father (the only true absolute and eternal god) has asked him to say (Jn 12:49-50).

Mainstream Christian doctrine teaches that Jesus's redemption and offer of salvation extend to all humankind (or to many or some), and all four gospels attest to his universal mission: *Go into the whole world and proclaim the gospel to every creature* (Mk 16:15, Lk 24:47, Mt 28:19-20, Jn 20:21-23). Given his words, it would be reasonable to conclude that Jesus desires that there be unity among his followers. To assert that his truth and his way can be interpreted in many ways, e.g., various orthodoxies, would be absurd. His saying, *I have other sheep that do not belong to this fold; these also I must lead, and they will hear my voice, and there will be one flock, one shepherd* (Jn 10:16), encapsulates his thorough desire for all sheep to be united under his teachings. Despite his wishes, Jesus realizes that not everyone might accept him, even though their refusal carries a heavy penalty: *whoever believes and is baptized will be saved; whoever does not believe will be condemned* (Mk 16:16, Jn 10:26, 15:6, 20:23).

The *unity* category is ranked as less significant according to content analysis results in Table 2, suggesting a disconnect with Jesus's stated objectives. Is it possible that Jesus was not that concerned with unity of belief and behavior, i.e., orthodoxy and orthopraxis? Ironically, lack of clarity and the difficulty in understanding some of his teachings (along with ill will and self-righteousness among Christians) seem responsible for Christianity's divisiveness.

Accepting the premise that Jesus's mission is to announce and lead the kingdom of God, his desire for unity becomes indispensable. Within this context, he issues a fateful warning, that while appearing to refute the scribes' contention that he takes orders from Satan, has direct relevance to the kingdom of God: *if a kingdom is divided against itself, that kingdom cannot stand; and if a house is divided against itself, that house will not be able to stand* (Mk 3:24-25, Lk 11:17, Mt 12:25). The message is powerful, logical, and unambiguous, and would appear to be germane to Christianity today. Adding to his concern for discord, Jesus even warns that impostors will come in his name attempting to deceive many; *do not follow them,* he tells his disciples (Mk 13:5-6, Lk 21:7-8, Mt 24:4-5, 11, 24), indicating that there is only one true messiah.

A reasonable disposition on Jesus's part to ensure unity is to assign someone to succeed him on earth, akin to a modern CEO of a major corporation or the head of a political party; someone responsible for keeping the flock together. Toward this end, he appears to name Peter as the head of his group (Mt 16:15-19), an assignation that, as history records, does not become authoritative until centuries later despite overt signals of his leadership role in the Gospels.[1]

Moreover, following his resurrection Jesus appears to confirm his decision by telling Peter three times to look after his sheep (Jn 21:15-17), a persuasive symbolic request indicating leadership. He even prays to the Father for unity among his disciples, *so that they may be one just as we are* (Jn 17:11), and for *those who will believe in me through their word, so that they may all be one* (Jn 17:20-21). Awkwardly, at some point, he says that he does not pray for the world, however; only for his disciples (Jn 17:9). Nonetheless, his insistence on the need for unity seems logical and evident. If his mission is to initiate a religious movement (the kingdom of God), its continuation requires a successor. This view applies to almost every single major temporal institution, both governmental and private.

Jesus's desire to keep the flock together fails despite his prayers to the Father. He even laments the many times God *yearned to gather* his people *together as a hen gathers her brood under her wings*. Since unity does not prevail among the Jewish people, Jerusalem becomes desolate (Lk 13:34-35). Christian divisiveness seems to follow the same direction. Have Christians become akin to the Israelite people that Jesus reprimanded?

Interestingly, as has been observed in previous sections, there are sufficient reasons that indicate that Jesus himself contributes to division. Although the authors of the Gospels portray Jesus as someone that speaks plainly, there are instances in which his sayings are not clearly understood, likely a reason for which various interpretations exist on diverse issues that have impeded Christian unity. He speaks in parables, some of which are meant to confuse while others are difficult to decipher. Some of his teachings seem to be contradicted by other sayings, and other teachings are simply incomprehensible. Supposedly, Jesus would want his teachings to be accepted, yet his mysterious ways of addressing even his disciples, and his lack of explanation regarding important themes, far from contributing to unity, reveal existing cracks within the kingdom of God. Thus, the lack of clarity in the texts contributes to creating disunity. As a result, each Christian denomination pretends that it can explain God's word better than Jesus himself. Such behavior is an embarrassment to the faith; Christian disunity reveals that his followers' claims that Jesus embodies the absolute truth is ludicrous.

Some may claim that Jesus contradicts himself by insisting that he wants to establish division into the world (Lk 12:51-53, Mt 10:34-36). The division Jesus refers to, however, is not among his initial followers; that much has been already established, although non-Christians may not necessarily interpret his words in the same manner as Christians do. Instead, setting the world on fire and creating havoc are the results he expects when others reject his teachings because they clash with the ways of the world. Somehow, it appears that the ways of the world have penetrated his followers, as they find themselves opposing each other. Their acrimonious dissent is seen today in their theological disputations and across socio-political and economic ideologies that vie to represent Christian values.

It appears incontrovertible that Jesus's teachings have two dimensions, the earthly or temporal and the spiritual. The former relates to social conduct, i.e., external behavior toward others, while the latter pertains to an internal disposition addressing the spiritual realm. Although we might not be able to easily ascertain one's internal disposition, overt human behavior is far easier to gauge and record. Furthermore, despite the view suggesting that Jesus is only concerned with individual behavior as the means to attain eternal salvation, it is difficult to deny the proposition that his teachings, by necessity, find their ultimate expression in society's social, political, cultural, and economic dimensions (as disparate as they seem to be). It is here where Christians clash the most, without realizing or caring that their opposing views reflect negatively on the teacher. This divisiveness is evidence that Christians' inability to attain unity has resulted in the faith's failure to set the world on fire à la Jesus.

There is one last question: besides his disciples, who does Jesus wishes to unite? The Gospels indicate that God sends his Messiah only to the Jewish people (Lk 2:11, Mt 2:6, 10:5-6, 15:24, Jn 1:11). Nonetheless, once baptized, Jesus begins his mission by recruiting a dozen men and (supposedly) instructs them to spread his teachings throughout the entire world. This world is made up almost entirely of Gentiles (non-Jews), whom Jesus at times does not seem to regard highly since they are the ones that will mock him and crucify him (Mk 10:33, Lk 18:32, Mt 20:19). He even refers to Gentiles pejoratively comparing them to tax collectors the Jewish people dislike intensely (Mt 18:17). Additionally, he belittles pagans, a term that is rarely used in the

Gospels, to denote idolaters that worship false gods (Mt 5:47, 6:7 6:32). Is Jesus aware that these pagans are the type of people he might be interested in gathering into his fold? Still, he instructs his disciples not to go into *pagan territory* (Mt 10:5), but only to the *lost sheep of the house of Israel* (Mt 10:6).

Since episodes in the Gospels are not often written in chronological order, there appears to be a contradiction regarding whom Jesus is seeking to unite; at times it is the Jewish people, at other times it is the Gentile and or the pagan world. There are several passages, including parables, suggesting that unity might include anyone who believes or eventually will believe in him or accept his teachings.

A most unique saying occurs in Matthew in which Jesus insinuates that the moment will come when *the times of the Gentiles are fulfilled* (Mt 21:24). The precise meaning of this passage lends itself to speculation. However, there is in the Book of Tobit (not among the best known in the Old Testament and excluded from the Protestant Bible) a passage indicating that after the land of Israel becomes desolate and burned, God will have mercy and rebuild Israel, after which *all the nations of the world will turn and reverence God in truth; all will cast away their idols, which have deceitfully led them into error* (Tob 14:6-8).

That the term *all the nations* is widely used in the Old Testament (approximately 159xt), referring to nations on earth, is exceptional in light that the texts represent the Jewish version of creation as well as the history of the Israelite people. In the New Testament, the phrase appears only 14xt.[2] The question may be raised whether the concept of *nations* includes the world that remained unknown to the Jewish people at the time the Old Testament was written as well as the world as we know it nowadays. Today's world, replete with non-Christian faiths and philosophies, is far more pluralistic (and relativistic) than ever before. Are these the *other sheep* that Jesus seeks to bring into his fold? Presuming they are, the task ahead is likely to remain elusive in the coming centuries; its first obstacle being the unity that Jesus may have wanted for his church.

Notes:
1. The name Peter appears 103xt in all four Gospels (without counting pronouns that reference him). No one, except for Jesus, whose name appears 643xt, is so publicly displayed in the texts. If Jesus is the main character in the Gospels (according to the numbers), Peter is clearly the second most important person.
2. *BibleGateway.com*.

Mystery in the Gospels

The term *mystery* aptly characterizes humanity's understanding of God. Other than our post-modern culture's avid desire to learn how and why the cosmos was created, nothing puzzles the human imagination more than knowing whether God exists, what he (she or it) is like, and what his purpose is in the creation of humankind.

Defined as something that cannot be fully understood and is beyond our current understanding, either because it is secretive or inexplicable,[1] *mystery* is a favorite and unavoidable word used in Christianity to denote that which God, and Jesus, leave unexplained regarding the kingdom of God.[2] The term seldom appears in the scriptures (depending on the English version), even though its reality is ascertained in the texts. Despite supposed divine revelation through scriptures, and other less germane and utterly subjective events (apparitions and personal visions or prophecies), God remains a mystery. This is problematic at a time when the Christian faith (as well as other religions) is becoming less relevant in secularized societies.

It is all too clear that humans (even righteous ones) are not clever enough to decipher God's message, while God, being aware of human limitations, fails or is unwilling to communicate with humans in a more specific or objective manner that we all can understand. Although it would not be presumptuous for humanity to attempt to understand that which embodies the infinite, it must be stated that, according to the scriptures, it is God who, after all, wishes to make himself known to his creatures.

Although it is not clear in Genesis, it is possible that in the Garden of Eden Adam and Eve may have seen God's face while enjoying friendly conversations. Nonetheless, the scriptures indicate that following their disobedience of God's directive, God has chosen to remain mysterious, seemingly to penalize humanity for the sins of their foreparents. But then, even Genesis and Exodus tell us that God refused to show his face (except perhaps to Moses, Ex 33:11) or communicate more openly with his creatures, except for holding non-visual talks with specific persons (Noah, Abraham, David, Solomon, Elijah, Job, Ezekiel, Jonah, Zechariah). According to the Gospels, not even Jesus holds face-to-face conversations with God, and God's audible remarks to Jesus occur only three times (Mk 1:11, Lk 3:22, Mt 3:17, first time, Mt 17:5, second time, Jn 12:28, third time).

Why is God so mysterious? If God rules human conduct, and it is important for him to convey that he is the Lord, transparency is vital. Presuming that understanding and knowing are basic elements of human behavior, it is difficult to behave righteously if, amid relativism, in which a variety of moral truths vie for legitimacy, humans must decide for themselves what is right and wrong. Hence, it appears that God's mysterious ways, far from contributing to righteousness, become a formula for confusion and moral relativism.

The only way to unravel a mystery is to acquire additional information. But in the case of getting to *know* God, the scriptures simply do not suffice because, despite the goodwill of many people, the texts, particularly the Gospels, are riddled with inconsistencies and teachings that are either archaic or simply difficult to understand or to accept. This reality places the Christian faith at risk of becoming inconsequential. Ironically, although part of Jesus's mission was to announce and make visible the kingdom of God, he was not cooperative, and even collaborated with God's desire to remain mysterious.

This category ranks low because we are only focusing on words and specific passages suggesting mystery. Nonetheless, if we were to include other "mysterious" categories such as Miracles, Holy Spirit, Divine Providence, Predestination,

Redemption, Devil, Grace, Jesus's Resurrection, and Supernatural Occurrences, among others, it would become the second or third highest after Righteousness.

Jesus's Teaching Style

At times, Jesus indicates that he prefers transparency over secrecy. He tells his disciples that a lamp is not to be placed under a bed but on a lampstand so that it would cast light; that *there is nothing hidden that will not become visible, and nothing secret that will not be known and come to light* (Lk 8:16-17 12:2-3, Mk 4:21-22, Mt 10:26-27). Although the saying appears in different contexts in the synoptics, it suggests that Jesus will not be more forthcoming, and that in the meantime part of God's truth will remain hidden.

It is Jesus who succinctly indicates the mysterious character of God's kingdom when he refers to *the mysteries of the kingdom of God* (Mk 4:11, Lk 8:10, Mt 13:11). Somewhat bewildering, in that same passage Jesus acknowledges that not everyone is entitled to know about God. He even praises God for keeping the mysteries of the kingdom hidden *from the wise and the learned* and reveal them only to the *childlike* (Lk 10:21, Mt 11:25). The remarks are troublesome, as we are left with the task of identifying who the wise, the learned and the childlike are, and having further to clarify that today many childlike people are religiously wise and learned, e.g., theologians, popes, bishops, rabbis, imams, Buddhist priests, and philosophers.

Even more disconcerting, Jesus acknowledges the exclusivity of God's kingdom by stating that no one knows God *except anyone to whom the Son wishes to reveal him* (Lk 10:22, Mt 11:27), suggesting the existence of a secretive circle to which most of humanity (or all of it) is not invited. As if the above statement is not confusing enough, we read that God himself hardens the heart of others to make it difficult for them to understand and be saved (Mk 4:11-12, Lk 8:10, Jn 12:40). Given that most of the world's population is not Christian, Jesus's remarks appear to concede not only the mysterious character of God's kingdom but God's perplexing behavior toward his many creatures that might be eager to know him.

Jesus is quite explicit when he tells his disciples that when it comes to understanding the mysteries of the kingdom there are several classes of people. In addition to the child-like and the wise and the learned, there are those he favors by confiding in them and those whom he does not. For example, he teaches the crowds in the form of parables, stories that enclose truths he wishes to impart. Parables are supposed to make the listener (or reader) think so that the teaching is understood and retained. But in the Gospels parables are a two-edged sword; while they deliver the teaching, they are also used to obfuscate and conceal. It is within this context that Jesus remarks to his disciples,

> *[T]he mystery of the kingdom of God has been granted to you. But to those outside everything comes in parables, so that 'they may look and see but not*

perceive, and hear and listen but not understand, in order that they may not be converted and be forgiven (Mk 4:11-12, Lk 8:9-10, Mt 13:10-15).

It appears that Jesus teaches the crowds in parables to fulfill a prophecy, supposedly from Isaiah (it stems from Psalm 78:2),[3] suggesting that his role is to unveil that which has *lain hidden from the foundation of the world* (Mt 13:34-35). Nonetheless, the above citation suggests that unveiling mysteries is not what Jesus does. Biblical experts agree that Jesus's approach is *enigmatic,* largely because he treats the disbelieving crowd differently.[4]

At one point his disciples acknowledge understanding three brief parables about the kingdom of heaven (Mt 13:44-51) that Jesus offers without further explanation. Immediately thereafter, they fail to comprehend the parable Jesus uses to defy the tradition of the elders (Mt 15:10-17). Nor his disciples can understand (until after the resurrection) his welcoming into Jerusalem as a king (Jn 12:12-16). Moreover, nothing is said in the Gospels about the disciples' reaction to Jesus's most enigmatic words. During his last supper, he expresses his desire to be remembered by having his followers eat his flesh and drink his blood. Additionally, despite Jesus informs his disciples (without further explanation) about his passion and resurrection on three instances, they fail to understand and are afraid to ask (Mk 8:31-33, 9:31-32, Lk 9:22, 44-45, 18:31-34, Mt 16:21-23, 17:22-23, 20:17-19, Jn 20:1-9). They also fail to apprehend the mysteries of the Parousia (that even Paul misconstrues), or the existence of the Holy Spirit, about whom his disciples do not even inquire.

The mysteries surrounding Jesus appear to trouble his disciples. They urge him to attend the Feast of the Tabernacles and manifest himself to the world; indeed, a sensible request. Although he attends the event, he does it, *not openly but [as it were] in secret* (Jn 7:2-4, 10). Not understanding Jesus's behavior one of his disciples finally asks him why he chooses to reveal himself to them but not to the world. This would be among the most consequential questions that we might want to ask Jesus today. Yet, his answer has little if any bearing to the question, indicating that it will be up to the Holy Spirit to teach them and remind them of all he has taught them (Jn 14:22-27). Hence, he remains mysterious even to his disciples.

Nonetheless, they are not the only ones who fail to grasp Jesus. Nicodemus, a member of the Sanhedrin and follower of Jesus, fails to understand Jesus's mystifying explanation about the need to be *born from above* to enter the kingdom of God (Jn 3:1-10). Moreover, Jesus cannot persuade the Jewish authorities who continue to reject him, largely because they cannot understand that he (a human being) comes from God who sends him to reveal God's truths (Jn 8;39-44). These passages from the Gospels indicate that Jesus's pedagogical approach was not effective at the time. Instead, it contributed to the creation of a Jesus mystique that can only be apprehended (by some) through faith. The mystery surrounding his person and his explanations about God has not been persuasive enough to reach the billions of people of other faiths or the highly educated that make up a sizable percentage of the population in post-modern secular society.

Jesus tells the Jewish authorities that he has *always spoken publicly to the world ... and in secret I have said nothing* (Jn 18:19-20). Nonetheless, the gospels narrate countless episodes in which Jesus meets privately with his disciples. Even Mark acknowledges that while Jesus only speaks to the crowds in parables, *to his own disciples he explained everything in private* (Mk 4:34). The shroud of mystery that Jesus tosses over God and his kingdom seemingly restricts human knowledge, making it more difficult to accept God. Disturbingly, Jesus proceeds to convict the world for not accepting him (Jn 16:8-11) and to suggest that Jerusalem will be punished for not recognizing his visitation (Lk 19:41-44). Are they to blame?

Although Jesus indicates that he fully explains the mystery of the kingdom of God to his disciples, it is obvious that he does not; otherwise, there would be no more mysteries. Additionally, it must be noted that his disciples (as well as the crowds) often do not understand his teachings, as seen in those instances in which he indicates that their inability to comprehend is due to their hard-heartedness (Mk 4:13, 6:52, 7:19, 8:14-21, 8:31-33, 9:31-32, Lk 9:44-45, 18:31-34, 19:41-44, Mt 13:10-15, 13:18, 16:5-12, 21-23, Jn 20:1-9). It is baffling that this is the same explanation he provides for not revealing the mysteries of the kingdom to outsiders. Inexplicably, Jesus's followers are tasked today with the absurd responsibility of having to explain what they do not fully understand to *those outside*.

Given the above, we need to ask the question, who is Jesus's version of the childlike today? How does the unquestionable acceptance of God and Jesus in heart and mind help humans to gain knowledge about God's kingdom? Have these qualifications moved us to a greater understanding of Jesus and God than the views upheld for thousands of years by Christian tradition, or is this tradition acting as a historical brake to increasing our understanding?

At the beginning of the book, I suggested that being aware of human limitations, God is either an abysmal communicator or he has chosen to remain mysterious and hidden for reasons unknown to us. The mystery surrounding the kingdom of God, and God's and Jesus's unwillingness to be more forthcoming, have had serious consequences for the future of Christianity, and even for all religions. Although Jesus tells his followers that they must be the *light of the world* and allow their righteousness to *shine before others* (Mt 5:14-16), it is difficult to accomplish his directive due to our limitations in understanding God's mysterious lack of transparency. As a result, we can only *know* about God through faith and reason in an exceedingly imperfect fashion. Hence, it ought not to be surprising that secularism and moral and religious relativism have arisen largely because of the vacuum created by God's own cryptic ways.

Notes:
1. *Merriam-Webster Dictionary, Cambridge Dictionary, Oxford Dictionary,* online, s.v. "mystery."
2. The following are some of the mysteries included in the Catholic Catechism under *Mystery*:

of Christ, 280, 512-60, 639, 654, 1067; of the Church, 770-76; of the Church's unity, 813-16; of creation, 287, 295-301; of the existence of evil, 309, 385, 395; of faith, 2558; of God, 42, 206, 234, 1028, 2779; of man, 359; of man's salvation, 122.

3. NEs' note, Matthew 13:35.

4. Ibid., note, Mark 4:1-34.

Miracles in the Gospels

A miracle is secularly defined as an extraordinary event that generates a positive outcome that supersedes human understanding and cannot be explained or reproduced within the confines of the laws of nature. Therefore, it is attributed to divine intervention.[1] In the Gospels, miracles, known as signs, wonders, works, or deeds, provide the most significant attestation that the kingdom of God is present in Jesus and that he is the promised Messiah.[2] This category is highly ranked according to content analysis results in Table 2. The high *sp* tally indicates that the authors of the Gospels sought to portray divine intervention prominently.

Why are Miracles Important to the Christian faith?

Miracles denote the existence of something or someone that stands above (and commands) the laws of nature. From a human viewpoint, miracles, whether performed by or through a human person, denote power; and power is indicative of authority. The Gospels suggest that Jesus is aware that for his mission to be credible he needs to persuade; he needs others to believe that he is who he says he is. Toward this end, he relies on miracles that no one has ever done before (Jn 15:24) as a means for others to accept his authority.

Although Jesus's miracles play a significant role in the faith of his disciples, this faith is different than the faith of generations of followers. The disciples' faith is not based on believing in works they have not witnessed; that is Christianity's faith today. The disciples' faith is rooted in empirical observation; they see that Jesus can do what no one else can, and they conclude that he is divine or that the divine operates through him. This faith is easier to acknowledge than having to believe without seeing.

Jesus's primary objective to be recognized as the Messiah and the Son of God is different than God's desire to be recognized by his creatures as the sole God. He seems to be aware that his miracles would play an even greater role in proving who he says he is because he chooses not to rely on negative or destructive power, such as plagues, to establish his authority. He must break the cycle of human incredulity by being kind, merciful, and forgiving instead of being a jealous, wrathful, and detailed lawgiver. Thus, in addition to conveying a sense of sacredness to the texts, it is understandable that without miracles Jesus might have been regarded as a righteous leader, a prophet, or an impostor, but not as a divine being.

The miracles reported in the Gospels are unlike the illusions created by a magician or a sorcerer, although at the time some people may have taken Jesus for a magician. Nonetheless, it may be recalled that people believe Jesus's deeds after having witnessed them with their own eyes, even though some opt to attribute Jesus's healing powers to works by the devil (Mk 3:22, Lk 11:15, Mt 12:24). Others are so terrified when they witness Jesus driving demons into a herd of swine and down a steep bank that they ask him to leave the area (Mk 5:1-17, Lk 8:26-38, Mt 8:28-34). Moreover, the Gospels do not indicate that people refuse to believe what they see; on the contrary, the texts indicate that people attest and react (positively and negatively) to Jesus's miracles.[3] A preliminary conclusion is that while the Gospels recognize that miracles happen, they do not always translate into acceptance of Jesus being the Messiah, except to a small group of Jews, his disciples. Despite witnessing his amazing powers many people still refuse to accept Jesus's authority.

Who Are the Recipients of Jesus's Miracles?
It is suggested that Jesus's miracles *reveal more and more his emphasis on faith as the requisite for exercising his healing powers*.[4] Indeed, Jesus's inability (not unwillingness) to perform mighty deeds in his native place *because of their lack of faith* (Mk 6:1-5, Mt 13:53-58) suggests there are limitations to his powers. Jesus's phrase, *your faith has saved you* (Lk 17:11-19, 18:35-43) following healing, suggests that faith is a requirement to be cured. Nonetheless, content analysis results suggest otherwise. There are cases in which faith means accepting that Jesus is the Messiah or the presumption that he simply has the power to heal without implying anything other than a desire on the recipient's part to be healed.

A review of miracles performed by Jesus indicates that faith does not always lie at the center of the deed. For example, at a synagogue in Capernaum Jesus drives an unclean spirit without asking the demoniac if he trusts him or if he even wants to be cured; Jesus simply does it (Mk 1:21-28, Lk 4:31-37). Nor does Jesus ask Peter's mother-in-law to believe prior to being healed (Mk 1:29-33, Lk 4:38-39, Mt 8:14-15). There is also the leper who asks him to restore his health, possibly because he wants to be healed (who doesn't?) and believes Jesus can do it (Mk 1:40-45, Lk 5:12-16, Mt 8:1-4). Furthermore, Jesus even performs miracles before his disciples, despite their unbelief (to show his power over nature), and then rebukes them for their lack of faith and hardness of heart (Mk 4:35-41, 6:45-52, Lk 8:22-25, Mt 8:23-27).

The total tally of passages attributing miracles to Jesus (90m, online) is most extraordinary in that they indicate that in sixty-one passages, i.e., 61 miracles, faith plays little if any role while in twenty-nine passages (29xt) they do (Table 2).[5] Even Jesus' resurrection does not demand faith; none of his disciples or Mary Magdalene believe he would be resurrected until after they see him alive following his crucifixion. Afterward, faith was not required. Jesus could have said to them what he said to Thomas, "you believed because you saw." Moreover, the miracle at Cana also does not require faith. Instead, the miracle itself engenders it; the disciples begin to believe in Jesus after they witness the transformation of water into wine (Jn 2:11).

The theological and religious implications of Jesus's possible motives for performing his wondrous deeds are considerable. There is little question that Jesus insists on showing the Jewish people (and others) that he is different than humans. In this regard, he is an empiricist. He does not say, *I will heal you (or feed you) if you believe in me.* In many cases he is moved by pity (Mk 8:1-9, Lk 7:11-16, Mt 14:13-21); in one instance, he forgives the paralytic man of his sins, perhaps aware that it would irk the religious authorities who consider this action blasphemy. His behavior would then allow him to relate his healing powers to his authority to forgive sins (Mk 2:1-12, Lk 5:17-26, Mt 9:1-7), or to alter the rules referring to the Sabbath (Mk 3:1-6, Lk 6:6-11, Mt 12:9-15), thereby manifesting himself as divine or proto-divine.

There are occasions in which the crowds become aware of his presence and bring the sick into the marketplace; others run frantically to him to touch the tassel of his cloak and be cured, without there being any mentioning of faith (Mk 6:53-56). At times too, Jesus performs miracles prior to belief; people appear to trust him because he can heal the sick (Mk 5:21-34, 7:24-30, 9:14-29, Lk 7:1-10, 8:40-48, 9:37-43, Mt 8:5-13). Nonetheless, it is not clear if those who wish to be cured are aware that they stand before the Messiah or the Son of God since no one tells them Jesus is divine. Although Jesus needs to provide empirical evidence of who he is (otherwise people might not believe in him), an important conclusion that may be derived is that he performs noble deeds regardless of faith, simply to set an example of caring for others.

The majority of passages relating to miracles involve healing the sick (68xt), followed by feeding the hungry (6xt), and various other miracles that denote his majestic skills (16xt), such as calming the seas, walking on water, transforming water into wine, acting as fish-finder, his transfiguration, and his resurrection. Given their noticeable differences, it might be pertinent to ask why Jesus emphasizes healing the sick. In healing the sick Jesus personifies the Good Samaritan; he shows compassion toward those in need while realizing that sickness stands as an impediment to a joyful life. It needs to be stressed that health is probably the most important aspect of human living; even more so than individual freedom, satisfying hunger, establishing law and order or attaining peace, all of which can best be managed in the absence of physical, emotional, or mental disabilities. Moreover, it is possible that given the belief at the time (now obsolete) that sickness was the result of sinful behavior, Jesus wishes to forgive sin by curing the sick to assert his divine prerogative.[6]

Could the Resurrection Have Happened?
The Gospels clearly indicate that Jesus's miracles are not simply good deeds done to entertain crowds; they are intended to manifest Jesus's divine power as well as his authority to dictate moral behavior. Had Jesus not provided empirical evidence through miracles, his commanding status, and his divine mission would have been severely undermined. Hence, his method of communication must be beyond the ordinary. Words would not be enough; rhetoric can persuade the credulous or people who are willing to be persuaded through reason, as Plato and Aristotle, for example, attempt to do through their dialogues. Jesus must be convincing; that is, miraculous. At risk is the religious movement Jesus creates. If he fails to stand out, his teachings would be considered simply one among many voices, each claiming to express the

authentic voice of God, as it happens today. But, can they all be factually correct? Can these voices be viewed as the various expressions of the same God despite their lack of harmony and their persecutions and warfare among each other?

Questioning the Miracles
Is it philosophically or scientifically worthy anymore to question the proposition that any material object thrown into the air might not eventually fall to the ground? Or that night will follow day as the earth rotates on its axis? Or to make it more problematic, that a tree falling to the ground will make a noise even if there is no one there listening? Perhaps someone with time on their hands might wish to embark on a fool's errand and attempt to negate any of the above.

The Gospels indicate that people, including Jesus's enemies, witness these deeds, i.e., they accept their occurrence. On the other hand, questions surround Jesus's resurrection because no one witnesses it. Jesus's trial and his crucifixion are a public affair. Although there are no witnesses to the act of the resurrection, the texts record events that occur before and after. Some of Jesus's disciples, Mary, Mary Magdalene, and a Roman centurion among others, are first-hand observers of his crucifixion and death; and Joseph of Arimathea and Nicodemus, friends of Jesus, retrieve the dead body and entomb it (Mk 15:39-47, Lk 23:47-56, Mt 27:54-61, Jn 19:25-26, 38-42). The day following the Sabbath, Mary Magdalene accompanied by other women go to the burial place and notice that the large stone that encloses the entrance to the cave-like tomb has been removed. In John's text, the resurrected Jesus appears before Mary Magdalene disguised as a gardener and reveals himself to her (Jn 20:11-18). In Matthew's text, an angel of the Lord is the one who removes the stone and tells Mary Magdalene of Jesus's whereabouts (Mt 28:1-7). According to Luke, *two men in dazzling garments* inform them about Jesus's resurrection (Lk 24:1-10) while in Mark's text it is a young man *clothed in a white robe* (Mk 16:1-8). The narratives are different, and apologists tend to set aside their significance not realizing that while oral transmission may account for these variations, it is the veracity or accuracy of divine revelation that is at stake.

Eventually, a resurrected Jesus appears before his disciples completing a cycle of events witnessed by people close to him: Jesus is crucified, he dies, his dead body is taken and buried, and days later he reappears and spends time with his disciples before ascending into heaven. Is this possible? If in the texts people acknowledge Jesus's other miracles, why should his resurrection be discarded? The Gospels, particularly Matthew's, raise a degree of doubt by pointing out that the religious authorities think that Jesus's followers could steal the dead body and then claim that he has risen from the dead (Mt 27:62-66). Nevertheless, the Gospels indicate that Jesus dies, is buried, and later comes back to life and meets with his disciples. If accepted, this assertion would negate the possibility of the body being stolen, giving way to other explanations.

But there is a lingering issue surrounding the Gospels' narrative; the resurrected Jesus is seen only by a few of his followers. It is reasonable that being with the resurrected Jesus is all that counts for them. There is no need to believe in that which is unseen; now they see the risen Jesus with their eyes. Mary Magdalene hugs him, and Thomas even puts his finger on Jesus's wound marks, leading him, not to believe, but to *know* that Jesus is once again alive (Jn 20:17, 26-27). Jesus's followers, however, are not impartial observers of the outside world. Outsiders now are placed in a position to have faith, not in Jesus, but in those who claim that the Gospels' narrative is accurate. On the other hand, while the disciples attest to what they see, why should outsiders (enemies of Jesus, and less gullible bystanders, philosophers, and historians) accept what to them represent oral stories, anecdotes, tales, or rumors that are put into writing decades later?

Jesus's Resurrection and the Historical Record
If Jesus knows that his mission relies entirely on his credibility and that his credibility lies in his miracles, why would he not leave a legacy for future generations to believe in him with the same ease as we accept the exploits of Alexander the Great or Napoleon? Suffice it to say that outside the New Testament, written by *Christian insiders* to educate newcomers into the faith, there is hardly any credible written record that corroborates Jesus's resurrection. Three Roman authors (two of them historians) make brief references to Jesus. Tacitus, writing in 109 C.E. about Nero's accusation against Christians for the burning of Rome and hatred of mankind, acknowledges that Christians were followers of Christus, who was executed during the reign of Tiberius by Pontius Pilate, but there is no mention of his resurrection.[7] In or around 110-112 C.E., Pliny the Younger, Roman Governor of Bithynia et Pontus province, writes to Emperor Trajan seeking advice regarding the measure he recommends for Christians who refuse to renounce their beliefs and practices and instead accede to curse the name of Christ to escape punishment. Pliny limits himself to mentioning Christ's name but without any additional information about who he was, what had happened to him, or why. In his reply to Pliny (Letter 97) Trajan simply acknowledges the existence of Christians while extending support for Pliny's measures, but without admitting anything else about Jesus.[8] And, Roman historian Suetonius, writing during the first decade of the second century, makes one brief reference that may or may not have any relation to Jesus. He writes about Emperor Claudius's expulsion of Jews from Rome, *who were continually making disturbances at the instigation of one Chrestus*. It is not clear if the reference is to Jesus Christ or whether these Jews may have been converted Christians who defied Roman laws. The phrase *at the instigation of Chrestus* might refer to Jesus if instigation means that these converted Jews were acting in accordance with his teachings. Nonetheless, it is important to emphasize that Suetonius could be referring to the existence of the historical Jesus without adding anything about the events that transpired in Jerusalem

at the time of Pontius Pilate's governorship.[9] None of these references, however, allude to the resurrection; only to Jesus's historical existence.

There is also Jewish historian Flavius Josephus, who is the most prominently referenced author regarding the historicity of Jesus on account of two passages in his *Antiquities of the Jews*. Josephus mentions the name Jesus (referring to Jesus Christ, as there are other Jesuses in the book) twice, once as an afterthought about James the disciple (*Jesus, who was called Christ*), and the name Christ, twice too, concerning Jesus. In the second passage, he characterizes Jesus as a *wise man* and *a doer of wonderful works* who brought Jews and Gentiles to his side. He calls Jesus *the Christ,* probably not as Paul would do it (signifying a risen Jesus), except that he mentions that he was crucified by Pontius Pilate at the behest of the Jewish religious authorities and resurrected on the third day as foretold by divine prophets.[10] Josephus's entries are closer to the Jesus event as he writes toward the end of the first century. Despite providing significant snippets, his information likely relies only on the Gospels. That a Jewish historian of Josephus's caliber writes about a dead person being resurrected would seem astonishing. Yet how is it possible that Josephus dedicates only a few lines to what may be the greatest historical human event ever recorded?

From the Gospels' perspective, the reader can tell that the accounts on the public life of Jesus were extraordinary and traumatic. These dramatic events, however, are absent in Josephus's writing. Moreover, while Josephus quotes the name *Jesus Christ* twice in his lengthy work, one of them rather insignificantly, the name of *Pontius Pilate* appears fifteen times (15xt) while describing in detail aspects of his public tenure as governor. This is indicative that outside the New Testament the public life of Jesus was but a footnote in the writings of non-Christians; granted, a footnote that somehow spreads like wildfire once Christianity is recognized as the official religion of the Roman Empire. Today, there are 2.3 billion people who have been baptized or call themselves Christians, accounting for one-third of the world's population,[11] and subdivided into numerous denominations due to religious schisms over beliefs. This means that two-thirds of the world's population does not believe or accept Jesus, much less that he was resurrected. Was there a disconnect between Jesus and his mission that led to this outcome? If Jesus (and God) needed to be an effective communicator for his mission to succeed, where lies the problem?

The Second Greatest Miracle That Never Takes Place
There is in Matthew a passage indicating that following Jesus's death an earthquake takes place, rocks are opened, and the bodies of many saints who had fallen asleep were raised. Coming forth from their tombs after his resurrection, they entered the holy city and appeared to many (Mt 27:52-53). This is an incredibly newsworthy event taking place in Jerusalem, the center of the Jewish people. But is this narrative a metaphor and symbolic of things to come, or did it really take place? There does not seem to be any outside source attesting to a most extraordinary event.

Jesus's claim that he is the God-sent universal Messiah and Son of God is not credible outside of Christianity. This may be attributed to the insufficient and problematic 'evidence' (dare I say Revelation?) there is about Jesus; hence, the need to rely on a faith that most of the world's population rejects. Questions about Jesus's historicity do not seem to be problematic; historically, even Muslims, Jews, and other non-Christians believe he existed as a human being. Still, the problem lies in Jesus's claim that he is the Son of God. We are talking about 'divine historicity,' which is different than Roman emperors' claims to divinity.

Going back to one of the initial theses in this book, if God wished to convey his message of salvation to humankind by presenting Jesus as his emissary, it would be up to him (and Jesus) to ensure intelligibility in the manner he communicates with his creatures at their level. Parting from the requirement that to be credible Jesus cannot afford to leave doubt about who he is or about his mission, can we even begin to fathom the magnitude and significance if, once resurrected, Jesus decides to appear before the Sanhedrin and before Pilate; if he walks the streets of Jerusalem accompanied by his disciples, and perhaps visits other nearby towns? Paul claims to have received information that Jesus appeared *to more than five hundred brothers at once, most of whom are still living*, then to James, to all the apostles, and lastly to him (1 Cor 15:6-8). However, how is it possible that the authors of the Gospels did not hear of such a miracle through oral transmission, or that God would not remind them to include it in their texts? Had it occurred, could Tacitus, Pliny, Suetonius, Josephus, and others have failed to record this event?

Appearing before those who doubted him would have enhanced Jesus's claim about being the Messiah and the Son of God. Furthermore, provided that the texts had been more lucid and less subject to misinterpretation, Jesus's historical record, his moral, religious, and political authority would have been exponentially magnified. Such a miracle, however, would not necessarily have cemented a universal faith in Jesus; humanity's flawed condition still allows some people to deny scientific evidence. Nonetheless, Jesus's resurrection would have been immensely more credible had it been effectively presented in the same manner he chose to perform his miracles by humbly showing to outsiders what he said he would do, overcome death. In effect, the miracle that never occurred would have been extraordinarily trustworthy news.

On what basis do the disciples believe in a resurrection that fails to persuade Jesus's opponents? There is no certainty, except that years before, Paul already had been preaching a resurrected Christ supposedly based on visions and revelations. If Jesus had appeared publicly before his opponents, there would have been no need for apologists to have written the Gospels; agnostic historians could have accurately written them more objectively. Instead, Christian theology had to depend on apologetic literature written decades after his death, and on Paul's previous account of his conversion based on a vision to enhance faith in Jesus.

Paul's emotional and radical psychological transformation seems to have been real; something must have occurred in his life that accounts for his turnabout after spending time persecuting Jesus's followers. Unfortunately, nowadays, a vision is a poor substitute for verifiable empirical evidence. Paul begins to write before the authors of the Gospels; thus, it may be inferred that Jesus reveals himself to Paul before God's revelation (or inspiration) led to the Gospels. The implication is that Paul takes it upon himself to write about his personal interpretation of Jesus's teachings based on a presumed personal revelation. However, given the disconnect between Paul's letters and the authors of the Gospel, the credibility of both texts is seriously undermined. In effect, is there a strong historical basis to accept Jesus's biographical data other than through an oral transmission that tends to suffer from mistakes, no matter how reliable it was thought to be at the time?

A New Jesus

Today, Christianity faces an enormous challenge from a 'secular Jesus' that already has outshined Jesus's miracles and eventually may end up stripping him, inadvertently, of his claims and authenticity. This challenge comes from human beings who, guided by reason, promise a better tomorrow with far more credible miracles that everyone will be able to witness. Human beings guiding science, technology, governments, formal and informal community groups, and countless non-governmental organizations are fashioning (albeit in a chaotic manner) a more inclusive humanitarian moral philosophy of life on earth, although with the assistance (and against the backdrop) of Christian teachings. The major difference lies in that this secular Jesus does not address eternal salvation or condemnation, and its moral teachings are anything but precise. On the other hand, the secular Jesus, while focusing on the temporal world, does not necessarily negate the afterlife.

Today, the secular Jesus can cure the sick and feed the hungry by the millions, reach the moon, allow the communion of humans from all four corners of the world in real-time, ensure human freedom and human rights, create the means to self-governing, and raise the standard of living of many people. Indeed, from a temporal standpoint, humans have outperformed Jesus. The path, however, has been arduous. These accomplishments have been attained despite great disparities, enormous suffering, and colossal mistakes. The greatest limitation this new Jesus presents is its lack of a coherent morality, precisely the problem that Jesus was supposed to solve. Instead, a humanitarian mindset is being expanded, although it has not been able to exert major influence over the secular Jesus. As a result, the existence of a vast moral vacuum is noticeable throughout the world. This may be observed in the immoral and illegal justification of preventive warfare by political leaders and their constituencies, the pursuit of power and wealth as ends in themselves, indifference toward the most vulnerable, the maximization of profits at the expense of ecological problems, political despotism and corruption of political leaders, and the want of respect toward human dignity. Nonetheless, despite its flaws (and in the absence of a supernatural miracle or human annihilation), the road is being mapped for the secular Jesus to eventually overcome the historical Jesus without a requirement for faith. What the outcome of the "new Jesus" might be, however, is difficult to say.

Notes:
1. *Merriam-Webster Dictionary, Cambridge Dictionary, Oxford Dictionary,* online, s.v. "miracle."
2. CCC 547. The Catholic Catechism does not provide a formal definition of the term *miracle.* It indicates, however, that miracles *are the most certain signs of divine Revelation* that provide *motives of credibility,* i.e., contribute to faith (156).
3. Jesus's reproach to the religious authorities and their followers' for refusing to believe in his works (Jn 10:25-26, 37-38) does not suggest that they refuse to accept the works that take place, but rather decline to acknowledge that the works they witness signify that he is the Messiah.
4. NEs' note, Mark 2:5.
5. Although evaluating passages to conform to specific themes involve a certain amount of subjectivity, in this case it may be fairly easy to notice that many miracles attributed to Jesus do not indicate that he makes faith a requisite for the deed. There are cases in which the recipient of the miracle begins to believe afterwards, not before; however, I give faith the benefit of the doubt and tally the passage as related to faith. The tally is as follows: miracles attributed to Jesus in which faith plays little or no role: Mark (13): 1:21-28, 29-33, 32-34, 40-45, 3:1-6, 7-12, 4:35-41, 5:1-20, 6:45-52, 53-56, 7:31-37, 8:1-9, 16:1-20. Luke (19): 4:31-37, 38-39, 40-41, 5:1-11, 12-16, 6:6-11, 17-19, 7:11-16, 18:22, 8:22-25, 26-39, 9:12-17, 28-36, 37-43, 11:14-20, 13:10-17, 14:1-6, 22:47-51, 24:1-53. Matthew (23): 4:23-25, 8:1-4, 8:14-15, 16-17, 23-27, 28-34, 9:1-17, 32-33, 35-36, 12:9-15, 12:22-28, 14:13-21, 22-33, 34-36, 15:29-31, 32-38, 17:1-9, 14-18, 19:1-2, 20:3-34, 21:14, 28:1-20. John (6): 2:1-11, 5:1-14, 6:1-14, 6:16-21, 9:1-39, 20:1-29. Miracles attributed to Jesus in which faith might be a requisite: Mark (12): 1:35-39, 2:1-12, 5:21-43x2m, 6:1-5, 6:7-13, 34-44, 7:24-30, 8:22-26, 9:3-8, 14-29, 10:46-52. Luke (9): 5:17-26, 7:1-10, 8:40-56x2m, 9:1-6, 10-11, 13:53-58, 17:11-19, 18:35-43. Matthew (5): 8:5-13, 9:18-25x2m, 27-31, 15:21-28. John (3): 4:45-53, 11:1-44, 21:1-23.
6. The belief is based on the Old Testament: Ex 20:5; Dt 5:9. NEs' note, Luke 5:20.
7. Tacitus, *The Annals,* Book XV, (109 C.E.), trans. Alfred John Church and William Jackson Brodribb, The Internet Classics Archive, http://classics.mit.edu/Tacitus/annals.html (accessed September 14, 2019).
8. Pliny the Younger, *Letter 96 to the Emperor Trajan,* Book 10, trans. J.B.Firth (1900), Attalus.org, http://www.attalus.org/old/pliny10b.html (accessed September 14, 2019).
9. C. Suetonius Tranquillus, *The Lives of the Twelve Caesars,* (In the chapter on Tiberius Claudius Drusus Caesar, XXV), The Project Gutenberg EBook, trans. Alexander Thomson, M.D., last updated 2016, https://www.gutenberg.org/files/6400/6400-h/6400-h.htm (accessed September 14, 2019).
10. Josephus, Book XX, Chapter 9, 1, and Book XVIII, Chapter 3, 3, (accessed September 14, 2019).
11. Conrad Hackett, David McClendon, "Christians remain world's largest religious group, but they are declining in Europe," Pew Research Center, April 5, 2017, https://www.pewresearch.org/fact-tank/2017/04/05/christians-remain-worlds-largest-religious-group-but-they-are-declining-in-europe/ (accessed September 14, 2019).

The Resurrection of Jesus

The section on the afterlife dealt primarily with the resurrection of humans. For comparative purposes, however, I decided to tally independent passages pertaining to the resurrection of humans and the resurrection of Jesus (Table 2). The results indicate that the Gospels wrote less about Jesus's resurrection. From a human perspective, however, Jesus's resurrection is the most awe-inspiring event recorded in the scriptures. Christians today believe in the resurrection of humans because they believe that Jesus rose from the dead. His resurrection moves Paul to affirm that without it the Christian faith would be worthless (1 Cor 15:17). This section focuses on aspects of Jesus's resurrection that may have been overlooked in the previous category.

The Gospels read as a written collage of sayings and events, set up as a condensed historical account of the life of Jesus. If all four texts were put together into one narrative, it would read like a novel filled with majestic deeds, conflict, and mystery, climaxing with a most improbable event. Jesus begins his public mission preaching the kingdom of God throughout Judea and other lands; in the course of his activities, he begins to tell his disciples that he will be killed but then will resurrect after three days. According to the sequence of events, Jesus's death is to be expected, namely because of his teachings and his conflict with the religious authorities, and because he keeps repeating it. It is what happens at the end that may bewilder the reader; is it possible for Jesus (a human being) to be resurrected?

The alleged resurrection of Jesus is the climax that encapsulates every saying, act, and event that surrounds his life. Interestingly, in journalism, a front-page story would be written in reverse. The headline would be 'Jesus is resurrected from the dead,' followed by his prediction that he would be killed and then resurrected, and his promise about the resurrection of humans. A sub-headline would then go into details of what prompted his execution along with biographical data and details of everything he said throughout his life.

On the other hand, content analysis results offer a different yet credible sequence of events that Jesus's mission makes abundantly clear. The fundamental objective of Jesus's teachings is not his resurrection, but to announce the kingdom of God. The centerpiece of the message is that eternal salvation is possible for humans who are willing to accept him. His resurrection becomes the validation of his teachings, which is why the authors of the Gospel devote considerable space to Jesus's sayings about the resurrection of humans.

According to the Gospels, Jesus rarely speaks publicly about his resurrection other than to his disciples. Nonetheless, four enigmatic passages deal with Jesus's possible public discussion of his resurrection. There is a brief sentence in which he tells his disciples about his death and resurrection, and Mark states that *he spoke this openly* (Mk 8:31-32). It is not clear if by *openly* Jesus meant that he told the crowd or that he was being open only with his disciples. In John's Gospel, Jesus replies to the crowd at the market area that wishes to know under what authority he disrupts their business saying, *destroy this temple and in three days I will raise it up.* The sentence that follows, however, indicates that the crowd did not understand what Jesus was saying.[1] Not even his disciples understood what he meant (Jn 2:18-22); eventually, they do, but only because they saw.

In another instance, the scribes and the Pharisees ask Jesus for a sign that might legitimize his teachings. Jesus replies enigmatically that just as Jonah was in the belly of the whale three days and three nights, *the Son of Man will be in the heart of the earth three days and three nights* (Mt 12:38-40). The religious authorities undoubtedly know the reference to Jonah (Jon 2:1), however, the passage does not suggest that they identify Jesus with the Son of Man or that Jesus is referring to his death and resurrection at that moment. Nonetheless, another passage provides more information suggesting that Jesus may have spoken publicly about his resurrection. Attempting to secure the burial site, the chief priest and the Pharisees tell Pilate, *Sir, we remember that this impostor while still alive said, 'After three days I will be raised up* (Mt 27:62-66). This remark indicates that Jesus's prediction about his resurrection had become public knowledge.

Jesus's private conversations with his disciples regarding his resurrection, however, are shown in at least seventeen passages.[2] Yet, despite these conversations the disciples fail to understand him (Lk 18:34). Hence, is it likely that the religious authorities would have a better understanding of Jesus's resurrection than his disciples who do not seem to grasp the essence of his remarks? The multiplicity of references to the resurrection of humans by Jesus in the four Gospels does not appear to be a random act. The authors of the Gospels understood that the most significant aspect of Jesus's teachings was the resurrection of humans. Jesus's death and resurrection, however, do not necessarily prove that he is divine, or that he is the Son of God. God simply may have wanted to raise Jesus from the dead to offer credence to the mission he undertakes on his behalf.

Are Jesus's Powers His Own?
Would it make a difference if Jesus resurrects himself through his own power as opposed to being raised by God? Yes, it does. The answer to this question has significant implications about Jesus's divinity and the interrelationship with the Trinity. The transfiguration of Jesus, in which he appears with Moses and Elijah in dazzling white clothes, his face changing in appearance, shining like the sun, is witnessed by three of his disciples (Mk 9:2-8, Lk 9:28-36, Mt 17:1-8), presumably to reveal Jesus's glory and to increase their faiths. The texts indicate that during the transfiguration a cloud casts a shadow over the disciples, and they hear a voice (supposedly God's) saying *this is my beloved son*. What is not clear from the synoptics (this event does not appear in John) is whether Jesus transfigures himself using his powers or whether it is God's doing. Moreover, why would he not want his other disciples to witness such an event, and why does he ask his three disciples not to reveal anything about it until after his resurrection? If the transfiguration had occurred in public, in full view of the religious authorities, perhaps it would have been the answer the scribes and the Pharisees were seeking from Jesus; a sign from heaven. Could many have doubted such an occurrence at the time; or if it were to happen today, particularly amid other deeds that Jesus performed? At the time, it may not have proven Jesus's divinity, but probably it would have legitimized his divine authority before the religious authorities.

We then come to a related matter, does Jesus resurrect himself or does God resurrect him? The answer is not trivial; if Jesus is as divine as God, he ought to have similar powers. As is, the Gospels present three distinctive versions of his resurrection. According to Mark's text, Jesus will be killed, but *he will rise* (Mk 9:31, 10:34); an ambiguous phrase suggesting the possibility that either Jesus or God has the power of resurrection. In Luke, Jesus will be killed and *raised* on the third day (Lk

9:22), hinting that he will be raised by someone else. But Luke states in another passage that *he will rise* after the third day (Lk 18:33), a vague remark regarding who will do the rising. In Matthew, Jesus is to be *raised* (Mt 16:21, 20:19), presumably by someone else.

In John's Gospel, Jesus's prediction of his passion is different. John presents two scenarios; in the first one, *the Jews* ask Jesus for a sign that would legitimize his authority, and he issues a metaphorical response: *destroy this temple and in three days I will raise it up,* insinuating that he will be resurrected through his own power. The Pharisees are confused, believing that he is referring to the Temple, although according to John, Jesus *was speaking about the temple of his body.* Yet, in the next sentence John writes, *therefore, when he was raised from the dead, his disciples remembered that he had said this,* indicating that someone raised him from the dead (Jn 2:18-22). Still, in another passage, John quotes Jesus indicating that the resurrecting powers are his alone: *I lay down my life in order to take it up again. I have power to lay it down, and power to take it up again* (Jn 10:17-18). Today, semantics would seem to matter, particularly when dealing with such an important question; but, as with other aspects of the Gospels, ambiguity prevails.

There seems to be no ambiguity, however, in the *Acts* (in both the Catholic and the King James Bibles). Numerous passages indicate that it is God who raises Jesus from the dead. Addressing the Israelites, Peter testifies that *God raised him up; God raised this Jesus; the God of our ancestors raised Jesus.* To the household of Cornelius, Peter refers to Jesus as a man, declaring, *this man God raised (on) the third day and granted that he be visible, not to all the people, but to us* (Acts 2:24, 2:32, 3:15, 4:10, 5:30, 10:40). Paul too, attests that God raises Jesus from the dead (Acts: 13:30, 34, 37).

Adding to the enigma, in other instances Jesus claims that it is *by the finger of God* (Lk 11:20) and *by the Spirit of God* (Mt 12:28) that *I drive demons*, thereby attributing his miraculous powers to God. Moreover, when he appears before the Sanhedrin, he intimates that the real power is God: *you will see the Son of Man seated at the right hand of the Power* (Mk 14:62, Lk 22:69, Mt 26:64). There is yet another passage that provides a different explanation, although its meaning is not clear. When Judas Iscariot decides to turn Jesus over to the religious authorities, John writes that Jesus is *fully aware that the Father had put everything into his power and that he had come from God and was returning to God.* (Jn 13:1-5). The passage, which does not seem to relate to either Judas or Jesus's act, suggests that God gives power to Jesus, and Jesus uses it as he deems proper.

The texts indicate that divine powers will be terrifyingly displayed at the end of time; wars, nations rising against nations, earthquakes, and famines will take place. Jesus calls them *labor pains*, although he does not say who is responsible for them (Mk 13:3-8, Lk 21:7-11, Mt 24:3-14). He adds that, following these tribulations, *all the tribes of the earth will see the Son of Man coming in the clouds with great power and glory, and then he will send out the angels and gather [his] elect from the four winds, from the end of the earth to the end of the sky* (Lk 21:25-27, Mt 24:30). The passage indicates that Jesus is a formidable being possessing intimidating powers; yet, are these powers his, or are they given to him by God?

What then are we to make of Jesus's resurrection? It is certainly confusing that the Gospels indicate both that Jesus will rise (Mk 9:31, Lk 18:33, Jn 2:19) and that he will be raised or has been raised (Mk 14:28, 16-6, Lk 9:22, Mt 16:21, 17:23, 20:19). Each phrase is subject to different interpretations; either he rises from the dead through his powers or God raises him, meaning that he either shares the same divine nature with the Father or that he is something less than the Father. The answer to the question is, as might be expected, a conundrum; one of the many mysteries that abound in the Christian faith.

In Mark, Jesus says that he must suffer greatly, be rejected, and be killed (Mk 8:31). It may be assumed that if Jesus *must* die, it is because he is following his mission or one dictated by someone else, supposedly the Father (Lk 22:42).[3] This passage suggests that despite having a choice, his death is inevitable and necessary if there is to be a resurrection. Jesus asserts that his death must happen in fulfillment of the scriptures (Mt 26:54), in which case his death seems determined by forces beyond him; or else, that he needs to fulfill the scriptures (still a matter of choice). The way his public life unfolds, however, suggests that no matter how it is analyzed Jesus puts himself in a position where death becomes inevitable. But why? A plausible explanation is that Jesus's death and resurrection are part of a divine plan that requires his death in order for him to be resurrected so that others may believe in his mission.

Although we are told that Jesus announces his passion (three times), given the scathing tone of his public criticism against his people, the religious authorities, and the fate of other prophets that preceded him, he must have realized that his behavior eventually would be met with strong opposition. Jesus seeks his own death, whether in obedience to the Father to make redemption possible, because of his temper or his conviction, or to fulfill the scriptures. His fate, however, had to be comforting because he knew that he would be resurrected almost immediately. For humans, death signifies the end to suffering, although the prospect of dying does not lessen human anxiety. However, Jesus's knowledge reduces his fear of physical death (Mt 10:28). His death, although real (he sweated blood), would be similar to a soldier being told that he will have to endure hardship and suffering for a worthy cause, but in the end he will emerge alive.

Notes:
1. In one instance, in Capernaum, many of Jesus's disciples (except the twelve) stop accompanying him because they cannot understand his teachings (Jn 6:52-66).
2. (Mk 8:31, 9-9, 9:31-32, 10:32-34, 14:27-28, Lk 9:22, 18:31-34, 24:6-7, Mt 16:21-23, 17:9, 17:22-23, 20:17-19, 26:31-32, 28:6, Jn 2:22, 12:23-24, 16:16-23).
3. Jesus states at least twenty times that his mission entails doing God's will while not mentioning any other motive.

Parousia

Although the term *Parousia* does not appear in the scriptures, it does not mean the issue is not present in the Gospels. Table 2 indicates that content analysis resolves rank this category among the less significant. Despite its ranking, the importance of the Parousia cannot be understated, as it represents the end of time on earth, according to the Gospels. As it shows in the Nicene Creed, the Parousia is the promise Jesus makes to humanity that he will come in glory to judge the living and the dead.

Although many believers regard it as a joyous occasion, the Parousia entails wars, famine, and natural and cosmic disasters. These cataclysmic occurrences, or *labor pains* as Jesus calls them, do not seem to be human-driven. Moreover, Jesus does not provide any explicit reason regarding why these labor pains will or must occur; only that they appear to be ordained by God before the end of the age.[1] Since the beginnings of the church, theologians have speculated the timing of the Parousia and the signs that will occur prior to it. Many of these signs have taken place already.[2]

There is no direct reference to the Parousia in the Old Testament either. Seemingly, in Matthew Jesus refers to the *desolating abomination* that Daniel said will occur, as a source for his Second Coming This passage, however, is based on the author's faulty interpretation of Daniel's prophecy.[3] Whether the Second Coming is foretold in the Old Testament depends on the extent to which 'prophetic experts' wish to extrapolate from passages that are not explicit (1 Chr 16:33, Psm 96:13, Joel 3:4, Amos 5:18, Is 2:11-21, Ezk 7:27, Dn 2:28, Zeph 1:18). These passages invariably refer to *the Lord,* i.e., God, not Jesus, as the one who will preside the Parousia. They do not indicate if this *Day of the Lord* signifies that God's action will take place in the near future against his people (the Israelites) or if it refers to the Day of Judgment of all humans that will take place at the end of time. In the Gospels, however, Jesus acknowledges that it is he, not the Father, that *all the tribes of the earth ... will see ... coming upon the clouds of heaven with power and great glory* on that day (Mt 24:30-31). Yet, somewhat incongruently, Jesus admits that no one knows when the Parousia will take place, *neither the angels in heaven, nor the Son, but only the Father* (Mt 13:26). The remark merits attention, as it denotes less than an intimate relationship between the Father and the Son that, along with the Holy Spirit, constitute the Trinity.

Hence, passages on the Parousia comprise a unique revelation by Jesus with little if any connections to the Old Testament. In the synoptics, he alludes numerous times to this cosmic event:

> - in the kingdom of God, a man (God) scatters seeds (the Word) and *when the grain is ripe, he wields the sickle at once, for the harvest has come* (Mk 4:26-29).
> - the Son of Man will [come] in his Father's glory with the holy angels (Mk 8:38).

- Jesus speaks to the Sadducees regarding what will happen following the resurrection of the dead (Mk 12:18-27, Lk 20:27-38, Mt 22:23-32).

- he tells the religious authorities that they will see the Son of Man seated at the right hand of the Power and coming with the clouds of heaven (Mk 14:62, Lk).

- he forewarns the unrepentant towns that *it will be more tolerable for Sodom on that day/the day of judgment* than for them (Lk 10:10-15, Mt 10:11-15, 11:20-24).

- addressing the crowds that are asking for a sign, Jesus tells them that *at the judgment* this evil generation will be condemned (Lk 11:31-32, Mt 12:38-42).

- he promises that he will acknowledge before the angels of God those who acknowledge him (Lk 12:8-9, Mt 10:32).

- he indicates that good deeds will be rewarded at *the resurrection of the righteous* (Lk 14:12-14).

- he wonders if upon his Second Coming he will find faith on earth, suggesting that by then many will have abandoned his teachings (Lk 18:8).

- he indicates that on the day of judgment people will render an account for every careless word they speak (Mt 12:36-37).

- he ascertains that as lightning flashes and lights up the sky from one side to the other, so will the Son of Man be [in his day] (Lk 17:24, 30).

John's Gospel does not present a detailed narrative of this event despite its magnitude and significance. There are several verses, however, suggesting that, eventually, Jesus will judge humanity. Speaking in the third person, he indicates that the Father gives him the prerogative to judge humanity (Jn 5:21-27), indicating that he will raise from the dead those who believe in him and condemn *on the last day* those who reject him (Jn 6:40-44, 54, 12:48-49). Martha, Lazarus's sister, believes that Jesus will resurrect the dead on the last day (Jn 11:23). Also, in Jesus's most explicit admission, he tells his disciples he will come back again (Jn 14:3, 16:22, 21:21-23).

Jesus (or the authors), however, introduces a confusing timetable by suggesting that the Parousia is imminent (Jn 5:28-29), a view that even Paul held once (Rom 13:11, Phil 4:5).[4] In Mark, Jesus is less than clear when he says that his return will occur soon, perhaps during their lifetimes: *Watch, therefore; you do not know when the lord of the house is coming, whether in the evening, or at midnight, or at cockcrow, or in the morning. May he not come suddenly and find you sleeping. What I say to you, I say to all: 'Watch!'* (Mk 13:35-37). Yet in the Parable of the Weeds among the Wheat and the Parable of the Fishnet, Jesus intimates that judgment will take place at *the end of the age,* supposedly in the distant future (Mt 13:24-29, 36-43, 13:47-50). He asserts that *the Son of Man will come with his angels in his Father's glory, and then he will repay everyone according to his conduct.* Then again, he says, *there are some standing here who will not taste death until they see the Son of Man coming in his kingdom* (Mt 16:27-28), suggesting that the Second Coming is rather imminent.[5] He even tells his disciples that their generation *will not pass away until all these things have taken place*; another allusion to the imminence of the Parousia (Lk 21:32-33, Mt 24:34-35) for which exegetes do not have a clear explanation.[6] Although he stands by his remark that no one knows when the Parousia will take place except God; in another passage, he suggests that he will return before the end of these ordeals (Mt 10:23).[7]

At some point, the authors of the Gospels seek to dispel believers of the imminence of the Parousia through the Parable of the Ten Lost Coins (Parable of the Talents in Matthew). Exegetes believe that these passages are an afterthought correction to the dilemma (Lk 19:11-27, Mt 25:14-30); [8] except that, who is doing the correction? It would not make sense for God to correct himself. No one seems to know when the Parousia will take place, and divine revelation does not appear to help clarify the issue.

A detailed description of the Parousia appears toward the end of each synoptic Gospel. All three are similar in content. Jesus warns his disciples not to be deceived by false messiahs; that there will be wars, insurrections, earthquakes, famines, and plagues. They will be persecuted, seized, and brought before the governing authorities; even be handed over by their close relatives, and some of them might be put to death. Amid his narrative, he tells them *not to be terrified*, since these events are to be expected, and there would still be more to come. His words, *not to be terrified,* following his description of future events, seem surreal; people are supposed to remain calm as if they are watching a display of fireworks at the beach.

Moreover, when apprehended by the religious and political rulers, Jesus tells his followers not to prepare their own defense since he will provide them with a type of wisdom that their opponents will not be able to refute. His followers will be hated, *but not a hair on* [their] *head will be destroyed* (Lk 21:5-36), Mk 1:1-23, Mt 24:1-26). Given that some or most of his disciples were persecuted and/or killed, the critically minded reader may surmise that this type of wisdom (if provided) was ineffective.[9]

In what many might describe as a horrific description of the Grand Finale of human history, Jesus assures his disciples that, *just as lightning comes from the east and is seen as far as the west, so will the coming of the Son of Man be* (Lk: 21:25-28, Mk 13:24-27, Mt 24:27-31). It is uncertain whether following the Parousia there might still be life on earth. Although Jesus indicates that people will die of fright, others will still see the Son of Man coming in a cloud. Nonetheless, in an Old Testament passage alluding to a type of Parousia against the people of Israel the prophet Zephaniah suggests that, *On the day of the LORD's wrath, in the fire of his passion, all the earth will be consumed. For he will make an end, yes, a sudden end, of all who live on the earth; because they have sinned against the LORD* (Zeph 1:18).

In Matthew, following his cataclysmic description, Jesus replies to his disciples' question regarding when the destruction of the Temple will occur. His answer wanders. He says, *stay awake! For you do not know on which day your Lord will come* (Mt 24:1-44). It appears that Jesus (or the author) conflates both events (the end of time and the destruction of Jerusalem by the Romans in 70 CE); therefore, it is difficult to know which occurrence he has in mind.

The Gospels represent the authors' version of what Jesus said to his generation; those who would die before the Second Coming. Given the supposed timeless nature of the Gospels, Jesus's words on the Parousia apply to future generations. Thus, in the metaphor about the narrow door, for example, Jesus intimates that eventually the master of the house (God) will lock the door and prevent anyone else from coming in, suggesting that time will run out for people to repent (Lk 13:22-30). Jesus stresses this point as he compares himself to a thief who comes unannounced in the middle of the night and breaks into the master's house. *So too, you also must be prepared,* Jesus tells his disciples *for at an hour you do not expect, the Son of Man will come.* Thus, *stay awake,* he tells them (Lk 12:39-40, Mt 24:43-44). The Parable of the Ten Virgins reinforces Jesus's metaphor about the narrow door. When the bridegroom shows up in the middle of the night, five maidens are caught unprepared and need to go out to buy oil for their lamps. Upon their return (on account of their negligence) they find that the bridegroom has shut the doors on them, and they are kept out of the feast, i.e., paradise. Once again, Jesus tells his disciples; *stay awake, for you know neither the day nor the hour* (Mt 25:1-13).

These passages suggest that for future generations death (not the Second Coming) is the thief that comes unannounced. Today, however, awaiting the Second Coming likely would become emotionally and mentally unbearable; it would be akin to constantly thinking about one's death, a reason for which many people would either reject or refuse to pay attention to these passages.

The above passages may be subject to misinterpretation because the authors of the Gospels use Jesus's words outside of their proper context. In Matthew, while speaking about the Parousia, Jesus appears to be counseling his followers to remain vigilant to his Second Coming and faithful to his teachings while he is away (Mt 24:45-51). But exegetes suggest that this teaching is used by Matthew to address the leaders of his church decades later following Jesus's death,[10] raising questions about the authors' use of literary license to transcribe Jesus's teachings in accordance with their circumstances, as opposed to the context in which Jesus taught them. Luke too, similarly uses Jesus's words to tell his followers that the Parousia may not take place imminently, in which case they cannot afford to become careless about God's will (Lk 12:35-48, 12:45).[11]

There is yet another discrepancy regarding the primary objective of the Parousia. Despite having said numerous times that he will come to judge everyone, Jesus tells his disciples that upon his Second Coming they will join him in *judging the twelve tribes of Israel,* without any mention about the rest of humanity (Mt 19:27-28);[12] still another insinuation that Jesus comes only for the people of Israel. In Matthew's passage on Judgement Day, however, Jesus reiterates that the purpose for the Second Coming is to judge all human beings (Jews and non-Jews), the living as well as the dead (Mt 25:31-46).

Beyond what the Gospels tell us about this calamitous and majestic event, what is the Parousia, other than the willful destruction of God's own creation? The non-believer might want to know why such an event needs to be so devastating. Why did Jesus have to leave instead of staying on earth doing battle with Satan on behalf of God's kingdom? Already, he had resurrected, thereby vanquishing Satan. But now he says he has to go to comply with the Father's wishes to prepare a place for his followers (Jn 14:2, 31); however, he would send them the Advocate or Spirit of truth to assist them and remind them of his teachings (Jn 14:16, 26). Within this context, the Jesus event seems like another of God's tests (this time a cosmic one) to see how humanity fares under the Son's teachings. But why?

If for illustration purposes we reduce God's creation to child-rearing, parents would not create life to prove if their children do well or not. They would be happy if their children turn out loving and loyal and probably become saddened if they do not. Good parents would sacrifice themselves to ensure that their children lead a good life and would regret not doing enough if their children run astray, even if they were not at fault. If parents were as omniscient as God and could foretell that their children would grow to become criminals, or if they could know in advance that they would suffer a great deal, would they still be willing to bring them to life? As real as the Parousia may be, it seems to lack a purpose that humans may understand.

What then is God seeking to accomplish by placing humanity on trial? A test may be reasonable if society is preparing students to be useful citizens, safe drivers, competent engineers, or honest and thoughtful public employees; otherwise, it would seem frivolous. The Parousia, seen through the lens of Original Sin seems pointless. Unwittingly, divine horror may weaken Christianity's interest among non-Christians.

Notes:
1. The Book of Daniel refers to *what is to happen in the last days* (Dn 2:28), but he provides no description. In chapter 7, Daniel refers to visions that include a Son of Man that *terrifies* him (Dn 7:15). NEs point out that the events narrated in Matthew refer to his *assurance that they must happen (see Dn 2:28 LXX), for that is the plan of God.* Note, Mt 24:6.
2. The following passages acknowledged the events that will precede the Parousia:
- the gospel shall be preached throughout the world; [this is taking place today and it is likely that it has reached all nations of the world through different venues].
- the conversion of the Jewish people; [although Jews convert to Jesus at times, mass conversions are not taking place].
- the return of Enoch and Elijah; [humans are not aware of a timetable although supposedly God may ordain their return on a moment's notice].
- many or most Christians will abandon the faith; [the process of secularization has contributed to a reduction in the number of Christians, although in some cases it does not mean they have entirely lost the faith].
- a person, group of people, or a force representing the antichrist will persecute the church; [different political regimes and rulers have persecuted the church and Christians throughout history, including popes; Protestantism traditionally has regarded the papacy as the antichrist too].
- there will be wars, famine, earthquakes; [these episodes have been taking place throughout history including today.

- false messiahs and false prophets will appear performing signs that will deceive even the chosen ones (Mt 24:24); [already humanity has had its share of them].
- there will be a general conflagration induced by God that will not annihilate creation; [it is difficult to determine what type of conflict this sign refers to].
- just prior to the end of time *the sun will be darkened, and the moon will not give its light, and the stars will be falling from the sky, and the powers in the heavens will be shaken.* People then will see *'the Son of Man coming in the clouds'* with great power and glory to judge the living and the dead (Mt 13:24-26, 25:31-46).
- following the above occurrences, the dead will be resurrected; [Jesus's disciples believed (including Paul, 1 Thes 4:15) that it would happen during their lifetime].
John McHugh, "General Judgment," *CE.* Vol. 8, http://www.newadvent.org/cathen/08552a.htm (accessed July 9, 2019).
3. NEs' note, Mt 24:15. Jesus points to the *desolating abomination* that the prophet Daniel said will occur as a sign pertaining (supposedly) to the Parousia. However, the *desolating abomination* refers to a previous event that takes place in the year 167 BCE, prior to the Book of Daniel (167-164 BCE). Mistakenly, Matthew uses Jesus's reference to the destruction of the Temple by the Romans in 70 CE as the fulfillment of Daniel's prophecy.
4. Ibid., note, 2 Thes 3:6. Paul's view of an imminent Parousia appears in Romans and Philippians, both written between 55-58 CE, according to NEs (Introduction). Paul then becomes aware that the Parousia is not imminent and writes in 2 Thessalonians that people cannot remain idle waiting for the Second Coming. Thus, he writes that those who do not work shall not eat. If this is a correction to his earlier letters, it must have happened after 58 CE. NEs indicate that 1 Thessalonians is said to be written between 51-52, but they do not suggest a date for the second letter. Paul's statement in 2 Thes 3:6-10 appears to be of dubious origins. NEs point out that confusion over the timing of the Parousia has to do either with Paul's *distorted thinking* or with a *forged letter.*
5. Ibid., note, Mt 16:28, 13:41. Deferring to biblical experts to solve the riddle, NEs indicate that *the coming* does not refer to the Parousia, but *the manifestation of Jesus' rule after his resurrection;* in other words, pointing out that the reference is to Jesus's kingdom as opposed to God's kingdom.
6. Ibid., note, Mt 24:34. *The difficulty raised by this verse cannot be satisfactorily removed by the supposition that this generation means the Jewish people throughout the course of their history, much less the entire human race. Perhaps for Matthew it means the generation to which he and his community belonged.*
7. Ibid., note, Mt 10:23. Even NEs find it difficult to understand what Matthew may have understood, suggesting that he may have been referring to the *"proleptic parousia" of Mt 28:16–20, or the destruction of the temple in A.D. 70, viewed as a coming of Jesus in judgment on unbelieving Israel.*
8. Ibid., note, Lk 19:11-27.
9. Factual data on the types of death the Apostles suffered is greatly lacking. A sample of the literature on the internet shows the following: apologists accept traditional beliefs that most of them were martyred for their faith: Brian Kelly, "How did the Apostles Die?" *Catholicism.org.*, April 12, 2016, https://catholicism.org/how-did-the-apostles-die.html (accessed July 12, 2019); Jack Wellman, How did the Twelve Apostles Die? A Bible Study," *What Christians Want to Know,* https://www.whatchristianswanttoknow.com/how-did-the-12-apostles-die-a-bible-study/ (accessed July 12, 2019); a less apologetic and more scrutinized article on the subject matter yet arriving at a similar conclusion, Sean McDowell, "Did the Apostles Really Die as Martyrs for Their Faith? By Sean McDowell," *OnePlace.com*, https://www.oneplace.com/ministries/bible-answer-man/read/articles/did-the-apostles-really-die-as-martyrs-for-their-faith-by-sean-mcdowell-17589.html (accessed July 12, 2019); a rather argumentative (even petulant), yet informative and reasonably persuasive piece, argues that there is not enough sound historical data that would allow us to assert that the Apostles died as martyrs for their faith, thus leading the already pre-disposed atheist author to question the belief, Richard Carrier, Ph.D., "Did the Apostles Die for a Lie?" April 7, 2016, *Richard Carrier Blogs,* https://www.richardcarrier.info/archives/9978 (accessed July 12, 2019); from a Catholic standpoint, a critic of the extent of Christian martyrdom questions the martyrdom of Peter and Paul; Candida Moss, "Nero, the Execution of Peter and Paul, and the Biggest Fake News in Early Christian History," *TheDailyBeast.com,* July 23, 2017, https://www.thedailybeast.com/nero-the-execution-of-peter-and-paul-and-the-biggest-fake-news-in-early-christian-history?ref=scroll (accessed July 12, 2019). In this article, as in her book, she argues that Nero could not possibly have persecuted Christians because there were no Christians at the time; only Jews who were followers of Jesus. Though technically correct (Jesus's followers might not have been publicly known as Christians yet), more than likely these "Jewish

Christians" would have been identified as a unique group according to the god they followed as well as by the way they worshipped him. Additionally, according to Paul's Letter to the Romans, there were Gentile Christian congregations in Rome alongside Jewish Christians. Hence, although Nero might not have persecuted "Christians" he may have persecuted "Jewish and Gentile Christians."

10. NEs' note, Mt 24:45-51.

11. Ibid., notes, Luke 12:35-48 and 12:45.

12. Ibid., note, Mt 19:28. According to NEs, *it is more likely that what the Twelve are promised is that they will be joined with Jesus then in judging the people of Israel.*

Parables

Jesus's mission requires him to instruct his followers about the kingdom of God; *let us go on to the nearby villages that I may preach there also. For this purpose have I come,* he tells his disciples (Mk 1:38). Quite often he would rely on figurative language to deliver a message or to impart specific teachings. As a form of speech, however, figurative language imposes additional effort on the part of the reader or the listener to grasp nuances, context, and allusions that often make it difficult to understand the essence of the message. Its purpose is to startle or jolt the mind so that the reader will make an extra effort to apprehend the message. Nowadays, figurative language is often used in daily conversations, speeches, and writing, because it is presumed that the average person, namely adult native speakers, is capable of understanding it.[1]

As an educational device, figurative language can be useful, provided the message is not too elaborate and the audience can readily grasp the substance of the message; otherwise, its main objective fails. Successful use of figurative language often depends on idiomatic expressions that are readily understood by audiences that know the native language being used. This means that non-natives may experience problems understanding figurative language if they are not used to these idiomatic expressions, if translations differ from the original text, or if the phrasing is too esoteric (even for native speakers).

Jesus's use of figurative language in the form of metaphors, similes, possibly hyperbole, allegories, and allusion, was extensive. Generally, we know the use of these devices in the Gospels as parables, although he relied on other devices too. The authors of the texts seemed to have been familiar with Jesus's pedagogical method. The word *parable* is used in the synoptics, 12xt in Mark, and 16xt in Luke and Matthew; however, it does not show up in John's Gospel, despite its use of figurative language.[2] The Parables rank relatively high among the less significant categories, largely because of space (*sp*) the authors allocated to each one. Bearing in mind that parables can be understood from different viewpoints, a breakdown according to topics suggests that most deal with descriptions or details about the kingdom of God, the wisdom of God's words, and with the Parousia; some of them also relate to Jesus himself. This section offers a few observations about the extent and circumstances of their use, the effectiveness of the method, and potential relevance to a secular world.

Jesus does not fully explain why he relies on parables as his preferred method of instruction, other than his explanation in Matthew. Some exegetes even describe Jesus's practice generously as being enigmatic.[3] Matthew indicates that Jesus speaks in parables to fulfill a prophecy, supposedly by Isaiah: *I will open my mouth in parables, I will announce what has lain hidden from the foundation of the world* (Mt 13:35). Nonetheless, although the passage is not taken from Isaiah but Psalm 78:2,[4] if Jesus's purpose is to reveal hidden mysteries, he often fails, as the mysteries remain in some of his sayings. Mark too, states that Jesus teaches the crowds and his disciples *at length in parables* (Mk 4:2). However, he clearly exaggerates when saying that *without parables he did not speak to them* (the crowds), *but to his own disciples he explained everything in private* (Mk 4:34). Much of Jesus's teachings to the crowds were literal. Moreover, he did not explain *everything* to his disciples, a reason for which he tells them that he will send them an Advocate to *teach you everything and remind you of all that [I] told you* (Jn 14:26). Additionally, many of Jesus's sayings, as recorded by the evangelists, were not in the form of parables. He addresses parables to the crowds that, likely, were easily understood because they related to their daily experiences while others were not. There are parables, however, that Jesus does not explain to his disciples as well as parables that his disciples fail to comprehend despite Jesus's explanations.

Hence, it is not surprising if the mystery in some of the parables remains hidden from believers today, given that there is no consensus on all of them. Throughout the ages, interpretations of some parables have eluded even students of the Bible because they lack considerable contextual background that experts have not been able to provide. It would not be surprising if first-time readers of the Gospels read parables literally, only to find them puzzling and un-Jesus-like.

Some parables, such as the Mustard Seed (Mk 4:30-34, Lk 13:18-19, Mt 13:31-32), the Good Samaritan (Lk 10:25-37), the Rich Fool (Lk 12:13-21), the Lost Sheep (Lk 15:3-7, Mt 18:12-14), the Lost Coin (Lk 15:8-10), the Prodigal Son (Lk 15:11-32), the Rich Man and Lazarus (Lk 16:19-31), the Pharisee and the Tax Collector (Lk 18:9-14), the Two Foundations (Mt 7:24-27), and the Fishing Net (Mt 13:47-50), are addressed to the crowds (while his disciples are present). They might seem easily understood in a literal sense, although the extent to which the message is fully comprehended may be questioned. Parables, even today, are susceptible to various interpretations that require specialized assistance that is seldom available to the reader. These conditions pose a problem since some claim that *without understanding the parables, it is impossible to fully understand Jesus and his teachings*; or that *a casual reading of the parables is not sufficient to discover the deeper meanings embedded in them.*[5] In short, Jesus's parables are not always easily understood, raising the question, why would Jesus rely on them to teach on matters of so much significance?

The act of understanding a parable lies not only in seizing the message in its literal form. Sometimes, the message is easily grasped only to be puzzled by its significance. The parable of the Seed that Grows Itself (Mk 4:26-29) suggests that the kingdom of God will continue to grow on its own, thus requiring no one to assist in its expansion; yet, Jesus recruits disciples precisely to extend the kingdom. The parable of the Good Samaritan must have left those who listened to it somewhat perplexed, since Jesus was proposing a Samaritan, i.e., someone Jews rejected, as an example of righteousness. This would be akin to a Christian preacher telling his flock, *do what he does,* while pointing out to a Muslim, a Jew, or an atheist who does virtuous deeds.

The unintelligibility and relevance of the Parable of the Friend at Night (Lk 11:5-8) and the Unjust Judge (Lk 18:1-8); the unforgiving tone of the Great Banquet (Lk 14:15-24, Mt 22:1-14); the unmerciful message in the Parable of the Ten Gold Coins/Talents (Lk 19:12-27, Mt 25:14-30); and the harshness of the Parable of the Ten Virgins (Mt 25:1-13) might be enough to deter potential converts. Enough has been said too about the Parable of the Weed (Tares) Among the Wheat (Mt 13:24-30), which is among the most incomprehensible teachings of Jesus when viewed from the standpoint of justice and law and order in a civilized society.

Jesus's pithy reply to people about the need to fast, *can the wedding guests fast while the bridegroom is with them?* followed by the Parable of Pouring New Wine into Old Wineskin (Mk 2:19-22, LK 5:33-38) may require strenuous mental effort to understand what Jesus is trying to tell the crowds nowadays since readers and listeners are not fully acquainted with their context at the time. Moreover, the Bible seldom provides contextual explanations following each parable. For example, the crowds might have found the ending to the Parable of the Lamp (Mk 4:21-25, Lk 8:16-17), *to the one who has, more will be given; from the one who has not, even what he has will be taken away*, disconcerting. Who is Jesus referring to as the one who has? What will be taken away from those who do not have anything? Read literally, it appears that Jesus's teaching is in contradiction with his preference toward the poor, sounding more like a ruthless capitalist or Marxist.

The Parable of the Unjust Steward (Lk 16:1-8) is equally baffling. In this parable Jesus counsels the children of light to be as cunning in dealing with salvation as the children of darkness are in their earthly tasks. Without further explanation, the parable suggests that the children of light should learn from the children of darkness and their undesirable vices.

Jesus's use of parables is unsettling because he opts for a double standard regarding non-believers. According to mainstream Christian interpretation of the parables, truth about the kingdom of God is hidden from those who have little or no faith, even though they would seem to require more remedial religious instruction than believers. Jesus, however, partially reveals the truth to his disciples,[6] suggesting favoritism on his part.

In the Gospels, the objective of the parables is not always to teach; in some cases, it is to hide the truth from those that need it most and to prevent them from believing. Unabashedly, he tells his disciples that the mystery of the kingdom of God is extended only to them, suggesting transparency; *but to those outside everything comes in parables, so that 'they may look and see but not perceive, and hear and listen but not understand, in order that they may not be converted and be forgiven* (Mk 4:11-12).

According to the Gospels, Jesus teaches according to people's ability to understand, which in the texts translates as their willingness to believe. The *gospel* he teaches, meanwhile, seeks to confuse those who refuse to believe in him as well as those who question or reject his teachings. Matthew quotes Isaiah that Jesus proceeds in this manner because peoples' heart is *gross,* and they are unwilling to hear with their ears or see with their eyes (Mt 13:15). This attitude on the part of unbelievers understandably exasperates Jesus. It is not only his teachings that they reject; in doing so, they refuse to accept his relationship with the divine that he legitimizes through his deeds. It seems that continuing to instruct them is a waste of time. If such events take place while people witness Jesus's deeds, what could he expect once he departs and those deeds no longer occur? Nonetheless, although it might be reasonable to give up on an obstinate audience at some point, is it fair to purposefully mislead people who (for various reasons) choose not to accept him?

If Jesus's objective is to teach his disciples about the mysteries of the kingdom of God through parables, at times they disappoint him. They fail to understand the Parable of the Sower (Mk 4:2-20, Lk 8:4-15, Mt 13:3-23), and Jesus becomes irritated: *do you not understand this parable? Then how will you understand any of the parables?* (Mk 4:13). He becomes annoyed at their failure to understand how sinfulness defiles a person (Mt 15:10-20). At times he follows a parable with a terse statement, *whoever has ears to hear ought to hear* (Mk 4:9, Lk 8:8, Mt 13:43) that perhaps might have been well taken at the time; today, this traditional saying tends to be used as a sarcastic remark, a riposte toward people he is less interested in persuading, e.g., if the shoe fits, wear it. Apologists are more lenient; they interpret Jesus's remark as meaning *Listen up!* or *pay close attention!* However, this type of phraseology does not appear anywhere in the Gospels.[7]

Returning to his Parable of the Sower, Jesus depicts four different situations relating to human conduct. In the first one, God grants his teachings to a group of seemingly good people, but *Satan comes at once and takes away the word sown in them [that they may not believe and be saved].* We may rightfully ask, who is to blame for this occurrence, humans for being weak and allowing an evil creature to seduce them, or a cunning Satan, in which case humans cannot be held responsible (or as responsible)? Could God be held accountable for allowing Satan to become the ruler of the world (Jn 12:31, 14:30, 16:11)?

In the second scenario, people who are given God's word appear to be righteous (they receive the word with joy), but they have a weak disposition, and when they are asked to be witnesses to the word they back down. But why do these people have a weak temperament? Did they raise themselves to become cowards? What circumstances may have played a role in their decisions to run away from the word? Would God condemn a person for being weak?

The third scenario depicts a most interesting situation; people who are conditioned by social structures to behave according to what Jesus might refer to as *the ways of the world.* These are passersby who casually hear the word but worldly ethos, i.e., anxiety, greed, and consumerism, prevent the word from bearing fruit. The causes for this behavior typically lie in political and economic ideologies and social structures that have been ignored by religious leaders for fear that their presence would diminish free will and moral responsibility; and because if opposed, it would undermine the political status quo that sustains such temporal values.

So far, Jesus has not referred to people in this parable as evil; they seem to be decent folks, even though they might be ignorant, weak, or superficial in their dispositions. Jesus then addresses those who *hear the word and accept it and bear fruit thirty and sixty and a hundredfold.* The primary reason the word is effective in these people is that they embody *rich soil.* Certainly, it must be asked, what makes these people a rich soil? Is it chance, divine nepotism, social conditioning? Jesus does not explain. He would declare only that those who repent and accept God's word are righteous, without saying what leads Mary, Elizabeth, Joseph, the Baptist, Simeon, or any of Jesus's disciples to become rich soil; or why do Herod, Pontius Pilate, many of the Jewish religious leadership, or Judas constitute poor soil? Jesus's lack of explanation suggests that he will not take into account a flawed human nature; instead, God will still hold people accountable even when their faith is stolen by the devil.

Peter fails to understand the Parable of the Faithful Servant, not knowing if it is meant only for the disciples or for everyone (Lk 12:35-48). Instead of explaining, Jesus answers him with another part of the parable; thus, it is not clear who is Jesus looking to address. On the other hand, in some cases, the religious authorities seem to grasp the meaning of parables that apply to them, including the Parable of the Tenants in which Jesus seems to threaten to take the kingdom of God away from the Jewish people. Their understanding of the parable leads them to plot his arrest (Mk 12:12, Lk 20:19, Mt 21:45).

Moreover, it is difficult to know how the disciples react to the Parable of the Fig Tree that deals with the Parousia (Mk 13:5-30, Lk 21:5-36, Mt 24:1-44). They do not ask him a most pertinent question: why should the end of time happen in such a catastrophic fashion? Nor does Jesus explain. Possibly, future generations resigned to the inevitable will rush to repent and accept the faith under duress; others might think that this prediction is maddening, and instead may opt to ignore his teaching.

John's use of figurative language is interesting because in some instances it becomes a dogma in the Catholic Church (less so among Protestants), e.g., *I am the bread of life*, he says (Jn 6:35-36), possibly referring to the Eucharist. Moreover, Jesus's use of figurative language fails to enlighten Nicodemus, a Pharisee friend who is greatly impressed by Jesus's deeds. He tells Nicodemus *that no one can see the kingdom of God without being born from above*, possibly referring to the heavens (Jn 3:3). Despite his religious training, Nicodemus does not understand what Jesus is saying. Jesus explains to him that *the wind blows where it wills, and you can hear the sound it makes, but you do not know where it comes from or where it goes; so it is with everyone who is born of the Spirit*. Again, Nicodemus does not understand, and Jesus slights him for not knowing things that a teacher of Israel ought to know (Jn 3:1-15). He insists on educating Nicodemus and begins to speak about the Son of Man, a cryptic term that Jesus never defines, and his disciples do not seem interested in asking him.

In another instance, Jesus finds a Samaritan woman and begins to speak to her about him being *living water*, i.e., eternal life that anyone who drinks it will never thirst. The credulous woman takes his words literally without grasping Jesus's message. Thus, she asks Jesus to give her this water so she would not have to come back to the well (Jn 4:15). Interestingly, Jesus is not using figurative language in this situation; he is describing the eternal nature of his mission.

When addressing a crowd, he tells them that he is the good shepherd whose sheep follow him because they recognize his voice. Yet, they fail to understand how the remark relates to him. He explains further, insisting that, as a good shepherd, he will give his life for his sheep, but his remarks lead to division, some saying that *he is possessed and out of his mind* (Jn 10:1-20). In another instance, he explains to his disciples (but not to the crowds) that he is the true vine and that without him they cannot do anything. Not being able to decipher the meaning of this saying, it has become one of Jesus's most perplexing and perhaps misleading statements in the Gospels, suggesting that, outside of him, no human being (not even the Samaritan?) is capable of a good deed. He does not provide any explanation for his remark, simply adding that anyone who does not remain in him will be cast into a fire (Jn 15:1-7).

The reader may wonder if Jesus's enigmatic approach to teaching about the kingdom of God might be effective, given that the true meaning of parables seems to elude even the disciples. John's Gospel, for example, is full of cosmic symbolism, and it is unlikely that much of what Jesus says can be understood without possessing blind faith in him; indeed, an obstacle to belief in an increasingly secularized world.

One may also want to ask if, pedagogically, parables are the most effective method to teach people. Many of Jesus's parables are narrated within the context of events that happened two thousand years ago when conditions and experiences were quite different than they are today. This means that to effectively extrapolate the significance of the parables into the present, the past must be readily understood. This is not the case with a newcomer to the Bible, which is why the historical-critical analysis (among other methods) becomes important. Rev. John Meier, a scholar in this field, has written five volumes on Jesus, the fifth one about the parables in the Gospels.[8] Without pretending to conduct an exegesis on the topic, he concludes that only four parables (out of dozens) may be legitimately attributed to Jesus: The

Mustard Seed, the Evil Tenants in the Vineyard, the Great Supper, and the Parable of the Talents. Meier suggests that other parables that appear in the Gospels were either created by the authors of the texts or else lack historical evidence. Meier's assessment, even if only partially correct, and there is no additional empirical confirmation of an opposite outlook, might require a redefinition of the theological term *divine revelation*. Some of the parables are, indeed, instructive; others, however, are confusing and frightening, while others, perhaps the ones we like the most, might have been invented.

Notes:
1. "Figurative Language," *LiteraryDevices*.com, http://www.literarydevices.com/figurative-language/ (accessed May 22, 2020); "Figurative Language," *The NROC Project,* https://content.nroc.org/DevelopmentalEnglish/unit07/Foundations/figurative-language.html (accessed May 22, 2020).
2. An approximate breakdown of figurative language in the Gospels is as follows: Mark (11xt): 2:19-20, 2: 21-22, 3:23-27, 4:2-20, 4:21-25, 4:26-29, 4:30-32, 7:14-23, 9:49-50, 12:1-12, 13:1-2, 13:5-31. Luke (27xt): 5:33-38, 8:4-15, 8:16-17, 10:25-37, 11:5-8, 11:17-22, 11:33-36, 11:39-44, 54, 12:13-21, 12:35-48, 13:6-9, 13:18-19, 13:20-21, 14:7-14, 14:15-24, 15:3-7, 15:8-10, 15:11-32, 16:1-8, 16:19-31, 17:7-10, 18:1-8, 18:9-14, 19:12-27, 20:9-19, 21:5-6., 2:29-33. Matthew (25xt): 5:13-16, 7:24-27, 9:14-17, 12:25-29, 13:3-23, 13:24-30, 13:31-32, 13:33, 13:44, 13:45-46, 13:47-50, 13:51-52, 15:10-20, 18:12-14, 18:21-35, 20:1-16, 21:28-31, 21:33-45, 22:1-14, 23:13-33, 24:1-2, 24:3-36, 24:45-51, 25:1-13, 25:14-30. John (6xt): 1:1-7, 4:7-14, 6:35-36, 10:7-17, 15:1-7, 16:20-22.
3. NEs' note, Mark 4:1-34.
4. Ibid., note, Matthew 13:35.
5. "The Parables of Jesus," *Christian Bible Reference Site,* https://www.christianbiblereference.org/jparable.htm (accessed May 22, 2020); Hampton Keathley IV, "Introduction to the Parables," *Bible.org,* https://bible.org/seriespage/introduction-parables (accessed May 22, 2020); R.T. Kendall, *The Parables of Jesus: A Guide to Understanding and Applying the Stories Jesus Told,* (Ada, Mi: Baker Publishing Group, 2008); Jay A. Parry, Donald W. Parry, *Understanding the Parables of Jesus Christ,"* Deseret Books, deseretbook.com/p/understanding-parables-jesus-christ-jay-parry-4334?variant_id=106513-paperback (accessed May 22, 2020); John P. Meier, *A Marginal Jew: Rethinking the Historical Jesus: Probing the Authenticity of the Parables*, Vol V, (New Haven: The Anchor Yale Bible Reference Library, 2016).
6. NEs' note, Mark 4:11-12 reads*: It is against this background that the distinction in Jesus' method becomes clear of presenting the kingdom to the disbelieving crowd in one manner and to the disciples in another. To the former, it is presented in parables and the truth remains hidden; for the latter, the parable is interpreted and the mystery is partially revealed because of their faith.*
7. "What did Jesus mean when He said, "He who has ears to hear"?" *Got Questions. Your Questions. Biblical Answers,* https://www.gotquestions.org/he-who-has-ears-to-hear.html (accessed May 14, 2019).
8. Meir, Vol V.

Supernatural Occurrences

The purpose of assembling narratives in the Gospels that deal with unearthly visions is to indicate to the reader the empirical presence of the supernatural on earth that the authors disclose in the texts. These passages are, purportedly, part of the initial oral tradition; the outcome of the research the authors prepared as they were gathering information about the public life of Jesus. This book assumes that everything that appears in the texts occurred as written. These incidents are supposed to be revelations by the divine, ways in which God sought to communicate his existence to humans.

Moreover, all passages tallied in this category suggest that the authors of the Gospels were witnesses to each occurrence or that they were told about them. Even

Jesus may have communicated his isolated moment in the desert to his disciples. His disciples may have witnessed the appearance of angels at Gethsemane. All this indicates that, either these events happened in some form, or that decades later through flawed oral transmission people passed along events they were told took place.

There is also the skeptical position that argues that the narratives are purposeful insertions intended to create belief in something that did not happen to deceive others. The deception hypothesis would require specific motives on the part of apparently good men and women who were willing to lead a life that entailed sacrifices and risks and led some or many of them to a violent death knowing or believing that what they wrote was false. On the other hand, it is, indeed, possible that the Gospels' authors' willingness to believe in Jesus may have led them to unintentionally accept, and thereby deceive, themselves and others.

These narratives figure temporal manifestations by God, the Spirit, the angel Gabriel, lesser angels, and even past prophets, all involved in a collective effort to support Jesus's legacy from his infancy to his death. Perhaps the most intriguing episode is that of Jesus being *led by the Spirit into the desert to be tempted by the devil*. It would be reasonable to ask: why would God want Jesus to be tempted in this manner? Was this more like a survivalist training to test Jesus overcoming the emotional and physical endurance required to accomplish his mission? What could God possibly be teaching human beings through this episode since we do not have a divine assistant next to us when we need it most to overcome temptation?

As incredible as these narratives are, the purpose of presenting them is not to affirm their truthfulness or to deny them, but simply to add to the descriptive character of the texts. As may be noted, neither Jesus's miracles nor supernatural manifestations of evil (Devil, demons, spirits) are included in this category despite being considered supernatural events as these are treated separately. This category merely indicates non-visible instances in which the supernatural interrelates with humans. Although this category ranks among the less significant, it is reasonable to include both Jesus's miracles and the Devil categories. When added together (manually), this category becomes among the Highly Significant ones tallying an overall score of 3007.

Below are examples of how God and its messengers appear in the Gospels adding to the supernatural dimension of the texts:

- The angel of the Lord appears before Zechariah to inform him about the role his son, John the Baptist, will play announcing the coming of Jesus (Lk 1:5-22).
- The Angel Gabriel is sent from God to announce to Mary she will become the mother of the Son of the Most High (Lk 1:26-38).
- Zechariah has been made mute by the angel and uses signs to provide his son's name (Lk 1:57).
- The angel of the Lord appears before Joseph to tell him not to be afraid to take Mary into his home despite her pregnancy since it was through the Holy Spirit that Jesus would be conceived (Mt 1:18-25).

- A star aids the magi to locate the birthplace of Jesus (Mt 2:1-2).
- The angel of the Lord appears to Joseph in a dream and warns him to take the baby to Egypt to keep him away from harm by Herod. Following Herod's death, the angel once again appears to Joseph in a dream and tells him to take Jesus and Mary back to Israel (Mt 2:13-23).
- The Holy Spirit reveals to Simeon that he will see the Messiah of the Lord before his death (Lk 2:25-32).
- The angel of the Lord appears before shepherds to announce the birth of Jesus. This is followed by a multitude of heavenly beings praising God (Lk 2:8-14).
- Jesus is given his name following the information previously provided by the angel (Lk 2:21).
- John the Baptist says he saw the Holy Spirit coming down like a dove and remain over Jesus (Jn 1:32).
- A voice from the heavens (God?) tells Jesus he is his beloved son (Mk 1:9-11, Lk 3:21-22, Mt 3:16-17).
- The Holy Spirit attends Jesus in the desert while being tempted by Satan (Mk 1:12-13, Lk 4:1-13); angels minister to Jesus after the encounter (Mt 4:1-11).
- Jesus's Transfiguration before Peter, James, and John (Mk 9:2-9, Lk 9:28-36, Mt 17:1-6).
- A crowd hears a voice from heaven, supposedly the Father, speaking to Jesus telling him that God's name has been glorified. Jesus tells the crowd that the voice is heard for their sake (Jn 12:28-30).
- At Gethsemane, an angel appears to strengthen Jesus's resolve to comply with God's mission (Lk 22:43).
- At the moment Jesus dies, there is an earthquake, tombs are opened, and bodies of the dead come alive and appear to many as they enter the holy city (Mt 27:50-53).
- A young man, supposedly an angel, appears before Mary Magdalene at the time of the Resurrection (Mk 16:18); two men in dazzling garments, supposedly angels, appear at the site of the tomb where Jesus is buried (Lk 24:1-8); an angel of the Lord speaks to Mary Magdalene and tells her Jesus has resurrected (Mt 28:1-7); two angels in white sit by the tomb on Resurrection Day and ask Mary Magdalene why she is crying. She then sees Jesus (20:12-13).
- Two men on their way to Emmaus tell a disguised Jesus that a vision of angels had told several women that Jesus was alive (Lk 24:22-23).

The discrepancy regarding the passages dealing with the resurrection is a characteristic of the Gospels that does not speak highly of the precision of oral tradition and/or revelation. Today, the absence of public supernatural occurrences, including by the devil, heightens human incredulity about the afterlife despite our realization that both good and evil exist in temporal life. Presumably, at a time when humanity might need God's visible presence most, Jesus's reticence may be perceived as a disappointment even to his most beloved followers.

(See Method Note for additional explanations)

God as Everyone's Father

The difference between the Jesus that the Gospels present, presumably as the Son of God, and the Lord God in the Old Testament is vast. At times, it appears as if Jesus is a different type of God, or else that God has given Jesus ample prerogatives to alter his dictates. Jesus's priorities, despite saying that he is simply doing the Father's will, are different, and often in contradiction to the Father. Jesus practically does away with Mosaic Law. He claims to come only for the Israelites but seems to change his mind; he says inside a synagogue that he will proclaim liberty to the captives and let the oppressed go free, the type of temporal messiah the Jewish people were expecting; however, he becomes an eschatological messiah less concerned about the temporal world while focusing on eternal salvation, something that hardly appears in the Old Testament. He modifies dozens of God's laws and regulations subsuming them into two basic commandments, love of God and love of neighbor (the Good Samaritan). He asks for mercy toward one another rather than sacrifices; his main concern is not with the righteous but with sinners. He teaches concern for the poor and preaches non-violence and forgiveness of one's enemies as behavioral indicators of his commandments. Some of his teachings are impractical; others seem absurd.

Nonetheless, perhaps, the most significant teaching, in contrast with the God of the Old Testament, is that he teaches people to call God *Abba* or father. Although the term *father* appears over 790xt in the Old Testament, God is not referred to as one's father in the Jewish texts. In the Gospels, Jesus refers to God as everyone's father 40xt, which raises its tally above the least significant categories. Despite the disparity in numbers (the Gospels are over eight times shorter than the Old Testament), the significance lies in the substance of Jesus's action. He personalizes an alien God, and teaches the crowds to call him *your heavenly father* who is pleased to give his *little flock* the kingdom (Lk 12:32). In effect, he is calling humans God's children while referring to God using the possessive pronoun *your Father* 20xt about God.

For unknown reasons, the same Jesus changes his attitude in John's Gospel. In John, it is no longer *your Father* but *the Father* (13xt). Whether it has to do with the translation or the audience it addresses, John's *Father* is at odds with the synoptics and constitutes an about-face that detracts from what Jesus was seeking to attain by regarding God more intimately. The term *abba* translates not only as *father* but as *dad* too. Although the Gospels do not expound on its significance at the time, referring to God as *our father* in an intimate manner would have been unheard of, perhaps scandalous, among the Jewish people who considered God as too impersonal and too holy to even use the complete name Yahweh; instead, God was YHWH or the Lord.

The Gospels do not indicate what the reaction of people accustomed to praying to a distant God might have been.

Nowadays, Christianity is trying to stress the more familiar term; someone that despite being unseen, unheard, and seemingly distant in space, is close to its children. Although God's presence on a personal level is felt by many, the overt result of God's intimate relationship with humans is more difficult to assess. God still appears far too remote from temporal life, raising the question, how can a distant God be a loving God?

(See Method Note for additional explanation)

Justification

Justification needs to be added to a list of obscure terms in Christianity, along with divine providence, grace, soul, Holy Spirit, and others. Justification, a declaration that God's creatures are made righteous by God, finds its roots in Paul's theology, not in the Gospels. Whether through faith, deeds, or both (it varies according to denominations), God justifies his creatures, i.e., makes them blameless, moral, virtuous, because of the actions of Jesus, namely his death, which atones for the sin of our foreparents in the Garden of Eden and in the process expiates humanity's sins, including those that will take place by future generations. God's pardon through justification, however, fails to have far-reaching protection since humans continue to sin. This means that despite being justified human beings may still end up being eternally condemned. Hence, what did God's justification accomplish?

Justification and the Gospels
When Martin Luther made public his Ninety-Five Theses in 1517, he was probably oblivious that conditions were being created for what became known as the Religious Wars in Europe. These wars, in which Christians fought against each other over their religious interpretations of the scriptures, lasted over two centuries. Millions of people died in these conflicts.[1] A primary reason for these wars was Luther's refusal to continue to render obedience to Pope Leo X because the pontiff did not merit Luther's respect, largely over the selling of indulgences.[2] But at heart were a series of objections by Luther over matters of beliefs, none perhaps more important than *justification by faith*. According to him, the term implies a freely ordained act by God through which sinners are pardoned for their misdeeds and become righteous on account of their faith in the redeeming death of Jesus. The dispute over which Christians senselessly killed each other has become a source of division that non-Christians might depict as "an irrational mess."

Perhaps, the most interesting aspect surrounding justification is the fact that it has nothing to do with Jesus since he does not address the issue in the Gospels. Once again, we notice the Gospels being undermined by Paul's musings over important doctrinal matters that God or Jesus forgot (or chose not) to pass on to the evangelists through oral tradition. According to Pauline doctrine, God sent Jesus on a mission to atone for Adam's and Eve's Original Sin that had affected all humankind. Paul indicates that Jesus was meant to be the new Adam: *For just as in Adam all die, so too in Christ shall all be brought to life* (1 Cor 15:22). His statement connotes that Jesus dies for all humanity and in the process redeems it; otherwise, human beings would have been eternally condemned or become non-existent following temporal death.

The problem with the term lies in that no one knows how justification works or how comprehensive it is. Although a gift from God, justification supposedly requires human assent, whether belief in Jesus and/or behavior in accordance with his teachings.

The term *justified/justification* appears only 4xt in the Old Testament, but possibly only once does it deal with Jesus. In Isaiah 53, the Lord places *the guilt of us all* upon the servant of the Lord (Is 53:6), perhaps alluding to a prototype Jesus. This means that it is God's will that his servant is to bear the pain *as a reparation offering* (Is 53:10), a rephrasing of the concept of atonement. Atonement was necessary, Christianity holds, because God had written humans off because they had 'offended' him. However, once God had a change of heart, the servant's reparation supposedly would serve to *justify the many* by bearing their iniquities (Is 53:11). As the servant surrenders himself to death, he is bearing the *sins of many* (Is 53:12). The passage, nonetheless, does not indicate that justification requires faith in the Pauline sense, i.e., that it merits eternal salvation.

Moreover, presuming there is an afterlife, no one knows who might be saved. The various Christian denominations are divided on this issue; is it only those who die while having faith in Jesus that will be saved? Will the type of life one leads on earth, sinful or righteous, influence God's decision? What happens to those who through no fault of their own do not believe in Jesus? Can non-Christians who act in accordance with Jesus's teachings be saved? And, since the various Christian denominations have their own interpretations of salvation, which one is correct, and how do we know? Most Christian denominations, however, tend to agree that it is God that freely grants justification (whether in a limited or unlimited scope), signifying that there is nothing humans can do to earn it through their own merits.

Although Jesus said that he wanted *to set the earth on fire* (Lk 12:49-51), likely he did not mean that Christians ought to engage in warfare over his teachings. That Jesus does not originate the concept of justification is reflected in the content analysis results in Table 2; *justification* is among the least significant of all categories tallied. The term appears only 3xt in the Gospels, all in Luke, and each one carries different meanings; hardly a crucial basis over which to develop a doctrine. Moreover, it is difficult to find passages or synonyms in the Gospels that could be tallied in this category. Thus, it falls upon Paul to become the primary exponent of *justification*; the term appears 29-30xt in his letters,[3] which leads to the question, why would Jesus fail to address such a noteworthy matter in his own words in the Gospels?

If justification were synonymous with being righteous, it might be possible to tally both words together requiring judicious consideration given how Jesus uses the terms. *Righteousness* in the Gospels means proper behavior in the eyes of God. It entails the summation of various categories regarding dos and don'ts, including repentance and a resolve to abstain from specific sinfulness; leading a life of faith and prayer; practicing charity in all its dimensions; being baptized and abiding first by Mosaic Law and afterward by Jesus's teachings. Righteousness comprises both belief in Jesus and behavior in accordance with his teachings.

Justification, as used by Jesus in Luke's Gospel, indicates something quite different. As a scholar of the law inquires on what is required to inherit eternal life, Jesus tells him that all he needs to do is to follow the Law. However, as Jesus notices that the scholar of the law wants to *justify* himself, i.e., appear righteous, he delivers the Parable of the Good Samaritan. In the parable, Jesus sets aside justification, i.e., God's forgiveness of sin, and instead focuses on his definition of righteousness in which he makes a Samaritan (much disliked by the Israelites) as the exemplary figure for being merciful to someone who has been robbed and injured. Furthermore, Jesus does not even specify if the victim is a Jew or not, suggesting that assistance to non-Jews may be considered an example of loving one's neighbor (Lk 10:25-37). In this passage, attainment of eternal life depends not on faith but on good works. Jesus reinforces the Parable of the Good Samaritan with his description of Judgment Day in Matthew, indicating (without referring to faith) that those who do good will be saved.

In a second passage in Luke, Jesus engages in a tirade against the Pharisees and tells them, *you justify yourselves in the sight of others.* Again, Jesus does not use the term *justification* to suggest God's forgiving action, since according to Christian doctrine humans cannot forgive themselves. Instead, he is being critical of the Pharisees' attempt to appear righteous before God and others. He tells them, *God knows your hearts; for what is of human esteem is an abomination in the sight of God.* (Lk 16:13-15). Once again, in this passage, Jesus defines justification in terms of righteousness.

The third passage, although confusing, deals mostly with righteousness too. It concerns Jesus's Parable of the Pharisee and the Tax Collector (Lk 18:9-14) that he addresses to *those who were convinced of their own righteousness and despised everyone else.* The parable contrasts two types of behavior in the eyes of God, the Pharisee's self-righteousness and the tax collector who humbly asks God for the forgiveness of his sins. Jesus concludes that the tax collector goes home *justified,* possibly meaning becoming righteous once he shows repentance for his sins. In the passage, it is belief in God (not in Jesus) that justifies (or forgives). Jesus's explanation that the tax collector becomes justified is followed by his saying, *everyone who exalts himself will be humbled, and the one who humbles himself will be exalted.* The term *exalted,* at least by today's standards, does not mean to be forgiven, but to be highly regarded or praised.[4]

Given the above examples, it may be difficult to conclude that Jesus uses the term *justify* as God's action to forgive; rather, he refers to a human decision to repent that is freely adopted, whether instigated by God or not. We may then ask again, how is it possible that a term Jesus seldom uses referring to righteous behavior could have unleashed a deadly conflict among Christians? Without getting into much detail, the answer lies in Paul's use of the term, which despite the numerous times it shows in his letters, its meaning remains ambiguous at best. While Paul definitively relies at times upon faith to be the sole saving element, in other instances he emphasizes righteous behavior by itself as being mandated by faith, his best example being when he compares faith, hope, and love, and indicates that, of the three, love (behavior) is the greatest (1 Cor 13:13). Moreover, if Paul's treatise on justification is so crucial, and he admits that he has explained his views to Peter, James, and the other disciples, how could oral tradition have missed it, in which case, what is the role of divine inspiration in the Gospels?

Justification by faith alone, suggesting salvation by faith, seems to find support in John's Gospel. The view that faith alone saves the believer shows up repeatedly (See *Faith* and *Salvation* categories). But John's Gospel lacks the human dimension of love that appears in the synoptics. Despite the term *love* and its synonyms (defined as an attitude and a type of behavior) appear 55xt in John, in most instances the term refers to love between the Father and Jesus and between Jesus and his disciples. The terms mercy, compassion, forgiveness, or examples of love of neighbor are mostly absent in John's Gospel. In the synoptics, meanwhile, the instances when Jesus says to a person *your faith has saved you,* refer to faith leading, not to eternal salvation, but to healing the sick.

The theological debate about the doctrine of justification has failed to resolve the conflict among Christians. Each side continues to stand firm in their positions resembling the Pharisee who self-righteously exalts himself before God, convinced of his truths. Fundamentally, it seems that Catholics and Protestants may have waged war incessantly over semantics, and those who held on to their positions probably perceived that killings in the name of their beliefs were 'justified.' It seems that the phrase *faith alone saves* becomes problematic only if it is literally taken to mean that Jesus will save regardless of how people lead their lives. To underline the absurdity of this proposition seems unnecessary; supposedly in Christianity, faith is not something to be believed but to be lived. In other words, faith ought to lead to good works.

Although this proposition seems rational enough, the dilemma regarding orthodoxy versus orthopraxis remains unresolved. Shall we assume that those who do not believe in Jesus, yet perform Jesus-like works would not be justified? All Christian denominations (except perhaps the most fundamentalist position) suggest that God could not possibly ignore virtuous deeds by non-Christians and non-believers. If they were to ignore such deeds, they would have to explain what accounts for their good behavior. Are humans able to perform righteous acts by themselves, or do these happen because God instigates them?

The Christian conflict would seem to lead the secular-minded person to repudiate the faith. As a Generation X and student of history with whom I debated this issue once told me: *if they* (Christians) *are so idiotic to fight over the meaning of a word whose substance only God knows, why would I even want to argue this matter! I don't care!* Hence, it appears inconceivable that strongly held beliefs based on interpretations of an imprecise term could have led to deadly conflicts among Christians.

Notes

1. "Selected Death Tolls for Wars, Massacres, and Atrocities Before the 20th Century," http://necrometrics.com/pre1700a.htm#30YrW (accessed October 29, 2019). This site provides various reference sources estimating the number of people that died during these wars.

2. Although the Catholic Church corrupted the practice, properly granting indulgences for the remission of sins is within the exercise of the Church's faculties *through the application of the superabundant merits of Christ and of the saints, and for some just and reasonable motive.* William Kent, "Indulgences," *CE*, Vol. 7, http://www.newadvent.org/cathen/07783a.htm (accessed October 29, 2019).

3. There is a discrepancy in the count of Paul's use of the term *justified/justification*. According to the NABRE version, my count shows 19xt in Romans while the Bible Gateway version shows 17xt; My count indicates 9xt in Galatians while Bible Gateway version shows 7xt; two other appearances of the term are 1xt in 1 Corinthian and 1xt in Titus.

4. *Merriam-Webster Dictionary,* online, s.v. "exalted."

Grace

According to Christian theology, grace is a gift; the free and undeserved call that God extends to all humans (or only to some, depending on the Christian denomination) inviting us to partake in his eternal realm. It is God's way of expressing his desire that we all become his children and eventually live eternally. Grace, however, is more than an invitation. The Christian faith would insist that since humanity developed a propensity to sin because of Original Sin, humans alone cannot attain salvation without God's intervention. If justification is humanity's side of the bargain, i.e., humans must believe that Jesus is Lord, grace is God's supernatural manifestation of his presence in their lives.

Grace not only justifies its recipient, i.e., erases sin, but also enables the acquisition of faith and allows the believer to participate in the life of God by leading a righteous life. It also accounts for those who respond to God's call to activities such as preaching and evangelizing, charisms, the gift of prophecy, and the ability to engage in specific services to others. Supposedly, grace is acquired through the merits of Jesus Christ's redemptive death and is either imputed or infused (depending on the denomination) by the Holy Spirit. In human terms, grace is like God whispering suggestions to humans that in turn may or may not require its free response.[1]

Despite lengthy volumes being written throughout history to explain the meaning of grace, the word appears only four times, all in John's Gospel.[2] Intriguingly, the authors do not provide a more concrete description of the term, and neither does Jesus.

Once again, the data points to the insufficiency of the most sacred texts in Christianity (the Gospels) to the understanding of the public Jesus. That a theology of grace exists at all is due to Paul who cites the word 81xt in his letters, acknowledging the existence of something while offering glimpses of what it means and what it can accomplish.[3] These numbers are yet another indication of God (or Jesus) speaking through Paul rather than being Jesus who teaches about this concept.

Grace in the Scriptures
In the Old Testament, the term *grace* seldomly appears (about 10xt), but its usage differs vastly from its Christian understanding.[4] At times, it suggests emitting a favorable or pleasant response from God, for example, in the King James 21 version, Noah finds *grace in the eyes of God* because he is a righteous man (Gen 6:8, KJ21); the NABRE Bible, instead, uses the term *favor*. This episode is interesting because, although grace is supposed to come from God, in this case, it appears to be sparked by Noah's behavior. Perhaps the most important distinction regarding grace is that in the Old Testament, finding favor with his people or with a specific Israelite meant God would reward them, not with the type of grace stipulated in Christian theology, but with material benefits, victories in battles as well as with riches, as long as they obeyed his rules. Genesis and Exodus indicate that Abraham and Moses (among others), were highly favored by the Lord (Gen 17:18-20, Ex 33:12-13, 17).

Grace may also be understood as God's reward for good behavior, as when Mary is chosen to become the mother of Jesus, the angel tells her that she has found favor in the eyes of the Lord (Lk 1:26-30, 39-48). Luke also recalls that Jesus is favored by God during his early years (Lk 2:40, 52) and later on during his public life, although this time he used the term *pleased* (Mk 1:9-11, Lk3:21-22, Mt 3:16-17, 17:5).

According to certain passages in the Gospels God wishes all to be saved (Lk 6:35, 14:13-15, 16-23, Mt 18:12-14, 22:1-4), indicating that grace is given to all since Jesus's death was meant to redeem humanity. Yet at the time of Jesus's birth, angels pray for peace on earth, not upon all humanity, but *to those on whom his* [God's] *favor rests* (Lk 2:13-14), suggesting that God picks winners and losers.

John's Gospel is the only one that deals (in most translations) with the term *grace,* but it provides little understanding. It states that Jesus is *full of grace,* i.e., fully favored by God; that from *his fullness we have all received, grace in place of grace,* indeed, a difficult phrase to understand,[5] and that *grace and truth came through Jesus Christ,* suggesting that whatever grace is, we receive it through Jesus (Jn 1:14-17). There is, nonetheless, a categorical and rather comprehensive assertion whereby Jesus attests that only by remaining in him can human beings bear much fruit because *without me you can do nothing* (Jn 15;5). His statement, taken literally, indicates that grace comes only upon those who have faith in him after they reply to God's call.

Paul offers a more ample understanding of grace. For example, we learn from him that something known as *grace* emanates from Jesus (1 Thess 5:28); human beings are *justified,* i.e., their sins are forgiven, by the grace of God as a result of Jesus's redemption (Rom 3:24); faith comes from God through Jesus (Rom 5:1-2); grace provides encouragement and hope (2 Thess 2:16); grace overshadows sin (Rom 5:20); grace is the root of gifts given to believers to expand the kingdom of God (Rom 12:6); believers' good deeds are the product of grace (2 Cor 9:8); and grace is but God's power acting in the believer (2 Cor 12:9), among many other details.

According to the Gospels, God *favors* some of the central personalities in the texts, including Mary, Zechariah, Elizabeth, John the Baptist, and Joseph, as well as people who find themselves in dire circumstances or who obey Jesus's commandments. In these instances, however, the texts use the term *blessed* instead of *favor* or *pleased.*

Ranking Grace in the Gospels

Since the Gospels do not provide a concise explanation that allows the reader to understand what is meant by *grace*, I focused on passages that are attuned to the above definition. Hence, in addition to the terms *grace, pleased,* and *favor,* the word *blessed,* insofar as it suggests finding favor in the eyes of God, or requesting favors, e.g., being blessed, are taken into account. This means that the Beatitudes in Luke and Matthew are tallied since the righteous acceptance of their conditions and behavior supposedly are the result of God's assistance; so too, are those who are blessed because of their good deeds in feeding the hungry, welcoming the stranger, and caring for the ill (Mt 25:31-34), presuming that good deeds are the outcome of God's grace.

There are also instances in which Jesus states, *blessed are those who hear the word of God and observe it* (Lk 11:28), or *blessed is the one who takes no offense at me* (Lk 7:23, Mt 11:6). The term presupposes the presence of God's grace without which believers would not be able to act accordingly. Additionally, there are passages in which Jesus clearly indicates that his disciples' insights are the outcome of God's grace, for example, when he says *blessed are your eyes, because they see, and your ears, because they hear* (Mt 13:16-17); and, perhaps, the most notorious passage in which Peter acknowledges who Jesus is, and Jesus replies *Blessed are you, Simon son of Jonah. For flesh and blood has not revealed this to you, but my heavenly Father* (Mt 16:17). God's grace also appears in the texts in Jesus's revelation of the truth about his kingdom, e.g., when he tells his disciples *the mystery of the kingdom of God has been granted to you* but not to others (Mk 4:10-11, Lk 8:9-10, Mt 13:10-11); these are included in the count. Nevertheless, despite considering other terms, grace remains a low-ranked category.

Grace in the Age of Secularization

Christian theology indicates that humanity does not ask for God's grace; he gives it to us gratuitously; to all or some, depending upon the denomination's interpretation. All we have to do is to respond. But what happens then? God provides humanity something mystical or spiritual that is neither visible nor rationally understood, hence, how can we detect that we enjoy God's grace? According to Jesus, if the tree is good it will bear good fruit, and a bad one bears bad fruit. (Mt 7:17). If so, does that mean that non-Christians also receive God's grace insofar as they act in accordance with Jesus's teachings, in which case, does faith matter?

Supposedly, God's grace does not alter the individuals' personality; it is only a whisper that somehow must be heard. God's grace presumes that we need to respond through rigorous self-discipline, i.e., *renunciation and spiritual battle*, seemingly against evil and sinful behavior.[6] This response becomes problematic as Christians find themselves divided over their interpretations. Moreover, an indication of enjoying God's grace is *living in the peace and joy of the Beatitudes*.[7] The Beatitudes, however, are not that joyful if you are poor, abused, persecuted, or have to mourn the death of your loved ones in acts of violence, and much less if one has to accept these conditions with meekness.

As a last observation, if grace comes from God through Jesus, and God wills the salvation of all humanity, it must be concluded that this grace must be made available to all. On the other hand, the gift of grace, according to the Gospels (and Paul) appears to be contingent upon having faith in Jesus. Since nearly two-thirds of the world's population is not Christian and has remained like that for centuries, given the sinful condition that humanity has endured throughout history, several conclusions may be inferred. If grace is supposed to work as intended, i.e., by providing faith (supposedly in Jesus) and by fostering a spirit of righteousness within believers,[8] a) God has not provided humanity or even Christians with enough grace; b) humans have disregarded grace or found it difficult to understand it, or c) sin has proven far stronger than grace. This condition negates Paul's saying that *where sin increased, grace overflowed all the more* (Rom 5:20). This is to say that, given the amount of prayer that Christians supposedly have engaged in throughout history, the efficacy of grace (as well as prayer) tends to be overvalued. From this perspective, the secularized mind would find it difficult to accept the significance (or even existence) of grace. Moreover, this view suggests that non-Christians may not attain salvation because, for numerous reasons, grace seems to have failed to reach them.[9]

But perhaps the greatest divergence between Christians and non-Christians is Jesus's attestation that without God's grace humans are incapable of good deeds. It is almost certain that non–Christians find this aspect of Christianity contemptuous, self-righteous, and in contradiction to the view that all human beings who exercise goodwill (to the best of their abilities and circumstances) may find favor in God's eyes. Thus, Christianity's version of grace constitutes a cultural and religious roadblock to greater human understanding, possibly the opposite of God's wishes.

Notes:

1. Nearly all Christian denominations accept the concept of grace as a supernatural element through which God touches and directly moves the heart of the person. Moreover, there is agreement that without grace human salvation would not be possible. Differences arise in terms of who receives grace from God and the extent to which grace may work on its own or whether it requires human cooperation.
2. There is not much variance in the numbers in other Bible translations; in some cases, some translations add the word once, in Luke, or use the term *kindness*. BibleGateway.com.

3. The numbers in Paul's letters are similar in other translations. For example, the term appears 80xt in the International Version of the Bible, 95xt in King James Version, 92xt in 21st Century King James Version, and 83xt in the Evangelical Heritage Version.

4. The term that is most used by the Protestant NKJ21 and the Catholic NABRE versions is *favor*, instead of *grace*. Still, there are considerable differences; NKJ21 uses *favor* 82xt while NABRE uses it 177xt. NKJ21 uses *grace* 37xt while in NABRE it appears 10xt.

5. NEs' note, John 1:16 states, *replacement of the Old Covenant with the New (cf. Jn 1:17). Other possible translations are "grace upon grace" (accumulation) and "grace for grace" (correspondence).*

6. CCC 2015. Seemingly, most Protestant denominations would agree with the statement.

7. Ibid. Likely, there are differing viewpoints among and within all Christian denominations regarding this statement.

8. Ibid., 1266.

9. This view was abrogated in the Second Vatican Council in its Dogmatic Constitution on the Church *Lumen Gentium* promulgated by Pope Paul VI in 1964. The Council declared *that the plan of salvation includes those who acknowledge the Creator; those who through no fault of their own do not know the Gospel of Christ or His Church, yet sincerely seek God and moved by grace strive by their deeds to do His will as it is known to them through the dictates of conscience; or those who, without blame on their part, have not yet arrived at an explicit knowledge of God and with His grace strive to live a good life,* http://www.vatican.va/archive/hist_councils/ii_vatican_council/documents/vat-ii_const_19641121_lumen-gentium_en.html (accessed on October 14, 2019). Some Protestant denominations share the updated version.

Redemption

Redemption has been reviewed in chapter 5 under the category *Savior/Redeemer*. This section briefly looks at *redemption* as it relates to the Old Testament, ancient Judaism, and the Gospels, and considers the results of content analysis.

As secularly defined, redemption/redeemer, and savior refer to the action of being freed from that which distresses or harms people, and/or to liberate or deliver from captivity by payment of ransom.[1] This definition would accord with the Christian concept whereby Jesus is the guiltless Messiah whose mission is to redeem or ransom humanity to satisfy God's anger because of the offense committed by Adam and Eve in the Garden of Eden.[2] Since there is a discrepancy among Christian denominations regarding whether Jesus dies for all, many, or only those who are predestined to be saved, the extent of Christian redemption is open to debate.

Another point that must be noted is that neither *savior* nor *redeemer* necessarily points to Jesus's resurrection; even from a Christian viewpoint, to redeem means only that Jesus's death atones for someone else's sins. Christianity would consider his resurrection a bonus to indicate that the divine is directly involved in the act, thereby making Jesus's teachings appear more credible.

Ancient Judaism's view of redemption was different than how Christianity eventually defined it. To Jews, the term meant several things: God's earthly rescue of the Jewish people from captivity;[3] personal spiritual atonement or repentance for one's sins through prayer, fasting, charity, and even suffering, as a means to become righteous in the eyes of God;[4] and the acceptance of God's word, signifying that no one redeems others, but it is up to humans to redeem themselves.[5] Other than these, references to redemption in the Old Testament are few. Awkwardly, they relate to property and financial transactions involving even human beings (Lev 25).[6]

In Judaism, redemption was unrelated to the view of a cosmic or supernatural ransom paid for the sins of humanity's original parents. This means that the term, as defined by the Christian faith, would have been a novel idea at the time; another departure by Jesus from the Old Testament. On the other hand, whether the Christian concept finds resonance in the Gospels is altogether a different question.

Given the profound significance of the terms *savior* and *redeemer* in the Christian faith, we would expect either of these words to appear numerous times in all four texts. Nonetheless, the title *savior* occurs only 3xt in reference to Jesus. On the other hand, there is no explicit reference to Jesus as the eschatological redeemer in any of the texts. The term *redemption/redeem* appears only 4xt, once alluding to God, twice to Jesus (as a temporal redeemer), and once in which Jesus mentions the term seemingly referring to the Parousia. Nonetheless, as previously mentioned in the *Savior/Redeemer* category in chapter 5, there are numerous passages, particularly in John's Gospel, in which Jesus claims to have the authority and the power to grant eternal life; these claims, however, are not related to Jesus's redemptive mission.

There are other passages in which Jesus refers to some type of redemption. In one instance he tells his disciples that *the Son of Man did not come to be served but to serve and to give his life as a ransom for many* (Mk 10:45, Mt 20:28). Moreover, during the Last Supper, he says only to them, *this is my blood of the covenant, which will be shed for many* (Mk 14:22-24, Lk 22:20). Jesus, however, does not explain what he means by those statements; who is asking him to undertake this action; who is to be ransomed, and why? What exactly was he trying to accomplish by shedding his blood? Soldiers have shed their blood in battle, although for specific causes. Since he provides no connection to Original Sin, Jesus's redemption, as it appears in the Gospels, lacks a purpose. Again, it is left up to Paul to devise a theology of redemption based on an eschatological savior (Rom 3:24, 1 Cor 1:18, 29-30, Phil 3:20, Eph 1:7), although even Paul has extraordinarily little to say about it.

All we know from the Gospels is that that a temporal savior is born to fulfill God's promise to free the Israelites from captivity. Nonetheless, despite prophesizing his death, we do not know why he must die, other than because the Father wills it, and because he must fulfill the scriptures. Hence, Jesus's eschatological outlook does not seem to have an unambiguous religious foundation. Overnight, this social and political redeemer and savior becomes apolitical, and a new religion is born.

The term *ransom* becomes significant in Christian theology despite it only appears twice in the texts without explanation. There is only one passage, in Matthew during the Last Supper, in which Jesus is more explicit regarding his purpose for redeeming humanity; he says that he will shed his blood *on behalf of many for the forgiveness of sins* (Mt 26:27-28). That no other Gospel narrative includes these words is perplexing. Nonetheless, ransoming many people for their sins connotes only that God will forgive someone's sins, but no necessary conclusion is warranted in which ransom is related to the afterlife.

Matthew's passage is similar to Zechariah's canticle in which Luke refers to John the Baptist as *a prophet of the Most High* (referencing God) because he will *go before the Lord to prepare his ways, to give his people knowledge of salvation through the forgiveness of their sins* (Lk 1:76-77). The phrase *salvation through the forgiveness of sins* does not connote redemption, and it seems to be out of context since the canticle refers to a temporal action by God in which he redeems his people from their enemies. Moreover, the term *Lord* is confusing, since it may refer to God as a divine being, or to the earthly title of respect given to Jesus.[7] Hence, is the Baptist going before God or before Jesus; and, is Jesus being portrayed as the human, i.e., temporal, Messiah the Jewish people have been waiting for, or as the Son of God?

A similar passage in Matthew portrays Jesus as a redeemer when the angel of the Lord appears to Joseph and announces that Mary will bear a son that is to be named Jesus *because he will save his people* (not humanity) *from their sins* (Mt 1:18-21). In the next chapter, however, there is a strange scene in which magi from the east (likely Gentiles) arrive in Jerusalem to pay homage to Jesus who is to become the ruler of the Israelite people, indicating that Jesus would be a temporal (not supernatural) messiah and redeemer (Mt 2:6). Moreover, every time Jesus acknowledges to be the king of the Jews (including people that welcome him in Jerusalem), he seems to be indicating his temporal (as opposed to a supernatural) role of redemption (Mk 15:1-2, Lk 23:1-3, Mt 27:11, Jn 12:12-13). Interestingly, in John's Gospel, as opposed to the synoptics, Jesus is non-committal about being the king of the Jews, even while admitting to the eschatological nature of his role when he tells Pilate, *my kingdom does not belong to this world* (Jn 18:36).

Perhaps the passage that more closely depicts Jesus as some form of redeemer does not show in the Gospels. Isaiah's chapter 53 succinctly traces Jesus's public life, including someone being pierced for our sins, healing our wounds, carrying *the guilt of us all,* and being slaughtered like a lamb as mandated by the Lord (Is 53:5-7). In Isaiah's passage, however, there is no resurrection and no reference of human iniquity being traced back to Genesis. Matthew refers to this passage while appearing to confuse the sins of humanity for physical diseases and infirmities that the character in Isaiah endures.[8]

There are, nonetheless, metaphorical passages in John's Gospel alluding to Jesus within the context of a possible cosmic redemption. For example, the Baptist refers to Jesus as *the Lamb of God*, connoting the sacrificial animal Jews offered to God to atone for their sins (Jn 1:29). Many Samaritans call Jesus *the savior of the world* (Jn 4:39-42), even though there are no unusual incidents on Jesus's part that would elicit this notion other than having spoken to them. He refers to himself as *the living bread that came down from heaven*, adding that this bread is his own flesh that he will give *for the life of the world* (Jn 6:51), insinuating that he dies for the entire world; a world that in several other passages he clearly despises (see Temporal World category). In John, Jesus states five times that, like a good shepherd, he will lay down his life for *the sheep* (Jn 10:11:18), although it is not clear who the sheep are. Then, in a separate passage, he indicates that once risen he will *draw everyone* to himself (Jn 12:31-32), suggesting an inevitable (magnetic-like) attraction to him.

In another passage, Jesus alludes to his death metaphorically suggesting that a grain of wheat produces much fruit once it dies (Jn 12:24). Finally, he says that he comes to save the world, but as the bearer of truth (Jn 12:46-50), not as a redeemer. These passages in John are like pieces of a puzzle that put together are supposed to point to an eschatological redeemer. Nonetheless, the image that emerges is disjointed, as if pieces are missing, requiring the reader to fill blank spaces with suppositions.

The lack of clarity in the Gospels is due, likely because the word 'sin' is introduced in some passages, thereby giving the terms redeemer/savior cosmic features. Since sinfulness occurs only regarding God, i.e., it is not part of a temporal/secular vocabulary, the perception is created that redemption is, somehow, an eschatological term. Nonetheless, we must bear in mind that in the Old Testament God asks his people to repent so he can redeem them by offering them temporal fortunes. Moreover, from a temporal standpoint, being a redeemer and a savior may entail having to die for causes that are not necessarily cosmic, but purely social or political. In Jesus's case, there was no need for an eschatological redemption or atonement. Faith in him and obedience to his teachings would have sufficed for humans to reach eternal life. Jesus's death and resurrection would certainly make his person and his teachings more credible without these acts being necessarily redemptive. The view that sending his son to die as God's sign of his love for humans that constantly fail him might be appealing and selfless, but still unnecessary to attain salvation. In the end, it is difficult to accept an eschatological redemption or atonement without establishing a direct connection to Original Sin, something that Jesus does not do.

The temporal nature of Jesus's redemption is even manifested in the two disciples on the road to Emmaus who believe that Jesus is to temporally *redeem Israel*. He seeks to correct them by referencing the Old Testament while alluding to a Messiah that needs to suffer before being glorified (Lk 24:26, 46). However, nowhere in the Bible does the concept of a suffering Messiah shows up prior to the New Testament.[9] Is it possible that Jesus could have been mistaken; or was it a case of a faulty oral transmission?

There is little doubt that Jesus is up to something. He claims to bring light to the world so that humanity may live in truth; he calls for repentance of sins; he says he will die to ransom someone, i.e., many, the world, his sheep, so that scriptures may be fulfilled (Mt 26:54); he associates some type of redemption with the Parousia (Lk 21:28) and indicates that he gives life to those that believe in him. But at no time does Jesus refer to a fallen humanity that needs to be ransomed through his death, or that his death will atone for humanity's sins to satisfy God's anger, the type of redemption dictated by the Christian faith based on the Pauline concept of Original Sin.

Content analysis results in Table 2 indicate the problems associated with this term; its context suggests both temporal and eschatological redemption. Altogether, the use of the term *redemption* and similar connotations occur 31xt; 11xt seem to pertain to temporal redemption, some ascribed to God and others to Jesus. All references to eschatological redemption, however, are imprecise, suggesting that they may be interpreted temporally too. The results offer a mixed picture that prevents ranking redemption as a distinct category. Instead, Table 2 shows the tallying of two categories, Eschatological and Temporal, each one ranked among the least significant.

Historically speaking, it appears that the Christian interpretation of redemption does not provide a sensible explanation for the human condition. In effect, if the price of redeeming humanity was the suffering and death of the Son of God, a reasonable cost-benefit analysis may show that the price was too high relative to its obtained benefit. Humanity remains as sinful as before, although slight progress on a consensus over ethics and morals is being attained within a secular environment. Nonetheless, increased worldwide fragmentation due to culture wars (being waged among Christians no less), selfishness, and self-righteousness as well as the risk of serious armed conflicts and ecological disasters may subvert the efficacy of a new morality. God may very well be questioning his actions once again, this time wondering why redemption has failed to attain his desired end.

Notes:

1. *Merriam-Webster Dictionary,* online, s.v. "redemption."
2. Joseph Sollier "Redemption." CE. Vol. 12, http://www.newadvent.org/cathen/12677d.htm (accessed November 20, 2019); CCC 613, 615. According to the Catholic Catechism, *the account of the fall in Genesis 3 uses figurative language but affirms a primeval event, a deed that took place at the beginning of the history of man* (CCC 390). Who exactly demands such ransom and to whom is it paid is open to interpretation among Christian denominations, although it is surmised that our foreparents' offense to God is being satisfied by the death of his son (CCC 602, 603, 604).
3. "Salvation," (redirected from Redemption), http://www.jewishencyclopedia.com/articles/12624-redemption (accessed November 20, 2019).
4. Kaufman Kohle, "Atonement," *Jewish Encyclopedia,* www.jewishencyclopedia.com/articles/2092-atonement (accessed November 20, 2019).
5. Rabbi Aron Tendler, "The Meaning of Redemption," October 27, 2005, http://torah.org/torah-portion/rabbis-notebook-5766-bereishis/ (accessed November 20, 2019).
6. *BibleGateway.com.*
7. NEs' note, Lk 1:76 suggests that the term *Lord* is most likely a reference to Jesus (contrast Lk 1:15–17 where Yahweh is meant). Such differentiation does not appear that clear to me as a reader, and the phrase *most likely* is not very reassuring.
8. Ibid., note, Matthew 8:17.
9. Ibid., note Luke 24:26.

The Soul

Secularly speaking, the soul refers to an incorporeal living feature residing within the human person often regarded as immortal.[1] In Christianity, it is defined as *the ultimate internal principle by which we think, feel, and will, and by which our bodies are animated.*[2] It represents *the innermost aspect of man, that which is of greatest value in him; that by which he is most* especially *in God's image,* suggesting that *it can have its origin only in God.*[3] These views are largely shared by most Christian denominations in one form or another.[4]

The term is rather common in the Old Testament, appearing more or less 157xt in the texts.[5] However, its meaning in Judaism is imprecise. The Catholic Catechism, for example, accepts that the term, as used in the Old Testament, is quite different from the manner it is defined today; in the Old Testament, it *refers to human life or the entire human person.*[6] Other scholars agree indicating the Israelites did not share the belief of a resurrected or immortal soul,[7] something that Jesus must have known.

Despite the discrepancy, the soul remains an integral part of the Christian faith; without an immortal soul there can be no reference to the resurrection of humans in body and soul; the death of a person would negate the Christian concept of an afterlife. Once again, we are facing a term that has been theologically developed in the post-Jesus era.

In Genesis, God seems to make an important distinction between *matter* and a unique process that leads to human life. First, God forms man from dust, and then he blows into his nostrils *the breath of life,* supposedly something different than matter. Genesis presupposes that God gives matter an exclusive element to humans that is not found in animal and vegetative life. The term *breath of life* seldom occurs in the Old Testament within the context of giving life to matter; per my count, only 7xt does it refer to God giving life to humans (Gen 2:7, 6:17, 7:15, 7:22, 1 Kings 17:21, 22, and indirectly in Dan 5:23). Nonetheless, God does not speak (clearly) of everlasting life in the Old Testament. The exception seems to be that since Original Sin is the primary cause of human death, Genesis suggests that, had there not been such a sin, humans, i.e., thinking matter, would have continued to live eternally.

Since the meaning of the term, as we understand it today, finds no basis in the Old Testament, and it is probably a Hellenic import from Platonic and Aristotelian philosophy,[7] why would Jesus use the word in the Gospels at all? Moreover, since it is so vital in Christianity, why did he use it infrequently, usually meaning physical *life* rather than an immortal soul? The term *soul* appears only 7xt in the Gospels, among the least significant categories according to content analysis results in Table 2. We find the word *soul* twice in Mark, once in Luke, and four times in Matthew. It is baffling that John's Gospel that deals with eternal life so often does not mention it. Even Paul seldom uses the term, in one instance making a distinction between spirit, soul, and body, thereby complicating the meaning of the term (1 Thess 5:23).

The phrase loving God with *all your soul, all your mind, and all your strength* in Mark and Matthew is standard in the Old Testament, but it does not suggest anything other than physical existence or life (Mk 12:30, Mt 22:37). When Mary says that her soul proclaims the greatness of the Lord, she is not inferring anything different than the Old Testament tradition she had been taught; likewise, when she adds that her *spirit rejoices in God my savior* (Lk 1:46-47) she is not engaging in theological distinctions. As previously mentioned, there simply was no understanding at the time of an immortal soul (or spirit). Moreover, since there is no clear explanation about the term in the Gospels, it is not apparent what Jesus is referring to when he says that his *soul is sorrowful even to death* (Mk 14:34, Mt 26:38). If anything, expecting to die soon, he may have been referring to the emotional stress his entire being was feeling at the moment.

The only instance in which Jesus provides discriminating information about the soul occurs in Matthew, when he says, *do not be afraid of those who kill the body but cannot kill the soul; rather, be afraid of the one who can destroy both soul and body in Gehenna* (Mt 10:28-33). Twice he distinguishes between the physical body and something called the soul, an element that can be destroyed, possibly suggesting that it can be eternally condemned along with the body or that it can continue to live after physical death, implying eternal life. It is mystifying that Jesus introduces a highly significant term, unknown in the manner it was understood at the time, yet he does not say anything else about it. Indeed, this is the sole passage in all the Gospels that deals with such a central theme in Christianity, giving rise to the possibility that the term is the product of human hands and not divine revelation.

Although today's understanding of the soul appears only once in the texts, might other terms add validity to its current meaning? It appears several terms connote the existence of the soul that for purposes of this study are not taken into account. For example, unless matter can think (and the question is still open for materialists), God is likely referring to the creation of the soul when he blows *the breath of life* in the nostrils of humans. Jesus, however, does not allude to the passage in Genesis. In the Gospels, nonetheless, references to *the resurrection of humans, the afterlife, salvation and condemnation, eternal life,* and *kingdom of God,* all highly significant categories in this work, connote the existence of an element that seems to be immaterial and can survive physical death; that element appears to enfold the characteristics of the soul.

The existence of the term *human soul* provides believers with the longing of being reunited with their loved ones, as well as the apprehension or disillusionment they would feel if they were to learn that there might be nothing else beyond life on earth. In this sense, Christian belief in the soul delivers a simple message: the possibility of eternal life. It is important to note, however, that outside the faith the term remains a theoretical notion lacking sufficient empirical basis that would allow science to render a definitive conclusion regarding its existence. From a Christian perspective, it signifies the hope (dream?) that in a secularized world, science might eventually validate faith. Materialist-minded persons, nonetheless, most likely would arbitrarily dismiss the existence of the soul,[9] despite questions about its existence remain scientifically unanswered. Once again, we find science and faith at an impasse.

Notes:
1. *Merriam-Webster Dictionary,* online, s.v. "soul."
2. Michael Maher, Joseph Bolland, "Soul," *CE,* Vol. 14, http://www.newadvent.org/cathen/14153a.htm (accessed November 2, 2019).
3. CCC 363, 33, 366.
4. A minority view (Jehovah's Witness, Seventh Day Adventist, and few others) holds that the soul of

those that are not saved will cease to exist.

5. *BibleGateway.com.*

6. CCC 363.

7. James Tabor, "The Jewish Roman World of Jesus," https://jamestabor.com/what-the-bible-really-says-about-death-afterlife-and-the-future-part-1/ (accessed December 14, 2013); Kaufmann Kohler, "Immortality of the Soul," *Jewish Encyclopedia,* http://www.jewishencyclopedia.com/articles/8092-immortality-of-the-soul (accessed November 2, 2019); also, the *Encyclopedia Judaica* indicates that *Jewish theology has no clearly elaborated views on the relationship between body and soul, nor on the nature of the soul itself. ... Whether the soul is capable of living an independent, fully conscious existence away from the body after death is unclear from rabbinic sources. Encyclopedia Judaica,* 2008, "Body and Soul," in *Jewish Virtual Library,* https:/jewishvirtuallibrary.org/body-and-soul (accessed November 2, 2019); also, NEs acknowledge that *Hebrew anthropology did not postulate body/soul dualism in the way that is familiar to us.* Note on John 12:25. The article on the Soul (above) in the Old Catholic Encyclopedia (1907-1914) makes the following statement that seems to contradict the Catechism: *it is evident that the Old Testament throughout, either asserts or implies the distinct reality of the soul.*

8. Mahler and Bolland; Kaufman Kohler, Isaac Broydé, Ludwig Blau, "Soul," *Jewish Encyclopedia,* http://www.jewishencyclopedia.com/articles/13933-soul (accessed November 5, 2019). See Hendrik Lorenz, "Ancient Theories of Soul," *The Stanford Encyclopedia of Philosophy* (Summer 2009 Edition), Edward N. Zalta (ed.), https://plato.stanford.edu/archives/sum2009/entries/ancient-soul/ (accessed November 7, 2019).

9. Neuroscientist George Paxinos suggests that the soul provides insufficient explanatory capability for human behavior because all cognitive and sensorial manifestations come from the brain. The statement, from a scientific viewpoint, seems correct. Nonetheless, it may be argued that such a view is the conclusion of a materialist inclination. Such an approach cannot definitively negate the existence of the soul, since it is possible that what resides inside the brain (commonly known as the mind) is a feature of the soul. "Why psychology lost its soul: everything comes from the brain," *Elsevier,* October 2016, http://scitechconnect.elsevier.com/why-psychology-lost-its-soul-brain/ (accessed November 5, 2019).

Sinfulness

The category *Sinfulness Total Space* as it appears in Table 2 is an artificial construct derived from the sum of two categories, *Sinfulness and Its Synonyms* and *Teachings about Specific Sins.* The two categories are grouped to indicate the importance of sinfulness to the authors of the Gospels. Indeed, the results suggest that Jesus's teachings on sinfulness are highly ranked. This section deals first with *Sinfulness and Its Synonyms* followed by *Teachings about Specific Sins.*

(See Method Note for additional explanation)

Sinfulness and Its Synonyms

According to the Christian faith, sinfulness relates to a human tendency to commit transgressions that God regards as offensive and evil. This definition applies not only to Christianity but to Judaism and Islam too. Secularly speaking, sinfulness is equivalent to wrongdoing according to social mores, ethos, values, or civil laws. While evil is defined as the calamitous outcome of a human or a natural act, the term *sin* or *sinfulness* applies to an evil act committed by a person responsible for such an act in the eyes of God.

In the Old Testament, it is God who dictates what constitutes evil and sinful behavior. (Ex 32, Lev 16, 20, Num 15, 16, 32). Nonetheless, throughout the ages, multiple aspects of the Old Law have been disregarded; many of them by Jesus, others by the hierarchies of the various Christian denominations, and still others by believers, while these denominations have generated, and rejected, new definitions of sinfulness in accordance with their interpretations of the Bible. The historical record suggests that what is evil and sinful comes down to pronouncements by each denomination, and ultimately to whatever the faithful wishes to believe.[1]

Christianity holds that there is a cause-and-effect relationship between sinfulness, evil, and what is sinful, at the center of which lies personal accountability. A deed is considered evil, thus sinful, because causing harm to another person or oneself constitutes an act of disobedience against God's commandments. Whether an evil deed is sinful, nonetheless, seems more complicated. In the temporal world, an evil act is encoded into law (whether fair or not), and any act that contravenes the law is a misdeed, or as we call it, illegal. Moreover, the act is illegal even if the person is not aware of the law that forbids the action. Hence, anyone who defies a law, steals, illegally crosses national borders, peddles one's body, traffics in drugs, or even kills, may be charged and convicted for breaking the law. But is that person guilty of sin in the eyes of God? According to most Christian denominations God judges human action according to, a) our internal motives; b) the extent of one's freedom to make decisions; c) whether there is sufficient knowledge, and deliberate consent to execute the action; and d) the stipulation that only God knows what lies inside of a person's heart (Lk 16:14).[2] Given these considerations, it might be presumptuous to judge one's moral guilt from God's vantage point.

Christian teachings tell us that humanity's fallen or weakened nature following Original Sin is responsible for unsettling the moral faculties, thus making us susceptible to yield to desires that result in evil deeds.[3] Setting aside natural disasters, evil is caused too by external agents, namely the devil or Satan that is constantly tempting a weakened human condition to offend God. Paul, himself a disciplined man, depicts the effects of sin upon him when mystifyingly he says, *What I do, I do not understand. For I do not do what I want, but I do what I hate ... So now it is no longer I who do it, but sin that dwells in me* (Rom 7:15, 17, 24).

Taking the human condition into account we may ask, what constitutes sinfulness according to the Gospels? Who are the sinners in the texts, and who are not, and which are the sins Jesus refers to? The answers in the Gospels reveal a rather comprehensive picture of sinfulness, though not without serious inconsistencies. Sinfulness is so malevolent that, according to the Christian faith, Jesus was willing to give his life *for the forgiveness of sin* (Mk 14:24, Lk 22:20, Mt 26:28), with the presumption that his death would atone for human sinfulness so that human beings could attain eternal salvation. Nonetheless, despite admitting that sinfulness is a disease for which there is no cure, Christianity asserts that it may still lead to condemnation. Oddly, Jesus makes repentance from one's sins and baptism for the sinner's rebirth a central part of his mission (Mk 1:14-15, Mk 6:12, Lk 3:3, 15:7, 10, 11-32, 24:47, Mt 4:17), seemingly indicating that through a combination of his atonement, repentance, and baptism sinfulness might no longer occur. However, as sin is likely to recur, repentance entails an endless psychological and spiritual struggle to do good and avoid evil. This reality, in effect, questions the effectiveness of Jesus's death, and the concepts of repentance and baptism.

Nonetheless, Jesus persists in preaching salvation while emphasizing its greatest obstacle: sinfulness. But, as he indicated, salvation is difficult to attain, i.e., the gate to enter into heaven is narrow. On the other hand, given his desire to save the world (Jn 12:47), it would be reasonable to expect that he would want to make salvation easier for a species that lacks the wherewithal to understand the mystery behind God's plan of salvation. A passage in all three synoptic texts, however, insinuates that Jesus purposefully makes it even more difficult for many to avoid sinfulness and be saved (Mk 4:11-12, Lk 8:9-10, Mt 13:10-13). His reply that the mysteries of the kingdom of heaven will not be granted to most people is altogether puzzling,[4] as it would seem to contradict his intention during the Last Supper when he says that his blood will be shed for the forgiveness of sins of all, most, or some people (Mt 26;28).

Despite sin's enduring nature, Jesus loathes sin. His parables of the Tenants, the Great Feast, and the Ten Gold Coins reveal that he is so offended by the human rejection of God that he punishes evildoers with death (Mk 12:1, Lk 14:15, Mt 25:14). His zeal for God even leads him to overreact as he angrily expels those doing commerce on temple grounds believing their activities offend God (Mk 11:15-17, Lk 19:45-46, Mt 21:12-13, Jn 2:13-16), despite their work is closely related to temple worship.[5] But, if sinfulness pervades humanity, would it not be more reasonable for God to be less mysterious and more forthcoming, and for Jesus to be less harsh and more forgiving of sinners? Yet, he continues to curse and to threaten those through whom sin occurs (Lk 17:1, Mt 18:7, 23:13-36) while at the same time meeting with them, because the healthy do not need to be healed; only the sick ones do (Mk 2:17, Lk 5:29-32, Mt 9:9-13). Ironically, by telling the Pharisees, 'I come for sinners, not for you,' he seems to regard the religious authorities as righteous when in fact they are among the greatest sinners according to the Gospels. This suggests that there are two types of sinners, those who repent and those who are not worth the effort to save because they will not accept their sinfulness, or because God does not grant them the ability to understand his mysteries.

Jesus is unwilling to provide a sign for an *evil generation,* suggesting that sinfulness extends beyond the religious authorities into people at large. (Lk 11:29, Mt 12:39). It may not be only the case that Jesus simply refuses to comply with their requests, but that, given their mindset, i.e., they see Jesus as evil, nothing will convince them.[6] But, is not this mindset the outcome of Original Sin and a flawed humanity that is not able to understand Jesus's teachings? Would that evil generation meet the criteria of sinfulness; that is, did it have perfect understanding and knowledge of the gravity of the matter? Have we not met people who are unwilling or incapable of understanding simply because they are ideologically blind with an unyielding mentality that allows no alternative explanations? Are such people pure evil? Yet, Jesus ignores that evil generation; he will not even alert the living relatives of the rich man who is suffering in hell, because he feels that they will not listen to Moses or to anyone that rises from the dead (Lk 16:31).[7] At the same time, he liberally forgives others' sins even though they might not have been interested in being forgiven, and instead were only concerned with being physically healed (Lk 7:44-50, Mk 2:2-12).

A noteworthy aspect of Jesus's take on sinfulness is his lack of explanation (there are exceptions) about why certain deeds are sinful and others are not. He presumes that people already are aware of what constitutes evil; a reasonable conclusion given the Israelites have been raised and educated under the Old Law. Hence, he identifies the types of righteous and sinful behavior that is expected of his people, in effect decreeing a new moral law. His presumption that people know what their sins are, however, is often not the case.[8]

In a secular society, Jesus's teachings are problematic. As the Gospels do not provide a concise theory of moral behavior based on reasonable explanations, but rather on God's dictates, 'Christian truths,' faith, prayer, love, repentance, cannot possibly be debated against competing values on religious grounds. All that a divided Christianity can do in the public square is to persuade opponents that its values can lead to a more ethical and just society by producing 'good fruits.'[9]

As a backup, Christianity has traditionally insisted on the concept of a Natural Law that God imprints in every human being that allows them to distinguish between right and wrong (precisely what God did not allow Adam and Eve to learn). Supposedly, this law would enable every individual to dispense with scriptures by relying on what 'their hearts tell them.' The historical reality, however, seems to question the efficacy of this law as there is nothing in it that could objectively assist the person to distinguish between right and wrong.[10]

Nonetheless, Jesus's teachings on sinfulness can still be useful. To reinforce his teachings, he promises eternal life to those who abide by them and condemnation to those who do not (Lk 10:1-16, Mt 11:20-24, 13:24-30). Although the Gospels indicate that Jesus is not as interested in temporal salvation, i.e., liberation, as he is in the afterlife (Mt 10:16-28), it is possible that conversion of hearts and minds in line with Jesus's teachings may enrich social institutions and structures that in turn may improve the lives of others. Accordingly, he identifies multiple sinful deeds while alerting us that we will be judged by our actions. He consolidates all divine laws and principles of behavior into two commandments, love of God and love of neighbor (Mt 22:36-40). Significantly, despite offering multiple examples of what it means to love thy neighbor, he does not provide a precise definition of what it means to love God *with all your heart, with all your soul, and with all your mind.*

Another interesting aspect of the texts is that Jesus appears to relate sinning and suffering. The synoptic texts include a passage in which Jesus forgives a paralytic man of his sins, and when questioned by the Pharisees he heals the man. While he proves the point that he has supernatural powers, he seems to equate infirmity with sin and physical healing with the forgiveness of sin (Mk 2:9-11, Lk 5:17-25, Mt 9:1-8). He tells a man he has just healed, *Look, you are well; do not sin anymore, so that nothing worse may happen to you* (Jn 5:14). Is this remark expressing a threat or a reasonable conclusion that causing evil may lead the doer into legal or physical problems? The view that sin leads to suffering ought not to be surprising since there are numerous passages in the Old Testament in which God punishes his adversaries, including their innocent offspring and his people when they misbehave.[11] God's remark, *Only the one who sins shall die* (Ez 18:20) convey the same message. Moreover, a passage in John in which Jesus cures a man blind from birth suggests that God tolerates suffering to allow Jesus to perform his healing miracles (Jn 9:2-3);[12] and, even Jesus indicates that Lazarus's death takes place so that *the Son of God may be glorified through it* (Jn 11:4). On the other hand, following Jesus's action of healing a crippled woman, he provides an opposite view, saying that it is Satan, not God, who has kept her suffering for eighteen years (Lk 13:16).

NABRE editors' conclusion that Jesus *never drew a one-to-one connection between sin and suffering*[13] is questionable and confusing if accepted as an overall explanation. Considering the above examples, several possible conclusions may be inferred: a) God punishes the sinner on earth; b) God allows human suffering of the innocent on account of the sins of others, or c) God uses human suffering for his own glory. A postmodern critique of Christianity could easily relate to the first conclusion since it is similar to human behavior on earth whereby human laws punish those guilty of misdeeds. Secular society could also accept the second conclusion since much human suffering of the innocent can be blamed on a minority of evil people. Nonetheless, regarding the third conclusion, the idea that God avenges sinful deeds by instigating his wrath against the innocent (despite passages in the Old Testament indicating it) seems perversely opposed to Jesus's admission that God loves the innocent and the righteous. This view is typical of some Christians who rely on specific passages in the Bible to paint a picture of God as a religious terrorist. While it might be difficult to disavow the Old Testament, much of Christianity today would attempt to erase such an image from the secular society.

Jesus's behavior toward sinfulness is puzzling in other ways. He forgives some who do not ask for forgiveness; he forgives those who crucify him; he forgives Peter despite his denial, but not Judas for betraying him. He forgives tax collectors and prostitutes if they repent but bypasses the Pharisees and their followers. Nonetheless, there is no criticism or denunciation of the Romans, presumably among the greatest sinners given their oppression of the Israelites. In contrast, cynically, a secular world would argue that the Romans could not have been that sinful, since their oppression generated those who mourn, the meek, those who hunger and thirst for righteousness, the merciful, and those who are persecuted and insulted for the sake of righteousness;

these are the types of behavior Jesus considers righteous and deserving of the kingdom of heaven, despite his condemnation of those who make others suffer.

Postmodern secularism likely will also question the Christian principle that all evil comes from human sinfulness or the devil. Without necessarily rejecting the belief in Original Sin or the possible existence of a malevolent supernatural being, it would be remissive of Christianity to ignore an evolutionary theory of good and evil that relies on the progressive improvement of human nature through reason and God's spiritual assistance. After all, the theory of evolution is accepted by many within mainstream Christianity, Judaism, Hinduism, and Islam, provided that God may have willed creation and human life to take place in such a manner.[14] Accordingly, at times human evil behavior can be the product of ignorance, flawed reasoning, structural, social, and religious conditioning, all of which may induce wicked actions among people who may not have a clear understanding that their behavior is sinful. This viewpoint would incorporate God's primary instrument to humanity, human reason and its fruits—philosophy and the sciences--and Jesus's insistence that humans ought to manage their affairs based on his teachings.

The alternative is to believe in the literal explanation of *creation* provided in Genesis that even John Paul II qualified as written in mythical terminology.[15] Post-Christian millennial generations are bound to reject the view that Original Sin is based on God's command not to eat from the Tree of the Knowledge of Good and Evil. Literally understood (as God did not provide footnotes), these passages in Genesis indicate God's unwillingness to allow humans to distinguish between good and evil, which might explain humanity's predicament today, and which is in contradiction with Jesus's mission to teach what is good and what is evil.

Although evolution is still a theory with its own limitations, it offers the best possible human explanation of creation. Evolution, of course, could still be refuted by other scientific discoveries or by empirical divine intervention. Insofar as the latter does not happen, human reason will continue to guide creation following God's directive in Genesis to build the earth. To withhold reason, the most significant feature that enables humans to follow God's wishes to subdue the earth and have dominion over it (Gen 1:28-31), would seem contradictory and unintelligible to humans.[16]

Nevertheless, problems remain. Postmodern secular society is characterized by its many faiths and philosophies. It is within this setting that Christianity needs to define sinfulness and evil by finding a modicum of agreement with its counterparts. Christians (hierarchy and laity) have been unable (or unwilling) to find consensus on this matter. Secularization concedes to them the freedom for each to go their own way, which unbeknown to each other dilutes the overall essence of the faith. The result is a Christianity with split personalities, each vying to prevail in a zero-sum game that insists on arguing their beliefs on religious grounds that would not be acceptable to those of different faiths or atheists. A plausible alternative left to Christianity would be to provide a rationale for its values in secular terminology, i.e., produce a common moral language that everyone might understand. Perhaps this might be a prospective venue to solving the problem the theological Tower of Babel created.

Notes:

1. There is hardly any difference between Catholicism and Protestantism regarding the role of conscience. Among Protestant denominations, the individual's conscience's understanding of the Bible is decisive in judging good and evil. Such understanding paves the way for an 'anything goes' type of individual decision-making in moral behavior. In Catholicism, the role of individual conscience is no less ambiguous. For example, a Catholic philosophy professor has argued that a "crisis of truth" prevails within the Church pitting divine law as interpreted by the hierarchy against individual freedom of conscience and religious freedom, suggesting that an autonomous conscience cannot be used to judge good and evil unless it is in line with the teaching authority of the Church; otherwise the prevalence of such "creative conscience" would seriously undermine the concept of natural law and the hierarchy's role in interpreting it; in effect, become Protestant morality. Dorothy Cummings McLean, "Saint JP II warned against 'creative conscience' that rejects God's laws: Angelicum prof," Lifesitenews.com, 23 May 2018, https://www.lifesitenews.com/news/saint-jp-ii-warned-against-creative-conscience-that-rejects-gods-laws-angel (accessed online 24 May 2018). The issue suggests a conflict without easy solutions. The discussion in Chapter 3 pointed to the difficulties the Teaching Authority of the Church faces in reaching absolute moral truths, particularly exegetes, upon whose expertise the hierarchy depends for its understanding of the scriptures. Moreover, the Catholic Catechism establishes that a person's conscience ought to be in line with or subordinated to a law (Natural Law) that God has inscribed in each human being (CCC 1776 -1782). However, the efficacy of human ability to discern Natural Law is questionable since this law may not be *perceived by everyone clearly and immediately* (CCC 1960). Hence, it cannot be argued that there is a sinful action behind every evil deed if the Catechism itself indicates that there are instances in which the person is not sinfully accountable for his action (CCC 1793). Additionally, the Catechism asserts that *Conscience is man's most secret core, and his sanctuary* (CCC 1776), adding that such conscience must be properly formed if it is to be effective. It does not say, however, whether a properly formed conscience requires degrees in theology and philosophy or Sunday catechism. The hierarchy's claim of infallibility (since before the dogma was declared) offers little assistance given that through the ages it has erred or made changes while dictating moral behavior. Thus, the directive that in the search of salvation the individual must abdicate personal responsibility to the teachings of the hierarchy even if his/her conscience opposes it, may be as unethical as it is absurd to presume that anyone can make an unqualified interpretation of the scriptures by themselves.

2. Such is the Catholic interpretation of sinfulness. CCC 1857, 1859.

3. Ibid., 2515. From a temporal standpoint, this is akin to holding a person accountable for not being able to walk or run properly because he/she became disabled after being pushed down a flight of stairs.

4. NEs' note, Mt 13:11 indicates that *To understand is a gift of God, granted to the disciples but not to the crowds. In Semitic fashion, both the disciples' understanding and the crowd's obtuseness are attributed to God. The question of human responsibility for the obtuseness is not dealt with, although it is asserted in* Mt 13:13.

5. Money exchange was necessary for foreigners to be able to purchase animals that were going to be sacrificially offered in the Temple. NEs' note, Mt 21:12-17.

6. Ibid., note Mt 12:38-42.

7. While it is possible that some people bent on ignorance and hatred will overlook tangible reality, it seems highly improbable today that most of humankind would ignore eternal peril if they were to witness Jesus's miracles.

8. When John the Baptist asks people to repent, they have no idea of their sins, so they ask him what they should do, and the Baptist has to tell them (Lk 3:10-14). A passerby (whom Luke identifies as a scholar of the law) appears not to know what to do to attain eternal life and has to ask Jesus who tells him to observe the commandments (Mt 19:16-20). And, in some instances, Jesus even charges his own disciples with hardness of heart.

9. I think it is possible for philosophy along with the assistance of the physical and social sciences to garner consensus on certain universal moral truths based on improved knowledge of human nature and behavior. Pope Francis's encyclical letter on Fraternity and Social Friendship, is a close example of elaborating a social and political philosophy based on secular realities behind which are moral values that humanity might be willing to explore. Pope Francis, *Fratelli Tutti,* Assisi, October 3, 2020, http://www.vatican.va/content/francesco/en/encyclicals/documents/papa-francesco_20201003_enciclica-fratelli-tutti.html (accessed October 6, 2020).

10. Despite its convoluted meaning, Natural Law has been utilized by church authorities, agnostic, and atheist philosophers to support their personal views while most believers and non-Christians tend to disregard it largely because they do not understand it. Natural Law has been used since the times of Aristotle and Cicero, and by Christians of various denominations and non-believers to espouse religious, social, political, and economic beliefs and theories, at times at variance with one another. For example, the American Founding Fathers based their concepts of rights by appealing to the existence of Natural Law and God. Without denying the possibility that such a nebulous concept can be apprehended by all humanity, its contentious and undiscriminating use to sustain almost any point of view suggests that, as a theory, Natural Law lacks any operational capability. Should anyone feel inclined to delve into this concept, a traditional primer is still Heinrich A. Rommen, *The Natural Law: A Study in Legal and Social History and Philosophy*, trans. Thomas R. Hanley O.S.B., Ph.D., (Indianapolis: Liberty Fund, 1998), http://oll.libertyfund.org/titles/rommen-the-natural-law-a-study-in-legal-and-social-history-and-philosophy (accessed 25 May 2018).

11. Exodus 20:5, *you shall not bow down before them or serve them. For I, the LORD, your God, am a jealous God, inflicting punishment for their ancestors' wickedness on the children of those who hate me, down to the third and fourth generation* (Ex 20:5). NEs' note on this passage indicates that *other Old Testament texts repudiate the idea of punishment devolving on later generations (cf. Dt 24:16; Jer 31:29–30; Ez 18:2–4). Yet it is known that later generations may suffer the punishing effects of sins of earlier generations, but not the guilt.*

12. NEs' note, Jn 9:2 indicates that the infirmity in this passage is providential.

13. Ibid, note on Jn 5:14.

14. An overall description of the various positions on evolution assumed by various religious faiths appears in, Pew Research Center, "Religious Groups' Views on Evolution," updated February 2014, http://www.pewforum.org/2009/02/04/religious-groups-views-on-evolution/ (accessed online October 2, 2018); the Catholic Church position accepting the theory of evolution appears in, International Theological Commission, *Communion and Stewardship: Human Persons Created in the Image of God*, 63, (the Vatican, 2004), http://www.vatican.va/roman_curia/congregations/cfaith/cti_documents/rc_con_cfaith_doc_20040723_communion-stewardship_en.html (accessed online October 2, 2018); Orthodox Christianity's views, however, vary: S.V. Bufeev, "Why an Orthodox Christian Cannot be an Evolutionist," trans. by Dr. Evgeny Selensky, http://www.creatio.orthodoxy.ru/sbornik/sbufeev_whynot_english.html (accessed online October 2, 2018); Fr. Lawrence Farley, "Evolution or creation Science?" Orthodox Church in America, 2012, https://oca.org/reflections/fr.-lawrence-farley/evolution-or-creation-science (accessed online October 2, 2018); Fr. George Nicozisin, "Creationism versus Evolution," Orthodox Research Institute, 2017. http://www.orthodoxresearchinstitute.org/articles/dogmatics/nicozisin_creationism.htm (accessed online October 2, 2018). Mainstream Protestantism tends to accept the main tenets of evolution similar to Catholicism, the exception possibly being Fundamentalist evangelical groups that rely on *Creationism* as an explanation of the origin of human beings: Ekklesia staff, "Churches Urged to Challenge Intelligent Design," February 20, 2006, http://www.ekklesia.co.uk/content/news_syndication/article_060220creationism.shtml (accessed October 2, 2018).

15. Christopher West, *The Theology of the Body Explained: A Commentary on John Paul II's "Gospel of the Body,"* (Boston: Pauline Books & Media, 2003), 67. John Paul II does not refer to myths as fables or stories of events that never happened; he defines the term in the context of modern thought, for example, as clarified by Giambattista Vico when stating that, *Myths are not false narratives, nor are they allegories. They express the collective mentality of a given age.* Alasdair MacIntyre, "Myth," *The Encyclopedia of Philosophy*, Vol. 5, (New York: Macmillan Publishing Co., 1967), 435.

16. In the "Pastoral Constitution on the Church in the Modern World, the Catholic Church indicates that," *God created man a rational being, conferring on him the dignity of a person who can initiate and control his own actions. "God willed that man should be 'left in the hand of his own counsel,' so that he might of his own accord seek his Creator and freely attain his full and blessed perfection by cleaving to him."* (CCC 1730). Quotation from the Pastoral Constitution appears in Gaudium et Spes 17; Sir 15:14.

Teachings About Specific Sins

While the previous section dealt with sinfulness as an ailment that affects humanity in its relation to God, i.e., a propensity toward evil in secular terms, this section refers specifically to attitudes and behavior that Jesus identifies as sinful at the time the Gospels were written. Based on the proposition that terms that appear more frequently in a document are more significant than those that show up less number of times, the content analysis approach suggests that while all sinful behavior may be evil in the eyes of God (or Jesus), some sins may be worse than others. This inference may be shocking even to Christians, which is why is precarious to assign to God responsibility for having inspired the Gospels. It is also possible that the fault lies with limitations of human oral transmission in which case God cannot possibly be blamed. Nonetheless, Christianity still maintains that the authors of the Gospels recorded what Jesus or God revealed to them. If so, how are we to understand that Jesus did not address slavery as sinful but as an existing tolerable institution, Roman oppression upon God's favorite people, and other forms of sins prevalent at the time?

It is reasonable (if moot perhaps) to ask why Jesus considers certain sins as being among the worst while today they are tolerated merely as flawed imperfections. This observation points to a radical change in Christian morality that many believers are unwilling to accept.

The recognition that Jesus did not provide a complete (and timeless) list of righteous and sinful behavior has resulted in the religious and cultural infighting we witness today among Christians in secular societies. This issue reflects the absence of an absolute universal moral code in Christianity. This is not to say that morality is necessarily relative to time and place, but rather that it is an evolving process in search of consensus. The question is whether Jesus provides enough detail to address current and future moral and ethical issues. The answer to this question is hindered by incongruences and contradictions in the texts that make this exercise cumbersome. It means that Jesus's teachings may enclose higher levels of truths that still need to be revealed, suggesting that revelation has not been made completely explicit despite the Catholic hierarchy's authoritative conclusion that there shall be *no further new public revelation* before Jesus second coming. There is a modicum of truth in John's Gospel about this view as Jesus signals that when the Advocate or Spirit of Truth comes, *he will guide you to all truth ... and will declare to you the things that are coming* (Jn 16:13). If the Holy Spirit is active, Jesus's words suggest that moral truth is still evolving.[1]

Notes:
1. The hierarchy adds a nuanced explanation: *even if Revelation is already complete, it has not been made completely explicit; it remains for Christian faith gradually to grasp its full significance over the course of the centuries.* Second Vatican Council, *Dogmatic Constitution on Divine Revelation Dei Verbum*, 4, Pope Paul VI, November 1965. www.vatican.va/archive/hist_councils/ii_vatican_council/documents/vat-ii_const_19651118_dei-verbum_en.html (accessed on October 4, 2018).

Anger and Hatred

Jesus points out that becoming angry toward others or offending them is sinful. This behavior is so serious that he instructs the crowd not to bring any offerings to God without first reconciling with the other person. Punishment for ignoring his teaching is severe; it may warrant condemnation (Mt 5:22-25).

Anger and hatred occur when the personal 'I' strongly disagrees with objective reality, e.g., when the actions of others are not in accordance with how one feels or believes they should be like. It is undoubtedly difficult to repress or sublimate anger on an everyday basis without perhaps becoming detached from the world. Anger affects all human relations. Living in a world culture that is fast acquiescing to social and political incorrectness, insulting or offending others becomes an acceptable norm. Anger may begin simply by becoming annoyed. Soon it may lead to insensitive and unpleasant behavior. As hatred seeps in, it transforms the differences we see in others into revolting and wicked behavior, hence the need to oppose them fiercely. Anger and hatred are components of self-righteousness and insensitivity. Potential outcomes are increased recrimination, polarization, and seeing the opposition as enemies, conditions that at times lead to physical violence. When these conditions ensue, conflict resolution becomes difficult; families and friendships are fragmented, and social peace becomes a scarce commodity.

Jesus's rules seem rather harsh. After all, anger and hatred are common human reactions. Interestingly, Jesus may have developed psychological insights that can be confirmed today by the social sciences. Anger, for example, stands for becoming exasperated and developing feelings of animosity and rage toward others. Hatred goes further, as it involves a deep sense of repugnance and abomination toward others that may lead to opposing that which is radically different from what we prefer.

The opposite behavior of anger and hatred is love, peacefulness, acceptance, goodwill, kindness, and friendship.[1] As seen in Table 2, the results of the content analysis rank the *Love and Its Synonyms* category highly significant while *Anger/hatred* is Jesus's most denounced sin followed by killing. It appears that Jesus notices what seems evident; anger and hatred lie at the base of conflict, murder, and war. His teachings point to a desire for humankind to lead a peaceful and cheerful life, the reason for which he transforms God's first commandment to include love of neighbor as a condition of loving God.

Jesus, however, is aware that there is (and will continue to be) hatred (Mk 13:7-13, Lk 21:12-19, Mt 10:17-19, 22-23, 24:7-12) insofar as the world refuses to abide by his teachings. Luke's Gospel indicates that the Israelites are surrounded by enemies (Lk 1:71, 74), so they await the consolation of Israel and the redemption of Jerusalem (Lk 2:25, 2:38); that is, peace. Jesus's teachings on anger and hatred seem to have been addressed namely to the Jewish people, and he must have realized that the behavior he condemns (Mk 12:1-8, Lk 12:45-46, 20:9-16, Mt 21:33-41) is being perpetrated by Roman authorities who are largely responsible for their abuse of power toward his people. Yet, while Jesus experiences these conditions, the Gospels do not explain why he claims himself to be *anointed to proclaim liberty to captives,* and *to let the oppressed go free* (Lk 4:18) but refuses to undertake such a task. Moreover, although he loathes anger and hatred, he awkwardly welcomes it upon his followers, telling them to be joyful *when people hate you ... exclude and insult you ... on account of the Son of Man. Rejoice and leap for joy on that day!* (Lk 6:22-23, Mt 5:10-12). Amid these conditions, he adds that, while rejoicing persecutions, his followers must still love one's enemies, do good to those who hate them, pray for those who mistreat them, and refuse to hit back when someone strikes them (Lk 6:28-29, Mt 5:43-44).

In a classroom, these ethical teachings may sound noble and bizarre. Jesus insists that there is no merit in only loving those who love us or those we like; after all, sinners and pagans do the same (Mt 5:46-48). The real test of love, according to him, lies in being different; caring for, and forgiving those who attempt to fashion a virtue out of hatred. However, today, these sayings would be strongly opposed by good people who fail to understand their rationale. From Jesus's perspective, his words would be regarded as a blessing in disguise by victims of genocide, including his own people, because he would welcome the slaughtered sheep with open arms. On the other hand, even if some of these killings and persecutions do not take place on account of him, would he still ask the victims to rejoice? Would they be welcomed in Paradise? Paradoxically, Jesus abhors hatred and killing as the greatest sins, shows compassion for a disabled woman who has been held captive by Satan, yet teaches that his followers must rejoice while enduring mocking, persecutions, and killings.

Is it possible to juxtapose Jesus's rejoicing under these conditions with his first commandment and conclude that there is no contradiction? Jesus teaches that the commandment to love one's neighbor entails defending others and caring for them in time of need, perhaps even while feeling angry toward those who do evil; nonetheless, doing so would require that we assist others without resorting to hatred and killing. Jesus's non-violent response toward the Jewish and Roman authorities offers the example of the sacrificial lamb that acts following God's will. In his role as son of God, Jesus's teachings and his behavior were meant for all humanity, although his followers likely would be required to set the example. It appears, however, that Christians have not taken these teachings seriously; a reason they mock and attack each other (verbally and physically) as well as people of other faiths.

John's Gospel
The reader may wonder why hatred is dealt with differently in John's Gospel. In John, love is not presented as the greatest of all commandments; the foundation that sustains *the whole law and the prophets* (Mt 22:36-40). There is no universal directive to love one's enemy or pray for those who persecute others, as there is in Luke and Matthew. Instead, the term *love,* which appears far more times in John than in the synoptics (55xt), is only offered as a commandment to Jesus's disciples (Jn 13:34-35, 14:21, 15:9-10, 17, 23, 26).[2]

In John's text, the term *hate* takes a new configuration; it shows up twice as many times as in the synoptics, but bewilderingly it relates mostly to the world. In John, *hatred* is used to identify evil people who belong to the world because they hate Jesus. The world hates him, he says, because he denounces their works (Jn 7:7). Subsequently, the world begins to hate the Father and his disciples because of their association with Jesus (Jn 15:18-25, 17:14).

Nonetheless, who constitutes this world Jesus keeps referring to? It appears that he was pointing to Gentile and Jewish people who rejected him. At the time, however, this was a small world, making up less than one percent; the rest of the planet did not know about Jesus or God's laws. To the reader, this must be confusing. In the synoptics, the world likely refers to the world's population whom Jesus wishes to reach with his message,[3] while in John, the reader is led to think that the entire planet hates Jesus (Jn 3:20). Since ninety-nine percent of the world did not yet know Jesus, could they still be condemned for their ignorance? The Spirit of Truth that would guide the disciples (not others?) *in all truth* had not arrived yet; and it appears that when it does it will be for their sole guidance (Jn 14:16-17, 15:26, 16:13-14).[4]

There is in John another use of the term *hate;* this one appearing only once but bringing forth a rather unpleasant and mystifying connotation. Prior to his death, Jesus says, *whoever loves his life loses it, and whoever hates his life in this world will preserve it for eternal life* (Jn 12:25). The synoptics include a similar passage although the wording is different. When Jesus says, *whoever wishes to save his life will lose it, but whoever loses his life for my sake and that of the gospel will save it* (Mk 8:35, Lk 9:24, Mt 16:25), he appears to be indicating that by giving up one's life for him the believer actually would be saving his life. In John, however, Jesus is indicating rather concretely that to attain eternal salvation the righteous must hate his temporal life. As human beings are for the most part accustomed to understanding words in their literal context, non-Christians would likely be flabbergasted when they read the passage; many Christians would too, regardless of their denominations. Although the world Jesus refers to is an inhospitable place where sin reigns, people today have a different understanding. The world is the temporal habitat that God created for humanity. Are Christians supposed to consider the world evil; and would it be appropriate for Christians to hate the life God has given them as a means to attain salvation?

Altogether, being told to hate one's life to gain eternal salvation would seem to go against the human psyche. The passages in the synoptics are akin to the belief held by Muslim jihadists suggesting that they would attain Paradise by purposefully engaging in physical violence.[5] Jesus's cry in John runs counter to Christian efforts to make life on earth a more hospitable abode in line with his commandment to love God and one's neighbor. The point Jesus likely wishes to make in John is confusing because he is teaching the need to counteract human attachment to a temporal life that God has created. The only way to attain this objective in its literal sense would require a high level of monastic asceticism that is unlikely to prevail in the next centuries unless cataclysmic disasters begin to occur.

Jesus's Attitude Toward the Roman Authorities

While anger and hatred are evident on the part of the religious authorities toward Jesus (and vice versa), there does not seem to be anger between Pilate and Jesus. Although he knows that Pilate oppresses his people, Jesus is not critical of the Roman official. There is an air of indifference between each other. The authors of the Gospels do not appear to be critical of Pilate, even though it would be difficult to read the texts and perceive him as an innocent bystander who attempts to hide his responsibility by washing his hands.

Roman soldiers' behavior is different. Since probably they do not know Jesus, there is no reason for them to hate him. Yet, according to the texts, they loathe Jesus; they flog him, place a crown of thorns on him; they mock, strike, and spit on him before they parade him to the place where he is to be crucified. Once nailed to the cross Roman soldiers mock him again, *if you are King of the Jews, save yourself,* they shout (Mk 15:16-20, Lk 23:36-37, Mt 27:27-31, Jn 19:1). Is it possible for humans to do these things to others without feeling anger or hatred? These soldiers seemingly enjoy hatred and killing, values that conditioned their training. It is inexplicable, however, that Jesus forgives them while he condemns these actions when done to others. There is at least one Gospel that indicates why he forgives his executioners; they do not realize the harm they do (Lk 23:34), perhaps because they have been conditioned throughout their lifetime to feel anger and hatred toward others.

Notes:

1. *Thesaurus.com,* online, s.v. "anger," "hatred."

2. Although in John Jesus refers to his 'commandments' while addressing his disciples, other than to love one another (which is never stated regarding other people), he does not identify any other commandment.

3. In the synoptics, the following passage appears, *You will be hated by all because of my name,* in a possible reference to the Parousia in Mark and Luke. Matthew, however, does not relate the passage to the Parousia. According to NEs, the phrase refers to each individual's death (Note on Mt 10:22). Altogether, it becomes difficult to estimate the number and kind of people that the phrase *hated by all* refers to (MK 13:13, Lk 21:17, Mt 10:22).

4. NEs suggest that the Spirit of Truth is a moral force put into a person by God, as opposed to the spirit of perversity. In John this Spirit is more personal; it will teach the realities of the new order (Jn 14:26) and testify to the truth (Jn 14:6). It is not clear how John's Spirit of Truth differs from Natural Law that is said to be infused in every human being since birth and is supposed to be intuitively recognized.

5. The cry of going to battle against Jesus's enemies inspired the Christian Crusades in the eleventh, twelfth, and thirteenth centuries. Relying on creative rhetoric, Pope Urban II delivered what Will Durant characterizes as *the most influential speech in medieval history.* Addressing his fellow French countrymen, Urban appealed to them to discard all hatred and quarrels and instead *enter upon the road to the Holy Sepulcher; wrest that land from a wicked race, and subject it to yourselves.... The royal city, situated at the center of the earth, implores you to come to her aid. Undertake this journey eagerly for the remission of your sins and be assured of the reward of imperishable glory in the Kingdom of Heaven.* The crowd replied *God wills it.* Citation in F. Ogg, *Book of Medieval History,* 1907, 282-8, in Will Durant, Vol IV, p. 587. For the most part, Christianity has overcome this behavior. Although Islamic culture and its ideological component lag seven hundred years behind Christian theology, it appears that part of its leadership is making strides toward a more fraternal, forgiving, and compassionate interpretation of the Quran.

Killing

Thou shall not kill (Mk 10:19, Lk 18:20, Mt 5:21). Jesus's views on killing are similar to a Kantian categorical imperative; under no circumstances is killing to be morally allowed.[1] In Judaism and Christianity, however, God's commandment is not interpreted in an absolute manner. The Old Testament shows that not only does God allow the Israelites to kill; God too prescribes killing of innocent people, including infants, as punishment for wrongdoing (Lv 20:10-15, 24:16-17, Dt 22:21-22, 23-25). Being familiar with the Jewish Bible, Jesus must have known about these godly acts, all of which appear to be in retribution for people disobeying God's wishes or while defending his people from their enemies.

In the Gospels, Jesus does not provide much explanation about killing being sinful, other than to restate God's commandment. Nonetheless, it is not clear whether he indicates that *murder* and *killing* are sinful according to the historical use of the words, i.e., unjust or illicit killing of innocent human life, or whether he extends the commandment to the taking of any human life. Either way, his words part ways with God's actions in the Old Testament.[2]

Killing ranks highly among sinful behavior, in part because all passages that relate to the killing of Jesus are included. The rationale for proceeding in this manner is that, in addition to Jesus's teachings, the Gospels depict the story of an innocent man who is killed simply because he teaches beliefs that are deemed threatening to the religious and political establishment. A breakdown of these two views (killings and the killing of Jesus) according to each author follows a similar pattern, particularly in the synoptics.[3]

Killing and the Value of Human Life in the Gospels
In the Gospels, Jesus does not engage in detailed discussions about the commandment *thou shall not kill*. The commandment assumes its absolutist character because it comes from God; and its disobedience precludes anyone from entering eternal life (Mk 10:17-19, Lk 18:18-20, Mt 19:16-18). Another aspect that reinforces its absolutism is that Jesus does not delineate a system of ethics regarding warfare or the legitimacy of law and order. For example, he does not object to killings by Roman soldiers, at one point overlooking Galileans murdered by Pontius Pilate. Instead, he relies on Pilate's action to threaten (or warn) others that they might face a similar death if they refuse to repent and accept him (Lk 13:1-5), an act that is akin to religious extortion. His harshest criticism regarding killing is directed at the Pharisees for the past murders of the prophets (Lk 11:49-51, 13:34-35, Mt 23:30-38). Cynically speaking, since Jesus forgives his killers, are enemies of Christians to understand that their killings will be forgiven too?

Despite the vagueness in Jesus's teachings, it appears that he views killing and murder as an offense to God. How serious an offense is difficult to assess because his emphasis on eternal life seems to undermine the commandment. His teachings, after all, indicate that ultimate happiness is not to be found on earth, but in the afterlife. This is the reason why, although he dreads his martyrdom, he is willing to die (Mt 26:39, Jn 10:17-18) as part of his mission. Moreover, he does not appear to mourn the horrendous decapitation of John the Baptist (Mt 14:12-13); instead, he considers him a martyr who gave his life for upholding God's honor (Lk 7:24-28, Mt 11:11). As previously noted, he does not dwell on those Galileans who died under Pilate. He casually speaks to his disciples about future persecutions in which families will kill each other (Mk 13:12, Lk 21:16), and seems unemotional when discussing the horrors that people will experience at the end of time.

Many of his parables are filled with slayings, murders, and a punishing God waiting to avenge the sinful killings of the just. It is amid such dreadful passages that Jesus tells his disciples *not* (to) *be afraid of those who kill the body but cannot kill the soul; rather, be afraid of the one who can destroy both soul and body in Gehenna* (Mt 10:28, Lk 12:4-5). How may his words be interpreted today? Instructing people not to be afraid to be killed or murdered is at odds with being human; most people are afraid of dying; they relish being alive even under dire conditions. His remarks suggest a disregard (perhaps indifference) toward temporal life (likely because of the eschatological nature of his message). It may be noted too that, with certain exceptions that indicate concern for the poor, there are no passages in the Gospels suggesting high regard for building the earth. This is not surprising. Jesus is an itinerant preacher who *has nowhere to rest his head,* and who calls on others to set aside burying their loved ones and instead follow him (Mt 8:20-22). He tells people not to *worry* about one's life or one's body, what to drink or eat, or what to wear, as God will fulfill these needs (Mt 6:25-34). There is an unmistakable dissonance in his message; although much of it addresses moral behavior on earth, it is meant to serve as a means to a higher end, eternity.

To suggest that the value of God's creation is insignificant in contrast with eternal happiness (which may be true for most people in terms of cost-benefit analysis) undercuts human attempts at creating sensible civil societies. Jesus's primary mission, as evidenced by the high tally of the term *kingdom of God* in the texts, is to announce eternal salvation. His moral dos and don'ts are the means, but there is a sensible built-in relativism in his teachings on account of their incongruences.

Given that the great Satan governs the world, what may we expect from Jesus's apparent incongruences? There are no directives on his part to engage evil forces and maintain a modicum of stability and law and order when crime and wars occur. Jesus indicates that as long as people have faith in him, being killed does not seem to matter much. As he teaches in the Parable of the Weeds among the Wheat, evil (the weed) is not to be removed from society (wheat field) for fear of killing (uprooting) innocent people. Instead, he will separate the weeds and burn them, and then gather the wheat into his barn on Judgment Day (Mt 13:24-30). The parable shows no concern for killings and murders that will occur while lawlessness reigns. Supposedly, it would justify passivity when crime, wars, and acts of genocide take place.

Christians, however, have long repudiated the way Jesus appears to undervalue temporal life. Along with non-Christians and humanists, they have taken it upon themselves to set parameters to minimize killings, realizing that having to live the Gospels' ideals while ignoring crime, corruption, poverty, political instability, and terrorism that today riddle major cities throughout the world, would be considered inhumane and possibly anti-Christian. It is telling that in studies ranking the worst quality-of-life cities in the world, more than half of them are in countries where Christianity is the principal religion; in the other half, Islam is the central religion.[4]

From a secular standpoint, another significant aspect within this category is the absence of any passage in the Gospels related to the killing of the unborn. It is significant because abortion has emerged as a controversial religious issue in the last few decades throughout the world. Given that the procedure has existed since the beginnings of recorded history,[5] Jesus must have been aware that abortion and infanticide were practiced at the time. His knowledge of the Old Testament as reflected through his pronouncements, however, indicates that he must have realized that God too had been responsible for acts of infanticide (Ex 12:29). Would this account for Jesus choosing not to speak about this issue? Even an ardent opponent to abortion as Pope John Paul II acknowledged an existing gap between two Old Testament passages that indirectly relate to the sinfulness of abortion (Jer 1:5, Psalm 139:15) and the time when the Church first begins to deal with the issue; there is nothing in between.[6] The doctrine on abortion as a sin and as a crime develops outside the Gospels as a *Christian reflection* on God's commandment *you shall not kill*. That it attains religious, cultural, and political prominence in the twentieth century is an example of the evolution, i.e., *a reflection,* of Christian doctrine throughout time.[7]

Thus, we must presume that Jesus left it up to humankind to decide on the application of the commandment *not to kill*. As a result, church officials and theologians, along with national governments and international bodies, have had to formulate moral and legal norms to fill the existing temporal moral vacuum. During the fourth century, the church hierarchy began to develop criteria for a Just War that would aid nations to evaluate the morality of international wars. Likewise, the Church (and all governments worldwide) has recognized, almost since its beginnings, the individual's right to self-defense against an attacker, and the moral duty of law enforcement personnel to kill when necessary to protect innocent life. Moreover, the doctrine condemns preventive warfare altogether as well as attempts by political leaders to conflate preventive and preemptive terminology to deceive citizens into supporting wars of aggression. Recent declarations by Pope Francis against the death penalty support the hierarchy's message in defense of human life.[8]

The Killing of Jesus

Although Jesus and the authors of the Gospel characterize his death as necessary (Mk 14:24, Lk 22:20, Jn 12:23-24), the texts suggest that it was an act of murder (Mk Lk 23:47, Lk 22:1-6, Mt 27:1-4, Jn 13:1-11). The term 'necessary murder' might evoke frowning among Christians and non-Christians alike. Not only is the term puzzling (it is best understood when signifying atonement); it led to Christian anti-Semitism and cries of deicide against Jews throughout history. The texts indicate that Jesus accepts the realization that he is going to be killed (Mk 10:33-34, Lk 9:22, 13:31, 33, Mt 16:21), a price he must pay for doing the Father's will to spread the message of God's kingdom (Mk 14:34-36, Mt 26:53-56, Jn 10:17-18).

The Jewish religious authorities see that Jesus's constant attacks against their character, i.e., pride, greed, hypocrisy, all of which tends to disfigure God's message (Lk 11:47-50, 13:34-35, Mt 23:13-36), threaten their status and their legitimacy as the voice of God. The texts suggest that these religious leaders have reasons to be skeptical of Jesus's claim to authority and believe (rightly or wrongly) that Jesus has committed blasphemy by forgiving sins and calling himself the Son of God (Mk 14:60-63, Lk 5:21, Mt 26:62-66, Jn 5:17-18). According to Mosaic Law Jesus deserved to be killed.[9]

The texts do not delve (explicitly) into whether the religious authorities make a judicial mistake. The narratives simply focus on their constant desire to kill him (Mk 3:6, 11:18, 14:1, Lk 19:47-48, 22:2, Mt 26:2-4, Jn 5:18, 7:1. 8:37-40), denoting that Jesus's trial is a mockery, at the end of which a disconcerted Pontius Pilate (not finding guilt in Jesus) accedes to their demands to ingratiate himself with them and to satisfy the crowd (Mk 14:55-56, 15:15, Lk 23:13-15, 22-25, Mt 26:59-60, 27:24, Jn 18:38, 19:4). The skepticism of the religious authorities, however, leads them to reject the evidence that Jesus provides through his miraculous deeds that attest to his relationship with God. This behavior on their part is disconcerting. Presuming these deeds happened, it is humanly difficult for reasonably intelligent unbelievers to discard empirical evidence in such a thoughtless manner.[10]

Notes

1. Kant's imperative is attained through pure practical reason, suggesting that whatever is deemed to be *good* is because it is good in itself without necessitating other explanations (a variation of Natural Law). In the Gospels, Jesus voices God's commandment that does not require any type of rational explanation since it is issued by divine mandate. Kant's detailed discussion of categorical imperatives is found in chapter 2, Immanuel Kant, *Groundwork for the Metaphysics of Morals,* 1785, online version in pdf, https://www.earlymoderntexts.com/assets/pdfs/kant1785.pdf (accessed October 13, 2018).

2. Instances of God killing humans abound in the Pentateuch and other parts of the Old Testament: Gen 6:5-8, 19:1-29, Ex 12:29-30, Lv 10:1-2, Nu 11:31-34, 16:30-32, 35, 21:2-3, 44-49, Deut 20:17, Joshua 6:17-20, in King James version.

3. In Mark, passages related to killing appear 32xt; 17xt relate to Jesus's killing and 15xt to criminal, thus sinful, acts. In Luke, 36xt, of which 16xt are about Jesus's killing and 20xt related to sinfulness. In Matthew, 47xt, of which 23xt are about Jesus's killing and 24xt concern sinfulness. In John, 30xt, of which 22xt are about Jesus's killing and 8xt concern his teachings. Overall, words related to this category appear 145xt; 78xt refer to Jesus's killing and 67xt to sinful behavior.

4. For current conditions in cities worldwide, see Lianna Brinded (Business Insider), "The 33 cities with the worst quality of life in the world," *The Independent*, May 20, 2016. Confirmation about the statement

that about half the cities were in predominantly Christian nations is found on the internet, https://www.independent.co.uk/news/business/the-33-cities-with-the-worst-quality-of-life-in-the-world-a7040516.html (accessed October 16, 2018). The research done in this study does not include countries in Latin America. Yet two reports indicate that conditions in this region are as bad as those in Asia, Africa, and the Middle East: Amanda Erickson, "Latin America is the world's most violent region. A new report investigates why," *The Washington Post,* April 25, 2018. https://www.washingtonpost.com/news/worldviews/wp/2018/04/25/latin-america-is-the-worlds-most-violent-region-a-new-report-investigates-why/?noredirect=on&utm_term=.bff3d6242864 (accessed October 16, 2018); "Latin America is the world's most dangerous region. But it is turning a corner," *World Economic Forum*, 14 Mar 2018. https://www.weforum.org/agenda/2018/03/latin-america-is-the-worlds-most-dangerous-region-but-there-are-signs-its-turning-a-corner/ (accessed October 16, 2018). For a similar study on Europe see Lianna Brinded (Business Insider), "The 17 most unsafe cities in Europe," *The Independent*, 25 February 2016, https://www.independent.co.uk/news/world/europe/the-17-most-unsafe-cities-in-europe-a6895511.html (accessed October 16, 2018). Regarding the United States, where a conservative type of Christianity prevails, a 1997 report found to have equal validity today indicates that *the United States clustered with other industrial countries in crime rate, but head and shoulders above the rest in violent death,* because of the number of guns. Zack Beauchamp, "America doesn't have more crimes than other rich countries. It just has more guns," *Vox,* updated February 15, 2018. https://www.vox.com/2015/8/27/9217163/america-guns-europe (accessed October 16, 2018). Studies also have been done about wars throughout history detailing the approximate number of deaths. Perhaps the most current detailed work on the subject is Matthew White, *Atrocities: The 100 Deadliest Episodes in Human History*, (NY: W. W. Norton & Company, 2013). For a quick online view, Lincoln Riddle, "Casualties of War – Deadliest Conflicts in Human History," War History Online, June 2017, https://www.warhistoryonline.com/instant-articles/casualties-war-ten-deadliest-conflicts-human-history-m.html (accessed on October 15, 2018). It is also significant that among the deadliest conflicts, several have taken place in Asia (particularly in China) where Christianity has been unable to make inroads.

5. Plato refers to the existence of abortion in his dialogue *Theaetetus* while describing the symbolic and actual role of the midwife: Plato, *Theaetetus,* trans. Benjamin Jowett, The Project Gutenberg EBook of Theaetetus, released online on November 17, 2008, www.gutenberg.org/cache/epub/1726/pg1726.txt (accessed October 25, 2018); *Abortion was practiced on a regular basis among the poor, slave, merchant and royal classes. To ancient peoples and the Romans an abortion was amoral. There was nothing in Roman law or in the Roman heart that said, "It is wrong to kill your baby in the womb."* Sandra Sweeny Silver, "Ancient Roman Abortions & Christians," *Early Church History, https://earlychurchhistory.org/medicine/ancient-roman-abortions-christians/* (accessed October 25, 2018); also, Thomas Bokenkotter, *A Concise History of the Catholic Church,* Doubleday, 1990, p. 51, taken from "What Does the Bible Say About Abortion?" *Christian Bible Reference Site, https://www.christianbiblereference.org/faq_abortion.htm* (accessed on October 25, 2018).

6. Pope John Paul II recognized the gap, writing that *the texts of Sacred Scripture never address the question of deliberate abortion and so do not directly and specifically condemn it. But they show such great respect for the human being in the mother's womb that they require as a logical consequence that God's commandment "You shall not kill" be extended to the unborn child as well. Evangelium Vitae:* on the Value and Inviolability of Human Life, 61, Rome, March 25, 1995, http://w2.vatican.va/content/john-paul-ii/en/encyclicals/documents/hf_jp-ii_enc_25031995_evangelium-vitae.html (accessed on October 25, 2018). *The Didache*, a rudimentary catechism for believers written anonymously between the late first and early second centuries, is the first document that mentions abortion as sinful behavior: *You shall not kill the embryo by abortion and shall not cause the newborn to perish,* 2,2, http://www.thedidache.com/ (accessed on October 25, 2018); also, the *Letter of Barnabas,* written between first and second centuries, considers abortion a crime: trans. J.B. Lightfoot, (19:5) *Early Christian Writings, http://www.earlychristianwritings.com/text/barnabas-lightfoot.html* (accessed on October 25, 2018). See CCC 2270, 2271.

7. The phrase *a Christian reflection* as applied to abortion appears in Pope John Paul II's encyclical *Evangelium Vitae:* on the Value and Inviolability of Human Life, 54, 55, given in Rome, March 25, 1995, http://w2.vatican.va/content/john-paul-ii/en/encyclicals/documents/hf_jp-ii_enc_25031995_evangelium-vitae.html (accessed on October 25, 2018).

8. The concept of a Just War doctrine is part of the Catholic Catechism 2307-2317. In 2016 a Vatican conference hosted by the Pontifical Council for Justice and Peace, however, called for the rejection of the doctrine; Joshua J. McElwee, "Landmark Vatican conference rejects just war theory, asks for an

encyclical   on   nonviolence,"   *National   Catholic   Reporter,*   Apr   14,   2016, www.ncronline.org/news/vatican/landmark-vatican-conference-rejects-just-war-theory-asks-encyclical-nonviolence (accessed on October 18, 2018). Despite its questioning by church authorities regarding its validity during the nuclear age, the doctrine remains in effect. The church's moral view on individual self-defense and its distinction from murder appears in the Catholic Catechism 2263-2269. For the Catholic Church's new position on the death penalty see, Chico Harlan, "Pope Francis changes Catholic Church teaching to say death penalty is 'inadmissible'," *The Washington Post,* August 2, 2018, https://www.washingtonpost.com/world/pope-francis-changes-catholic-church-teaching-to-say-death-penalty-is-inadmissible/2018/08/02/0d69ef5e-9647-11e8-80e1-00e80e1fdf43_story.html?utm_term=.509c3e2e2db8 (accessed on October 18, 2018).

9. In Leviticus 24:10-16, God authorizes a blasphemer to be stoned to death. The texts do not point out that the religious authorities judged Jesus according to this passage; only that members of the Sanhedrin indicate that Jesus is blaspheming by taking upon himself prerogatives that belong to God, which they consider blasphemous.

10. The same attitude is observed among reasonably intelligent persons that, as a result of cognitive dissonance or ideological stubbornness, reject the evidence provided by the overwhelming majority of the scientific community regarding climate change.

Selfishness

This category identifies passages that relate to selfish and self-centered behavior according to contemporary definitions: *seeking or concentrating on one's own advantage, pleasure, or well-being without regard for others*; and being *concerned solely with one's own desires, needs, or interests in disregard of others.*[1] The words tallied under this category convey the desire to gain material possessions or accrue personal benefits through illicit means or as a result of human insensitivity. They include fraud, theft, stealing, robbery, extortion, tax collection, falsehood, deceit, greed, envy, embezzlement, or calumny, and other behavior that, although legal, does not consider the wellbeing of others.

Christian doctrine considers all sins acts of selfishness since it presumes the person chooses to do his/her will rather than God's. Jesus condemns several types of selfish behavior, directly and indirectly, numerous times (Mk 7:20-22, 10:19, 14:48, Lk 12:33, 39, 16:1, Mt 6:19-20, 15:18-19, 19:16, 19, 24:4, 24, 26:55, Jn 10:1, 8, 10, 12:6). In the Gospels, selfishness is characterized by two observable behaviors, greed and callous indifference to human suffering. Greed applies not only to the rich but to those whose main concern in life is to accumulate material possessions (Lk 12:13-21, 16:13-15).

Jesus regards greed as being so addictive that it requires God's assistance to free oneself from it (Mk 10:17-31, Lk 18:18-30, Mt 19:16-30). He confronts greed in a most perplexing passage that appears in all three synoptic texts. As a young man asks Jesus how to attain eternal life, he replies, *just follow the commandments.* When the man replies he already does that, Jesus suddenly changes the rules. In Mark and Luke, he tells the young man that he needs to give up all his possessions and follow him. In Matthew, Jesus's teaching to surrender his possessions is only conditional, i.e., if he wants to be perfect. Disappointed by Jesus's remark, the young man goes away because he does not wish to part with his wealth.

In the Parable of the Rich Man and Lazarus (an example of today's 'trickle-down economic policies), he condemns greed and selfishness because such behavior makes the rich man insensitive to Lazarus's plight (Lk 16:19-31). John the Baptist too, condemns selfishness by demanding the sharing of material goods as an indication of repentance and righteous behavior (Lk 3:10-11). Likewise, theft, extortion, embezzlement, deception, and fraud find grounds in greed and callous indifference (Lk 3:12-14, 6:26, 18:20, 21:8). Jesus specifically points to tax collectors as sinners, as it was well-known that, to amass wealth, they unfairly collected more taxes than necessary (Mk 2:13-17, Lk 5:30-32, 7:29, 7:34, 15:1, Mt 5:46, 9:9-13, 18:17).

Jesus does not explain why he considers this type of behavior evil; once again, he is merely stating that the conduct goes against God's commandments. From his viewpoint, it appears that he thinks that his teachings on sinfulness are self-evident. Ideally, Jesus's best explanation would have taught that God meant for all human beings to love and care for each other since the Father provides the bounties of the earth for all to enjoy. Hence, Jesus would have taught that sharing these resources was a prerequisite of the commandment to love one another. Jesus establishes this relation in his Parable of the Samaritan while he explains to a scholar of the law interested in attaining eternal life that love of God and love of neighbor imply aiding those in need (Lk 10:25-37). Moreover, he reiterates his teaching dramatically pointing out that his ruling on who will be saved or condemned will be based on who comes to the aid of those in need of care and support.

We may surmise that his teachings applied only to the Israelites. But, as people began to regard Jesus as divine and his teachings were preached throughout the world, Christianity now considers that these sins apply to all humanity, including non-Christians and atheists. Since these two groups do not believe Jesus is divine, it is questionable how they may be found liable for their behavior.

It is interesting, nonetheless, that secular society has legally codified behavior that Jesus generally condemns as sinful, including theft, fraud, embezzlement, extortion, deception, and usury.[2] This legal understanding might not have been a direct outcome of Jesus's teachings, although we need to consider the impact that centuries of Christian teachings have had upon the codification of these laws. Likely, human society has recognized that curbing these activities provide financial and commercial stability and safeguard (to some extent) the interests of citizens in their capacity as consumers. This probably was not Jesus's rationale. He saw selfishness as being the opposite of loving one's neighbor, an implied violation of human equality before God, and a principle dictating that no one is entitled to take advantage of others.

It is noteworthy that selfishness is not well-looked upon in secular society.[3] Even people who act selfishly, whether consciously or not,[4] do not relish being called selfish. In the Gospels, this type of behavior is related to self-centeredness or what we refer to today as being self-absorbed, a term denoting behavior so involved with oneself that it precludes thinking about anyone else.[5] This definition dovetails with

Jesus's parable of The Good Samaritan, in which he condemns the unconcerned attitude of a priest and a Levite[6] toward a man who is robbed and left on the road half-dead (Lk 10:30-37). He denounces those who think of themselves as being righteous because of their superficial piety, insisting that he demands mercy toward others instead of ritualistic sacrifices (Mt 12:1-7).

Being self-absorbed robs love and caring of their purposes; it implies one self's conscious or subconscious indifference toward others. It blinds us from seeing the good in others, appreciating their needs, or the necessity to forgive. This is the case of the Pharisees who condescendingly demean people they consider sinners while boasting about their own self-righteousness (Lk 7:36-50, 18:11-12). Often, unknowingly, this behavior engenders human apathy, a conduct that Jesus will condemn on Judgment Day (Mt 25:41-43). Often, this is an outcome of structurally induced sin, something that Jesus hardly speaks about because of his emphasis on morality being mostly an interpersonal matter.

Postmodern culture tends to legitimize (and subliminally encourage) attachment to material possessions, rampant individualism that neglects the common good, avarice, and the profit motive as foremost ends and as justifiable economic behavior. These activities tend, not only to ignore Jesus's teachings but are used to confirm sinful behavior. Although secularism consents to these types of behavior in the name of freedom, ultimately, they are humanly created (with the backing of Catholic and Protestant notions);[7] they have become acceptable in capitalist-oriented societies and are claimed to be compatible with Christian values. None of these attitudes are illegal, despite they were the foremost instigators of the 2008 catastrophic worldwide economic recession and the resulting induced inequality and poverty in many countries.[8]

Institutionalized sinfulness is hardly spoken about today because most economic studies are not conducted from a Christian point of view;[9] that is, they do not deal with unique 'sinful' behavior that may lead to specific consequences. Instead, they apply the so-called 'rational economic behavior' known as self-interest, under the unsubstantiated truism that *the best economic benefit for all can usually be accomplished when individuals act in their own self-interest.*[10] These ideas are studied in college courses in economics, finances, and marketing (among others), likely (or perhaps knowingly) without recognizing that they refer to the economic definition of selfishness. This realization suggests that society stands to benefit if the social sciences empirically test the validity of Jesus's teachings in terms of their outcome in economics and standards of living.

Jesus's teachings presumably would oppose the creation of social, political, economic, and cultural structures that induce people toward unbridled riches and material possessions. Nonetheless, it is important to bear in mind that until a new economic order is established, along with their corresponding values that respond to the needs of all human beings, the current largely unrestrained capitalist-oriented, production/consumption cycle is the only engine available to sustain physical life on earth. The effort to create a new economic order likely will create strong opposition by Christians themselves, unless there is an *en masse* hearts and minds conversion in accordance with Jesus's teachings on selfishness.

Selfishness has a similar outcome in the world of politics where the same behavior leads to power struggles and the intemperate desire to win at all costs. Again, none of this behavior is illegal, although it is legitimized by variations of a normative concept known as *Realpolitik,* better known as the pursuit of the National Interest interpreted in terms of nationalism.

Arguably, it might be difficult to codify greed, callous indifference, and selfishness in a secular society, particularly when economic and political concepts of freedom nurture these tendencies. Thus, what might be required to offset this behavior are principles or norms of conduct that once they are empirically validated can be socially taught and individually internalized.

Notes:

1. *Merriam-Webster Dictionary,* online, s.v. "selfishness," "self-centered." Some schools of thought regard selfishness as virtuous; Ayn Rand, *The Virtue of Selfishness,* (New York: Signet/Penguin Random House, 1964); or as a natural, i.e., 'normal' human behavior, Thomas Hobbes, *Leviathan,* originally published in 1651, (New York: Penguin Classics, 2017). As everything one does is usually done to attain desired ends, it is easy to conflate any type of behavior with acting selfishly; however, proceeding in this manner distorts the precise meaning of the term. In Christianity, selfishness considers other people almost exclusively as being less important or inferior to a selfish person. There is in selfishness an almost complete disregard for the wellbeing of others that is aptly described as caring only about oneself. This does not mean that it would be sinful to care about or be concerned with one's desires, needs, or interests; such daily concerns are the trait of a self-sustaining responsible person.

2. Although usury, long considered among the worse sins, is still unlawful in the United States and other countries, it has become legalized usury through political schemes. For example, in the United States, federal usury laws set limits to interest rates on borrowed money; however, laws and Supreme Court decisions allowing each state to write its own laws are used as legal means to circumvent limitations to interest rates charged by credit card companies and nationally chartered banks by registering in states where the highest interest rate is legally allowed. By these standards, the most usurious state in the United States is likely Delaware. *Investopedia,* "Usury Laws," https://www.investopedia.com/terms/u/usury-laws.asp (accessed on October 6, 2018).

3. Robert A. Stebbins, "The Social Psychology of Selfishness," *Canadian Review of Psychology,* Vol 18, Issue 1, February 1981, 82-92, Wiley Online Library, onlinelibrary.wiley.com/doi/pdf/10.1111/j.1755-618X.1981.tb01225.x . The author writes, *Selfishness is an imputation hurled at perceived self-seekers by their victims.... It may be understood as a violation of certain rules of etiquette or courtesy that relate to fairness and consideration of others.... In terms of common sense the moral standing of selfishness is clear: 'It is one of the most generally agreed judgments of ordinary morality that unselfishness is to be commended and selfishness condemned* (Downie and Telfer, 1969: 39).

4. William Berry, LMHC., CAP., "You're So Selfish," *Psychology Today,* 16 April 2016, https://www.psychologytoday.com/us/blog/the-second-noble-truth/201604/youre-so-selfish. Berry indicates that often *people are unaware of selfishness.* Along the lines of an evolutionary theory of human sinfulness, he points out that: *Recent research indicates no decisive conclusion regarding whether humans are "fundamentally generous or greedy and whether these tendencies are shaped by our genes or environment." (Robison, M; 2014). Studies seem to indicate we are both, and the reasons are genetic, evolutionary, and environmental.*

5. *Cambridge Dictionary,* online, s.v. "self-absorbed."

6. The priest and the Levite were religious representatives of Judaism who would have been expected to be models of "neighbor." NEs' note, Lk 10:31-32.

7. Max Weber identified the ascribed relationship between Protestant values and capitalism early in the twentieth century in his book, *The Protestant Ethic and the Spirit of Capitalism,* (London: Penguin

Books, 2002); regarding Catholic apologists of American capitalism see Michael Novak, *The Spirit of Democratic Capitalism,* (New York: December 1990); George Weigel, ed., *A New Worldly Order: John Paul II and Human Freedom,* (Lanham: February 1992).

8. While a macro-level outlook suggests that living standards are gradually increasing worldwide, multiple studies have concluded that economic inequality has risen as well. Increasing the inequality gap, aside from exacerbating inequities in health, education, mortality, environmental sustainability, and social upheavals, slows down economic growth and the process of lifting people out of poverty. "Reward Work, Not Wealth," *Oxfam International.org,* January 2018, www.oxfam.org/sites/www.oxfam.org/files/file_ attachments/bp-reward-work-not-wealth-220118-summ-en.pdf; "Fiscal Monitor: Tackling Inequality," International Monetary Fund (IMF), Washington, October 2017, http://www.imf.org/en/Publications/FM/Issues/2017/10/05/fiscal-monitor-october-2017; Era Dabla-Norris, Kalpana Kochhar, Nujin Suphaphiphat, Frantisek Ricka, Evridiki Tsounta, "Causes and Consequences of Income Inequality: A Global Perspective," *International Monetary Fund,* (Washington, D.C.: 15 June 2015), https://www.imf.org/en/Publications/Staff-Discussion-Notes/Issues/2016/12/31/Causes-and-Consequences-of-Income-Inequality-A-Global-Perspective-42986; "World Inequality Report 2018," *The World Inequality Database,* http://wir2018.wid.world/ (all accessed 11 June 2018).

9. In many countries under the semblance of being 'just a game,' children are subliminally taught about greed and avarice through games such as Monopoly, Monopoly Deal, Acquire, or the Game of Life.

10. "Self-Interest," *Investopedia, https://www.investopedia.com/terms/s/self-interest.asp.* An interesting take on economic behavior appears in David R. Henderson, "Income Inequality Isn't the Problem," *Hoover Institution,* 20 February 2018, https://www.hoover.org/research/income-inequality-isnt-problem (accessed 11 June 2018). Henderson argues that the trickle-down approach (that Jesus denounced in his parable about Lazarus and the Rich Man, Lk 16:19) is a most effective way to reduce poverty, or at least not to make it worse. He delves into economic behavior by observing that (based on self-interest economic behavior), if governments were to tax high incomes or wealth there would be *fewer people trying to make high incomes and get wealthy.* This rationale suggests that people would prefer to opt out from making $10 million if they knew they would be left with only $6 million. This is akin to saying that the person would prefer not to eat an apple pie unless it can eat as much as he/she want to. This rationale indicates that self-interest as a driving force of progress may be also self-destructive. The study by Oxfam listed above, for example, illustrates that the wealth accrued by an insignificant number of billionaires in 2017 ($762 billion), would be sufficient to end extreme poverty (those earning less than $1.90 per day) seven times over. p 10. Henderson, however, adds, seemingly complacent, that poverty worldwide has declined, so that *fewer than one billion people now live in extreme poverty.* Presumably, these must be great numbers; after all, it's only one … billion, that live while earning, about $2.15 daily, a number that makes the use of the Gini coefficient approach economically pleasing, although physically, emotionally, and morally unsuitable.

Refusal to Accept Jesus or God's Kingdom

It is difficult to overlook Jesus's condemnation in the synoptics of those unwilling to accept him as God's messenger; or as is the case in John's text, as the Son of God. Many of his parables, such as the Tenants, the Faithful Servant, the Great Banquet, the Talents, the Wedding Feast, the Bread of Life, the Shepherd, and the True Vine relate to the sinful consequences of rejecting Jesus or God.

Jesus condemns his own generation of Israelites as being faithless, sinful, perverse, and evil precisely for their unwillingness to believe in him (Mk 8:38, Lk 9:41, 11:29, Mt 12:45, 16:4). Mark goes as far as quoting Jesus saying that, *whoever believes and is baptized will be saved; whoever does not believe will be condemned* (Mk 16:16). Jesus's impatience is visible as he becomes irate, presumably with his own disciples, over their inability to drive out an evil spirit from a mute boy. Because of their failure, he chastises an entire generation for lacking faith, wondering how long he will have to endure these people (Mk 9:19, Lk 9:41). He lacks tolerance for those who are ashamed of him (a normal human feeling in a secularized culture), saying that the Son of Man will be ashamed of them on Judgment Day (MK 8:38, Lk 9:26).

When placing together these selected passages, Jesus's anger at his generation is evident. The word *generation,* referring to the Jewish people of his time, is mentioned 26xt in the synoptics, nearly all of them in negative terms. Jesus is particularly exasperated by the conduct of the religious authorities. They demand a sign (credentials) that may authenticate who he says he is. Their attitude seems to be a reasonable request to someone who is critical of them and who calls God his Father; after all, it is not as if the Son of God visits the earth every day. But exactly what kind of sign they are demanding is somewhat unclear. Are Jesus's miraculous deeds not enough? Could it be that some or all the Pharisees and scribes have not witnessed any of his deeds? According to John's text, on two occasions the Pharisees hear about (but do not witness) the healing of a paralytic and a blind man (Jn 5:1-12, 9:1-33). In Matthew, the Pharisees hear about (but do not witness) Jesus driving out demons (Mt 12:24). Some scribes and Pharisees witness his miraculous deeds (Mk 2:1-12, 3:1-6, Lk 5:17-26, 6:6-11, 14:1-6, Mt 12:9-14), but at times they do not, and he gives *strict orders* to those present not to say anything about his actions (Mk 5:42-43, 7:35-36, Lk 5:13-14, 8:54-56, Mt 8:1-4).

Why would Jesus want to keep his wondrous public deeds secret? His reluctance contributes to people's continued unbelief. Does he think that it would have been possible to keep his actions from becoming public even though many of his deeds (his miracle at Cana, the healing of a royal official's son, the blind man, and Lazarus's resurrection), had taken place publicly with the specific intention that people would believe? (Jn 2:1-11, 4:48, 9:1-3, 11:1-4). His strict orders are in vain; he cures two blind men, then tells them, s*ee that no one knows about this. But they went out and spread word of him through all that land.* It seems that people are so excited that they defy his directives, and by word of mouth (a primitive version of the internet) his deeds become known all over the land: (Mk 6:53-56, Lk 7:11-16, Mt 8:16-17, 9:29-31).

He insists that *no sign will be given to this generation* (Mk 8:12, Lk 11:29, Mt 12:38-39), despite he has provided them with many signs already. In some instances, he is stubbornly reluctant to satisfy their demand. He expects to be listened to and be accepted at faith value. Jesus goes even further and turns down a crowd's request for a sign, claiming that he does not need to do it because he will be vindicated in the future. He claims that since he is superior to Jonah and Solomon, he shall grant no sign (Lk 11:29-32, Mt 12:38-42).

The religious authorities seem as unreasonable as Jesus. On the one hand, it is sensible for people, particularly nowadays, to ask for evidence of issues that may be transcendental. But, supposedly, Jesus has fulfilled their request, in which case, what else do they want? On the other hand, Jesus's obstinacy in providing additional signs would not make a good case for his mission. If his teachings are to be obeyed, his deeds serve to validate them. Nonetheless, while these miraculous deeds may have been enough to create faith at the time within a rather credulous culture, as time passes, believing in Jesus's miracles becomes difficult, because time has created an enormous gap that, along with secularization, scientific and technological progress, Christian relativism, divisiveness, and rejection of his teachings, have contributed to people's skepticism today.

Jesus's remark that *whoever is not with me is against me, and whoever does not gather with me scatters*, today would sound authoritarian (Lk 11:23), something that would not endear him to people living in highly individualistic societies that consider freedom to be paramount. In his parable about him being the true vine, Jesus's words become eerier as he warns, *anyone who does not remain in me will be thrown out like a branch and wither; people will gather them and throw them into a fire and they will be burned* (Jn 15:6). He declares himself to be the absolute moral truth; thus, he considers everyone who is not with him to be a conspirator that attempts to impede the progress of God's kingdom on earth.

Initially, it appears that Jesus addresses his message only to the Jewish people, hence, it would have been understandable if Gentiles had not paid attention to him. At the end of the Gospels, however, there are passages in which Jesus directs his disciples to spread the Good News to all nations (Mk 16:15, Lk 24:45-48, Mt 28:19-20, and less precise in Jn 20:30-31) that, naturally, includes Gentiles. But the textual evidence that Jesus wanted his message spread to all nations is at best mixed. Despite obscure passages in the Old Testament that refer to Jesus as the Messiah and redeemer, in Acts, the evidence illustrates that a degree of religious appropriation takes place when Paul convinces Peter, James, and others, that Gentiles, i.e., all humankind, ought to be included in Jesus's salvific plan (Acts 15:2-35). Jesus's insistence that he only comes for the lost sheep in Israel, and his failure to explain his change of heart, suggest that the endings in the synoptics are questionable at best. These endings take place only after Paul is able to persuade the disciples in Jerusalem about the need to seek the conversion of Gentiles. From then on, conspiring against the kingdom that Jesus preaches applies to all humankind.

Jesus's dogmatism poses a problem for Christianity. Several conditions outlined above contribute to society's questioning the legitimacy of his claim, notwithstanding the possibility that he may be divine. The rapid pace of secularization, a decline in fear of hell and credibility regarding Jesus's message, long unresolved questions about the veracity of certain aspects of the scriptures, in addition to the 'distractions' that temporal life now provides, compete today with allegiance to Jesus's teachings. Unless there is a more explicit intervention by God, Jesus's teachings will likely become a historical relic.[1]

Notes:
1. Every poll that appears in this work has outlined the toll that Christianity has taken on account of secularization in the United States and Europe. In 2020, most people living in the most prosperous nations, Western and Eastern Europe, the United States, Canada, South Korea, Japan, and Australia felt that it is not necessary to believe in God to be moral; the opposite holds in less prosperous nations.

Christine Tamir, Aidan Connaughton, Ariana Monique Salazar, "The Global Divide," *Pew Research Center,* July 20, 2020, https://www.pewresearch.org/global/2020/07/20/the-global-god-divide/ (accessed October 30, 2020). Already in 2015, Millennials in the United States (ages 22 to 37 in 2018) regarded Christmas as more cultural than a religious holiday, (forty percent of Millennials saw Christmas as a religious holiday compared with fifty-six percent for Baby Boomers): Michael Lipka, "Many Millennials see Christmas as more cultural than a religious holiday," Pew Research Center, December 18, 2015, http://www.pewresearch.org/fact-tank/2015/12/18/many-millennials-see-christmas-as-more-cultural-than-religious-holiday/ (accessed on December 13, 2018). Another Pew poll is indicative of this trend: "Americans Say Religious Aspects of Christmas Are Declining in Public Life," Shrinking majority believes the biblical account of the birth of Jesus depicts actual events, December 12, 2017. https://www.pewforum.org/2017/12/12/americans-say-religious-aspects-of-christmas-are-declining-in-public-life/ (accessed December 13, 2018).

Egotism

As opposed to the Selfishness/Self-centeredness category that focuses on the desire to gain material possessions or accrue personal benefits through illicit means, greed, or human indifference, the *egotism* category centers on passages in the Gospels that relate to the relationship between the 'person' and 'others.' Jesus would disapprove of an attitude that fosters the belief or feeling that 'I am better than the rest,' namely because it negates the proposition that (despite obvious passages in the texts), nowadays all humanity enjoys the same dignity in the eyes of God, and equally deserve God's love and mercy. From Jesus's standpoint, to distort God's conception of his creatures by treating others as inferior beings signifies denying them their equal human value. This view is illustrated in Jesus's saying that he came not to be served but to serve (Mk 10:45, Mt 20:28), and manifested in the washing of his disciples' feet and his directive to them to *do as I have done to you* (Jn 13:1-17).

Defined today as *an exaggerated sense of self-importance,*[1] the term *egotism* does not appear in the Gospels. It is used here to encompass three distinct attitudes that are reflected in the texts: pride, self-righteousness, and hypocrisy. Egotism refers to someone proud, conceited, and ostentatious. This person tends to be arrogant while showing an offensive attitude of superiority. Having an exaggerated sense of oneself that borders or falls into narcissism, the egotist engages in self-worshipping, has an over-inflated ego, and exhibits pompous behavior. Considering himself/herself above others, the egotist tends not to accept criticism well and translates weaknesses or vices into hypocrisy to appear virtuous.[2]

Pride, Self-Righteousness, Hypocrisy

The word *pride* does not show up in the Gospels, and yet since Early Christianity, it has been considered one of the seven deadly sins. Thomas Aquinas, citing Pope Gregory I, rates pride as *the queen of all vices.*[3] Although it appears that it was sinful pride, i.e., to become like God, that led the first humans into Original Sin, and was first regarded as self-destructive by the Greeks (hubris), pride seemingly has lost its sinful characterization in postmodern times. Today, *pride/proud* has become a positive attitude in many instances; *be proud of yourself and your accomplishments*, parents, and teachers tell children that feel dejected for failing to meet others' standards. On the other hand, we observe parents' bumper stickers boasting that their children are honor students at *XYZ* school; or adults 'proudly' announcing their beliefs and values to the world. Indeed, pride is a double-edged sword that, positively viewed, stands for a measured sense of self-worth that can be appreciated by others. Negatively viewed, pride signifies obnoxious arrogance or a pretentious feeling of self-importance that postmodern democratic societies tend to find distasteful.[4]

The term *self-righteousness* also does not show up in the Gospels; however, several passages relate distinctively to this behavior (Lk 6:26, 10:26-37, 18:9-14, 20:21, Mt 6:1-4, 23:28-33) by contrasting those who humbly acknowledge God's commandments and behave accordingly with those who boast and pretend to be righteous. Self-righteous behavior is associated with being conceited and overly preoccupied with social standing. As such, it is not perceived to be sinful nowadays, despite being equated with a *showoff* behavior that 'down to earth' common people dislike. Jesus is explicitly clear when he speaks about this attitude: *I tell you ... for everyone who exalts himself will be humbled, and the one who humbles himself will be exalted* (Lk 18:14). Interestingly, secular democratic societies shun feelings of superiority or self-righteousness because these attitudes place people in a condition of self-imposed inferiority.[5]

Hypocrisy as a sinful attitude, on the other hand, shows up in the synoptics 21xt, although John's Gospel inexplicably avoids it altogether. The term's connotation today relates highly to its usage in the Gospels. Jesus refers to hypocrisy as a conscious or subconscious attempt to disfigure God's message through behavior that is antithetical to his teachings. His words are directed mostly toward the politicians of the day, i.e., the Jewish religious authorities (Mk 7:5-7, Lk 12:1, Mt 16:5-12, 23:1:39). However, on one occasion, for unknown reasons he becomes angry and refers to the crowds he is preaching to as hypocrites (Lk 12:56).[6] Although hypocrisy is nowadays regarded as highly obnoxious,[7] it appears that the general population has become oblivious to the fact that it implies deception. Hypocrisy is a manifestation of egotism insofar as the self intends to behave in a purposefully deceitful manner. Its sinfulness, as observed in the Gospels, lies in that hypocrisy poisons the public discourse, lowers expectations of good behavior in society, establishes false role models, and clouds the citizenry's understanding of public affairs (Lk 11:37-54, Mt 23:13-39).

Jesus's sayings on this matter would seem to relate closely to the divisiveness that currently exists within Christianity and in secular societies. He finds hypocrisy and arrogance among those who pay more attention to the letter of the law while neglecting *the weightier things of the law: judgment and mercy and fidelity* (Mt 23:23); and in those that focus more on rituals and offerings of sacrifice rather than on mercy (Mt 9:13). He is willing to break the rule of the Sabbath to do good, to cure a disabled person, or to save a life (Mk 3:4, Luke 13:10-16, 14:2-5, Mt 12:1-12, 13:10-17, Jn 5:1-14), because, as he says, authoritatively, that *the sabbath was made for man, not man for the Sabbath* (Mk 2:27).

He refuses to follow the tradition of the elders requiring the cleansing of the hands prior to eating meals because he considers it hypocritical to rely on human precepts while ignoring God's commandments (Mk 7:1-13, Mt 15:1-9). He is critical of the Jewish authorities who attempt to ensnare him by acting condescendingly toward him regarding the payment of the census tax to Caesar (Mk 12:15-17, Mt 22:17-21). He calls out their pretentiousness and their attempts to show off their superficial religious devotion: performing self-righteous deeds by giving alms to the poor, praying in public for the sake of showing off their religiosity, and neglecting their appearance when fasting so that others can see their sacrificial behavior (Mk 12:38-40, Lk 16:14-15, 20:45-47, Mt 6:1-8, 6:16-18). He warns about the danger of becoming self-righteous when *all speak well of you* (Lk 6:26), and he tells the Parable of the Good Samaritan to a scholar of the law who is seeking to justify his righteousness (Lk 10:25-37). He distinctly defines hypocrisy as being critical of others' actions while behaving similarly: *You hypocrite! Remove the wooden beam from your eye first; then you will see clearly to remove the splinter in your brother's eye* (Lk 6:41-42, Mt 7:1-5).

When a Pharisee invites Jesus to dine at his home and becomes judgmental of Jesus for not following the washing of the hands, he engages in a tirade against all Pharisees for their self-righteousness, their pride, and their hypocrisy (Lk 11:37-52). Jesus shows his anti-establishment posture by not being willing to be religiously correct. Nowadays, his insults would debase the political and cultural discourse in a polarized society, unless the one voicing them is extraordinarily righteous, credible, and non-ideological. Under current conditions in which religious, political, and cultural values are heatedly contested in the public arena, harsh ideological criticism against opposing values likely will lead to hatred, violence, and further polarization. Today, it might be difficult to find someone with impeccable credentials that may be culturally accepted while recriminating society at large.

Notes:
1. According to the Merriam-Webster Dictionary, the term (with a slightly different meaning) was first used in 1714. *Merriam-Webster Dictionary,* online, s.v. "egotism."
2. *Merriam-Webster Dictionary,* online, s.v. "hypocrisy," "pride," "self-righteousness."
3. Joseph Delaney, "Pride," CE, Vol 12, (New York: Robert Appleton Company, 1911), http://www.newadvent.org/cathen/12405a.htm (accessed online November 2, 2018).
4. The kernel of democracy (in its broadest sense) lies in the conception that all citizens are equal before the law. Hence, whether through memes, ethos, or long-standing norms, citizens in a democracy abhor anyone (particularly public elected officials or wealthy people) who boasts of being superior to them. In this sense, the term *elitism* is understood to be synonymous with snobbishness and is disliked too.
5. The relationship between U.S. President Donald Trump and his most ardent followers appears to be an exception to this view. President Trump, more than any other president in the history of the nation, boasted about being superior to anyone else, whether military leaders, politicians, elites, scientists, or financiers. He might be considered the most conceited politician in US history as indicated by his populist speeches. Nonetheless, boasting about his supposed superiority appears to have pleased his followers who seemed thrilled to feel inferior to him.
6. Jesus possibly meant to say, "do not be like the hypocrites," as in (Mt 6:2, 5, 16).
7. Jillian Jordan, Roseanna Sommers, Paul Bloom, David G. Rand, "Why Do We Hate Hypocrites? Evidence for a Theory of False Signaling," *SSRN* (formerly Social Science Research Network), January 11, 2017, https://papers.ssrn.com/sol3/papers.cfm?abstract_id=2897313 (accessed online November 3,

2018). For an interesting study about hypocrisy seen from a series of scientific behavioral studies see, Olga Khazan, "Inside the Mind of a Hypocrite," *The Atlantic,* June 21, 2017, https://www.theatlantic.com/science/archive/2017/06/mind-of-a-hypocrite/530958/ (accessed online November 4, 2018).

Sinful Sexuality

This section discusses issues the Gospels consider sinful in matters of sexuality: divorce, adultery, lust, licentiousness, and prostitution; there are no others. Table 2 presents a breakdown of each one.

Sexuality in the Scriptures

From the moment God creates two types of similar physical human beings, capable of feeling mutually strong physical and emotional attraction, then gives them the consent to *be fertile and multiply* (Gen 1:28), a potential sexual upheaval becomes unleashed. According to Christian teachings, the sexual urge becomes more forceful given human proclivity toward the flesh because of Original Sin, or speaking in secular terms, due to our biological makeup.

It appears that God is aware of the consequences of his decisions given the many restrictions he places in the Old Testament to regulate sexual behavior. The volatile mixture of these two creatures, better known as concupiscence in moral terminology, has been responsible for the creation of its own theology, passionate drama, poetry, crime, a morally questionable financial industry, romantic as well as bawdy songs and films, broken and righteous families, poverty, disease, anguish, heroic love, and the power at times to alter the course of history. Hence, it might be pertinent to ask, did God think that given the intense desires that sexuality evokes among frail beings he could curb its impact by legislating its behavior? Did he think his laws would be enough to regulate what is simply a biological function that humans share with animals?

Christianity treats sexuality as sacred placing emphasis on righteous or proper moral behavior. Interestingly, the Old Testament contains rather explicit passages about sexual behavior that God seems to allow (some of which are sinfully regarded today), others that are questionable by today's standards, and still other behavior that exudes erotic bliss.[1] Perhaps unbeknownst to many Christians, the Gospels' pronouncements on sexuality are rather negligible, particularly when contrasted to strong Christian condemnation of unacceptable sexual behavior throughout much of its history.

Divorce and Adultery in the Gospels

The reader may be surprised to note that Jesus includes divorce as sinful behavior. His declaration in Mark and Matthew sounds compelling. He relies on Genesis 2 to indicate that it was God's will to create male and female, and that each would leave their respective parents to become one flesh (Mk 10:6-8, Mt 19:4-6). However, while refuting the Pharisees on the issue of divorce, Jesus appears to repudiate Moses, and presumably God too, saying that Moses had been too lenient in granting a divorce. Still, he authoritatively declares that *what God has joined together, no human being must separate* (Mk 10:9, Mt 19:6). These are words that do not appear in Genesis. Hence, it means that it is Jesus who sees divorce as sinful because he believes that it defies God's initial design. Interestingly, this declaration continues to be relevant to all major Christian denominations even when, in one form or another, they allow the mutual or one-sided dissolution of marriage).[2]

In Genesis, God does not provide counseling when marital problems creep into the relationship. God simply wishes man and woman to lead a happy and fruitful life, in which case he would prefer for couples not to break their union. Jesus goes further. It is noteworthy that while in other instances he shows himself to be forgiving of human weakness and sinfulness, including those whom he pardons without visibly asking for forgiveness (the paralytic in the synoptics, and the Samaritan woman, and the prostitute in John's Gospel), Jesus does not seem willing to understand the complexity of marriage and divorce.

Jesus could have spoken about the goodness of love in marriage as the foundation of society. Nonetheless, he does not present a rationale for his teachings; he is dogmatic, citing God's commandments (while adding words to it) that must be obeyed without being questioned. Hoping to learn about the positive side of marriage, the reader might prefer to read Paul's letters dealing with love in marital relations.

Other than the above passage regarding the union between man and woman that God has ordained, the texts' dealings with divorce relate specifically to the sin of adultery: the case of the Baptist's admonition to Herod for divorcing his wife and marrying his brother's wife (Mk 6:17-18, Lk 3:19, Mt 14:3-4); Joseph's intention to divorce Mary before being told by the angel that he could take her into his home (Mt 1:18-25); and Jesus's brief and in some cases awkward denunciations about adultery. In life, divorce occurs when the union between man and woman is broken (for innumerable reasons including adultery) and each partner, wishing to find companionship and happiness once again, decides to remarry. In these circumstances, adultery occurs (in one or both parties), and in the eyes of Jesus this behavior leads to eternal damnation (Mk 7:22, 10:19, Lk 18:20, Mt 15:19, 19:17-18). In the Old Testament, adultery entailed death by stoning (Lev 20:14).[3]

Among Jesus's teachings, anyone may commit adultery with the eyes: *everyone who looks at a woman with lust has already committed adultery with her in his heart* (Mt 5:27-28). Presumably, the teaching applies to women too. This teaching, however, seems perplexing; a lustful look, i.e., visualizing a woman with emotional desire, is equivalent to committing adultery. Given the emotional and carnal attraction that God places among human beings, Jesus is imposing a hardship that becomes difficult to uphold, particularly since sexual attraction plays a significant role in pre-marital stages and the creation of a family.

While lust may lead to sinful behavior according to Jesus, Thomas Aquinas, citing St. Augustine (an expert on the matter of sexuality), indicates that the sins of the flesh are the most difficult to combat, *wherein the fight is a daily one, but victory rare.* Aquinas relies on St. Isidore of Seville who reminds us that '*mankind is subjected to the devil by carnal lust more than by anything else,*' for which *the vehemence of this passion is more difficult to overcome.*[4] Thus, the Fathers of the Church were able to grasp through carnal experience and scholastic reasoning what Jesus apparently was not able to understand.

In other instances, however, Jesus is ambivalent about adultery. As strict as he is about this behavior, he shows his forgiving side by not condemning the Samaritan woman who has had five husbands (Jn 4:7-25) and pardoning the prostitute the scribes and the Pharisees want to stone to death (Jn 8:3-11). In these passages he emphasizes the need to forgive, and although he appears to weaken his case against adultery, ironically, and contrary to his previous remarks, he seems to grasp his understanding about the sins of the flesh.

It is puzzling that the Gospels pay scant attention to sexual sinfulness, given that it was so important in the Old Testament and today has become part of the culture wars. Aside from divorce and adultery, other sexual sins rank exceptionally low. Jesus refers to prostitution only three times in passing, indicating that upon repentance, they would be welcomed into the kingdom of God. Although the afterlife side-effects of lust are horrific, the term appears only once in the texts (Mt 5:28). Similar words such as, licentiousness and unchastity appear only once as an evil that comes from the heart (Mk 7:22, Mt 15:18-19).

Overall, Jesus focuses more on the evils of sexuality than on its goodness. In so doing, he does not offer an understanding of God's designs. In that respect, his teachings are sorely limited and incongruent if they were to be used for educational (including moral) courses on matters of sexuality. Setting aside the loss of sexual inhibitions that a long-running, worldwide sexual revolution has brought about, postmodern society has acquired more realistic and beneficial information about human sexuality than God and Jesus have ever provided, disagreements among mainstream Christian denominations over its content notwithstanding. This does not mean that Jesus's teachings on divorce, adultery, lust, and licentiousness are absent of any moral value. He conveyed a moral foundation that places human sexuality above being simply an animal drive. Nonetheless, difficulties in his endeavor are noticeably seen as Christianity has discarded substantial portions of Old Testament regulations.

Notes:
1. Chapters 15 and 18 in Leviticus are the prototypes of God's attempt to regulate sexual behavior by divine edicts that provided harsh penalties including death by stoning and strangulation. Such deterrence seems to have had little effect on human behavior (or perhaps it may have slowed down its ill effects). Some of these regulations and punishments possibly have done more to create anxiety disorders than to eliminate the proscribed behavior. Practices dealing with sexual cleanliness dictated in Leviticus 15, for example, today would likely lead to an obsessive-compulsive disorder, or to abstinence if sexuality were to be regarded as filthy and indecent under all circumstances. Leviticus 18 deals mostly with the prohibition of incest or sexual intercourse with close relatives, adultery, and bestiality, but does not

mention pedophilia. Today, Christian heads would spin upon learning that the allegory in Ezekiel 16:3-8 suggests that a girl entering puberty (between 10-12 years) may have sexual intercourse. Among the regulations, cross-dressing is forbidden (Deut 22:5). In Exodus, God tolerates bigamy as Sarah, Abraham's wife who is unable to have children, gives her maid, Hagar, to him as a wife, and advises him to have intercourse with her; Abraham and Hagar paid dearly for following her recommendation (Gen 16), after which God decides to miraculously impregnate Sarah and continue with the Jewish branch of descendants (Gen 21:1-8). The Song of Songs is another allegory, detailing the beauty of love. Chapter 7, dealing with the splendor of woman and lovemaking upgrades eroticism to virtuous levels, although it may very well be forbidden in today's Christian and public high schools.

2. Because of the importance ascribed to the institution of marriage, all Christian denominations likely prefer that divorce would never happen. Cultural reality, however, has imposed changes in the regulation of marriage. Protestant Christianity allows divorce, some denominations being laxer than others. The Catholic hierarchy consents to a *de facto* or civil divorce insofar as none of the spouses remarry without first having the marriage annulled. Annulment, however, is a post-Jesus formulation that seeks to find a human aspect that might have invalidated the union, hence a decision that sacramental (not physical or emotional) marriage never existed in the first place. Nonetheless, despite consenting to a civil divorce, Catholicism considers divorce a *grave offense* and *immoral,* although like other denominations, it does not equally blame the spouse that is unjustly abandoned by the other. CCC 2384-2386.

3. In Matthew, Jesus leaves room for divorce if the previous marriage is unlawful (Mt 19:9).

4. Thomas Aquinas, "Question 154, Article 3, The parts of lust," *Summa Theologica,* II/II, http://www.newadvent.org/summa/3154.htm#article3 (accessed online December 6, 2018).

Betraying Jesus

This section focuses on Judas's betrayal of Jesus and contrasts it with Peter's denial. Given the timeless nature that Christianity ascribes to the texts as the word of God to all humanity, distinguishing Jesus's response to Judas's and Peter's actions serves as a frame of reference that applies to all believers. This category ranks among the less significant, although still higher than divorce, adultery, or even blasphemy (Table 2).

Being betrayed by a person one has trusted tends to elicit deep feelings of anger and resentment. Trust is both a conscious and a sub-conscious action through which the betrayed person practically places one's life in the hands of another. Trusting is as noble an act as it is ignoble not to reciprocate.

All four authors of the Gospel record Judas's betrayal in a similar fashion (Mk 14, Lk 22, Mt 26, 27, Jn 13, 18). Mark and Luke report the incident in classic journalistic fashion (who, what, when, where, why). Judas Iscariot, one of the initial twelve disciples, decides to betray Jesus, days before his death. He conspires with the chief priests and later leads a crowd with swords and clubs to the location where Jesus is. He identifies Jesus to his captors with a kiss in exchange for money. Matthew indicates that Judas is to receive thirty pieces of silver in exchange for delivering Jesus (Mt 26:14-16). But having *deeply regretted* what he had done, Judas throws away the money upon finding out that Jesus had been condemned and hangs himself (Mt 27:3-5). Matthew's and John's narratives use the term *betray* more often while Luke and John indicate that it is the devil or Satan that induces Judas to betray Jesus (Lk 22:3, Jn 13:2).

By far, the most condemning statement comes from Jesus himself in the synoptics: *woe to that man by whom the Son of Man is betrayed. It would be better for that man if he had never been born* (Mk 14:21, Lk 22:22, Mt 26:24). His pronouncement makes Judas's action more reprehensible. The Son of Man being betrayed for money is similar to Jesus's statement about the sin of blasphemy against the Holy Spirit; it is serious enough that it should never be forgiven (Mk 3:28-30, Lk 12:10, Mt 12:31-32). On the other hand, is Judas aware of what Jesus means by the Son of Man? Is he aware that he is betraying the divine Son of God? Likely not, as the Gospels do not associate the terms Son of Man and Son of God.

None of the synoptic texts depict Judas as being greedy; the thirty pieces of silver would not have been a sizable amount[1] unless Judas needed the coins for other purposes. Instead, the synoptics characterize him as a betrayer without even insinuating a personal motive. John, on the other hand, indicates that Judas is a thief who steals the temple contributions (Jn 12:6). He explicitly writes that Judas is a hypocrite who pretends to care for the poor by being critical of Jesus when he allows a woman named Mary to anoint a costly perfume on his feet (Jn 12:5).[2]

There is, however, a different view of the incident in which Judas's critique of Jesus's behavior appears reasonable. Jesus has been quite consistent in aiding the poor through his teachings and his deeds. It would have been shocking for Judas (or any of the other disciples) to see an expensive perfume being used on Jesus's feet instead of being sold and its proceeds being given to the poor, and even more shocking to see Jesus approving its use. Is Jesus not contradicting himself in front of them? Although it would have been unkind to refuse the woman's act of love, Jesus's remark that soon he will die while there will always be other times to help the poor may disturb even the sensibility of a caring believer.

Perhaps the most salient point in this category is the way Jesus refers to Judas's betrayal as opposed to Peter's denial. Interestingly, the space given by the authors of the Gospels to Judas's betrayal of Jesus is almost the same as that given to Peter's denial, suggesting that publicly denying Jesus is similar to betraying him. They are not, however; Peter may attribute his behavior to fear for his life (a normal human feeling) while Judas seems either jealous of Jesus or possibly has other intentions in mind such as being more concerned with Jesus's social justice teachings.

Nonetheless, Jesus's response to each case is as dramatic as it is incongruent. In the texts, Jesus does not forgive Peter explicitly for his denial, despite Peter's braggadocio telling Jesus that he would never deny him (Mk 14:31, Lk 22:33, Mt 26:33). Jesus assures him that he will disavow knowing him three times prior to his death. Once Peter denies Jesus he cries in remorse. On the other hand, Judas is instrumental in handing Jesus to his executioners, certainly a wicked act. However, he so *deeply regretted* doing it that he atones for his action by killing himself.[3] Although suicide is condemned by most mainstream Christian denominations, Judas's feeling that he did not deserve to be alive following his betrayal of Jesus seems far more remorseful than Peter's crying repentance. Moreover, if the timeline of events in Matthew is correct, it appears that despite Jesus knowing that Peter would deny him publicly, already he has pardoned him (*ex-ante*) by granting him innumerable powers, including the keys to the kingdom of heaven, and making him the foundation of his church (Mt 16:18-19).

How did Jesus know that Judas would betray him? Was it omniscience, a feature that humans attribute to the divine? If so, why would Jesus choose him as one of the twelve? Did he choose Judas (whom he will condemn), to fulfill God's will? This would be a nefarious plan on Jesus's part; not the type of behavior Christians would ascribe to their God. If Jesus forgave his executioners, perhaps Pontius Pilate too, all of them without having repented, why was he so unforgivable of Judas? Jesus must have known that Judas was going to be remorseful in the same manner he knew that Peter would deny him. *I have sinned in betraying innocent blood*, he said (Mt 27:4), before he threw away the thirty pieces of silver and hung himself. Hence, to what extent the authors of the Gospel, not divine revelation, needed to make an example of Judas as the ultimate betrayer?

Notes:
1. A rough evaluation based on today's American silver dollar (99.93 percent silver weighing oz.) suggests that at 2020 prices averaging $12 per ounce, thirty silver coins would fetch around $360.
2. In John's Gospel, Mary appears to be Lazarus's and Martha's sister. In the other Gospels, the woman is not named and is described as a sinful person. NEs' note, John 12:1-8. Once again, the oral transmission fails to deliver as the voice of God.
3. In the Acts of the Apostles, Luke provides a different account, indicating that Judas died an accidental death: *He bought a parcel of land with the wages of his iniquity, and falling headlong, he burst open in the middle, and all his insides spilled out* (Acts 1:18). Still, another instance of divine revelation being revealed differently.

Blasphemy

Blasphemy is secularly defined as something said or done that shows disrespect toward God or religion.[1] The meaning is similar in Christianity, although it is regarded as a grave offense, particularly when done in public.[2] The content analysis results rank this category among the least significant.

The term is seldom found in the Old Testament. Its most notable and ancient passage dealing specifically with blasphemy appears in Leviticus 24:10-23, whereby the son of an Israelite woman involved in a fight curses God. The punishment that God prescribes is death (Lev 24:16). Other passages associated with the crime, some of which do not mention blasphemy, suggest similar behavior, such as despising God or cursing a religious leader (Ex 22:27), or defying God and his statutes (Nm 15:22-31, Isa 37:6, Ezek 20:27).

Interestingly, in the Gospels, the religious authorities and Jesus use the term differently. Several times the Pharisees accuse Jesus of blasphemy because *You, a man, are making yourself God* (Jn 10:33), whether by forgiving sins (God's attribute) or by asserting that he is the Messiah and the son of God (Mk 2:7, 14:64, Lk 5:21, Mt 9:3, 26:65, Jn 10:33). Additionally, they accuse Jesus of driving demons by the power of Beelzebul (Satan). In contrast, Jesus takes the latter remark quite seriously, claiming that they have blasphemed against the holy Spirit (supposedly by attributing evil deeds to the divine). It is for this reason that Jesus states that such a sin is unforgivable (Mk 3:28-30, Lk 2:10, Mt 12:31-32), except it is the texts, not Jesus, that provide the explanation. Paradoxically, Jesus forgives perhaps the worst sin that any human being may commit, his crucifixion.

There is the view that the reason that blasphemy is unforgivable is that the sinner does not wish to repent from his action,[3] although this explanation does not appear in the texts. It seems logical, however, that he/she who does not wish to be saved and actively refuses salvation cannot be saved. On the other hand, it is difficult to comprehend that someone with a perfect understanding of both the sin and the extent of the punishment would still consent to the sin. Moreover, Thomas Aquinas writes that, although unpardonable, God can pardon the sin simply because he can do anything he wishes, including forgiving the unforgiven, whether out of mercy or because of his understanding of the human heart.[4]

While blaspheming sounds appalling and spiteful, the Gospels hardly establish the connection between the religious authorities' behavior and the unforgiving character of the sin. The religious authorities seem perplexed by Jesus's unorthodox teachings and deeds. Their charges of blasphemy are expressions of anger as well as true accusations given their understanding of the Law. From Jesus's standpoint, however, their remarks are nonsensical, e.g., the Son of Man driving demons by the power of the devil.

The passages dealing with blasphemy reveal that Jesus and the religious authorities are trading the same charges, and neither one perhaps understands what the other is saying. It is likely that the religious authorities do not understand Jesus's charge against them. In Judaism, blasphemy is a largely unfamiliar concept in biblical thought. In broad terms it refers to *any act contrary to the will of God or derogatory to His power,*[5] something that in Christianity would amount to any sinful deed. The religious authorities claim that Jesus makes himself God by forgiving sins, calling himself the Son of God and the Messiah, and driving demons in the name of the devil.[6] Except for the last accusation that Jesus regards as absurd, the other charges seem to be correct, at least from their own interpretation of Mosaic Law. Jesus, however, responds that the scribes and the Pharisees blaspheme because they address an untruthful remark at the holy Spirit; he tells them that he drives demons, not by his own powers (which is inexplicable, since he is the second person of the Trinity), but as the Son of Man and by the power of the holy Spirit.

The religious authorities, on the other hand, likely have no idea who the Son of Man or the holy Spirit is. At this point neither side understands the other, and a power struggle ensues for religious legitimacy and credibility over the use of the same term.[7] Exchanging charges of blasphemy do not get either side anywhere. Miscommunication does not allow the possibility of a dialogue, which makes Jesus's mission that more difficult. In the end, he is unable to persuade the religious authorities who, despite their recalcitrance, seem convinced of their righteousness. Once again, Jesus's credibility hinges on whether others believe he is who he says he is. His teachings alone do not serve him; he depends on his miraculous deeds. Is it possible the religious authorities witness his deeds and still reject him?

Notes:

1. *Merriam-Webster Dictionary, Cambridge Dictionary, Oxford Dictionary,* online, s.v. "blasphemy." Synonyms include denigrate, disparage, bad-mouth, or deprecate.

2. The Catechism of the Catholic Church considers blasphemy to be *gravely illicit, in and of (itself), independently of circumstances and intentions* (CCC 1756) as it is contrary to the second commandment. Depending on the situation, all Christian denominations probably would regard blasphemy as a serious sin. It must be said, however, that throughout the ages some cultures have incorporated phraseology that disparages religions, God, or Jesus to the extent that people might not even be aware that they are 'bad-mouthing' the divine.

3. Pope John Paul II dealt with the specificity of this sin in *Dominum et Vivificantem – On the Holy Spirit in the Life of the Church and the World,* no. 46, Rome: May 18, 1986. http://w2.vatican.va/content/john-paul-ii/en/encyclicals/documents/hf_jp-ii_enc_18051986_dominum-et-vivificantem.html (accessed on December 15, 2018).

4. Thomas Aquinas, "Question 14 - Of Blasphemy Against The Holy Ghost, Article. 3 - Whether the sin against the Holy Ghost can be forgiven?" *Summa Theologica,* II/II, p 2778 in pdf format. http://www.ccel.org/a/aquinas/summa/cache/summa.pdf (accessed online September 25, 2018).

5. "Blasphemy," *Jewish Virtual Library,* https://www.jewishvirtuallibrary.org/blasphemy (accessed on December 15, 2018).

6. In Matthew, the Pharisees call Jesus an agent of the demon (Mt 12:24); in Mark, it is the scribes; and in Luke is someone among a crowd (Lk 11:15). This is another example of the inaccuracies that God has allowed to permeate the Gospels.

7. According to John's Gospel, the religious authorities accuse Jesus of blasphemy for making himself the son of God. Jesus engages them saying, *Is it not written in your law, 'I said, "You are gods"'? If it calls them gods to whom the word of God came, and scripture cannot be set aside, can you say that the one whom the Father has consecrated and sent into the world blasphemes because I said, 'I am the Son of God'?* (Jn 10:34-36). The Jewish authorities fail to understand (or reject) this point, and there is mutual recrimination.

The Lesser Sins

This category comprises sins that are almost insignificant according to content analysis results, namely because they are not highly mentioned in the Gospels. The results suggest that either Jesus, God, or the authors of the texts did not think or believe they merited greater attention, despite the significance of some of these sins and the seeming incongruence of others.

Inducing Others to Sin

Inducing others to sin seems to be a very serious offense, as it refers to someone who persuades another person (or others) to engage in sinful behavior. In a secular society, this act is similar to aiding and abetting in the commission of a crime. In Matthew, Jesus is uncompromising when he tells his disciples, *whoever causes one of these little ones who believe in me to sin, it would be better for him to have a great millstone hung around his neck and to be drowned in the depths of the sea.* (Mt 18:6-7). This passage, because of its location in the text, and because it deals with *little ones,* may suggest a connection with sexual sins, although that might not be the case since Jesus refers to adults in some cases as children of God.[1] Jesus stresses inducement to sin as being sinful again when he indicates that at the end of time his angels will collect all who cause others to sin and *throw them into the fiery furnace* (Mt 13:41-42).

It might be important to recognize that today, this sin has acquired a social dimension it did not have at the time: structural sinfulness, i.e., humanly created social structures whose values and desires contribute to those immersed in them to engage in sinful behavior. Christianity has paid scant attention to this issue in the past, largely under the assumption that it would diminish human responsibility and free will while being concerned that it would lead to social upheavals in defense of the poor. In Latin America, Catholic liberation theologians and bishops have written about this topic for decades but received limited support from Popes John Paul II and Benedict XVI. Pope Francis, however, has shown an increased understanding of the issue.[2] At the same time, secular leaders, including public elected officials (most of them Christians), have failed to speak out, despite they are primarily responsible for the creation of these structures. Likely, politicians have not seriously challenged these structures because they tend to favor the ideologies that sustain them and because they are afraid of running against the values they represent.[3]

Among these sinful structures the most recognizable are the following: those that favor the rich and are responsible for the inequality that exists in the world; the low regard for human life, whether expressed through war, genocide, the gun culture, abortion, or religious, ethnic, racial, and sexual discrimination; corrupt politicians' indifference toward the people they represent; cultural structures that lead to dependencies, either through the need to cope with stress and anxiety (drugs and alcohol), or to increase personal gratification (pornography and lack of commitment in relations); the claimed 'rightful' desire to accumulate wealth and material possessions, and the profit motive as primary human values; and social and political 'incorrectness' that allow disrespect, divisiveness, and a lowering of standards in public discourses. These issues have become major points of contention in modern politics and culture wars.[4] Given Christian relativism, i.e., divisiveness over issues of right and wrong in society at large, it is likely that inducing others to sin has become a major issue without easy solutions insofar as they continue to recriminate each other.

Notes:
1. NEs point out that it is the location of the passage relative to the previous one dealing with children (Mt 18:1-5) that may lead the reader to make such a connection. NEs add that, *it is difficult to know how Matthew understood the logical connection between these verses* (Note on Mt 18:8-9). In Mark and Luke, there is no such connection although both authors stress the seriousness of inducing others to sin (Mk 9:42-48, Lk 17:1-2).
2. Although John Paul II and Benedict XVI sought to silence and disregard some notable Liberation Theology writers, Pope Francis has rehabilitated some of them, personally meeting with Gustavo Gutierrez, among the first ones to write on the issue of sinful structures.
3. Andrew Basden, "The Variety of Structural Evil in Western Society," abxn.org/discussion/structural. evil.html (accessed on December 19, 2018).
4. Sinful social structures existed, and continue to exist, in dictatorial countries with a communist past. Scarcity of resources, due to planned misallocations and corruption resulted in the flourishing of the black market, in which people were 'forced' to engage in lying and stealing to lessen their impoverished conditions.

Sinning with the Hand, Foot, or Eye

Among the most bizarre of Jesus's sayings is one in which he tells the crowd that if one's hand, foot, or eye leads to sin, *cut it off and throw it away. It is better for you to enter into life maimed or crippled than with two hands or two feet* [or two eyes] *to be thrown into eternal fire.* (Mk 9:43-48, Mt 18:8-9). According to Jesus, sin seems to originate in the heart, or is induced by the devil; it seems too that body limbs act as agents of sinful behavior, such as greed, acts of violence, sexual offenses, or theft.

Possibly, Jesus was speaking hyperbolically, having in mind the severity of sinfulness, i.e., sinning is so severe it is worth mutilating a limb than to risk eternal damnation. Nevertheless, history does not seem to have recorded cases in which righteous people have seriously harmed their bodies (flagellation is less than serious) to avoid sinful behavior. The question arises whether someone with no religious instruction who reads this passage will be capable of understanding what Jesus means, or if his remarks might be dismissed as being as inexplicable as having to eat his flesh and drink his blood. If sinfulness is inevitable, as Jesus admits, e.g., the spirit is willing, but the flesh is weak (Mt 23:41), these remarks suggest that his yoke is not as easy or his burden as light as he says. Hence, it appears that the door keeps getting narrower, and that even with God's help, salvation becomes a stressful process.
(See Method Note for additional explanation)

Harboring Evil Thoughts

This behavior refers to thinking or desiring to commit any kind of sinful behavior without doing it. It applies to any possible act that usually requires the planning of the act, be it theft and murder, desire to taint someone's reputation, or the thought of rape or the abuse of children. Probably, Jesus proscribes this behavior because he realizes that harboring evil thoughts may ultimately lead to the act itself. However, he does not elaborate. It is likely, that this teaching has more to do with his unrealistic desire that his disciples *be perfect, just as your heavenly Father is perfect* (Mt 5:48), despite inevitable human tendencies toward sin.

The term appears three times (Mk 7:21-23, Mt 9:4, 15:19), although other passages reveal similar behavior. When the scribes accuse Jesus of blasphemy, he becomes aware of their thinking and says to them, *why are you thinking such things in your hearts?* (Mk 2:5-8, Lk 5:20-22, Mt 9:2-4). Lust also refers to harboring evil thoughts (Mt 5:28). This is a behavior that seems difficult to eradicate and tends to produce anxiety since God is aware of what dwells in the heart, so evil thoughts cannot be hidden from him. The alternatives are, either to repress or to sublimate these thoughts. These are processes that entail emotional struggles, and Jesus does not teach what to do to prevent such temptations other than to pray. Despite his recommendation (Mt 26:41), however, history indicates that prayer does not offer flawless protection. His prayer at Gethsemane was not helpful. And, in the desert, he avoids succumbing to Satan's temptations because he receives supernatural assistance.

Conditions in today's world, given the desires that cultural structures stimulate, e.g., greed, indifference, revenge, power, and sexual dominance, the task of being perfect becomes more difficult.

(See Method Note for additional explanation)

Dishonoring One's Parents

In Christian culture, the family has been a long-standing institution. Honoring father and mother appears as one of the Ten Commandments. Nonetheless, some of Jesus's sayings are, at best confusing, while at worst he seems to contradict himself. Stressing the importance of marriage, he indicates that man and woman leave their respective parents to become one flesh (Mk 10:6-8, Mt 19:5). Leaving their parents, however, does not mean abandoning them; the children must still honor them. The commandment's significance is noted in the synoptics, including one instance in which Jesus is critical of the religious authorities for ignoring it in favor of their tradition (Mk 7:8-13, Mt 15:3-7), while on another occasion he makes it clear that honoring father and mother is essential to *inherit eternal life* (Mk 10:17, Lk 18:18, Mt 19:16).

Yet, in the Gospels, he appears to belittle his mother by ignoring her presence in favor of doing God's will (Mk 3:31-35, Lk 8:19-21, Mt 12:46-50). His reply to his mother's request at a wedding in Cana is also perplexing for its lack of affection (Jn 2:4), suggesting instead a degree of hostility or indifference.[1]

It is significant too that despite the commandment and the Gospels' recognition of Joseph's arduous efforts to keep the family out of harm's way, the texts pay scant attention to him once Jesus begins his public life. Moreover, it is difficult to understand Jesus's wishes to be a source of discord that will set *a man against his father, a daughter against her mother* (Mt 10:35, Lk 12:53). His lack of explanation for this behavior may be unacceptable by those inquiring about the faith today. After all, it is parents that educate and condition children in the love of God and in observing Jesus's teachings.

Besides, seeking to accentuate his authority over his disciples (and supposedly over those who will follow him in future generations), he declares in an awkwardly autocratic fashion that regardless of how much parents need to be honored, those who love their parents more than they love him are not worthy of his attention (Mt 10:37). Interpreting this saying literally would probably disappoint many people nowadays because, since God represents a higher authority, his saying does not conform with a Jesus that inspires righteousness. The saying might best be understood as suggesting that, if there were conflicts over Jesus's teachings among family members or friends, his commandments would take precedence. Instead, Jesus comes across as an egocentric person who *demands* to be worshipped in return for eternal life. (Mk 10:29:30, Mt 19:29). The teaching seems more appropriate if addressed to those who freely have chosen a different call in life, e.g., monks, nuns, priests, or if it is interpreted as a form of the first commandment, *you shall love the Lord, your God, with all your heart, with all your soul, and with all your mind* (Mt 22:37, Mk 12:29-30). In a secular society, however, this saying may sound unnecessarily arrogant and in contradiction with the meaning of honoring one's parents. Such incongruences make Jesus's teachings and his person difficult to understand.

Notes:
1. In their note on John 2:4, NEs point out that although the term *woman,* is *a normal, polite form of address*, it is highly unusual (*unattested*) *in reference to one's mother*. Jesus's reply, *How does your concern affect me?* is a *Hebrew expression of either hostility* (Jgs 11:12; 2 Chr 35:21; 1 Kgs 17:18) *or denial of common interest* (Hos 14:9; 2 Kgs 3:13). Cf. Mk 1:24; 5:7 *used by demons to Jesus.*

Making False Oaths

In denouncing false oaths, Jesus indicates that making a false oath in the name of God signifies placing God as a witness to a sinful act. At the time of Jesus, it appears that oaths were quite common, highly appropriate in some circumstances, and they seemed to carry some weight. At times, false oaths were accompanied by curses that were tantamount to taking the Lord's name in vain; behavior that merited serious punishment by God (Ex 20:7, Lev 19:12). One's oath was so important that. seemingly, it led Herod to comply with Herodias's daughter's wish to behead John the Baptist to save his credibility (Mk 6:26, Mt 14:8-11).

Keeping one's oath, however, is not always an easy task or they might come with an expiration date. In Genesis, God takes an oath saying that never again will he *curse the ground because of human beings* or that he will *ever again strike down every living being* (Gen 8:21). It appears that God did not keep either oath as he cursed and struck down upon human beings in many instances. God also swears an oath to Abraham to rescue the Israelites from their enemies (Lk 1:68-75), but that would not happen at times, as they are defeated by their enemies, even with God's consent (2 Kings 18:13, 24-10, Judith 5:17-18, 1 Samuel 4:1) and their Temple destroyed twice, supposedly as punishment for their sins.

Swearing, (not to be confused with using foul language) was an adaptation of the oath and stood as a guarantee of one's word. Swearing in vain was considered a desecration of God, denying the perjurer *access to God's holy places and his blessings.*[1] Thus, Jesus accuses the Pharisees and the scribes of falsely swearing by the Temple, the altar, and by heaven (*the throne of God*) (Mt 23:16-22). He curses them, calling them serpents and brood of vipers, and he suggests that their actions will land them in Gehenna (Mt 23:33).

Suggesting that at times the flesh is weak, we recall that, none other than Peter, who earlier had vigorously indicated that he would not deny Jesus, swears and denies him *with an oath* when confronted by bystanders who accused him of being one of Jesus's followers (Mk 14:70-71, Mt 26:72-74). On the other hand, Jesus takes this principle quite seriously. With his life at stake, he could have lied about being the Messiah and the Son of God. However, when he is asked in the presence of the entire

Sanhedrin, *to state under oath before the living God whether you are the Messiah, the Son of God*, he says yes, and as a result he is crucified (Mt 26;62-64).

Today, Jesus's teaching has undergone a subtle transformation. While the church hierarchy acknowledges Jesus's words, it relies on Paul and the tradition of the institution to signify that it allows oaths *made for grave and right reasons (for example, in court)*.[2] Basing itself on Christian tradition, it is customary in many countries and for persons acquiring citizenship or appearing in courts of law as witnesses, or for public officials, to take an oath by swearing on a Bible that ends with the phrase *So help me God.*

In a secular society, taking the name of God in vain has become ordinary behavior, likely without any intention of offending God. In effect, swearing for trivial behavior, e.g., 'I swear that I didn't take your shirt' or 'I swear I will pay you back,' have become common figures of speech that have made inroads into society, likely even among believers.[3] There is little doubt that many believers will frown on the use of the term *God* in vain. Viewed differently, however, by mentioning God in vain people are instinctively appealing to something they consider higher than themselves, a compliment that might be pleasing to the Almighty in today's secular culture.

Notes:
1. *Swearing by YHWH could be used as a synonym of adhering to Him.* Menachem Elon, "Oath," *Encyclopedia Judaica, in Jewish Virtual Library*, https://www.jewishvirtuallibrary.org/oath (accessed on December 28, 2018).
2. *An oath,* says the Catholic Catechism, *is the invocation of the divine name as a witness to truth, and cannot be taken unless in truth, in judgment, and in justice.* CCC 2153, 2154.
3. In 1975 Frankie Valli and the Four Seasons recorded the pop song *Swearin' to God* to high acclaim; OMG (Oh my God) has become part of texting acronyms nowadays; and the expression *oh god,* supposedly referencing the Almighty, has become a casual manifestation denoting sexual ecstasy.

Folly

Nowadays, the term *folly* signifies lacking good sense or foolishness, stupidity, or even tragic criminal conduct. At one time, the term stood for evil, wickedness, and lewd behavior.[1] From a religious standpoint the term is probably outdated. If *folly* were truly a sin, it would be among the most significant sinful behavior, given the amount of foolishness that takes place in the world today. Interestingly, not even the Catholic Catechism includes the word in its index.

The term would be ranked almost as irrelevant since it is mentioned only once in the Gospels when Jesus outlines a series of evil behavior that comes from the heart and defile the person (Mk 7:21-23). However, searching beyond the term itself, content analysis uncovers meaningful passages suggesting behavior that is opposed to reason and wisdom. Jesus gives several examples of folly as sins that carry serious consequences. When the Pharisees accuse him of driving demons in the name of Beelzebul, he tells them that their claim is non-sensical since harming one's own kingdom will only lead to its downfall (Mk 3:23-27, Lk 11:18-22, Mt 12:25-29). In a parable, he focuses on the foolishness of the man who wants to gain wealth by storing his belonging in his barns and enjoy life, when suddenly he is reminded that he will soon die and lose everything (Lk 12:16-21). In another parable, Jesus denies access to the wedding feast, i.e., eternal life, to five virgins (likely bridesmaids) who decide to act foolishly instead of vigilantly awaiting the return of the groom (Mt 25:1-13). Moreover, when an imprudent servant does not comply with the responsibility his master gives him and becomes drunk and abusive of his other servants, he meets severe punishment (Mt 24:45-51).

Perhaps Jesus's most precise definition of folly pertains to people who choose not to heed his words, liking them to fools who build their houses on sand, incapable of withstanding floods and wind (Mt 7:24-27, Lk 6:47-49). John's Gospel, on the other hand, does not include specific references to folly. As in other instances, the text seldom refers to sinful behavior in the manner the synoptics do.

Notes:
1. *Oxford Dictionary,* online; *Cambridge Dictionary*; *Merriam-Webster Dictionary,* online, s.v. "folly."

7 - Contemporary Significant Categories

This section pertains to an examination of significant moral issues that do not find their roots in the Gospels. The categories outlined below owe their views to a combination of Christians and non-Christians exploring diverse ways to confront social issues that had been facing humanity for centuries. Their activism created an awareness that slowly has transformed modern and post-modern societies. In the wake of what remained of Christendom, i.e., European nations where Christianity had become the established religion, a humanist sense[1] focusing on temporal rather than supernatural matters began to filter into philosophy, theology, the arts, and politics. The intellectual roots of this humanism are found in sixteenth-century Renaissance philosophy, the Rationalists in the seventeenth century, and the Enlightenment in the eighteenth century.

Christian hierarchies' continued attempts to expand their influence and authority, resulted in a surge of anti-clerical sentiments among secular and religious philosophers and theologians willing to assume responsibility for the affairs of humankind. They rejected aspects of institutional religion and many of the temporal values it stood for such as privileges accrued to social and religious standing, economic and political inequalities, and strong monarchical sentiments. The outcome evolved into a struggle between modern secularism and Christian hierarchies (both Catholic and Protestant). The most notable lesson during this period was how secularist forces contributed to the significant development of new social values and their adoption by institutional Christianity. Certainly, this process of cultural evolution raises the question of whether there might be intrinsic Christian values embedded in modern secularism, and whether the rapid pace of secularization is leading present and former believers (both Catholics and Protestants) to reexamine the basic tenets of Christian theology. It is nothing short of incredible that Christian hierarchies have accepted secularism as a mainstream value (not that they had a choice) while working alongside non-Christians to make considerable moral and socio-cultural advancements. Some of the categories examined in this section are interrelated, dealing mostly with values that for centuries were anathema to Christianity, namely social and individual human rights.

We may surmise that if God had wanted for there be peace on earth, he might have arranged for human uniformity; the same language, same religious and socio-political and cultural beliefs, and one racial and ethnic background. He could have prevailed over evil, and for purposes of reproduction God could have eliminated sexual differences through self-procreation. Instead, God seems to have opted (or allowed) for a radical design of humankind resulting in many of today's conflicts that have arisen from diversity. These conflicts, according to Christian belief, have to do with the consequences of Original Sin that in retrospect might have caused more disruption to *creation* than God may have anticipated. We must recall that God had second thoughts about his own creation (Gen 6:6).

There is too the secular explanation that, interestingly, is accepted by some mainstream religious denominations; that God's plan for humanity proceeds through an evolutionary process that involves not only biological but socio-political and cultural transformations. Whether God's direct hand or working through evolution, i.e., *the gradual development of something, especially from a simple to a more complex form,*[2] it is noticeable that today humanity is characterized by a multiplicity of racial and ethnic makeups, genders, languages, religious beliefs, cultural likes and dislikes that make human life rather colorful, and conflicting. Amid this reality, Jesus is asking humanity, particularly his followers, to overcome human differences no matter how unpalatable or difficult. This is not to say that uniformity, although helpful, will necessarily guarantee peace and understanding on earth. Evil, aside from a possible real entity, seems to be deeply rooted in human imperfections, whether covetousness, greed, distrust, hatred, insecurity, selfishness, or mental illness, among others. Nonetheless, the alternative to not being able to overcome acceptance of each other would be continued polarization, discrimination, injustices, and armed warfare. Attempting to alter reality by eradicating the differences we dislike probably will lead to various forms of mutual annihilation.

It might be possible to conclude that some of Jesus's teachings impede peace and good relations among humans. His desire to set the world on fire, create divisions among family members, and recommend inaction amid conflict is not exactly conducive to social wellbeing when interpreted literally. On the other hand, a rereading or total reinterpretation of the Gospels leading to their adaptation to the type of world we live in might contribute to considerable moral and social progress. Although an elaborate theory of the good society might not be precisely detected in the Gospels, some of its foundations may be found in the texts.

For example, reason and goodwill are two important features that humans possess that Christians believe are God-given. Hence, simply because the clear hand of Jesus does not show in social progress does not mean that Jesus does not will it. It is here that secularism and secularization show both its worthy and its ugly faces. The ugly face refers to verbal attacks against institutionalized religion, some of it understandable and justified, although enormously disliked by believers, and to physical violence against various faiths and social groups that cannot be justified and can only be understood as the outcome of ignorance, prejudice, and the absence of goodwill. The good face, on the other hand, has been in some cases extraordinarily beneficial to humanity despite its dislike by various ideologies within Christianity.[3]

Notes: As may be noticed in Table 2, the Contemporary Significant Categories are not tallied or ranked, namely because they do not owe their origin to the Gospels. Instead, they emerge due to later developments led in many instances by non-Christians. Nonetheless, the case can be made that certain passages or values observed in the texts present indirect parallels suggesting that Jesus's teachings may not necessarily oppose the temporal recognition of these categories.

1. A distinction is made between Christian humanism that while focusing on temporal matters does not negate the supernatural, i.e., God, and secular humanism that rejects its existence.

2. Oxford Dictionary, online, s.v. "evolution."

3. The Gospels, and the rest of the New Testament, cannot be considered either progressive, liberal, conservative, or traditionalist by today's standards. These seem to be ideological positions that Christians assume based on preferences related to their understanding of the scriptures, their fears and insecurities, their self-righteousness, and above all, because of the incongruences found in the texts that lead each group to their own interpretations.

Temporal Freedom

Secularly speaking, individual *freedom/liberty* may be described as the ability to act, move, think, feel, speak, and write as we may desire. This definition entails the absence of physical, emotional, or psychological constraint, oppression, and/or repression by other individuals, social institutions, or governments. Most Christian denominations, however, traditionally have defined the term from a moral standpoint, the internal act to become righteous, i.e., to live in accordance with God's design (as interpreted by each denomination).[1] Historically, Christian ethics bypassed secular considerations, as they were deemed less important, namely because they left little or no room for God. For centuries, this approach led to Christianity ignoring and rejecting an understanding of the fundamental external freedoms and liberties that humankind enjoys today.

Ironically, because individual freedom and liberties have become highly desirable, their individualistic and amoral tendencies have persuaded human civilizations to impose necessary restrictions, relying upon the axiom that absolute individual freedom inevitably leads to endless chaos and conflict. As a result, freedom and liberty manifest themselves within the constraints of (supposedly) fair or just laws and regulations; the purpose of these laws being to prevent people from infringing upon the personal freedom and liberties of others.

Individual Freedom in the Old Testament

Achieving temporal freedom and liberties has been a historically lengthy process lasting thousands of years, involving in most (if not all) instances bloody conflicts. Individual freedoms in the Old Testament varied according to God's design. Initially, the first generation of humans seemed to enjoy almost absolute freedom in the Garden of Eden with one exception: they were not to eat from the Tree of Knowledge of Good and Evil (Gen 2:16-17). Following the Fall of humankind, God punishes humanity by making life more difficult (Gen 3, 4, 6, 7), although later he regrets his actions and tries to mend relations with his earthly creatures (Gen 8:20-22). Seemingly, God allows humankind limited freedom of action given the numerous regulations he imposes. Yet, he allows human enterprise to flourish, but upon noticing humanity's ingenuity, i.e., the Tower of Babel, God reacts, seemingly jealous, and once again punishes his creatures by creating chaos (Gen 11:1-9). Immediately afterward, the history of humanity shifts directions, and so begins God's intimate and roller-coasting relations with the Jewish people.

God's rules and regulations regarding temporal freedom were meant solely for the Israelites. Other nations do not appear to be subjected to God's laws. Thus, it may be surmised that the rest of the nations on earth enjoyed only the types of freedom that leaders would allow their people, which history tells us was not extensive and was mostly dependent on the leader's personal interests.

The freedom God offers to the Israelites is strictly regulated, dealing for the most part with his worship and with rules of moral behavior toward one another, and in some instances including foreigners. Throughout, the Old Testament is the history of God's caring for his people, and his willingness to constantly liberate them from oppression and grant them freedom to worship him without fear *in holiness and righteousness before him all our days* (Lk 1:46-55, 72-55). Thus, one fundamental type of individual freedom emerges from the Old Testament, freedom of oppression to worship God in the manner he wishes. Presumably, along with religious freedom, the Israelites would also be free to earn their living in accordance with the regulations that Mosaic Law imposed.

Jesus and Freedom
Jesus's teachings in the Gospels did not lead to an extensive elaboration of a temporal theory of freedom; they were only meant to instruct Jesus's disciples in his own version of what is meant to be free. In his confrontation with the religious authorities regarding the payment of the census tax to the Roman Emperor, Jesus decides to sidestep the issue. Whether inadvertently or not, in his reply to *repay to Caesar what belongs to Caesar and to God what belongs to God*, he points to the existence of two contrasting authorities, the secular and the divine, and allows (at least by default) for their distinctive separation (Mk 12:17, Lk 20:25, Mt 22:21). His terse reply suggests that he is unwilling to confront the issue. He also does not provide an answer to a significant question: how the two realms, the secular and God's kingdom, ought to interact, and what are the implications for temporal freedom. Such a responsibility, supposedly, would fall upon *the Advocate ... that the Father will send ... [to] teach you everything and remind you of all that [I] told you* (Jn 14:26); and *will guide you to all truth ... and will declare to you the things that are coming* (Jn 16:13). We may assume that this event has taken place, although, given the many denominations that have arisen within Christianity alone, and their different interpretations of Jesus's teachings, one must wonder if Christians have been listening.

Some important passages in the Gospels allow us to delineate Jesus's preferred model of God's kingdom on earth. The texts clearly indicate that the Jewish people are awaiting a temporal Messiah (Lk 1:49-55, 67-79, 2:25, 38, Mt 2:6). Initially, Jesus seems willing to assume this role as he announces that he is anointed by God to bring good news to the poor, proclaim liberty to the captives, and let the oppressed go free, all of which have socio-political connotations that require specific laws to protect their liberties (Lk 4:16-21). In the Lord's Prayer, he instructs his followers to ask, *thy kingdom come,* and *thy will be done on earth as it is in heaven*, strongly suggesting that temporal rule ought to be fashioned in accordance with God's, i.e., Jesus's teachings. By telling Pilate that all temporal power comes from God (Jn 19:11), he reinforces his preferred option in the Lord's Prayer. Here, Jesus seemingly indicates that, insofar as his teachings are not implemented, temporal ruling might take divergent paths that might harm humanity.

Paul initially would borrow what eventually became Jesus's view on political power in the Gospels, and (naively or out of expediency) directs Christians to submit to their respective governing authorities. This directive, coming from Paul in a divine text, provides indiscriminate legitimacy to temporal political rulers (no matter how ruthless) under the assumption that political power will always reside in *God's servants* who will have the best interests of the people at heart (Rom 13:1-6). Hence, we must ask, was this view a revealed truth or Paul's personal musings about Jesus's teachings? Given that reality has differed from Paul's views, his words have inflicted serious mischief to the concept of temporal freedom throughout history, and they even can be used today to justify authoritarianism.

By far the most important aspect of Jesus's model is that he does not tell his disciples to conquer foreign lands by force, but to *go into the whole world and proclaim the gospel to every creature* (Mk 16:15, Lk 24:47, Mt 28:19-20), and to feed his lambs, not to slaughter them (Jn 21:15-17).

However, Jesus's reluctance to become actively involved in socio-political matters as the Messiah the Jewish people awaited retards the evolution of individual freedoms and liberties. By opting not to confront Jewish or Roman unjust and oppressive structures, he leaves his followers in the dark on relations between the two types of authorities. In his (confusing) plea to the Father, Jesus prays not *for the world* (that he insists he wants to save) *but for the ones you have given me,* while at the same time asking the Father not to take them out of the world, despite they do not belong to the world (Jn 17:6-16). Instead, he delegates his intention to save the world to the holy Spirit that will tell them how to act.

As they disperse throughout the Roman Empire, Christians bring forth a new set of values and a different type of behavior: there is to be no more greed; love of neighbor will compel believers to practice charity toward the poor and the sick; they would not steal, cheat, kill, or be adulterous; and while awaiting the end of time they would resign themselves to accept in Jesus whatever misfortune befalls them, knowing that the outcome of everyone's lives would be sorted out on Judgment Day. Jesus's followers become mindful that it would be their responsibility to extend God's kingdom, which they do, somehow persuading others to follow Jesus's values. For nearly three hundred years the kingdom grows despite popular opposition and without the aid of temporal rulers. The freedom Christians enjoy is limited to one existential choice; their willingness to worship their God instead of the empire's pagan gods or having to reject their faith. Refusal to follow paganism earns Christians the dislike of the Roman authorities and the people, and some (or many) suffer persecution.[2]

Persuasion, non-violence, repentance, love, and faith are Jesus's trademarks in the expansion of the kingdom of God, all of which point to an alternative model: coexistence and tolerance amid the diversity of beliefs. Insofar as the world has not become Christian yet, good and evil will reside together. This, however, is not what takes place. Initially, Jesus's followers retreat into isolated small communities and begin to gain adepts. Then, extraordinary events ensue that would affect the destiny of Christianity and change its historical and theological course drastically in the fourth century. Emperors who by now have converted to Christianity grant the new religion certain privileges, including legitimization of Christian worship, until finally, they designate Christianity as the empire's official religion. Jesus's disciples then decide to organize a hierarchical theocracy with the pope as their leader. Believing that the temporal realm is to be an extension of God's kingdom, the hierarchy engages in struggles for divine and temporal powers with Christian monarchs who also believe to have been entrusted with the authority to govern temporal affairs (Paul's doing). Church and state become one, leading the institution to acquire earthly powers that are necessary to govern.

Interestingly, in his *City of God* Augustine points out that the powers and legitimacy extended to the faith were merely spiritual and had nothing to do with political power.[3] It appears that being confronted by popular accusations that Christians were responsible for the fall of the Roman Empire, Augustine was merely offering the best possible defense of the faith. However, he had to realize that Christianity has not only a vertical (spiritual) relation with the heavens but inevitably has to manifest itself horizontally through the overt interpersonal expression of Jesus's teachings. The conflict between the two realms that Augustine depicts in his book occurs precisely because Christian behavior ends up clashing with pagan values. It is only a matter of time until Christianity, realizing by now that its authority over the temporal realm is affirmed by earthly rulers, would necessitate a comparable structure on earth with laws and rights geared to protect the Christian faith. Thus, begins Christendom and its version of freedom; a theocratic state that would restrict temporal liberties by opposing all sorts of heretical views that could jeopardize the souls of believers and the legitimate authority of the hierarchy. Political power also would need to be strengthened to deter existential threats that now were becoming common occurrences. With some exceptions, the leaders of the church were probably operating in good faith to comply with Jesus's mandate to establish God's kingdom on earth. In effect, the implication is that the Son of God assigns such a task to flawed human beings with a limited understanding of his teachings.

Whether acting as guardians of God's kingdom and/or deviating from Jesus's teachings, popes and bishops become entangled in power struggles with their lay counterparts seeking to establish God's will on earth. To protect their acquired temporal authority from external threats, popes seek protection from anyone that would provide it. They engage in the art of military warfare and alliances, extending moral legitimacy to monarchs they think would protect their interests best. At this stage, Jesus's design for God's kingdom appears to have become compromised. Defending the faith requires bloody crusades against infidels. Since the infidels remain, it may be asked on whose side is God now. Centuries later, convinced of what seems self-righteous truths, the leaders of Jesus's church become divided and conduct warfare among themselves. The history of Christendom, as dazzling and fascinating as the movies portray them today, seems to be a reprise of God's relations with the Israelites in the Old Testament.

As it has been shown, the Gospels point to Jesus not being significantly interested in temporal affairs except as a means to extend the kingdom of God to save souls (and supposedly the world). He appears to be less concerned with temporal freedom than God in the Old Testament.[4] He fails to carry on temporal duties he claimed he was anointed to implement. His statement to the religious authorities regarding the payment of the census tax to Rome further indicates his refusal to be dragged into temporal affairs.

Perhaps, Jesus's best interpretation of the term *freedom* as it applies to temporal affairs is shown when he heals a woman on the sabbath. He conveys to the religious authorities that the sabbath (a religious regulation) ought not to be an obstacle to set her free from Satan's bondage (Lk 13:10-16). By bondage, however, he is not referring to slavery, but the woman's illness, awkwardly suggesting that the devil had made her sick. Thus, at least in this instance, Jesus's concept of freedom means being freed from sickness.

Something similar occurs in John's Gospel when Jesus tells a group of people that by adhering to his teachings, they will get to know the truth, *and the truth will set you free* (Jn 8:31-32). It would be reasonable to suppose that he is saying that truth would set people free from moral ignorance, indeed, a higher level of truth: ignorance about sin. That this is his main concern is indicated by his use of a temporal metaphor in which he compares being set free from sin to set free a slave and a son, likely an allusion to Ishmael and Isaac (Jn 8:35-36).[5] Jesus's prototype of freedom is linked to his desire to free humanity from sin.

Free will

Free will is an important component of personal freedom, referring to the idea that humans enjoy the ability to choose between good and evil without their decisions being influenced by external considerations. Interestingly, although the term does not show up in the Gospels, it has not prevented Christianity from vouching for its existence in humans. On the other hand, every time that Jesus asks people to repent of their sins, he is, in effect, indicating that humans are endowed with free will; that they can reject evil if they wish. Nonetheless, Jesus's horrific threats of eternal condemnation of those who refuse to abide by his teachings probably exert undue pressure to repent and start believing. This is not an argument in favor of or against humans' capability to exercise free will. A significant problem facing free will is that science has not been able to devise methods to detect its existence. Whether a person might be able to do good as a moral imperative without any temporal consideration for a reward or punishment; or the opposite, to do evil while being fully aware of intentions and consequences remains a significant question in search of an answer.[6]

At the same time, how much free will can there be within human beings if Jesus insists that *even the smallest things are beyond* [one's] *control* (Lk 12:26-28)? Although Jesus's use of the carrot and stick approach may dilute free will, his teachings are geared to induce flawed human beings to do good and avoid evil, similar to the effect of laws in civil society.

Jesus's teachings did not lead to the elaboration of a workable political theory based on individual rights and liberties, despite he was aware of the theological pluralism, heresies, and moral relativism that existed during his lifetime. More than likely, these were the conditions that he sought to eliminate through his teachings; the 'truths' that, if accepted, would have set humanity free from mortal sin. Neither were the Fathers of the Church able to articulate such a theory, largely because they had been thrown into a temporal vortex that constantly called for the survival of the institution and for defending the identity of the faith they deeply believed in. The price they paid was their need to acquiesce to temporal power and the ways of the world. The necessity to defend faith also becomes a major source of political conflict within the empire. Throughout the Middle Ages, popes become zealous defenders of the faith. They engage in military conflicts, seemingly reflecting that the faith had lost sight of the true essence of the Gospels. Its triumphalist behavior while being co-opted by the strappings of temporal power, eventually would lead to Christianity's erosion as the source of moral influence in temporal world affairs.

Nonetheless, it is ironic that by allowing for the separation of church and state Jesus tolerates secularism, freedom of religion, and moral relativism in the temporal world. Hence, he is *de facto* defining types of temporal freedoms that he is willing to tolerate, at least until his followers can persuade humanity of his teachings. By choosing not to call for a holy war against those who reject him, Jesus is sensitive and respectful of individual liberties on earth, e.g., freedom to worship in accordance with one's beliefs and freedom of expression (notwithstanding his threats of eternal condemnation). Moreover, he had to realize, as Augustine did, that insofar as Christians are unable to persuade humanity of Jesus's truth, relations between the two realms would be characterized by disorder and moral confusion. Once again, it appears that either the Holy Spirit did not speak loud enough, or Christians failed to pay close attention.

Christian Revisionism

For centuries, people lived under autocratic rule in which the notion of individual rights dealing with freedom and liberty nattered little to popes and Christian monarchs. Being regarded as subjects of the temporal realm, citizens enjoyed as much freedom as their rulers would allow, which was not extensive. Individual liberties would have posed a threat both to the moral authority of the institutional church and to monarchs. Obedience to spiritual and temporal authority had been imprinted in the minds and the culture of peoples since Jesus's time, and the notion that power is exercised by rulers in the name of God continued to retard individual freedoms. Change would come slowly, spurred by Christian and secular thinkers, largely as a reaction to historical events and the writings of theologians and philosophers. In the seventeenth and eighteenth centuries, these writers become concerned with issues that acquire great significance: the plight of humanity as well as the undesirability of autocratic rule; a spiritual world that could not be explained empirically; the emergence of science and the laws of the physical world; and a desire by secularized philosophers to attempt to discover social laws that govern humanity in the same manner as physical laws do.

But first, there were a few daring thinkers and religious leaders whose writings and declarations bring about unintended consequences to the cause of individual freedom. Among the most renowned thinkers is Thomas Aquinas, a Dominican Friar writing during the thirteenth century who, although his views are well cemented within the Christendom of the era, begins to formulate a theory of temporal government based on human laws extracted from the old concept of *Natural Law,* and through an old human artifact: reason.

While reason is still constrained by faith, Aquinas postulates that humans can (and ought to) enact positive laws toward the common good. By articulating these views from within the church he gives *de facto* credence to the idea that temporal freedom, although a human reality, needs to be regulated for the wellbeing of society. His focus is not on individual freedom, but insofar as human laws become a requirement for governing the temporal kingdom, Aquinas's concept of laws represents humanity's emancipation from divine revelation. It is not God who now rules peoples but temporal rulers who must exercise power in accordance with laws that stem from Natural Law.

The unintended effect at the time was that if humans are born with free will, and they are free to act as they wish, their only constraints are domination or coercion by religious and monarchical authority. This (subliminal) recognition that human beings are by nature free, now begins to evolve. Until then, the church hierarchy had maintained that real freedom existed only within the internal expression of the self. Paul could declare that there are no longer slaves, but only because internally they are freed in Jesus. Paul's view, however, legitimizes the imposition of physical chains. Aquinas argues that human beings need more than just free will to govern themselves; they require the promulgation of laws that emanate from reason, aimed at the common good and enacted by public officials.[7] In its intended purpose, positive law restricts not only the autocratic exercise of power but the chaotic freedom of behavior that otherwise would prevail. As Aquinas's conception of laws is accepted within Christendom, philosophers and theologians begin to reflect on the notion of positive laws: are they just or unjust; who originates them and based on which criteria; and, how can these laws be changed if necessary? In Aquinas, positive law represents (as with any type of law) control and guidance of conduct that is expressed through individual behavior. It is through this concept that the notion of temporal individual freedom (perhaps inadvertently) begins to emerge.

The notion of temporal freedom acquires prominence at the time of the slave trade in the fifteenth century. Once this horrible practice becomes known, the papacy (not all popes) and prominent theologians begin to denounce it, thereby furthering the theoretical and moral belief in the existence of individual liberty.[8] The significance of these pronouncements and denunciations ought not to be underestimated. Human beings considered to be at the lowest social and political stratum because of their pagan beliefs or racial differences are now deliberately deemed to enjoy the same dignity as anyone else. The initial outcome is that slavery is no longer judged to be humanity's proper moral condition. Eventually, these pronouncements would constitute the official moral recognition that all human beings are entitled to their individual freedom.

Opposition to Religious Views Leads to the Origins of Temporal Freedom
Christian beliefs begin to be scrutinized when the faith spreads in the second and third centuries. Jesus's followers, struggling to consolidate and protect their religious views, oppose the questioning of their beliefs, fearing that it would weaken the faith and undermine their authority. Its most significant opponent is Manicheism, whose gnostic doctrine believes that salvation may be accomplished through knowledge rather than faith. In the fourth century Arianism surges. Arius, a Libyan presbyter, has views on God and Jesus so radically opposed to Christian doctrine that the Council of Nicaea, convened by Emperor Constantine in 325, declared him as a heretic and was exiled.

In 1054 a true schism occurs between Eastern and Western Christianity, allegedly not so much provoked by issues of theology as by animosity and ill will conditioned by cultural differences within the same faith. Ultimately, it leads to the mutual separation of the Catholic and the Eastern Orthodox Churches.

In the eleventh and twelfth centuries, a series of religious movements and personalities continue to question Christian doctrine. The Cathars/Albigensians focus on perfection through a life lived in poverty. They hold a dualist view of *creation*, i.e., two gods, one good and the other evil, that runs contrary to Christian doctrine. They are vigorously persecuted, and hundreds are burned at the stake. There is also the Waldense Movement led by Peter Waldo (1140-1205), who might be regarded as a precursor to Francis of Assisi in his devotion to the poor. Reacting to the wealth and splendor of Renaissance Christianity, he takes a cue from Jesus, *if you wish to be perfect, go, sell what you have and give to [the] poor, and you will have treasure in heaven* (Mt 19:21-25), gives up his possessions and organizes a lay movement to preach poverty as a way of life. The pope excommunicated the movement, not so much for its heretical views as for the implementing a parallel church.

John Wycliffe (1328-1384) is perhaps the best earliest exponent of the sixteenth-century Protestant Movement. An English priest and theologian, he is a firm believer in evangelical poverty but dares to question traditional Christian dogmas, including the transubstantiation, i.e., the change of bread and wine into the body and blood of Jesus during the Mass, clerical wealth, and the authority of the pope. Jan Hus (1372-1415), a Czech priest and theologian, and defender of Wycliffe becomes the leader of the Hussite movement. After years of expressing strong opposition to the doctrine of the Church and refusing to recant, he is burned at the stake. His followers are enraged by his execution; they revolt and are persecuted by a papal army.

Girolamo Savonarola, a Dominican friar, is another victim of the excesses of Renaissance popes. He dares to criticize corruption within the Church, preaches against frivolity and extravagance while predicting a possible earlier return of Jesus. He is excommunicated in 1497 and burned at the stake a year later, not because of heretical pronouncements as much as because of his fanaticism and disobedience.[9]

The most significant common denominator among the above opponents to the Church (other than most of them arise from within the Catholic Church) is their claim to their individual freedom of thought and expression in matters of religious doctrine. None of them were advocating public recognition of religious freedom, tolerance, or freedom of expression as individual rights; they were merely practicing it. But in the process, they were planting ideas that, like seeds, would take time before sprouting.

Centuries of questioning papal and monarchical authority find an outlet in a devout German Augustinian monk convinced of his belief that *justification by faith* is the only way to salvation. The selling of indulgences at the time had become a source of real scandal in the Church, and Martin Luther's (1483-1546) 95 Theses that he presents for academic disputation become the fuse that ignites the conflict.

Likely, Luther did not anticipate that his litany of complaints would provoke a strong reaction. Its content, however, concealed the basis for questioning fundamental tenets of Catholic doctrine in many respects. A compromise was necessary to avoid a split with the Church, but neither side acted with evangelical demeanor toward each other. The disputation of several of the Theses that was about to take place between the pope's emissary and Luther became an acrimonious event filled with invectives. Pope Leo X was one among several popes that at the time was more attuned to the imprudent lavishness and corrupt politics of the Renaissance than to Jesus's teachings. Conditioned by dubious cultural values, he failed to heed calls to reform the institution, remaining steadfast in his position regarding the supreme power of the papacy. Luther, who supposedly becomes a monk to escape the suffering he experiences at the hands of his parents (or out of fear of death in a storm), is consumed with obsessive sinfulness and his unworthiness of salvation. He struggles with bouts of depression and anger toward God. The future of Christianity lies in the hands of these two obstinate and most imperfect personalities, making conciliation impossible. In retrospect, Luther's actions represent the eruption of a religious volcano that had been (actively) dormant throughout centuries; its eruption was inevitable. Luther's 'enough is enough' anger leads him to attack the papacy with vehemence.

The effect of his actions is similar to Thomas Aquinas's dissertation on the Laws. Luther does not wish to advocate religious freedom; he becomes as intolerant as the pope. He becomes a Protestant pope, the first among several who appear alongside him, including Philip Melanchthon, Huldrych Zwingli, John Calvin, William Tyndale, Martin Bucer, Andreas Karlstad, Thomas Cranmer, John Knox, King Henry VIII, his daughter Queen Elizabeth I, and others. Ironically, Luther's fundamental claim that the human person is justified by faith alone, finds as much foundation in the scriptures (it is negligible in the Gospels) as those who believe the opposite. Nonetheless, his act of defiance gives vigor to the right of the believer to come to his/her conclusions regarding the faith. This is the practical definition of freedom of thought. Hidden too, in his defiance of papal authority is his belief that the scriptures are the only source of divine knowledge; an admission and *de facto* personal demand for individual freedom of expression and freedom of worship.

The view that Martin Luther changes the world with his revolutionary ideas of individual liberties, however, is unfounded. It suggests that Luther knowingly and willfully sought to underscore the concept of personal liberties and set the foundations for democracy. It is known, however, that Luther and his contemporaries denied these freedoms to others during the religious wars that followed the Protestant Reformation. That the process in time would germinate in the concept of secular liberties is an unintended historical outcome, similar to a wildfire ignited by lightning that, unknown to science until recent decades, would eventually prove to be ecologically beneficial to the ecosystem in accordance with laws of nature.[10]

Luther does not set out to change the world; his motive is to attempt to wreck the Catholic Church prompted by his justifiable anger at corruption within the hierarchy, his self-righteous beliefs, and his hatred toward a self-righteous pope (Luther called him the anti-Christ) that would not yield to him. The bloody wars that ensue are evidence that the teachings of Jesus are ignored by contemptuous behavior on both sides.[11]

Meanwhile, the Age of Reason, culminating in the French Enlightenment, constitutes a philosophical and secular reflection on autocratic authority, the Christian faith, the Catholic Church, and on presumed rights of man that are said to exist either through social contracts or in natural laws. In North America, Deism, a mixture of rational Christianity and the rejection of divine revelation, expands on the ideas of these secularly-minded thinkers (John Locke, Baruch Spinoza, Jean-Jacques Rousseau, Thomas Hobbes, Baron of Montesquieu, Voltaire, and other Encyclopedists) who are in opposition to the Catholic hierarchy's spiritual dogmas and freedom of thought, and to the hierarchy's close association with the nobility and the absolutism of monarchs. These thinkers had been endorsing the separation of church and state, religious liberty, tolerance, and restrictions on monarchical power through the consent of the governed, ideas that ran against the will of a recalcitrant French monarchy, and of a Catholic hierarchy that for centuries had opposed any type of popular individual freedoms and liberties that could erode its authority on temporal and spiritual matters.[12]

In North America, men of the Enlightenment are strongly manifesting themselves against monarchies, expressing instead a preference for a republican form of government. Nothing is more representative of this view than the American Declaration of Independence, drafted by Thomas Jefferson and approved by the Founding Fathers of the new nation. The document makes its appeals based on history (the course of human events), suggesting that no longer are the smallest things on earth beyond human control, as Jesus had stated (Lk 12:26-28). The Declaration calls upon Laws of Nature, Nature's God, and to opinions of mankind, rather than to the Bible, to assert that there are truths that are self-evident (supposedly emanating from reason and/or Natural Law) that indicate that all human beings are created equal and given certain inalienable rights by God, including life, liberty, and the pursuit of happiness, and their right to form a democratic government.

Other than the admission that life is created by God, none of the other rights or grievances in the Declaration of Independence are explicitly envisioned in the Gospels as applying to temporal affairs. Even happiness, which in the Gospels is the product of faith in Jesus, is now the result of humans governing their own affairs. The numerous complaints that constitute the reasons for breaking up relations between the colonies and England were of a political and economic nature that would have been inconceivable in the Gospels. Nonetheless, the signatories appeal to God to legitimize their intentions and to the divine Providence to protect them.[13] Regardless of its wording, the secular nation-state is born.

Meanwhile, in Catholic France and other parts of Europe, the anti-clerical and secularist Enlightenment has been more powerfully felt. Ironically, in 1789 none other than a French Catholic abbé, Emmanuel Sieyès, who objects to the privileges of the nobility and the church's association with it, helps to draft the French Declaration of the Rights of Man and of the Citizen with the assistance of Thomas Jefferson and the Marquis de Lafayette.[14] The declaration expounds on the ideas contained in the American Declaration of Independence, itself a philosophical child of an anti-clerical Enlightenment. There were other lesser-known writers who despite their Catholicism expressed astounding independence from traditional values and the culture of the time whose views were likely drowned by the dramatic political events in North America and France.[15]

The papacy strongly rejected these and other ideas that went against established Catholic doctrine. Pope Benedict XIV already had condemned various writings of the Enlightenment, including Montesquieu's *Spirit of the Laws*. He continued the practice of placing books deemed to oppose the doctrine in the *Index of Forbidden Book*, created in 1557, decades following the Protestant Reformation.[16] Pope Clement XIII placed Rousseau's *Emile* in the Index, largely because, while dealing with individual liberties, it offered an alternative (secular) education to that of the church.[17] The anger of the leaders of the French Revolution against the Catholic hierarchy reached its culmination one year following the storming of the Bastille when its leaders approved a document reorganizing the church's French clergy and made them salaried employees of the state. Pope Pius VI broke relations with France and condemned the state's ordination of bishops as being sacrilegious. Unsuccessful in his opposition, Pope Pius VI died in jail, having been incarcerated by Napoleon in 1799.[18] These events give birth to a second secular nation-state.

As the forces of secularism advance, they propel perhaps the greatest moral contribution to humanity from the standpoint of temporal individual freedoms and liberties: the codification of the rights and duties of individual persons and nation-states universally adopted by the United Nations General Assembly following World War II. These include the *Universal Declaration of Human Rights* (1948), the *International Covenant on Civil and Political Rights* (1966), and the *International Covenant on Economic, Social, and Cultural Rights* (1966). These documents manifest the highest aspirations of peoples and their governments for the type of *modus vivendi* and *modus operandi* called for in modern times. They read like a list of dos and don'ts about the individual person and his/her relations with their respective states and other world entities. The values these documents embody represent a moral evolution of the human conscience.

Interesting common denominators are observed in these documents. Their foundation, found in their Preambles, is the inherent dignity and the equal and inalienable rights of all members of the human family [as] the foundation of freedom, justice, and peace in the world. In principle, there are no 'chosen' people in these documents as there are in some passages of the Gospels. All human beings, simply by nature of being human, are entitled to the same highest aspirations of the common people, without distinction of race, ethnicity, sex, language, religion, political or other opinions, national or social origin, property, birth or other status.[19] Along with their call to fraternity, these documents represent humanity's temporal emancipation from God, from Christian spirituality and other religious faiths, and instead emphasize the secular aspirations of the human person, including its individuality and its communal relationships. In effect, the documents constitute a secular counterpart to Jesus's teachings, although applied to temporal morality since they relate heavily to socio-political, economic, religious, and cultural behavior.[20]

Lest too much may be made of their contribution to the city of man, it must be admitted that compliance, in this case by governments and their leaders, has left a great deal to be desired. The abuse and corruption that reign in the poorest nations continues unabated. Moreover, the major powers' indifference toward the values promoted by these declarations regarding warfare, civil and political rights, unequal trade and commerce resulting in maldistribution of resources, and their often disregard for persecuted minorities and genocides, indicate a disregard of Jesus's commandment to care for one another. Under the heading of Human Rights, questionable liberties too are being claimed. Nonetheless, overall, the value of these documents to the post-modern world represents intermittent progress. At the very least, they have served to ensure the survival of the Christian faith (and other religions) in many countries.

Notes:

1. The Catholic Catechism defines freedom as *the power, rooted in reason and will, to act or not to act, to do this or that, and so to perform deliberate actions on one's own responsibility*, thus referring to it as *free will*, by which *one shapes one's own life* (CCC 1731). Temporal freedom is defined in its last paragraph in the section as the respect that all humans owe to each other to the *right to the exercise of freedom, especially in moral and religious matters, as an inalienable requirement of the dignity of the human person* that *must be recognized and protected by civil authority* (CCC 1738). Martin Luther also saw freedom, not in terms of its external behavior, but as originating internally as a desire to do God's will, for which the self needs to be disciplined by subjugating anything that detracts from Christ's teachings. Rev. Travis Loeslie, "On the Freedom of a Christian," *LutheranReformation.org,* March 20, 2016, lutheranreformation.org/theology/on-the-freedom-of-a-christian/ (accessed January 10, 2020).

2. Bernard Green, *Christianity in Ancient Rome: The First Three Centuries,* (London: T & T Clark, 2010); an overview of the period is presented by James W. Ermatinger, *Daily Life of Christians in Ancient Rome,* (Westport: Greenwood, 2006); for reasons and extent of persecutions see Will Durant, Vol. III, Chapter XXX; as for the scale of martyrdom by early Christians see Candida Moss, *The Myth of Persecution: How Early Christians Invented a Story of Martyrdom,*(San Francisco: Harper One, 2014).

3. Aurelius Augustine, *The City of God,* trans. Rev. Marcus Dods, M.A., (Edinburgh: T & T Clark, 1871), Project Gutenberg's, www.gutenberg.org/files/45304/45304-h/45304-h.htm (accessed January 10, 2020).

4. There are three instances in the Gospels (Lk 15:11-14, Mt 20:1-16, Jn 2:9-10) in which the word *free* appears. The word seems to be used colloquially, i.e., without impediments, in Luke and John. However, in Matthew, Jesus's Parable of the Workers in the Vineyard places God in the position of acting freely to choose between being generous with his money if he so chooses. This seems to be the only indication of free will in the Gospels.

5. NEs' note, John 8:35. Ishmael was the son of Abraham and Hagar, a slave woman, who eventually is set free. Isaac was Abraham's son with Sarah; he was set to be sacrificed under God's orders to test Abraham's faith but was set free from his binding at the last minute.

6. Temporally speaking, there is little doubt that even if free will is humanly impossible, civil society would have had to create it (as it has done), since without it there would be no accountability for human behavior and laws would be rendered meaningless, in effect returning humanity to a beastly state of nature.

7. Thomas Aquinas, *Summa*, Part I-II, Q 90, A 4.

8. Popes Eugene IV in his bull *Sicut Dudum* in 1435 is critical of the enslavement of black natives, and Paul III in a pontifical decree *Sublimis Deus* in 1537 addresses the human condition of the Indians in

South America. Other popes, including Gregory XIV in 1591, Urban VIII in 1639, Innocent XI (1691-1700), Benedict XIV (1741), Pius VII (1815), and Gregory XVI (1838) continued their denunciations of slavery. Fr. Joel S. Panzer, "The Popes and Slavery: Setting the Record Straight," *EWTN.com*, https://www.ewtn.com/catholicism/library/popes-and-slavery-setting-the-record-straight-1119 (accessed January 5, 2020). Francisco de Vitoria, a Catholic theologian writing in the sixteenth century (way before the Golden Age of the Enlightenment), follows in the footsteps of Aquinas but makes unprecedented inroads in the concept of temporal freedom by writing (still within the confines of Natural Law) about popular sovereignty or the natural freedom of the peoples, and arguing in favor of the rights of aborigines in the Americas to be free from slavery. Francisco de Vitoria (1557), *De Indis De Jure Belli,* Relectiones Theologicae XII; Part 2 - On the Indians Lately Discovered, ed ca. 1917 James Brown Scott, (New York: Wildy & Sons Ltd, 1964), https://en.wikisource.org/wiki/De_Indis_De_Jure_Belli/Part_2 (accessed January 14, 2020). Francisco Suarez, another theologian, writing in the seventeenth century defends the right of aborigines not to be coerced into accepting the Christian faith (although heretics could), and rejects the power of the temporal monarch and that of the pope to *abrogate any proper precept of natural law, nor truly and essentially restrict such a precept, nor grant a dispensation from it.* He goes further to declare that *by virtue of the very fact that he is created and has the use of reason—possesses power over himself and over his faculties and members for their use,* man is naturally free possessing too *the faculty of self-government, in consequence whereof it also possesses power and a peculiar dominion over its own members.* Francisco Suarez, *A Treatise on Laws and God the Lawgiver* (1612), first quote from Ch 14.8, 15; second quote from Ch 3.6, (Indianapolis: Liberty Fund, 2015), https://oll.libertyfund.org/titles/selections-from-three-works (accessed January 14, 2020).

9. John Arendzen, "Manichæism," CE, Vol. 9, http://www.newadvent.org/cathen/09591a.htm (Accessed January 19, 2020); William Barry, "Arianism," CE, Vol. 1, http://www.newadvent.org/cathen/01707c.htm (accessed January 14, 2020); Adrian Fortescue, "The Eastern Schism," CE, Vol. 13, http://www.newadvent.org/cathen/13535a.htm (accessed January 14, 2020); Nicholas Weber, "Cathari," CE, Vol. 3, http://www.newadvent.org/cathen/03435a.htm (accessed January 14, 2020); Weber, Nicholas, "Waldenses." CE, Vol. 15, http://www.newadvent.org/cathen/15527b.htm (accessed January 14, 2020); Francis Urquhart, "John Wyclif," CE, Vol. 15, http://www.newadvent.org/cathen/15722a.htm (accessed January 14, 2020); Joseph Wilhelm, "Jan Hus," CE Vol. 7, http://www.newadvent.org/cathen/07584b.htm (accessed January 14, 2020); Johann Peter Kirsch, "Girolamo Savonarola," CE, Vol. 13, `http://www.newadvent.org/cathen/13490a.htm (accessed January 14, 2020);

10. Joan Acocella, How Martin Luther Changed the World," *The New Yorker,* October 23, 2017, https://www.newyorker.com/magazine/2017/10/30/how-martin-luther-changed-the-world (accessed January 21, 2020). On the unintended effects of wildfires, Laurie L. Dove, "How does a forest fire benefit living things?," *Science.HowStuffWorks.com,* https://science.howstuffworks.com/environmental/green-science/how-forest-fire-benefit-living-things-.htm (accessed January 20, 2020); T. J. Blackman, "The Ecological Benefits of Forest Fires," *EarthEasy.com,* https://learn.eartheasy.com/articles/the-ecological-benefits-of-forest-fires/ (accessed January 20, 2020).

11. On the Protestant Reformation in general, see Durant, *The Reformation,* Vol VI, Books I, II; Hans J. Hillerbrand, *The Reformation: A Narrative History Related by Contemporary Observers and Participants,* (Grand Rapids: Baker Publishing Group, reprint edition 1981); Henry Ganss, "Martin Luther," CE, Vol. 9, http://www.newadvent.org/cathen/09438b.htm (accessed January 14, 2020); Klemens Löffler, "Pope Leo X," CE Vol. 9, http://www.newadvent.org/cathen/09162a.htm (accessed January 14, 2020); Richard P. McBrien, "Leo X, *The Lives of the Popes,* pp. 272-274, (San Francisco: Harper San Francisco, 1997).

12. Leo Gershoy, *The French Revolution and Napoleon,* Chapters 2, 3, (New York: Appleton-Century-Crofts, 1964).

13. *Declaration of Independence: A Transcription,* National Archives, www.archives.gov/founding-docs/declaration-transcript (accessed January 15, 2020).

14. Jennifer Llewellyn, Steve Thompson, "The Declaration of the Rights of Man and Citizen," Alpha History, July 26, 2020, https://alphahistory.com/frenchrevolution/declarations-rights-of-man-and-citizen (accessed January 16, 2021).

15. There is Spanish writer Josefa Amar (1749–1833). *on Economic, Social, and Cultural Rights*, Josefa Amar y Borbón, "Discourse in defense of the talent of women, their aptitude for governing, and other positions in which men are employed," 1786, *Antología del Ensayo,* Edición de Carmen Chaves Tesser (basada en la versión publicada en Memorial Literario VIII, No. 32 [Agosto de 1876]: 400-430), publicada en Dieciocho 3.2 (1980): 144-159, https://www.ensayistas.org/antologia/XVIII/amar-bor/

(accessed January 16, 2020); Luigi Muratori (1672-1750), Catholic priest and theologian who was regarded as a thorn in Rome for his views, showed his independent-minded attitude by questioning limitations posed by the papacy on freedom regarding religious matters. Johann Peter Kirsch, "Luigi Antonio Muratori." CE, Vol. 10, www.newadvent.org/cathen/10641b.htm (accessed January 16, 2020); and theologian Ferdinand Sterzinger who along with a few others led a crusade against superstition, namely the belief in the existence of witches and the possibility of humans making pacts with the devil. These and other prominent members of a Catholic Enlightenment are the subject of a book: Ulrich L. Lehner, *The Catholic Enlightenment: The Forgotten History of a Global Movement,* (New York: Oxford University Press, 2016.)

16. McBrien, "Benedict XIV," p. 323.

17. Ibid., p. 325.

18. Ibid, pp. 329-330.

19. United Nations, *Universal Declaration of Human Rights,* https://www.un.org/en/universal-declaration-human-rights/ (accessed January 3, 2020); *International Covenant on Civil and Political Rights,* https://www.ohchr.org/en/professionalinterest/pages/ccpr.aspx (accessed January 3, 2020); *International Covenant on Economic, Social, and Cultural Rights*, https://www.ohchr.org/en/professionalinterest/pages/cescr.aspx (accessed January 3, 2020).

20. For decades the Catholic hierarchy viewed the rights being approved in these documents with distrust. Although temporal freedoms were defended during the Second Vatican Council in 1965 in *Gaudium et Spes* (nos. 26, 41, 60, 68, 71, 73-76, 88), and Christianity owes its earthly existence in no small part to legalized protections promoted by secular bodies, there is no mention whatsoever of the term *human rights* in the pastoral constitution. The Catholic hierarchy made a turnabout years later by fully endorsing the Universal Declaration of Human Rights. In his address to the General Assembly in 1979, Pope John Paul II called it *the "fundamental document," the "basic inspiration and cornerstone of the United Nations Organization," and a "milestone on the long and difficult path of the moral progress."* Statement by H.E. Archbishop Bernardito Auza, Apostolic Nuncio, Permanent Observer of the Holy See, on "The Universal Declaration of Human Rights at 70: Foundations, Achievements and Violations," United Nations Headquarters, New York, 4 December 2018, Mission of the Holy See to the United Nations, https://holyseemission.org/contents/events/5c09a2d66d950.php (accessed January 13, 2020). In 2020, Pope Francis's encyclical letter on Fraternity and Social Friendship added to the Catholic Church's teachings on social and political philosophy based on secular realities. Pope Francis's thinking seems to be that there are moral values within secular society that might be worth exploring. Pope Francis, *Fratelli Tutti,* Assisi, October 3, 2020, http://www.vatican.va/content/francesco/en/encyclicals/documents/papa-francesco_20201003_enciclica-fratelli-tutti.html (accessed October 6, 2020).

Anti-Slavery

Among the greatest consequences of Jesus's disinterest in temporal freedoms was the continuation of slavery for centuries. That the weak may be enslaved because of their condition is considered secular anathema, deemed collectively to be among major crimes against humanity. This recognition, however, is not found in the Bible, even though God himself acknowledges that the practice of slavery is evil the moment he frees his people from Egyptian domination, realizing the cruel conditions under which they are living (Ex 1:13, 6:5-6). Nonetheless, numerous passages in the Pentateuch indicate that God allows the practice of slavery and even codifies it. Supposedly, the purpose of these laws is to prevent injustices, but some of them are so appalling (by today's standards) that their motives seem questionable despite superficial sensitivities and instances of favoritism (Ex 21, Lev 25:39-46).

Although God allows slavery to take place, he does not always look down on them. For example, despite Sarah's jealousy of Abraham's slave mistress, Hagar, God says that regardless of her position he will make a nation of her son Ishmael *since he too is your offspring* (Gen 21:12-13). However, it is no less true that slaves in the

Pentateuch are considered inferior beings; they are property to be possessed and gifts that God offers to those he favors along with camels and donkeys (Gen 24: 34-35).

Christian apologists do their best to defend God as a considerate practitioner of slavery, alluding in some cases that in the Bible slaves are not considered property (chattel slavery), but that due to prevailing cultural conditions, and to sin, God allows it *to help the poor survive.*[1] Reasonable thinking, however, would ask why an all-powerful God could not legislate a different socio-economic system that did not require what some refer to as 'benevolent slavery' to deal with poverty? Awkwardly, modern-day labor practices advanced by non-Christians, including atheists, and religious sentiments have improved the conditions of workers, suggesting that the practice of slavery is historically conditioned. Throughout history, the pervasiveness of slavery has been the outcome of people who called themselves Christians; supposedly honorable men and women that failed to see injustice in the practice.

Moreover, if the type of slavery outlined in the Old Testament is not as harsh as chattel slavery (a form of indentured servitude), why is it no longer favored by Christianity and allowed in modern capitalist societies? Perhaps it may have something to do with how God regulates the practice. In a passage that would horrify most believers today, God dictates how human property is to be acquired: if anyone refuses to make peace with his people, every male should be killed, and *the women and children and livestock and anything else in the city—all its spoil—you may take as plunder for yourselves, and you may enjoy this spoil of your enemies, which the LORD, your God, has given you* (Deut 20:10-14).

Jesus and Slavery

Content analysis tally of the various terms used in the Bible for slavery, e.g., slave, servant, or bondage, shows great variations according to each Bible version.[2] Nonetheless, the existence of slavery at the time (mostly as the result of war bounties) cannot be historically refuted. The Gospels' and Jesus's uses of the term indicate acceptance of slavery as a socio-political and economic institution no different than what appears in the Old Testament. Its acceptance is similar to *de facto* consent to mercantilism, colonialism, totalitarian socialism, or coldhearted capitalism as earthly stages, all of which are characterized by self-centered, nationalistic, and individualistic zero-sum approaches toward people. It appears that having noticed God's ambiguity in the Old Testament regarding slavery, Jesus does not feel the need to implement changes to the practice. Jesus might have realized that slavery is averse to the kingdom of God. Yet, although he dares to question large portions of Mosaic Law, he fails to inquire about the morality behind slavery.

Despite standing before his people inside a synagogue and proclaiming himself to being anointed to *bring glad tidings to the poor*, including liberty to captives and freedom to the oppressed (Lk 4:6-21), Jesus decides not to confront the structures and values that sustain slavery. Instead, as he does with the issue of the census tax, he dodges the condition. Given that the nature of Jesus's mission changes radically from being the expected temporal liberator and king to an eschatological messiah, the passage may be interpreted as indicating that according to him the poor and the oppressed would find their happiness fulfilled in heaven, as indicated in the Beatitudes. This view is reinforced by a passage in Luke in which Jesus heals a woman of her infirmity referring to her sickness as the type of *bondage* he deems to be evil (Lk 13:10-16). Hence, it is not surprising that slavery is to be tolerated, as shown in his Parable of the Weed Among the Wheat (Mt 13:24-30) whereby he teaches that temporal ills are to be borne until Judgment Day.

Still, there is a difference between Jesus and God in the Old Testament. While God institutes his version of slavery, Jesus is indifferent to the practice. At times he uses the term *slave* to mean *servant*, i.e., household staff, or to urge his disciples to imitate his role as the Son of Man who comes to serve others (Mk 10:42-45, Mt 20:25-28). He uses the terms *slave* and *servant* positively numerous times to indicate conformity or docility to his teachings (Mk 9:33-35, Mt 23:11-12, Jn 15:14-15). It must be noted, nonetheless, that in some of his parables the relationship between master and servant tends to be contentious, at times involving the master killing useless servants (Lk 12:35-48, 19:11-27, 20:0-19, Mt 24:45-51, 25:14-30).

Jesus uses the term *slave* within the context of what it meant at the time, bondage or servitude; however, he ascribes a different connotation to the word: being of service to others. By the mere fact that he utters the word *slave* and hears others mentioning it, he is acknowledging the existence of the practice (Lk 7:1-10, Mt 8:5-13, 10:24-25, 13:24-28, Jn 4:51). Nonetheless, although a slave is understood to be inferior to the master, he says, *no slave is greater than his master,* to indicate that if he, the master, dares to humble himself in washing his disciples' feet, so should they too humble themselves while being in service to others (Jn 13:2-17).

In Matthew, Jesus's words are difficult to understand by temporal standards. While repeating that no slave is above his master, he adds that it is enough for the slave that he become like his master (Mt 10:24-25). In Luke, while referring to the disciple/teacher relations, he says that no disciple is superior to the teacher; but when fully trained, every disciple will be like his teacher (Lk 6:40). Jesus appears to indicate that in God's kingdom such differences ought not to exist. Nonetheless, at no time he is critical of temporal slavery.

While accepting slavery, in his parables Jesus suggests that the slave is to be treated with the same consideration as the master. At no time does he make exceptions regarding his commandment to love one's neighbor if the neighbor is a slave. When he cures the Roman centurion's slave (Lk 7:1-10), a servant in Matthew (Mt 8:5-13), he indicates that he would assist anyone regardless of faith or socio-economic status. Jesus's sayings become more complicated when he acknowledges that adherence to his teachings is a yoke, a symbol of harsh servitude that God would not hesitate to use against those who disobey him (Deut 28:45-48). Relying on the nomenclature that prevailed at the time, he says that his yoke is easy and its burden light, suggesting that, as enslaving as his teachings may be, they are less severe than God's punishment.

The term *slave* has another meaning in the Gospels; it refers to human servitude to sin (Jn 8:33-35). This view is significant. From an eschatological perspective, Jesus appears to be more concerned with the negative consequences of being enslaved to sin than with the afflictions brought about by the lack of personal freedom that humans endure under bondage. Paul echoes this view in a manner that appears to sanction slavery for the sake of Jesus (Eph 6:5-8). By indicating that in Jesus there are no slaves or free men since all humanity enjoys the same dignity in his eyes, Paul suggests that physical slavery can be bearable provided that the master treats his slave as a brother in Christ (Gal 3:28, Phil 1:7-22). Nonetheless, it is difficult to ignore Paul telling slaves to *obey your human masters in everything ... in simplicity of heart, fearing the Lord* (Col 3:22). From early on, popes focus upon the spiritual dimension of Paul's theme and either ignore the issue or are indecisive (along with some Fathers of the Church that distinguish between just and unjust types of slavery).[3] It is important to notice that, at the time, slavery did not necessarily have racial, religious, or ethnic overtones. Slaves were acquired as the bounty that conquerors would gain in wars.

Change Begins to Emerge
Opposition to all forms of slavery (including calls for its abolition) is absent in Christianity for centuries. Christian nations had been mostly responsible for race-based slavery as they embarked on trade and colonialism in Africa and the Americas. When the trade of slaves on account of race begins in the fifteenth century, the papacy begins to emit its opposition, inconsistent as it may have been, and notwithstanding deaf ears by bishops in areas in which slave trade was taking place.[4] Nonetheless, the slave trade continues unabated throughout most of the eighteenth century. The absence of human sensitivity is seen in 1789 in Catholic France; the Chamber of Commerce of Bordeaux is quoted as saying that *France needs its colonies for the maintenance of its commerce, and consequently it needs slaves in order to make agriculture pay in this quarter of the world ...until some other expedient may have been found.*[5]

Sensing that its denunciations had not been well heeded, the Catholic hierarchy gathering in Rome in mid-twentieth century for the Second Vatican Council (1962-1965), seems compelled to promulgate its Pastoral Constitution on the Church in the Modern World, *Gaudium et Spes,* in which it officially calls on *human institutions, both private and public, ... to put up a stubborn fight against any kind of slavery, whether social or political, and safeguard the basic rights of man under every political system.*[6]

There seems to be scant information about the initial leaders of the Reformation regarding slavery. Martin Luther does not appear to say much, although he opposes the rights of peasants as promoting overbearing equality and quotes the Old Testament in support of slavery. Moreover, he considers freedom, as Paul does, to be found only within a man who has faith in Christ.[7] John Calvin seems to follow a combined version of Paul's and the Founding Fathers' view of slavery, i.e., submission and adequate treatment to ensure their productivity. Although he dislikes the practice, Calvin too regards slavery as a consequence of sin, and thus permitted by God. He believes that slaves are entitled to equal treatment, presumably among themselves, otherwise, equality among all human beings would have required slavery to be abolished.[8] At least through its reticence, Protestantism was more supportive of slavery than Catholicism throughout the eighteenth and nineteenth centuries.[9]

Eventually, there is an awakening in the Protestant conscience in parts of Europe. In England, opposition to slavery begins, tracing its thoughts in some cases to the Enlightenment, in others to Christian piety. Among opponents of the practice are George Fox, founder of the Quakers, poet Alexander Pope, ecclesiastic and moral philosopher William Paley, Scottish Enlightenment figures, such as Francis Hutcheson and Adam Smith, Anglican poet Samuel Johnson, and the Puritanical, anti-rationalist, anti-Catholic, and pro-monarchy leader of the Methodist movement, John Wesley.[10]

Why did it take so long for Christian leaders to overturn God's design in the Old Testament and Jesus's apparent indifference to slavery? A probable answer is that popes and monarchs did not wish to upset the socioeconomic status quo upon which the Church hierarchy depended. Christian monarchs also seem to have been persuaded about the goodness of black and Indian enslavement in the Americas, because it would bring about the faith to them. But perhaps an even greater reason is the burden of tradition and the legitimacy it provided to the Church. The hierarchy had not elaborated a detailed moral doctrine on slavery before the fifteenth century; instead, it accepted the same reality that Jesus experienced, and which Paul explained. It would have been quite difficult to contradict God in the Old Testament, Jesus and Paul in the New Testament, and the Fathers of the Church. On what grounds, theologians may have asked, could a pope possibly dare to challenge divine scripture? Another probable reason was existing warfare norms. Slavery was the price defeated nations would pay in war; to the victors, it proved to be economically profitable, as it would help to defray the costs of wars.

Race and Ethnic-Based Slavery Become a Turning Point

Seemingly, a series of epiphanies occur as the sign of the times begin to unearth cultural values that would enlighten the human conscience that slavery is detestable simply because it offends human sensibility. In other words, this revision is the product of men relying on a God-given instrument, reason, who realized that the scriptures and tradition required extensive re-examination.

Meanwhile, as the Age of Reason leads Europe into the Enlightenment, we notice a radical change in the culture. *Reason is for the philosopher what grace is for the Christian,* Diderot would joyfully claim.[11] Reason among the *philosophes* was the means to focus on the various natural sciences that were flourishing (ironically, silently allowed by the clergy). It became weaponized as an instrument to attack superstition and was used to counter religious dogma and censorship while arguing in favor of individual liberties. However, its record on the abolition of slavery is mixed.

Throughout the Enlightenment we notice that some of its leaders dislike the idea of enslaving human beings, and thus would oppose it; others entertain the view that some people are more equal than others and allow it in some instances. Respected men driven by a sense of benevolent prejudice, hypocrisy, and ignorance hold slaves. There are even those that are actively involved in the trade of slaves who argue the issue in terms of positive economic benefits, individual political liberties, and Bible Christianity, i.e., Paul's views. It is argued that the dualism found in the minds of the Enlightenment, e.g., humanity, justice, and benevolence (notwithstanding the violent excesses of the French reign of terror) standing next to economic progress and utilitarian business models, prevented a more cohesive and stronger opposition.[12]

Perhaps reacting to anything coming from the various Christian hierarchies, men of the Enlightenment did not consider the various pleas by the popes. John Locke, for example, was an opponent of slavery, to a point. He states: *Slavery is so vile and miserable an estate of man, and so directly opposite to the generous temper and courage of our nation; that it is hardly to be conceived, that an Englishman, much less a gentleman, should plead for it.*[13] Somehow, his arguments are weakened by his distinctions (and elusive views) between legitimate and illegitimate slavery, and contradicted by his active participation in the race-based trade of slaves in the American colonies.[14] Others, including Spinoza, Montesquieu, Hume, Rousseau, Kant, and Thomas Jefferson exhibit similar views, as they are not vigorous abolitionists despite their intellectual dislike of the practice.[15] On his part, Jefferson's rationalism leads him into one of the most egregious contradictions in political theory. Along with other American Founding Fathers, he makes it palpable in the *Declaration of Independence* that the self-evident truth that *all men are created equal* and *endowed by their Creator with certain unalienable Rights* somehow does not include enslaved Negroes. That these men were not able to recognize their glaring inconsistencies can be easily overlooked because their moral ignorance and the economic advantages derived from slavery led them to hardened convictions based on prejudice.

Philosopher Chris Meyns calls attention to the neglect of victims of slavery that write during the eighteenth century, including women, but whose writings are obscured, because, at the time, philosophy and science were being used deceptively to justify enslavement.[16] Nonetheless, in what seems an abrupt upturn, science begins adding its voice to repudiate slavery and discrimination by suggesting that race is nothing more than a social construct that can be used to validate prejudice.[17]

Although denounced and persecuted, slavery continues today under the term *human trafficking*. About forty million people are *trapped in modern-day slavery,* much of it occurring under repressive regimes, but also under democratic-styled systems of government.[18] Secular societies appear to have been persuaded that slavery based on race, age, ethnicity, gender, or religion, however, is a secular sin that needs to be eradicated. Such an awareness did not stem from the Gospels, and certainly not from Christian hierarchies until much later. Instead, change comes about as the result of an evolving determination by Christian and non-Christian individuals, governmental entities, and secularized humanist considerations that consider slavery a dreadful system.

Notes:

1. "Why was slavery allowed in the Old Testament?" *CompellingTruth.org.,* www.compellingtruth.org/slavery-Old-Testament.html (accessed January 4, 2020).

2. A cursory search in *BibleGateway.com* shows that in the NABRE version, which is the one being utilized in this work, the term *slave* occurs 21xt in the Gospels while the term *servant* shows up 85xt; in the 21st Century King James Version, however, the term *slave* is non-existent while *servant* shows up 97xt (results for the traditional King James Version are similar). Other versions show similar results: in the Christian Standard Bible the term *slave* in the Gospels occur only 6xt while the number for *servant* is 102xt; in the Evangelical Heritage Version the results are 5xt for *slave* and 110xt for *servant*; in the International Children's Bible, 7xt for *slave* and 140xt for *servant;* in the American Standard Version, 0xt for *slave* and 92xt for *servant.* Differences are notably more striking when contrasting *slave* and *servant* in the Old Testament. In the Old Testament version of the American Standard Bible, the term *slave* appears only 3xt; in the King James Versions, *servant* occurs 739xt. A reason many Bible versions prefer not to use the term *slave* and instead rely on *bondage* or *bondservant* may be that today they do not seem to have the same evil connotation as slavery, hence, they are used apologetically to soften the image of the Christian God. Note: Content Analysis results in this work are not based on numbers provided by *BibleGateway.com.* Instead, I rely on my own process that eliminates the terms from headings and subheadings, thereby making my count more accurate.

3. Augustine, for example, follows in the steps of Paul acknowledging the reality of slavery as being a punishment for sin enforceable by natural law. Although he argued against cruel treatment, he added that, despite being physically enslaved, humans can nevertheless remain spiritually free. Margaret Mary, "Slavery in the Writings of St. Augustine," *The Classical Journal,* vol. 49, no. 8, 1954, pp. 363–369. JSTOR, www.jstor.org/stable/3292914 (accessed January 5, 2020); John Chrysostom argues that slavery is the product of sin too, *the fruit of covetousness, of degradation, of savagery,* and preaches against unfair treatment, though he does not call for its abolition. "Homily XXII, Ephesians vi. 5–8," https://www.ccel.org/ccel/schaff/npnf113.iii.iv.xxiii.html (accessed January 5, 2020); Thomas Aquinas adds to Augustine's views. He states that *slavery is a condition of the body, since a slave is to the master a kind of instrument in working.* He indicates that some types of slavery are ordained by nature (through positive law), although slaves in some circumstances possess some rights. Thomas Aquinas, *Summa Theologica,* "Question 52. The impediment of the condition of slavery," CE, http://www.newadvent.org/summa/5052.htm (accessed January 5, 2020).

4. Initial denunciations begin with Pope Eugene IV in his bull *Sicut Dudum* in1435 on the enslavement of black natives, and Pope Paul III in a pontifical decree *Sublimis Deus* in 1537 on the human condition of the Indians in South America. However, between these two papacies, Nicholas V issues a bull in 1452, *Dum Diversas,* to the king of Portugal in which he supposedly authorizes the enslavement (or imprisonment) in perpetuity of all Saracens conquered in North Africa. *"Dum Diversas (English Translation)" Unam Sanctam Catholicam,* February 5, 2011, http://unamsanctamcatholicam.blogspot.com/2011/02/dum-diversas-english-translation.html (accessed January 21, 2020); Gregory XIV in 1591, Urban VIII in 1639, Innocent XI (1691-1700), Benedict XIV (1741), Pius VII (1815), and Gregory XVI (1838) furthered their denunciations of slavery against Christian traders despite opposition to the latter by the American hierarchy. Fr. Joel S. Panzer, "The Popes and Slavery: Setting the Record Straight," EWTN.com, ewtn.com/catholicism/library/popes-and-slavery-setting-the-record-straight-1119 (accessed January 5, 2020). Fray Bartolome de las Casas, a Dominican Friar, persuaded Emperor Charles V in 1542 to approve the *New Laws of the Indies for the Good Treatment and Preservation of the Indians,* although the laws were met with stiff resistance by slaveholders in the Americas and eventually were abrogated. Christopher Minster, Ph.D., "Spain and the New Laws of 1542," *ThoughtCo.com,* September 3, 2018, https://www.thoughtco.com/the-new-laws-of-1542-2136445 (accessed January 21, 2020).

5. English, French, Dutch, and Portuguese shipping companies participated in the selling of African blacks. The Treaty of Utrecht (1713) allowed Spain to transfer the rights to supply Spanish colonies with slaves from France to England. The English took *over two million negroes to America* between 1680 and 1786. Durant, Vol. 9, pp. 67-68. Slavery is abolished in Portugal in 1773 but allowed to continue in its colonies. Durant, Vol 10, p. 269. In Denmark, slavery was legal within the country until 1792, becoming the first European nation to abolish it in its territories. Ibid, p. 649. The French Chamber of Commerce quote is found in Durant, Vol. X, p. 935.

6. Pope Paul VI, *Gaudium et Spes,* no. 29, http://www.vatican.va/archive/hist_councils/ii_vatican_council/documents/vat-ii_const_19651207_gaudium-et-spes_en.html (accessed January 5, 2020).

7. *Sheep, cattle, men-servants, and maid-servants were all possessions to be sold as it pleased their masters.* Durant, Vol. VI, P. 449. Martin Luther, "The Freedom of a Christian Man," *The Protestant Reformation,* Hans J. Hillerbrand ed., (New York; Harper & Row, 1968), pp. 4-28.

8. "'All Things Turned Upside Down'" – Calvin on Slavery," *Political Theology Network*, January 30, 2014, https://politicaltheology.com/all-things-turned-upside-down-calvin-on-slavery/ (accessed January 21, 2020).

9. Somewhat detached from the Reformation Movement, Katharine Gerbner presents the concept of *Protestant Supremacy,* a mixture of Bible Christianity, politics, and economics, that leads to support of the practice in the Americas. Slaveholders even oppose the religious conversion of slaves because they deemed them unworthy of the faith. Missionaries seeking their conversion end up becoming entangled in the practice in order to accomplish their objectives. Katharine Gerbner, *Christian Slavery: Conversion and Race in the Protestant Atlantic World*, (Philadelphia: University of Pennsylvania Press, 2018).

10. Durant, Vol. X, pp. 732-733; on Wesley, Vol. IX, pp. 133-137.

11. Ibid, p. 645.

12. This point is well argued in Thomas N Tyson, David Oldroyd, "Accounting for slavery during the Enlightenment: Contradictions and interpretations," *Sage,* March 19, 2018. https://journals.sagepub.com/doi/full/10.1177/1032373218759971 (accessed January 7, 2020). They indicate that *slave owners endorsed those Enlightenment principles which stressed national well-being, moral development, economic progress, and work discipline to sustain their business models, maintain their lavish lifestyles, bolster their views on the superiority of the White race, or simply to counter abolitionists. Alternatively, the clear majority of those calling for the end of slavery consistently prioritized the principles of humanity, justice, benevolence, and virtue. Slave owners invoked the utilitarian/pragmatic side of the Enlightenment in the abolition debates, whereas abolitionists emphasized the more abstract humanist/moral dimension. The Enlightenment ideal of the natural rights of man played a key role in the abolition of the slave trade by Britain and the United States toward the end of the period (1807) and in the later abolition of slavery altogether (1834 in the British Empire and 1863 in the United States); notwithstanding that, former slaves were rarely afforded the rights and opportunities that were commensurate to those of the White citizenry.*

13. John Locke, *Two Treatises of Government,* ed. Thomas Hollis (London: A. Millar et al., 1764)., LibertyFund.org, oll.libertyfund.org/pages/john-locke-two-treatises-1689 (accessed January 6, 2020).

14. Stanford Encyclopedia of Philosophy, "John Locke," revised May 1, 2018, https://plato.stanford.edu/entries/locke/ (accessed January 7, 2020).

15. Rousseau states, seemingly unequivocally, that *from whatever aspect we regard the question, the right of slavery is null and void, not only as being illegitimate, but also because it is absurd and meaningless* (Ch 4). However, he argues his views from the perspective of natural law and political submission to authority, without expressing opposition to race-based slavery. On the other hand, he is forgiving of the Christian religion for not opposing other types of slavery (indicating his lack of awareness to denunciations by the popes), since *Christianity as a religion is entirely spiritual, occupied solely with heavenly things* (Ch 8). Jean-Jacques Rousseau, *The Social Contract and Discourses,* trans G.D.H. Cole (London and Toronto: J.M. Dent and Sons, 1923, https://oll.libertyfund.org/titles/rousseau-the-social-contract-and-discourses (accessed January 7, 2020). Montesquieu is critical of slavery, indicating, *the state of slavery is, in its own nature, bad. It is neither useful to the master nor to the slave; not to the slave, because he can do nothing through a motive of virtue; nor to the master, because, by having an unlimited authority over his slaves, he insensibly accustoms himself to the want of all moral virtues, and from thence becomes fierce, hasty, severe, choleric, voluptuous, and cruel* (Book XV.1). Despite being critical of racism by Christian predators (Book XV.4), he nonetheless favors a form of natural slavery that is *to be limited to some particular parts of the world, since in all other countries, even the most servile drudgeries may be performed by freemen* (Book XV.8), while arguing that the system

ought to be regulated to prevent abuses (Book XV.10). For references to Hume, Spinoza, and Kant, see Chris Meyns, "Why Don't Philosophers Talk About Slavery?" Essays, October 2018, Philosophersmag.com, www.philosophersmag.com/essays/173-why-don-t-philosophers-talk-about-slavery (accessed January 7, 2020). Marxism also had little influence in advancing the abolition of race-based slavery in Europe and the United States in the nineteenth century, largely because it did not oppose it on moral grounds. In its analysis, Marxism incorporates its denunciation of slavery in terms of a nefarious socio-economic component of rogue capitalist structures that contributed to wealth. Furthermore, its atheist underpinnings and its attacks on private property were seen as challenging the very ideological and political foundations of these countries. A sample writing of Marxist denunciation of slavery appears in Ken Lawrence, Karl Marx on American Slavery, SojournerTruth.net, http://www.sojournertruth.net/marxslavery.pdf (accessed January 7, 2020).
16. Meyns.
17. Megan Gannon, "Race is a Social Construct, Scientists Argue, Live Science, February 5, 2016, ScientificAmerican.com, https://www.scientificamerican.com/article/race-is-a-social-construct-scientists-argue/ (accessed January 7, 2020).
18. The Thomas Reuters Foundation indicates that human slavery takes different forms today, such as prostitution, forced labor, begging, criminality, domestic servitude, forced marriage, and organ removal. India has the largest number of slaves globally, with 8 million, followed by China (3.86 million), Pakistan (3.19 million), North Korea (2.64 million), Nigeria (1.39 million), Iran (1.29 million), Indonesia (1.22 million), the Democratic Republic of the Congo (1 million), Russia (794,000) and the Philippines (784,000). Arantxa Underwood, "Which countries have the highest rates of modern slavery and most victims?" *Thomas Reuters Foundation,* July 30, 2018, https://news.trust.org/item/20180730000101-aj7ui/ (accessed January 7, 2020).

Equality

This section inquires what if any features or conditions might account for all human individuals being considered equal to the extent that they would be entitled to the same temporal rights and freedoms that are important nowadays. Or, the opposite, whether certain characteristics might account for denying equality to some human beings, suggesting that certain peoples are entitled to be morally and legally superior to others, be it based on age, sex, gender, race, religion, nationality, wealth, or other considerations.

There is no denying that a penchant for superiority has existed throughout history among peoples. The origins of slavery, autocracy, colonialism, and imperialism find their basis in the belief that some people regard themselves to be superior, and thus feel empowered to subjugate others. This conduct likely is based on the view that the 'high and the mighty' possess natural conditions that enable the imposition of their will upon others. These beliefs or ideologies find commonality with wild creatures in the animal kingdom that are driven by a desire or instinct for survival and sheer supremacy. Although members of the same species cohabitate together, animals are not exempt from attacking members of their own species, including wolves, lions, elephants, alligators, or even hummingbirds.[1]

The legal prohibition of slavery and the universal codification of freedoms and human rights appear to have settled the question of whether some human beings deserve to regard themselves as superior to others. The proposition that all human beings are equal, however, is, on its face, flawed. Human equality cannot even be anatomically justified, given the obvious physical differences between men and women. Physically, emotionally, and psychologically, there seem to be significant differences in the sexes, for example, regarding gender and personality traits, and scientific research has not been able to aptly detect what accounts for these differences.[2] Among men and women there are striking differences; we come in different sizes, colors, shapes, physical power, intelligence, skills, languages, and beliefs. Moreover, can there be anything that makes each one of us more different from others than having unique fingerprints and DNAs? Hence, if humans are so different from one another, on what basis can we demand equality?

Despite our differences, humans may claim to be equal either because we have a common Creator or because we have evolved into the same species, say, as opposed to chimpanzees. Interestingly, despite the difference in the respective genetic codes of humans and chimps is rather small (1.2 percent),[3] such a difference is vast, at least until chimps can learn to read, write, think, and build societies as complex as ours. But can these claims to equality overcome and justify the enormous differences that exist among us? Probably not, the reason being that the proposition that all humans beings are equal is nothing more than a temporal convention subject to its acceptance and enforcement through laws, government, and moral values. This is to say that, insofar as rulers and people are complacent with human inequality or unequal treatment on the basis of a multitude of features, e.g., sex, gender, religion, socio-economic background, race, ethnicity, or nationalities, unchristian-like discrimination would continue unabated around the world.

As we read in the Old Testament, God's concept of freedom following Original Sin is rather limited, to the point of allowing slavery to prevail for centuries. Given God's favoritism of one group of people over others, the claim to freedom and equality based on divine revelation, or its intuition from an abstract Natural Law that has never been transcribed into stone, is weak at best. Nonetheless, the term *equality* seems to evoke a magical dimension, a yearning, like freedom, that something inside many of us suggests that all human beings deserve to be equal (despite their differences), and thus be entitled to the same temporal rights and freedoms.

The enchantment with human equality began to take hold just prior to and throughout the Enlightenment. It was propelled by men and women (many of them atheists or agnostics) who strongly opposed the papacy and the French hierarchy for their positions in favor of autocratic monarchies and the wealthy classes that had been responsible for creating extraordinary levels of social, political, and economic inequality. Ironically, those who wrote the American Declaration of Independence and the French Declaration of the Rights of Man and the Citizen based their claims to equality on a Supreme Being as humanity's Creator (even while they were denying it to others). It appears that at some point in history the human conscience was able to 'invent' equality, probably after noticing that both slavery and the denial of freedoms were considered repulsive. Whether a moral gene is internalized in humans, or the concept of equality is so attractive that it becomes a cultural, or even a religious meme is worth considering, because in and of itself, temporal equality is nothing but a human convention.

Does Jesus Regard All Human Creatures Equal?

The words *equality* or *equal* referring to the temporal convention that has been internationally recognized as legitimate, both legally and morally, seldom appear in the Gospels. There are a few passages that, if we were to stretch the imagination, could conceivably relate to equality as a human condition. Hence, we need to ask ourselves if Jesus regards all human beings equal, and if he does, under which circumstances.

Jesus indicates on two occasions that he gives his life and sheds his blood for *many* (Mk 10:45, 14:22-24, Mt 20:28, 2:26-28), although in Luke, blood is shed only *for you* (Lk 22:20), i.e., his disciples. However, if the term *many* is translated as signifying *all,* as it appears in most English versions of the Bible, it is possible to suggest that Jesus regards all humanity worthy of his death and redemption.[4] Of course, to accept this view, the reader would have to quibble over passages in the Gospels in which Jesus indicates that he comes only for a chosen few Christians or for the Jewish people, in which cases he would be disregarding the Father's mandate.

Those who believe that only some people are chosen or elected by God to be saved, find reasons to negate the conception that God regards all his creatures as being equal, i.e., deserving his love. Additionally, numerous passages indicating that Jesus comes only for the Jews also reiterate a selective view of redemption that favors inequality. On the other hand, a brief sentence in Luke by the righteous Simeon indicates that God's salvation represents *a light for revelation to the Gentiles* (Lk 2:30-32), suggesting that Jesus's message extends to people other than Jews.

In Matthew's Parable of the Workers in the Vineyard, Jesus narrates a story in which the master of the vineyard (God) consents to unequal treatment by paying the same wages to those who join the labor force late as those who have worked longer hours. Insisting that he is free to do as he wishes with his money (Mt 20:1-15), the master appears to be a practitioner of economic inequality. However, the parable may be seen from a different angle; the master seems to leave his doors opened to anyone who needs a job even if they should arrive late. In other words, Jesus might be referring to God's generosity; a view that possibly many unforgiving people might object to in some circumstances, e.g., the possibility that God may forgive a criminal.

There is an even more explicit passage in which Jesus seems to have changed his mind, and instead of coming only for his people (the Israelites), he now wants to extend his teachings and the kingdom of God to all. This view is indicated in similar passages that appear toward the end in the synoptic texts: *Go, therefore, and make disciples of all nations* (Mt 28:19, Mk 16:15, Lk 24:46-47).[5] Furthermore, two passages in Matthew express a degree of commonality among humans that relate to the view that all people are equal in the eyes of God. The heavenly Father, Jesus says, makes the sun rise on the bad as well as on the good, and causes rain to fall on the just and the unjust (Mt 5:44-45). Speaking in general terms, he adds that people are more important to God than the birds in the sky that he feeds or the grass he makes grow that provides bread for all (Mt 6:26-33). Although Jesus is not explicitly connecting equality to temporal rights, he is implying that God grants equal access to the kingdom to all; that anyone who wishes to join may do so as long as they abide by his teachings. Despite Jesus's convoluted remarks, it is possible that he believes that in the eyes of God all human beings enjoy the same special dignity, an intrinsic personal value that rejects any feeling or belief of superiority or supremacy by a group of peoples over others.

There is another brief passage by the authors of John's Gospel, attesting that in the beginning … *all things came to be through him* (Jesus), and … *what came to be through him was life, and this life was the light of the human race; … the true light, which enlightens everyone, was coming into the world* (Jn 1:1-4). Literally speaking, the term 'human race' suggests (at least today) all of humanity. The message the authors would send decades later (following the Council of Jerusalem in 50 CE), once the disciples decided that Christianity would be expanded throughout the world to the Gentiles, appears to support the view that in John's view, Jesus's mission encompasses all humankind.

The references to human equality in the Gospels are few, and their relationship to its temporal connotations needs to be established with utmost care. These references convey the impression that human beings are equal in the eyes of Jesus (who claims to speak on behalf of God). Nevertheless, is it possible to extrapolate from these passages that Jesus would favor a concept of human equality that could eradicate all types of discrimination that may lead to the revocation of individual liberties and human rights? If Jesus says that God loves all humans alike; that he dies to ransom all humanity; and that his teachings constitute a *light for the revelation of the Gentiles*, his case for human equality seems to have a relatively strong foundation. But again, is he referring to temporal or supernatural equality, or both?

Before answering the question, we may want to inquire into another approach to equality in the Gospels. The words, *whoever, anyone,* and *everyone* are among the most inclusive terms in the English language, and assuming they are translated correctly from the existing copies of the Gospels, their inclusivity makes them universal. These three words are relevant to the category at hand. Jesus uses these terms numerous times to indicate that a particular teaching applies to whoever, everyone, or anyone. The question is whether these words refer only to the Jewish people, or if it includes anyone who is listening to him since he preaches to Gentiles too. Or we may ask if he is aware that he is addressing all nations; nations that neither he nor even Roman emperors knew existed?

Content analysis results show that the few instances that appear to be relevant to the equality category in the Gospels total 18xt times, 19p passages, and occupy 138sp spaces, thus making for a lowly ranked category. On the other hand, a cursory count of the three aforementioned words (*whoever, anyone,* and *everyone*) account for 189xt. The estimated number of passages likely would have been over 100p, and the estimated space occupied in the texts would have amounted to over 1500sp spaces, making this a significant category.[6] Without negating the possibility that through his teachings Jesus seeks to imply that all of God's creatures are created equal, such equality would signify that God considers all of his children as deserving of his love simply because he creates them.

Jesus, however, does not address temporal socio-political structures and conditions (except through the love of others and his condemnation of temporal sins) to the extent that temporal rights might be inferred from his teachings. Hence, it has taken centuries for Christianity, through its various denominations, to acknowledge human equality as the foundation of individual liberties and human rights. Therefore, it would be difficult to conclude that Jesus's teachings apply to temporal equality. It is not even clear from the Gospels whether eternal salvation might entail differences in honors (similar to Dante's levels of heaven) depending on how righteous the person lives his/her life.

It may be argued that Jesus's strong denunciations of sinfulness along with his commandment to love one another (two of the major significant categories) attest to any wrongdoing as sinful, precisely because no one has the right to inflict harm upon others. Nonetheless, although these teachings are meant to be applied on earth, their basis is not temporal equality. Instead, it is the path that Jesus dictates for eternal salvation. Hence, if anything, it reinforces the view of supernatural equality

This means that the type of equality implied in Jesus's teachings relates primarily to equality of opportunity for the salvation of all, provided they adhere to his teachings. Thus, Christianity can make the case for equality by indicating that all humans possess an equal dignity they share because they were created by God and redeemed by Jesus. At the same time, humanists may rely on science and draw from evolution theory the implication that human beings are (by far) the most valuable, worthy, or dignified species in the animal kingdom on account of their attributes. Possessing the same basic biological characteristics, and these being superior to other species, all humans would be entitled to the same fundamental liberties and rights. Together, these views lend themselves to the foundation of human equality, without which it would have been impossible to lay down universal principles, laws, and codes of ethics to govern human behavior in secular societies. Hence, it may be concluded that the concept of temporal equality does not emanate from the Gospels; instead, it has been humankind's accomplishment, a significant social construct that Christianity has had to accept regardless of Jesus's intentions, and whose rejection humans may not favor.

Notes:
1. Joseph Castro, "Do Animals Murder Each Other," *Livescience.com,* September 16, 2017, https://www.livescience.com/60431-do-animals-murder-each-other.html (accessed July 31, 2020).
2. *Sex differences in personality and behavior are real,* argues psychologist David P. Schmitt, "The Truth About Sex Differences," *Psychology Today,* November 7, 2017,

https://www.psychologytoday.com/us/articles/201711/the-truth-about-sex-differences (accessed August 1, 2020); Diane F. Halpern, past president of the American Psychological Association, agrees in, *Sex Differences in Cognitive Abilities: 4th Edition,* (not read), (London: Psychology Press, 2013); Bruce Goldman, "Two Minds – The cognitive differences between men and women," https://stanmed.stanford.edu/2017spring/how-mens-and-womens-brains-are-different.html (accessed August 1, 2020). The research on this topic on the internet is extensive as well as some of its conclusions.
3. "What does it mean to be human," *Smithsonian National Museum of Natural History,* January 17, 2020, http://humanorigins.si.edu/evidence/genetics (accessed January 23, 2020).
4. The Catholic Church affirms that *Christ died for all men without exception: "There is not, never has been, and never will be a single human being for whom Christ did not suffer."* CCC 605.
5. In John's Gospel the message is somewhat different but the authors directed it (decades later) to everyone, not only to the Jewish people: *Now Jesus did many other signs in the presence of [his] disciples that are not written in this book. But these are written that you may [come to] believe that Jesus is the Messiah, the Son of God, and that through this belief you may have life in his name* (Jn 20:30).
6. Based on the xt count of the three words, I took an average of other categories exhibiting as high as 190xt and as low as 100 xt to suggest possible numbers for *p* and *sp.* Additionally, as a real tally, utilizing the term *whoever* in John's Gospel alone, its numbers would increase from 5xt/4p/18sp to 44xt/24p.100sp. Nonetheless, it does not change the view that equality in the Gospels is for the most part a supernatural and not a temporal term.

Democracy

According to the Gospel of John, Jesus is *the true light of the human race that enlightens everyone* (Jn 1:1-4). We may need to inquire, however, if this light provides clear indications about the type of political system humans ought to establish to manage their temporal affairs. If Jesus is said to represent moral truth, it might be possible to elaborate a just political system based on his teachings. Nonetheless, imperfect or sinful humanity seeking to decipher the mysteries in his teachings prevent such an undertaking. While Jesus departs considerably from the Father's initial code of ethics and regulations, his teachings remain an inadequate instrument to comply with God's command *to subdue the earth* (whatever he may have meant by that). It appears as if God expected that as his creation was to become more complex, it would be up to humanity to decide how his power and authority were to be used on earth.

The Emergence of the Body Politic
Throughout history, humans have congregated into groups to ensure their physical survival as individuals. And since humanity has not been known for gathering together into a single group (with the exception perhaps of the mythical Tower of Babel), human beings have congregated separately according to shared characteristics and purposes that provide them with a common social identity of who they are. Among these are language, similar background and values, and an individual desire and will to rely on others and to trust that, being like-minded, those others would agree to mutually support each other. Surges in population, diversification of labor, natural disasters, and an array of increased demands to satisfy additional needs to further safeguard their survival, have led to a type of organization known today as the body politic, also known as *polis* in Ancient Greek and Roman political theory, in reference to peoples who agree to live under a common system of government.

Fundamentally, the body politic is a humanly created enterprise set up to regulate social, cultural, economic, religious, and other types of affairs in which people involve themselves. The body politic can be differently configured; it can be a village or a town, a legal corporate entity, an empire, or a nation-state. Nowadays, the nation-state prevails as the most internationally accepted social organization upon which other institutions depend for their existence. Its essence or lifeline is politics.

The term *politics*[1] has acquired a negative connotation, suggesting self-interest, corruption, partisanship, and endless conflicts. All of this does happen. However, the term has a positive meaning that cynicism has managed to obscure. In this work, *politics* refers to the process through which human beings engage in managing their domestic and international affairs. It entails having to find solutions to problems created by complications that life presents, e.g., scarcity of resources, military conflict, natural disasters, injustice, disease, poverty, and other dissimilar values and desires among actors (individuals, institutions, and governments), each of which seeks to conduct their affairs in accordance with their understanding of right and wrong, or simply by abiding by their desires. In brief, politics emerge when divergent virtues and vices converge within the body politic. Within this framework, nothing escapes politics, even if its people (at their own peril) wish to insulate themselves from it.

The Rise of Democratic Republics

Among nation-states, the concept of a democratic republic has emerged as the most preferred one so far. Many nations that call themselves democracies, however, do not embody its essential attributes. For purposes of this work, a democratic republic is defined as self-government by its people, as opposed to a single individual or political party that wields absolute authority. In this political model, citizens are guided by a written social and political contract, i.e., a constitution, that spells out the rules (rights and duties) by which it operates, with the understanding that the exercise of political authority rests upon the consent of the governed.

A democratic republic has constitutional powers to protect itself from anything that may unjustly impair the freedoms and rights of citizens and other peoples living within their territories through a series of mechanisms and procedures, e.g., separation of powers, establishment of law enforcement and military personnel under civilian authority, and the explicit declaration of individual rights. Democratic republics seek to uphold certain fundamental values, including freedom of religion, thought, expression, and assembly, the right to life, liberty, and the pursuit of happiness within the confines of the law, tolerance toward diverse views, equal respect for the dignity of the individual person, equality of opportunity, protection of every citizen and others within its territory before the law, freedom of movement, and freedom to elect those that will represent the citizenry based on one equal vote per person without discrimination.[2]

The ideal democratic republic seeks to be inclusive. Since equality is its foundation, this model would not make exceptions to the worth of the individual person based on political influence, wealth, religion, gender, sex, race, intelligence, or other differences. Conflicts do arise, however, when particular ideologies, or secular or religious morality, question the types of people whose rights ought to be protected. Such a political system, nonetheless, safeguards personal liberty by acknowledging that freedom is not (and cannot be) absolute, leading to the realization that it needs to be constantly monitored by the government to prevent being violated. Moreover, recognizing the equal and intrinsic dignity of each person, this model of self-government abhors the view that some citizens, regarding themselves as superior to others, claim exceptions from the law. Hence, it becomes the government's duty to protect individual dignity and freedom by ensuring that its actions attain the common good and not the good of a portion of society. Moreover, a democratic republic ensures that the laws are just, transparently legislated, and faithfully executed and adjudicated. Precisely because it embodies so many of human nature's values and desires, the case can be made that a democratic republic is the highest and most noble form of government that has existed so far, and which despite its flaws, might represent the last stage (or next to last) in the history of political philosophy.

Jesus's Political Philosophy

Jesus's disproportionate concern with humanity's ultimate destiny in contrast with temporal values (Mk 8:35, Lk 9:24, 12:4-5, Mt 10:28, 39, Jn 12:25) appears to be the foundation of what might have been his political philosophy. His lack of vocal opposition to Roman oppression and injustice, in addition to some of his parables, and the significance of the Beatitudes suggesting that evil must be endured while on earth, may have unintentionally legitimized temporal authoritarian and unjust practices. There are other passages, however, including his commandment to love one's neighbor and his healings that indicate his dislike of injustice and suffering. At the very least, it seems that Jesus would favor any political system that follows his teachings. But what would that system be like?

Despite his insistence that there is no salvation outside of him, Jesus exercises his mission amid opposing religious views, e.g., Pharisaic Judaism and paganism. Nonetheless, rather than calling for violent crusades to eliminate those that refuse to believe in him, he chooses to tell his followers to persuade all nations of the truth in God's teachings. This is significant because it indicates tolerance on his part toward people whose views he opposes. He accepts the separation of church and state by declining to confront the authority of the Roman Empire. Although he views equality as a supernatural concept, his teachings call for the utmost respect of all people no matter their differences (except for the Jewish religious authorities). Interestingly too, Jesus's model of governing the institution that he founds depends on the consent of each of his disciples, even accepting one of his own to betray him (Jn 13:21-26), and the others to desert him if they choose (Jn 6:66-68).

Jesus, however, might have been concerned with a flawed body politic tainted by sin exercising its independent freedom of thought and expression to decide what is right and wrong. He would think that without acceptance of his teachings (absolute truth) humanity's moral compass would not stop whirling, unable to find its proper course, as, in fact, has happened. So far, reason has not proven sufficient to find humanity's moral destiny on earth. Nonetheless, Jesus cannot be critical of reason (God's gift to humanity), since without it faith would not be possible (that we know of, animals cannot detect the presence of God). As his followers understood throughout Christendom, reason needs to stay within the confines of faith, regulated by and subordinated to faith, as indicated by Thomas Aquinas. While relying on his philosophical method truth can be debated, affirmed, and expanded but only insofar as certain tenets derived from divine revelation are accepted *a priori.* The outcome of the Aquinas method was to prevent unfettered reasoning from straying away from divine revelation and lead souls to eternal damnation. Yet, despite this concern, Jesus was willing to accept the risk by not calling for the elimination of diverse ways of thinking or the establishment of an authoritarian theocracy. His directive, *go and make disciples of all nations* (Mt 28:19), favors persuasion; although in the Gospels it carries a major incentive: eternal condemnation (Mk 16:16).

This picture brings us to the realization that incongruences depicted in the Gospels concerning Jesus's teachings, and their reaffirmation by Christian theology and hierarchical authorities, impeded the emergence of democratic republics. Although the initial democratic model had been widely discussed and experimented with by the Greeks, humanity had to wait centuries for a combination of self-described deists, agnostics, humanists, and anti-church philosophers and practitioners of politics to draw a model that most closely would resemble human aspirations. It is to be understood, however, that as an ideal, democratic republics reflect the shortcomings of its participants, including the Christian churches that opposed this system as being incompatible with its teachings. The clergy, both Catholic and Protestants, did not trust the perceived irrationality of uneducated mobs that could represent a threat to the faith and their authority. At the time, they did not realize that centuries later their faith and their authority would be defended and upheld by the same political system they resisted.[3]

Although the democratic model has expanded slowly while making further refinements well into the twenty-first century, an unvarnished version of this system is different than its ideal. This model is meant to be contentious because human beings are not alike in their values, or even in their understanding of the process and/or of the issues. At times, differences of opinion ignite emotions that lead to a polarization that a divided Christianity is unable to overcome. It is ironic that divisiveness in well-established democratic republics occurs over issues that have strong moral overtones, precisely the turf of the Christian faith. Christians find themselves divided over racism, warfare, crime, taxation, corporate or individual welfare, abortion, big or small government, illegal migrations, drugs, human trafficking, the ecological debate, and gay rights, among others.

Another obstacle to the realization of democratic exceptionalism is that the model openly favors freedom and rights at the expense of the duties of citizens toward one another and the government. Moreover, incessant cries for freedom obscure the concept of equality, thereby forgetting that equality is based upon the need to restrict the freedom of each so that each may enjoy a share of their own freedom.

Many Christians do not seem to be aware that while totalitarianism annuls individual dignity, unmitigated individualism masks the reality that each person is ultimately dependent on someone else for their accomplishments. The body politic begins to disintegrate unless each member agrees to abide by a social or communal agreement that prevents endemic legalized injustices such as laws affirming the existence of structural organizations that exempt its leadership from becoming accountable to the judicial system, well-preserved systemic inequalities, or the protection of special interests that operate against the wellbeing of the common good.

Nonetheless, Christian hierarchies did not notice the values embodied in democratic republicanism until the seventeenth, eighteenth, nineteenth, and twentieth centuries. The formulation of this experiment was initiated by the unintended (and perhaps detrimental) effects of the Protestant Reformation and Catholic reactionary attitudes toward each other. Nonetheless, its direct contribution came from humanists, deists, and a mixture of Jewish and Christian philosophy, all focusing on the temporal world; another instance in which those who were perceived as enemies of the faith were able to gift the democratic model to humanity.

Notes:

1. *Politics* is being defined in this work akin to Harold Laswell's classic, *Politics: Who Gets What, When, and How,* (New York: The World Publishing Company, Twelfth printing 1972); however, the definition in this work goes beyond Laswell's study of specific elites as influencers. The involuntary role of the masses, the media, foreign and domestic events, and random groups that appear in the political scene as reactions to social issues, among others, in my view find little consideration in Laswell's work, yet they wield considerable influence in the political process.

2. This is a description of values observed within most democratic republics, and does not apply to a specific nation.

3. Catholics and Protestants objected to the democratic model, as they all opposed any political system that could dilute their theocracies in Europe. Pope Gregory XVI (1832) condemned freedom of conscience, freedom of the press, separation of church and state, and religious liberty while supporting temporal monarchical authority, despite denouncing slavery and the slave trade. McBrien, pp. 338-339. In 1864, Pope Pius IX reiterated Gregory's denunciations and created the *Syllabus of Errors,* a compendium of statements deemed to be erroneous, such as rationalism, liberalism, religious liberty, secularism, and Protestantism. Ibid., p. 346. In Europe, Catholics and Protestants established Christian theocracies that favored the faith of the ruler. It should be noted that the first signs of democratic principles appear in the United States, Britain, and France in the nineteenth and twentieth centuries when slavery is abolished, women's suffrage becomes legalized, and all (adult) citizens are allowed to vote. In the United States, the basis of democracy expressed as one man or woman, one vote, does not take place until the passing of the 13th Amendment (1865) forbidding slavery, the 14th Amendment (1868) granting citizenship to all persons born or naturalized in the United States, the 15th Amendment (1870) denying the right to vote on account of race, color, or previous condition of servitude, and the 19th Amendment (1920) guaranteeing women the right to vote.

LGBTQ Rights

Gay rights have become among the most divisive issues worldwide nowadays. LGBTQ people are facing an uphill battle for social acceptance while generations imbued in traditional religious and cultural beliefs, feeling that their own values are being threatened, are resisting changes. This issue is best seen against the backdrop of serious problems the LGBTQ world community shares with Jesus and his disciples at the time; they suffer harassment, persecution, discrimination, and violence in various parts of the world. Hence, it seems reasonable to inquire what the public Jesus might say about gay behavior and the rights of gay people.[1]

The inquiry is both uncomplicated and problematic; Jesus does not address gay behavior, unions, or relationships in the Gospels. As a result, content analysis results indicate that the issue of *gay rights* in the texts seems insignificant. If the Gospels constitute divine revelation about absolute truths, it may be tentatively concluded that Jesus did not address this matter because there were more pressing problems that needed his attention, or that the authors had failed to capture the issue through oral transmission, or even because the issue had not become prominent enough throughout Jesus's public life. Presumably, it is highly unlikely that God might have forgotten to raise the issue at the time he inspired the authors of the Gospels.

Unless Jesus led a secluded life and became impervious to his surroundings, he must have been aware of same-sex behavior. There are two regulations in the Old Testament prohibiting men (presumably women too) from having sexual intercourse with members of the same sex, suggesting that Jesus, being knowledgeable of the Jewish Bible, must have been aware that the behavior probably existed (Lev 18:20, 20:13). Moreover, at least two instances dealing with gay behavior in the Old Testament likely displeased God because the intention was through force (rape) (Gen 19:4-11, Judg 19:22-23). Additionally, homosexual behavior had become acceptable practice within the Greek World and the Roman Empire,[2] two cultures that prevailed during Jesus's time that suggests that he may have been familiar with this issue. Nonetheless, it appears that Christian influence on matters of sexual practices objecting to homosexuality is not discussed by the Church Fathers until the second and fourth centuries CE, after changes in Roman morality began to emerge.[3] By the fourth and sixth centuries CE, Christian emperors already had issued decrees (death by flames) against homosexuality.[4]

Jesus Approach to Gay Behavior

Jesus does not address gay behavior, except by default, through his teachings on marriage. As examined under the *Righteous Sexual Behavior* category, Jesus does not have much to say about marriage that is of relevance today, or even at the time. He discusses marriage mostly from the negative consequences of divorce and adultery. In nearly all instances, when the term *marriage* appears in the Gospels, the passages seem immaterial, either because the word is insignificantly mentioned or because it relates mostly to divorce and adultery.

His views on marriage are limited to God's account in the Old Testament: *from the beginning of creation, God made them male and female. For this reason a man shall leave his father and mother [and be joined to his wife], and the two shall become one flesh. So they are no longer two but one flesh* (Mk 10:2-8, Mt 19:3-5). The passage does not concern marriage; it is Jesus's reply to the Pharisees on divorce. He is merely expressing God's narrative saying that God creates man and woman for companionship, to populate the earth, cultivate the land, and to manage their affairs (Gen 1:27-28, 2:18-24). Jesus, however, goes further than God and issues a decree prohibiting divorce, saying that, once they become one body, no human being must separate what God has joined together (Mk 10:9, Mt 19:6).

By amending God's doing, Jesus pronounces himself on the inviolability of marriage between a man and a woman while declaring divorce and adultery as sinful. Since he only contemplates marriage between a man and a woman, Jesus would likely have regarded gay sexual behavior in the same manner. His firmness regarding divorce, however, seems to lack understanding about the complexity of marriage, a reason perhaps why he does not elaborate further on this issue. It is noteworthy that the sanctity of marriage is not included among the Ten Commandments other than in a negative manner, e.g., *thy shall not commit adultery,* and *thy shall not covet your neighbor's wife.* Given that Jesus's teachings on marriage and divorce are so disappointingly limited, all Christian denominations have found ways to circumvent the issue of divorce, likely as a necessity to a problematic human issue.[5]

Additionally, although Jesus practically obliterates Mosaic Law, he offers no teaching moment regarding marriage. It is the Fathers of the Church who take over this task. There are no teachings in Jesus about the undesirability of divorce itself, such as the impact on children and the spouses, or the lasting emotional traumas that every member of the family experiences. These refinements have been the result of human learning led by the social and biological sciences. He does not refer to divorce as being painful, but sinful, because it may lead to adultery, and thus to a violation of God's commandment. His emphasis is on sin rather than on the unfortunate separation of what God has joined together. While the passages in Mark and Matthew present marriage as an inviolable contract, nothing is said about its goodness, about love and commitment, the personal and social worthiness of having children, or about the value of the family. Although Joseph (along with Mary) provides a good example of being a loving and caring father and husband while Jesus is a young child, soon he disappears from the narratives. Only Mary is left, and in two of the three instances in which she appears in the Gospels prior to Jesus's crucifixion, she is ignored by her son.

It is puzzling, however, that despite Jesus's concern with divorce and adultery as possible causes of sin, in the only two instances in which he confronts adulterous women, he does not condemn them (Jn 4:16-18, 8:3-5). These passages suggest that

Jesus's understanding of sinful humanity leads him to forego Mosaic Law that called for death by stoning. Nonetheless, while he is more forgiving about adultery, he is unbending when it comes to marriage or divorce. Thus, given his limited teachings on sexuality (ranked as less and least significant in the content analysis results), it is not surprising that gay behavior finds no space in the Gospels.

Is There an Alternative Christian Approach?
If marriage can take place only between a man and a woman, where does that leave gay people? Despite obvious differences in behavior, gays have similar sexual desires as heterosexuals; the same longings to be socially accepted as human persons, same yearnings to love and to be loved, and they seek the same equal protections and rights that are offered to heterosexuals. Moreover, it is evident that gays can be as religiously devout, honest, patriotic, and productive citizens as heterosexuals. Hence, since Jesus did not deal with the issue, what solutions may Christianity provide the worldwide gay community if it appears that the only difference lies in their sexual orientation?

It must be understood that neither science nor religion have definitive explanations about the roots of gay sexual orientation. Some, without sound empirical evidence, suggest that sexual orientation is a matter of personal choice; others, relying on solid scientifically peer-reviewed studies, indicate that gay behavior might not be a simple matter of personal preference, although they cannot account for what causes this behavior or for its historical origins.[6] Since gay sexual behavior has existed for a long time, given what has been said so far, the LGBTQ community awaits an answer from the Christian faith. Conditions around the world seem to be demanding an answer too, as gay people are being persecuted, killed, and threatened with imprisonment.[7] Currently, the world is divided over this issue, there being *greater acceptance in more secular and affluent countries* and far less in Africa, Asia, and the Middle East.[8] The number of countries throughout the world granting legal recognition to same-sex marriages is increasing.[9] Meanwhile, in the United States, major religious denominations are sorely divided over the issue.[10]

It is highly unlikely that continuous prayers, novenas, or traditional exorcism might prove effective in changing gay behavior. It is also humanly understandable that many people tend to dislike what seems unnatural to them. But what if what people dislike is not anyone's fault? Should the LGBTQ community be treated as modern lepers? Should they be forcefully sent into isolation, imprisoned for violating God's design, subjected to shame to force them back 'into the closet,' mandated to undergo so-called conversion therapy to modify gay behavior, electroshocks, or implantation of hormones or cells to reverse their sexual orientation? Or how about considering more advanced methods of eugenics? Granted, these are radical propositions that most people may not find palatable; but are there reasonable alternatives? Could Jesus condemn gay people to eternal damnation without knowing how or why it occurs? We know of people that suffer physical and mental disabilities or deformities, yet they are allowed to marry, provided their partners are of the "proper" sex. Would it be appropriate to ask gays what they might not be able to deliver? What would Jesus do? We do not know because Jesus does not say, but it would seem highly unlikely that he would resort to any of the above practices.

Christians understand that God forbids gay behavior in the Old Testament; Paul does too, in the New Testament, and so do the Church Fathers. The question is, why does Jesus fail to mention this prohibition, in which case we may want to ask what motivates Paul to go further than Jesus? Possibly, Jesus never had the opportunity to meet gay people to either scold, forgive, or heal them. Moreover, there are no lapses in the Gospels regarding adultery, killing, selfishness, theft, denial of faith, or hypocrisy. Perhaps Jesus spoke about same-sex behavior, but not loud enough for oral tradition to incorporate the issue in the texts. While we could add a myriad of possibilities, Christians face two alternatives: either the faith and its followers continue to foment harassment and persecution of gay people because they dislike how they behave (it is not as if they can turn their internal gay switch off), or they may try to understand, adapt, and tolerate differences, despite their irritation, fear, and anger. Continued condemnation of gay people would provoke increased hatred and violence, none of which are considered Christian values.[11] Ironically, gay people belong to an exclusive club they would rather not be a part of--those that Jesus includes in the Beatitudes who on account of being persecuted and discriminated will be rewarded in heaven.

What emerges from this picture is that, according to Christian theology, gay people are human beings created by God and redeemed by Jesus. The difficulty in dealing with this issue is that opposition to social recognition and acceptance of gays as human beings that deserve the rights given to heterosexuals is being driven by religious conviction as well as by social phobia and hatred, the product of cultural conditioning.

The issue of gay rights, however, is gaining acceptance among heterosexuals motivated by a desire to make gay people part of God's creation. After disregarding God's rules in the Old Testament and Paul's views, some mainstream Christian denominations, non-Christians, and non-religious people, inspired by their sense of humanity are leading the struggle for gay rights. Other Christian denominations that oppose same-sex marriage tend to be supportive of civil rights, including civil unions.[12] If the mission succeeds, could it be that Satan is winning the culture war, or that, as Jesus once said, the Holy Spirit blows where it wills?

Notes:
1. In writing this section I have had to carefully navigate through the maze of new terms used to deal with the issue of gay rights. I realize that the term *homosexual* has been used in the past in a derogatory fashion and have sought to avoid it except when I am extracting the term as it is discussed in a publication. Neither English dictionaries nor the thesauruses have been updated regarding proper terminology. It is understood in this work that gay sexuality, for sake of simplicity, refers to lesbian, bisexual, and transgender persons as expressed through the acronym LGBTQ.
2. *Ancient Greece and Rome have often been invoked as models of advanced civilizations that accorded same-gender relations considerably higher status and freedom of display than most subsequent Western societies did until very recently*, writes Thomas K. Hubbard (ed.) in his Preface. *Homosexuality in Greece and Rome: A Sourcebook of Basic Documents*, First Edition, (Berkeley: University of California Press, 2003); he argues, however, that acceptance did not mean there were no disagreements among writers,

orators, artists, poets, and philosophers regarding the issue. His book discusses each period followed by actual documents that were written at the time, containing depictions of art expressing gay behavior, including pederasty (accessed August 21, 2020).

3. Craig A. Williams, *Roman Homosexuality: Second Edition,* (Oxford: Oxford University Press, 2010), p 307, note 34.

4. Ibid., p 393, note 182.

5. See footnote 2, Sinful Sexuality category.

6. If sexual orientation were to be a matter of personal choice, heterosexual people could easily choose to become gay, however, it does not seem to happen. The question of sexual orientation has been the subject of numerous scientific studies. Among the most recent ones regarding the historical data is, Julien Barthes, Pierre-André Crochet, and Michel Raymond, "Male Homosexual Preference: Where, When, Why?" *PLos One,* August 12, 2015, https://www.ncbi.nlm.nih.gov/pmc/articles/PMC4534200/ (accessed January 29, 2020); another study, this one attesting to the non-existence of a 'gay gene,' was led by Andrea Ganna, a geneticist at the Broad Institute of MIT and Harvard in Cambridge, Massachusetts. Jonathan Lambert, No 'gay gene': Massive study homes in on genetic basis of human sexuality," August 29, 2019, https://www.nature.com/articles/d41586-019-02585-6 (accessed January 29, 2020). Neither the Catholic Church's Pontifical Academy of Science nor its Pontifical Academy of Social Sciences has issued scientifically-peer reviewed conclusions on the issue.

7. Aengus Carroll, "State-Sponsored Homophobia: a World Survey of Sexual Orientation Laws: Criminalization, Protection, and Recognition," 11th ed., October 2016, International Lesbian, Gay, Bisexual, Trans and Intersex Association, https://ilga.org/downloads/02_ILGA_State_Sponsored_Homophobia_2016_ENG_WEB_150516.pdf (accessed January 29, 2020).

8. *The Global Divide on Homosexuality*, Pew Research Center, June 4, 2013, pewresearch.org/global/2013/06/04/the-global-divide-on-homosexuality/ (accessed January 29, 2020).

9. *Same-Sex Marriage Around the World,* Pew Research Center, October 28, 2019, https://www.pewforum.org/fact-sheet/gay-marriage-around-the-world/ (accessed January 29, 2020).

10. David Masci, Michael Lipka, "Where Christian churches, other religions stand on gay marriage," Pew Research Center, Fact Tank, December 21, 2015, https://www.pewresearch.org/fact-tank/2015/12/21/where-christian-churches-stand-on-gay-marriage/ (accessed January 29, 2020).

11. Some people believe that Satan is behind the rise of homosexuality, and link the threatening advance of Islam too, to the spread of homosexuality. Steve Jalsevac, "MUST VIEW: Peter Kreeft on the simultaneous rise of homosexuality and Islam," November 30, 2018, www.lifesitenews.com/blogs/must-view-peter-kreeft-on-the-simultaneous-rise-of-homosexuality-and-islam (accessed January 29, 2020).

12 In 2020 Pope Francis indicated that while the Catholic doctrine regarding same-sex behavior as sinful continues to be upheld, he favors legalizing civil unions for the sake of gays being able to enjoy equal rights protections. Chico Harlan, Michelle Boorstein, Sarah Pulliam Bailey, "Pope Francis calls for civil union laws for same-sex couples," *The Washington Post,* Oct 21, 2020, www.washingtonpost.com/world/europe/pope-francis-civil-unions/2020/10/21/805a601c-139e-11eb-a258-614acf2b906d_story.html (accessed November 11, 2020). Although his words seemed to raise eyebrows and concern throughout the Christian world, already he had gone even further on his visit to the United States in 2015. In full view of television cameras inside the Vatican Embassy in Washington, DC, he embraced a long-time friend who is gay as well as his partner. The moment, transmitted throughout the world later, was as close a papal blessing as a pope could offer since it visually changed the optics about the issue.

Feminism

Feminism as a social and political movement concerns discussion about the proper place of women in society and the rights they deserve. It is a recent phenomenon in Western history, despite bursts of activism at the turn of the twentieth century. The movement precedes the gay movement, becoming prominent in the early to middle 1960s. Feminism appears to have been retarded, as was the case with the gay movement, by strong Christian and non-Christian religious opposition, and by a male-propelled secular backlash, the product of a long-lasting patriarchal world society. Feminism has raised relevant questions regarding the cause of women's true worth, to the point that leaders of all Christian denominations have been forced to confront, and in many cases, accept its main tenets.

At the heart of the discussion is whether feminism poses positive or negative religious and social outcomes. The answer depends on the human lenses used to judge the changes it has brought to society. World cultures for the most part have been patriarchally structured since late prehistoric times. Although biological differences likely played a role in establishing patriarchal societies, there seem to be no scientifically peer-reviewed studies (that I know of) indicating that men's cultural predominance is biologically (genetically) dictated. Rather, patriarchally-established structures appear to have created ethos, mores, and a cultural system of values throughout history that have reinforced its continued existence.

The question of whether patriarchalism should continue to prevail is probably a moot issue. World cultures are undergoing deep transformations that may not be easily reversed, although we do not know what the outcome will be hundreds of years from now. Challenging patriarchalism means that traditional roles that have been socially dictated to women are now being probed. Although the role of women in overseeing the household and in raising children is noble and dignified, the question being asked by feminism is, can they do more? Can women partake in roles traditionally reserved to men, presuming they have the wherewithal to do them as efficiently and effectively as men, if not better? Is it possible that women's maternal instincts (and their household and child-rearing experiences) may lead to less warfare and to increased political and economic stability than men's predispositions have demonstrated? Or do the disruptions brought about by feminism, e.g., male insecurity, gender discrimination, social and personal depression, family break-ups, single parenting, abortion, questions over gender identity, and issues concerning the wellbeing of children, among others, far outweigh addressing the issue?

Among the most influential factors delaying the rise of feminism, has been a strong Judeo-Christian patriarchal tradition that fostered a culture throughout centuries that was inimical to the contributions that women would bring to society. Probably being the most read book in history,[1] it would appear that the Bible has been influential in the permanence of this cultural system.

Biblical Judaism initially seems to have contributed to dictating the role of women and men in society. According to Genesis, and following Adam's and Eve's disobedience, God decided that women would bear children in pain (and supposedly bear the obligation to raise them). Women were to become man's object for sexual gratification too while being subjected to his authority (Gen 3:16) while men would have to do arduous work for a living throughout their entire lives (Gen 3:17-19).

Culturally speaking, God's punishment initiated the outcome of the division of labor from its beginnings in Judea and its expansion throughout Europe, and the North American continents. Other religions, e.g., Judaism, Islam, and Hinduism, that stress patriarchalism also have played a significant role in perpetuating this system.

Interestingly, Jesus not only has little to say about these conditions; tacitly, he appears to affirm them.

Paul, however, goes beyond Jesus, dictating that it would be righteous for Christians to abide by God's dictate in Genesis, so he proposes a series of recommendations regarding women's conduct, none of which appear dictated by Jesus in the Gospels. Although Paul acknowledges their worth as he praises a group of women for their laborious work on behalf of Christ (Rom 16) and maintains that in Christ there is no longer male or female (Gal 3:28), theological parity does not necessarily translate into temporal equality in some of Paul's letters. He dictates how women ought to dress, *with modesty and self-control, not with braided hairstyles and gold ornaments, or pearls, or expensive clothes*; they must receive instruction from men while remaining in silence, and without ever permitting a woman to have authority over a man. After all, man is formed first, then woman; and it was the woman who was responsible for Original Sin, not man. However, motherhood, he adds, would save her if she perseveres in faith and love, and with self-control (1 Tim 2:9-15). Inside the church, Paul says that women are to remain silent; *they are not allowed to speak, but should be subordinate, as even the law says. But if they want to learn anything, they should ask their husbands at home. For it is improper for a woman to speak in the church* (1 Cor 14:34-35). They must be subordinate to their husbands in everything, namely because, *as is proper in the Lord*, the husband *is head of his wife* (Col 3-18, Eph 5:22-24).

Such opposite views have elicited scholarly discussions inquiring which sayings may be attributed to Paul and which ones might have been written by someone else and inserted in his letters.[2] However, from the standpoints of moral conduct and a literal interpretation of what constitutes divine revelation, this line of thinking is immaterial insofar as Paul's letters have the canonical imprimatur of all major Christian denominations. In terms of space (sp) and the number of passages (p), Paul's passages on the subordination of women to men outrank their equality. Quantifying Paul's views does not signify that one view prevails over the other as much as it confuses. However, it is a historical fact that passages relating to women's secondary status within the Christian churches and in society have withstood the test of time. This is not to say that the Christian interpretation of the role of women has been the only contributing element to their unequal treatment, only that given the influence of Christianity, divine revelation has played a significant role in predisposing cultural subordination of women to men.

Since the Gospels were written decades after Paul's letters, and not knowing the extent of their influence in the writings of the Gospels, it should not be surprising that women play a less significant role than men in the Gospels, notwithstanding several events that denote the importance of women. For example, Mary and Elizabeth conceive by divine will, thereby reversing the standing of women vis-à-vis the account in Genesis; in Mary's case the divine male now is born of woman, and so does John the Baptist, Jesus's precursor. In theological terms, these events enhance the importance of women in the supernatural redemptive process. Moreover, the role of nurturing the Son of God enhances Mary's image. And, judging by the number of times her name shows up in the texts (second only to Mary), Mary Magdalene's role suggests that her relationship with Jesus may have been far more significant than what the Gospels detail (without necessarily suggesting intimate relations).

Nonetheless, a tally of the words *man/men, woman/women* in the Bible, indicates that the Judeo-Christian biblical history is male-dominated. Without relying on pronouns, the count in the Old Testament for men is 2149xt and 523xt for women. In the New Testament, the words *man/men* appear 732xt while *woman/women* occur 161xt.[3] Thus, the content analysis approach based on a simple word count, exposes and confirms the patriarchal culture and mentality that existed at the time.

There is an instance in which Jesus becomes overtly partial in favor of men; his disciples that he alone selects are all men. This action is significant. In the Catholic Church, it seems to be the primary symbolic reason that women are being denied the priesthood, even though there is nothing in the texts that explains Jesus's behavior, other than him being conditioned by the patriarchal culture in which he lived.

The texts describe Jesus's relations with women positively, even though passages in which women are the focus of attention are few. As he heals and feeds many, it is reasonable to presume that women are among the crowds. He exalts individual women for their faith (Mk 5:27-34, 7:24-30, Mt 9:20-22, 15:21-28) and their selflessness (Mk 12:41-44, 14:3-9, Lk 21:1-4, Mt 26:6-13, Jn 12:1-8). His friendship with Mary and Martha, in which Jesus allows Mary to seat *at his feet* (a disciple's posture uncharacteristic of women at the time) to listen to the teacher, suggests that he welcomes it (Lk 10:38-42).[4] Mary Magdalene's closeness to Jesus is shown following his resurrection, as he appears to her before his disciples. His forgiveness of the adulterous woman (Jn 8:3-11) constitutes one of the best teaching moments in the Gospels. The narrative about the Samaritan woman in John's Gospel illustrates the activist role of someone disliked by Jews who, following her conversation with Jesus, runs to her people to announce that she may have met the Messiah (Jn 4:28-30). And, during Jesus's crucifixion, it is significant that while the disciples disappear out of fear, a group of devoted women follow him on the road to the Calvary (Lk 23:27-29). On the other hand, passages in which Jesus appears in the company of his disciples abound; the term 'his disciples' show up 135xt in the four Gospels.[5] Additionally, a quick breakdown of miracles in which individual persons are healed indicates that narratives about men far outweigh those about women (38xt men, 12xt women).[6]

A Possible Omission

Since the Gospels are the product of an oral tradition that went over for decades before the original Gospels were written, there were elements in the life of the public Jesus whose implications the authors overlooked; or else, we would have to conclude that God did not think it was important to include additional passages while inspiring the writing of the texts. One of these elements appear in a short passage in Luke:

> *Afterward he journeyed from one town and village to another, preaching and proclaiming the good news of the kingdom of God. Accompanying him were the Twelve and some women who had been cured of evil spirits and infirmities, Mary, called Magdalene, from whom seven demons had gone out, Joanna, the wife of Herod's steward Chuza, Susanna, and many others who provided for them out of their resources* (Lk 8:1-3).

The substance of this seemingly insignificant passage lies not in the names of women that accompany Jesus and the disciples (that in itself is noteworthy) but rather in the ending phrase, *and many others who provided for them out of their resources.* Its significance lies in that Jesus not only recruits women to proclaim the good news, but that he recruits *many,* and these *many* use their own resources, something that the texts do not mention about the disciples. If many women committed their own resources to the expansion of the kingdom of God, why do the Gospels not expand on their activities? Why is the role of women minimized in the texts, particularly when Jesus is willingly ignoring patriarchalism (a deeply ingrained Judaic value) through his actions?

Centuries following Jesus's death and resurrection, it appears as if the Holy Spirit's role as the Advocate remained limited. Nothing the Fathers of the Church wrote opposed the patriarchal views in the New Testament. The cultural weight of Christian dogma, theology, and religion in reinforcing this system cannot be overlooked. It is within this religious context (that has prevailed despite secularization), that self-reflection and activism among women begin to ponder about their legitimate worth as human beings. Simply put, the Women's Movement begins to ask if there are sufficiently moral, cultural, physical, and psychological reasons that prevent them from attaining goals in their lives that men have historically denied women. As many women began to prove themselves successful in a variety of careers, e.g., government, business, the arts, sports, and other vocations, it seemed inevitable that social disruptions that characterize mass movements would occur.

Despite disruptions, women's persistence and their contributions to society in all professional fields in the last decades have led Christian hierarchies to question their traditional positions. This outcome, led in part by some mainstream Protestant denominations, has paved the way to increasing equality as society recognizes women's personal and social worth. Nonetheless, it is the leading role of secularized elements that deserve the recognition for the rights women have attained so far in society.

Notes:
1. Jennifer Polland, "The 10 Most Read Book in the World," *Business Insider,* December 27, 2012, businessinsider.com/the-top-10-most-read-books-in-the-world-infographic-2012-12 (accessed November

11, 2020); "Best-Selling Book," GuinnessWorldRecords.com, www.guinnessworldrecords.com/world-records/best-selling-book-of-non-fiction (accessed November 11, 2020).

2. Barbara E. Reid, "Women and Paul: Was Paul an egalitarian or a chauvinist?" *America,* November 10, 2008, www.americamagazine.org/issue/675/article/women-and-paul (accessed November 12, 2020).

3. *BibleGateway.com*

4. NEs' note, Luke 10:39.

5. *BibleGateway.com.*

6. Numbers may easily be extracted from within the Miracles category data online.

Abortion

Abortion has remained a polarizing issue in postmodern societies, mainly because it has been politicized at a time when the cultural influence of Christianity has slowly but steadily declined in most advanced countries while education, science, and technology have become highly valued, suggesting an upswing in the process of secularization. While abortion has become both socially acceptable and legally permissible in many countries it still faces opposition throughout the world. Most recent polls allow a panoramic view on the issue:

- In nearly all nations (96%) women are allowed to terminate their pregnancies for one or more reasons. Most permissive legislation regarding abortion (including abortion on request) exists in 58 of 196 countries, among them countries with a traditional Christian background. There are regulations, however, in many of these countries that do not allow women to terminate their pregnancies after a certain point, e.g., 20 weeks.[1]

- Major religious groups are divided worldwide regarding the permissibility of abortion.[2]

- In the United States there is both support and opposition to abortion among (and within) all religious faiths, including non-Christian faiths, agnostics, and atheists.[3]

- The vast majority of abortions occur in response to unintended pregnancies, which typically result from ineffective use or nonuse of contraceptives.[4]

- Access to safe abortion has been established as a human right by numerous international frameworks, the UN Human Rights Committee, and regional human rights courts, including the European Court of Human Rights, the Inter-American Court of Human Rights, and the African Commission on Human and Peoples' Rights. According to the UN Population Fund, addressing the unmet need for family planning would both considerably reduce maternal mortality and reduce abortion by up to 70 percent in the developing world.[5]

Abortion, the Bible, Science, and Politics

The basic biblical premise upon which abortion is opposed within Christianity is centered on the concept expressed in the *Yahwist* account of Genesis (and in Ezekiel) that God initiates human life by blowing into the man's nostrils *the breath of life* after which *man became a living being* (Gen 2:7, Ezek 37:5, 9:10). Some Fundamental

Christian denominations accept this narrative literally. Non-fundamentalists, on the other hand, do not accept a literal interpretation, although they uphold the belief that God is the author of life.[6] There are additional passages in which the Lord says to Jeremiah *before I formed you in the womb I knew you* (Jer 1:5); or where Job tells the Lord, *your hands have formed me and fashioned me* (Job 10:8-12); and in Psalms, where David says to the Lord, *for you drew me forth from the womb* (Psalm 22:10), all attesting to the view that God is the creator of human life.

In past epochs, humanity had not been able to gather sufficient scientific data to indicate when biological life began. Today, there is a clear scientific consensus that biological life originates somewhere between conception and the implantation of fertilized eggs in the mother's uterus.[7] As it pertains to abortion, what is undetermined in the biblical account is the question, when does God create human (not biological) life; is it at the moment of conception, following implantation, at any specific time throughout the gestation period, or after the birth of the baby? The answer lies at the base of the abortion debate, and although it is no longer dependent on theology or science, it seems to have profound moral and philosophical implications.

Civil laws regarding the recognition of the unborn as a *human person* vary considerably, between conception and the moment just before the baby is born. These laws have allowed abortion for various reasons: if the life of the mother is in danger, rape, incest, bodily autonomy, social taboos, physical appearance, economic reasons, or simply a desire not to have a child. The types of laws that are enacted have depended on the lobbying strength of various secular and religious groups upon state officials. These battles (as in the case of gay rights) have been acrimonious, as people subordinate their beliefs to political ideologies, bringing out into the open personal inconsistencies within their faith (Christian and non-Christian).

Abortion in the Old Testament
The issue of abortion is further complicated because the few related passages in the Bible express different views whose interpretations are not clear. For example, in Exodus, we find a law stating that if a pregnant woman suffers a miscarriage as the result of a fight between two men, the law of retaliation, i.e., an eye for an eye and a tooth for a tooth, would apply (Ex 21:22-25). Equal punishment for equal injury is similarly stated in Leviticus (Lev 24:18-21) and Deuteronomy (Deut 19:21). Interpreted literally, the accidental death of the unborn would require the deliberate injury to the guilty party's pregnant wife (presuming there is one) that conceivably may result in the death of the unborn and would constitute a deliberate abortion. The passage in Exodus indicates at the very least that a separate life exists during pregnancy and possesses a value of its own. Its significance, however, seems diminished as the law appears among other regulations demanding similar punishment for damage to animal property (Ex 21:33-36).

In Genesis, Judah, founder of the Israeli tribe of Judah, was willing to kill Tamar, his daughter-in-law, despite knowing that she was pregnant. This account, however, is merely a narrative in which God does not appear to judge Judah's intention (Gen 38). In Hosea, on the other hand, the wording suggests that because of the sins of the Israelites, God will punish them by allowing *a miscarrying womb, and dry breasts!* If they were to bear children, God *would slay the beloved of their womb* (Hos 9:14, 16). Moreover, when the Samaritans rebel against God, he threatens them, saying that *their pregnant women shall be ripped open* (Hos 14:1). In another passage, Hazael, anointed by God through Elijah as king of Syria, and Menaham, king of Northern Israel, commit these atrocities too (2 Kings 8:12, 15:16), although it is not clear that God is behind these crimes. However, God seems to reverse his views and punishes the Ammonites because *they ripped open pregnant women in Gilead, in order to extend their territory* (Am 1:13). Although the Old Testament does not provide clarity about the issue, there is no doubt that in these texts, God is capable of directing his wrath at will, particularly against those who disobey him, even if they were his favorite children, the Israelites.

Abortion in the New Testament and Beyond
As with the gay rights issue, Jesus must have been aware of the practice of abortion. Throughout ancient Greece and the Roman Empire, abortion was a contested topic. In Greece, it was morally opposed, while philosophically, both Plato and Aristotle expressed views in its favor. Generally, abortion was regarded as being in opposition to the Hippocratic Oath. Nonetheless, Soranus, a famed Greek physician in the first century CE believed that abortion could be allowed if there is danger to the life of the mother.[8] Among the Romans, the moral view on abortion was similar. But once the Stoics expressed the notion that the unborn was not considered a person until it took its first breath of life outside the woman's womb, it became more acceptable.[9]

Judaism, on the other hand, did not have a clear stance on abortion, other than the few passages outlined in the Jewish Bible.[10] Hence, for Jesus, abortion did not attain the significance it has today, a reason for which there are no references in the Gospels. Some argue that opposition to abortion is found in one instance in Paul's Epistle to the Galatians (Gal 5:20). Paul states that among the sinful works of the flesh is *sorcery,* which at the time might have related to the Greek term *pharmakeia* that alludes to the use of medicinal drugs, the suggestion being that he must have been referring to drugs that induce abortion.[11] This interpretation is questionable, however, because Paul does not clarify or define the various sins of the flesh or their relation to abortion, much less through the use of drugs.

An explicit condemnation of abortion appears for the first time in the *Didache,* a concise version of the teachings of Jesus that served as the first Christian Catechism to newcomers to the faith. Its writing dates anywhere from the end of the first century to the beginning of the second century. Chapter 2 states clearly that abortion is among the sinful activities that are to be avoided.[12] Following the *Didache,* the Early Fathers begin to speak out in opposition to abortion throughout the second and third centuries.[13] It is evident that a swift evolution of the doctrine on abortion occurs despite its absence in the New Testament. The inference can be made that, once again, the human conscience evolves without taking into account written divine revelation. This is to be expected in some instances. For example, Jesus amends God's law of retaliation (Mt 5:38-40), leaving it up to humankind to find alternative forms of punishment.[14]

Seeking a Reasonable and Humane Solution
The process of secularization, feminism, a divided Christian laity, traditionalists imbued with the spirit of Christendom, and the formation of ideologies politicizing the issue, likely account for abortion becoming a contentious religious and political issue. In the 1960s, the women's rights movement began its support for abortion through its insistence on bodily autonomy, organizing a support organization (Pro-Choice) that would appeal to religious people while omitting the term *abortion*. Its counterpart, the Pro-Life movement, tacitly then overtly, narrowed down the term *life* to opposition to abortion and engaged in the public shaming of women that favored abortion. Given that by then, Christians were supporting each movement, debates and exchanges were characterized by the absence of cordiality, charity, and most important, caring. Once the issue became polarized, profound inconsistencies within the Christian and humanist beliefs of both, the Pro-Choice and Pro-Life movements, began to appear.[15]

Religion (or God) offers little help in providing a moral or political clarification to the issue of abortion; even believers of non-Christian denominations and humanists are divided over its resolution. At the beginning of this section, it was noted that the issue of abortion revolves, not around the question of when human life begins, but when life attains personhood. Hence, a more germane question is, when does a human being become a person? Since words do matter, and communications tend to deal with semantics, we could begin by proposing a definition of what is meant by a human person. A simple definition suggests that, fundamentally, a person is a mortal human being that, given its characteristics, is different than animals. It is a being capable of abstract reasoning (regardless of whether it uses it or not) and complex behavior that no other species in the animal kingdom can equate. We may add that a person is an individual being, meaning that it is uniquely distinctive from other persons, i.e., it possesses a different genetic code from others, despite belonging to the same classification or grouping.

Ultimately, it is important to note that the term *person* is nothing but a title, a designation that we humans assign only to ourselves. This means that the definition of personhood the Stoics offered at the time was as arbitrary as that provided by the United States Supreme Court in *Roe v Wade* in 1973, or the various definition given by pro-abortion or anti-abortion groups. A reasonable conclusion is that a person is what we want it to be; to attempt to extend the argument would result simply in circular debating.

The issue of abortion has rational and emotional foundations. As with other important issues, abortion involves mindsets, i.e., established views hardened by deeply- held attitudes and beliefs. Mindsets predispose human behavior in magnet-like fashion to feel and accordingly, which is why they are difficult to change. Mindsets, however, can be modified, suggesting how the issue of abortion might evolve in the future.

The enlightened minds that founded the United States as an independent nation-state, sought *to establish a more perfect Union, establish Justice, insure domestic Tranquility, provide for the common defence, promote the general Welfare, and secure the Blessings of Liberty to ourselves and our Posterity.*[16] Previously, they had come to the conclusion that the self-evident truths that were to hold the nation together centered around the concepts that *all men are created equal, that they are endowed by their Creator with certain unalienable Rights, that among these are Life, Liberty and the pursuit of Happiness.*[17] Yet, the mindset of these judicious Founding Fathers firmly believed that men and women of African descent were not entitled to the same rights as white men and women; hence they could be enslaved because they were considered less than being inferior; they were considered physical property. This conception led to a black slave being counted as three-fifths of a white freedman under the U.S. Constitution.[18] This mindset was not limited to the United States; it prevailed among the European colonial powers too. It took a civil war, constitutional amendments, Supreme Court decisions, and a series of federal laws to overcome this way of thinking. As the slavery mindset evolved, a new one took over that led to greater (though still inadequate) equality of blacks.

Another example of a mindset change occurred as democracies began to flourish throughout the world in the nineteenth and twentieth centuries. At that time, women were ineligible to vote in elections. A mindset prevailed ultimately implying that men regarded women not to be competent enough to decide upon the affairs of their nations, largely because of their assigned household obligations. Worldwide, women gradually pushed back. In the United States there was no civil war this time; however, democracy, i.e., freedom of expression and assembly, persuaded the nation (and other countries) that the prevailing mindset was outdated and immoral (as in the case of racial slavery) because it denied equal political participation to women. The new mindset even had to overcome opinions of women who wanted to deny suffrage to themselves (anti-suffragists) because they believed that civic and religious morality demanded it, and because of their self-entitlement due to their socio-economic status.[19] As the new mindset prevailed, women today can vote as men do, and their numbers in higher public office are steadily increasing.

It may be observed that despite changes to the laws, blacks and women continue to be discriminated against politically, socially, and economically. We should expect the same to happen to gay people despite their newly acquired rights. This suggests that overturning Roe v Wade might result in fewer legal abortions, but it is likely to fuel increased resentment by the other half of the population that feels its rights being taken away. Since Roe v Wade was a judicial compromise to solve a moral and political question, i.e., the arbitrary declaration of personhood based on bodily autonomy, its reversal would turn the issue upside down. Just as Roe v Wade divided the unborn baby into three parts, reversing the decision signifies that the human worth of the unborn might be divided according to decisions by each of the fifty states.

Eventually, a new mindset will become necessary to resolve such a complex moral and political issue. The dilemma may have nothing to do with faith, religion, or theology since these cannot add any more to the discussion. Furthermore, it is unlikely that God will explicitly intervene in this issue. Hence, in abortion, the solution comes down to a question about fairness: whether women ought to have the right to control their bodies and terminate a distinct and individual life; or whether that distinct and individual life ought to be given the same right to be born that was once given to those who now favor abortion.

Notes:

1. Angelina E. Theodorou, Aleksandra Sandstrom, "How abortion is regulated around the world," Fact Tank, Pew Research Center, October 6, 2015, https://www.pewresearch.org/fact-tank/2015/10/06/how-abortion-is-regulated-around-the-world/ (accessed January 31, 2020).
2. David Masci, "Where major religious groups stand on abortion," Fact Tank, Pew Research Center, June 21, 2016, https://www.pewresearch.org/fact-tank/2016/06/21/where-major-religious-groups-stand-on-abortion/ (accessed January 31, 2020).
3. Masci, "American religious groups vary widely in their views of abortion," Fact Tank, Pew Research Center, January 22, 2018, https://www.pewresearch.org/fact-tank/2018/01/22/american-religious-groups-vary-widely-in-their-views-of-abortion/ (accessed January 31, 2020).
4. Susheela Singh, Lisa Remez, Gilda Sedgh, Lorraine Kwok, Tsuyoshi Onda, "Abortion Worldwide 2017: Uneven Progress and Unequal Access," *Guttmacher Institute*, March 2018, https://www.guttmacher.org/report/abortion-worldwide-2017# (accessed August 6, 2020).
5. Rachel B. Vogelstein, Rebecca Turkington, Abortion Law: Global Comparisons, *Council on Foreign Relations*, Updated October 28, 2019, https://www.cfr.org/article/abortion-law-global-comparisons (accessed August 6, 2020).
6. Pope John Paul II indicated that the Genesis narrative is a mythical story in the modern philosophical sense of the term, i.e., it does not mean that it is a fable, but *merely an archaic way of expressing a deeper content.* Christopher West, *The Theology of the Body Explained,* (Boston: Pauline Books and Media, 2003), p. 67. The analogy is that of a movie that is based on real events.
7. There are no peer-reviewed scientific studies concluding that human life, i.e., biological life, does not begin between conception and fertilization. "Life Begins at Fertilization," *Princeton.edu,* https://www.princeton.edu/~prolife/articles/embryoquotes2.html (accessed August 6, 2020); Maureen Condic, Ph.D., "A Scientific View of When Life Begins," *Charlotte Lozier Institute,* June 11, 2014, https://lozierinstitute.org/a-scientific-view-of-when-life-begins/ (accessed August 6, 2020).
8. W. den Boer, *Private morality in Greece and Rome: some historical aspects*, (Leiden: Leiden E. J. Brill, 1979), chapter 12, pp 272-75. Aristotle, *Politics,* Book VII, Part XVI, trans By Benjamin Jowett, The Internet Classics Archive, Classics.mit.edu., http://classics.mit.edu/Aristotle/politics.html (accessed November 12, 2020); Plato refers to the existence of abortion in his dialogue *Theaetetus* while describing the symbolic and actual role of the midwife: Plato, *Theaetetus,* trans. Benjamin Jowett, The Project Gutenberg EBook of Theaetetus, released online on November 17, 2008, http://www.gutenberg.org/cache/epub/1726/pg1726.txt (accessed October 25, 2018). On a different view, Sandra Sweeny Silver says that *abortion was practiced on a regular basis among the poor, slave, merchant and royal classes. To ancient peoples and the Romans, an abortion was amoral. There was nothing in Roman law or in the Roman heart that said, "It is wrong to kill your baby in the womb."* Sandra Sweeny Silver, "Ancient Roman Abortions & Christians," *Early Church History, earlychurchhistory.org/medicine/ancient-roman-abortions-christians/* (accessed October 25, 2018).
9. den Boer.
10. "Issues in Jewish Ethics: Abortion," *Jewish Virtual Library,* https://jewishvirtuallibrary.org/abortion-in-judaism (accessed August 7, 2020).

11. Joe Kral, "Dear Whoopi Goldberg: What the Bible Has to Say about Abortion," *Truth and Charity Forum.org.*, academia.edu/16998237/What_the_Bible_Has_to_Say_About_Abortion (accessed January 31, 2020).

12. *You shall not commit murder, you shall not commit adultery, you shall not commit pederasty, you shall not commit fornication, you shall not steal, you shall not practice magic, you shall not practice witchcraft, you shall not murder a child by abortion nor kill that which is born.* In this chapter, abortion appears separate from magic and witchcraft. On the other hand, chapter 5, "The Way of Death," which lists several types of evil behavior that appear in Chapter 2, and considerably expands the list to include other sinful behavior, does not mention abortion again. *The Didache*, EarlyChristianWritings.com, various translations in English, earlychristianwritings.com/didache.html (accessed January 31, 2020).

13. Michael J. Gorman, "Abortion and the Early Church," *Ancient Faith Store*, store.ancientfaith.com/abortion-and-the-early-church-by-michael-j-gorman/ (accessed January 31, 2020).

14. NEs' note, Exodus 21:22.

15. The issue has split our understanding of human life. Those who identify as being Pro-Life regard themselves as being deeply religious (and politically conservative), which is why they fiercely oppose the termination of the life of the unborn baby. And yet, many among them tend to favor (or not oppose) preventive military conflicts (that are morally wrong by Christian standards and illegal by international law). They also tend to be less concerned about the plight of poor migrants, defamation and discrimination of minorities, or racial, economic, and political inequalities, all of which relate directly to living human beings. Those who favor the Pro-Choice position, on the other hand, including Christians and humanists, tend to identify with liberal or progressive causes that defend the dignity of living humans, including minorities, poverty, and social justice programs; they are also less eager about engaging in military conflicts that kill lives. Yet, their concern for living humans does not extend to the life of the unborn baby, basing their positions on their unwillingness to force their views upon others (despite having done so on issues involving slavery, women's suffrage, and gay rights). Interestingly, I have read about activists who defend the rights of animals more eloquently than the rights of the unborn.

16. Preamble, The Constitution of the United States: A Transcription, *National Archives*, archives.gov/founding-docs/constitution-transcript (accessed August 7, 2020).

17. Preamble, The Declaration of Independence: A Transcription, *National Archives*, https://www.archives.gov/founding-docs/declaration-transcript (accessed August 7, 2020).

18. Negro slaves were regarded either as property, particularly by southern states where slavery had become an economic institution, or as persons of lesser value for purposes of a compromise at the constitutional convention. The three-fifths clause was inserted in the U.S. Constitution, under Art 1, Sect 2. Some authors seeking to camouflage racism as being at the roots of the Declaration of Independence and the U.S. Constitution suggest that, since the terms *race* or *slavery* do not appear in either document, the argument cannot be advance that the documents were racist. David Azerrad, Ph.D., "What the Constitution Says About Race and Slavery," December 28, 2015, *The Heritage Foundation*, *https://www.heritage.org/the-constitution/commentary/what-the-constitution-really-says-about-race-and-slavery* (accessed November 18, 2020). To be sure, racism is not necessarily motivated by hatred. However, the definition, as it applied to Negroes, indicates the cultural, religious, political, and economic tolerance and legitimization of slavery on account of race. The fact that neither term appears in the documents is irrelevant and specious, since both documents while taking slavery as a given, dealt with other significant political issues. Nonetheless, both documents upheld the physical and human reality of slavery. Many of the most illustrious Founding Fathers were slave owners and did not notice, or chose not to notice, the incongruence between slave ownership and their convictions regarding human freedom. For an opposite view, Paul Finkelman, "Slavery in the United States, Persons or Property?" *Scholarship.Law.Duke.edu.*, https://scholarship.law.duke.edu/cgi/viewcontent.cgi?article=5386&context=faculty_scholarship (accessed November 18, 2020); Roy W. Copeland, "The Nomenclature of Enslaved Africans as Real Property or Chattels Personal: Legal Fiction, Judicial Interpretation, Legislative Designation, or Was a Slave a Slave by Any Other Name." Journal of Black Studies, vol. 40, no. 5, 2010, pp. 946–959. JSTOR, www.jstor.org/stable/40648615, (accessed 18 Nov. 2020).

19. *Woman does not wish to turn aside from her higher work, which is itself the end of life, to devote herself to government, which exists only that this higher work may be done. Can she not do both? No!* Lyman Abbott, "Why Women Do Not Wish the Suffrage," *The Atlantic,* September 1903 issue, https://www.theatlantic.com/magazine/archive/1903/09/why-women-do-not-wish-the-suffrage/306616/ (accessed August 8, 2020); Linton Weeks, "American Women Who Were Anti-Suffragettes," NPR, October 22, 2015, https://www.npr.org/sections/npr-history-dept/2015/10/22/450221328/american-women-who-were-anti-suffragettes (accessed August 8, 2020).

Climate Change

Climate change presents a most difficult challenge to the survival of the planet. As defined in this work, the term refers to the increasing global warming of the planet to the point whereby the changes it brings to land, air, freshwater, and oceans begin to pose an existential threat to human life if nothing is done to reverse the process. A mostly secular, non-sectarian, worldwide, scientific community has been responsible for creating awareness about climate change as an issue that has deep moral implications. Its scope would appear to be imbued with Christian teachings, namely concern for one's neighbors. Concern for the planet, however, finds little support in the Gospels. The Old Testament, nonetheless, is less reticent.

Jesus, we recall, was far more concerned about the afterlife and salvation, demonstrating a certain disdain for temporal matters, including *the world*. Somehow, his priorities overlooked God's creation that he found to be *very good* (Gen 1:31). From a biblical perspective, God's words to humankind, *be fertile and multiply; fill the earth and subdue it. Have dominion over the fish of the sea, the birds of the air, and all the living things that crawl on the earth* (Gen 1:28), imposes upon humanity the responsibility to protect God's habitat for his creatures on earth

Human mistreatment of the planet seems too real to be ignored. Not being a climatologist, I must defer to science to sound the alarm. Hence, it is important to realize that denying climate change, regardless of whether it is humanly induced or not, without incontrovertible empirical evidence is pointless. Science, a premier product of human reason, is the only process that may credibly speak about scientific matters, and the only process that may credibly be allowed to commit errors, if only because it is on that basis, i.e., research, testing, mistakes, failure, and more testing, that reliable data is accumulated, problems identified, and solutions provided. Within this framework, what appears to be irrational is to use non-science to oppose science. Such an attitude would only invite social calamities.

If it were to be proven that the planet finds itself beyond a point of no return; that there is nothing that humans can do to alter the course of climate change, the only alternative would be to adapt to its effects and await whatever consequences the process may bring. We must bear in mind, however, that a catastrophic event may truly result if we were to assume an 'every nation and human person for itself' survival scenario; fear and chaos tend to be the enemies of human sensibility and moral behavior.

So far, the consensus that climate change is mostly humanly produced, and its course probably still can be altered, is practically indisputable within the scientific community.[1] Nonetheless, there is another side to the crisis that needs to be acknowledged. The effects of global warming are the result of human endeavor that, otherwise, has sustained and improved life on the planet for centuries. This means, not that industrial and technological work must be stopped, but transformed so that humans may continue to build the earth[2] taking into account ways to overcome potential catastrophic injury to human life.

The appropriate mindset to confront climate change, however, is not yet present, although it is growing. A PEW Research Center survey indicated that *majorities in most surveyed countries say global climate change is a major threat to their nation.*[3] Non-scientific deniers (many of them Christians) have set back the agenda in the last couple of decades allowing precious time to elapse while insisting on continuing with outdated methods based on carbon emissions. It suggests, once again, that political ideologies, on both sides, have prevented solutions that may benefit present and future generations that will be responsible for reversing conditions that in many cases were willfully exacerbated. Fortunately, perhaps, several Christian and non-Christian denominations have realized the significance of climate change to humanity and are actively contributing to this endeavor.[4]

It would be hyperbolic to state (today) that climate change is the beginning of the end of time as Jesus predicted. At any time, accidental or willful nuclear warfare, a devastating pandemic, or any other unforeseen combinations of natural and human disasters could result in immediate and long-lasting ecological desolation. What tends to be overlooked is that while nuclear warfare may be avoidable, and solutions to pandemics eventually appear, there exists in climate change a point of no return beyond which damage to the environment becomes irreversible,[5] which in some cases already has happened.[6] If the climate change crisis is eventually resolved, it would be in large part due to the active participation of a common humanity (believers and non-believers) that has thrived within a secular society.

Notes:

1. National Aeronautics and Space Administration (NASA), "Climate Change: How Do We Know?" https://climate.nasa.gov/evidence/ (accessed August 15, 2020); IPCC, 2014: *Climate Change 2014: Synthesis Report. Contribution of Working Groups I, II, and III to the Fifth Assessment Report of the Intergovernmental Panel on Climate Change* [Core Writing Team, R.K. Pachauri, and L.A. Meyer (eds.)]. IPCC, Geneva, Switzerland, ipcc.ch/site/assets/uploads/2018/02/SYR_AR5_FINAL_full.pdf (accessed August 15, 2020). The Intergovernmental Panel on Climate Change was created in 1988, endorsed by the United Nations General Assembly, and tasked with providing *policymakers with regular scientific assessments on climate change, its implications and potential future risks, as well as to put forward adaptation and mitigation options.* It gathers peer-reviewed scientific studies from all over the world as the basis to formulate recommendations for all nations.

2. *Building the Earth,* by Jesuit Catholic priest Pierre Teilhard de Chardin, was among the earliest work praising the temporal human endeavor; (Wilkes-Barre: Dimension Books, 1965).

3. Moira Fagan, Christine Huang, "A look at how people around the world view climate change," Pew Research Center – Fact Tank, April 18, 2019, https://www.pewresearch.org/fact-tank/2019/04/18/a-look-at-how-people-around-the-world-view-climate-change/ (accessed August 15, 2020).

4. Yale School of the Environment, *Yale Forum on Religion and Ecology,* https://fore.yale.edu/Climate-Emergency/Climate-Change-Statements-from-World-Religions, (accessed August 15, 2020). The topic received the backing of the Catholic Church in Pope Francis' encyclical, *Laudato si'- on Care for Our Common Home,* May 2015.

5. "Only 11 (10) Years Left to Prevent Irreversible Damage from Climate Change, Speakers Warn during General Assembly High-Level Meeting," United Nations General Assembly, Seventy-Third Session, March 28, 2019, https://www.un.org/press/en/2019/ga12131.doc.htm (accessed August 15, 2020).

6. Bryan Walsh, "Antarctic Glacier Loss Is 'Unstoppable,' Study Says," *Time,* May 12, 2014, https://time.com/96173/antarctic-glacier-loss-is-unstoppable-study-says/ (accessed August 15, 2020);

(NASA), "Is it too late to prevent climate change?" https://climate.nasa.gov/faq/16/is-it-too-late-to-prevent-climate-change/ (accessed August 15, 2020).

On Secularism and Secularization

It may be argued that the process of *secularism* does not belong in this section since the categories listed are those that do not owe their origins to the Gospels. Properly speaking, although secularism has flourished in modern and postmodern times, the process is not only noticed in the Gospels; Jesus may be said to be its precursor in Christianity. Whether he was aware or not of how his teachings were going to be utilized by future generations, his refusal to engage the Jewish religious authorities when asked about paying tribute, i.e., taxes, to the Roman Emperor, along with his foundation of a separate kingdom of God, became the groundwork of the secular state. His visible objections to getting involved in temporal politics, e.g., his lack of criticism of Roman ruling or its laws, affirmed his disposition. Moreover, his recognition that God's kingdom (Jesus's kingdom) is not of this world, signified that Jesus was accepting the existence of two realms, the sacred and the profane, that would coexist until the end of time.

Yet, secularism was politically and culturally abolished in the fourth century by the catholic, i.e., Christian, Church with the support of Christian emperors. In its place, a theocracy was instituted that lasted for centuries, before its unity was fragmented by Christians themselves while arguing over their interpretations of Jesus's teachings. Throughout Christendom, pope, emperor, and monarch left hardly any space between the church and the state, since a theocracy blends the two entities into one. Anything remotely deemed secular, such as non-Christian governmental or commercial entities that attempted to wield power in opposition to the church/state institution, had their influence curtailed. The expansion of Muslim rule over vast portions of today's Spain might be considered an exception, although for nearly eight hundred years Christians were living under the authority of another theocracy.[1]

Based on the historical record, we may attribute the emergence of secularism and the concept of the secular state to ideas that begin fermenting during the seventeenth and eighteenth centuries in the minds of men like Baruch Spinoza, Thomas Hobbes, John Locke, Montesquieu, Jean Jacques Rousseau, and others. The Enlightenment, or the Age of Reason, as it is known too, rose under the shadow of a humanist Renaissance movement that during the fourteenth, fifteenth, and sixteenth centuries gradually freed itself from the spirit of Catholicism by turning toward the temporal world. There was an incipient Catholic Enlightenment at the time that supported temporal reforms, but ultimately failed during the French Revolution.[2]

Secularism, a child of the Enlightenment, advocated for the separation of church and state as a means to liberate the temporal realm from religious authorities that were opposed to the ideas of human freedom and equality. But, perhaps, secularism's greatest contribution to humanity was the concept of religious tolerance and toleration, considered anathema both by Catholicism and Protestantism following the

Reformation and the Counter-Reformation. The religious wars that ensued at the time, despite their senseless manifestation of Christian values, were deemed proper and necessary by both sides, as each was following deep religious convictions that saw the opposition as the Satanic enemy of Jesus's teachings that required its annihilation.

Religious tolerance was the Enlightenment's sensible philosophical and political invention. Although Jesus remained invisible throughout, his teachings and deeds were now being expressed in secular terms by progressive Christians, non-Christians, agnostics, and atheists, the likes of Voltaire, Diderot, Spinoza, and Hobbes, as an alternative to religious persecution and wars caused by opposing religious beliefs.[3]

Religious tolerance and its enforcement, i.e., toleration, were not meant to serve as justification or personal acceptance of opposing views, particularly if those views went against one's religious faith and their own salvation. Instead, it signified enforced coexistence for the sake of survival. The execution of laws became necessary to promote order and the continuation of civil society, despite the values that went into the concept were grounded on Christian principles, namely love of neighbor, love of enemy, forgiveness, and forbearance. Namely, for this reason, toleration is considered a religious and temporal value that is ultimately based on civil law under the principle of freedom of expression; the type of freedom that, ironically, can culminate in exacerbating one's limits on tolerance.

Religious toleration evolved slowly over time, finding in quasi-Christian men, like Montesquieu, Thomas Jefferson, and John Stuart Mill, ideas that added to the concepts of liberty, religious freedom, freedom of expression, and representative government. By the end of the eighteenth century, the secular state had been established in the United States. The First Amendment of the U.S. Constitution, forbidding the government from establishing religious preferences while safeguarding the free exercise of religion, freedom of speech, the press, and the right of people to peacefully assemble, was responsible for guaranteeing the physical survival of all Christian denominations. It formalized tolerance as a constitutional virtue. A significant consequence of the First Amendment, however, was that it led to moral relativism by allowing religious pluralism. Nonetheless, today, all Christian denominations, perhaps to their dislike, have accepted the proposition that they must work within the parameters of the secular state after recognizing that it is in their interests to do so.

As for *secularization*, the process owes its origins to the appeal and enjoyment the postmodern world provides through the marvels of science, technology, and education; a rising standard of living; massive discontent with organized religion, ironically because of the conduct of religious institutions and Christian laity that have 'underperformed' in terms of their observance of Christian values. Nonetheless, regardless that some believers consider it an evil concept, secularization has imposed a great responsibility upon Christians to salvage their faith. Whether they will succeed is difficult to answer. The disappointing behavior of Christians and the various Christian authorities throughout history, eventually brought about their division, the Enlightenment, democracy, and human progress that in turn have accelerated the cultural demise of Christianity, as Christians are slowly focusing more on temporal affairs over a heavenly kingdom. History might be the preeminent witness that Christian behavior has been a major contributor to the process of secularization. And yet, the idea that non-Christians would see Jesus reflected in Christians may have been too much to ask of sinful people. Whether humanism, science, reason, and technology might be able to provide adequate answers to humanity's most profound existential questions remains to be seen. Christians themselves, constituting one-third of the world's population certainly have not been able to accomplish Jesus's mission.

Notes:

1. Brian A. Catlos, *Kingdoms of Faith: A New History of Islamic Spain*, (New York: Basic Books Publishers, 2018).

2. Ulrich L. Lehner, *The Catholic Enlightenment: The Forgotten History of a Global Movement,* (Oxford, Oxford University Press, 2016).

3. Ironically, John Locke, considered to be among the forefathers of religious tolerance, excluded Catholics and atheists from being tolerated in his *Letter Concerning Toleration* (1689). Mark Goldie, ed., *John Locke: A Letter concerning Toleration and Other Writings,* (Indianapolis: Liberty Fund, 2010) https://oll.libertyfund.org/titles/2375 (accessed August 10, 2020).

Chapter 8 - Toward a Conclusion

The question raised at the beginning of this book, who is the public Jesus? must be answered while recurring not only to the Gospels but to history; that is to say, to empirical reasoning. The texts alone reveal that Jesus had a perplexing personality. He was both easy and difficult to comprehend, which in the end does not advance our understanding of him. He was a *sign of contradiction* in the literal sense of the term,[1] at times appearing to present teachings and act in ways that clashed with his kind demeanor. Sometimes, he seemed to understand the limitations of human behavior; at other times he appeared indifferent. While scrutinizing the Gospels the reader sees signs suggesting that he was truly a good man, a quality that even Jewish historian Josephus affirmed. He insisted on wishing to save the world from itself; a world that (at least today) seems indifferent to wanting to be saved. In that respect, perhaps Jesus was too good, or maybe even too naïve (he expected too much of us mere humans), a trait that does not speak highly of the divine.

The Gospels reveal that Jesus did not feel comfortable living in a world he seemed to disdain. Claiming to be the Son of God, he probably felt more at home with the Father. His yoke has neither been easy nor has his burden ever been light. The evidence lies in the way he dies. His teachings reflect righteousness, but also incredible incongruences; a seemingly forgiving understanding of human nature accompanied by horrific threats should we not follow his commandments. And even if humanity were to accept him, he indicated that he would still make a cosmic entrance that entails the destruction of the world.

Among Jesus's most extraordinary features was his disposition to break with much of God's teachings while claiming that he was doing the Father's will. His profile in chapter 5 best summarizes his demeanor. Jesus's supernatural mission finds no basis in the Old Testament despite apologetic contortions to show him in the texts. No other Jewish prophet would have dared to call himself Lord of the Sabbath, Son of Man, or ask his followers to eat his flesh while overriding the Father so often. Moreover, no one has expressed such an intimate relationship with God (including being part of God) or spoken so authoritatively in its name.

The quantitative results in Table 2 allow us to assess the issues that were important to Jesus at the time and the extent to which the Gospels differ from the postmodern world; likely, it is one reason that much of the texts seem irrelevant to Christians, and to an increasingly secularized society. It may be inferred from these results that if Jesus were to appear publicly today, his emphasis on issues would be completely different; not to mention that, at the very least, we would be able to record him as opposed to having to accept a dubious version of oral transmission guided by a divine hand. Otherwise, how may we explain Jesus's indifference to the positive aspects of marriage, or his lack of exposition about human sexuality, redemption, grace, the soul, baptism, his unwillingness to deal with issues such as war and peace, slavery, abortion, or human rights! A 'today Jesus' probably would be more attuned to the temporal world he appeared to deride while preaching God's kingdom.

Divested of its incongruences, contradictions, and the irrelevance of large portions of the texts, what remains of the Gospels is a beautiful and majestic story. However, what does this story tells us about Jesus? That he was a good man? He was. That he may have been a prophet? Yes, that too. That he was the Messiah the Israelites had placed their hopes on? Certainly not. That he came to save humanity? Perhaps, but we do not know how, since there is no clear reference to this type of savior in the Old Testament or the Gospels. That he is the Son of God? It is possible, but he certainly could have made it easier for humanity to believe it.

The history of Christianity illustrates that Jesus's affirmation that he defeated Satan through his resurrection does not seem to have had palpable ramifications when juxtaposed to his desire to save the world. The world still appears to be well under Satan's control. After two thousand years, two-thirds of the world's population still does not acknowledge that Jesus is the Son of God, and while Christianity seems to be increasing in poor, uneducated, and less advanced countries, it is fast becoming the symbol of a glorious historical past in the more advanced nations that gave birth to the faith. The remaining one-third of the world that is labeled as Christian is still divided within itself, and large numbers of them (judging by conditions on earth) carry the Christian tag merely as a cultural relic after being baptized. These conditions reveal that whatever Jesus claimed to have accomplished must have happened at a cosmic level, in which case humanity still awaits the implications of his triumph.

The different narratives about the same events, whose importance apologists tend to minimize, signal a weak link in the Gospels, and present a more credible scenario about how human oral transmission would have worked (even when it is alleged that memorizing details at the time was a cultural trait). The alternative would be to hold God responsible for literally guiding or inspiring a transcript of Jesus's message that includes errors and personal insertions. The various incongruences, contradictions, and bizarre teachings add to a healthy skepticism of the texts. Moreover, Jesus's decision to reveal himself to Paul, thereby allowing him through visions or inspirations to be his interpreter on fundamental doctrinal issues (as opposed to him being the teacher) considerably weakens the Gospels' credibility. Is there a sensible reason that prevented Jesus from saying what Paul said in his letters? In effect, it signifies that Paul becomes a distant and secondary source of information on Jesus. The fact that scholars today accept that various associates other than the named authors may have taken part in the writings of the texts makes it difficult to distinguish Jesus's sayings from human hands.

Despite its limitations, the Christian faith has gained billions of adepts throughout history, many of them because they have chosen to concentrate on teachings that they find righteous, and possibly many more because of Jesus's most effective incentive to accept him, the desire for eternal salvation or the fear of condemnation. Nonetheless, it is ironic (though not surprising) that despite lacking an adequate understanding of Jesus and his teachings, people still have faith; after all, millions of people with no understanding of physics still dare to fly in an airplane. There is a difference, though; we notice that most airplanes do not crash, hence there is empirical validation that allows us to have 'faith' in science. Meanwhile, not having other alternatives, Christianity has to rely on having 'faith in faith.'

In the postmodern world, the advance of secularization is a setback to Jesus's eschatological teachings, and it is forcing Christianity to come to terms with the temporal world (as it seems to be doing). Nonetheless, its inability to persuade other faiths and its continued preference for disunity has further eroded its faculty to permeate social structures and overcome perceived sinfulness in them. Although Jesus promised to send his replacement to remind the world about God's truth, it appears as if Christians and non-Christians have become impervious to the whispering of the Advocate. As a result, in an increasingly secularized age, humankind has no choice but to institute basic moral norms to confront the issues that beset it. On the other hand, we do not know if such are the circumstances that God has chosen at this time.

In the end, it may be asserted that secularism is an inevitable asset to the Christian faith (given the times in which we live) since at least it allows it to manifest itself publicly. Moreover, the so-called pernicious effects of secularization present a challenge that can only be met by Christians themselves should they decide to confront it through their actions. This means that Christianity will have to survive within a temporal world permeated by moral relativism and offer proof that its teachings provide better possibilities for peace, kindness, and justice than any other philosophies. After all, those critics of secularization cannot continue to blame the process itself while pretending that it has nothing to do with how Christians behave.

Living in an age characterized by various freedoms and by secularism has encouraged humanity to proceed on its own at elaborating moral philosophies independent of Christian teachings. Jesus's loss of cultural influence, a consequence of Christians defaulting to pagan values (in the classic Roman interpretation), partially accounts for this effort, although it cannot be denied that education, the sciences, and technology, have led to the expansion of secularization, much to the irritation of some church authorities. Nonetheless, any attempt to counter secularization by adopting instead a traditionalist mindset that finds solace in the past is folly. Unless the divine intervenes, the world will continue its course, and those who stand in its way will find in their lament the senselessness of their behavior.

Even in its most basic formulation, the world has remained the same over its more than four thousand years of 'civilized' existence. Good and evil are still the major contenders. The Christian version of the good continues to be selfless love, caring for others, peace, justice, restraining impulsive individualistic and authoritarian tendencies, and a major emphasis on duty and respect toward the rights and dignity of others. Its opponent, evil, is characterized by egotism, greed, selfishness, disregard for others, raw ambition for power, and the individual desire to survive at the expense of others. The crisis Christianity faces becomes more acute because the lines between good and evil have become blurred to the point where Christians see evil among themselves. In a postmodern secular society, it appears that self-righteousness and pride have permeated Christianity. Ironically, these were the same vices that Jesus claimed to have prevented the Israelites from discerning the real God.

Fear too seems to be hindering the distinctive paths that humankind looks for nowadays. Amid a more complex yet organized world, uncertainty prevails, leading to increased levels of social apprehension and personal stress. Older generations, resentful and longing for the way they were raised, object to a new enemy, diversity, which in turn is spurring a conflict between exclusiveness and inclusiveness. Nativism has given way to a pernicious nationalism that threatens to destroy the world's social fabric, while lack of foresight among the world's political leaders seems to be leading to a fateful arms race and power struggles as only alternatives.

It is still possible, although not easy, to extract a human understanding of the public Jesus from the Gospels. Perhaps, my friend's advice to ignore most of the Gospels and concentrate on only a few of Jesus's words is correct. Nonetheless, how can we be sure that even humans did not write those words? Without an adequate understanding of the texts, it is not surprising that Christians seem confused and divided between orthodoxy and orthopraxis that in the end leads them to believe and behave in any manner they choose. Literally understood, it is more realistic to perceive the public Jesus as a supernatural being (or someone detached from earthly life) who tells humankind how to attain eternal salvation, even if his teachings seem not to be aligned with human nature at times. Although Jesus is supposed to be a source of joy, such a joy refers mostly to what comes at the end of time; otherwise, it is difficult to find joy in the Beatitudes, or his yoke and his burden. His various titles seem to confuse more than enlighten our understanding of him. His mission (or missions) seems filled with contradictions. It is no wonder that he disappointed the Jewish people who were waiting for someone more in line with their expectations. Without offering any explanations he extends the possibility of salvation to Gentiles despite his disparaging comments about them. And, it is Paul, not Jesus, who has to enlighten the disciples.

The observations in this work tend to confirm the conclusions noted by a group of knowledgeable scholars about the Bible, namely, that its interpretation is often difficult to understand. Such statements ought to tell us something about God. Exactly what, I do not know. I leave that part to the experts who likely will continue to be divided over the meaning of Jesus's teachings. Nonetheless, continuing to act as if we understand God, accepting a faith whose elaboration appears to be humanly contaminated, does not make sense. Nor does it make sense to dismiss it altogether. It is far more difficult (at least to me) to accept the proposition that creation finds its origins in nothingness than in its counterpart, a superior something that wishes to remain anonymous and whose existence is, for practical purposes, seemingly inconsequential despite its possible concealed significance.

In the end, it is puzzling how God benefits by remaining mysterious and not communicating more effectively with human beings. If God rules human conduct, and it is important for him to convey that he is the Lord, transparency is vital. Presuming that understanding and knowing are basic elements of human behavior, it is difficult to behave righteously if, amid relativism, humankind must decide for itself what is right and wrong. Thus, it appears that God's mysterious ways, far from contributing to righteousness, creates confusion and moral relativism.

Such confusion may be observed today in the understanding gap that prevails within the Christian faith. Even after taking into account inordinately high levels of incongruous statements found in the texts, if there is an incontrovertible result in this work, is that the highest category regarding what the Gospels are about is *Righteousness* or appropriate moral behavior in the eyes of God. Today, polarization is taking place among Christian hierarchies and the laity over questions regarding what is morally right and what is morally wrong. This attempt to define moral righteousness has given way to the struggle that peoples, governments, and institutions are waging in the temporal world over the values of the Kingdom of God. Some, however, depict this struggle as implying that the kingdom of this world is more important than the Kingdom of God; that dogma, the sacraments, and ministry are being set aside allowing polarization to occur on account of trivial political-ideological issues.[2] It appears that church authorities are not being cognizant that these ideologies are but a symptom of the real problem: the values of the Kingdom of God are being fought within the confines of the kingdom of this world. At stake are issues that find their roots in Jesus's teachings, in addition to other issues that humankind is elevating to Gospel-like levels of significance.

A Final Caveat

Once again, it must be noted that not everything that Jesus said and did is likely compiled in the texts. The Gospels are only a summary of what God and/or its human authors considered to be the most significant aspects that were to be passed along through oral tradition and/or direct revelation. It must be remembered that there is an enormous biographical gap in Jesus's life. We do not know what he does prior to beginning his public life, including the events that shape his adolescence and his early and middle adulthood life, or what prompts him to begin teaching about repentance and the kingdom of God or his tirades against the religious authorities. This means that, historically speaking, we do not know if omissions in words and deeds could have shaped the Christian faith differently. The issue, however, is moot since there is nothing we can add unless new information is unearthed or a more emphatic (public) revelation takes place.

Notes:
1. Pope John Paul II wrote a book titled *Sign of Contradiction* referring to Jesus as someone who encountered opposition and hostility despite being a holy man.   Karol Wojtyla, *Sign of Contradiction*, (New York: Seabury Press, 1979).
2. Inés San Martín, "Papal Preacher says divisions have 'wounded' Catholic Church,' *Crux*, April 2, 2021,https://cruxnow.com/vatican/2021/04/papal-preacher-says-divisions-have-wounded-catholic-church/ (accessed April 10, 2021). The article refers to words enunciated by Catholic Cardinal Raniero Cantalamessa on Good Friday, 2021. The cardinal expressed views indicating that the Second Vatican Council *entrusted laypeople with the task of translating the social, economic, and political implications of the Gospel into practice in different situations,* perhaps forgetting that the hierarchy is required to lead the flock instead of simply providing a blank check to the laity. The cardinal appears to be correct, however, in his observation that the hierarchy is also divided on this issue.

Appendix A – Implementing Content Analysis in This Work

Outside of academic circles, content analysis is not widely known, although it is often used in an oversimplified manner in political journalism and even in articles on religion. Hopefully, this section might make it easier for the average reader to understand how it is used in this work.

Quantifying the data begins by identifying diverse categories that are intrinsic to the Christian faith, such as love, sin, salvation, hell, poverty, justice, redemption, marriage, or faith, and other (invisible) categories that are not addressed in the texts that, nonetheless, are important to Christianity. Overall, this work identifies over one hundred categories that together may provide an outlook of how Christianity has evolved, either by ignoring certain of Jesus's teachings, continuing to affirm others, or by formulating new ones.

The next step is to rummage through the texts and identify and group passages according to each category. Afterward, each category is tallied and ranked according to the number of times it is referenced in the texts. There are three types of ranking, i.e., three distinctive levels of examining the texts: (1) the number of times that words or terms associated with each category appear in the texts, labeled (xt); (2) the number of passages that relate to a category, expressed as (p); and (3) the total space that each category occupies in the Gospels, calculated by the number of lines, and indicated by (sp). Finally, their overall significance is established according to the weighted sum of each ranking mode. The results appear in Table 2.

Additionally, each category is examined seeking to infer similarities, nuances, incongruences, and the relevance each may have for Christianity in postmodern times, by allowing passages to speak by themselves. By grouping passages from the Gospels according to specific categories (rather than to simply read throughout the texts or study certain passages isolated from others), the reader will be able to view the public Jesus from different perspectives. These inferences, which constitute the bulk of the reading material, may reveal traces of the mental and emotional dispositions of the authors of the Gospels, and about the man many call the Son of God that otherwise may remain obscure. We may even find concepts, rules, and moral norms that have failed the test of time and consequently have been disregarded or ignored by believers today. Ultimately, an examination of the results of this approach will seek to find out the degree of relevance of the Gospels in a highly secularized temporal world characterized by an unlimited diversity of competing norms, values, ideologies, and philosophies. Below, I describe the steps I have taken in organizing the data and explain both the quantitative and the qualitative aspects of the work. The raw data used to quantify the results appear online at www.RicardoPlanas.com/notes.

Preparing the Framework for Quantitative Analysis
I began by acquainting myself with all four Gospels through a thorough reading without paying attention to details. Along the way I devised the following steps:

- identified initial terms, words, or concepts that led to the selection of potential categories to be examined.
- identified other categories by re-reading the texts to detect concealed terms I believed existed and were relevant to the Christian doctrine.
- broke down major topics into manageable ones that would widen the scope of both the quantitative and qualitative portions of the method.
- identified categories that were going to be tallied and ranked. Because of their significance to the reader, I decided to treat sub-categories as independent categories fully aware of their overall minor role once they were disaggregated. Categories were selected subjectively under the assumption that each one is relevant to the Christian doctrine.
- defined the scope of the categories by describing the methodological approach of each one, i.e., specific words/terms chosen and how they were to be tallied.
- identified and selected three levels of analysis: totals for the number of words/terms, number of passages, and space allocated to each category by author.
- coded selected passages under each category, highlighting tallied words/terms, passages, and allocated space, by author, then adding the totals.
- tallied number of words (xt), number of passages (p), and space of each passage (sp) and ranked each one accordingly per author. Due to its length, this information is posted online.
- re-counted totals in each category by author for possible errors; did this several times.
- re-examined the content of each category to eliminate (when possible) excess passage space.
- selected a method, i.e., 'leveling the playing field,' to prevent numerical disparities due to the nature of each level of analysis. This method is explained below.

- posted a final tally according to each author and added the three levels of analysis to come up with three weighted totals. This information is also posted online.

- the approach used to quantify Table 1, Profile Database of Jesus based on titles accorded to him in the Gospels, were limited to xt or the number of times each title would show up. Each title is broken down according to how others see Jesus, and how Jesus sees himself. This approach is explained in the body of this work.

- grouped categories in Table 2 according to xt, p, and sp follow, but they are not ranked numerically. Once weighed, the three values, xt, p, and sp are added together. It is based on these totals that the categories are finally ranked in Table 2.

- ranked each category according to their overall scores and label a level of significance according to their final ranking. Their designation in terms of significance is subjective, i.e., based on their numerical separation from each other, which seemed reasonable as opposed to using more complicated mathematical approaches such as expressing mean, median, and mode, or cluster analysis that might have confused the reader. A separate term, *contemporary significant categories*, was reserved for issues that arose at a later time and have minimal if any connections with the Gospels, although their individual significance was not quantified in Table 2.

Steps Undertaken to Do the Qualitative Analysis:

- drew inferences from the content of each category by establishing and discussing (when relevant) the category's relation to the Old Testament, including (when pertinent) word count and contrasting them among the authors.

- examined the usage of each category in the Gospels, seeking to find conformity, incongruence, and/or possible contradictions with other passages or categories; examined consequences for Christianity.

- examined each category's relevance considering contemporary secular norms and values that prevail today and the role they may play within a secularized world and with future generations of Christians and non-Christians.

- discussed the background of each of the Contemporary Significant Categories as major contributions by secularized and non-sectarian elements.

Quantifying the Data

There are various levels of measurement and explanation for each category; these levels are akin to looking at an object from different angles. Each level presents its own characteristics and limitations, but together they provide a more objective understanding of the texts. Three levels of analysis were selected and tallied:

1) Identifying categories according to xt, signifying the number of times a word, term, or concept appears in the texts. This is done for each of the Gospels, and a total is then recorded for all four texts. Quantitatively speaking, this is the easiest and more accurate level of explanation. For example, selecting "salvation" as a term, the researcher would locate the number of times the word occurs within the texts. This is a simple and more accurate procedure once the texts have been transformed into a Word or Pages document, or any other program with a Search function. The researcher would scan the texts looking for specific or related words that relate to each category and highlight them. The search would focus on the term's roots (prefixes and suffixes); related synonyms if applicable; on other terms whose definitions express a close relation to the main term; and on its opposites (when relevant) as evidence that the category does exist.

For example, hypothesizing that the word *love* is central to Christianity, it is then identified as a primary category. There are, nonetheless, additional terms that describe Christian love, such as mercy, compassion, forgiveness, and others. The above-described procedure is then followed for each of these terms. Tallying the term love within each Gospel and adding their totals to its related terms would show how significant the Love category is relative to others and relative to the texts themselves.

2) Identifying concealed categories and label them as p, indicating the number of passages that relate to a category. Despite how laborious the search for words might be, the method is suitable for analyzing only certain categories that are obvious to the naked eye (the PC Search function). Other categories require a methodological twist. As an example, the term divine providence does not appear in any of the Gospels. This term refers to specific examples Jesus provided to describe God's intervention in the lives of humans. In this case, the researcher would have to scrutinize the document searching for passages that relate to our understanding of divine providence. No simple PC program would be of help in searching for this category. Extensive knowledge of the scriptures would be useful in identifying relevant passages. Not being able to vouch for this knowledge, it is conceivable I may have omitted certain passages. Nonetheless, I can safely predict that the number of passages that may have been left out would affect only the particular category and to a small degree but would not invalidate its significance or the overall results when placed on a ranking scale.

The same approach is used to unearth categories that are hardly mentioned in the texts, such as, justice, power, sexuality, attributions of divinity, anger, temporal world, that otherwise would remain ignored and left unexplained. Proceeding in this manner provides us with a quantitative measure of how significant these less visible categories were to the authors. Additionally, it allows us to qualitatively analyze their meaning and relevance for a postmodern mindset conditioned and educated under secular forces (tolerance and diversity of beliefs), and by a healthy and critical skepticism of human events.

Once again, totals by p would be ranked for each Gospel according to the number of times these concealed or less visible categories appear in the texts. Tallying categories according to the number of passages is simply an approach to viewing it from a different angle and has as much empirical validity as identifying terms and concepts by xt. In some cases, xt and p coincide simply because there is no other alternative than to treat a passage as a single xt.

3) Identifying space allocated to each category, sp, indicating the amount of space each author devoted to a category. Quantifying space is a different, yet meaningful level of explanation. It requires bridging the gap between what can be quantitatively measured and what can be qualitatively apprehended. This approach entails deciding how much of a passage ought to be accorded to a specific category. Inevitably, it brings me to what I would call subjective objectivism—using one's judgment to decide what to retain in a passage and what to leave out. Although personal judgment may affect the results of the specific category one way or another, since space decisions are a matter of small chunks of the text, the overall reliability of the results will likely be sustained, particularly after leveling the playing field. The aim is to measure space by providing as little as necessary for the reader to understand the passage. Sometimes, however, entire passages are necessary; for example, when dealing with the category of miracles and parables.

This approach is particularly relevant since the authors may have quoted Jesus at length on a specific term while mentioning it once or twice. For example, the term power appears infrequently in the Gospels, and yet numerous passages relate to the term. Once the category is defined and relevant passages identified, they are tallied within each of the Gospels, added, and ranked. Quantifying sp would be as significant as tallying xt and p, if done judiciously.

Tallying sp is straightforward. Each Gospel is pasted in a Word program without spaces separating paragraphs from each other in print layout format with 0 to 7" margins. All sentences are linked together in Calibri font, size 11, without subtitles, as if each Gospel constitutes one lengthy paragraph. Each line has been arbitrarily assessed two points (it could have been 5 or 10 points). If the end of a passage goes beyond half the line (3.5 inches more or less as measured by Word), it counts as a complete line and given two points, otherwise, it does not. Applying this procedure throughout the entire work allows for the overall results to average themselves out. The number in red or blue xt that appears at the end of each tallied passage (online) constitutes an approximation of sp or space allocated to the passage. Once the results of each category within the individual Gospel are identified, they are added into a single total, and ranked.

In a few instances, I added a sensible dimension. When dealing with Pharisees, Jewish people, and Gentiles, I categorized the terms as positive, negative, or neutral to indicate the tone in which the authors referred to them to find out if there were veiled or transparent traces of animosity or even the possibility of anti-Semitism in the texts.

In addition to tallying specific words, there are passages, such as parables, that may fit more than one category. In these cases, the same parable may be coded under various categories, e.g., sin, salvation, condemnation, or forgiveness, and approximately the same space is assigned to every single one.

Leveling the Playing Field

Categories are tallied according to three levels of analysis: xt, p, and sp. This may require assigning weight to each one because each approach recognizes the texts differently. Xt presents reliable empirical results that are indisputable. At times, however, it will be noticed that tallying passages (p) offer valid empirical results; a tallied p indicates that a passage has been identified as relating to a specific category and is given a value of 1. Thus, a category may include 10 individual passages related to it, and p will be tallied as 10. There may be instances, for example when dealing with Miracles, Justice, Parables, or Predestination, in which no words match the category even though there are several passages relating to the term. In these cases, xt is given the same value as p, as opposed to ignoring it altogether. Since the xt tally in these instances will be less than if the words were to appear several times, xt will be undervalued.

P is also a credible measure of an existing category. Nonetheless, it is undervalued too, when contrasted with sp. Sp will almost invariably report higher counts than xt and p because what is being tallied is the number of lines in a passage. Given the subjective element introduced when the researcher chooses how much of a passage to include in its tally, sp may record inordinate high numbers that may affect the overall results. Consequently, sp requires a lesser value to minimize disproportionate counts. Hence, the field is leveled by multiplying xt by a factor of 2; p by a factor of 3; and dividing sp by 2. Once leveled, the three levels of analysis, xt, p, and sp are added together to obtain an overall score. Subsequently, categories are ranked according to their scores, and labeled according to the significance they may represent.

Altogether, the process is quite tedious but verifiable, insofar as the reader accepts the premises of the method. Accepting or discarding the results and/or the findings ought not to be a matter of simply liking or disliking them because they are not within one's expectations. The approach stands on its own and ought to be rejected either by flaws in its usage or if a sufficient number of errors warrant questioning the overall results.

The choices of over one hundred categories were personal, but after several readings of the texts, I think the reader may find the selection reasonable. I chose categories over which there has been much debate; others that caught my interest along the way as they are relevant to the meaning of Christianity today; and yet others that are breakdowns of major categories or routine terms that may be useful for comparison purposes. In all instances, I have identified the location of the word and/or passage that pertain to each specific category according to traditional biblical citations. This is done to allow others to review the results.

Quantitative Data

The data I selected to assign a numerical value to each category is too extensive to be published in a book, although it is necessary to allow readers to see for themselves if the qualitative inferences are justified and the quantitative numbers are valid. I published the raw data on the internet at www.RicardoPlanas.com/notes. In the case of xt, readers will be able to notice tallied words highlighted in yellow. The number of passages or p may be manually counted. As for sp, the process is more tedious; it requires verifying the value given at the end of each passage by multiplying the number of lines x 2. The totals for each passage are expressed as a number followed by sp.

Table 1 Profile Database of Jesus Based on a Breakdown of Titles Accorded to Him

Table 1A Titles by xt (number of times)

Gospels' Portrayal of Jesus by Others and by Himself	Totals	Total Gospels	Rank
Son of God (term plus references to divinity)	239xt		
Others perceive Jesus as Son of God	38xt	**254xt**	Extremely Significant
Jesus perceives himself as Son of God	216xt		
Lord (word), God or Jesus	171xt/ 93xt Jesus 70xt God		
Others perceive Jesus as Lord	90xt	**150xt**	Highly significant
Jesus perceives himself as Lord	60xt		
Teacher/Rabbi/Master (words)	91xt		
Others perceive Jesus as Teacher/Rabbi/Master	70xt	**145xt**	Highly significant
Jesus perceives himself as Teacher/Rabbi/Master	75xt		
Son of Man (term)	82xt		
Others perceive Jesus as Son of Man	3xt	**82xt**	Significant
Jesus perceives himself as Son of Man	79xt		
Savior and Redeemer as one term (includes allusions)	6xt		
Others perceive Jesus as Savior and/or Redeemer (temporal or eschatological)	14xt	**68xt**	Less Significant
Jesus perceives himself as Savior and Redeemer (temporal or eschatological)	54xt		
Messiah (word and allusions)	50xt		
Others perceive Jesus as Messiah	31xt	**57xt**	Less Significant
Jesus perceives himself as Messiah	26xt		
King (word)	52xt		
Others perceive Jesus as King	28xt	**52xt**	Less Significant
Jesus perceives himself as King	24xt		
Prophet (word and allusions)	92xt		
Others perceive Jesus as prophet	23xt	**46xt**	Less Significant
Jesus perceives himself as prophet	23xt		
Powerful Master (from the Parables)	40xt		
Others perceive Jesus as Powerful Master	0xt	**40xt**	Less significant
Jesus perceives himself as Powerful Master	40xt		
Son of David (term)	15xt		
Others perceive Jesus as Son of David	13xt	**21xt**	Insignificant
Jesus perceives himself as Son of David	8xt		
		915xt Jesus known under 10 titles	

Table 1B

How Gospels Portray Other People's Image of Jesus	Totals	Rank
Opponent of religious authority *	134xt	Highly significant
Jesus as Lord +	90xt	Significant
Jesus as Teacher/Rabbi +	70xt	Significant
Jesus as Son of God	38xt	Less significant
Jesus as Messiah +	31xt	Less significant
Jesus as King +	28xt	Less significant
Jesus as prophet +	23xt	Less significant
Jesus as Savior and/or Redeemer +	14xt	Less significant
Jesus as Son of David +	13xt	Less significant
Jesus as Magician, superman, ghost	8xt	Less significant
Jesus as knowledgeable religious teacher	4xt	Insignificant
Jesus as Son of Man +	3xt	Insignificant
Jesus as Insane/possessed/Agent of Beelzebul	3xt	Insignificant
Jesus as divisive and disruptor of family institution	2xt	Insignificant
Jesus as Enigmatic person	2xt	Insignificant
Jesus as Famous healer	2xt	Insignificant
Jesus as Being Favored by God	2xt	Insignificant
John the Baptist Being Uncertain Who Jesus is	1xt	Insignificant
Jesus Being Misunderstood by his disciples	1xt	Insignificant
Jesus Seen as Being Fearless, by Pontius Pilate	1xt	Insignificant
Jesus as Master (not teacher) +	0xt	Insignificant
*134xt is based on number of times Jesus is depicted as being critical of religious authorities	470xt	

Table 1C

How Gospels Portray Jesus's Image of Himself	Totals	Rank
Jesus sees himself as Son of God	216xt	Extremely significant
Jesus sees himself as Son of Man	79xt	Highly significant
Jesus sees himself as Teacher (Rabbi) Master	75xt	Highly significant
Jesus as Lord	60xt	Significant
Jesus sees himself as Savior and Redeemer	54xt	Significant
Jesus sees himself as Powerful Master	40xt	Significant
Jesus sees himself as Messiah	26xt	Less significant
Jesus sees himself as King	24xt	Less significant
Jesus sees himself as prophet	23xt	Less signficant
Jesus sees himself as Son of David	8xt	Insignificant
Total	605xt	

Table 1D (Source: Word count)

Word count of the terms Jesus, Christ, and Jesus Christ in the Gospels. See FN 1 below	Jesus 593xt Christ 1xt JC 5xt

Table 1E (Source: Word count)

How Paul refers to Jesus in Romans	J 6xt, C 34xt, JC 16xt, CJ 14xt
How Paul refers to Jesus in 1, 2 Corinthians	J 16xt, C 82xt, JC 18xt, CJ 7xt
Christ name in Paul's 8 Letters	386xt

FN1: [Jn 17:3] This verse was clearly added in the editing of the gospel as a reflection on the preceding verse; Jesus nowhere else refers to himself as Jesus sChrist.

Chapter 5 - Method Note to Tables 1A, 1B, 1C: The quantitative results appear in Tables 1A, B, and C. The first column in Table 1A shows a list of titles ascribed to Jesus that appear in the Gospels. Each one displays three subheadings: the title, how others perceive Jesus, and how Jesus perceives himself according to the title. Table 1B is a breakdown of how others perceive or address Jesus per title; and Table 1C, how Jesus perceives himself according to how he refers to himself or consents others to call him. Quantifying how Jesus perceives himself was complicated because it involved not only instances in which Jesus refers to himself explicitly by the title, but also having to assess when he implicitly acknowledges it by not refusing to be addressed by the title. The second and third lines in the second column are most relevant for comparisons. The third column adds together the second and third lines and provides a powerful indicator of how the public Jesus interacted with others. This sum is used to rank the titles according to their significance warranted by disparities among the numbers themselves (last column).

Unless noted, all numbers are expressed as (xt) indicating instances in which the titles are mentioned in the Gospels. The tally was done by separately copying and pasting each Gospel from the NEs' Bible online in Word. The count that appears in BibleGateway.com is less accurate for purposes of this study because it tallies words that appear in headings as well as counting the same two words in one sentence as only one. In some cases, title totals include sayings that allude to the title itself. This happens in Son of God, Messiah, Savior, and Redeemer, or Prophet, in which cases the passages are identified according to verse numbers. Other titles, such as Lord, Teacher, or Son of Man are much simpler to count. I search the title, assess if it refers to God or Jesus, assess if others or Jesus call out the title, and reasonably assess if Jesus acknowledges the title by not rejecting it or by continuing the conversation. When the results are extensive, these are provided online with the breakdown total per gospel author.

*The category *Opponent of religious authority* is stated in terms of *p* or passages in which Jesus's opposition to the Jewish religious authorities is noticeable. For practical purposes, the numbers are similar to *xt* or number of times.

Table 2 – Overall Results

Categories	Total xt	Total p	Total sp	Overall Score	Significance
Righteousness (includes dos and don'ts in the texts)				24038.7	Supremely significant
Faith Plus	3950	2331	3451	9732	Extremely significant
Sinfulness Total Space	2236	1326	1578	5080	Remarkably significant
Teachings About Specific Sins Total Space	1692	999	1042	3733	Highly significant
The Afterlife, Existence of the Supernatural (see Method Note)	1844	735	976	3555	Highly significant
Jewish Religious Authorities	2038	426	901.5	3365.5	Highly significant
Religious Authorities Evaluation (Positive, Negative, Neutral)	+ 53sp	- 1713sp	=68sp		
Power	1186	738	1344	3268	Highly significant
Jewish People (excludes Jewish authorities)	1772	645	822	3239	Highly significant
Jewish People Evaluation (Positive, Negative, Neutral)	+754sp	- 822sp	= 66sp		
Love Total Space (Jesus's Miracles Included)	728	747	1535	3010	Highly significant
Reason	872	897	1136	2905	Highly significant
Joy (when added to miracles)	502	519	1162	2183	Significant
Prophecy	898	423	592	1913	Significant
Gentiles	1150	192	532	1874	Significant
Gentiles Evaluation; Positive, Negative, Neutral	+ 455sp	- 529sp	= 80sp		
Poverty and Wealth	294	441	1085	1820	Significant
Church	392	360	1056	1808	Significant
Mosaic Law	682	378	695	1765	Significant
Faith (without supernatural categories included)	638	372	636	1646	Significant
Temporal World	556	390	637	1583	Significant
Justice	260	390	854	1504	Significant
Devil/Satan	460	690	250	1400	Significant
Miracles in the Gospels Total Space	206	297	874	1377	Significant
Love and Its Synonyms (Jesus's Miracles Excluded)	502	402	462	1366	Significant
Sinfulness and Its Synonyms (no discussion of specific sins)	544	327	476	1347	Significant
Kingdom of God/kingdom of heaven	326	348	640	1314	Significant
Miracles by Jesus in the Gospels Total Space	182	264	861	1307	Significant
Attributions of Divinity to Jesus by him and others	482	297	509	1288	Significant
Humility	204	306	738	1248	Significant
Violence Non-Violence in Jesus	194	291	659	1144	Significant
Resurrection of humans	468	264	310	1051	Less significant
Jesus's Mission	176	264	555	995	Less significant
Parables/Similes/Metaphors	140	210	623	973	Less significant
Jesus Conflicting Personality	176	264	504	944	Less significant
Prayer	356	294	270	920	Less significant
Truth	338	240	313	891	Less significant
(Sin) Hatred/Anger	430	216	244	890	Less significant
Joy (miracles excluded)	326	255	300	881	Less significant
Mystery in the Gospels	236	222	333	791	Less significant
Repentance	186	165	412	763	Less significant
(Sin) Killing/Murder	294	252	186	732	Less significant
Divine Providence	122	183	364	669	Less significant
God's will	138	180	330	648	Less significant
Forgiveness/Unforgiveness	150	135	294	579	Less significant
Parousia/Judgment Day	90	135	343	568	Less significant
Gospel/ Word of God/Good News *	206	171	181	558	Less significant
(Sin) Egotism/Hypocrisy/arrogance/pride/self-righteousness	206	105	245	556	Less significant
(Sin) Selfishness Self-centeredness	220	177	158	555	Less significant
Hell (excludes Satan-related terms)	172	135	198	505	Less significant
Sexual Behavior in the Gospels (righteous and sinful)	256	108	139	503	Less significant
Grace	156	168	157	481	Less significant
War and Peace	208	96	168	472	Less significant
Love as a Term Only (synonyms excluded)	182	135	146	463	Less significant
Heart	122	144	182	448	Less significant
Christianity as Opium	78	117	245	440	Less significant
(Sin) Refusing to accept Jesus/Conspiring against God's kingdom	120	114	206	440	Less significant
Pontius Pilate	256	42	114	412	Less significant
Mary (Jesus's Mother)	200	54	117	371	Less significant
Holy Spirit/God's Spirit	108	108	153	369	Less significant
Resurrection of Jesus	100	69	199	368	Less significant
Predestination	98	93	170	361	Less significant
Righteous Sexual Behavior	166	75	110	351	Less significant
Blessedness	116	117	112	345	Less significant
Marriage	152	66	84	302	Less significant
Supernatural Occurrences	52	78	170	300	Less significant

Categories	Total xt	Total p	Total sp	Overall Score	Significance
(Sin) Sinful Sexual Behavior	116	108	70	294	Less significant
Baptism	112	51	123	286	Less significant
Hope (Hope Plus, not shown, is more significant)	116	66	99	281	Less significant
Unity	104	78	88	270	Less significant
Pity	46	54	145	245	Less significant
God as Everyone's Father	80	69	81	230	Less significant
Mary of Magdala (MM)	130	30	63	223	Less significant
(Sin) Betraying Jesus (Judas's case)	96	63	57	216	Less significant
Jesus's Crucifixion (weighed) No narrative. For comparison only	n/a	n/a	225	n/a	n/a/
Redemption/eschatological	40	45	59	144	Less significant
Peter's Denial of Jesus	68	27	48	143	Least significant
(Sin) Divorce	56	48	33.5	137.5	Less significant
Redemption/temporal	34	33	55	122	Less significant
(Sin) Adultery	44	48	26.5	118.5	Less significant
(Sin) Folly	34	30	46	110	Less significant
Mercy	28	30	44	102	Less significant
(Sin) Blasphemy	34	33	32	99	Least significant
(Sin) False Oaths/Swearing by God	34	12	16	62	Least significant
(Sin) Harboring Evil Thoughts	20	27	13	60	Least significant
Compassion	8	12	34	54	Least significant
Soul	14	18	19	51	Least significant
Celibacy, Virginity, Chastity	14	9	26	49	Least significant
Caring	10	9	29	48	Least significant
(Sin) Dishonoring One's Parents	10	15	21	46	Least significant
(Sin) Inducing Others to Sin	14	18	13	45	Least significant
(Sin) Sinning with the Hand, Foot, or Eye	16	12	13	41	Least significant
Justification	6	9	25	40	Least significant
(Sin) Prostitution	8	9	4	21	Least significant
No Marriage or Sex in Heaven	6	9	6	21	Least significant
(Sin) Licentiousness/Unchastity/Lust	8	9	3	20	Least significant
Generosity	2	3	15	20	Least significant
Marriage (Disabilities preventing intercourse)	4	3	2	9	Least significant
Miracles in which faith plays a role (Total in Gospels)				29 mir	
Miracles in which faith does not play a role. (Total in Gospels)				61 mir	

Contemporary Categories in Which Gospels Play No Role (Categories are not quantifiable)

Temporal Freedom/Liberty	N/A	N/A	N/A	N/A	Highly significant
Anti-Slavery	N/A	N/A	N/A	N/A	Highly significant
Temporal Equality	N/A	N/A	N/A	N/A	Highly significant
Democracy	N/A	N/A	N/A	N/A	Highly significant
LGBTQ Rights	N/A	N/A	N/A	N/A	Highly significant
Feminism	N/A	N/A	N/A	N/A	Highly significant
Abortion	N/A	N/A	N/A	N/A	Highly significant
Climate Change	N/A	N/A	N/A	N/A	Highly significant
Secularism & Secularization	N/A	N/A	N/A	N/A	Highly significant

Table 3 - Overall Results by Gospel

Note: Table 3 is not setup according to the final ranking; only Table 2

Categories	Mark (13,546 words)	Luke (23,745 words)	Matthew (21,932 words)	John (18,025 words)	Total xt weighed x2	Total p weighed x3	Total sp weighed/2	Overall Score (Add for Total Rank)
Righteousness								18008.7
The Afterlife, Existence of the Supernatural	136xt/39p/304sp	273xt/76p/616sp	292xt/79p/732sp	222xt/51p/300sp	1844	735	976	3555
Sinfulness Total Space	171xt/72p/426sp	260xt/120p/1014sp	348xt/139p/1058sp	171xt/84p/558sp	1900	1245	1528	4673
Jewish Religious Authorities	179xt/29p/389sp	273xt/40p/498sp	304xt/39p/531sp	263xt/34p/385sp	2038	426	901.5	3365.5
Religious Authorities Evaluation of Passages	+18 - 363 = 8	+24 - 468 = 6	+0 - 501 = 30	+11 - 350 = 24		+53 -1713 = 68		
Teachings About Specific Sins Total Space (Sinfulness excluded)	139xt/77p/430sp	181xt/106p/796sp	265xt/139p/990sp	116xt/75p/370sp	1692	999	1042	3733
Jewish People (excludes Jewish authorities)	Jew 6xt 161xt/37p/277sp	Jew 4xt 320xt/64p/455sp	Jew 5xt 284xt/55p/334/sp	Jew 58xt 248xt/42p/348sp	1772	645	822	3239
Jewish People Evaluation of Passages (ex-cludes authorities)	Pos 169sp Neg 92sp Ntrl 14sp	Pos 258sp Neg 175sp Ntrl 22sp	Pos 184sp Neg 134sp Ntrl 16	Pos 146sp Neg 166sp Ntrl 36	Pos 754sp Neg 567sp Ntrl 88sp			
Power	129xt/57p/640sp	161xt/71p/764sp	191xt/80p/744sp	112xt/38p/540sp	1186	738	1344	3268
Faith	52xt/25p/248sp	55xt/26p/278sp	69xt/33p/246sp	143xt/40p/500sp	638	372	636	1646
Love Total Space (Jesus Miracles Included)	60xt/50p/570sp	123xt/83p/1006sp	108xt/75p/820sp	73xt/41p/674sp	728	747	1535	3010
Mosaic Law	76xt/24p/278sp	88xt/35p/398sp	114xt/39p/490sp	68xt/28p/224sp	692	378	695	1765
Reason: understanding, knowledge, wisdom (includes Parables)	76xt/54p/412sp	101xt/85p/796sp	105xt/64p/612sp	154xt/96p/452sp	872	897	1136	2905
Poverty and Wealth	36xt/36p/532sp	53xt/53p/730sp	46xt/46p/598sp	12xt/12p/310sp	294	441	1085	1820
Temporal World (world as term per Gospel in xt)	World 4xt 38xt/18p/200sp	World 9x 74xt/35p/314sp	World 13x 88xt/40p/444sp	World 78x 91xt/37p/316sp	556	390	637	1583
Love and Its Synonyms (Jesus's Miracles Excluded)	33xt/23p/110sp	86xt/47p/336sp	69xt/31p/286sp	63xt/33p/192sp	502	402	462	1366
Attributions of Divinity to Jesus by Him and Others	15xt/12p/106/sp	27xt/18p/210sp	39xt/26p/184sp	160xt/43p/518sp	482	297	509	1288
Kingdom of God/kingdom of heaven	20xt/13p/152sp	42xt/40p/468sp	59xt/40p/526sp	42xt/23p/134sp	326	348	640	1314
Sinfulness and Its Synonyms (no discussion of specific sins)	33xt/13p/102/sp	92xt/36p/328sp	90xt/37p/296sp	57xt/23p/226sp	544	327	476	1347
Prayer	24xt/15p/78sp	57xt/36p/210sp	46xt/25p/122sp	51xt/22p/130sp	356	294	270	920
Miracles in the Gospels Total Space	27xt/26p/428sp	34xt/33p/576sp	32xt/30p/372sp	10xt/10p/372sp	206	297	874	1377
Miracles in the Gospels Involving Jesus	25m/24p/454sp	28xt/28p/522sp	28xt/27p/348sp	9xt/9p/402sp	182	264	861	1307
Prophecy	78xt/22p/206sp	138xt/41p/334sp	132xt/47p/406sp	101xt/31p/238sp	898	423	592	1913
Violence Non-Violence in Jesus	12xt/12p/168sp	35xt/35p/452sp	30xt/30p/520sp	20xt/20p/178sp	194	291	659	1144
Church	42xt/27p/312sp	77xt/43p/618sp	52xt/33p/666p	25xt/17p/516sp	392	360	1056	1808
Jesus Conflicting Personality	19xt/19p/218sp	25xt/25p/294sp	25xt/25p/380sp	19xt/19p/116sp	176	264	504	944
Jesus's Mission	20xt/20p/184sp	34xt/34p/428sp	22xt/22p/350sp	12xt/12p/148sp	176	264	555	995
Gentiles	119xt/13p/198sp	138xt/22p/282sp	160xt/22p/362sp	158xt/7p/222sp	1150	192	532	1874
Gentiles Evaluation of Passages	+93 - 91 = 14	+137 - 131 = 14	+123 - 191 = 48	+102 -116 = 4	+455	- 529 = 80		
Parables/Similes/Metaphors	12xt/12p/182sp	27xt/27p/514sp	25xt/25p/464sp	6xt/6p/86sp	140	210	623	973
Devil/Satan	58xt/16p/146sp	86xt/21p/168sp	64xt/19p/124sp	22xt/11p/62sp	460	690	250	1400
Justice	20xt/20p/206sp	45xt/45p/688sp	45xt/45p/666sp	20xt/20p/148sp	260	390	854	1504

Categories	Mark (13,546 words)	Luke (23,745 words)	Matthew (21,932 words)	John (18,025 words)	Total xt weighed x2	Total p weighed x3	Total sp weighed/2	Overall Score (Add for Total Rank)
Joy (miracles included)	38xt/34p/506sp	105xt/66p/818sp	65xt/46p/454sp	43xt/27p/546sp	502	519	1162	2183
Resurrection of humans	33xt/10p/100sp	48xt/20p/180sp	78xt/32p/232sp	75xt/26p/126sp	468	264	319	1051
Truth	14xt/8p/70sp	33xt/18p/160sp	41xt/20p/194sp	81xt/34p/202sp	338	240	313	891
Predestination	7xt/4p/44sp	15xt/13p/136sp	12xt/7p/106sp	15xt/7p/54sp	98	93	170	361
God xt only	51xt	122xt	53xt	83xt	166			na
Humility	20xt/20p/244sp	41xt/41p/544sp	32xt/32p/492sp	9xt/9p/196sp	204	306	738	1248
Parousia/Judgment Day	4xt/4p/82sp	13xt/13p/228sp	19xt/ 19p/324sp	9xt/9p/52sp	90	135	343	568
(Sin) Selfishness Self-centeredness	21xt/9p/48sp	33xt/18p/132sp	44xt/28p/124sp	12xt/4p/12sp	220	177	158	555
Divine Providence	8xt/8p/102sp	23xt/23p/256sp	22xt/22p/286sp	8xt/8p/84sp	122	183	364	669
Miracles (faith not required)	13m	19m	23m	6m				
Repentance	9xt/8p/80sp	41xt/24p/418sp	25xt/16p/232sp	18xt/7p/94p	186	165	412	763
Sexual Behavior in the Gospels	22xt/5p/42sp	47xt/18p/130sp	53xt/10p/94sp	6xt/3p/12sp	256	108	139	503
Forgiveness/Unforgiveness	13xt/8p/64sp	29xt/17p/200sp	28xt/16p/222sp	5xt/4p/102sp	150	135	294	579
Love as a Term	8xt/5p/32sp	14xt/7p/78sp	14xt/9p/44sp	55xt/24p/138sp	182	135	146	463
Heart	15xt/11p/130sp	20xt/18p/90sp	20xt/14p/130sp	6xt/5p/14sp	122	144	182	448
Miracles (faith required)	12m	9m	5m	3m				
God's will	6xt/6p/90sp	17xt/17p/232sp	18xt/18p/270sp	28xt/19p/68sp	138	180	330	648
Mystery in the Gospels	19xt/14p/120sp	31xt/20p/168sp	34xt/20p/214sp	34xt/20p/164sp	236	222	333	791
Holy Spirit/God's Spirit.	6xt/5p/32sp	17xt/12p/114sp	11xt/8p/90sp	20xt/11p/70sp	108	108	153	369
Blessedness	7xt/6p/28sp	30xt/20p/114sp	18xt/10p/54sp	3xt/3p/28sp	116	117	112	345
(Sin) Killing/Murder	33xt/22p/90sp	37xt/19p/98sp	47xt/25p/108sp	30xt/18p/76sp	294	252	186	732
Joy (excluding miracles)	13xt/9p/52sp	77xt/38p/300sp	38xt/19p/104sp	35xt/19p/144sp	326	255	300	881
Grace	9xt/8p/38sp	38xt/27p/134sp	23xt/15p/102sp	8xt/6p/40sp	156	168	157	481
Resurrection of Jesus	11xt/6p/72sp	8xt/3p/108sp	13xt/9p/82sp	18xt/5p/136sp	100	69	199	368
Pontius Pilate	23xt/1p/34sp	24xt/5p/54sp	30xt/5p/56sp	51xt/7p/84sp	256	42	114	412
Hell related (Excludes Satan related terms)	10xt/4p/26sp	20xt/11p/104sp	34xt/18p/206sp	22xt/12p/60sp	172	135	198	505
(Sin) Egotism/Hypocrisy/arrogance/pride/self-righteousness	13xt/4p/58sp	29xt/12p/148sp	47xt/9p/150p	14xt/10p/134sp	206	105	245	556
Mary (Jesus's Mother)	4xt/2p/14sp	61xt/7p/126sp	24xt/6p/62sp	11xt/3p/32sp	200	54	117	371
Mary of Magdala (MM)	17xt/2p/32sp	20xt/4p/36sp	10xt/2p/30sp	18xt/2p/28sp	130	30	63	223
Christianity as Opium	6xt/6p/56sp	12xt/12p/154sp	15xt/15p/228sp	6xt/6p/52sp	78	117	245	440
Jesus's Crucifixion sp only (not weighed) For comparison only	68sp	76sp	110sp	196sp				450 (not weighed)
(Sin) Refusing to accept Jesus or God	4x/4p/28sp	17xt/9p/130sp	15xt/11p/172sp	24xt/14p/82sp	120	114	206	440
Pity	6xt/5p/106sp	5xt/4p/62sp	12xt/9p/122sp	0xt/0p/0sp	46	54	145	245
Righteous Sexual Behavior (marriage, celibacy, chastity, virginity)	21xt/4p/40sp	22xt/10p/68sp	31xt/8p/100sp	9xt/3p/12sp	166	75	110	351
(Sin) Hatred/Anger	45xt/14p/92sp	60xt/21p/112sp	58xt/18p/108sp	52xt/19p/176sp	430	216	244	890
Sinful Sexual Behavior (divorce, adultery, licentiousness, prostitution, lust)	15xt/9p/30sp	12xt/10p/20sp	24xt/15p/60sp	7xt/2p/30sp	116	108	70	294
(Sin) Betraying Jesus (Judas' case)	11xt/4p/24sp	8xt/4p/20sp	13xt/5p/28sp	16xt/8p/42sp	96	63	57	216
Peter's denial of Jesus	9xt/2p/24sp	10xt/2p/24sp	9xt/2p/24sp	6xt/3p/24sp	68	27	48	143

Categories	Mark (13,546 words)	Luke (23,745 words)	Matthew (21,932 words)	John (18,025 words)	Total xt weighed x2	Total p weighed x3	Total sp weighed/2	Overall Score (Add for Total Rank)
(Sin) Divorce	8xt/4p/18sp	5xt/4p/8sp	12x/6p/33sp	3x/2p/8sp	56	48	33.5	137.5
(Sin) Adultery	5xt/4p/10sp	5xt/4p/8sp	8xt/6p/13sp	4xt/2p/22sp	44	48	26.5	118.5
Mercy	0	9xt/6p/58sp	5xt/4p/30sp	0	28	30	44	102
Compassion	1xt/1p/30sp	2xt/2p/12sp	1xt/1p/26sp	0	8	12	34	54
Celibacy, Virginity, Chastity	0	3xt/1p/24sp	4xt/2p/28sp	0	14	9	26	49
Caring	0	2xt/1p/18sp	2xt/1p/32sp	1xt/1p/8sp	10	9	29	48
(Sin) Dishonoring One's Parents	2xt/2p/18sp	1xt/1p/6sp	2xt/2p/18sp	0	10	15	21	46
(Sin) Blasphemy	6xt/4p/22sp	2xt/2p/6sp	6xt/4p/26sp	3xt/1p/10sp	34	33	32	99
No Marriage or Sex in Heaven	1xt/1p/4sp	1xt/1p/4sp	1xt/1p/4sp	0xt/0p/0sp	6	9	6	21
(Sin) Inducing others to sin	1xt/1p/4sp	1xt/1p/4sp	5xt/4p/18sp	0	14	18	13	45
(Sin) Sinning with the hand, foot, or eye	3xt/1p/10sp	0	5xt/3p/16sp	0	16	12	13	41
(Sin) Licentiousness/unchastity/lust	2xt/1p/2sp	0	2xt/2p/4sp	0	8	9	3	20
(Sin) Harboring Evil Thoughts	2xt/2p/4sp	2xt/2p/6sp	5xt/4p/14sp	1xt/1p/2sp	20	27	13	60
Generosity	0xt	0xt	1xt/1p/30sp	0xt	2	3	15	20
(Sin) Prostitution	0	2xt/2p/4sp	2xt/1p/4sp	0	8	9	4	21
(Sin) False Oaths/Swearing by God	2xt/1p/6sp	0	15xt/3p/26sp	0	34	12	16	62
Marriage (disability preventing intercourse)	0	0	2xt/1p/4sp	0	4	3	2	9
(Sin) Folly	3xt/2p/10sp	5xt/4p/38sp	9xt/4p/44sp	0	34	30	46	110
Baptism	13xt/4p/60sp	15xt/5p/74sp	11xt/3p/60sp	17xt /5p/52sp	112	51	123	286
Justification	0xt	3xt/3p/50sp	0xt	0xt	6	9	25	40
Supernatural Occurrences	4xt/4p/42sp	11xt/11p/158sp	8xt/8p/116sp	3xt/3p/24sp	52	78	170	300
Soul	2xt/2p/10sp	1xt/1p/2sp	4xt/3p/26sp	0	14	18	19	51
Marriage	21xt/4p/40sp	19xt/9p/44sp	27xt/6p/72sp	9xt/3p/12sp	152	66	84	302
Gospel/ Word of God/Good News	24xt/14p/86sp	26xt/16p/116sp	22xt/9p/56sp	31xt/18p/104sp	206	171	181	558
Redemption/eschatological	2xt/2p/6sp	3xt/3p/28sp	3xt/3p/28sp	12xt/7p/60sp	40	45	59	144
Redemption/temporal	1xt/1p/4sp	12xt/6p/80sp	2xt/2p/18/sp	2xt/2p/8sp	34	33	55	122
Hope (Hope Plus not shown)	3xt 3p/10sp	27xt/10p/116sp	24xt/6p/62sp	4xt/3p/10sp	116	66	99	281
War and Peace	13xt/3p/34sp	50xt/18p/190sp	32xt/6p/88sp	9xt/5p/24sp	208	96	168	472
Unity	5xt/3p/18sp	8xt/5p/28sp	14xt/8p/50sp	25xt/10p/80sp	104	78	88	270
God as everyone's Father	2xt/2p/14sp	4xt/4p/24sp	21xt/11p/90sp	13xt/6p/34sp	80	69	81	230

Contemporary significant Categories

Categories	Mark	Luke	Matthew	John	Total xt	Total p	Total sp	Overall
On Freedom/Liberty/Liberation	n/a	n/a	n/a	n/a	n/a	n/a	n/a	n/a
On Slavery	n/a	n/a	n/a	n/a	n/a	n/a	n/a	n/a
On Temporal Equality	n/a	n/a	n/a	n/a	n/a	n/a	n/a	n/a
On Democracy	n/a	n/a	n/a	n/a	n/a	n/a	n/a	n/a
On LGBTQ Rights	n/a	n/a	n/a	n/a	n/a	n/a	n/a	n/a
On Feminism	n/a	n/a	n/a	n/a	n/a	n/a	n/a	n/a
On Abortion	n/a	n/a	n/a	n/a	n/a	n/a	n/a	n/a
Climate Change	n/a	n/a	n/a	n/a	n/a	n/a	n/a	n/a
On Secularism and secularization	n/a	n/a	n/a	n/a	n/a	n/a	n/a	n/a

Chapter 6 - Method Notes to each category follow the order in which they appear in the chapter.
Gospel – Method Note: The following terms were used to tally this category: gospel of Jesus Christ, gospel of God, gospel of the kingdom, the word, word of God, my words, words of mine, words of the kingdom, good news, good news of the kingdom of God, seed, the Word, and words of eternal life. Xt refers to the number of times these terms appear in the texts, and it is different from p, which refers to the number of passages.
Righteousness – Method Note: This super-category includes: Sinfulness, Sins, Faith, Baptism, Repentance, Love, Mosaic Law, Forgiveness, Prayer, Poverty and Wealth, Non-violence, Humility, God's Will, Righteous Sexuality, and Parables.
The Temporal World – Method Note: References to the category Temporal World were searched by tallying terms such as world, flesh, human, natural, body, earth, and others closely related. Their total distribution is as follows: flesh 18xt, human 28xt, body 40xt, earth 47xt, world 104xt.
The Afterlife – Method Note: Terms tallied suggesting the existence of an afterlife included the following: eternal life, redemption, rescue, shed blood, ransom, resurrection, rise(n), salvation, save, secure life, save a life, lose life, live, paradise, enter, heaven, kingdom (of God), angel, voice of God, repentance, baptism, Spirit, condemnation (eternal), hell-related terms (fire, grinding of teeth), and Satan-related words (evil one, devil, ruler of the world). Additionally, the term *God* was counted (only as xt) while excluding it from the term *kingdom of God* (already above), to accentuate references to the divine in the texts. This approach still underestimates the true relevance of this category. Some passages focus on the afterlife in the Faith and Prayer categories and were included in the tally only when referring to a supernatural God; the term *faith* is not included if it simply means human trust that Jesus can heal the sick. Moreover, the term *Father* (standing for God) and *Son of Man* (that has divine characteristics) could have been added, all of which likely would have elevated the ranking of this category second to Righteousness. Adding these, however, ran the risk of double counting.
Love and Its Synonyms (miracles excluded) – Method Note: The category *Love Total Space* is an all-encompassing artificial construct that adds together *Love as a Term*, *Love and its Synonyms,* and *Miracles Total Passages*. The *Love as a Term* category accounts only for instances in which the word *Love* and its rooted terms, e.g., loving, loved, appear in the texts. Initially, I hypothesized that if *Love* lies at the center of Jesus's teachings today it would be among the highest tallied themes. It turned out that it does, and it does not. *Love as a Term* ranks as a less significant category. Nonetheless, there are other words, such as *blessed, generosity, pity, mercy, compassion, caring,* and *forgiveness* that are manifestations of love. When these words are added, they present a more accurate picture of the role of love in the Gospels; hence, *Love and Its Synonyms (Jesus's Miracles Excluded)* category. The category *Love Total Space* includes all miracles in the texts performed by Jesus, including his resurrection. It is based on the assumption that, although the primary purpose of Jesus's purported miracles is to create faith and validate his existence as God's son or messiah, miracles are also an expression of Jesus's love for the *least ones*. Although there is a separate *Miracles* category, I chose to concentrate on the *Love and Its Synonyms (Jesus's Miracles Excluded)* category, leaving it up to the reader to decide if miracles ought to be considered for purposes of ranking. Miracle passages are not included in this category to avoid excessive double-counting. The count and rankings of the terms *blessed, generosity, pity, mercy, compassion, caring,* and *forgiveness* also appear individually in Table 2. Their totals in some cases may not add to the Total Love Space category. Although double counting was inevitable from a practical standpoint, having done the counting several times indicated that it would not have altered the tally or the ranking significantly.
Jewish Religious Authorities – Method Note: Terms searched in his tally include, *scribes, Pharisees, Sadducees, scholars of the law, Sanhedrin, chief priest, high priest, Jews* (when related to the religious authorities), *elders of the people, Caiaphas, Nicodemus, Joseph of Arimathea,* and other terms and passages that relate to the Jewish religious authorities. To establish an evaluation of how the texts refer to this group (positive, negative, or neutral), the tally included pronouns and other nouns that directly relate to the religious authorities. This evaluation appears underneath the category in Table 2. The content analysis tally indicates that the term *Pharisee* appears (89xt) followed by *scribe* (66xt), then *Chief Priest* (54xt), *High Priest* (29xt), *elder* (21xt), and *Sadducee* (9xt). That the Gospels refer so often to the Pharisees relative to the others is not surprising. Luke himself in his Acts of the Apostles indicates that the Christian faith emerges directly from Pharisaic Judaism, or as a reaction to it (Acts 21:20; 22:3; 23:6–9; 24:14–16; 26:2–8, 22–23).
Jewish People – Method Note: Searched terms included *Jewish, Jew, Israeli(te), Israel, Judea, Jerusalem,* or inhabitants of other Jewish towns Jesus visited. Additionally, the terms 'crowd,' and 'people' were included if they refer to the Jewish people. To establish a more realistic assessment of how

the terms are used, the tally also included other words, pronouns, and phrases that refer to Jewish people. To establish an evaluation of how the texts refer to this group (positive, negative, or neutral), the tally included pronouns and other nouns that directly relate to the Jewish people. This evaluation appears underneath the category in Table 2. The geographical terms are tallied only if they indicate Jesus's presence to preach to the people.

Gentiles – Method Note: For purposes of content analysis, and to obtain a broad picture of the role of Gentiles in the Gospels, the tallying takes into account the terms *gentile* and *pagan* as well as non-Jewish persons and groups of people Jesus ministers to (including pronouns), the names of non-Jewish towns and other geographical areas he visits that are inhabited mostly by Gentiles, parables, miracles involving Gentiles, and passages related to his trial and execution at the hands of the Romans. To assess the Gospels' attitude toward Gentiles, all passages in this category were subjectively evaluated as being positive, negative, or neutral from the viewpoint of the authors' and Jesus's views toward Gentiles. The negative count corresponding to Gentiles is high, partially because of the inclusion of passages dealing with Jesus's trial and crucifixion by the Romans.

Mosaic Law – Method Note: The words that were searched in this category were the following: Moses (39xt), law (referring to Mosaic Law, 73xt), righteousness, i.e., abidance to the law (36xt), tradition (originating within the context of the law, 40xt), fasting (practice pertaining to the law, 20xt), Sabbath (one of the commandments, 50xt), baptism (practiced originated by Jesus, 30xt), commandment (related to Mosaic Law, 23xt), blasphemy (contravention of the law, 15xt).

Reason – Method Note: The words used in this search included *reason, understand, think, wisdom, mind, know, comprehend, explain, learn, and realize.* The Parables category is added since parables constitute teaching lessons through which Jesus appeals to human understanding and wisdom. NEs' note, Matthew 13:11 indicates that parables demand *reflection for understanding,* even if such understanding is a gift that God gives only to a few. Each parable is tallied as 1xt and added to the above words or terms to express Total xt, except when the above words appear in a parable, in which case the parable is not counted as xt. All parables, however, are added to the total as (p) and (sp). The distribution of these terms in the synoptics seems proportionate to their length, although all four authors show a preference for three words: *think, know,* and *understand* account for about eighty-six percent of all terms related to the category. The term *know* appears 245xt, by far the most, but largely because of the lopsided use in John's Gospel, (113xt), as opposed to (30xt) in Mark, (53xt) in Luke, and (49xt) in Matthew. In the Gospels, *Reason* appears 12xt only; however, other terms are more numerous: *think* 38xt, *understand* 43xt, *realize* 25xt; altogether terms related to this category appear 440xt in the Gospels.

Faith – Method Note: There are in Table 2 two distinctive categories for faith. The content analysis tally initially sought to isolate faith from other categories to explain its nature. It searched for the terms, *faith, belief/ve, accept, embrace, acknowledge, persevere, remain,* etc., insofar as they point to Jesus's request to trust God, and him, because of his close relationship with God. The term *faith* appears by itself in Table 2 as a highly ranked category. In the Gospels, however, *faith* is much broader than what its synonyms may indicate, because almost everything that appears in the texts is, ultimately, a matter of faith. Hence, I added eight supernatural categories—Afterlife, Faith, Kingdom of God, Resurrection of Humans, Prayer, God's Will, God as Everyone's Father, Resurrection of Jesus—and came up with a super-category for comparison purposes that focuses on faith from a wider perspective. Nevertheless, each of these categories is separately tallied in Table 2.

Prayer – Method Note: The words searched for this category include pray/prayer, worship, ask (as in petitioning), knock (as in calling on God), may (as part of prayer), blessing (as in giving thanks to God or asking for God's grace), praise (to God), glorify, and instances of actual praying in the texts. The word that is mostly used in the synoptics is *pray* (61xt) followed by *blessing* (55xt) while John's Gospel relies more on the terms *glory* (34xt), *worship* (13xt), and *ask* (12xt).

Church – Method Note: The search for this category concentrated on the words *synagogue, temple, church, assembly* (if referring to a gathering of believers), *house* or *room,* i.e., a dwelling, house indicating a community or nation of believers, and deserted or open areas (where Jesus often prays and teaches), all suggesting church ministry.

Divine Providence – Method Note: There are no particular words or phrases that point to divine providence. Generally defined as God's active participation in human affairs, the search focused on passages that allude to instances in which the texts suggest that God is, indeed, involved in his own creation.

Predestination – Method Note: Specific words, such as *predestined, preordained, destined, determined, predetermined, chosen, the elect,* were searched in this category as well as any passage that connotes the view that human salvation is predetermined or predestined by God since creation.

Repentance – Method Note: Searched words included repentance, conversion, baptism, rebirth, transform, acknowledge sins, crying, and forgiveness (if related) since at the time these terms presumed an attitude of repentance.

Forgiveness – Method Note: Searched words were those rooted in *forg,* e.g., forgave, forgiving, unforgiving, etc. Passages that relate to the act of forgiveness are included even if the term is not present. Miracles that appear in passages dealing with forgiveness are not included in tallying (sp) since they are counted in the overall category of Total Love Plus Miracles.

Kingdom of God – Method Note: The terms that were searched for this category included any specific word or phrases such as *kingdom of God, heavenly kingdom,* or *kingdom* (when referring to God's kingdom), *enter into,* i.e., entering into eternal life, *eternal life,* and *salvation* (suggesting entrance into the kingdom), *eternal dwellings,* and *life* (in John's Gospel when referencing salvation or entering into the kingdom). Parables referencing God's kingdom, even when the term does not appear, are included. Indirect references, *such as You do not enter yourselves, nor do you allow entrance to those trying to enter* (Mt 23:13) are also counted. Luke uses *kingdom of God* (32xt), far more than the others. Matthew is the only one who uses the term *kingdom of heaven* (32xt), in deference to devout Jewish audiences who avoided the name "God" (NEs' note, Mt 3:2). John's Gospel hardly uses the term kingdom (5xt). Instead, the text uses the terms *life* (18xt) and *eternal life* (17xt).

Jesus's Mission – Method Note: There are specific phrases in the texts that relate to Jesus's mission. Passages denoting reasons, needs, or duties he is asked to fulfill, were selected for this category. As there are no specific words to be searched, the same number of passages (p) is assigned to xt. The formula for (sp) remains the same.

Jesus's Conflicting Personality – Method Note: This category focuses on passages from the Gospels in which Jesus's behavior and teachings differ from the apologetic view as explained in the text. Passages are equally tallied in xt and p columns while sp is tallied according to rules of space.

Hell – Method Note: The tally in this section includes words and phrases that stand for, allude to, or are more or less the Gospels' equivalent of hell. They include wailing and grinding of teeth; condemnation (pertaining to eternal damnation); eternal fire; eternal punishment or eternal life; fire (pertaining to hell); fiery furnace; Gehenna; netherworld; outer darkness; save his life or forfeit his life or a variation of any of these terms that suggest eternal condemnation.

Devil – Method Note: Terms searched in this category were *devil,* Satan, Lucifer, Beelzebul, Baal, Legion, demon, tempter, the one, power of darkness, the evil one, unclean spirit, ruler of the world, or 'possessed.' The search includes pronouns and other direct references, such as quotes by the devil.

Truth – Method Note: The words that were searched in this category include *truth/true; falsehood* and *lie/liar* as behavior he condemns; *honesty, the way* (when applicable), *light* as a synonym for truth, and *darkness* implying falsehood. *Hypocrisy* is included since it is a form of deception of truth.

Heart – Method Note: Tally of this category was based on searching the word *heart* in the Gospels.

Power – Method Note: This section identifies and includes every specific miracle attributed to Jesus in the Gospels as symbols of his power. Their totals appear in Table 2. Words searched include the following: power, might, authority, command, follow, order, rule(r), drive out, speak languages, pick up serpents, drink deadly drinks, heal, sign, wealth/riches. The word *signs* (48xt) is unique in John's text; it stands for mighty deeds or miracles done by Jesus, while in the synoptics, in most instances, the word does not indicate deeds but signals of things to come, e.g., wars, earthquakes, stars falling from the sky, etc., and few instances in which the Pharisees ask Jesus to do a miraculous deed to legitimize his claim. Other passages suggesting any of these words are identified, counted as a single *xt,* and added to the totals. Each passage describing a miracle, no matter its length, is tallied as 1xt and is equivalent to 1p as well. The category ranks high, mostly because of space (sp) allocated to miracles narrated in the texts.

Justice and Divine Retribution – Method Note: Searching for Jesus's conception of justice requires combing through the texts for words or instances that denote justice or injustice such as, *judge/judgment, righteous, sin/sinner, reward, punishment, save/salvation,* or *condemn.* The texts are replete with these words, particularly sin, salvation, and condemnation. Adding all these terms to the *justice category* would result in a disproportionate count that would meaninglessly affect its ranking. Instead, I opted to focus primarily on passages that reflect the above terms, counting each passage as (1xt), as I have done with other categories. Although this approach reduces the number of *xt,* it still indicates how prominent Jesus's conception of justice is in the Gospels, as it ranks quite high among all categories.

Poverty and Wealth: Method Note: The objective in this category is to find out how much the Gospels refer to the matter of poverty and wealth and what they say about it. The words *poor/poverty, hungry/hunger, suffering, persecution, oppression, wealth/riches, ailment,* are included as well as passages in which he praises material detachment and is critical of greed. There are other passages related to wealth and poverty that are difficult to dissect. I chose to count each passage as 1xt, hence the numbers of xt correspond to the numbers of p. This method will diminish xt, however, it will be offset by increased sp. The tally includes passages involving miracles that Jesus does on behalf of the poor. Nothing in the gospel indicates that Jesus's healing miracles were intended for poor or rich people. Given that the wealthy have more resources at their disposal to deal with their sickness, it is presumed that most miracles were geared toward poor people. Indeed, some among them were not poor, for example, Jairus, who was a ruler at a synagogue. In most instances, positive remarks concerned the poor but also included moneyed tax collectors who have repented, and at least two possibly affluent members of the Sanhedrin, e.g. Nicodemus and Joseph of Arimathea, who befriended Jesus.

Mary and Pilate – Method Note: Searched words for the Mary category included *Mary, mother,* and *wife* when referencing Jesus's mother, *virgin* as well as pronouns referring to her. Searched words for the Pontius Pilate category included his name and *governor* in addition to pronouns referring to him.

Joy – Method Note: Words searched included joy, rejoice, *happiness, cheerfulness, laughter, pleasure, pleasing, satisfaction,* and *blessed*; and passages that convey a sense of joy or happiness or provide a feeling of *hope* and inner *peace,* both of which are manifestations of joy. The words *happiness, bliss, cheerfulness,* and similar terms do not appear in the texts. Instead, *joy, rejoice, blessed, pleased, satisfied, peace, gladness,* and *laughter* do, although the terms have both a positive and negative connotation at times.

Holy Spirit – Method Note: : Tallying this category was based on searching the terms *Spirit, holy Spirit,* and *Advocate.* In Table 2, *xt* represents the number of times these words appear in the texts.

Baptism – Method Note: Tallying was conducted by searching the terms *baptism/baptize, born of water,* or other passages denoting the practice and effects of baptism.

Sexual Behavior in the Gospels: This category tallies and ranks anything denoting righteous or sinful sexuality, and other sex-related matters such as pregnancy, birth, purification, circumcision, eunuchism, or erectile dysfunctionality, and the absence of marriage and sex in heaven. There is no narrative for this category since it is broken down into two, *Righteous Sexual Behavior,* which discusses marriage, celibacy, chastity, and virginity (that appears below), and *Sinful Sexual Behavior* that shows under the Sinfulness category. Tallying marriage entails the word itself as well as passages indicating the union of two persons or a wedding. Additionally, it includes passages where divorce and adultery are discussed since these cannot happen unless one of the parties is married. In these cases, each passage that mentions adultery or divorce (but not marriage) is counted as 1xt for each. Tallying Celibacy, Virginity, and Chastity focused on the specific terms or passages indicating abstention from sexual intercourse.

Hope – Method Note: As the term seldom appears in the Gospels, the Content Analysis search focused on other words that closely suggest similar connotation, such as *promise, await, reward, and longing,* that relate to the kingdom of God or the afterlife regardless of whether their intent is temporal or eschatological.

Prophecy – Method Note: The Content Analysis approach to this category searched for the words *prophecy* and *prophet, fulfill, as it is written,* and *scriptures* (insofar as they lead to a prophecy); and the names of prophets that appear in the texts (if indirectly or directly relevant to prophecy), including Jesus when he issues a prophecy. At times, the prophecy shows up in the texts without mentioning the prophet, in which case the name is obtained by going to the Old Testament. To avoid double-counting in statements such as, *as it is written by the prophet Isaiah,* rather than to count it *as it is written, prophet* or *Isaiah,* only the name of the prophet is tallied along with the prophecy itself. A prophecy is taken into account when its fulfillment spans decades, centuries, or more. Thus, Elizabeth's statement of revelation in Luke regarding Mary being *the mother of my Lord* (Lk 1:42-43) and Mary's pious evocation of God's prowess in her canticle (Lk 1:46-55) do not appear in the count. There is an exception to this rule in John the Baptist that is briefly explained in the section. Although in some instances the names of prophets appear without being referenced to a prophecy, they are counted (including pronouns) to indicate the scope of their significance in the texts, and because they work to validate Jesus's authority on basis of his relationship with the Old Testament.

God's Will – Method Note: Search for the term *will of God* is part of the tally as well as other passages that may refer to the category. Accordingly, except for John's Gospel (due to the numerous sayings about Jesus doing God's will), (*xt*) and (*p*) receive the same values while (*sp*) is independently tallied according to allocated space in the synoptics. In John's Gospel, each saying is tallied as 1xt).

Christianity as the Opium of the People – Method Note: Following the physical effects of opium as a drug, this category searched for passages in the Gospels that denote parallel side-effects in human behavior on account of Jesus's teachings and contrast them with Marx's critique.

Violence and Non-Violence in Jesus – Method Note: The ranking in Table 2 is the outcome of passages (not words) depicting violence and non-violence in the texts. As done with other categories, the numbers for (*xt*) conform to the number of passages (*p*) while (sp) depicts space allocated to the category. Data used to rank violence and non-violence in Jesus by author appears online at www.RicardoPlanas.com/notes.

Humility – Method Note: This category searched for words that denote humility in the texts, such as, *humble, meekness, slave, servant, children*, and *poverty*; terms suggesting an opposite attitude such as arrogance, pride, hypocrisy, rich, and wealth; and passages denoting humility. The xt count in Table 2 tallies passages as 1xt each.

War and Peace – Method Note: Searched words and terms included *peace, war, nations rising against nations, persecutions, insurrections*, and passages connoting violence, domestic disturbances, or civil wars.

Unity – Method Note: The words that might disclose Jesus's desire for unity include *one, divided, united, together*, and *remain*, insofar as they relate to his presumed need of the sheep being under one shepherd. Other passages that imply unity (or division as being undesirable) are included too.

Mystery in the Gospels – Method Note: Tallying this category is done according to (*p*) and (*sp*). The search seeks to identify words and passages denoting the mysterious nature of the kingdom. Some keywords include *hidden, conceal, secret*. There are also passages implying restrictions that either God or Jesus place on revelation that keep human beings in the dark, and passages indicating failed attempts by the disciples and others to understand Jesus's teachings.

Miracles in the Gospels – Method Note: The tallying in this category was not based on searching for the term *miracle*; instead it recorded the total number of times that miracles are said to take place in the texts in terms of (*xt*) and (*p*) followed by a complete description of each miracle (*sp*).

The Resurrection of Jesus – Method Note: These words searched in this category include *rise, risen*, and *raise* as well as other terms related to Jesus's resurrection, such as, *appear, met them, greeted them, look at my hands, touch me* (to see he is real), *recognized him*, and *I will see you again*. Passages in which Jesus seems to predict his passion and the grain of wheat metaphor in John are also part of the count, along with the lengthy passages dealing with the resurrection and post-resurrection at the end of each Gospel. The purpose is to gauge how much interest the authors devoted to this event.

Parousia – Method Note: Terms and phrases that stand for the *Parousia*, known also as the Second Coming, were used to tally and rank this category. They include, *harvest, comes in glory, has come in power, the Son of Man, gather the wheat, on that day, final test, day of judgment, end of the age, last day*, and *until I come*, in addition to certain parables that address the Parousia. The Resurrection of Humans category would fit the Parousia since it is at the end of time that the resurrection will occur. However, I chose to limit this category to passages that strongly allude to Jesus's Second Coming. Passages tallied as (xt) will be the same as (p).

Parables – Method Note: The search in this category focused on actual parables (rather than on the word itself) and includes any type of figurative language, i.e., similes, metaphors, allegories, and similar narratives that Jesus utilizes to instruct his disciples or the crowds. Passages in which Jesus explains the use of parables are included too. Therefore, as previously done with other categories, each passage (*p*) is treated as 1xt.

Supernatural Occurrences – Method Note: The search is limited to God's attempts to communicate with humans on earth. If we were to manually add both Jesus's miracles and the Devil category to Supernatural Occurrences it would increase its tally to a Highly Significant level (3007) in Table 2. Xts are tallied in correspondence with p.

God as Everyone's Father – Method Note: The search in this category focuses on the ways Jesus refers to God as everyone's father. Terms such as *your heavenly Father, your Father, our Father, the Father.*

Justification – Method Note: The search in this category was limited to the term *justified/justification* to distinguish the term from redemption or righteousness.

Grace – Method Note: In addition to searching for the word *grace*, tallying this category included other terms that amounted to a similar meaning, such as *blessed, favor, pleased*, or passages that indicate the presence of grace.

Redemption – Method Note: The words that were searched included *redemption/redeem, savior, ransom, shed blood, liberate/liberty, rescue*, and other passages that connote these terms, regardless of whether they pertain to Jesus or God.

Soul – Method Note: Only the word *soul* was tallied in this category. Categories such as *the resurrection of humans, the afterlife, salvation and condemnation, eternal life*, and *kingdom of God*, suggest the presence of an element that continues to exist after death, presumably the soul. It would not be methodologically wrong if the reader wishes to add these categories to the *soul,* in which case it would increase its ranking considerably. Nonetheless, it would signify a big leap since the process entails the presupposition that the Gospels are referring to the soul in each of the above categories.

Sinfulness – Method Note: The *Sinfulness Totals* category is all-encompassing, comprised of the sum of the categories *Teachings about Specific Sins* and *Sinfulness and Its Synonyms. Sinfulness and Its Synonyms* includes all occurrences in which the term *sin,* its root, and words analogous to sin show up in the texts. The following words were tallied in this category: sin-rooted terms (sin, sinful, sinner), evil (as in deeds), wickedness, wrongness, darkness, iniquity, defile, transgression, repentance, forgiveness, and baptism (insofar as the terms relate to sins). On the other hand, *Teachings about Specific Sins* incorporates every instance in which an identifiable sin, e.g., hypocrisy, murder, blasphemy, adultery, etc., appears in the Gospels. Each sin is discussed in this work, then tallied and ranked separately. For ranking purposes, it seemed reasonable to add these two categories together, not only because both relate to sin, but also to indicate how important sinfulness was to the authors of the Gospels.

Sinfulness and Its Synonyms – Method Note: The tally for this category included synonyms of terms such as sin, evil, defile, repentance, forgiveness and baptism if related to sinfulness, transgression, wrongness, darkness, goats (in Matthew), and iniquity. The term *sinfulness* and its synonyms appear 261xt, as opposed to love 276xt (Table 2 online). Overall, this category ranks slightly lower than the Love and Its Synonyms category. However, once the tallying of specific sins is added, Total Sinfulness becomes much more significant than Total Love even when miracles are added (Table 2).

Teachings About Specific Sins – Method Note: This section incorporates exact words/terms (xt) that constitute sins, e.g., theft, killing, adultery, hypocrisy, and others that appear in the Gospels with their corresponding passages (p) and total space (sp). This category is the second of two independent categories that together comprise *Sinfulness Total Space.* The results in Table 2 show that Teachings about Specific Sins is also among the most significant categories after Righteousness, Faith, and Totals about Sinfulness. Tallying specific sins presents problems. There are passages in the Gospels indicating attitudes and behavior that Jesus does not identify by specific names despite being sinful. This is the case with the *Selfishness/self-centeredness* category; neither term appears in the texts, and yet Jesus regards both as among the worst sins. There are also specific behavior patterns that are related to selfishness/self-centeredness, for example, theft, greed, or tax collectors (whose sin is greed). At times, passages (p) count as 1xt, thus, xt and p often will be the same. This approach diminishes xt to a degree, but it appears to be the best possible method to tally each sinful behavior. Moreover, some passages that appear in this category may have shown up under *Sinfulness and Its Synonyms* category. In such cases, to avoid double-counting such passages have been eliminated. Hence, the total for this category is the sum of each sin as they appear in Table 2 minus passages that have been eliminated to prevent double counting. Whenever the texts refer to specific sins, they are tallied and ranked by their names as independent categories.

Anger and Hatred – Method Note: This category involves words and passages that denote anger, hatred, cursing, mistreatment, despising, mocking, insulting, wounding, persecuting, arraigning, handing over, beating, kingdoms, and nations against each other, and similar instances. Despite their close relation, murder and killing constitute a separate category that may be added together to hatred if the reader so wishes, although in this section they are treated as separate categories. This section also includes passages that relate to the level of hatred and anger by the Pharisaic religious authorities and their followers, and by the Roman authorities toward Jesus as well as his anger (perhaps even hatred) toward the Pharisees (Mk 3:1-5). It includes anti-Semitic sentiments shown by the authors of the Gospels. This behavior is included because the texts' authors thought it was important to disclose that Jesus's death is the result of these attitudes. The authors never say that Jesus's crucifixion is sinful, although they implied in graphic terms the extent to which hatred can drive humans.

Killing – Method Note: A Content Analysis of the category included words such as murder, killing death, blood, crucify, and perish, in addition to passages related to Jesus's death. The tally of this category does not include instances that pertain to killings that Jesus attributes to God in his parables. Such retribution or punishment by God for sinful behavior is examined under the *Violence/non-violence* and *Justice* categories.

Selfishness – Method Note: This category is an abstract construct. It brings together passages denoting selfishness and self-centeredness as observed in the Gospels that are in accordance with contemporary definitions. Unless specific words such as greed or envy appear, passages suggesting selfishness are tallied as 1xt. The (p) and (sp) tallies in this category are lower since they have been excluded to avoid double-counting, as they appear in the Sinfulness as Term category.

Refusal to Accept Jesus or God's Kingdom – Method Note: This category, like the previous one, is constructed not based on specific words but rather on passages denoting Jesus's denunciation of two sinful behaviors: refusal to accept Jesus or God and conspiring against God's kingdom. As a result, in this category (as with other constructs) the number of (*xt*) is the same as the number of (*p*); space (*sp*), however, still refers to the total number of lines that selected passages occupy in the text. The term *unbelief,* suggesting a refusal to accept Jesus, and actively seeking to oppose God's kingdom, are typical behaviors identified in this section. In the synoptics the term *unbelief* plays a minor role; not so in John's Gospel where "to believe" or not is central to the text. I identified passages that indicate unbelief, and a few others that suggest that belief is necessary, thereby indicating that unbelief in John's Gospel is considered sinful. To avoid duplicating the count, passages already included in the *Sinfulness* category are omitted in this section, a reason for which, likely, *Refusal to accept Jesus or God/Conspiring against God's kingdom* will be undercounted in the overall ranking.

Egotism – Method Note: Searched words included, *hypocrite,* and instances that denote pride, arrogance, or self-righteousness. In cases where the word does not appear each passage is tallied as 1xt, 1p, and whatever line space it occupies at 2sp per line.

Sinful Sexuality – Method Note: This category considers attitudes and behavior (including thought or feelings) that Jesus deemed to be sinful, such as divorce, adultery, lust, licentiousness, and prostitution, each of which appears in Table 2. No other act, such as premarital sex, orgies, rape, masturbation, sadomasochism, child molestation, incest, oral sex, anal sex, or bestiality are mentioned in the Gospels. Terms searched included words or passages denoting divorce, adultery, lust, licentiousness, or prostitution.

Betraying Jesus – Method Note: This section searched passages showing how Judas Iscariot was characterized in the Gospel in contrast with Peter. Mark's passages about Judas's betrayal are 3:19, 14:10-11, 14:17-21, 14:42-46; Luke's passages are 6:16, 22:1-6, 22:21-23, 22:47-48; Matthew's passages are 10:4, 26:14-16, 26:21-25, 26:47-49, 27:3-5; John's passages are 6:64, 6:70, 12:4, 13:1-2, 13:10-11, 13:21-27, 18:1-5, 21:20. Mark's passages about Peter's denial are 14:28-31, 14:66-72; Luke's passages are 22:31-34, 22:54-62, Matthew's passages are 26:31-35, 26:69-75; John's passages are 13:36-38, 18:15-18, 18:25-27.

Blasphemy – Method Note: Search on this category was limited to the term *blasphemy* and passages depicting instances of the act.

Inducing Others to Sin – Method Note: Tallying this category is limited to passages in which Jesus specifically mentions this type of sin.

Sinning with the Hand, Foot, or Eye – Method Note: Tallying this category is limited to passages in which Jesus specifically mentions this type of sin.

Harboring Evil Thoughts – Method Note: Tallying this category is limited to passages that cite the specific sin.

Dishonoring One's Parents – Method Note: Tallying this category is limited to passages that cite the specific sin.

Making False Oaths – Method Note: Tallying this category is limited to passages that cite the specific sin.

Folly – Method Note: Tallying this category entails identifying passages that depict the sin of folly.

Index

www.ingramcontent.com/pod-product-compliance
Lightning Source LLC
Chambersburg PA
CBHW081142270326

41930CB00014B/3010